3610043900

D1349605

THE FRENCH SECOND EMPIRE
AN ANATOMY OF POLITICAL POWER

This book is about a major historical figure, Napoleon III, and a political regime. It is both about great figures in history and the contexts–the political institutions and social networks – within which they were located.

First the book examines 'the circumstances and relationships that made it possible for a grotesque mediocrity to play a hero's part' (Karl Marx); how the disorder caused by the 1848 Revolution, and the introduction of male suffrage, enabled Louis-Napoleon Bonaparte to secure election as president of the Republic and subsequently to launch a *coup d'état*. The book then considers the ways in which power was exercised by the new imperial regime, by analysing the institutions of state and the mechanisms through which these interacted with society.

The eventual growth of opposition, reflecting alternative political loyalties, led Napoleon III to contemplate the transition from an authoritarian towards a more liberal rule, a process fraught with difficulties and social and political tension. Nevertheless, the establishment of the Liberal Empire appeared to have secured the regime's future; but at the point of success, the decision was taken to go to war against Prussia, which resulted in a catastrophic defeat and the destruction of Napoleon III's empire.

This is the most throughly researched book on the Second Empire in any language, which makes a contribution to our knowledge of a vitally important period of French history following the 1848 Revolution and the intense mid-century crisis.

ROGER PRICE is Professor of History at the University of Wales, Aberystwyth. His books include *The French Second Republic: A Social History* (1972), *Revolution and Reaction: 1848 and the French Second Republic* (1975), *The Modernisation of Rural France: Communication Networks and Agricultural Market Structures in Nineteenth-Century France* (1983), *A Social History of Nineteenth-Century France* (1987), *The Revolutions of 1848* (1988), and *A Concise History of France* (1993).

NEW STUDIES IN EUROPEAN HISTORY

Edited by

PETER BALDWIN
University of California, Los Angeles

CHRISTOPHER CLARK
University of Cambridge

JAMES B. COLLINS
Georgetown University

MIA RODRÍGUEZ–SALGADO
London School of Economics and Political Science

LYNDAL ROPER
Royal Holloway, University of London

This is a new series in early modern and modern European history. Its aim is to publish outstanding works of research, addressed to important themes across a wide geographical range, from southern and central Europe, to Scandinavia and Russia, and from the time of the Renaissance to the Second World War. As it develops the series will comprise focused works of wide contextual range and intellectual ambition.

THE FRENCH SECOND EMPIRE

An Anatomy of Political Power

BY

ROGER PRICE

CAMBRIDGE
UNIVERSITY PRESS

PUBLISHED BY THE PRESS SYNDICATE OF THE UNIVERSITY OF CAMBRIDGE
The Pitt Building, Trumpington Street, Cambridge, United Kingdom

CAMBRIDGE UNIVERSITY PRESS
The Edinburgh Building, Cambridge CB2 2RU, UK
40 West 20th Street, New York, NY 10011-4211, USA
10 Stamford Road, Oakleigh, VIC 3166, Australia
Ruiz de Alarcón 13, 28014 Madrid, Spain
Dock House, The Waterfront, Cape Town 8001, South Africa

http://www.cambridge.org

First published 2001

Printed in the United Kingdom at the University Press, Cambridge

Typeface Baskerville Monotype 11/12.5 pt.   *System* LATEX 2$_\varepsilon$ [TB]

A catalogue record for this book is available from the British Library

Library of Congress Cataloguing in Publication data
Price, Roger, 1944 Jan. 7–
The French Second Empire: an anatomy of political power /
Roger Price.
p.   cm. – (New studies in European history)
Includes bibliographical references and index.
ISBN 0 521 80830 8
1. Napoleon III, Emperor of the French, 1808–1873.   2. France – Kings and rulers – Biography.
3. France – History – Second Empire, 1852–1870.   I. Title.   II. Series.
DC280.P74   2001
944.07′092 – dc21   2001 025954

ISBN 0 521 808 308 hardback

In memory of my father, Godfrey David Price (1908–1968) and of my mother, Martha Price (1916–2000)

Contents

vii

Acknowledgements

I have accumulated an enormous number of debts since beginning work on this history. The raw material was largely provided by the archivists and librarians of the Archives nationales; Service historique de l'Armée de Terre; Bibliothèque nationale; University of East Anglia; University of Wales, Aberystwyth; and National Library of Wales. Research grants and study leave were generously awarded by both of the universities mentioned above and further indispensable funding by the British Academy, Leverhulme Trust, and Wolfson Foundation. I am grateful to William Doyle, Richard Evans, Douglas Johnson, Gwynne Lewis, and Vincent Wright for supporting various grant applications. Christopher Johnson, John Merriman, Sylvie Eyrich, Robert Frugère, and Jane Frugère offered encouragement and friendship. Colin Heywood was brave enough to take on the task of critically reading the original manuscript. Heather Price, more than anyone, improved its readability.

I am extremely grateful to William Davies and to the Syndics of Cambridge University Press for agreeing to publish the book as well as for the constructive criticism offered by the readers appointed by the Press, one of whom did me a great favour by suggesting the subtitle. Jean Field very efficiently copy-edited the text.

Above all I have to thank Richard and Luisa, Siân and Andy, Emily and Luke, Hannah, and my beloved Heather, who make life such a pleasure.

Abbreviations

AHG	Archives historiques du Ministère de la Guerre
AN	Archives nationales
APP	Archives de la Préfecture de Police
BN	Bibliothèque nationale
DM	Division militaire
(G)OC	(General) officer commanding
jp	juge de paix
MI	Minister of the Interior
MJ	Minister of Justice
NLW	National Library of Wales
PG	Procureur général
PI	Procureur impérial
PR	Procureur de la république
TP	Travaux publics

Introduction

This is a book about a major historical figure, Napoleon III, and about a political regime – the French Second Empire. It is a book both about great figures in history and the contexts, the political institutions and social networks, within which they were located. It is a study of the exercise of power, of the institutions of the state and the mechanisms through which these interacted with the enveloping society. Part I examines the circumstances which made it possible for Louis-Napoleon Bonaparte to secure election as president of the Republic and subsequently to launch a *coup d'état*, as the prelude to an Imperial restoration. Historians have frequently presented this Second Empire as a political drama in two acts – authoritarian and liberal – focusing on high politics and the character of Napoleon III.[1] The regime's ignoble origins in a *coup d'état* and the tragedy of its final ignominious collapse in the war of 1870 have loomed large. At first the dominant trend, as republicans struggled to secure the Third Republic, was one of bitter hostility. The combination of a carefully researched political narrative with moral indignation – the construction of the 'black' legend – was exemplified by Eugène Ténot's studies of the *coup d'état*, published even before the empire had disappeared. By the 1930s and 1940s the Second Empire was described as a precursor of fascism. However, more positive assessments were also beginning to appear. Thus, from the inter-war years of the twentieth century and during the period of reconstruction which followed the devastation of the Second World War, historians' interests shifted to reflect a concern with French 'backwardness' and 'stagnation'. They looked for inspiration to the Imperial regime's 'technocratic' achievements and particularly the reconstruction of Paris, the creation of a modern transportation infrastructure, and, more broadly, the establishment of the conditions for rapid economic growth. This 'revisionism' culminated in 1990 in

[1] On the historiography see S. Campbell, *The Second Empire Revisited. A Study in French Historiography* (London 1978).

I

the publication of *Louis-Napoléon le Grand* written by the conservative politician Philippe Séguin, a work inspired by the search for a populist politics capable of attracting disillusioned voters from both the far right Front National and the socialist and communist left. On 13 June 1990 Séguin, at the inauguration of the Place Napoléon III in Paris and flanked by Jacques Chirac – then the city's mayor – and the Prince Napoleon, insisted that the much-disparaged Emperor had indeed been a great head of state.[2]

Narrative political history has served as an important means of understanding the period. Historians have repeatedly described the regime's growing political difficulties and the exhaustion and increasing irresolution of the Emperor. The seemingly inexorable rise of opposition has appeared to offer a clear linear vision of inevitable collapse. This perspective, however, underestimates the very real problems of regime transition once its leading figure had taken the decision to adapt to changing political circumstances through liberalisation. Moreover, whilst the study of political leadership is undoubtedly of crucial importance, so too are questions about the nature of social and political systems. Thus a more thematic, analytical approach also has its attractions. If the objectives political leaders set for themselves need to be identified, so also does the context within which they operate. Social structures and relationships, both formal and informal, regulate the ways in which political authority can be exercised, and influence the creation of a more diffuse political culture. Various factors serve to reinforce or to restrict the authority of governments. Our knowledge of the period has been enlarged considerably by social historians working at the level of the community and region. The 'top-down' vision associated with a traditional political history has been neatly supplemented by 'bottom-up' perspectives much more concerned with the experience of the rural and urban masses.

Governmental effectiveness depends in part on institutional design but additionally on personal and political relationships, on economic and social circumstances, and frequently on the impact of largely uncontrollable external events. It should be borne in mind also that governments are far from being unitary enterprises, but are frequently riven by internal rivalries which affect their capacity to define and achieve their objectives. The debate on the nature of the Second Empire, and indeed on the state in general, continues to be informed by the contribution of Karl Marx.

[2] R. Gildea, *The Past in French History* (London 1994), pp. 88–9.

In *The Manifesto of the Communist Party* he contended that 'the executive of the modern state is but a committee for managing the common affairs of the whole bourgeoisie'. It was the product of class rule at a particular stage of social development. His stress on the repressive role of the state was supplemented by an insistence on the state's employment of religion and patriotism, and on its recourse to war, as a means of reinforcing its position – an emphasis foreshadowing Gramsci's notion of hegemony. Louis-Napoleon Bonaparte's seizure of power caused problems for Marx.[3] It represented an apparent renunciation of power by the 'ruling classes' and a step back from bourgeois liberalism to absolute monarchy, to a situation in which 'the executive power with a host of officials numbering half a million, besides an army of another half a million, [an] appalling parasitic body ... enmeshes the body of French society like a net and chokes all its pores.'[4] The state had apparently achieved autonomy. However, this contradiction could be resolved by stressing that the state continued to favour the interests of some social groups rather than others. It remained the guarantor of the established social order. Marx assumed that in the longer term state policy had to remain compatible with the interests of economically and socially powerful interest groups and particularly of those from which ministers, bureaucrats, and army officers were recruited.[5] Part II will shed light on these issues by focusing on the machinery of state, on the personnel involved, on policy formulation and upon its impact. Its primary concern will be with state–society relations but viewed from the perspective of the state. Its concerns will include some of the central issues of socio-political history including the identity of those individuals and social groups enjoying privileged access to the state apparatus. After all, to a large extent 'the action of the state as an institution depends ... on the people who direct it.'[6] The first chapter will examine the institutions of the Second Empire and the roles of the Emperor himself, of his courtiers, ministers, and officials. Succeeding chapters will consider the practical workings of the machinery of government in four crucial areas – electoral management; the preservation of public order; the establishment of 'moral order;' and the creation of the conditions for socio-economic modernisation and public prosperity. They will consider the means by which state agencies sought to

---

[3] A. Gilbert, *Marx's Politics* (Oxford 1981), pp. 220f.

[4] K. Marx, *The Eighteenth Brumaire of Louis Bonaparte* in *Marx-Engels Selected Works*, 1 (Moscow 1962), p. 284.

[5] *Ibid.*, pp. 340–1.

[6] P. Birnbaum, *The Heights of Power. An Essay on the Power Elite in France* (London 1982), p. 1.

legitimise their authority and how effective they were in penetrating societies combining *archaïsme et modernité* (Corbin) and in achieving their goals.

Awareness of context is all important. The rulers of a nineteenth-century authoritarian state could deal harshly with opponents, but were neither willing nor able to engage in the forms of extreme and sustained brutality which were employed to ensure compliance during the twentieth century. Whilst those who had shared political power during the Restoration and July Monarchy might be willing to accept a temporary dictatorship at a time of extreme crisis, in the fashion of the Roman Republic with whose history these classically educated elites were so familiar, in the longer term they would favour a return to 'normal' and a renewed fragmentation of political power. In effect the boundaries to state action were defined partly by power centres – social groups, political alliances, institutional bodies – capable of political organisation. Stability depended upon accommodating their special interests. As a result of the introduction of manhood suffrage, greater attention than hitherto also had to be given to the concerns of socially subordinate groups, to the small businessmen, professionals, peasants, and workers, all increasingly anxious to influence state policy. Indeed, one of the central questions to be considered will be the degree to which these various groups might have lost or benefited from changes in the (unequal) balance of power. Another concern will be the ways in which state power impinged upon the various groups and how they perceived its diverse activities – as class oppression or as the benign exercise of authority. How would people react, not only to governmental activity, but also to social change on a previously unimagined scale? Whilst continuities with the past will need to be stressed, contemporaries could hardly fail to be aware of the tearing down and reconstruction of city centres, of the railway lines and telegraph wires extending their tentacles across the landscape, affecting the capacity of the government machine to penetrate society, and creating new opportunities for enrichment albeit within a far more competitive environment. More than ever before people were on the move in search of a better life. What were the relationships between economic and social change, the 'formal' establishment of manhood suffrage, and the evolution of local and national political cultures? Certainly historically based expectations conditioned individual political behaviour to a large degree. The Second Empire is of particular interest, however, because in a relatively short time radical changes in economic structures and political institutions forced people to adapt their life strategies.

The primary responsibility of every political regime is the maintenance of order. However, definitions of what constitutes 'order' and the systems constructed and methods employed to achieve this objective will vary both between regimes and, in the case of the same regime, over time, as situations and personnel change. Political repression can be regarded as a 'normal' feature of governmental activity although its intensity and form vary with both perceptions of the threats posed as well as the capacity of the administration to conduct 'police' measures. The 1848 Revolution led to increasingly intense counter-revolutionary repression. Most regimes would, however, probably prefer to exercise power through consensus-inducing forms of social control with a clearly defined moral and legal basis. This explains the importance of securing cultural hegemony through the religious or educational institutions which provide means of socialisation, designed to induce conformity to essentially conservative norms. In this context, both the criteria employed for defining potential threats and ensuing policy decisions – as between repression or concession – tell us a great deal about a regime and its relationships with the wider society. During the Second Empire the state also assumed a far more substantial economic role than its predecessors. The Emperor was determined to promote modernisation along the lines suggested by the British model. How did this perceived need to promote economic development affect the regime's agenda?

Another distinctive feature of the regime was its capacity for adaptation. Inevitably, in a society which remained profoundly inegalitarian, the scope for political mobilisation varied considerably. The Emperor's freedom of action varied to an important degree according to the willingness of elites to accept his dominant position. Efforts to reinforce his authority and appeal over their heads to the 'sovereign people,' employing such devices as the plebiscite and electoral manipulation, enjoyed only limited success. As a result some degree of agreement with, as well as substantial cohesion within the political elite, would appear to be a prerequisite for effective state action. Unlike his predecessors, Napoleon III was prepared to contemplate adapting to circumstances. Liberalisation and the institutionalisation of protest could be seen as representing either the creation of a slippery slope towards regime collapse, or else an effective method of moderating opposition and of more effectively ensuring long-term stability. The transition from an authoritarian to a liberal regime was to be fraught with difficulties. To what extent did it involve concessions freely made, and to what extent was it a response to growing pressure and the rise of opposition? To what extent did liberalisation occur as the result of competition for power between rival elite groups and to what extent did it represent a challenge, from below, to the established social order? These questions will be at the heart of Part II and also of Part III, which concentrates on the rise of opposition. The final section (Part IV) will bring some of these threads together by means of an analysis of the interaction between internal and external politics and of the causes of military defeat and the regime's rapid collapse.

The sources for this book are many and varied, and all of them have their shortcomings. An effort has been made to consult as wide a range of sources as possible, including private papers, memoirs, administrative reports, official and private economic and social enquiries, and the newspaper press. A massive amount of information was gathered by more or less zealous and competent officials operating within the various administrative hierarchies (especially those reporting to the Ministers of the Interior, Justice, and War). Complaints about the quality of reports were frequent. There was especial concern about the unwillingness of those at the bottom of the hierarchy – mayors, justices of the peace, and gendarmes – to spare the time and effort. As always, the directly expressed views of the masses are greatly under-represented. Much of the extant information on these groups is derived from the observations of members of other social groups and is distorted inevitably by their particular concerns and prejudices. Reporters from the social elites tended to focus in particular on novelty and whatever appeared to be threatening to their interests. Government officials frequently told their superiors what it was presumed these wanted to hear, in the hope of enhancing their own career prospects. The quality of reporting obviously varied according to the skills and commitment of individual reporters. Experience suggests that the recruitment, training, and professional concerns of the judicial administration resulted in more objective and frequently more comprehensive reports than those emanating from the parallel prefectoral hierarchy. If this book has a claim on the reader, it will be based on the exceptionally wide range of primary and secondary sources employed – in critical fashion – as well as on the complex of questions raised. I hope that it adds up to a well-informed and searching study of the historical role of the Emperor Napoleon III, of the workings of the French state, and of the inter-relationships between state and society during an important period of political and social 'modernisation'.

PART I

The rise of Louis-Napoleon Bonaparte

CHAPTER I

President of the Republic

MID-CENTURY CRISIS

In the preface to *The Eighteenth Brumaire of Louis-Napoleon Bonaparte*, Karl Marx described his purpose as being to 'demonstrate how the class struggle in France created circumstances and relationships that made it possible for a grotesque mediocrity to play a hero's part'. Alexis de Tocqueville similarly insisted that 'a dwarf on the summit of a great wave is able to scale a high cliff which a giant placed on dry ground at the base would not be able to climb'. The 'great wave' was the intense mid-century crisis – economic, social, and political – lasting from 1845 until 1852, and marked by widespread popular protest, revolution, civil war, and the prospect (or threat) of a démocrate-socialiste electoral victory in 1852. These were the circumstances – widespread deprivation and misery combined with disappointed expectations and social fear – that made it possible for the nephew of Napoleon I to exploit the potency of the Bonapartist legend – 'this deplorable prestige of a name' which, according to the exiled republican Victor Schoelcher, 'entirely made the incredible fortune of M. Bonaparte'[1] – by ensuring that large sections of the population were tempted to look for a 'saviour'.

At the middle point of the nineteenth century France might be defined as a transition society. Substantial continuities with the past survived. The economy remained predominantly agrarian. Within the manufacturing sector most workers were employed, using hand tools, in small-scale enterprise. However, there were clear signs of structural change, most notably with the development of growth 'poles' characterised by advanced, large-scale industrialisation and, from the 1830s to 1840s, the broader development of an industrial economy as coal and steam power came

---

[1] Marx, *Eighteenth Brumaire*, p. 244; A. de Tocqueville, letter to Beaumont, 29 Jan. 1851 in *Oeuvres complètes* (Paris 1959), vol. VIII, p. 369; V. Schoelcher, *Histoire des crimes du deux décembre* (London 1852), p. 402.

to replace wood and water as the primary sources of energy and power, and the first railways were added to the developing road and waterway networks. Appreciating that this was a world in flux is vital to an understanding of the complex and intense nature of the economic difficulties, which from 1845 to 1847 combined the features of a traditional subsistence crisis with those of over-production/under-consumption and loss of confidence in financial markets more typical of an industrial society, as well as the fears and aspirations which informed political activity.[2]

To most informed observers the July Monarchy, created by the 1830 Revolution, had seemed secure. The various oppositions, ranging from the Legitimist supporters of another Bourbon restoration on the right, to the republicans on the left, were weak and divided. The regime's leading personalities insisted on the finality of 1830. Personalities were all important in the absence of a stable party system. Alexis de Tocqueville likened the July Monarchy to an 'industrial company all of whose operations are designed to benefit the shareholders'.[3] The historian A.-J. Tudesq has defined a social elite, of men with national power, made up of *grands notables* each paying over 1,000f a year in direct taxes (in 1840) and including landowners (65.3%); bureaucrats (11.7%); liberal professions (5.9%); and businessmen (15.9%).[4] These groups shared similar lifestyles and belonged to the same or contiguous social networks. In whatever way they are categorised, most members of this social elite possessed land as a source of both income and status, had received a similar classical education and a grounding in the law, and had served the state at some stage in their lives. Virtually all were anxious to share in lucrative new investment opportunities. Candidates for election to the Chamber of Deputies were wealthy – paying at least 500f in taxes, whilst voters, contributing 200f, were at least moderately well off. There were roughly 250,000 of them by 1846. If debate in the cities with their large electorates was politicised, in rural areas a small electorate resulted in highly personalised electoral campaigns dominated by the competition for power and status between a few wealthy families and their clienteles.[5] This was an elite possessing power through control of the institutions of state, and by means of the

[2] R. Price, *An Economic History of Modern France, c. 1730–1914* (London 1981) and *A Social History of Nineteenth Century France* (London 1987), ch. 1.

[3] A. de Tocqueville, *Souvenirs* (Paris 1964), p. 79.

[4] A.-J. Tudesq, *Les grands notables en France (1840–49): Etude historique d'une psychologie sociale* (Paris 1964), I, p. 429.

[5] *Ibid.* p. 365f ; T. D. Beck, *French Legislators* (Berkeley, Calif. 1974), p. 127.

local social and economic power conferred by the ownership of property and control of access to employment and scarce resources. They supported a regime which had appeared fully committed to maintaining social order and the conditions for continuing prosperity.

The regime's most articulate critics were drawn from the ranks of the so-called 'dynastic' opposition. Although they proclaimed their loyalty to their king, opposition politicians returned to the language of 1789 to attack the dominant *aristocratie bourgeoise*. Former ministers, like Adolphe Thiers, condemned the corruption of the parliamentary process through the abuse of government influence in elections and, particularly following the opposition's dismal failure in 1846, sought to change the rules of the electoral game through franchise reform. The objective was certainly not to enfranchise the masses which, liberal politicians agreed, would lead to anarchy, but rather the wider enfranchisement of the educated, property-owning middle classes. The government was associated with scandals in high places, electoral corruption, and the use of patronage to control deputies. It was blamed for the economic crisis and for the widespread popular protest, which suggested that the authorities were unable to safeguard public order. The corrosive impact of competition for power amongst the landowners, financiers, senior civil servants, and wealthy professionals who made up the political elite was thus reinforced by the concerns of businessmen faced with bankruptcy, workers threatened with unemployment, and the mass of urban and rural consumers faced with the spiralling cost of food. The image of prosperity and order cultivated by the July Monarchy was shattered. Political agitation multiplied.[6]

It would culminate on 22–24 February 1848 in a demonstration in Paris which, as a result of ineffective government crisis management and military incompetence, turned into an insurrection and finally a revolution with the establishment of a Second Republic. To their own great surprise a small group of republicans had been able to take advantage of governmental collapse and to assume power. It was then that their problems really began. The sense of expectancy amongst the crowds in Paris ensured that even these cautious men felt bound to take such decisive steps as the introduction of manhood suffrage, conceived of as 'universal' because of contemporary assumptions that by their nature women were unsuited to roles in public life and were thus best represented by their

---

[6] H. Collingham, *The July Monarchy: A Political History of France* (London 1988), pp. 398–402; J. Gilmore, *La République clandestine* (Paris 1992), pp. 302–15.

men folk.[7] The economic situation remained desperate. A plentiful harvest in 1847 had stimulated recovery when, as a result of the revolution, 'confidence disappeared and work with it'.[8] The financial system was thrown into chaos as banks suspended payments and interest rates rose.[9] In Paris unemployment rose to around 54 per cent of the work force, reaching 64 per cent in the building trades and 74 per cent in furniture manufacture.[10] In Lyons up to three-quarters of silk looms remained idle.[11] National Workshops were established. Intended by the government merely as a means of offering temporary work-relief, they were seen by many radicals as the first step in a socialist re-organisation of society. In agriculture, in place of poor harvests and high prices, almost the whole period from 1848 to 1851 was to be characterised by substantial harvests of grain and wine, over-supply of markets, and the collapse of prices, creating a particularly serious situation for the numerous farmers who had incurred debts: whether to purchase land or survive the earlier crisis. The sense of malaise was almost universal.

The introduction of manhood suffrage, which at a stroke increased the electorate from 250,000 to close on 10 million, was the realisation of a dream for radicals. For the first time the entire male population of a major European state would be able to vote, to elect a Constituent Assembly. How would the masses use their new-found political power? Their political education proceeded apace in the host of newspapers, political clubs, and workers' associations created to take advantage of the new freedom. These were only the institutionalised expression of a ferment which spread into the streets and cafés. Probably only a minority of workers and peasants conceived of politics in terms of a formulated ideology. Particularly in the major cities, slogans in favour of the 'organisation of work' and the République démocratique et sociale were popular, representing the demand for state assistance in the creation of a network of producers' co-operatives to replace capitalist exploitation. The discourse in Parisian clubs like Blanqui's Société républicaine

---

[7] See e.g. A. Verjus, 'Le suffrage universel, le chef de famille et la question de l'exclusion des femmes en 1848' in A. Corbin, J. Lalouette, and M. Riot-Sarcy (eds.), *Femmes dans la cité* (Paris 1997), pp. 401–7.

[8] Chambre consultative de Roubaix, AN F12/7600.

[9] See e.g. Ministre de Finance to Ministre de l'agriculture et du commerce, 16 Oct.1848, AN F12/7600.

[10] Paris Chambre de Commerce, *Statistique de l'industrie à Paris résultant de l'enquête faite ... pour les années 1847–48* (1851), I, p. 41; 16 June 1848 in AN F12/7600; see also Comité des constructeurs mécaniciens, 12 July 1848 in AN F12/2337–8.

[11] M.-L. Stewart-McDougall, *Artisan Kingdom: Revolution, Reaction and Resistance in Lyon, 1848–51* (Gloucester 1984), p. 58.

centrale or Barbès' Club de la révolution was frequently extreme. The latter's manifesto announced that 'we have the Republic in name only, we need the real thing. Political reform is only the instrument of social reform.'[12] The propertied classes were terrified, afraid that granting the vote to the propertiless would lead to the re-distribution of property. They feared anarchy, a blood-bath worse than the Terror of 1793. Alexis de Tocqueville was concerned about the impact of enfranchising a population characterised by its 'prodigious ignorance' and the challenge to the authority of established elites this represented.[13] Social fear helped create a sense of common interest, a sort of 'class consciousness' amongst notables, particularly in the cities and their hinterlands, where the threat appeared greatest. Democrats were to be disappointed. In the absence of organised parties the choice of candidates in most areas, and especially in rural constituencies, remained dependent on the activities of small groups of politically experienced notables. Conservative organisation and propaganda were better resourced and more effective.[14] Most of the deputies elected on 23 April – perhaps 600 out of 900 – were to be conservatives, and former monarchists, even if, reflecting a continuing crisis of confidence, they adopted the republican label. Around 300 appear to have been republicans before the revolution and only 70 or 80 would reveal a clear sympathy for measures of social reform. This was an assembly made up mainly of well-off provincial notables – landowners and professional men determined to resist the pressure of the Parisian 'mob.'

Inevitably the election results caused great dissatisfaction amongst urban radicals. They felt betrayed by the votes of those they saw as ignorant and priest-ridden peasants. In Paris itself, on 15 May, a mass demonstration in favour of social reform and support for the Polish rebels against Russian rule, which would of course have provoked a general European war, culminated in the chaotic invasion of the Assembly's meeting place and the call for a committee of public safety to levy a wealth tax to finance the immediate creation of producers' co-operatives. This strengthened the government's determination to restore order and was followed by the arrest of such luminaries of the left as Blanqui and Barbès and the closure of some political clubs.[15] According to Tocqueville, 'an

---

[12] Quoted by P. Bastid, *Doctrines et institutions politiques de la Seconde République* (Paris 1945), II, p. 168.

[13] Letter to Nassau William Senior, 10 April 1848, in *Oeuvres complètes*, VI (1991), p. 101.

[14] E.g. M. Bernard, 'Les populations du Puy-de-Dôme face à la nouvelle république', *Cahiers d'histoire*, 1998, pp. 207–8.

[15] M. Traugott, *Armies of the Poor. Determinants of Working-Class Participation in the Parisian Insurrection of June 1848* (Princeton 1985), pp. 24–5.

indescribable disappointment, terror and anger seized the Assembly and the nation'.[16] The National Workshops, which to radicals symbolised the hope of a better world, for conservatives increasingly came to represent the threat of renewed revolution. Men, unable to find work because of the economic crisis, were constantly denounced as 'scroungers'.[17] Thiers warned that by denying the principles of 'property, freedom of labour, emulation [and] competition' the association of workers would inevitably lead to communism and slavery.[18] On 22 June their closure was announced. They had provided work for around 117,000 workers, with a further 50,000 awaiting entry.[19] The announcement was followed by another mass insurrection. Over a thousand barricades were constructed throughout the densely populated and impoverished eastern *quartiers* of the capital. Estimates vary, but a substantial number of men and women (perhaps 20,000 to 30,000) felt sufficiently disappointed with the outcome of the revolution to risk their lives – with varying degrees of commitment and enthusiasm – to establish a regime more responsive to their needs. They believed they were fighting for justice, in defence of the République démocratique et sociale which they were convinced would transform their lives, against its 'monarchist' enemies.[20] These were not the rootless vagabonds so beloved of conservative publicists but mostly skilled workers, well integrated into their craft and neighbourhood communities. Against them were ranged the forces of 'order,' including National Guards from the wealthier western *quartiers* and members of the Mobile Guard recruited from amongst young, unemployed workers for whom institutional loyalties appear to have outweighed those of class.[21] The most important role in combating the insurrection was played by the 37,000 men of the regular army, commanded by the republican General Cavaignac, which became in the eyes of the propertied classes the 'saviour of civilisation'. Subsequently there were 12,000 arrests. The Parisian left was to be decapitated for a generation.

The conservative press depicted the events as an outbreak of mindless savagery, as a rising fought for 'pillage and rape'. The initial cry of triumph at the 'victory gained by the cause of order, of the family, of humanity, of civilisation' (*Journal des Débats*, 1 July) was followed by demands from conservatives and many traumatised moderate republicans for

---

[16] *Souvenirs*, p. 115.   [17] *L'Assemblée nationale*, 17 May 1848.

[18] Quoted Traugott, *Armies*, p. 149.

[19] Prefect of Police reports of 23 May, 12 June 1848, AN C930.

[20] Price, *The French Second Republic. A Social History* (London 1972), pp. 162f.

[21] Letter from E. Foulquier delegate of *club des clubs* to Garde Mobile in AN C940; Traugott, *Armies*, pp. 44–5; Price, *Second Republic*, p. 185.

sustained repression (*Le National*, 29 June). For the latter the insurrection had represented an intolerable attack on popular sovereignty represented by the Constituent National Assembly. The brutal crushing of the June insurrection was thus to be followed by a long period of increasingly intense political repression, first under the republican government headed by Cavaignac. Existing legislation, in abeyance since February, could be used to eliminate or restrict the activities of political clubs, workers' associations, and the press. New measures were also introduced. Public meetings were subject to prior authorisation. Police officers could halt any discussion 'contrary to public order'. Censorship was imposed on newspapers. Having alienated many of their supporters on the left, the ruling moderate republicans more than ever were determined to prove their commitment to social order. Nevertheless, they were regarded as too moderate by conservatives, for whom republican institutions had been discredited irreparably.[22] On 4 November the Constituent Assembly approved a constitution for an essentially liberal democratic republic bereft of welfare institutions. Nevertheless, the retention of 'universal suffrage' ensured the continuation of political agitation, providing some hope to supporters of social reform and maintaining high levels of anxiety amongst conservatives. Significantly the constitution also provided for the election of a president, ultimately responsible to the elected assembly, but nevertheless provided with substantial executive power, in the interests of social order.[23]

THE ELECTION OF A PRINCE-PRESIDENT

On receiving news of the February Revolution, Louis-Napoleon Bonaparte, still in exile in London, had announced to his cousin Marie that 'I'm going to Paris, the Republic has been proclaimed. I must be its master', only to be told that 'You are dreaming, as usual'.[24] Arriving in Paris on 28 February he was immediately expelled by the republican authorities. Nevertheless, in by-elections held on 4 June, and without the support of a single important newspaper, he was elected as a deputy in the departments of the Seine, Yonne, Charente-Inférieure, and Corsica, to the amazement of the political elite. Louis-Napoleon was the beneficiary of a sentimental cult of Napoleon kept alive by an outpouring of books,

---

[22] See e.g. letter from M. Marc to Benoist d'Azy, 2 July in R. Locke, *Les fonderies et forges d'Alais à l'époque des premiers chemins de fer* (Paris 1978), p. 145; Bugeaud to Thiers, 29 June in BN naf 20617.

[23] E.g. J.-Y. Mollier, 'De l'orléanisme à la République conservatrice, la volonté de pouvoir de M. Thiers' in M. Agulhon *et al.*, *Monsieur Thiers d'une république à l'autre* (Paris 1998), p. 25.

[24] L. Girard, *Napoléon III* (Paris 1986), p. 83.

pamphlets, plays, songs, the lithographs which decorated so many poor homes, and, perhaps most potently, the stories told by old soldiers keeping alive the myth of a more prosperous, happy, and glorious epoch in sharp contrast to the misery and strife which appeared to accompany the Republic.[25] He had assumed the role of Bonapartist pretender following the death in 1832 of the Duc de Reichstadt, son of Napoleon I and Maria-Louisa. His claims had been reinforced through otherwise farcical attempts to seize power at Strasbourg in 1836 and at Boulogne in 1840. In 1839 he had presented his *Idées Napoléoniennes* in a pamphlet, which would sell half a million copies by 1848. In it Louis-Napoleon insisted that

the Napoleonic idea is not an idea of war but a social idea – an industrial, commercial, humanitarian idea. If to some men it always seems to be surrounded by the thunder of combat, this is because indeed it was enveloped for too long in the smoke of cannon and the dust of battle. But today the clouds have vanished, and one can see beyond the glory of arms a civil glory which was greater and more lasting.

Imprisonment in the fortress of Ham gave him time to produce a work on *L'Extinction du paupérisme* (1844), which with its vague promises of social reform again attracted considerable interest. The year 1848 would give him the opportunity to realise the 'destiny' in which he so firmly believed.

Louis-Napoleon's electoral success stimulated a further explosion of Bonapartist sentiment. Unwilling to be associated with the growing tension and disorder in Paris, however, he resigned and returned to London, a move which coincidentally ensured that he was able to avoid compromising himself during the June insurrection.[26] He was easily re-elected anyway in five departments on 18 September. Increasingly it was becoming evident that, as a candidate for the presidency, Bonaparte was likely to attract considerable support. Tocqueville commented on the strange and disturbing procedure by which 'in the degree to which the popular movement pronounces itself in favour of Louis-Napoleon, it drags along the parliamentary leaders ... Thiers began by being violently opposed, then violently in favour. The Legitimists will hesitate until the last. Most will finish by giving way to the torrent; the tail of society definitely leads the head.'[27] Unable themselves, because of personal and ideological

[25] See e.g. B. Ménager, 'La vie politique dans le département du Nord de 1851 à 1877', Doctorat d'Etat, Université de Paris IV (1979), I, pp. 81–2.

[26] A fact on which he congratulated himself in a letter to his friend Mme. Cornu on 30 June 1848 – in AN 400 AP 41.

[27] *Souvenirs*, p. 279.

differences, to agree on a candidate likely to defeat him, conservative politicians were increasingly, even if reluctantly, drawn towards an opportunistic and qualified adherence. Bonaparte appeared to be fully committed to the restoration of order and was even prepared to promise to re-establish the temporal power of the Pope, expelled by revolution from Rome, as a means of winning over Catholic leaders.[28] Moreover, for conservatives like Molé, Barrot, and most notably Thiers, as a result of his ineffective performance in parliamentary debate and reputation as a womaniser, Louis-Napoleon appeared to be weak, a clown they could use. Marshal Bugeaud's warning to Thiers that the peasants would be voting not for a president but for an emperor went unheeded.[29] The conservative caucus gathering in the rue de Poitiers appears to have reached an unanimous decision to support Bonaparte on 4 November.[31] The only real alternative was Cavaignac. He had proved his commitment to social order in June and would attract some conservative support. However, as the former prime minister Guizot declared, 'Cavaignac is the Republic, Louis-Napoleon is a step away from the Republic.'[31] For many republicans Cavaignac was the 'butcher of June', whilst the great Emperor had defended the work of the revolution and enhanced the glory of the nation.[32] This was the strength of Bonapartism – to be able to appear as 'all things to all men', as a credo above party struggles. One Bonapartist manifesto appealed to suffering France where:

The unfortunate die of hunger;
The worker is without work;
The cultivator is no longer able to dispose of his crops;
The merchant sells nothing;
The proprietor no longer receives his rents;
The capitalist no longer dares to invest, lacking security

and promised that 'The nephew of the great man, with his magic, will give us security, and save us from misery.'[33]

Louis-Napoleon's electoral victory in December 1848 was to be overwhelming (see table 1).[34] Even Thiers had to admit that, if the candidate

[28] E. Beau de Lomenie, 'L'arrivée de Louis-Napoléon au pouvoir' in *L'esprit de 1848* (Paris 1948), p. 207.
[29] Letter of 4 Nov. 1848, BN naf 20617.   [30] *Gazette de France*, 5 Nov. 1848.
[31] Quoted G. de Broglie, *Guizot* (Paris 1990), p. 397.
[32] See e.g. G. Duveau, *La vie ouvrière en France sous le Second Empire* (Paris 1946), p. 56; and P. Goujon, 'Les révélations du suffrage universel: comportements électoraux et politisation des populations de Saône-et-Loire sous la Seconde République', *Cahiers d'histoire* (1998), pp. 279–80.
[33] Enclosed with report from PG Metz, 1 Dec. 1848 in AN BB18/1471.
[34] Price, *Second Republic*, pp. 208–25.

Table 1. *Presidential election, 10 December 1848*

Candidate	Votes	Share (%)
Bonaparte	5,534,520	74.2
Cavaignac	1,448,302	19.5

he had supported had been only the 'least bad' alternative, he had shown that in spite of his inexperience he was well informed and not unintelligent.[35]

In Paris Louis-Napoleon gained 58 per cent of the vote, in Lyon 62 per cent. Support for the author of the supposedly socialist *Extinction du paupérisme* was highest in the popular *quartiers* where before and even during the June Days there had been plenty of evidence of popular Bonapartist sentiment.[36] However, it was peasant support which was to remain the basis of Bonaparte's electoral strength for decades to come. According to Marx this was 'the day of the peasant insurrection',[37] and represented both a vote against the republic, which had brought tax increases instead of prosperity, and for the man of providence whose election heralded a better future. Paradoxically, whilst notables supported Bonaparte as the guarantor of social order, in some regions – especially in the south of the Paris basin, the Alps and departments in the centre like Creuse and Puy-de-Dôme – existing social tensions ensured that the peasant vote represented a questioning of the authority of these very notables. The prefect of the Isère concluded that 'for the first time, the rural vote has entered politics with its own will. Henceforth the rural element will have its full weight in the political movements of our society.'[38] According to the socialist writer Proudhon: 'France has named Louis Bonaparte President of the Republic because she is tired of parties.'[39] The Austrian diplomat Apponyi told conservative leaders that, in this situation, 'if they believe themselves able to do anything with him and to dominate him, they are badly mistaken'.[40] More dramatically, the journalist Martinelli warned that 'whether you wish it or not', Bonaparte would be 'king in opinion first, and later in reality. The logic of facts

---

[35] Letter of 3 Dec. 1848, AN AB XIX 3321.   [36] Police report, 21 June, AN C930.
[37] 'Class struggles in France', *Selected Works*, p. 173.
[38] Quoted P. Vigier, *La Seconde République dans la région alpine* (Paris 1953), I, p. 57.
[39] P.-J. Proudhon, *Les confessions d'un révolutionnaire* (Paris 1929), p. 277.
[40] R. Apponyi, *De la révolution au coup d'état* (Geneva 1948), p. 68.

leads there. In a review some regiments will cry: *Vive l'Empereur*! The suburbs will reply to them and all will be said; we will be just like Spanish
America, subordinate to the pleasures of the multitude and the soldiery.
A glorious and fortunate destiny!'[41] This unique election of a monarchical pretender, of a man with complete faith in his historical 'mission'
and, once having gained power, determined to retain it, had made a *coup
d'état* almost inevitable.

This was the point at which the construction of 'the political system
of Napoleon III' (Zeldin) might be said to have commenced. In the
immediate aftermath of his election, however, the new president's
behaviour was re-assuring. The appointment on 20 December 1848
of a ministry composed of monarchist notables led by Odilon Barrot,
with Léon Faucher at the key Ministry of the Interior and the Comte
de Falloux responsible for education, symbolised his commitment to
counter-revolution. The constitution was, however, ambiguous on the
question of ministerial responsibility. Barrot caused immediate offence
by holding meetings in the President's absence and by withholding
diplomatic despatches.[42] Gradually, and following a series of ministerial
crises, Bonaparte would, by 31 October 1849, replace those ministers
who saw themselves as primarily responsible to parliament with men
dependent on himself. In a message to the National Assembly justifying
his dismissal of the Barrot ministry Louis-Napoleon warned about the
danger represented by the 'old parties,' and insisted that a 'community
of ideas' between the President and his ministers was essential for
the effective conduct of government, concluding: 'A whole system
triumphed on 10 December, for the name of Napoleon is itself a
programme. At home it means order, authority, religion and the welfare
of the people; and abroad it means national self-respect. This policy,
which began with my election, I shall, with the support of the national
assembly and of the people, lead to its final triumph.'[43]

The Constituent Assembly elected the previous April had voted its
own dissolution on 29 January 1849. Its members were aware of their
growing political isolation and subject to pressure from the new government. In the elections, which followed on 13 May, the failure of
Bonapartist candidates – poorly organised, divided on strategy, and unacceptable to other conservatives – seemed to emphasise the President's
continued political weakness. However, especially in the provinces, the

[41] J. Martinelli, *Un mot sur la situation* (Bordeaux 1848), p. 26.
[42] Louis-Napoleon to Barrot n.d. but early 1849, AN 271 AP 4.
[43] *Compte rendu des séances de l'Assemblée nationale législative* (Paris 1849), III.

electoral campaign was far more politicised than that of April 1848. A clear right–left division emerged, between a reactionary conservatism and a radical republicanism, with the centre, the moderate republicans, squeezed in between. The real victors were conservatives, with some 500 successful candidates. They had been supported effectively by Faucher and his prefects as well as by the clergy. Many peasants accepted the conservative view that socialism was a threat to their property and to the renewal of prosperity. Contemporaries, however, were struck more by the success of 200 representatives of the démocrate-socialiste or Montagnard movement, the first attempt to create a 'modern' national party,' and incorporating both democrats like Ledru-Rollin and socialists determined to defend the Republic and work for genuine social reform. It was the social fear generated by this and continued démocrate-socialiste agitation, which eventually would provide Louis-Napoleon with circumstances propitious to his seizure of power.

Although the victories of the left compared badly with conservative successes, the latter were alarmed by such unexpected radical strength. Overall some 35 per cent of the votes had been cast for 'reds'. In the larger cities, support for the left survived amongst the lower middle classes and workers, groups which felt threatened by the development of commercial capitalism and inspired by the dreams of greater social justice. Even more alarming, voters in some parts of the supposedly 'incorruptible' and conservative countryside had also supported the left – in much of the Massif Central, the Alps, the Rhône-Saône corridor, and Alsace, with substantial minorities in the Midi.[44] In spite of their election victory conservative leaders were increasingly anxious, afraid that their mass support might eventually be eroded. Following by-election defeats in March 1850, they determined to change once again the rules of the political game. It was intolerable, according to the procureur-général at Rouen, that 'the communists [be offered] the possibility of becoming kings one day through the ballot. Society must not commit suicide.'[45] In May 1850 a new electoral law removed around one-third of the poorest voters from the rolls, with much higher proportions in the larger cities and industrial centres. In Paris the electorate was reduced from 225,192 to 80,894.[46] Adolphe Thiers saw this as the means by

[44] J. Bouillon, 'Les démocrates-socialistes aux élections de 1849', *Revue française de science politique*, 1956.
[45] 13 June 1850, AN BB30/334.
[46] R. Balland, 'De l'organisation à la restriction du suffrage universel en France' in J. Droz (ed.), *Réaction et suffrage universel en France et en Allemagne (1848–50)* (Paris, 1963).

which the 'vile multitude that has ... delivered over to every tyrant the liberty of every Republic' might be excluded from politics.[47] Significantly, however, Louis-Napoleon Bonaparte, elected President of the Republic with massive popular support in December 1848, carefully distanced himself from this legislation.

Conservative leaders, listening to the presidential address to the Academy of Moral and Political Sciences in 1849, were reminded that the physical suppression of revolt was 'not enough'. It was necessary to 're-establish moral order to protect society and civilisation'.[48] Safety lay in punishing the wicked and in protecting those, the vast majority, who were simply weak and easily led astray. They had to be taught to respect a social hierarchy which reflected the natural and God-ordained fact that some people had more ability and moral strength than others. The task was difficult and would take time. Above all it depended on saving the younger generations through moral instruction.[49] The object of the 1833 Guizot law on primary education had been to internalise respect for social order. Now, in reaction against the proposals for free, universal, obligatory, and secular instruction previously prepared by the republican education minister Hippolyte Carnot, a committee chaired by Adolphe Thiers prepared legislation which would reinforce the dominant position of religion in the school curriculum. A notorious anticlerical, Thiers was determined to hand primary instruction over to the Roman Catholic church, accepting that it had become 'the great social rampart which must be defended at all costs'.[50]

The apparatus of the police state was also being constructed. Ever more intense action was directed at surviving left-wing newspapers and organisations. Prefects were instructed to implement the July 1849 law on clubs, in order 'to prohibit ... in an absolute manner any clubs or public meetings in which political affairs are discussed'. Relatively few political clubs had anyway survived the persecution beginning in June 1848. Political activists were harassed constantly.[51] Particular animosity was shown by the authorities towards *bourgeois* radicals perceived to be acting as 'class traitors.' Montagnard deputies were especially closely watched.

---

[47] Quoted J. Bury and R. Tombs, *Thiers, 1797–1877. A Political Life* (London 1986), p. 126.
[48] *Séances et travaux de l'Académie des sciences morales et politiques*, 16 (1849), p. 353.
[49] See e.g. Montalembert speech, 20 Sept. 1848, Assemblée nationale, *Compte rendu*, IV, p. 41.
[50] See G. Chenesseau (ed.), *La Commission extraparlementaire de 1849* (Orleans 1937), pp. 30–78; A. de Falloux, in Assemblée nationale, *Compte rendu*, I, 18 June 1849; Comte Beugnot, parliamentary *rapporteur*, 6 Oct. 1849, *ibid.*, II, p. 268.
[51] J. Merriman, *The Agony of the Republic: The Repression of the Left in Revolutionary France, 1848–51* (London 1978), p. 31.

When in November 1851 Martin Nadaud met between twenty and thirty *démocrates* in a café in Limoges, police spies were clearly present, and a subsequent meeting with 300 workers was dispersed quickly. In addition the homes of his known associates and those of friends and relatives were searched as part of a process by which his contacts were restricted and his influence undermined.[52] The attack on the press, so vital both as a means of propaganda and an organisational base, had begun after the June insurrection. Although censorship had not been re-introduced formally, it was an offence to attack the sacred principles of religion, the family, and property. The costs of publication were increased substantially by the re-establishment of caution money deposited to ensure that fines could be paid. The effect was to reduce the number of démocrate-socialiste newspapers. Between 12 December 1848 and the end of 1850, 335 court cases were heard against 185 republican newspapers. A local paper like *L'Egalité* of Auch (Gers) had its print run seized five times in four months (May–August 1849) for criticising the government or social system. In October it succumbed to the financial strain.[53] The distribution of the republican message through almanacs, pamphlets, and lithographs was obstructed similarly, with the peddlers who distributed this material throughout the countryside obliged to obtain licences and approval of their wares. Also under attack were the voluntary associations, which provided cover for illicit political activity. This policy drove even the more persistent activists into the back rooms of cafés and secret societies where, of course, their activities were more difficult to detect. The official response was the closure of suspect drinking places, which moreover offended against 'a moral code that rejects debauchery and protects family life'.[54] Songs, seditious shouts, the wearing of emblems like red scarves or dresses, the politicisation of funerals or traditional festivals were all prosecuted. Such acts as the symbolic execution at Vidauban (Var) of a dummy on Ash Wednesday 1850, a traditional means of expressing dissatisfaction with a member of a community, but which was now directed at the mayor and his Legitimist supporters, was followed by the arrest of those who in employing a guillotine had re-awakened memories of an earlier Terror. [55] These were the barbarians who threatened society.

The forms and effectiveness of repression reflected official perceptions of the danger, the efficiency of the agencies of repression, the scale of public support for police action, and the degree to which legal rights

[52] M. Nadaud, *Mémoires de Léonard* (Paris 1948).   [53] Merriman, *Agony*, p. 39.
[54] Prefect, 22 Jan. 1850, AN F1 cIII Gers 8.
[55] M. Agulhon, *The Republic in the Village* (Cambridge 1982), ch. 15.

were respected, as well as the left's own capacity for resistance. The future shape of opposition was determined by the surviving opportunities for political action, the manner in which local social networks and the means of mass communication facilitated organisation, the commitment and willingness of individual militants to risk prosecution, and the extent to which their propaganda inspired support. A social programme was presented, based upon a few simple, egalitarian slogans, which linked the solution of the pressing, day-to-day, problems faced by so many people to the political objectives of the démocrate-socialiste movement. As a means of escape from the burden of debt and the threat of expropriation, and of guaranteeing their dignity and independence, [56] peasants and artisans were promised cheap credit once the République démocratique et socialiste had been established and, together with propertiless workers, the right to work, free justice and education, and support for the establishment of producers' and consumers' co-operatives. These were the means of liberation offered to the *prolétariat*. Employment and the enjoyment of the fruits of one's labour were to be recognised as basic human rights. The appeal was to the *Peuple*, to the *Petits*, against the *gros* or the *blancs* – the Legitimists presented as partisans of a return to the *ancien régime*. An effort was made by the more moderate Montagnards to reassure the wealthy that their right to property would be respected. But clearly it was the *gros* who would pay for reform through progressive taxation, together with the nationalisation of the railways, canals, mines, and the insurance companies.[57] In the historical context this was a very radical programme. The ideal of a society of small, independent producers, that of the *sans-culottes* of 1793, was to be reconciled with a modern capitalistic economy.

Songs like the *Chant du départ* and the *Marseillaise* inherited from the first revolution along with new works like Pierre Dupont's *Chant du vote* or *Chant aux paysans* were especially effective means of inculcating slogans and diffusing a sense of unity. The first identified the democratic vote with the voice of God. Social justice was to be achieved through electoral victory in 1852.[58] Republican traditions were reinforced through appeals to the memory of the struggle against the aristocracy and the tyranny of kings. A sense of popular Jacobinism was revived, rich in symbols,

[56] See e.g. P. Jones, *Politics and Rural Society. The Southern Massif Central c. 1750–1880* (Cambridge 1985), pp. 318–22; P. Lévêque, 'Les campagnes françaises et la deuxième république. 50 ans d'historiographie', *Revue d'histoire du 19e siècle* (1997 / 1), pp. 83–4.

[57] See e.g. P. Dupont, E. Sue, and V. Schoelcher, *Le républicain des campagnes* (Paris 1849).

[58] P. McPhee, *The Politics of Rural Life: Political Mobilisation in the French Countryside, 1846–52* (Oxford 1992), p. 240; Price, *Second Republic*, pp. 264–5.

words, and images, in anniversaries and heroes. As repression intensified, weakening the démocrate-socialiste movement, it also encouraged a shift away from 'modern' electoral politics, from institutionalised protest, back to conspiratorial politics and the threat of violence. The more radical, although affirming in a confused and perhaps half-hearted fashion their confidence in victory in 1852, were impatient with a parliamentary system hijacked by conservative politicians. Some devoted themselves to the organisation of secret societies. They were willing to contemplate insurrection if the restrictions on voting rights were not lifted, or to head off a conservative or presidential *coup d'état*. They accepted that it might be necessary to vote with 'ballot in one hand and a gun in the other' in order to establish finally *la Vraie République*. Whatever their intentions, for many workers and peasants 1852 began to acquire millenarian overtones. The shouts of *vive la guillotine*, and songs and graffiti promising *vengeance finale* might have largely been bravado but the frequent brutality of popular language certainly frightened 'honest' citizens – all those with whom accounts might be settled finally in 1852. Where might this lead? Amongst conservatives an apocalyptic perspective of an eventual socialist electoral victory began to develop.

Recruited from the upper classes, senior officials and judges were certainly committed to the preservation of social order. As the president of the assizes at Montpellier pointed out in January 1849 the 'holy mission of the magistrate' was both to 'assure the reign of law [and] to defend ... the religion of our fathers, the family and property' against the assaults of anarchy and mad utopian dreams.[59] The concept of the rule of law, in these circumstances, effectively served to legitimise police activity. The larger towns with resident representatives of the central administration, commissaires de police, gendarmerie and usually military garrisons were relatively easy to control. However, there remained serious limits to the efficiency of political policing. These included legal procedures, which would not allow indefinite detention of suspects without reasonable evidence. Faucher's term as Minister of the Interior was brought to a premature end by parliamentary disquiet about his apparent contempt for legality and in spite of his welcome efforts to purge the administration and improve the policing of Paris.[60] Although efforts were made to select jurors carefully, on occasion they were unaccountably sympathetic towards those accused of political crimes. The numerical weakness of the

[59] Quoted J.-P. Royer, R. Martinage, and P. Lecocq, *Juges et notables au 19e siècle* (Paris 1982), p. 68.
[60] M. Papaud, 'La répression durant le ministère de Léon Faucher' in P. Vigier *et al.*, *Maintien de l'ordre et police en France et en Europe au 19e siècle* (Paris 1987), p. 100.

bureaucracy was another problem as was the frequent negligence, and even opposition, of subordinate officials, particularly the elected mayors of the numerous small towns and villages, who served as the key intermediaries between the state and community, controlling National Guard units and the village police. These amateur officials were often reluctant to 'betray' their neighbours and afraid of reprisals if they did. As a result, repressive legislation might not be implemented and higher authority could be starved of vital information. Frequent purges were necessary and illustrate the scale of the problem. Thus between 18 April 1849 and 20 February 1851 the Conseil d'Etat agreed to revoke 852 mayors and deputy-mayors and dissolved 276 municipal councils.[61]

Increasingly, the favoured solution to all these problems was the imposition of martial law. Thus, after disorders at Chalon (Saône-et-Loire) in May 1849 during which National Guards had remained inactive, the decision to disarm this force was followed by the deployment of 5,000 troops and a house-to-house search for arms. On the eve of the *coup d'état*, eight departments were already subject to martial law – five in the Lyon area, together with Ardèche, Nièvre, and Cher.[62] In most areas and particularly in Paris and Lyon, formerly the major centres of démocrate-socialiste activity, the level of coercion and the climate of fear it engendered were sufficient to ensure a substantial political demobilisation. Much of what remained was forced underground and rendered less effective. In the absence of a permanent organisational structure, the left fragmented. Yet it survived, particularly in relatively under-policed regions of the centre and south-east in which substantial mass support had previously been built up. In such regions the domiciliary searches and arbitrary arrests and the interference in communal affairs, which characterised sporadic police repression, were likely to provoke anger and encourage affiliation to secret societies.[63] As the 1852 legislative and presidential elections came closer, rumours of socialist plots abounded.

Conservative confidence was further threatened by the tension which continued to exist within the political elites. In spite of the death of Louis-Philippe in August 1850 and the likelihood that the childless Legitimist Pretender, the Comte de Chambord, would accept the late king's grandson as his heir, Legitimists and the more liberal Orleanists remained divided by personal loyalties and differing political and social programmes. When in March 1851 Adolphe Thiers suggested that the Orleanist Prince de Joinville stand for election to the presidency in 1852, the collective

---

[61] Merriman, *Agony*, p. 113.   [62] *Ibid.*, pp. 125–9.   [63] Price, *Second Republic*, pp. 266–8.

response of Louis-Philippe's sons was that they were unable to accept the terms proffered by the Legitimists and moderate republicans.[64] The well-informed English visitor Nassau William Senior recorded Tocqueville's despairing observation that 'everyone is plotting against everyone'. Although the constitution debarred him from a second term of office, the failure of royalist 'fusion' left Louis-Napoleon, as the incumbent president, in an increasingly strong position. The conservative factions, unable to agree on an alternative, were frightened increasingly by the prospect of a démocrate-socialiste electoral victory in 1852.[65] Thiers' correspondent and fellow-historian Mignet conceded that the prospect terrified everyone.[66] The *spectre rouge* was coming to seem very real. There was a growing willingness to accept ever more extreme measures to safeguard social order.

Bonaparte himself was determined not to hand over power with his historic 'mission,' the regeneration of France, unachieved. Carefully orchestrated provincial tours and Bonapartist propaganda sought to increase popular support. In a speech delivered at Dijon in May 1851 the president observed that

France neither wishes for a return to the old order of things, in no matter what form that may be disguised, nor for ventures into dangerous and impractical utopianism. It is because I am the most natural enemy of both these alternatives that France has given me its confidence .... Indeed if my government has not been able to bring about all the improvements it had in mind, that must be blamed on the devious conduct of the various factions. For three years ... I have always had the support of the Assembly when it has been a question of combating disorder by repressive measures. But, whenever I have wanted to do good and improve conditions for the people, the Assembly has denied me its support.'[67]

Most conservative deputies had come to favour revision of the constitution to allow Bonaparte a second term of office. However, when constitutional revision was approved by the National Assembly by 446 votes to 270 this fell short of the three-quarters majority required. The president was forced to conclude that he would have to mount a *coup d'état*. This is what many conservatives had come to desire. Odilon Barrot's son-in-law, Treilhard, confirmed that almost all his acquaintances, bankers and landowners – both noble and bourgeois – whilst

---

[64] 'Note' from Princes d'Orléans to Thiers, n.d., but probably March 1851, in BN naf 20618.
[65] N. W. Senior, *Journals kept in France and Italy from 1848 to 1852* (London 1871), I, p. 275 – 7 July 1850.
[66] BN naf 20618.
[67] Quoted E. Ténot, *Paris en décembre 1851: Etude historique sur le Coup d'Etat* (Paris 1868).

ridiculing Louis-Napoleon's imperialist pretensions nevertheless considered him as 'the man around whom we need to rally, until things are sufficiently stable to move to a definitive form of government, which will most certainly not be his'.[68]

THE COUP D'ETAT

As head of the executive of a centralised state, in which officials and army officers were committed to passive obedience, Louis-Napoleon was well placed to mount a *coup d'état* on 2 December 1851. The decisive factor was the army. Success depended on moving trusted personnel into strategic positions. The new War Minister, General Saint-Arnaud, was a *déclassé* aristocrat extremely hostile to any form of democracy and with a complete contempt for politicians.[69] The *coup* was carefully planned. On 30 November a practice alert permitted a dress rehearsal in major provincial centres. Contingency plans existed to deal with a possible *guerre des rues* in the capital.[70] General Magnan, commanding in Paris, was promised a written order, in effect absolving him of personal responsibility, as were the twenty generals who swore their loyalty to the President in his office on 26 November.[71] Although senior officers were predominantly monarchist rather than Bonapartist, and some generals were unwilling to become directly involved, they would obey orders.[72] Their conservative and anti-parliamentary reflexes made it all the easier.[73] In implementing the *coup*, control over the semaphore telegraph system would allow the government a crucial time advantage in terms of the dispatch of instructions and the receipt of information.[74] Preventative arrests removed potential leaders of monarchist opposition like Adolphe Thiers and the generals Changarnier, Bedeau, and Lamoricière, as well as republicans who might organise resistance. Although directed against both the monarchist groups represented in the National Assembly and

---

[68] Undated letter in AN 271 AP 4.

[69] W. Serman, 'Le corps des officiers français sous la deuxième république et le second empire', Doctorat d'Etat, Université de Paris-Sorbonne 1976, p. 1291.

[70] O. Pelletier, '*Figures imposées*. Pratiques et représentations de la barricade pendant les journées de décembre 1851' in A. Corbin and J.-M. Mayeur (eds.), *La barricade* (Paris 1997), pp. 253–5.

[71] G. Bapst, *Le Maréchal Canrobert* (Paris 1896), I, p. 525.

[72] See e.g. MacMahon letter to Pélissier, 10 Dec. 1851, AN 235 AP 3.

[73] See e.g. Colonel de Beaufort de Hautpoul to Pélissier in P. Guiral and R. Brunon (eds.), *Aspects de la vie politique et militaire en France au milieu du 19ᵉ siècle à travers la correspondance reçue par le Maréchal Pélissier* (Paris 1968), p. 227.

[74] See e.g. H. Gachot, 'Le rôle politique du télégraphe à Strasbourg en 1851 et 1852: le règne des dépêches politique', *Annuaire de la société des amis du Vieux-Strasbourg* (1983), p. 122.

the radical republicans, the fact that only the latter offered resistance would give the *coup* an essentially anti-republican character. In this respect it could be seen as the culmination of a long period of repression directed at the left.

In Paris only very limited resistance occurred, due to preventative arrests, and to obvious military preparedness. The predominantly conservative deputies, including Guizot, Thiers, and Tocqueville, who gathered at the town hall of the 10th arrondissement, refused to rally to the president, but were unwilling to contemplate more than symbolic resistance to a *coup d'état* which promised to establish the strong, authoritarian government which they believed the situation demanded. As the Legitimist Paul Benoist d'Azy wrote to his father Denys, one of the four vice-presidents of the now dissolved National Assembly:

we are caught between the regime of the sabre which has violated the constitution it was sworn to uphold and the hideous socialists. There is really no choice, and just as we supported the Republic we will accept the existing government … if it can persuade us to forget its origins by means of energetic action against the socialists and vigorous encouragement of business.[75]

In spite of the appeals of a group of around sixty Montagnard deputies – including Victor Hugo, Carnot, Favre, Michel de Bourges, Schoelcher, and Flotte, as well as Jules Leroux and August Desmoulins on behalf of a *comité central des co-opérations* – few workers were prepared to risk a repetition of the June insurrection to defend the rights of a conservative assembly against a president who now promised to restore manhood suffrage, who presented himself as the defender of popular sovereignty, and who enjoyed still the prestige that went with the name Bonaparte.[76] Nevertheless, some seventy barricades were constructed in the rue du faubourg Saint-Antoine and the streets adjoining the rues Saint-Denis, Rambuteau, and Transnonain. The army repeated its tactics of June 1848 and again deployed large, well-supplied columns. Perhaps 30,000 troops faced 1,200 insurgents. [77] The unequal struggle was short-lived. Subsequently the official *Moniteur universel* announced that 27 soldiers and 380 insurgents had been killed, although the latter figure was inflated by the volleys fired by nervous troops at peaceful, and mainly

---

75 R. R. Locke, and R. E. Cubberly, 'A new *Mémoire* on the French *coup d'état* of December 1851', *French Historical Studies* (1982), p. 584.

76 Price, *Second Republic*, pp. 288–9.

77 Baron Cochet de Savigny (editor of *Journal de la gendarmerie*), *Notice historique sur la révolution du mois de décembre 1851* (Paris 1852); Pelletier, 'Figures', pp. 256–7.

middle-class, civilian spectators.[78] Only short-lived demonstrations occurred in other cities. In Lille, the republican newspaper *Messager du Nord*
called for resistance on 3 December. The workers who gathered on the
grande-place that evening were easily dispersed. News of the failure of resistance in Paris discouraged further efforts.[79] In Dijon a crowd of 400
to 500 gathered outside the railway station in the afternoon waiting for
news from the capital. In the meantime the local démocrate-socialiste
leaders were arrested whilst waiting at a printer's for leaflets calling for
resistance. As a result the militants of Beaune and other little towns in
the region, who habitually followed the lead of Dijon, would also remain inactive. Their hesitation was in marked contrast with the obvious
determination displayed by the authorities.[80] Troops had been concentrated in the larger towns and once their security had been assured were
deployed in mobile columns in potentially disaffected rural areas. The
disadvantage of this tactic was that it allowed time for insurrection to
develop in some under-policed parts of the countryside.

Unexpectedly, the situation for the government was to prove much
more serious in rural areas than in the cities. Thus around 100,000 men,
in some 900 rural communes and small towns, mainly in the centre (Allier,
Nièvre), south-west (Lot-et-Garonne, Gers), and especially the south-east
(Drôme, Ardèche, Basses-Alpes, Hérault, Var), were involved in some
form of protest and as many as 70,000 from at least 775 communes
actually took up arms, with over 27,000 becoming involved in acts of violence. The insurgents came from regions of predominantly small-scale
peasant farming in which the difficulties caused by growing population
pressure on resources had been intensified by the persistent problems
of market-oriented activities like vine and silk cultivation, forestry, and
rural industry. Insurgent zones were not generally the most backward and
isolated but were located on the plains and in river valleys where effective
communications had provided access to markets in places like Béziers
(Hérault) a centre of the wine trade, or the southern textile towns of
Lodève, Mazamet, and Bédarieux, with their extensive hinterland links
through the 'putting-out' organisation of the woollens industry.[81] In the
north, north-east, west, and most of the Paris region, in contrast, there
was little disorder. These were, in the main, either the economically most

---

[78] See e.g. L. Girard, 'La troupe face aux insurrections parisiennes (1830–48)' in Vigier *et al.*,
Maintien de l'ordre et police, pp. 57–60.
[79] Commission mixte. Dépt. du Nord n.d., AN BB30/398.
[80] Report OC gendarmerie at Dijon, 4 Dec. 1851, AHG F1/51; see also e.g. PG Nancy for long
reports on similar incidents, 22 Jan. and 1 Feb. 1852, AN BB30/381.
[81] T. Margadant, *French Peasants in Revolt: The Insurrection of 1851* (London 1979), chs. 1 and 10.

advanced regions of commercial farming in which industrial development was beginning to relieve population pressure and/or areas in which
traditional elites, supported by the church, remained dominant. Of considerable significance in determining whether resistance took place was
the extent to which clandestine démocrate-socialiste organisations had
survived. These offered the means by which mobilisation could occur in
defence of the République démocratique et sociale and the new era of
security and happiness which had been promised for 1852. Only where
a clandestine organisation, with a hierarchical structure based on local
towns and market centres, survived was large-scale mobilisation possible. The ease with which this occurred in some areas, suggests that the
notion of resisting a *coup* or, more likely, seizing the vote, arms in hand,
in 1852, was a familiar one. It makes it easier to comprehend why, initially, insurgents were convinced that an easy victory was assured. If, as
they were told, the same thing was happening in countless communities throughout France and the army would not resist, how could they
fail? The greatest determination was to be found amongst artisan and
peasant militants. Probably they were less aware of the danger than the
middle-class leaders who, now that the crisis had arrived, often had to
be pressed into taking action against their better judgement. The desire
of these middle-class leaders to defend democratic politics was inhibited
by legalism and a fear of unleashing anarchic popular violence. They
would have preferred to await instructions from Paris. Bad news soon
confirmed the wisdom of their hesitation.[82]

One obvious characteristic of the insurrection was its localism. Previous repression had fragmented démocrate-socialiste organisation and
almost certainly prevented the development of more widespread resistance. Preventive arrests had the same effect. Typically risings occurred
when *démo-soc* majorities, well organised in *Montagnard* societies, were
able to dominate small communities through village and kin-based social networks, and where a shared belief in the justice of their cause,
and an initial enthusiasm based on incomplete and misleading information, created contagious feelings of unanimity. Following the arrival of
messages from leaders in nearby towns, gatherings of local leaders occurred in cafés or in public spaces and decided to call out their followers
by ringing the alarm (*tocsin*) on the church bells or beating the *générale*
on the communal drum. Emissaries were sent to outlying farms and
hamlets to call or if necessary coerce the *frères et amis* into gathering, arms

---

[82] See e.g. M. Vigreux, *Paysans et notables du Morvan au 19ᵉ siècle* (Château-Chinon 1987),
pp. 341–4.

in hand. Frequently *bourgeois* leaders appear to have been desperate to retain control of a popular uprising they were afraid might turn into a violent *jacquerie*. At any rate, as in the Gers, where some 150 to 200 militants were able to mobilise 8,000 to 10,000 members of secret societies, large groups of young men gathered, with whatever weapons they could find, and marched off behind the communal flag and drum towards the arrondissement and departmental *chefs-lieux* apparently inspired by the belief that the same thing was happening throughout France. Such rumours were typical of the distortion caused by the oral transmission of information. Thus on 4–5 December, as the 'news' spread, columns moved off in military order, often led by National Guard officers or former soldiers, to assume authority in captured town halls and government offices. In Basses-Alpes 7,000 to 8,000 men occupied Digne, the departmental capital. At Clamecy (Nièvre) and Bédarieux (Hérault), where social relations were inflamed already, violent action was taken against gendarmes and 'men of order.' Elsewhere, 'class enemies' were frequently disarmed. In all, only nine gendarmes, nine soldiers, and four civilians were killed by provincial insurgents. The casualties were mainly on their side. Insurgent columns were no match for the military forces belatedly sent against them. Most melted away without fighting, their morale shattered. They had been assured that the soldiers would join them. Some 6,000 men marching on Béziers shouted *Vive la ligne* on encountering troops. The latter responded with a volley which killed or wounded 70. The 300 insurgents who attacked 30 soldiers protecting Crest (Drôme) were dispersed by canon fire, which left 6 or 7 dead.[83] It is hardly surprising if initial euphoria turned to demoralisation once insurgents became aware of their isolation and inevitable defeat

Misery and disappointed expectations, although major causes of unrest, had not in some deterministic sense led to insurrection. The likelihood of resistance reflected the ways in which these discontents were perceived and explained. It depended on popular conceptions of justice, informed by démocrate-socialiste propaganda, as well as on previous experience of collective action and of the costs imposed by state repression. The naïveté of the beliefs of many of the insurgents should not be allowed to detract from their very real faith in progress and the triumph of democracy. If their resistance to the *coup* had much in common with 'primitive' traditions of popular protest it was inspired nevertheless by political ideology. *La Bonne, la République démocrate et sociale* had been presented as the means of establishing an egalitarian and just society.

[83] Price, *Second Republic*, p. 307.

For many miserable people 1852 had represented hope of escape from poverty and insecurity. The under-employed rural artisans and agricultural labourers, the impoverished weavers of Bédarieux, the *flotteurs* and forestry workers around Clamecy (Nièvre) exploited by the wood merchants supplying Paris, the harshly treated sharecroppers of the Allier, and the small peasant farmers afraid of expropriation for debt, were defending an ideal of *liberté* conceived of less in terms of abstract ideals than of measures meaningful in relation to their everyday lives. They were certainly not defending the republican constitution of 1851 but rather the ideal Republic of 1852.

The insurrection was followed by a settling of accounts. Over 26,000 suspected republican militants were arrested. The authorities were able to complete the work of repression without paying too much attention to the rule of law. The fright they had received, their bitter hatred of the démocrate-socialistes and their utter inability to understand their motives is clear from the insulting phraseology contained in the police interrogation records.[84] The civil and military authorities offered a moral explanation of the insurrection in terms of the poor and ignorant being led astray by the greedy, envious, and perverted. Official policy was to concentrate on punishing the ringleaders and the more active participants. Of those arrested, 10.6 per cent belonged to the middle-class professions (including 1,570 *rentiers*, 325 doctors, 225 lawyers) and only a minority were peasants (5,423 *cultivateurs*, 1,850 *journaliers*). The majority were artisans and workers in the traditional trades (building workers, shoemakers, tailors, etc.). Peasant participation in the insurrection was undoubtedly far more significant than these figures suggest.[85] If arrested, many of the rank and file were soon released. Subsequently, and taking advantage of their personal and family contacts, many middle-class professionals were also able to secure their own release to the great disgust of the police authorities.[86] Most had been frightened anyway into political quiescence – at least for the immediate future – throwing themselves on the mercy of the authorities as the only way of protecting themselves against the essential arbitrariness of the police and military.[87] The contrast with the dream of 1852 was only too marked. What was left of the démocrate-socialiste press was closed, as were the *cabarets*, which had so often served as *rendez-vous des individus dangereux*.

[84] See e.g. sessions of Premier Conseil de guerre de la 10e Division militaire séant à Montpellier, session 25 May 1852, *Affaire de Bédarieux*, 1852, pp. 26–7.
[85] For detailed analysis see Price, *Second Republic*, pp. 292–6.
[86] See e.g. Prefect, 8 July 1852, AN F1 cIII Jura 14.
[87] See e.g. GOC 8th DM, 11 Jan. 1852, AHG F1/69.

In most regions the *coup* was received with indifference or positively welcomed. Amongst notables, initial objections to the replacement of a liberal parliamentary regime by a Bonapartist dictatorship soon ceased. For a wide cross-section of the population, after long years of crisis the promise of strong government was very attractive. The acts of resistance to the *coup* seemed to confirm its necessity as a means of preventing socialist revolution, of avoiding 'a dictatorship of brigandage and blood' (*Courrier de la Drôme et de l'Ardèche*, 9 Dec. 1851). According to the new Interior Minister, the Comte de Morny, the insurrections were clear evidence of 'the social war which would have broken out in 1852'. An editorial in the *Courrier du Tarn-et-Garonne* is equally revealing in admitting that its author had not previously believed official warnings about secret-society activity – 'we thought in our naïve way that, apart from the very natural excitement of the election, the year 1852 would pass by very quietly ... But when we saw the peasants of Var, Ardèche, Basses-Alpes up in insurrection, then we did see the real menace to the country.' (18 Dec. 1851). Conservatives had been badly frightened by grossly exaggerated accounts of 'red' atrocities, of the murder and mutilation of gendarmes, rape and pillage, and the official presentation of the risings as a form of mindless *jacquerie*. Now they thanked God for their deliverance. The church itself gave thanks in solemn *Te Deums*. According to the Bishop of Nancy in an address to the President, the 'triumph of your cause ... is that of France and Religion ... God wishes to use you for his own purposes.'[88] Salvation seemed to be offered by the police state. Although the *coup* was undoubtedly an illegal act, which caused widespread terror and considerable suffering for many of those arrested, as well as their families,[89] it nevertheless hardly bears comparison with the brutality of twentieth-century dictatorship. This was 'dictatorship' understood in the Roman sense by a classically educated elite, as a short and exceptional period when the rule of law was suspended. Bonaparte himself subsequently confirmed this at the opening session of the new Corps législatif on 29 March 1852 when he announced that 'the dictatorship that the people had conferred upon me ends today'.[90] Martial law, which had been imposed on thirty-two departments, had ended two days previously.

Of course this did not end the process of repression. A complex of old and new laws, and especially their more rigorous enforcement, effectively

---

[88] 10 December 1851, AN AB XIX 173.
[89] See e.g. V. Wright, 'The *coup d'état* of December 1851: repression and the limits to repression' in R. Price, *Revolution and Reaction. 1848 and the Second French Republic* (London 1975).
[90] Procès-Verbaux de la séance d'ouverture de la session et du Corps législatif pour l'année 1852, AN 400 AP 93.

deterred political opposition. The authorities remained nervous, responding in exaggerated fashion to drunken outbursts and gatherings of 'suspicious' persons.[91] In many communities tension survived. When the prefect of the Hérault visited the graves of murdered gendarmes in Bédarieux, the streets were lined with silent and hostile workers. Government supporters remained frightened and intimidated.[92] Village mayors, the essential representatives of 'authority' at local level were instructed to display greater firmness.[93] Lists of political suspects were to be maintained in each department and regularly updated, to facilitate arrests should these ever be judged to be necessary. Detailed military contingency plans were prepared to deal with mass insurrection in Paris and Lyon.[94] Surveillance of the press and of former militants and their likely meeting places continued. Domiciliary searches, for concealed arms or subversive literature, were frequent. The wearing of red clothing could still lead to arrest.[95] Control of the press was a major preoccupation. Conservatives blamed its corrupting influence for much of the disorder since 1848. The new press law of 17 February 1852 codified the legislation introduced since 1814 – prior authorisation, caution money, stamp duty, suspension, etc. – and reinforced the discretionary powers of the administration, forcing editors to engage in rigorous self-censorship if their newspapers were to survive.

On 20 December 1851 a plebiscite was held to sanction the extension of the Prince-President's authority. The electorate was asked to vote on whether 'the people wish to maintain the authority of Louis-Napoleon and delegate to him the powers necessary to establish a constitution'. This appeal to popular sovereignty was to be a characteristic of the new regime. Louis-Napoleon was determined to secure a large majority as a means of legitimising his actions. It was made clear to all officials that their continued employment depended upon enthusiastic campaigning. The basic theme was the choice between 'civilisation and barbarism, society and chaos'.[96] In place of the era of disorder which opened in 1848, a new period of order, peace, and prosperity was

---

[91] See e.g. GOC 9th, DM 26–31 March 1852, AHG F1/69.

[92] AN F1 CIII Hérault 15.   [93] See e.g. prefect, 3 April 1852, AN F1 CIII Saône-et-Loire 13.

[94] See G. Carrot, *Le maintien de l'ordre en France depuis la fin de l'Ancien Régime jusqu'à 1968* (Paris 1986), II, p. 560.

[95] E.g. PG Montpellier, 26 April 1852, AN BB 30/403.

[96] See e.g. anon, *La solution donnée par le Président de la République aux sinistres complications politiques qui pressaient la France avant le 2 décembre 1851, peut-elle être considérée comme définitive?* (Paris 1852), AN AB XIX 687 Collection Duménil.

promised. At the same time every effort was made to eliminate signs of opposition. The result was predictable. Coercion was employed but primarily the result was due to the immense popularity of the Prince-President in the countryside. He was perceived to be the only safeguard against renewed revolution and additionally offered protection against the restoration of the *ancien régime*. The strength of latent Bonapartist sentiment was clearly evident. Even areas which had voted 'red' in 1849, like the Nièvre and Cher, were distinguished now by their ardent Bonapartism.[97] Nationally, 7,500,000 voted 'yes', 640,000 'no', and 1,500,000 abstained. Ominously, opposition was concentrated in the major cities. In Paris, 132,000 voters registered their approval, whilst 80,000 rejected the proposal and 75,000 did not vote. Rejection was evident especially in the working-class *quartiers*. In the industrial Nord significant opposition was registered in Lille, although in the mining and metallurgical centres of Anzin and Denain 79 per cent and 84 per cent respectively of an overwhelmingly working-class electorate voted in favour. Two forms of opposition manifested themselves: a vote 'no' mostly in areas of strong republicanism and amongst the middle classes and skilled workers in the towns of the east and south-east which had not been involved in the insurrection and thus managed to avoid the most intense repression; and abstention, particularly in parts of the west and Provence where popular Legitimism survived. Many Legitimists voted 'yes', as did many former republican supporters either in the perceived interest of social order or from fear of official reprisals.[98] The conservative newspaper *L'Union bourguignonne* typically warned that 'those who vote NO declare themselves accomplices in the crimes of the demagogues' (16 Dec. 1851). The future Marshal Niel represented senior army officers in expressing both unease about the arrest of conservative deputies and the workings of the military courts, and the belief that 'in present circumstances, a reasonable man cannot vote *non*: that would be to side with the bandits'.[99] The representatives of big business also welcomed the *coup* as the essential means of restoring confidence and as a prelude to a renewed wave of investment. Relieved of their terror, the upper classes celebrated carnival in 1852 with great enthusiasm.

[97] See e.g. B. Ménager, *Les Napoléons du peuple* (Paris 1988), pp. 112–14; F. Bluche, 'L'adhésion plébiscitaire' in F. Bluche (ed.) *Le prince, le peuple et le droit. Autour des plébiscites de 1851 et 1852* (Paris 2000).

[98] Price, *Second Republic*, pp. 321–3; Bluche, 'L'adhésion plébiscitaire', and L. Tilmant, 'Les gens du nord: l'illusion d'une résistance et la réalité de l'adhésion' in Bluche, *Le prince*.

[99] J. Lacombe de la Tour (ed.), *Correspondance inédite* (Paris 1912), p. 208, letter of 17 Dec. 1851.

CONCLUSION

The introduction of manhood suffrage in 1848 represented an important stage in mass politicisation. It had encouraged widespread political mobilisation. In spite of subsequent repression, it was during these years that the idea of the republic gained precision and mass support. This had aroused fear of social revolution. The *coup* had, however, smashed republican aspirations. For the second time a Bonaparte, supported by the army, threatened to destroy a republic. Indeed, within a year, in far less dramatic circumstances and following another carefully orchestrated campaign, a second plebiscite (on 21–22 November 1852) was held. In October, in a widely publicised speech made at Bordeaux, the Prince-President had promised peace, order, and reconciliation. Returning to Paris he was welcomed at the Gare d'Austerlitz by enthusiastic crowds and processed to the Tuileries Palace along boulevards strewn with flowers, passing under a succession of triumphal arches. In all, 7,824,000 voters approved the re-establishment of the hereditary empire which was proclaimed on 2 December, the anniversary of the Battle of Austerlitz.

The political solution to the threat of revolution has often been described as Bonapartist. As Marx suggested, this involved abdication of political power on the part of both traditional elites and their liberal bourgeois competitors for power, in return for protection of their vital interests – most notably private property, the basis of their social power – by the state. According to Marx, the new regime was 'not like its predecessors, the legitimate monarchy, the constitutional monarchy, and the parliamentary republic, one of the political forms of bourgeois society, it is ... its *ultimate* form. It is the state power of modern class rule.'[100] Gramsci's prison notebooks suggested a variant of this – *Caesarism* – 'in which a great personality is entrusted with the task of "arbitration" over a historical-political situation characterised by an equilibrium of forces heading towards catastrophe.'[101] Once organised opposition had been crushed using military force, that is, 'the manifest use of violence,' a shift occurred to 'the pervasive use of administrative power'[102] employing growing numbers of civil servants, policemen, clergy, and schoolteachers. The popularity of the head of state was enhanced by the 'invention' of ritual and by the provincial tours, facilitated by railway travel, which

[100] K. Marx and F. Engels, *Writings on the Paris Commune* (New York 1971), pp. 37, 46.
[101] Q. Hoare and G. N. Smith (eds.), *Selections from the Prison Notebooks of Antonio Gramsci* (London 1971), p. 219.
[102] J. Gledhill, *Power and its Disguises. Anthropological Perspectives on Politics* (London 1994), p. 19.

sought to 'personalise the bonds between ruler and common folk'.[103] Subsequently, and more dangerously the Emperor, invariably wearing military uniform, would pose as the symbol of national unity and as the supreme warlord. This resurgence of the monarchical state in the second half of the nineteenth century was exemplified daily by its judicial and police activities and glorified in school, church, and in the developing mass media. These were measures more appropriate to the emerging mass society created by industrialisation and urbanisation. In practice, much of the support offered to Bonaparte was conditional. Thus the liberal Catholic Comte de Montalembert insisted that 'To vote against Louis Napoleon is to support Revolution ... To vote for Louis Napoleon, is not to approve everything he has done, it is to choose between him and the total ruin of France.'[104] The independence of the state would continue to be circumscribed by the power and influence of social elites and its own recruitment of key personnel from within their ranks. The dominant positions they retained would thus ensure that they preserved the 'ability to set the terms under which other groups and classes would operate'[105] and the likelihood of a revival of opposition to the Bonapartist regime.

[103] D. Barclay, *Frederick William IV and the Prussian Monarchy 1840–61* (Oxford 1995), p. 12.
[104] *L'Univers*, 14 Dec. 1851.
[105] G. Domhoff, *Who Rules America Now?* (Englewood Cliffs, N.J., 1983), p. 2.

PART II

State and society

CHAPTER 2

Napoleon III and the Bonapartist state

THE CONSTITUTION OF THE SECOND EMPIRE

The *coup d'état* was followed by a period of rule by decree, of dictatorship in the ancient Roman sense of the word, when the normal rule of law was suspended with the assent of the population, given by plebiscite on 21 December 1851. Continuing repression completed the identification of the new regime with the political right, giving it a reactionary image from which it would never escape. During the four months that followed, its institutional structures were established. The constitution of 14 January 1852 transformed the government of the Republic and would require little further modification before becoming the constitution of the Second Empire. It was drafted mainly by Rouher, by-passing the consultative commission originally established as a means of attaching leading political figures to the regime. However, the President himself laid down its basic structure. The model followed was the Napoleonic constitution of the Year XII. Indeed, in a proclamation of 14 January 1852 Louis-Napoleon insisted that

I have taken as models the political institutions that once before, at the turn of the century, in similar circumstances, gave a new strength to a shaken society and raised France to the height of prosperity and grandeur. I have taken as models the institutions that, instead of vanishing at the first outbreak of popular disturbances, were toppled only by the coalition of all of Europe against us. In short I asked myself: since France has been functioning for the past fifty years only thanks to the administrative, military, judicial, religious and financial organisation of the Consulate and Empire, why should we not also adopt the political institutions of that period? As the creation of the same mind, they must surely embody the same national character and the same practical usefulness.

According to the first article, 'The Constitution recognises, confirms and guarantees the great principles proclaimed in 1789 and which are the foundations of French public law.' In thus recognising the Rights of

Man and equality before the law the regime clearly distinguished itself
from both reactionary conservatism and revolutionary republicanism.
The constitution also sought to combine the exercise of personal power
with manhood suffrage. It provided for a head of state to be elected for
ten years with the right to present his successor. As the elect of the nation,
the president was to be responsible directly to the people through the
mechanism of regular elections and plebiscites. He would be responsible for the initiation and promulgation of legislation, for declaring war,
negotiating treaties, and for appointing ministers and officials. Ministers
were to be responsible to the head of state alone. Legislation was to be
prepared by the Conseil d'Etat whose forty to fifty members, nominated
and revocable by the President, would present legislative proposals to an
elected Corps législatif. This would be composed of 275 deputies specifically representing their constituents and not the nation, with the right
to discuss and vote on legislation. Provision was also made for a Senate,
which was envisaged as playing a moderating role as well as ensuring
respect for the constitution and public liberties. This would be made
up of 80 to 150 members including King Jérôme, the first Napoleon's
surviving brother, and his son Prince Napoleon, together with cardinals, admirals, and marshals and nominated members who would be
irremovable subsequently as a guarantee of their independence.

This was indeed a strange republic! In symbolic promise of things to
come, the republican device 'Liberty, Equality, Fraternity' was effaced
from public buildings. The image of the Prince-President stared from
coins and stamps. On 1 January 1852 a solemn *Te Deum* was celebrated
in Notre Dame at which the Archbishop of Paris chanted the *Domine
salvum fac Ludovicum* as though the Empire already existed. On 10 May
new flags and imperial eagles were distributed at a parade of 60,000
troops on the Champ-de-Mars, watched by some 400,000 spectators, to
shouts of *Vive l'Empereur*. However, Louis-Napoleon remained to be convinced that an imperial restoration was the popular will. During a tour
of southern and central France in October, which took in such centres
of opposition as Lyons, Marseilles, and Toulouse, the Prince-President
and his military entourage processed along streets covered in flowers,
under triumphal arches inscribed with the imperial 'N'. The crowds
acclaimed him. This was partly the result of instructions from the devotedly Bonapartist Interior Minister, Persigny, to his prefects ordering
them to organise pro-Empire demonstrations in the hope of forcing the
President's hand, but additionally because much of the population welcomed the prospect and saw this new Bonaparte as the personification

of aspirations for order and prosperity.[1] At Bordeaux on 9 October, undoubtedly impressed by the reception organised by Haussmann the local prefect, Louis-Napoleon finally committed himself to the restoration of the Empire and to national reconciliation:

Never has a people proved in a more direct, more spontaneous, more unanimous fashion its determination to free itself from concerns about the future, by consolidating power in a single hand ... It knows that in 1852 society would have rushed to disaster, because every party was willing to risk shipwreck in the hope of hoisting its flag over the debris which floated. I am glad to have been able to save the ship and hoist the national flag ... France appears to want to return to the Empire. Some distrustful people say: the Empire means war. Myself, I say: the Empire means peace ... I admit, though, that like the Emperor, I have conquests to make. I want, like him, to work for the conciliation of dissident parties. We have immense uncultivated territories to clear, roads to open, ports to excavate, rivers to render navigable, canals to finish, our railway network to complete. We have opposite Marseilles, a vast kingdom [Algeria] to assimilate ... Everywhere we have ruins to restore, false Gods to overthrow, truths to make triumphant.[2]

Through the procedure known as a *sénatus-consulte* on 7 November the senate formally revised the constitution – 'the imperial dignity is re-established. Louis-Napoleon Bonaparte is Emperor of the French, under the name of Napoleon III.' The proposal was sanctioned by another plebiscite on 21 November with 7,824,000 positive votes, an increase of 400,000 over the vote in December 1851, and only 253,000 against, although with nearly 2 million abstentions. Further constitutional modification on 25 December sought to reinforce the power of the executive in areas in which the Corps législatif had already dared to challenge government policy – the modification of customs tariffs, financing of public works, and presentation of the budget.[3]

THE EMPEROR NAPOLEON III

The negative assessments of the new Emperor handed on to posterity by Marx and Tocqueville have already been referred to. They were shared widely within the political elite. In part this was because he was an adventurer who, in terms of background, education, and experience, did not fit into conventional moulds. Charles de Rémusat pointed out that 'He lacks so many of the qualities of an ordinary man of merit,

---

[1] Bluche, 'L'adhésion plébiscitaire', pp. 3–16.   [2] Girard, *Napoléon III*, pp. 181–2.
[3] See N. Blayau, *Billault, ministre de Napoléon III* (Paris 1969), p. 219.

judgement, education, conversation, experience, all these are subject to so many gaps that one is easily tempted to class him as utterly mediocre', and then added:

> But this idiot is endowed with a rare and powerful ability ... His presence has changed the course of history ... Whoever is able to decide to intervene in the affairs of the world, and produce or modify events as he might wish, possesses an indefinable gift of boldness or strength which distinguishes him from the crowd and raises him to the rank of an historical personality.[4]

As a result of his family background and upbringing Louis-Napoleon Bonaparte possessed an intense sense of personal destiny and faith in his historical mission. In his determination to become guardian of the Napoleonic tradition he combined the outlook of a romantic mystic with the instincts of a political opportunist. Understanding him is not easy and requires the close analysis of his writings and speeches as well as of the views of those few relations and collaborators who managed to get close to this very private person. His friend from childhood, Mme Cornu, in conversation with the well-connected British political economist Nassau William Senior, described his 'mission' as 'a devotion first to the Napoleonic dynasty, and then to France ... His duty to his dynasty is to perpetuate it. His duty to France is to give her influence abroad and prosperity at home.'[5] Even when he relaxed with such old friends his manner made it impossible for them to forget his rank. Moreover he rarely spoke openly and unambiguously, and outside this narrow circle political critics provided most contemporary assessments.

Louis-Napoleon's objectives would be spelled out in a letter to his cousin Prince Napoleon: 'when one bears our name and is head of government, there are two things to do: satisfy the interests of the most numerous classes, attach to oneself the upper classes'. This would require a constant juggling act. His basic ideas were stated quite early in his career in a series of pamphlets. These included most notably *Les Réflections politiques* (1832), *Les Idées napoléoniennes* (1839) – based closely on Napoleon I's writings and on Las Cases' *Mémorial* – and *L'Extinction du paupérisme* (1844). Although the presentation was vague and imprecise and replete with contradictions, these writings, reflecting the utopian optimism of the 1830/40s, were to serve as his 'guiding ideas'.[6] They

---

[4] Quoted Girard, *Napoléon III*, p. 104.

[5] N. W. Senior , *Conversations with M. Thiers, M. Guizot and other Distinguished Persons during the Second Empire* (London 1878), II, p. 115.

[6] See A. Plessis, *The Rise and Fall of the Second Empire* (Cambridge 1985), p. 9; J. Bury, *Napoleon III and the Second Empire* (London 1964), p. 49.

were characterised by a determination to eliminate the party divisions, which he believed were responsible for political instability. Although sharing with conservatives a determination to safeguard social order Louis-Napoleon was, however, distinguished by his apparent commitment to 'democracy'. Periodic plebiscites would serve to ratify the regime's general policies, as well as to re-affirm the 'mystical link between Emperor and people'.[7] Through its vote the people delegated power to the Emperor and legitimised his authority.[8] The powers of representative assemblies – representative only of the particular interests of deputies[9] – were to be reduced to a minimum. Only the Bonapartist dynasty, he assumed, could effectively represent the twin principles of order and democracy.

Constitutional structures were one thing, the actual workings of the regime quite another. Hereditary monarchy linked the ruler's personal, family life to public, constitutional concerns. In the first instance the question of the succession appeared to require urgent resolution. Prince Napoleon, the immediate heir, had little to commend him. The Emperor, in his urgent search for a suitable bride, however, caused great surprise by selecting a Spanish aristocrat, Eugénie de Montijo, Countess of Teba, rather than a member of another royal family. He appears to have fallen in love, although this would not spare the Empress from continued resentment by members of the Bonaparte family who felt that the Emperor had married beneath himself. Their marriage would provide another occasion, on 30 January 1853, for a splendid celebration of the dignity of empire. Provincial tours, making use of the growing railway network and often associated with the opening of new stations, and carefully organised displays of imperial munificence including the distribution of medals to faithful servants of the First, as well as the Second Empire, signified the re-establishment of the *fête impériale*.[10] These, together with printed propaganda, presented an image of Napoleon III as a saviour, a monarch to be both feared and respected, and as the source of growing prosperity. The birth of the Prince-Imperial in the night of 15–16 March 1856 and his baptism on 14 June led to an extraordinary round of fireworks and festivities in celebration of the apparent securing of the dynasty.

[7] S. Campbell, *The Second Empire Revisited. A Study in French Historiography* (London 1978.), p. 4.
[8] M. Emerit (ed.), *Lettres de Napoléon III à Madame Cornu* (Paris 1937), p. 198.
[9] Letter to Hortense Cornu quoted Girard, *Napoléon III*, p. 30.
[10] See Voyages de l'Empereur, AN F70/422; also V. Robert, *Les chemins de la manifestation 1848–1914* (Lyons 1996), pp. 140f.

A further characteristic of monarchy was the existence of a court, facilitating the – often undocumented – influence on policy-making of individuals in close contact with the Emperor.[11] Indeed, a glittering court was judged to be essential to the regime's prestige, an act in the theatre of power. If the primary function of the court was to provide a public spectacle, and serve as a symbol of French civilisation, its political importance should not be ignored. The court's style and protocol, and the ceremonies presided over by the Duc de Cambacérès, were borrowed from the First Empire. On special occasions such as the New Year ball in the Tuileries the palace filled with men in glittering uniforms or evening dress, women in silk and lace crinolines. On other occasions the court might be moved by train, followed by an army of domestics and its baggage, to Saint Cloud on the outskirts of the capital – the favoured residence from spring to mid-August; to the palaces of Fontainebleau or Versailles or, during the autumn for hunting, to Compiègne. The receptions for visiting dignitaries like Queen Victoria in 1855, or the numerous state visits during the international exposition in 1867, were incredibly luxurious affairs, attended by three or four thousand of the regime's leading figures including the Emperor's relatives – the old King Jérôme and his children, Prince Napoleon and the Princess Mathilde, Walewski, the natural son of Napoleon I, and Morny, the Emperor's half-brother and accomplice in the *coup d'état*, who together with Napoleon's old companion Persigny was raised to a dukedom. Alongside these were the imperial nobility and some former Orleanists, as well as leading figures from the administration and army, politicians, representatives of the arts and letters and of big business. Most Legitimists continued to avoid the court as a matter of principle. Invitations to the smaller and more intimate balls and dinners were particularly sought after. The Tuileries Palace, considerably extended, nevertheless, offered little basic comfort. Much of it was unheated, and the palace lacked running water. Packed full of officials and servants, it resembled a rabbit-warren. The Imperial family occupied the southern wing between the Seine and the pavillon de l'Horloge. In addition to the services controlled by a minister responsible for the imperial household – first the financier Achille Fould and from 1860 Marshal Vaillant – there was also a military household and indeed the male members of the Imperial family frequently appeared to be part of a military pageant. Military equerries provided a staff responsible both for transmitting instructions and carrying out a variety

---

[11] E.g. L. Girard,'La cour de Napoléon III' in K.Werner (ed.), *Hof, Kultur und politik im 19. Jahrhundert* (Bonn 1985), pp. 155f; W. Smith, *Napoleon III. The Pursuit of Prestige* (London 1995), ch. III.

of private and public missions. Along with the omnipresent police they also contributed to ensuring the security of the Imperial family. In the 1850s this establishment cost around 8 million francs to maintain, out of a civil list of 25 million. Court expenditure made a substantial contribution to the prosperity of the fashion and luxury trades.

An exhausting round of festivities and massive feasts was interspersed with long and boring evenings when women embroidered and men played whist. At any time court etiquette imposed a reserve quite unlike the orgiastic behaviour described by republican pamphleteers. The status of the Empress, rapidly established as a model of elegance, was particularly enhanced by her central position in the life of the court. In spite of its stifling etiquette, the Imperial court was probably less formal than those of most European kingdoms. Nevertheless, to escape this formality and enjoy a rest, the Imperial family favoured taking the waters at Plombières and then Vichy or visiting the seaside at Deauville or Biarritz. Official tours, private visits, trips to the opera, or society balls added further variety as well as providing for regular gatherings of the people who mattered socially and politically. This all helped to create a public image of the model family, although after the first days of his marriage the number of mistresses favoured by the Emperor continued to grow, and with it a certain detachment between himself and the Empress.

To be close to the monarch was to enjoy influence. The Emperor's private office – presided over by Mocquard, until his death in 1864, and then by Conti – was a crucial part of the machinery of government. The surviving documentation offers little information on the day-to-day relationships between the Emperor, ministers, and unofficial advisors, especially his former co-conspirators, his democratic and anticlerical cousin, Prince Napoleon, and courtiers like General Fleury. Institutional character was given to gatherings of the Emperor's intimates through the establishment of the Conseil privé following Orsini's attempt to assassinate the Imperial couple in January 1858. This included some ministers and conferred ministerial rank on all its members. Former ministers, like Persigny after his dismissal in 1863, or later Rouher when out of office during the Liberal Empire, would thus be able to continue to exert considerable influence. The Empress also seems to have developed a taste for politics, particularly after serving as regent during her husband's absence with the army in Italy in 1859, and exercised her influence in favour of authoritarian and clerical policies. As her husband's health declined she regularly attended ministerial meetings from 1867 and would be subject to considerable criticism for moving beyond her 'womanly role'.[12] The deteriorating health of the Emperor was to be of considerable significance given the personal character of monarchical authority. Rumours concerning Napoleon's health were a potent means of demoralising the regime's supporters and encouraging its opponents to believe that the end was in sight.[13] A *très-confidentielle* Interior Ministry circular dated 6 June 1859 would order that in case of the sudden death of the Emperor the news should be kept secret until the civil and military authorities had time to swear an oath of allegiance to his heir. If necessary, martial law should be declared and suspects arrested.[14] During the 1860s it would become obvious that the Emperor was ageing rapidly. Chain-smoking and an unsuitable diet hardly helped matters. In 1864, aged fifty-six, he suffered the first serious illness caused by stones in his bladder, which would lead to his death eight years later. Fatalistic, and unwilling to face surgery, he depended on increasing doses of morphine to ease the pain.[15] Poor health reinforced Napoleon's natural indolence. He became increasingly hesitant. This apparent loss of confidence inevitably created a leadership vacuum. The regime appeared to many observers to be in a state of decay. This sick man, his decision-making ability severely impaired, was the leader who would take France into war in 1870. The confidence of ministers and senior officials whose careers depended on the Emperor's longevity must have been shaken. The prospect of a regency until the Prince-Imperial came of age – he was eight in 1864 – added to a growing sense of uncertainty. Although the Empress, devoted to her only child, and desperate to safeguard the succession, made considerable efforts to prepare herself, her growing prominence within ministerial councils only added to her unpopularity.[16] To some extent the Emperor's willingness to accept political liberalisation and the diminution of his own authority might have resulted from an awareness of his declining physical and intellectual capacity.[17] However, he had spoken of an eventual liberalisation almost from the beginning of his reign, and most notably in a speech to the Corps législatif in February 1853.[18]

---

[12] V. Bidegain, 'L'origine d'une réputation: l'image de l'impératrice Eugénie dans la société française du Second Empire' in Corbin, Lalouette, and Riot-Sarcey, *Femmes* pp. 63, 66.

[13] See e.g. PG Rouen 15 Oct. 1863, AN BB30/387.

[14] *Pièces saisies aux archives de la police politique de Lyon. Publiée par ordre du Conseil municipal* (Lyons 1870), p. 35; see also circular, 26 Sept. 1861, *ibid.*, p. 38

[15] See e.g. M. Remy, 'Le mauvais calcul de l'empereur Napoléon III', *Annales de l'Est* (1993), pp. 31f.

[16] See e.g. report from OC 1st Legion of gendarmerie, 30 Sept. 1869, AHG G8/166.

[17] See e.g. General du Barail, *Mes souvenirs* (Paris 1896), III, pp. 106–7.

[18] J. Rougerie, 'Le Second Empire' in Duby (ed.), *Histoire de la France* (Paris 1972), III, p. 72.

CONSTITUTIONAL REVISION

On constitutional matters Napoleon, an admirer of British institutions, appears to have been willing to be flexible, as even the hostile liberal politician Adolphe Thiers recognised.[19] Unlike his predecessors the Emperor was prepared to adapt to changing political circumstances, accepting the precedent he believed his illustrious uncle had established with his *Actes additionels* during the Hundred Days in 1815. Certainly the initial liberalising measures in 1860/1 were not conceded under pressure. They represented concessions by a regime at the height of its power and caused considerable surprise.[20] Quite what the Emperor intended remains open to debate. The form of authoritarian government introduced in response to the mid-century crisis had inevitably come to appear less justifiable as the threat of revolution diminished. In this situation he was presented with contradictory advice. Persigny, more than a little irritated by his despatch to the London embassy, made full use of the direct access to the Emperor that their old friendship permitted to observe in June 1858 in response to his master's complaints about growing unrest, that 'that which afflicts me the most is to feel carried along, in spite of myself, by that torrent of opinion forming from all sides against the theory of unlimited power, without advice, without counter-balance, without control, power which you certainly exercise with the purest and noblest conscience, but which is beyond the capacity of a single human being'. Accepting the need for change, he recommended the establishment of a council of ministers which would enjoy greater authority as a result of recognition that it was collectively, rather than individually, responsible to the Emperor. This would 'guarantee the Emperor against the seductions to which the person of the sovereign might be subject, surround him with the necessary wisdom, and assure ... by means of their public responsibility the independence and dignity of his councillors'. According to Persigny the system of individual responsibility sanctioned by article 13 of the constitution only encouraged the intrigues of the former Orleanists with whom he had chosen to surround himself.[21] The Emperor would prove unwilling to accept this particular recommendation. Nevertheless, in a letter of 12 November 1860, published in the official *Moniteur*, he responded to disquiet about the government's finances with a major, and revealing, concession:

[19] Senior, *Conversations*, II, pp. 111–12.   [20] See e.g. PG Limoges, 12 Jan. p. 1861, AN BB30/378.
[21] BN naf 23066.

For some time ... my preoccupation has been to contain the budget within strict limits ... The only means of achieving this is to abandon my right to authorise new credits when the chambers are not sitting ... In renouncing this right, which has always belonged, even to the constitutional monarchs who preceded me, I intend to provide for the better administration of our finances. Faithful to my origins, I am not willing to regard the prerogatives of the crown as a sacred trust, or as an inheritance, which I am bound to transmit intact to my son. Elected by the people, representing its interests, I will always abandon, without regret, any prerogative damaging to the public interest.[22]

Additionally, both the Corps législatif and the Senate were invited to vote an address in response to the annual speech from the throne. Assembly sessions would also be graced by the presence of three commissaires du gouvernement, ministers responsible for explaining – and defending – government policy. Furthermore, a full account of debates would be published in the *Moniteur* and might be reproduced by other newspapers. The problem was how to liberalise the regime without destabilising the system of government. The Emperor's closest advisers, with the notable exceptions of Morny and Walewski, were generally opposed to these concessions and the Emperor himself was reluctant to go too far. In a major speech on 18 June 1861 he insisted on the need to preserve the prerogative powers conferred on him by popular plebiscite, and which alone guaranteed social order.[23] In a rather heated conversation with Prince Napoleon the following day, he would insist that 'The country already has too much liberty.'[24] His ideal would probably have been a parliament without parties, offering loyal support for his various initiatives. The prospect of a 'faction'-ridden assembly on the model of those of the July Monarchy, together with freedom of the press, filled him with horror. As late as the state opening of the Corps législatif in 1866 Napoleon condemned the parliamentary regime in an eulogy on the 1852 constitution.[25] The concessions made from 1867 were much less voluntary.

A further series of reforms was announced in a letter printed in the *Moniteur* on 19 January 1867. The debate on the address was replaced by the right of *interpellation* with ministers required to participate in debates. These were concessions made in an effort to win over disaffected liberals and under pressure from Walewski, president of the Corps législatif,

[22] Quoted F. Barbier, *Finance et politique. La dynastie des Fould* (Paris 1991), p. 207.
[23] Quoted Blayau, *Billault*, pp. 331–2.
[24] 'Note sur une conversation entre l'Empereur Napoléon et moi, le 19 juin 1865 ... ' in E. Hauterive (ed.), *Napoléon III et le prince napoléon. Correspondance inédite* (Paris 1936), p. 377
[25] J. Maurain, *Un bourgeois français au 19ᵉ siècle: Baroche, ministre de Napoléon III* (Paris 1936), p. 377.

himself influenced by Adolphe Thiers.[26] The reform was presented as necessary 'to correct the imperfections which time has revealed and to accept progress compatible with changing customs'.[27] The liberalisation process was reinforced further by May 1868 laws that recognised substantial freedom for the press and meetings, and provided the means for a spectacular revival of public political life. Even then, and as if to illustrate the confusion in the Emperor's mind, the speech from the throne at the state opening of parliament in January 1869 was authoritarian in tone. Napoleon condemned those 'adventurous and subversive spirits determined to upset public tranquillity'. Rouher reinforced the point when, during a debate on the freedom of the press in the Senate, he insisted that there was no question of a return to parliamentarism.[28] Administrative reports complained about the confused signals being given to the public. The procureur-général at Aix went so far as to suggest that 'the voluntary renunciation by the Head of state of his personal power might be the only means of ending the general discontent of the middle classes, of rallying to the regime all those who ought naturally to support it ... of persuading the moderates to return to the Empire, [and] of substituting ... for the old Party of Order, inactive for some years but now tired of its long inertia, the great party of conservative liberals'.[29] A *Note sur les élections de 1869* prepared for the Emperor pointed out that not only had 116 deputies in the new Assembly signed a motion in favour of reform but that even *les bons candidats* had presented liberal electoral manifestos. It concluded that further concessions were unavoidable: 'It is essential that the government clearly states that it will accept all those reforms which will, without destroying its authority, enlarge the functions and control exercised by the Corps législatif.'[30] A *Note* from Prince Napoleon spelled out the options: (1) a reactionary policy, which might succeed in the short term, but for only as long as the Emperor lived; (2) maintenance of the *status quo, la politique d'indécision* as the Prince tactfully put it, but this would mean gradual but inevitable decline; (3) *la conciliation ou l'initiation* which demanded that the Emperor put behind him previous false starts and take a decisive lead in liberalisation.[31] According to this view authoritarianism had proved to be a short-term expedient whilst liberalisation provided the means of reinforcing the legal–political foundations of the regime, and was essential to its survival.

[26] Barbier, *Finance*, p. 241.   [27] Letter from Napoleon to Rouher, 19 Jan. 1867, AN 400 AP 42.
[28] R. Schnerb, *Rouher et le Second Empire* (Paris 1949), pp. 247–8.
[29] PG Aix, 4 Oct. 1868, AN BB30/378.   [30] AN 400 AP 54.
[31] 'Note sur les élections générales de 1869, 28 mai 1869' in Hauterive, *Napoléon III*, pp. 389–90.

In a letter to Rouher on 9 June 1869,[32] the Emperor accepted the need to take the initiative and to prepare legislation which would increase the powers of elected departmental and communal councils and substantially extend the right of deputies to ask questions and propose amendments to legislation. The Corps législatif would also acquire the right to vote on the contentious issue of commercial treaties. There appeared to be a real prospect of a rejection of the 'free trade' treaties negotiated at the Emperor's behest, and which had aroused such alarm amongst economic interest groups. For the elites represented in the Assembly even this remained too little, too late. It was increasingly apparent that in place of piecemeal reform thoroughgoing change was becoming necessary. The Empress Eugénie, usually described as a convinced authoritarian, agreed, in a letter written from Egypt on 27 October 1869 that 'it is necessary to prove to the country that one has principles and not expedients', adding that 'I am convinced that *coups d'état* are not possible twice in the same reign.'[33] The formation of the Ollivier ministry on 2 January 1870, a possibility discussed since early 1867, represented the real beginnings of a liberal Empire. Ollivier, a former moderate republican, like most liberals saw a strong executive as essential to the maintenance of public order and appreciated the continued potency of the Napoleonic legend. Additionally he wanted the Emperor to rule with the support of public opinion.[34] Detailed proposals for constitutional reform were presented to the Senate on 20 April. The rights of parliament to initiate debate, to vote the budget, and decide on customs tariffs, were enlarged. Ministers were to be responsible to both the Emperor and parliament. According to article 19 'the Emperor appoints and revokes ministers. They are responsible.' They remained his ministers, but it would be difficult for him to retain individuals who did not enjoy the confidence of parliament. The Senate would now lose its powers as a constituent assembly to become an upper house with powers similar to those of the Corps législatif. The Emperor's own power to determine constitutional development was, however, preserved by article 13 of the new constitution: 'The Emperor is responsible to the French people to whom he retains the right of appeal.' As the elect of the people, Napoleon retained ultimate responsibility. He had the right to dissolve parliament and appeal to the country. He retained considerable prerogative power, including the authority to negotiate treaties and declare war. It was this

[32] AN 400 AP 44.
[33] *Papiers secrets et correspondance du Second Empire*, P. Poulet-Malassis, ed. (Paris 1873), pp. 220–1.
[34] Report of meeting with Ollivier by Clément Duvernois to Emperor, 8 Nov. 1869, *ibid.*, p. 268.

retention of the right to consult voters through the plebiscite – opposed by Ollivier – which more than any other provision symbolised the survival of Napoleon's personal power. In the plebiscite on the new constitution held on 8 May 1870, 7,350,000 voted in favour, 1,538,000 against, and 1,900,000 abstained.

Following this definition of the political role of the Emperor, the next step is to examine the workings of the system of government, beginning with the complex relationships between Napoleon and *his* ministers, and then considering the shifts in the balance of power between the Emperor, ministers, the elected deputies, and key decision-makers within the bureaucracy.

CHAPTER 3

The system of government

MINISTERS

Under the terms of the 1852 constitution, ministers were to be appointed and dismissed at will by the Emperor. They were not to be members of the Corps législatif and were not required to defend the government's policies before it. Napoleon's conception of their role was spelled out in his letter dismissing General Espinasse as Interior Minister in June 1858: 'Ministers are an important part of the machinery of state and I change them whenever I believe it to be necessary for the public good ... I have no need to offer further explanation to a minister than to thank him for his services.'[1] Furthermore, ministers were responsible to the Emperor as individuals and not on a collective basis. The Emperor convoked ministerial meetings once or twice a week. At these, ministers presented dossiers. There was no real discussion and generally Napoleon postponed decisions, to give himself time to reflect.[2] The real influence of ministers depended a great deal upon their personal relations with Napoleon and on face-to-face meetings or personal correspondence. In this the Emperor's private office and his secretaries, Mocquard and later Conti, played an important part, controlling access and the flow of information. Unfortunately its archives have not survived. It is clear, nevertheless, that the Emperor intervened frequently in the working of such key ministries as Interior and demanded regular and detailed reports on the state of public opinion. Considerable stamina was required on the part of ministers like Billault and Rouher who were frequently expected to attend on the Emperor and to appear at an exhausting round of official and private functions. These were the essential means of acquiring social and political credit, building client networks and accumulating and diffusing information in the rarefied world of high politics. In an autocratic system

---

[1] Quoted F. Caron, *La France des patriotes de 1851 à 1914* (Paris 1985), p. 23.
[2] See e.g. M. de Maupas, *Mémoires sur le Second Empire* (Paris 1884), II, p. 19.

with, at its heart, the small world of the court, personal rivalries could all too frequently influence policy. However, in the last resort the Emperor assumed responsibility.

As he told Prince Napoleon, 'No-one must take policy decisions without consulting me, however sensible they might be.'[3] The irritated tone of a letter to Persigny, however, suggests that matters were not so simple. Napoleon again insisted that 'it is essential that ministers appreciate the spirit of the constitution which renders them responsible to me alone, and attributes to me responsibility for their actions. They must then do nothing important without my assent.'[4] On the eve of the 1863 elections, when he felt it necessary to dismiss his Foreign Minister, Thouvenel, to conciliate clerical opinion, Fould, Baroche, and Billault actually threatened to resign. Their affirmation of ministerial responsibility was, however, short-lived. In a letter to Fould, the Emperor insisted that 'I will never consent to be dictated to by my ministers.'[5] He additionally reprimanded Rouher, informing him that

You seem to misunderstand our institutions and negotiate with me as if you were the Prime Minister of a parliamentary government instead of being my representative before the chambers. I am in fact and by law responsible for the acts of the government; the policy followed by the foreign minister is mine. Ministers receive their impetus from me ... I invariably welcome your observations and would never refuse to discuss my acts and intentions with you but I will never accept that the Minister of State should adopt practices and policies of his own.'[6]

It might be tempting to assume that ministers were simply technicians, executants of the Emperor's will. In practice, however, ministerial powers were quite considerable. The regime was characterised by relative ministerial stability, with some ministries, like Finance, dominated by strong and experienced ministers like Magne (1855–60; 1867–70) and Fould (1851–2; 1861–7). Long periods in office, and accumulated expertise, ensured that they enjoyed considerable influence over colleagues and within the bureaucracy. Although until around 1860 the Emperor worked hard, reading and annotating reports, he was never as assiduous as his uncle had been. He lacked interest in the detailed implementation of policy. As his health declined so did his capacity for work. Amongst ministers the practical need to co-operate and the habit of holding informal weekly dinners, from which the Emperor was absent, created a limited sense of unity, sufficient to persuade Napoleon, at times,

[3] Prince Napoleon, 'Note sur une conversation', 19 June 1865, in Hauterive, *Napoléon III*, p. 376.
[4] Letter of 9 Feb. 1863 in Duc de Persigny, *Mémoires* (Paris 1896), p. 185.
[5] 7 April 1864, AN 400 AP 44.   [6] Napoleon to Rouher, 4 April 1864, AN 400 AP 44.

that he was in danger of being marginalised.[7] Even so, ministers were never able to develop the sense of collective responsibility, which might have compensated for the Emperor's declining ability to coordinate government policy. They were often left uncertain about his intentions. A growing loss of cohesion as well as serious divisions between ministers was the inevitable result. After complaining in March 1859 about ministers who 'agree to your face ... and then oppose you, expose you, and slander you behind your back', Prince Napoleon added: 'I believe that the worst thing about your government, which weakens it, is internal dissension ... The more power is concentrated in the hands of the Emperor, the more indispensable is unity amongst those who serve him.'[8] In this instance he recommended the replacement of men he judged to be without principles like Fould, Walewski, and Baroche.[9] Death added to the problems. Billault, exhausted, died in October 1863, to be replaced by Rouher in the key position of Minister of State and chief government spokesman and target for parliamentary attacks. More obviously, the situation of ministers had begun to change from 22 November 1860 when the Emperor agreed to appoint ministers without portfolio to take on the increasingly difficult task of defending government policy in the Corps législatif. Constitutionally, ministers remained solely responsible to the monarch, but it would be difficult for a minister who lost the confidence of the Assembly to remain in office.

As the political situation changed, the Emperor's freedom to select ministers was thus reduced. As his health deteriorated, government was increasingly subject to intrigue, both as a result of quarrels between ministers and the intervention of individuals without formal authority but who belonged to the Imperial entourage. Thus in the 1860s Walewski and Morny pressed for liberalisation and Persigny attacked the surviving authoritarian features of the regime as much out of personal hostility towards Rouher, Baroche, and Fould as from political conviction. Rouher and Morny had quarrelled in 1857 over the latter's treatment of his mistress, the Countess Le Hon. Morny's questionable speculative activity intensified their mutual dislike.[10] Conflicts over status and responsibilities were also frequent. Even if Billault, when Minister of the Interior, generally supported Haussmann, the prefect of the Seine, who, at least technically, was his subordinate, the latter's strong

[7] See e.g. Maurain, *Baroche*, p. 238.
[8] Letter from Prince Napoleon to the Emperor, 5 March 1859, in Hauterive, *Napoléon III*, pp. 139–40.
[9] 20 April 1859, *ibid.*, pp. 162–3.   [10] Schnerb, *Rouher*, pp. 122–3, 151.

personality, privileged relationship with the Emperor, and constant demands for resources inevitably caused difficulties. When Billault accused
him of insubordination in 1857 Haussmann went straight to the monarch
for support.[11] A system which encouraged favouritism did not always
attract the best-qualified personnel. Emile Ollivier's judgement of La
Valette, Interior Minister in 1865-6 and subsequently Foreign Minister
in 1866 and again in 1868-9, is revealing. According to Ollivier this
eminent figure was 'a mediocre personality, ignorant, lazy, a man of
pleasure'. With his polished, aristocratic manners he had proved to be
a 'superior courtier, skilled at making the most of court factions, at flat-
tery, and taking whatever course of action might profit him personally
... To consolidate his situation he informed the Emperor about the internal situation in much the same way as Bazaine informed him about
the state of affairs in Mexico: he left disagreeable facts in the shadows.'
In Ollivier's opinion, the Emperor needed to find new and younger
men urgently, otherwise there was a danger of the regime turning into a
gérontocratie.[12]

Against this background, around twenty ministers at any one time
sought to carry out their duties, with varying degrees of success. They
were a disparate group, with Persigny almost unique in his commitment
to Bonapartism. The majority came from solid *haut bourgeois* families and
previously had been socially conservative and anti-democratic supporters of the parliamentary institutions associated with Orleanism. Although
they were personally loyal to the Emperor they were not always in tune
with his policies. The key figures included Bineau, Magne, Fould – who
at various times served as finance minister, the three lawyers – Billault,
who succeeded Persigny at Interior in 1854, Baroche, President of the
Conseil d'Etat and Rouher, Minister of Commerce and Public Works
in the 1850s. Other former Orleanists included Walewski, the clerical
illegitimate son of Napoleon I, and Morny the Emperor's half-brother,
arch-speculator and president of the Corps législatif at a crucial time.
Their shared experience of the July Monarchy resulted in a certain uniformity of approach. The other experience, which unalterably shaped their
outlook, was the 1848 Revolution. The social fear this provoked certainly
reinforced the commitment of Baroche and Rouher to the authoritarian
Empire which had rescued France from the chaos to which it had been
reduced by parliamentary regimes.[13] During the 1850s it was probably

[11] See e.g. G. E. Haussmann, *Mémoires* (Paris 1893), II, pp. 156–8, 222–5.
[12] E. Ollivier, *L'Empire libéral* (Paris 1895–1918), VII, p. 503 and IX, p. 176.
[13] See e.g. *ibid.*, II, p. 324; Schnerb, *Rouher*, p. 161.

Baroche, working in close harmony with Rouher and Fould, who was the most influential figure. As President of the Conseil d'Etat he was responsible for the preparation and presentation of legislation to the Corps législatif. A liberal on economic issues, he was politically conservative and a Gallican on religious matters – in marked contrast to the clericalism of Magne and Walewski. The onset of liberalisation saw Baroche, together with Magne and Billault, acting as government spokesmen in the assembly. Although his status was diminished by these reforms, Baroche served as Minister of Justice and Religious Affairs from 1863 to 1869 and remained an influential critic of moves towards further liberalisation. His successor as the single most influential minister would be Rouher.

Rouher had been an extremely successful Minister of Public Works. However, it was Billault who was appointed to the important new office of Minister of State and government spokesman in the Corps législatif in 1863, with Rouher as his assistant. His performance there was described by that experienced English observer Nassau William Senior as in 'tone and manner [that] of a lawyer, not of a statesmen. He speaks, in fact, avowedly as a mere advocate ... he does not pretend to utter sentiments of his own.'[14] Prince Napoleon made much the same point about his lack of vision, pointing out additionally that 'he concentrates all his attention on the means of attenuating difficulties. We live from day to day.'[15] Following Billault's death in 1863, Rouher took over and rapidly made himself almost indispensable – *almost*, because, as Rouher was only too aware, Napoleon was determined not to accord even his most trusted subordinate too much authority. In a climate of growing political tension he became the symbol of authoritarian government and of devotion to the Emperor. Personally a convinced free-trader, he also opposed the determination of the propertied classes to re-establish the political power they had enjoyed during the July Monarchy, afraid that this would lead to renewed political instability. By 1869, serving as Minister of State and of Finance, he was overworked and tired and increasingly discredited in parliamentary circles.[16] His problems were increased substantially by the Emperor's indecision.

Ministers remained at their posts out of a sense of personal loyalty to Napoleon but also from a desire to retain power with all its trappings, including high salaries and the gifts showered on them by a grateful master. In a far more nepotistic age, there were also opportunities to

---

[14] *Conversations*, II, pp. 19–20.
[15] Quoted Caron, *La France*, p. 24; similar observation by Barail, *Mes souvenirs*, III, p. 109.
[16] See e.g. Schnerb, *Rouher*, p. 212.

establish family and friends in well-remunerated official positions. Ministers enjoyed a basic salary of 40,000 francs as well as accommodation and carriages, with further rewards for those nominated to the senate or Conseil d'Etat. Access to privileged information also permitted most ministers to engage in highly profitable financial speculation.[17] The loyalty of the Emperor to his ministers, together with their reluctance to leave office, resulted in a significant ageing. The average age of ministers increased from forty-eight in 1852 to fifty-nine by 1867. Membership of this small group was altered mainly by death (Saint-Arnaud in 1854; Fortoul 1855; Billault 1863; Morny 1865; Thouvenel 1866; Fould 1867; Walewski 1868). Finding adequate replacements became a matter of growing concern.[18]

The death of Morny, who as president of the Corps législatif had encouraged its growing assertiveness, certainly represented a setback for the process of liberalisation. Concerned by opposition successes in the cities in the 1863 elections, he had suggested a new approach to the Emperor. Concluding that 'the elections have left only two forces, the Empire and democracy', he had advised that 'it is time to immediately extend political liberty ... and to study social problems. The Emperor should, as a matter of urgency, avoid causing surprises, and no longer leave his advisors in a state of complete ignorance concerning his foreign policy.'[19] Prince Napoleon, who similarly favoured abandonment of the system of official candidature, together with the election of mayors and the replacement of ministers and prefects too closely associated with the authoritarian regime, proved to be an unsatisfactory substitute. He also enjoyed easy access to the monarch, but lacked tact and political sensitivity. In May 1865 the Emperor felt obliged to disassociate himself publicly from the liberal and anticlerical sentiments expressed by his cousin, although meetings and correspondence between the two continued and one should not discount the influence of the Prince entirely. Certainly, in comparison with these two advocates of reform, Emile Ollivier, for all his idealism and influence as a parliamentary orator, would cast rather a pale shadow. From as early as 1863, encouraged by Morny, and with the support of his republican colleague Darimon, Ollivier had been willing to search for a compromise with the regime. By 1865 his role had changed from that of an outright opponent of the regime to that of a

---

[17] See e.g. Barbier, *Finance*, pp. 192, 199.
[18] See e.g. 'Note pour l'Empereur', written by Rouher, 15 Oct. 1867 in *Papiers et correspondance de la famille impériale*, ed. R. I. Severs, I, pp. 132–3.
[19] Hauterive, *Napoléon III*, pp. 379–80.

member of the loyal opposition. Offered a place in government as early as January 1867, Ollivier had concluded that to enter a government alongside Rouher would destroy his credibility as a reformer. He believed that it was essential to combine a radical change in policy with that of personnel. The old war-horses must be replaced by the representatives of a younger generation, which, previously, had felt excluded. Rouher also rejected collaboration.[20] Nothing less than a clear commitment to the establishment of parliamentary government by the Emperor together with a request to assume responsibility for forming a new administration would satisfy Ollivier. His own political programme was outlined in a book, *Le 19 janvier*, published in 1869:

The Emperor's responsibility is for the overall direction of government, that of ministers is for their share in determining that direction and for the detailed execution of policy. The Emperor's responsibility cannot be denied except by a plebiscite or a revolution. It represents the constitutional recognition of popular sovereignty; ministerial responsibility which depends on the support of a majority [of deputies] recognises the political rights of the Assembly.[21]

Clearly Ollivier was willing to concede a major role to the Emperor, accepting privately that the government should not include individuals to whom Napoleon objected, recognising in effect an Imperial veto.[22] The balance of power was shifting, nevertheless. The Emperor accepted, however reluctantly, following the 1869 elections, that decisive constitutional change had become necessary. On 27 December Ollivier received the following request from the Emperor: 'I request that you nominate those individuals who might form, with you, a homogeneous cabinet, faithfully representing the majority in the Corps législatif.'[23]

Acceptance of the need for change was primarily in response to pressure from conservative liberals, both those in opposition and, more significantly, from supporters of the government anxious to restrain some of the Emperor's wilder impulses. The pressure had been building up for some time. Even the banker Achille Fould, responsible for the Imperial household until December 1860 and thus in especially close contact with the Emperor, and then finance minister from September 1861 until January 1867, a man personally devoted to the monarch and to the

[20] Ollivier to Napoleon, 12 Oct. 1869 in Poulet-Malassis, *Papiers secrets*.
[21] Quoted Girard, *Napoléon III*, p. 437.
[22] Letter from Ollivier to Duvernois, the Emperor's intermediary, 24 Oct. 1869 in Poulet-Malassis, *Papiers secrets*.
[23] Quoted Pinol, 'L'exercice du pouvoir' in Y. Lequin (ed.), *Histoire des français 19e–20e siècles* (Paris 1984), III, p. 113.

authoritarian regime, accepted the need to restrain his master. Conservative financial precepts and the ideal of the balanced budget were his guiding principles. In a *Mémoire* written, presumably at the Emperor's behest, whilst out of office in September 1861, Fould was extremely critical of the development of extraordinary and supplementary expenditures. His solution was the reinforcement of the budgetary controls exercised by the Corps législatif. At a joint meeting of ministers with the Conseil privé on 12 November, Rouher and Baroche – also liberal in financial matters and authoritarian in politics – supported Fould.[24] The Emperor himself, aware of disquiet in the financial circles upon whose support his public works programme depended, decided that Fould's highly critical memo should be published and its author appointed Minister of Finance with instructions to implement the reforms he had proposed.[25] The explanation subsequently offered by the Emperor to a ministerial meeting on 22 November is of considerable interest.[26]

Engaging in useful expenditure is a considerable temptation. As a result I would like to impose on my ministers, and on myself, a barrier that will not be exceeded without careful reflection.

In addition I would like to destroy the impression which appears to prevail abroad that my government is so absolute that I hold in my hand the entire wealth of France and that I can dispose of it as I wish, whether for my personal needs or the reconstruction of Paris.

This is one of the causes of that hostility, of the fear which France inspires, because it is assumed that suddenly, without warning, I can, from one day to the next, mobilise enormous funds ... for military preparations. I would like everyone to know that is impossible.

In addition to representing a major step in the re-assertion of parliamentary control, these changes would do much to restore the central governmental role of the Finance Ministry and its ability to exert control over the budgets of other ministries. This had declined in the 1850s in relation to such centres of expenditure as Haussmann's Paris prefecture and Rouher's Public Works Ministry. The presence of Fould in government would be seen now as a guarantee of greater financial orthodoxy. His dismissal in January 1867, because of his lack of sympathy with political liberalisation, would be a severe blow to the regime's financial credibility.[27] In the same month the government's authority was further weakened by the savaging of the proposals for military reform

---

[24] See Maréchal de Castellane, *Journal* (Paris 1897), III, p. 155, for account of discussion at dinner at Fould's.
[25] Barbier, *Finance*, pp. 205–6.   [26] Maurain, *Baroche*, p. 226.   [27] Barbier, *Finance*, pp. 241–3.

introduced by Marshal Randon. This revealed strong disenchantment amongst many of the regime's normal supporters. Rouher, who was afraid that they might alienate both conservative deputies and the peasant support on which electoral success depended, defended the measures only half-heartedly.[28]

The Emperor accepted the final moves towards a parliamentary regime with considerable reluctance. He did not want to abandon trusted ministers. In his own inimitable way, Persigny had warned Napoleon against the temptation to retain established figures.

The danger comes from those two men [Rouher and Baroche] who personify the unpopularity of the regime in the eyes of the public, of whom the public is tired, bored and almost ashamed, from two men who are the real causes of the regime's demoralisation, who represent precisely the kind of petty-minded bourgeois system, with its trickery, its unprincipled little expedients, lack of conviction, of morality, and of *grandeur*, which characterised the government of Louis-Philippe ... With these two men, public contempt and the dissatisfaction of honest men will increase at the same time as the audacity of the regime's enemies and public disaffection. Unless you have the courage somehow to get rid of them, everything is impossible, and your regime is condemned.[29]

Prince Napoleon was similarly forthright, pointing out the adverse consequences for public opinion of the retention of ministers like Rouher as spokesmen for the government when they were notorious for their opposition to its new policy of liberalisation.[30] Only the disastrous election results in 1869, followed by the signature by 116 deputies of a petition in favour of reform and their obvious hostility to the Emperor's ministers, finally ensured the replacement of an obviously tired and dejected Rouher. Even then he was compensated with the presidency of the Senate, and would remain influential. In the meantime a transition ministry was formed to prepare a new liberal constitution before handing over to a properly constituted parliamentary ministry headed by Ollivier.

The ministry formed on 2 January 1870 was to be collectively responsible to both parliament and the monarch. In accepting this situation, according to General Fleury, one of his closest confidants, the Emperor had two main objectives. These were, firstly to 'disarm the monarchist and parliamentary oppositions and bring them into our camp' and to use the fact that the new ministry 'cannot be accused of being too closely

---

[28] See e.g. J. Casewitz, *Une loi manquée, la loi Niel, 1866–68. L'Armée française à la veille de la guerre de 1870* (Paris 1960), pp. 52–5.

[29] Quoted Schnerb, *Rouher*, pp. 255–6.

[30] Letter from Prince Napoleon to the Emperor, 24 Jan. 1867, in Hauterive, *Napoléon III*, pp. 280–2.

attached to the person of the Sovereign ... to employ the most energetic repression'.[31] Napoleon was determined to use Ollivier to his own advantage. Fleury insisted that under the new system there should be: 'Liberty yes, but not licence; discussion yes, but respect for the Sovereign, respect for the army, for without that we are lost.'[32] The Ollivier ministry was not to last long. Faced with dissatisfied liberals and republicans as well as a hard core of authoritarian Bonapartists, it was never going to have an easy time.[33] In terms of its composition it was not quite the renewal of government personnel for which Ollivier had asked.[34] It included the liberal representatives of a centre-left committed to a parliamentary regime but who would shortly resign (Buffet, Daru, Talhouët) in protest against the decision to hold a plebiscite, as well as those of a centre-right, supporters of a liberal monarchy. Ollivier's personal position was weak. Of eight civilian ministers, six were pronounced clericals (Buffet, Chevandier de Valdrôme, Daru, Parieu, Segris, and Talhouët). Most were economic protectionists and Ollivier was forced to concede a major enquiry into the effects of the 1860 commercial treaty. He would remain an isolated figure in an essentially centre-right government divided over major issues and riven by personal differences.[35] Thiers, undoubtedly the leading figure in the liberal opposition, would perhaps have been a more appropriate choice as chief minister, and the possibility had been considered. However, it was decided that he was too domineering and would have threatened the Emperor's remaining prerogatives. At any rate Napoleon appears to have had little confidence in his new government,[36] whilst the successful outcome of the plebiscite in May only encouraged the authoritarian Bonapartists in their determination to obstruct the process of liberalisation. In these circumstances the lack of coherent policy-making was hardly surprising. The first reverses in the war of 1870 lent weight to criticism of Ollivier by the Empress, Persigny, Rouher, and Fleury. In the Corps législatif there were demands on 9 August for a 'cabinet capable of organising the nation's defence'. That evening a government formed entirely by the right was established. It was led by the hero of punitive missions in China, General Cousin-Montauban, Comte de Palikao. This victory by the authoritarians was reinforced by the decision that in future members of the Conseil privé would participate in meetings

---

[31] General Fleury to Duvernois, 7 Feb. 1870, AN AB XIX 173.   [32] Maurain, *Baroche*, p. 491.

[33] See warnings from Clément Duvernois to Napoleon on 8 Nov. 1869 in *Papiers et correspondance*, I, pp. 267–9.

[34] Ollivier to Napoleon, 12 Nov. 1869, *ibid.*, pp. 271–2.

[35] See e.g. Ollivier, *L'Empire libéral*, XII, p. 226.

[36] Report of conversation with Emperor on 13 June 1870 in Haussmann, *Mémoires*, II, pp. 563–5.

of the council of ministers.[37] Doubtless aggrieved, Ollivier saw this as the restoration of the 'vice-emperor' – Rouher. However, this was to be the final victory of the representatives of the authoritarian Empire over the proponents of parliamentary government.

THE CORPS LEGISLATIF

One of Napoleon's original objectives had been to weaken considerably the authority of parliament, which he perceived to be a divisive forum for political dispute and party particularism. From its origins the regime had sought legitimacy by appealing directly to popular sovereignty. The device of the plebiscite was used on three occasions. On 21 December 1851 to confirm the outcome of the *coup*; on 21 November 1852 to approve the restoration of the hereditary empire; and finally in May 1870 to confirm the liberal reforms. On each occasion popular support provided a means of re-affirming the empire's legitimacy. Only the Emperor was the elect of the nation. In contrast, parliamentary deputies were elected by particular, geographically confined, constituencies.

The constitution provided for a Senate, the role of which was to reject legislation or acts of the administration which were judged to be contrary to the constitution, to religious morality, individual liberty, and equality (*les grands principes proclamés en 1789*), or which threatened the sanctity of private property, the independence of the magistrature or the security of France. By means of a procedure known as the *sénatus-consulte* it would consider amendments to the constitution, although major changes were to be submitted to a plebiscite. Theoretically, then, its powers were immense, but in practice this guardian of liberty showed little desire to oppose the government. This was hardly surprising when, in addition to members of the Bonaparte family, cardinals, and marshals, its members were selected carefully and richly endowed by the Emperor. The Senate was to be a means of rewarding loyal servants of the regime, retired deputies and soldiers, the occasional businessman and intellectual. Nomination as a senator was the culminating event in a successful career. Very occasionally there were faint signs of opposition. In January 1857 many senators were aggrieved by the loss of their power to debate commercial treaties, a threat to a variety of economic interest groups. A commission actually drew attention to 'the disquiet of many major industries which ... have developed in the shelter of protection and

---

37 See e.g. Maurain, *Baroche*, p. 491.

whose very existence might be threatened by a commercial treaty.'[38] If the commission's members finally acceded to the Emperor's wishes they continued to insist on the principle of parliamentary control over credits for public works and over the budget. Considerable dissent would again be voiced within this, the most Bonapartist of the regime's institutions, over the question of liberal reform in 1869, but once more this was not sustained.

The lower house, the Corps législatif, was to be elected by all adult (over twenty-one) males, with the exception of criminals, including those guilty of political crimes. Around 92 per cent of those qualified actually registered as voters. The Emperor had the exclusive right to convene, adjourn, or dissolve the Assembly, although in case of dissolution he was required to convene a new Assembly within six months. Voting would be organised on the basis of single-member constituencies, with roughly one deputy for every 35,000 voters. The *scrutin de liste* system favoured by the Republic was abandoned because it seemed to favour the expression of political opinions. Candidates were required to obtain an absolute majority of the votes cast on the first ballot or else submit to a second ballot. The consent of the Corps législatif would be required for all laws and taxes. Its role, however, was viewed as primarily consultative. It would discuss legislative proposals prepared by the Conseil d'Etat, which would be presented by its president (Baroche until 1860). Deputies would not be permitted to initiate legislation. They would not be able to bring down governments, whose ministers were not allowed to become members of the legislature or even to appear before it. Although they would have the right to approve or reject legislation this could only occur en bloc and without amendment. As a result, deputies would be very reluctant to contemplate a total rejection of budgetary proposals in case this would lead to the complete paralysis of the state.[39] Moreover the Corps législatif would sit for only three months each year (May–July) and ministers quickly appreciated that if legislation was presented only towards the end of this period there was little chance of it being examined rigorously, although such tactics as submitting a law to regularise extraordinary financial credits on the very last day of the parliamentary session in June 1854 did arouse too much criticism to be repeated.[40] Legislative proposals, approved by the Conseil d'Etat, were submitted to the seven

[38] Quoted *ibid.*, pp. 129–30.
[39] See e.g. L. Girard, *Problèmes politiques et constitutionnels du Second Empire* (Paris n.d.), pp. 75–6; Rougerie, 'Second Empire,' pp. 65–6.
[40] Maurain, *Baroche*, pp. 149–50.

bureaux into which deputies were divided. Following discussion, each of these elected a *rapporteur* who presented suggested amendments to the Conseil d'Etat. The final bill, incorporating any changes accepted by the Conseil was presented to the Corps législatif. Although this complex procedure was intended to reduce the importance of parliamentary debate some sessions were serious affairs. Around fifty deputies (the *budgétaires*), including men devoted to the regime like Gouin, Devinck, or Larrabure, might be expected to criticise 'excessive' expenditure on public works and to express their alarm at any hint of reductions in protective customs tariffs. Deputies delivered warning shots after proposals to abolish the prohibition of certain imports were presented in June 1856. This kind of criticism focused, however, on detail rather than major political issues. Nevertheless, it proved to be such an irritant to the Emperor that a *sénatus-consulte* was convoked on 25 December 1852, which conferred on him the right to modify tariffs and initiate public works, by decree.[41] Another cause of dissent was a series of proposals to increase the powers of the government in education, at the expense of the church. Initially, however, genuine discussion was confined to the privacy of parliamentary committees, especially those dealing with budgetary questions. Publicity was limited. The press was not allowed to reprint debates in full, but only the official, truncated account.

In spite of the existence of manhood suffrage the Corps législatif remained an assembly representative almost solely of the wealthy social elites determined to defend their vested interests. In 1852, eighty-one appear to have had claims to nobility. Most deputies were landowners or members of the liberal professions, particularly lawyers. Many of those classified as landowners had formerly been in the service of the state and most deputies, whatever their supposed occupation, were landowners. Continuity was more evident than change, although the number of businessmen continued to increase and a growing proportion of these were industrialists rather than merchants or bankers.[42] Serving government officials were now barred, so that the new regime was unable to pack the lower house with its dependents on the model of the July Monarchy. Nevertheless, a significant proportion of deputies had previously served in the bureaucracy or army (see table 2) and might be expected to sympathise with the interests of the state.

---

[41] A. Darimon, *Histoire d'un parti. Les cinq sous l'empire (1857–60)* (Paris 1888), entry of 9 May 1858, pp. 259–60.
[42] T. Zeldin, *The Political System of Napoleon III* (Oxford 1958), p. 62; Plessis, *Second Empire*, pp. 36f.

Table 2. *Occupations of deputies elected in 1852 and 1869*[a]

	1852	Percentage	1869	Percentage
Landowners, without other profession	97	37	85	30
Former civil servants	29	11	53	18
Businessmen	57	20	65	22
Lawyers	30	12	44	15
Other professionals	25	10	28	10
Former military	22	8	13	5

[a] Based on E. Anceau, *Les députés du Second Empire* (Paris 2000), p. 62.

A similar structure of membership was characteristic of the departmental conseils généraux, although often, in rural regions in particular, these bodies were characterised by a growing social exclusiveness as nobles sought to reinforce their local status.[43] In many respects the Second Empire marked the apogee of an exclusive class of *notables*.

Politically, amongst the 260 deputies elected in 1852 there were around 70 self-affirmed Bonapartists. Their views varied considerably. Forty were newcomers to politics; another 25 had formerly been identified with the Orleanist dynastic opposition. Amongst the remaining 190 deputies there was a powerful current of gratitude and of loyalty to the regime.[44] There were only three declared Legitimist opponents. Three republicans (Hénon in Lyon, Carnot and Cavaignac in Paris) were elected, but refused to take the oath of allegiance and were unseated. Only in 1857/8 would an effective group of republicans secure election and accept the necessity of taking the oath – Hénon in Lyon, and Ollivier, Darimon, Picard, and Favre in Paris. Although Haussmann denounced them as representing the 'old army of insurrection, always with us',[45] in reality these were moderates, legalistic in their opposition. Even so, they were ignored or treated with contempt by their parliamentary colleagues.[46] Additionally, perhaps a quarter of deputies were to show occasional signs of independence. The leading Catholic layman, the Comte de Montalembert, who had greeted the *coup d'état* with enthusiasm, soon launched into denunciations of a political system which reduced parliament to a rubber stamp. He won little support and would complain

[43] See e.g. L. Girard, A. Prost, and R. Gossez, *Les conseillers généraux en 1870* (Paris 1967), p. 52.
[44] Zeldin, *Political System*, pp. 28–32.   [45] Quoted Caron, *La France*, p. 166.
[46] Darimon, *Les cinq*, entry 29 Jan. 1858, p. 103.

of 'the tireless complacency and boundless self-abasement' of this assembly. This was perhaps a little unfair. The Corps législatif was, after all, made up of men of independent means, many of them with substantial political experience, who were always likely to resent and eventually to resist government tutelage. As Darimon pointed out: 'the seed of the liberal Empire was present in the Constitution of 1852, because ... as long as there existed an elected chamber, voting on the budget and the military contingent ... there was no despotism. Sooner or later the official candidatures would transform themselves into independent candidatures'.[47] The 'authoritarian' decade thus saw the partial emergence of a mixed and rather muted opposition – predominantly conservative, liberal, protectionist, and clerical. This process would be encouraged by Morny following his appointment as President of the Corps législatif in 1854. Indeed the Emperor himself declared before the assembled senators and deputies on 14 February 1853: 'To those who regret that a greater share has not been allotted to liberty, I reply: liberty has never helped to found a lasting edifice; it crowns it when time has consolidated its existence.'[48]

Not all deputies were willing to wait. The presence in the Corps législatif of a large number of experienced parliamentarians, self-confident notables, with essentially liberal views, made it inevitable that a challenge to the authoritarian regime would emerge once their fear of revolution declined. The regime's Italian policy in 1859 and the commercial treaty with Britain in 1860, which appeared so contrary to their perceived interests, provided the occasions. Unlike his predecessors Napoleon would be prepared to offer concessions. The Emperor was an admirer of the British and Swiss constitutions, although he insisted that revolution had created a very different context in France. In a speech on 19 January 1858 he insisted that 'liberty without limits is impossible whilst there exists in a country a faction determined to disregard the fundamental bases of the constitution, because then liberty, instead of serving to enlighten, control, and improve government, is nothing but a weapon in the hands of parties determined to overthrow it'.[49] Again, a few days after the opening of the 1863 parliamentary session, speaking to French exhibitors at the London Exposition, the Emperor observed that 'You have been struck by the existence in England of an unrestricted freedom to express every opinion and to develop every interest. This exists because English liberty respects the foundations on which society

---

[47] Ollivier, *L'Empire libéral*, v, p. 86.
[48] Quoted Girard, *Les libéraux français, 1814–75* (Paris 1985), p. 202.
[49] Quoted by Duc de Persigny, 'Note sur la situation intérieure' (Aug. 1865), AN AB xix 175.

and the state are built. France will enjoy similar freedom once we have consolidated the indispensable base for the establishment of a complete liberty.' Morny felt a greater sense of urgency. Motivated by a terror of revolution and the belief that only concessions would head it off, he spoke of the need for 'the gradual establishment of liberty in order to establish the Imperial dynasty on permanent foundations'[50] and worked to enhance the powers of the Corps législatif. Advised by Walewski and Thiers, he planned and promoted the 1860 reforms and insisted on the need to restore civil liberties. In his speech at the end of the 1863 parliamentary session he claimed that 'a government without control and without criticism is like a ship without ballast. The absence of argument leads the government astray and fails to re-assure the country. Debate has done more to increase security than a deceptive silence.'[51] He believed that the gradual extension of liberty was the only means of avoiding foreign policy disasters and of securing the dynasty. In practical terms a widening of parliamentary debate would provide a better understanding of public opinion.[52]

The decree of 24 November 1860, introduced against ministerial advice, had allowed the Corps législatif and Senate to debate the address from the throne which accompanied the opening of each parliamentary session. As a practical measure and because of the poor performance of the *conseillers d'état* who had previously introduced legislation, the decree also created ministers without portfolio, initially Magne, Billault, and Baroche, to explain and defend government policy. In future the verbatim publication of debates would also be allowed, giving much-needed publicity to parliamentary activity. According to Persigny the objective was 'to encourage ... the development of the habit of free debate'.[53] From 1863 a Minister of State was appointed as spokesman for the government. First Billault and, after his death in October, Rouher occupied this key post. Due to his ability to conciliate and cajole deputies and his dogged loyalty to the Emperor, Rouher would rapidly become the regime's dominant minister. Thiers, who had analysed the reforms for Louis-Philippe's son, the Duc d'Aumale, pointed out in a letter of 8 January 1861 that as the 'fear of the reds' had declined, the Corps législatif had become inevitably less manageable. He concluded that through these reforms

[50] Ollivier, *L'Empire libéral*, VI, p. 132. [51] Girard, *Napoleon III*, pp. 358–9.
[52] Memo, Morny to Emperor, June 1863, copied to Ollivier, in Ollivier, *L'Empire libéral*, VI, pp. 501–2.
[53] 7 December 1860, quoted Maurain, *La politique ecclésiastique du Second Empire de 1852 à 1869* (Paris 1930), p. 486.

the Emperor, to some degree followed his own inclinations, and to some extent the pressure of circumstances. His inclination always has been to believe, as he often told me, that repression was by its nature a passing phase. He assumed that sooner or later it would be necessary to make concessions to the renewed desire for independence and believed that it was preferable to avoid waiting until they ceased to be voluntary.

Additionally, Thiers believed that Napoleon was preparing the way for his son, and had accepted that preaching liberty to the Pope and other foreign potentates whilst refusing to extend it at home was too much of a contradiction. He accepted the sincerity of the Emperor's intentions but doubted whether these were supported by a 'clear and complete understanding of what has been done ... The Emperor believes that he has got away with an annual debate ... following which he will remain in control of the state.' The manner in which the reforms were implemented would be decisive. 'If he makes concessions in a dignified manner, the regime will be able to gain in longevity what it loses in absolute power; otherwise he will return to the era of revolutions, because the course of action he has entered upon is one along which one can march slowly but never stop, much less reverse.' A decisive step had been taken. 'He has been remarkably wise if he is serious in the measures he has taken; but extremely imprudent if he has only given in to a momentary whim in response to circumstances and the desire to be applauded.'[54] Thiers concluded that liberals should welcome these concessions and use them to engage in constructive criticism. He recognised that this might lead to an eventual accommodation with the Empire but accepted that compromise was better than continued conflict, which might well lead to another revolution.[55] In contrast, Darimon, from the moderate republican point of view, was concerned that concessions made to clericals and protectionists heralded a compromise between the Emperor and conservative politicians and might well represent something retrograde.[56]

These were indeed concessions made to the Corps législatif from a position of strength. At this stage ultra-Catholic and protectionist criticism hardly represented a threat to the regime. Nevertheless, they were symptomatic of a growing current of unrest. In this respect, and with the longer term in view, these reforms were made out of a sense of necessity and probably with the hope that further substantial concessions would be rendered unnecessary. Additional reforms nonetheless followed. The

[54] 8 Jan. 1861, BN naf 20618.   [55] Darimon, *Les cinq*, entry of 27 Nov. 1860, p. 415.
[56] Letter from Darimon to Proudhon, 2 Jan. 1861, in A. Darimon, *L'opposition libérale sous l'Empire (1861–63)* (Paris 1886), p. 10.

official *Moniteur* on 15 November 1861 published a letter from the former minister and banker Fould to the Emperor, probably written at the latter's request, together with the monarch's response, which accepted Fould's criticism of the government's financial management and appointed him Finance Minister. The *sénatus-consulte* of 31 December ended the government's power to levy extraordinary credits by decree and reinforced parliamentary controls over expenditure. This satisfied many of the criticisms made previously in private sessions of the Corps législatif's budget commission. The Emperor's objective was to restore business confidence and assuage conservative anxiety concerning possible tax increases and even the introduction of an income tax. Explaining his motives to ministers at Compiègne on 22 November Napoleon stressed both the need to impose a check on the instinct to spend on useful projects and to re-assure foreign powers about levels of military expenditure.[57] This did not entirely end sharp practices. Even Fould would conceal the heavy costs of the intervention in Mexico. Nevertheless, Haussmann would be complaining soon about the financial conservatism of the likes of Fould and Rouher, of the predominance of 'the narrow, routine ideas of the Paris middle class ... completely and instinctively hostile to our great work'.[58]

The essential problem for the regime in making piecemeal concessions from 1860 was that liberals would never be satisfied with anything less than a return to a parliamentary system similar to that of the July Monarchy, in which deputies enjoyed the right to question ministers, reject their proposals, and to initiate legislation. In addition they wanted a substantial increase in press freedom. It was maintained that only this would allow them to defend their vital interests. Clericals, protectionists, *budgétaires*, critics of the regime's foreign policy, all those made anxious by the arbitrary and seemingly erratic character of government, wanted change. The Emperor's personal initiatives had to be brought under control. Concessions, which left the Emperor's prerogatives largely intact, failed to satisfy his critics. At the same time they demoralised supporters of authoritarian government. Persigny complained, in July 1865, with an air of despair, that 'for the last three years, every day has brought a victory for [the opposition], every day has engaged us more and more in a parliamentary regime and on the road towards the ruin of the Empire'.[59] Furthermore, and in spite of the Emperor's denials, there appeared to be every prospect of additional change. Morny's proposals,

[57] Quoted Maurain, *Baroche*, p. 226; see also Barbier, *Finance*, pp. 205–6.
[58] Maurain, *Baroche*, p. 212.   [59] Persigny to Emperor, 27 July 1865, BN naf 23066.

early in 1865, that deputies should be given the right to initiate legislation
and amendments and to question ministers were nevertheless rejected
after his death in March, on the advice of a joint meeting of ministers
and the Conseil privé.[60] Advice of this kind invariably confirmed the
Emperor's own misgivings[61] and helped give the process of reform a
hesitant appearance. Typically, in the address from the throne in 1865,
Napoleon declared: 'France dreads the excesses of liberty as much as
the excesses of power. Let us be content to add each day a new stone
to the edifice.' The following year the speech made a renewed commitment to the constitutional principles of 1852, profoundly discouraging
the liberals.[62] The view of Prince Napoleon, close to the Emperor in spite
of their sometimes bitter disagreements, was that his cousin would not
willingly extend political liberty but that 'if opinion demands it, he will
give in.'[63] It was, indeed, the further development of liberal opposition,
which explains the concessions made in 1867.

The 1863 elections had seen the return of seventeen republican and
fifteen independent deputies. Morny, in a note to the Emperor, insisted
that 'the elections have left two forces face to face: the Emperor and
Democracy. The forces of democracy grow without cease and it is urgent
to satisfy them to avoid being swept away.' The alternative – another *coup
d'état* – would enjoy little public support.[64] Control of parliament became
increasingly difficult. Public interest was increased by a series of brilliant
and linguistically violent debates involving notably Thiers and Rouher,
with the former formulating a coherent liberal programme in two major speeches in January 1864 in which he demanded *les libertés nécessaires*
and condemned the government's financial policy. Reproduced in the
press, these were to inform and mould public opinion and propel the
regime on a parliamentary course. The growing signs of independence
and sympathy for liberal ideas amongst government supporters, together
with the failure to secure support for military reform in the aftermath
of the Prussian victory over Austria in 1866, convinced ministers that
the government's majority in the Corps législatif was in danger of disintegrating. Given the regime's unwillingness to make the kind of policy

---

[60] See e.g. Maurain, *Baroche*, p. 373.
[61] See e.g. Prince Napoleon, conversation with Ollivier, reported in Ollivier, *L'Empire libéral*, VII,
p. 272.
[62] Printed *ibid.*, VII, pp. 562–4.
[63] Discussion with Ollivier, 27 Jan. 1865 – *ibid.*, VII, pp. 269, 272; the view also of Emile de Girardin
following conversation with the Emperor in December 1863 and reported by A. Darimon,
Le tiers parti sous L'Empire (1863–66) (1887), entry of 19 Dec. 1863, p. 65.
[64] Quoted Girard, *Napoléon III*, p. 365.

shifts which would have allowed an opening to the left, it was forced into an effort to restore the conservative alliance and to conciliate its liberal, clerical, and protectionist critics. As a result, in a letter published in the *Moniteur* on 19 January 1867, the Emperor conceded the right to question ministers in place of the very restricted right of debate on the address. There was also the promise of new laws on the press and public meetings. In May 1868 the preliminary authorisation formerly required before newspapers could be published was abolished, as was the system of warnings to editors. The press would in future be subject to the jurisdiction of the courts although without the further safeguard of jury trial. The need for official permission to hold non-political and non-religious meetings was also abolished, as was that for electoral gatherings. These were measures which caused considerable concern amongst conservatives but represented a realistic response to public resentment of arbitrary government. They would contribute to a spectacular revival of political life and especially republican agitation in the cities. The retention in office of Rouher and those other stalwarts of authoritarianism who had so recently and vehemently opposed reform,[65] however, continued to weaken public confidence in the regime's commitment to the reform process.[66] By the last session of the Corps législatif elected in 1863 there was a widespread conviction that only substantial further liberalisation, together with a guarantee of peace, would save the dynasty. During the 1869 electoral campaign an influential figure like Chesnelong, standing in the Basses-Pyrénées, would express the mixture of 'realism' and anxiety so common amongst government supporters by insisting that 'the Empire, in spite of its faults, remains the basis of order in France and in Europe. We must know how to defend it in resisting it, in developing in it if possible ... the spirit of conservatism seasoned by a sincere and prudent liberalism.'[67]

These elections revealed a marked decline in support for the regime and were followed by serious disorders in Paris and other cities. The meeting of the new Corps législatif was to be decisive. On 6 July, 116 deputies, all supporters of the dynasty, signed an amendment requesting that the government consider 'the need to satisfy the aspirations of the country in associating it more completely with the direction of affairs'.

---

[65] See e.g. letter from Ollivier to Emperor, 8 April 1867 – Ollivier, *L'Empire libéral*, VIII, pp. 414–15; and Rouher's response to proposals made by 43 deputies, *ibid.*, VIII, p. 596.

[66] See letter from Prince Napoleon to Emperor, 24 Jan. 1867, in Hauterive, *Napoléon III*, pp. 280–1.

[67] Quoted Girard, *Questions politiques et constitutionnels du Second Empire* (Paris n.d.), p. 108.

This forced the pace of change. Clearly it represented the determination of most deputies to finish with the constitution of 1852, although a substantial majority still favoured the dynasty as the necessary means of protecting social order. The author (almost certainly Prince Napoleon) of an unsigned *Note sur les élections générales de 1869* found amongst the Emperor's personal papers and judged by him, in a marginal annotation, to be 'very important,' insisted that all the opposition parties – including the strongest – the republican, were weakened by internal divisions or a lack of popular support. The real threat to the dynasty came from disillusionment amongst its own supporters. It followed that liberal concessions were the only means of restoring support. Certainly disorder ought to be suppressed but a politically reactionary response would only reinforce the republican and revolutionary threat. The Emperor was reminded that this menace was concentrated in the cities, above all in Paris, and that 'to live in the middle of an immense capital, the majority of whose inhabitants dream, to a certain degree, of overthrowing the regime, is for the government a considerable problem'. The key recommendation was that the Emperor should 'put himself at the head of the liberal movement, vigorously impose a sense of direction on it, and achieve dominance over it'. Already too many opportunities had been wasted. It was important to remember the experience of previous regimes, which had resisted for too long and finally been overwhelmed.[68] In receipt of similar advice from such pillars of the regime as Fleury and Persigny, if with very little enthusiasm, the Emperor agreed to present a programme of major reforms. Even Rouher had recommended that, instead of further piecemeal change, a general reforming measure, in effect a new constitution, should be presented to the nation for approval by plebiscite.[69] The situation at least contained the *potential* for a revolution in government and, judging by a letter written on 12 January 1870 to Ollivier, the Emperor seemed at last willing to grasp the opportunity. He announced that 'to impress opinion with decisive measures, I would like, finally, to complete what has been referred to as the crowning of the edifice. I would like to do so in an irreversible manner because it is important that the nation enjoys stability.'[70]

According to these proposals, in future the Emperor and the Corps législatif would share the initiative in the presentation of legislation. Ministers would remain responsible to the Emperor but it was clear that for

---

[68] AN 400 AP 150.
[69] See also report of Magne to Emperor, 20 July 1866, in *Papiers et correspondance*, I, p. 242.
[70] Quoted Jardin, *Histoire du libéralisme politique* (Paris 1985), p. 397.

the government to work they would need to retain the confidence of a majority of deputies. Deputies would be free to question ministers, propose amendments to legislation, and consider the budget in detail. Parliamentary approval would be required for customs treaties, presaging a rapid return to protectionism as treaties came due for renewal in the 1870s. The Senate would lose its constituent power, becoming simply an upper house with responsibilities similar to those of the Corps législatif. These proposals were approved by a *sénatus-consulte* on 20 April 1870. Rather than a concession to democracy they represented a renewal of the power of the notables, of the elites represented in the Corps législatif, a restoration of the Party of Order of the Second Republic, in a similar situation of political polarisation. Both the Emperor and conservatives were clearly alarmed by the rise of republicanism and revolutionary agitation.[71] Once more Napoleon was able to take advantage of social fear. In a speech to the Corps législatif on 29 November 1869 he had insisted that 'France wants liberty with order; I accept responsibility for order; help me gentlemen to save liberty.'[72] Officially inspired articles in *La France* and *Le Pays* spread the message. As well as responsibility for protecting order, the Emperor reserved to himself the authority to negotiate treaties of alliance, to command the armed forces, and to declare war. He also retained the right to dissolve parliament and to appeal to the nation, over the heads of parliamentarians if need be, through the plebiscite. This was of considerable symbolic and practical significance. It preserved the direct link between the Emperor and the electorate and ensured that only Napoleon could take constitutional initiatives. Thiers wanted to insist on the need for parliamentary approval for the holding of a plebiscite. However, both he and Ollivier had been privately warned by the writer and courtier Prosper Mérimée that this, 'the essential attribute, in his eyes, of a Napoleonic regime', was a concession the Emperor would never make.[73] It was an issue which aroused strong feelings. The moderate republican Ernest Picard warned, in his newspaper *L'Electeur libre*, that 'the sovereignty of the nation has no more dangerous enemy than the plebiscite. The plebiscite invokes national sovereignty the better to confiscate it. Through the plebiscite, the executive power retains for itself ... the formidable personal appeal to the people which results in the surprise votes which precede or follow *coups d'état*.'[74]

---

[71] The view of Darimon after audience with Emperor, 4 March 1869, in *Les irréconciliables sous l'Empire (1867–69)* (Paris 1888), pp. 385–90.

[72] L. Girard, 'L'Empire libéral (1860–70)' in L. Hamon, *Mort de dictature* (Paris 1982), p. 35.

[73] Ollivier, *L'Empire libéral*, VI, pp. 407–8.   [74] Quoted Girard, *Questions politiques*, p. 131.

In certain key respects parliamentary government had been grafted onto the authoritarian constitution of 1852. It would not be easy to ensure the smooth working of this new system. This was immediately clear from the experience of the ministry formed, after lengthy negotiation, by Emile Ollivier on 2 January 1870. Ollivier, a former republican and idealist and romantic in the tradition of 1848, had welcomed the regime's gradual liberalisation and had worked for its continuance. His journal entry for 25 November 1860, reacting to the initial reforms, is revealing: 'I do not think that these measures will undermine the Empire; they will consolidate it. And yet I rejoice that this is a beginning ... I rejoice all the more, even if this is only an expedient, because we have gained another means of attack.'[75] Asked some days later by Morny if he was satisfied, Ollivier responded: 'if this is an end you are lost, if it is a beginning you are re-established'.[76] It seems clear that Ollivier, faced by the reactionary clericalism of fellow deputies like Keller, was coming to believe that the Empire represented the essential safeguard against counter-revolution at home and abroad. In a speech on 14 March 1861 he had shocked his republican colleagues by promising support for the regime provided that it established wider liberty.[77] Ollivier had come to be seen by Morny and eventually by the Emperor himself as a potential advocate and eventual successor to ministers like Rouher, too closely associated with authoritarian government.[78] Nevertheless, Olliver would frequently be discouraged. Following the Imperial speech from the throne at the opening of the 1866 parliamentary session, for example, when Napoleon had linked the prospect of further reform to 'the improvement of public morality', he had complained to the Empress that her husband 'had postponed liberty until we become religious, virtuous, and learned: it will be a long wait. He has taken away all hope.'[79] He had consistently refused to compromise himself by joining an administration committed to no more than piecemeal reform. The isolation of the reformist Education Minister, Duruy, within the government was sufficient warning.[80] He made this clear once again in a letter to Duvernois, the Emperor's intermediary, on 24 October 1869, in demanding the avoidance of war, final abrogation of the *loi de sûreté général*, of the system of official candidature, and the introduction of administrative decentralisation. Given that the freedom

75 Ollivier, *L'Empire libéral* V, p. 95.
76 Darimon, *L'opposition libérale*, entry of 8 June 1861, pp. 88–9.
77 *Ibid.*, p. 37, entry of 14 March 1861; Ollivier, *L'Empire libéral*, V, p. 141.
78 Ollivier, *L'Empire libéral*, VI, pp. 430–2.
79 Darimon, *Le tiers parti*, entry of 27 March 1865, p. 253.
80 Ollivier, *L'Empire libéral*, VII, p. 569.

recently accorded to the press and public meetings was serving to discredit the republicans, and that the authoritarians were demoralised, the essential need, Ollivier assumed, was to win over the liberals, the political centre. Although, he now conceded, eventually it might be possible to serve alongside Rouher, he insisted that in the short term such a combination would only discredit the process of reform as well as threatening the harmony of government.[81] A thoroughgoing political renewal was necessary. Writing to the Emperor himself, Ollivier insisted that 'Your *sénatus-consulte* has transformed the situation; it is essential that my appointment represents a transformation of personnel', adding that 'it is essential that you make every effort to attract the largest possible number of young men, and give to those who are not immediately employed every hope of being used later on'.[82] Ollivier was, however, certainly prepared to associate himself with reforms on the scale proposed in 1870 and to participate in the formation of a ministry made up of deputies likely to enjoy the confidence of parliament. This was nothing less than the 'regeneration' of the regime for which he had worked.[83]

In practice Ollivier's position was weaker than he would have hoped. Napoleon believed that his lack of strong party support would ensure that he remained dependent. Indeed, in supporting the regime's proposals Ollivier had given numerous hostages to fortune. Despised by his former republican colleagues, as well as by the authoritarian Bonapartists, he was distrusted by most of those liberals on whose support he would have to depend.[84] They were divided themselves, between a centre-right, mainly made up of liberal Bonapartists, and a centre-left, composed of liberals who accepted the Empire, many of whom were hostile to the retention of substantial prerogative powers by the Emperor as well as to the practice of plebiscites. Their anxiety was further stimulated by Ollivier's vague suggestion that social 'reform' might be necessary and they bitterly rejected his advocacy of free trade and his anticlericalism.[85] The new chief minister appears to have rapidly become devoted to the Emperor. He later admitted to being 'charmed' at their first meeting[86] and, according to Duvernois in a report to Napoleon, he 'will not accept

[81] *Ibid.*, VI, pp. 502–3.
[82] Duvernois to Napoleon, 8 November 1869, in Poulet-Malassis, *Papier secrets.*
[83] Letter of 12 Nov. 1869, *ibid.*
[84] See especially Ollivier to Napoleon, 12 Nov. 1869 in *Papiers et correspondance*, I, p. 271 and to Duvernois, 2 and 5 Oct. 1869, *ibid.*, pp. 257–8.
[85] See e.g. Darimon, *Le tiers parti*, entry of 2 May 1864, p. 152 and *Les cent seize et le ministère du 2 janvier (1869–70)* (Paris 1889), entry of 29 Dec. 1869, p. 221.
[86] Ollivier, *L'Empire libéral*, XII, p. 226.

that the Emperor should play a self-effacing role, nor that the throne should become an empty chair. He would like the Emperor to govern in the sense of public opinion. He does not wish at any price to diminish the prestige of the Emperor which he considers ... one of the best guarantees of order.'[87] Parliament was subject to the whims of the moment. Deputies needed guidance from a powerful head of state.[88] In this respect he clearly distinguished himself from Adolphe Thiers, the leading liberal politician.

Undoubtedly, the Emperor was delighted to have been able to avoid calling on Thiers, whose intellectual arrogance and egotism he found intolerable,[89] sharing perhaps Persigny's view of him as 'the most extraordinary moral monstrosity one was ever likely to encounter.'[90] Paradoxically, however, Ollivier's parliamentary majority would depend on the so-called Tiers parti whose most eminent figure was Thiers. More generally, Ollivier had to contend with fellow ministers and a parliamentary majority made up of political liberals who were also clerical, protectionist, and socially conservative, and shared, above all, a determination to preserve social order, and smash the revolutionary threat which, once again, appeared to be posed by the people of Paris. Significantly, whilst Haussmann was rapidly removed from office Pietri the authoritarian Prefect of Police remained. Additional concessions to the particular interests of conservative liberals were also necessary and in February 1870 three commissions were appointed, chaired by such Orleanist luminaries as Guizot and Odilon Barrot, and with the mission of liberalising the administration of Paris; of increasing administrative decentralisation; and providing greater freedom from state control for higher education, the last a measure particularly desired by clericals. If the regime had survived, probably additional reforms would have been unavoidable, particularly in the event of conflict between the Emperor, his ministers, and the majority in the Corps législatif. Many liberals certainly believed that 'liberty' could be safeguarded only if ministers were made unambiguously responsible to the elected chamber. At the same time the authoritarian Bonapartists gathered around men like Baroche, Jérôme David, and the journalist Granier de Cassagnac, and meeting as the Cercle de la rue de l'Arcade, were to be encouraged greatly by the result of the May 1870 plebiscite. With support from the

---

[87] *Ibid.*, VII, p. 406; see also Persigny's remarks made at a reception given by Prince Napoleon and reported by Darimon, *Les cent seize*, entry of 4 Jan. 1870, p. 226.

[88] Letter of 8 Nov. 1869 in *Papiers et correspondance*, I, pp. 267–8.

[89] See e.g. Ollivier, *L'Empire libéral*, VI, p. 509, repeating Morny's comments on Thiers.

[90] *Mémoires*, 1896, p. 8.

Empress and court they persuaded themselves easily that they could manage without Ollivier.[91] The political situation thus remained inherently unstable. Who can tell what might have happened if war had not brought this experiment in liberalisation to a dramatic and premature end?

We have been considering the question, Who rules? Logically this needs to be followed by an analysis of How? This requires consideration of the role of government officials and of their contribution to complex processes of policy formulation and implementation.

ADMINISTRATION

The regime established by the *coup d'état* did little to alter the basic structures of the administrative system, but its leading figures were determined to reinforce the authority of the state. This required a substantial increase in the numbers of state employees at both central and local levels – from 122,000 to 265,000 – largely due to the rising numbers of policemen, teachers, and postal workers.[92] Together with the Emperor's determination to depoliticise government, these developments have led to the Second Empire being described as a *régime administratif*. However, in analysing the workings of the state, the historian must recognise that a considerable gulf exists between the legal principles upon which administration is based and its daily practice.[93] Howard Payne identified the following restraints on executive power – 'the constitutional and legislative law as interpreted by the judiciary, public opinion, the executive's own sense of political expediency and, not least, administrators' attitudes towards their own proper functions'.[94] The rules guiding administrative action were the product of parliamentary legislation, of ministerial decree, the writings of jurists and the decisions taken by the Conseil d'Etat and the Cour de Cassation, the highest court of appeal in matters of civil law. The particular role of the Conseil d'Etat should be noted, its importance varying inversely with that of the Corps législatif. It prepared legislative drafts and administrative regulations and discussed amendments proposed by deputies. During the 1850s it was members of the Conseil who defended government policy both in the Corps législatif

---

[91] See e.g. Darimon, *Les cent seize*, entry of 2 March 1870, pp. 273–4.
[92] Plessis, *Second Empire*, pp. 42–3.
[93] G. Thuillier and J. Tulard, 'Conclusion' to *Histoire de l'administration française depuis 1800* (Geneva 1975), p. 112.
[94] H. Payne, *The Police State of Louis-Napoleon Bonaparte, 1851–60* (Seattle 1966), p. 6.

and the Senate. The Conseil served, additionally, as the supreme administrative tribunal, the final court of appeal in administrative matters.[95]
Its forty to fifty members were appointed by the Emperor and could
be dismissed from their lucrative positions at will. In practice dismissals
were rare, following a thorough purge of thirty-one of its forty members
in 1852.[96] The Conseil would prove itself adept at using legal techni-
calities to thwart the Emperor's will. On the issue of the compulsory
purchase of property necessary for the renovation of Paris, for example,
its President, Baroche, faithfully reflected its members' overwhelming
respect for private property and determination to provide for generous
compensation. The ensuing delays and cost led an exasperated
Haussmann to observe that 'as an administrator [Baroche] is a bourgeois,
imbued with the narrow, unimaginative conceptions of the Paris middle
classes and completely and instinctively hostile to our great work'.[97] On
this, and other key matters such as the 1864 law legalising strikes or the
1867 military law, the Conseil would employ technical legal arguments
to limit the impact of the Emperor's reforms. Darimon, the normally
well-informed republican deputy, confided to his diary on 16 January
1860 that 'In the Conseil d'Etat, Napoleon III passes for an utopian.
Whenever a project arrives bearing the seal of the Emperor's private
office, it is trimmed, cut back, castrated, it is re-drafted in such a fashion that it is bound to fail. How many projects have thus remained dead
letters!'[98] That ministers bitterly resented this and sought to subvert control over their activities by the Conseil d'Etat goes without saying, and
perfectly illustrates the conflicts of interest within the administrative machine. Although the existence of conseillers d'état en service ordinaire
hors sections, senior civil servants who were not allowed to participate
in the day-to-day work of the Conseil but could take part in its general
assemblies, allowed the government to push through such projects as the
loi de sûreté générale, this facility was rarely used. Otherwise, more discrete
pressure might succeed, and certainly great care was taken in the appointment of the Conseil president as well as those of its various sections.
They would include such close confidants of the Emperor as Baroche,
Rouher, Magne, and Parieu.

In terms of structural change within the administration, the main
initial focus was on efforts to improve the co-ordination of police activity

95 V. Wright, 'Les directeurs et secrétaires généraux des administrations centrales sous le Second
Empire' in F. de Baecque *et al., Les directeurs de ministère en France* (Geneva 1976), pp. 76–8; Maurain,
Baroche, p. 114; C. Bigot, 'Le Conseil d'Etat, juge gouvernemental' in Bluche, *Le prince*, pp. 171f.
96 Plessis, *Second Empire*, p. 34.   97 Quoted Maurain, *Baroche*, p. 212.
98 Darimon, *Les cinq*, p. 102.

through the creation of a Ministry of General Police on 23 January 1852. In a revealing note to Maupas, the new minister, the Emperor instructed him to 'make certain that the truth, which one often tries to keep from those in power, reaches me.'[99] The new system proved unworkable and the Ministry was abolished in June 1853 as a result of jurisdictional conflicts with the other ministries responsible for policing – Interior, Justice, War – and with the Paris Prefecture of Police. The Ministry of the Interior thus was restored to its position at the centre of the state security apparatus, with three main subordinate branches – the Paris Prefecture of Police responsible for the capital and its suburbs; the Sûreté générale for the provinces; and the prefectoral corps. Second in importance was the War Ministry, responsible for the gendarmerie which policed small towns and the countryside, and for supporting the civil authorities with troops where this was judged to be necessary.[100] Efforts were made to stimulate efficiency by exhortation, promotion, and constant supervision, which involved the local representative of one ministry reporting on those of the others. Conflicts of interest or mere personality were not uncommon. Civil servants were very conscious of hierarchy and precedence and quite naturally were anxious to enjoy the professional success represented by promotion to more responsible and better-rewarded posts. Social networking, which required a substantial private income, was generally a prerequisite for a successful career in the higher administration. In 1846 a maximum of 1,316 officials (of the then total of 188,000) might be considered to have been *hauts fonctionnaires*, a level attained between the ages of forty-five and fifty-five.[101] Generally their profession offered an interesting means of occupying their time and of reinforcing their social status rather than the means of earning a living. Nevertheless, a salary of over 10,000f must have represented an useful supplement to a private income. At a time when a successful Paris barrister might earn around 50,000f a year, the salary of director of a ministry was 15,000 to 25,000f (in 1860), of a state prosecutor with substantial legal and administrative responsibilities around 30,000f, and a prefect between 20,000 and 40,000f.[102]

The world of ministers, senators, deputies, senior civil servants, and military officers was a small one. The fact that members of this political-

99 Quoted V. Wright, 'Les préfets de police pendant le second empire: Personnalités et problèmes' in J. Aubert (ed.), *L'Etat et sa police en France (1789–1914)* (Geneva 1979), p. 93.
100 *Ibid.*, pp. 93–4; C. Emsley, *Gendarmes and the state in 19th Century Europe* (Oxford 1999), p. 126.
101 C. Charle, *Les hauts fonctionnaires en France au 19ᵉ siècle* (Paris 1980), p. 17; V. Wright, 'Les directeurs,' p. 56.
102 V. Wright, 'Les directeurs', pp. 49–50; Charle, *Les hautes fonctionnaires*, p. 21.

Table 3. *Social origins of prefects 1852–70*[a]

	1852	1860	1870	Total	Percentage
Modest origins	3	—	—	3	1
Lower middle class	12	12	10	38	17
Bourgeoisie	26	40	45	91	42
Nobility	46	34	31	88	40

[a]B. Le Clère and V. Wright, *Les préfets du Second Empire* (Geneva 1973), p. 181.

administrative elite frequently met at private social, as well as official, occasions undoubtedly reinforced the perceptions and objectives which they held in common. The nomination of directors and secretaries-general in the central administration was mainly in the hands of ministers. Nepotism was quite common. Rouher appointed his nephew; Rouland and Baroche their sons, although the latter's was brought down by suspect links with the financial speculator Mirès; Duruy, a son-in-law; Chevreau, his brother; and Persigny his cousin. To which might be added a substantial number of more distant relatives, friends, and acquaintances.[103] The ubiquitous prefects, each responsible for the administration and policing of a department, were drawn mainly from aristocratic or *haut bourgeois* (particularly Parisian) backgrounds, often from families with traditions of public service (see table 3). They were well educated, usually in the law, and cultivated men. The cost of education alone, of course, would have limited the opportunities for entry into the upper civil service.

Although not as aristocratic as the Foreign Office or the army general staff, the prefectoral corps nonetheless counted six marquis, twenty-five counts, twelve vicomtes, and at least thirty barons, although three-fifths of these titles originated from the First Empire.[104] During the Second Empire, promotion to the rank of prefect occurred largely from within the corps itself and through merit. However, if success generally required talent and determination it also very much depended upon the support of a powerful patron. In the early stages of a career individual potential was defined largely by family origins. An accumulation of familial and friendship links, of social capital, could be extremely useful. Some officials were, of course, more important than others. A select few, due to their functions, personalities, and Imperial favour, exercised more power than

[103] V. Wright, 'Les directeurs', p. 41.   [104] Le Clère and Wright, 'Préfets', p. 183.

ministers. Haussmann at the Seine prefecture, the brothers Pierre-Marie and Joseph Pietri as Prefects of Police in Paris from 1852 to 1858 and from 1866 respectively and at the same time directors of the Sûreté générale at the Interior Ministry, and General Fleury, nominally director-general of the Imperial stud, but often employed for confidential political missions at home and abroad, were clearly in this situation. Even less-eminent civil service *directeurs* could play major roles. Franqueville, responsible for both roads and railways at the Ministry of Public Works between 1855 and 1876 was a case in point, owing his position to his technical knowledge, capacity for hard work, and ability to get on with ministers.[105] Such eminent figures were richly rewarded with decorations and membership of the Senate. More generally, the existence of an authoritarian regime reinforced the power and status of civil servants. Formally, a decree of 25 March 1852 had increased the authority of prefects over the various state agencies represented in their departments and at the same time reduced the rights of departmental and communal councils. Although the advent of the Liberal Empire would see the removal of two symbols of authoritarianism, Haussmann and Saint-Paul, the senior civil servant at the Ministry of the Interior, the perceived need for administrative continuity limited the number of changes Ollivier felt able to make.[106]

Politically, at the beginning of the regime, most senior officials and army officers were monarchists rather than Bonapartists, with Legitimist sympathisers particularly numerous amongst the magistrature, due to the social origins of its recruits and in spite of the dismissal of 132 (a small proportion) supposedly irremovable judges in March 1852.[107] Following the *coup d'état*, six prefects were dismissed and eight resigned, the latter mainly Orleanists unable to stomach the arrest of leading politicians. Certainly, the purge was not as thoroughgoing as that which had followed the February Revolution but a change of personnel had been under way since December 1848. Of the sixty-seven prefects remaining in post, only nine appear to have been Bonapartists (and these were divided between authoritarians and liberals), five were former republicans, eight were Orleanists, and the remainder conservatives committed to the defence of the family, private property, and religion. Most would rally to the new order.[108] At local level, in 1853 Migneret, the prefect of Haute-Garonne, estimated that of 985 functionaries only 53 were

[105] V. Wright, 'Les directeurs', p. 63.   [106] Le Clère, and V. Wright, *Préfets*, pp. 210–11.

[107] Royer, Martinage, and Lecocq, *Juges et notables*, p. 72.

[108] V. Wright, 'Les épurations administratives de 1848 à 1885' in P. Gerbod *et al.*, *Les épurations administratives, 19ᵉ–20ᵉ siècles* (Geneva 1977), pp. 69f; Le Clère and Wright, *Préfets*, pp. 23–4.

committed Bonapartists, whilst 629 were Legitimist and Catholic in sympathy, 241 Orleanist liberals, 53 republicans, and 9 unknown.[109] Proportions varied but the message was the same, namely that the regime would be well advised to take account of the often contrary opinions of its own officials. On the other hand, these appreciated the need to behave with reserve, if they valued their careers. Moreover, they were committed to obeying their hierarchical superiors and above all to the preservation of 'order'. An increasingly professional mentality ensured a basic loyalty to the state[110] but it remained possible to serve the Empire without loving the Emperor. Typically, members of the Conseil d'Etat remained overwhelmingly committed to political liberalism and the conservative economic and social ideas typical of Orleanism rather than to the Orleans family itself. Few Legitimists obeyed the Pretender the Comte de Chambord's instructions to refuse to accept employment under the new regime. Income and status would have suffered. Increasingly also they were led to justify their continued administrative roles as being in the interests of the church and the protection of moral order. Appointments policy would subsequently take account of political allegiance, but this was slow to take effect.

How effective were these administrators? The 'Notes sur les préfets' prepared in the Ministère de la Police générale some time between July and October 1852 paint a very mixed picture. Few earned the notation *Très-dévoué, très intelligent*. In all, five were described as 'incapable' and recommended for dismissal. Transfers were suggested for another eighteen, due to laziness, involvement with local factions, lack of tact, excessive zeal, or the financial parsimony which resulted in a failure to mix in society. D'Epercy in the Vosges was described as entirely unsuitable, given his bad manners and the serious error of judgement which had led him to marry his housekeeper. Haussmann, then prefect of the Gironde, was described as 'an intelligent and capable administrator, loyally devoted to the head of state; but the coarseness of his features gives him an unsympathetic appearance'. He needed to be replaced because of his excessively close links with local families and the speculative activity which further threw his impartiality into question. Amongst the others, several earned the label 'mediocre' but with the surprising recommendation that they could do little damage if left, at least

---

[109] Payne, *Police State*, p. 169.
[110] See e.g. letter from Colonel de Beaufort d'Hautpoul to General Pélissier in Guiral and Brunon, *Aspects*, p. 51.

temporarily, in office.[111] This reflected the attitude expressed by the Emperor himself to Persigny in 1862: 'I attach the utmost importance to the stability of prefects in their departments. A mediocre prefect, but one who has a long acquaintance with the area, is better than a distinguished and transient prefect.' In practice, twenty-four prefects would remain in post for over ten years, including most notably Haussmann who occupied the Seine prefecture from 1853 to 1870 and Vaïsse, resident in Lyon between 1853 and 1863.[112] Given the small size of the state bureaucracy, prefects depended on the co-operation of local notables. They were expected to develop an informal network of acquaintances. The ideal prefect was something of a diplomat. He represented the regime in local society and acted to conciliate its various interest groups. He needed the manners and affability of a man of the world and was expected to entertain regularly, something for which a presentable and preferably well-connected wife was regarded as essential.[113]

The demands made on prefects were certainly considerable. They were expected to cope with crises and take initiatives, but Paris was suspicious of prefects who were too independent. Prefectoral autonomy would inevitably decline as communications improved and the potential for central control was enhanced.[114] The decree of 25 March 1852, although presented as a measure of decentralisation, both increased the authority of the central administration over its prefects and considerably reinforced their authority over all the public services in their departments and over municipal councils.[115] The object was to ensure that the prefect, as the government's representative, would become the source of all patronage, in place of the deputies elected by the department. This would never entirely be realised. Prefects were far from being the omnipotent despots denounced by their opponents. Where deputies elected by manhood suffrage were able to construct formidable local or national power bases they had to be handled with care.[116] The authority exercised by magistrates and military commanders also diminished prefectoral power. Furthermore, the supposedly subordinate representatives of Finance or *ponts et chaussées* were able to appeal to their technical competence as a means of resisting prefectoral 'interference'. It was easy for a prefect to cause offence. The state prosecutor (procureur-général) at Nancy reported in 1857 that the good impression initially created by the recently

---

[111] *Papiers et correspondance*, II, pp. 4–12.   [112] See J. Tulard, *Dictionnaire du Second Empire* (Paris 1995).
[113] J. Charbonnier, *Un grand préfet du Second Empire: Denis Gavini* (Nice 1995), p. 121.
[114] See e.g. Maupas, *Mémoires*, vol. I, p. 434.   [115] Charbonnier, *Un grand préfet*, p. 91.
[116] See especially V. Wright, 'Préfets de police,' pp. 87f.

appointed prefect of the Meuse had been dissipated by his wife – 'Mme
Rogniat treated the elite of Bar with an aloofness which has wounded
pride and sensibilities of all sorts. Numerous names have been struck off
the old invitation lists, imprudent words, places thoughtlessly distributed
at official receptions, whims, arrogant and unappreciated witticisms have
caused numerous recriminations.'[117] Magistrates and the representatives
of the financial administration appear to have been particularly irritated
by prefectoral efforts to employ them as electoral agents.[118] Prefects and
state prosecutors generally were able to work closely together in the
prosecution of crime and especially 'political' offences. Judicial impartiality went by the board when Christian civilisation itself appeared to be
threatened:

> when revolution is at the door, the magistrate would ill-understand his mission
> if, in the middle of an universal peril, he retained a stoic disdain for events, and
> refused to throw himself into the midst of the struggle ... using the pretext that
> politics was outside his competence ... In the presence of a social order under
> threat ... abstention becomes more than a weakness; it is absolutely criminal.[119]

Conflicts over responsibilities were especially likely in Paris between
the Prefect of the Seine and the Prefect of Police,[120] as well as between
these powerful bureaucrats and the ministers to whom they were nominally responsible. Baroche was genuinely shocked by Haussmann's arrogance and irregular procedures and would prove to be a half-hearted defender of the prefect's financial arrangements before the Corps législatif
in May 1859.[121]

In a situation in which electoral manipulation and restrictions on the
press and on parliamentary debate deprived the government of means of
assessing public opinion, the effectiveness of official information gathering and reporting was of crucial importance. The government's understanding of what was happening and its decision-making depended on
the quality of the information it received. Technically, considerable improvements in reporting procedures were evident. The communications
revolution brought about by the completion of the primary rail and
electric telegraph networks made it much easier to travel and to transmit information. Supervision by the centre was more evident and less
room was left for prefectoral discretion than in the days of post horses,

---

[117] PG Nancy, 19 June 1857, AN BB30/350.   [118] See e.g. Ménager, 'La vie politique', p. 609.
[119] Quoted J.-P. Royer, *La société judiciaire depuis le 18ᵉ siècle* (Paris 1979), p. 299.
[120] See e.g. Blayau, *Billault*, p. 250; R. Price, 'Poor relief and social crisis in mid-19th-century France',
European Studies Review, 1983, p. 444.
[121] Haussmann, *Mémoires*, vol. II, p. 233.

mail coaches, and the semaphore.[122] The quality of reporting obviously varied according to the powers of observation and the perspicacity of individual reporters and the efficiency of hierarchical reporting procedures. The frequent repetition of commonplaces, which characterised regular situation reports, represented both administrative attitudes and those of the social groups from which administrators were recruited. In general prefects, informed by local police commissaires and mayors, and by the sous-préfets, appear to have been anxious to provide reassurance to ministers. The tone of their reports tended towards optimism, with the overall presentation securely contained within the rubrics laid down by the ministry.[123] The caution of career bureaucrats is hardly surprising. Pessimistic assessments such as that by Joseph Pietri, then prefect of the Cher, in April 1858, following the Orsini assassination attempt – which claimed that the political calm was only on the surface – provoked an irritated marginal comment on his report by the minister to the effect that 'the most effective means of restoring confidence is by showing it one-self ... Vague declamations succeed only in revealing the feebleness of those who make them,' a view subsequently communicated to the unfortunate prefect.[124] The senior schools inspector in the Nièvre warned later that year that 'Unfortunately the Government is forced to see the country through the Prefect's reports. However, every prefect affirms that he holds his department in his hand, that he has been successful in winning the love of his department for the Emperor, his dynasty and his government. Such reports breed a fatal sense of security which needs to be held in check.'[125] A circular from Interior Minister La Valette in 1865 suggested a degree of dissatisfaction with the information actually provided. In addition to regular situation reports, he invited prefects to submit 'other communications of a more confidential nature' so that 'the Government is left ignorant of nothing which, to any degree whatsoever, affects its policies. It must be informed without delay; it is essential that it knows the entire truth, all the details of a particular situation. Whenever an event of some importance occurs in your department, do not hesitate to signal it to me and without any reticence.'

---

[122] See Lavialle de Lameillène, *Documents législatifs sur la télégraphe électrique en France* (Paris 1865), pp. xiv, 59–60, 74–8, 221; and 'Note confidentielle demandée par M. A. Fould' – on importance of postal and telegraph facilities – in AN 45 AP 23.

[123] Le Clère and Wright, *Préfets*, pp. 52–9.

[124] Report of 8 April 1858; minister to prefect Cher, 23 April 1858, AN F1 cIII Cher 9.

[125] Academic rector Dijon, 21 Oct. 1858, enclosing reports of Inspecteurs d'Académie, AN F17/2649.

These reports would be *pour moi seul*.[126] From the historian's point of view, these at least remain in the archives, whilst the oral reports made to ministers by senior officials on their frequent visits to Paris are lost forever.

Dissatisfaction encouraged ministers to look for alternative sources of information. These included the parallel hierarchies of the Ministries of Justice, War, and Education whose officials were instructed to offer political situation reports as well as reporting on each other.[127] In 1864, doubts about the competence of the prefect of the Gironde, Bouville, led to the dispatch of a senior police commissaire to Bordeaux to gather information.[128] The quality of reports made by the procureurs généraux (on the basis of information provided by procureurs impériaux and juges de paix) was generally regarded as being superior to those from the prefects.[129] They were longer, and apparently prepared with greater care. A circular from the Minister of Justice on 11 March 1859 typically insisted that 'It will not be enough to observe and report on the state of public opinion in a general way; it is absolutely necessary that I find in your reports evidence of personal effort and a clear and exact appreciation of everything characterising the period in question and of anything revealing the tendencies and demands of the population.' Information on economic conditions and the material situation of the population was also required.[130] In response, the sort of attitude expressed by the procureur général at Paris was not untypical – 'should I adopt the usual formula of official reports and say that the situation is satisfactory, from the moral and political point of view as well as the economic? Surely it is my duty to insist on the symptoms of malaise and discontent?'[131] It was hoped that co-operation and the regular exchange of information would occur at all levels between the agents of the various hierarchies. The repeated reminders suggest that inter-departmental rivalries and personal and political differences frequently obstructed the smooth

---

[126] 15 April 1865, in *Documents pour servir à l'histoire du Second Empire: circulaires, rapports, notes et instructions confidentielles* (Paris 1872).

[127] See e.g. circular from Rouland, Ministre de l'Instruction publique, 19 March 1858, in AN F17/2649; PG Grenoble, 29 April 1867, on the prefects in his judicial *ressort* in AN BB30/378; Minister of War to Interior relaying comments by GOC's military divisions on prefects in Le Clère and Wright, *Préfets*, p. 365.

[128] Gohier, commissaire divisionnaire de la police des chemins de fer to Directeur général de la sûreté publique, 4 Dec. 1864, AN AB XIX 173.

[129] See also C. Seignebos, 'Les documents inédits des Archives nationale sur la réaction de 1848–58', *Bulletin de la Société d'histoire moderne*, 1907, p. 266f; L. Case, 'New sources for the study of French opinion during the Second Empire', *South Western Social Science Quarterly* (1937), p. 163.

[130] In AN BB30/367.   [131] PG Paris, 10 April 1862, AN BB30/384.

workings of the bureaucratic machine.[132] Another major problem was the reluctance of those at the bottom of the various administrations, and particularly village mayors, to provide information, which might damage their standing in their communities. This affected not only the collection of economic and demographic data, which it was feared might influence tax liability[133] but also the reporting of crimes and political activity.[134] It was at this local level that the greatest gap existed between administrative theory and practice.

The mayor occupied a key position in the administrative–political system.[135] The mayors of communes with populations of under 3,000 were selected by prefects. Elsewhere, the responsibility would rest with the Minister of the Interior.[136] Appointment from above represented official insistence that mayors were the representatives of the state rather than of the interests of their communities. They might therefore be selected – and increasingly were, at least until 1865 – from outside the elected councils. In a confidential circular in July 1855 the Interior Minister in fact instructed prefects to persuade sitting mayors not to stand for election.[137] In practice mayors were selected from amongst respectable and influential local worthies, normally after soliciting the advice of local deputies and notables.[138] In the mass of rural communities they were usually landowners (*propriétaires-rentiers*).[139] Appointment by the prefect was to be their badge of independence of local pressures. The constant concern of the regime was to ensure their reliability.[140] The prefect of Bas-Rhin justified his recommendation in August 1852 of M. Coulaux as mayor of Strasbourg in the following terms: 'I looked for a new man, a stranger to the old parties, a man exclusively and sincerely devoted to the Prince-President, a man with status in the community because of his wealth and connections, sufficiently influential to attach the city to us, sufficiently devoted never to constitute a force against us.' In a

[132] See e.g. circular MJ to PGs, 3 March 1858, on reluctance of magistrates to co-operate with prefects.

[133] See e.g. Léonce de Lavergne, *L'agriculture et la population* (Paris 1865), p. 306.

[134] See e.g. prefect, 5 Sept. 1855, AN F₁ cɪɪɪ Isère 10.

[135] E.g. C. Caron-Deneufeglise, 'Le personnel politique bonapartiste du Pas-de-Calais sous le Second Empire,' *Revue du Nord*, 1993, p. 539.

[136] J. George, *Histoire des maires, 1789–1939* (Paris 1989), p. 141.

[137] Reprinted in Maurain, *Baroche*, p. 273.

[138] See e.g. E. Constant, 'Le départment du Var sous le Second Empire, et au début de la 3ᵉ République', Doctorat ès Lettres, Univ. de Provence-Aix 1977, pp. 804–5.

[139] George, *Histoire des maires*, p. 152.

[140] See e.g. circulars MI to prefects, 10 December 1851 and 15 July 1867, in *Documents pour servir*, p. 19.

city divided by religious affiliation, it was important for the mayor to be 'Catholic without being intolerant, so that the Catholic majority will view his nomination with favour, without inspiring apprehension amongst the dissident cults'. Although Coulaux had no administrative experience, he would be provided with competent assistants.[141] The mayor would be expected to preserve order and to provide for the efficient administration of his commune. This involved the submission of regular reports, preparation of the communal budget for submission to both the municipal council and the prefect, conduct of marriages, supervision of conscription, the safeguarding of public hygiene, provision of public assistance to 'deserving' cases, supervision of school teachers and constables, and the establishment of good working relationships with the local clergy, as well as preparation of the electoral register and ensuring that his *administrés* voted for official electoral candidates. A competent and, above all, loyal mayor, assisted in rural communities by the village schoolmaster who frequently occupied the strategic post of secretary to the mayor,[142] might do well for his community in terms of securing a share of the growing state subsidies to improve schools, churches, and roads.

Finding competent and loyal candidates for mayoral office was, however, not always easy, especially in small communities riven by personal or factional disputes.[143] Administrative continuity was certainly valued.[144] The local notable, selected because of his presumed influence, might harbour Legitimist, Orleanist, or even republican sympathies, providing that these had little impact on the performance of his duties.[145] In some small communities, and in the poorer regions, the shortage of suitable candidates ready to take on these onerous and unpaid responsibilities might even lead to the appointment of 'semi-literates, incapable for the most part of taking any initiative, often not understanding the responsibilities with which they are charged, and only appreciating the personal advantage they are able to gain from the functions they exercise.'[146] Complaints about the inability of mayors to divorce themselves from purely local concerns and their fear of giving offence to

---

[141] Prefect, 5 August 1852, AN FI CIII Bas-Rhin 15.

[142] B. Singer, *Village Notables in 19th Century France, Priests, Mayors, Schoolmasters* (Albany, N.Y., 1983), p. 75.

[143] See e.g. C. Muller, 'Les rapports de Georges de Golbery sur la situation morale et politique dans le canton de Kayserberg (1853–58)' in *Annuaire des quatre sociétés d'histoire de la Vallée de la Weiss*, 1991, p. 131.

[144] See e.g. prefect, 12 April 1855, AN FI CIII Haute-Saône 12.

[145] See e.g. PG Rouen, 10 July 1862, AN BB30/387.

[146] Prefect, 15 Jan. 1857, AN FI CIII Lozère 6.

their neighbours were particularly frequent.[147] In spite of a succession of purges from 1849, and especially following the *coup*,[148] the suspension or revocation of mayors or even entire municipal councils remained a not-infrequent procedure. Following the 1863 elections, 126 mayors were dismissed in the Puy-de-Dôme and 128 in Bas-Rhin, usually for lack of zeal, and doubtless others were 'persuaded' to resign quietly.[149] Prefects were sent a reminder of the need to make appointments with greater care in future.[150] In a more normal, that is non-electoral, year like 1864, only 94 out of over 76,000 mayors and deputy-mayors were revoked.[151] As their responsibilities grew in such matters as roads, education, sanitation, and public assistance, greater efforts were necessary to select competent personnel and to provide them with basic guidance. Specialised publications such as the *Ecole des communes* published by the Interior Ministry from 1853 or the *Journal des maires et du secrétaire de mairie* (1863) were provided, as well as an annual calendar laying out their responsibilities on a monthly basis.[152] Considerable efforts were also made to supervise mayoral activities, although 'excessive' interference could be counter-productive.[153] Careful attention was increasingly given to local election results as the growth in municipal activity and expenditure increased their importance. In an atmosphere of fear and repression in 1852, most elections were regarded as satisfactory by the government. In the arrondissement of Riom, for example, only 6 of 128 communes elected an opposition majority, and 22 were divided, whilst in 100 government supporters were dominant. Unfortunately for the prefect, the town of Riom itself passed completely to the opposition.[154] The gradual revival of opposition inevitably in later years had an effect on local opinion and on the smooth operation of municipal administration.[155] Growing resentment of the imposition of un-elected mayors ensured that decentralisation would become a major political issue.[156] The strength of feeling was recognised eventually by the Emperor in his speech from the throne in

---

[147] See e.g. PG Bordeaux, 3 Feb. 1854, AN BB30/374.
[148] See e.g. prefect, 3 April 1852, AN F1 cIII Saône-et-Loire 13.
[149] Vigreux, *Paysans et notables*, p. 427.
[150] Ministerial circular, 15 July 1863 in *Documents pour servir*, p. 115.
[151] E. Constant, 'Emile Ollivier et la décentralisation sous le Second Empire' in A. Troisier de Diaz (ed.), *Regards sur Emile Ollivier* (Paris 1985), p. 169.
[152] F. Igersheim, *Politique et administration dans le Bas-Rhin, 1848–70* (Strasbourg 1993), p. 303; C. Thibon, 'L'ordre public villageois: le cas du pays de Sault' in Vigier *et al.*, *Maintien*, p. 315.
[153] See e.g. PG Riom, 14 April 1866, re situation in the Puy-de-Dôme, AN BB30/386.
[154] PG Riom, ?October 1852, AN BB30/386.
[155] See e.g. PG Paris, 26 Nov. 1861, re Yonne, AN BB30/384.
[156] See e.g. PG Riom, 10 Oct. 1865, AN BB30/386.

1865 promising 'greater independence' and in La Valette's circular recommending prefects to select mayors, wherever possible, from amongst the ranks of elected councillors. Mayors were now to be encouraged to stand for election, a clear reversal of previous policy. It was agreed that to attain their own objectives prefects needed to select mayors whose authority was respected in their communes. Finally, the Emperor would adopt, in February 1870, the formula – 'Universal suffrage proposes, the executive power nominates' – recognising the right of communities to elect their municipal administrators and at the same time that of the government to select the mayor, from amongst these councillors.[157] This, in effect, legislated for existing practice and firmly rejected opposition demands that communal councils should be left free to select their own mayors.

Judgements about the efficiency or even honesty of these local officials are difficult. At best they engaged in a difficult balancing act, anxious to avoid alienating their fellow citizens, and at the same time attempting to retain the confidence of the prefectoral administration, often by adopting its authoritarian style. In any community, but especially in the larger towns, faction rivalry might develop, more or less politicised according to the strength of local traditions often dating back to the first revolution. Municipal elections, orchestrated by sous-préfets and mayors, although generally non-political, might in such circumstances be contested bitterly.[158] Close prefectoral control over such a multiplicity of communes was clearly impossible, given the resources available. It was at this level that political opposition could most easily, and safely, be expressed. The prefect of the Var would continue to complain about local elections which 'keep hatreds and divisions alive', and served as 'the last refuge of the government's enemies'.[159] Within the community opponents could preserve an informal organisation and through local elections both assess their own support and challenge the regime.[160] Far more common, however, was the sort of situation described by the procureur-général at Rouen: 'Rivalry for influence, jealousy for position, faction rivalry, individual grievances, disagreements concerning the propriety of police or administrative decisions; these are the most common cause of those local quarrels about which candidates and their supporters have made so much noise during the last few days, and which will

---

[157] Constant, *Var*, p. 185.
[158] See e.g. P. Gonnet, 'La société dijonnaise au 19ᵉ siècle. Esquisse de l'évolution économique, sociale et politique d'un milieu urbain contemporain (1815–90)', Doctorat d'Etat, Université de Paris IV, 1974, V, p. 988.
[159] 7 July 1854, AN F1 CIII Var 7.   [160] See e.g. prefect, 24 July 1852, AN F1 CIII Dordogne 5.

be utterly forgotten within a few hours.'[161] In rural communities, what mattered was 'practical questions, of local concern, and capable of rapid solution, such as the completion of a road or the revision of labour ser-vice [*prestation*]'.[162] The exceptions were comparatively rare, although increasing as the general political situation grew more combative in the later 1860s.[163] Unfortunately, from the government's point of view, these exceptions tended to include the major centres of population. In the Loire in 1865, for example, the municipal elections were deemed to be satisfactory or simply involve local disputes in 314 communes. The remaining seven, however, were the most important industrial centres – Saint-Etienne, Roanne, Montbrison, Saint-Chamond, Rive-de-Gier, Le Chambon, and Firminy.[164] One thing that is certain is that the growing independence of mayors in the cities ensured that their effectiveness as the regime's electoral agents declined.[165] More generally, for govern-ment to be effective, its officials, at all levels, had to be convinced of the value of its policies.

It seems clear that relationships between the head of state, minis-ters, deputies, and officials were frequently more complicated than the constitution, laws, and administrative regulations would suggest, and in-deed that in practice they required repeated informal re-negotiation. Even then it was not always possible to overcome opposition and inertia. Furthermore, the Emperor's distaste for administrative detail restricted his ability to control subordinates. Something of the resulting frustra-tion was revealed in the text of a projected newspaper article found amongst the Emperor's private papers and written probably around 1865:[166]

One fact that is certain is that the Emperor is as popular as he was fifteen years ago, whereas his government is not.

What explains this anomaly?

It is that the representatives of the government, instead of imitating the benevolence displayed by the Head of State, his modesty and simplicity, have become infatuated with the powers delegated to them, and are not sufficiently occupied with its interests.

The administration has retained the same spirit as under Louis-Philippe, arrogant and set in its ways.

---

[161] 13 Oct. 1860, AN BB30/387.   [162] PG Douai, 5 Jan. 1865, AN BB30/377.
[163] Point made by PG Metz, 7 Oct. 1865, AN BB30/380.
[164] Prefect, 31 May 1865, AN F1 cⅢ Loire 9.
[165] A point made as early as 4 Aug. 1865 by PG Paris re by-election in Marne, AN BB30/384.
[166] *Papiers et correspondance*, I, pp. 387–8 includes projects, in the Emperor's handwriting, for articles to be planted in subsidised newspapers.

The prefects have wanted to behave like pashas and impose their will on the population.

The Emperor's reign is the most honest that has ever existed, but it has allowed itself to be contaminated by men who, without holding office, have maintained close relations with the government and compromised it through their speculative activities.

The practical limitations on Imperial power were clearly substantial. The effectiveness of the administration might further be judged from a review of its performance in achieving its main objectives – the management of elections, the preservation of public and moral order, and the establishment of the conditions for sustained prosperity.

CHAPTER 4

The management of elections

THE ELECTORAL SYSTEM

The decision to retain manhood suffrage clearly distinguished the Second Empire from previous monarchical regimes. This was a monarchy which owed its legitimacy not to divine right but to the popular will. The constitution required occasional plebiscites to sanction major constitutional change, together with regular elections to the Corps législatif, each of them, in effect, a quasi-plebiscite on the regime itself. Electoral failure would have heralded collapse. As the Prince-President had insisted, 'if I no longer possess your confidence, if your ideas have changed, there is no need to make precious blood flow, it is enough to place a negative vote in the ballot box. I will always respect the people's judgement.'[1] A dangerous promise from someone intending to found a dynasty. Therefore, the regime made every effort to ensure that such a defeat did not occur. Morny insisted on the crucial importance of the 1852 election – 'a grave affair which will be either a corollary or a contradiction of the vote of 20 December' legitimising the *coup d'état*.[2]

The electoral system adopted, voting procedures, and candidate selection were all designed to reinforce the government's position. The *scrutin de liste* system of the Second Republic, which had provided for multi-member constituencies in the hope of diluting the influence of traditional notables, was abandoned in favour of the *scrutin d'arrondissement* with its single-member constituencies, a system giving more weight to personalities than programmes, and justified on the grounds that deputies would be better known to their constituents. For the regime, the danger was that this would promote rivalry between local notables, forcing the government to choose between them and thus destroying the preferred image of unanimity. Constituencies were established with care. The objective

---

[1] Quoted L. Puech, *Essai sur la candidature officielle en France depuis 1851* (Mende 1922), p. 58.
[2] Circular, ?Jan 1852 in Albiot, *Les campagnes électorales 1851–69* (Paris 1869), p. 75.

was to divide the country into units which each included around 35,000 voters. It followed that their limits would not necessarily coincide with existing administrative boundaries and that they would regularly be sub-ject to revision to accommodate population movements. In addition, as the Minister of the Interior advised prefects in a circular of 18 January 1852, 'you need to be aware of how the more or less intelligent drawing of constituencies will influence election results'.[3] The first *circonscription* of the Nord, quite typically, was drawn to include part of working-class Lille, linked, however, to three rural communes whose votes in 1857 'an-nihilated those given in Lille'. The allocation of an additional deputy to the department in 1863 provided the opportunity for a further creative re-modelling of boundaries.[4]

As with other forms of manipulation, taken to excess this could have an adverse impact on public opinion. The possibilities for electoral fraud were extensive, however, beginning with the registration of voters. The practical problems of registration were evident especially in large cities with their mobile populations. The prefect of the Seine complained that the citizens of Paris constantly failed to inform the authorities about changes of address and deaths.[5] Double counting was a frequent con-sequence. In preparation for the plebiscite on the re-establishment of the empire, prefects were instructed to ensure that the dead had been removed from the registers, in order to prevent an inflated number of abstentions. Official concern with registration procedures was aroused again by the 145,070 abstentions recorded in 1857. Subsequently ef-forts were made to update the Parisian electoral registers using tax and National Guard records. The result was to reduce registered voters from 360,615 to 314,923 in 1858. The number would rise slightly to 325,712 following further revision in 1862, making use of the 1861 census re-turns. Inevitably opponents complained that these fluctuations were the product of fraud. The republican newspaper *Le Siècle* received an official warning in 1862 for making just that suggestion. The prefect's response was that every citizen had the right to check the electoral lists kept at the various arrondissement town halls and that the administration was determined that the process be seen to be fair. There were in fact 43,829 appeals recorded in 1862 of which 38,489 were accepted.[6] Neverthe-less, republicans felt bound to establish a committee to assist voters to

3 MI circulars 18 and 20 Jan. 1852 in *Documents pour servir*.
4 Prefect, 26 June 1857, AN F1 cIII Nord 15; PG Douai 2 Jan. and 29 Oct. 1863, AN BB30/429.
5 Prefect, 3 Feb. 1863, AN F1 cIII Seine 12.
6 L. Girard, *Nouvelle histoire de Paris. La deuxième république et le second empire* (Paris 1981), p. 119.

claim their rights, as well as publishing an advisory *Manuel électoral.*[7] Such efforts could make a significant difference in closely fought elections.[8] Furthermore, the formalities for the practice of the secret ballot were rarely respected. The candidates or their supporters generally presented voters with ballot papers. Only official candidates were able to use white paper. It was thus possible to gauge a voter's loyalties at a glance. To ensure this the juge de paix at Mèze (Hérault) recommended before the 1852 plebiscite that 'it would be preferable not to send the ballot papers to voters' homes, because the voters who would not dare vote openly against the administration, would be able to cross out the "yes" and write in a "no" ... modifications they would not dare make under the eyes of those present at the vote if they only received the ballot papers in the town hall itself just as they were about to vote.'[9]

Another feature of the system was the nomination by the government of its preferred candidates, who could expect the wholehearted support of all state employees at the same time as their opponents were subjected to every form of obstruction. Systems with officially nominated candidates were as old as elections themselves.[10] It was unthinkable that any government should abandon the right to defend its policies and to secure a parliamentary majority.[11] With a mass electorate, the involvement of the administration in electoral management had to be refined and enlarged. To a large degree, this was the work of Persigny as Minister of the Interior responsible for preparing the elections in 1852 and again in 1863. He insisted that the government was doing now openly merely what its predecessors had done surreptitiously.[12] There would remain, however, a marked contrast between what was officially defined as legitimate electoral activity and what actually happened before and during polling day.

At constituency level the key figures were the prefects. They were forcefully reminded of their obligations by ministerial instructions prior to every election, and were only too aware of the adverse effect failure was likely to have on career prospects. In the system conceived by Persigny, the prefect, representing the Emperor, would replace the

---

[7] Darimon, *L'opposition libérale*, p. 145.
[8] PG Paris, 4 May 1868, AN BB30/384 re election at Saint-Germain (Seine-et-Oise).
[9] Quoted Puech, *Essai*, p. 126.
[10] See e.g. circular from the Duc Decazes to prefects, 12 Dec. 1817, and from Duchâtel, 7 Sept. 1846 – both quoted Puech, *Essai*, pp. 12–13.
[11] See report on discussion between Emperor and ministers on 29 March 1856 in H. Fortoul, *Journal* (Geneva 1989), II, p. 284.
[12] Persigny, 'Note sur la situation intérieure', Aug. 1865, AN AB XIX 175.

deputy, the representative of particular interests, as the essential intermediary between the local community and the state. The prefect should become the fount of all patronage, upon whom even the deputy must depend. According to a circular of 6 March 1852, 'deputies must be considered as *les obligés* of the government which has selected them, and supported their appeal to the electorate with its patronage'. Competing influences were to be combated. Thus 'every request made by a deputy directly to Paris must ... be returned immediately to the prefect for consideration'.[13] According to the state prosecutor at Toulouse the role of the administration must be to 'destroy the power' of existing notables, 'and substitute its own influence'.[14] For a committed Bonapartist like Migneret, prefect of Haute-Garonne, this meant that the administration must 'eliminate everything that might give importance to party and faction leaders and, at the same time, associate itself with that direct communion between the Prince and the People, which requires no intermediaries'.[15] To facilitate this, the supervisory power of the prefects over all agents of the state as well as municipal councils was reinforced by a series of decrees and circulars which contributed to the creation of the myth of prefectoral omnipotence within a centralised, hierarchical administrative system.[16] That the reality was, of course, very different should not lead us to ignore the importance of the prefect's role, nor indeed the power of the myth.[17]

The realities were spelled out in a report from the prefect of the Ain in February 1852.[18] He was concerned to point out that whereas 'in Paris the political question dominates all others ... when you are on the spot, when you live among the landowners of the region, when you feel local interests at every step, it is very difficult not to take them into account'. Prefects inescapably depended on the co-operation of local elites. Socially they were themselves members of these elites. There was also a clear contradiction between the objective of securing dominance over notables and the frequent ministerial circulars, which urged a policy of reconciliation.[19] Not all ministers were as supportive of prefectoral authority as Persigny.[20] In the competition for influence and patronage, deputies and other notables with access to ministers and the Imperial court retained an advantage. Informal influence clearly modified the

---

[13] Copy in AN F1 cIII Haute-Saône 12.   [14] 4 Dec. 1852, AN BB30/388.
[15] 12 July 1854, AN F1 cIII Haute-Garonne 9.   [16] E.g. 25 March 1852; 13 April 1861.
[17] See e.g. Le Clère and Wright, *Préfets*, p. 45.   [18] 8 Feb. 1852, AN F1 cIII Ain 9.
[19] See e.g. circular MI to prefects, 5 Dec. 1860, AN 45 AP 11.
[20] See e.g. complaints by Haussmann concerning Fould and Billault quoted Le Clère and Wright, *Préfets*, p. 114.

official distribution of power. Prefects were obliged to be cautious in their dealings with such people. A relationship of interdependence was the most likely outcome. When, in 1852 Pron, prefect of the Sarthe, managed to alienate a senator and three deputies, his removal – to the less prestigious Manche – could not be postponed for long. His adversaries had complained of his arrogance, whilst he accused them of seeking to restore their dominance in order to *exploiter le pays*.[21] A great deal depended on local circumstances and personalities.

OFFICIAL CANDIDATES

In the sphere of electoral management the first necessity was to choose an official candidate. Morny, during his brief period at the Interior Ministry, set the pattern. In a circular of 8 January 1852, issued in preparation for the elections to be held on 29 February and 1 March, Morny instructed prefects to 'let me know as soon as possible the names of the notables of your department whom you believe it would be desirable to see elected to the Corps législatif'. The essential qualification was the 'sincerity and energy of the support they would offer to the Prince-President'.[22] On 20 January, Morny further advised prefects that

as the government is determined never to use direct or indirect corruption and to respect the freedom of conscience, the best method of conserving popular confidence in the Corps législatif is to nominate men who are entirely independent by their situation and character. When a man has made his fortune by work, industry, agriculture, and if he has made himself popular through the noble use of his wealth, he is preferable to those who might have reputations as politicians, because he will bring a practical sense to the preparation of laws and support the Government in its work of pacification and reconstruction.

This apparent call for new men was difficult to put into practice. Although the minister insisted that electoral committees were unnecessary and that it was the prefect's responsibility to make recommendations, some prefects did organise comités napoléoniens.[23] Even they, however, were unable to ignore leading local notables who were likely to present them with requests to be considered, together with lists of services rendered.[24] In practice, concerned as they were to ensure success, and given the paucity of Bonapartists amongst notables, prefects

---

[21] Igersheim, *Politique*, pp. 580–1.   [22] Circular, 20 Jan. 1852, AN 116 AP 1.
[23] See e.g. prefect, 5 Nov. 1852, AN F1 cIII Tarn 12; P. Lévêque, 'La Bourgogne de la Monarchie de Juillet au Second Empire', Doctorat d'Etat, Université de Paris I, 1976, p. 1153.
[24] See e.g. letter to MI from mayor of Sarlat (Dordogne), 16 March 1852, AN F1 cIII Dordogne 5.

generally had little alternative but to oblige established members of elite
social networks and those already involved in politics during the July
Monarchy,[25] especially former members of the dynastic opposition, but
also Legitimists. Persigny, Morny's successor, advised prefects that 'the
Government is not interested in the political antecedents of candidates
who openly and sincerely accept the new order of things'.[26] Only the
irreconcilable or leaders of the former parties should be excluded. The
selection process had turned into an effort to win over existing social
elites. As a result, only around a third of official candidates were to be
Bonapartists, with the others essentially conservatives who had rallied
to the regime. Outside the cities most candidates would be notables
with local roots – châteaux, land, or businesses.[27] In this process few
concessions were made to popular Bonapartism. The electoral committees established in many areas for the plebiscite, with their largely lower
middle-class membership, were dissolved.[28] Electoral success was more
important than the creation of a genuine Bonapartist party.

Moreover, social hierarchy was to be respected. As a result the re-
introduction of 'universal' suffrage had little effect on membership of
the Corps législatif. The Second Empire ensured the restoration of the
grands notables, rich men able to bear the costs of representation and to
satisfy contemporary perceptions of the necessary social and educational
qualifications. In the selection of official candidates, wealth, social status,
political opinions, likelihood of winning, age, religion, and personality
were all relevant factors. Over time the number of nobles would decline
slightly and that of businessmen increase, to include such symbols of the
regime's economic achievements as the rail magnate Talabot in the Gard
and the Pereire brothers at Perpignan and in the Tarn. Overall, however, the regime continued to prefer the representatives of the traditional
landowning and office-holding elites and its efforts to integrate members of the middle classes were limited. Whilst many former adherents
of the deposed Legitimist and Orleanist monarchies rallied to the new
order, their support was clearly conditional and related to the strength of
their fear of revolution and the degree to which they felt that the Empire
would respect their special interests. There was an obvious danger that
official candidates with strong local bases of support might subsequently

[25] E.g. Caron-Desneuféglise, 'Le personnel', pp. 530–5.
[26] Circular of 11 Feb. 1852 in J. Albiot, *Les campagnes électorales 1851–69*, p. 75.
[27] See e.g. J. Goueffon, 'La candidature officielle sous le Second Empire: le rôle des considérations locales', in A. Mabileau (ed.), *Les facteurs locaux de la vie politique nationale* (Paris n.d.), pp. 377–8; Igersheim, *Politique*, p. 512.
[28] Ménager, *Les Napoléons*, pp. 199–202.

be able to assert their independence from prefectoral control.[29] Persigny would be sufficiently disturbed by the results of this selection process to complain that 'we who only have friends amongst the lower classes ... have handed the Corps législatif over to the upper classes'.[30] Even at this early stage the authorities were aware of the potential for opposition within the 'political classes'.[31]

Something like two-thirds to three-quarters of those selected as official candidates appear to have been nominated by prefects.[32] In making recommendations, however, they were not always sufficiently aware of competing currents of opinion and personal rivalries within constituencies. In the Var, Pastoureau was so embarrassed at having to choose between rival local notables that an impatient minister made the selection for him.[33] There was also frequently pressure from the Emperor, ministers, or courtiers in favour of one potential candidate rather than another. This might lead to the selection of candidates who lacked local roots. Although the imposition of an outsider was frequently resented within a constituency, this was not always the case, provided that the outsider was able to call on a useful range of contacts in defence of his constituents' interests. When Billault was adopted as official candidate in the Ariège the prefect pointed out that this was 'a poor and disinherited area, which needs a powerful protector'. Billault did not even bother to visit his constituency before the election although, subsequently, he would take the waters at Ax-les-Thermes and prove very adept at ensuring that rural roads were improved.[34] According to the prefect of Charente-Inférieure the choice tended to be between 'a powerful notable from whom everyone might expect favours, or a wealthy and well-connected local man, easily accessible and from whom individuals might occasionally be able to solicit and expect services'.[35] Public confidence in the selection of official candidates was especially likely to be threatened where prefects recommended a candidate and then changed their minds. In the arrondissement of Parthenay (Loiret) the unfortunate Dr Morin was unceremoniously dumped when the prefect decided that he needed to conciliate Legitimist nobles. Morin sustained the

---

[29] E.g. E. Phélippeau, 'La fin des notables révisitée' in M. Offerlé (ed.), *La profession politique* (Paris 1999), p. 75.

[30] Letter to Falloux, 25 Feb. 1852, quoted Maurain, *Politique ecclésiastique*, p. 26.

[31] See e.g. reports to MI from a well-informed secret agent known only as P.P., 9 Feb. 1852, AN 116 AP 1.

[32] Zeldin, *Political System*, p. 22.   [33] Constant, *Var*, p. 43.

[34] Blayau, *Billault*, pp. 211, 221.   [35] 5 Dec. 1866, AN F1 CIII Charente-Inférieure 9.

discord by deciding to stand as an independent 'Napoleonic' candidate.[36]
Disappointed expectations could easily lead notables, eventually, into opposition. For this reason, amongst others, the system carried the seeds of
its own destruction.

The problems inherent in the system of official candidature were to
become increasingly evident. Prior to the 1857 elections, only nine sitting deputies lost government support as a result of their less than whole-
hearted support for its policies, or else because prefects believed that their
re-election might be difficult. The liberal Catholic Montalembert was the
only significant figure amongst them. Whilst rewarding the faithful, this
continuity obstructed the renewal of the political elite through the entry
of ambitious young men into what was anyway a very restricted caste. It
assumed also that voters, out of a sense of loyalty to the Emperor, would
continue to support official candidates whose political or social backgrounds rendered them unpopular, that, for example, middle-class and
peasant voters would vote for clerico-Legitimist official candidates whom
they suspected of favouring a restoration of the *ancien régime*.[37] Some
deputies were absentees, virtually unknown in their constituencies, like
the Parisian bankers Calley Saint-Paul and André in the Haute-Vienne
and Gard respectively.[38] The government's determination to support
such candidates risked alienating those local notables who felt excluded
not only from the candidacy itself but also even from the consultation
process leading up to the selection. Inevitably this impinged upon competition for local influence and power not only between aspiring deputies
but also between those who, lacking adequate wealth, status, and contacts, restricted their ambitions to municipal or departmental office. In
any case, the sense of exclusion might well weaken their support for the
prefect's initiatives.[39] Another weakness of the system was the inability of prefects to prevent deputies, whose status was enhanced through
election by 'universal' suffrage, from re-claiming their pre-eminent place
as intermediaries between the locality and central power. The prefect
of Mayenne complained that they 'interfere in minor administrative
matters, impede official business and spirit away, for their own profit, the
gratitude the population owes to the government for each new favour'.[40]
Even during the authoritarian years, ministers were more interested in

---

[36] PG Poitiers, 9 March 1852, AN BB30/403.   [37] See e.g. Vigreux, *Paysans et notables*, p. 455.
[38] A. Corbin, *Archaïsme et modernité en Limousin au 19e siècle* (Paris 1975), II, p. 868; R. Huard, *Le
    mouvement républicain en Bas-Languedoc, 1848–81* (Paris 1982), p. 121.
[39] See e.g. OC gendarmerie Côtes-du-Nord, 30 April 1869, AHG G8/165.
[40] ?April 1857, AN F1 CIII Mayenne 6.

conciliating deputies and in winning over members of the social elite than in protecting prefectoral authority.

Nevertheless, the loss of official support could represent political suicide for a deputy. Thus Carayon-Latour, elected in the Tarn in 1857 with 83.9 per cent of the votes cast, was abandoned by the administration because of his opposition to the regime's Italian policy and found his share of the vote in 1863 reduced to 25.1 per cent. This was in spite of the support of the clergy who were hostile to the new official candidate, the financier Eugène Pereire, whom they denounced both as an outsider and a Jew.[41] Notables with strong local roots might, however, successfully assert their independence. In the industrial Nord, conservative liberals had already gained 44 per cent of the votes in 1857. The subsequent alienation of both Catholics and protectionists in 1859/60 substantially reinforced the determination of critics of the regime, like the Catholic businessman Kolb-Bernard, to declare their opposition. The problem for the prefect in 1863 was whether to tolerate a man who, whilst affirming his loyalty to the regime condemned its policies, or risk electoral defeat by opposing him. Dropping the sitting member always risked opening up vicious competition between potential successors and nothing could be worse than the sitting member, with strong local support, successfully standing as an independent. Thus, in the case of Kolb-Bernard it was decided to adopt a 'neutral' stance.[42] There were major problems in Paris and Lyon and, to a lesser degree, every significant urban centre. In the capital, eminent supporters of the regime were unwilling to risk defeat and the administration was forced to select secondary figures like the businessmen Devinck, Fouché-Lepelletier, and Koenigswarter, the sugar refiner Constant Say, or the wood merchant Frédéric Levy, to stand against such well-known opposition leaders as the liberal Adolphe Thiers and the republicans Darimon, Favre, or Simon.[43]

The 1863 elections provided the occasion for a particularly thoroughgoing renewal and purge of forty-eight 'disloyal' deputies. Persigny explained that this was due to their lack of devotion to the dynasty and constitution. That they were mainly clericals of course ensured that the religious issue was revived during the campaign, although the government continued to judge it necessary to select clericals as official candidates in many constituencies. Thus of the eighty-four deputies who on 15 April 1865 voted for an amendment favourable to the protection

[41] J. Faury, *Cléricalisme et anticléricalisme dans le Tarn* (Toulouse 1980), p. 56.
[42] Ménager, *Nord*, I, p. 246; II, p. 568.   [43] Girard, *Nouvelle histoire*, p. 369.

of the Pope's temporal power, seventy had been elected with government support.[44] Nevertheless, whilst the official vote remained at around
5 million, that for the various oppositions grew to 2 million. Thirty-two
opposition deputies were elected, including seventeen republicans and
fifteen independents. Persigny was dismissed. His attempt to purge the
Corps législatif had clearly failed. In a note written in 1865 Rouher asked
whether 'nomination of candidates ... by the voters themselves' might
not be preferable, 'thus reducing the responsibility of the administration, and strengthening its influence by requiring it to support popular
nomination, instead of imposing a name on recalcitrant voters'.[45] His
establishment of local election committees presaged substantial changes
in the electoral process. In effect, it was proving impossible to sustain
the pressure on electors established in the aftermath of the *coup d'état*.
Increasingly it was becoming evident that greater care would have to be
taken to ensure that official candidates possessed more of the qualities
which recommended them to voters. It was clear by 1863 that a perhaps
more mature electorate resented the imposition of outsiders as well as
the pressure necessary to secure their election.[46] There was growing suspicion of those deputies, imposed by the administration, who evinced a
willingness to support every and any government decision.[47]

INFLUENCING THE ELECTORATE

The second necessity of electoral management, intimately related to the
choice of an official candidate, was indeed the ability to influence the
electorate. In this respect the era of managed elections had effectively
commenced in 1849. In the aftermath of the démocrate-socialiste successes in May, Ferdinand Barrot, the Interior Minister, had insisted that
'it is the government's duty to demand from each of its officials ... an
energetic and sincere devotion to the cause of order ... But in such a
profoundly disturbed period, when the struggle is often violent and has
as its clear objective either the overthrow or the preservation of social
order, the duty of officials is to be more active, their obligations are more
extensive and urgent. They are the foremost soldiers of Order.'[48] This
was not yet the 'political system of Napoleon III' but a more fundamental

---

44 Maurain, *Politique ecclésiastique*, pp. 634–5, 666.   45 Schnerb, *Rouher*, p. 175.
46 Point made by Falloux in letter to Thiers, 7 July 1866, BN naf 20619 and by prefect, 29 Jan.
    1864, AN FI CIII Saône-et-Loire 13.
47 See e.g. Ed. Ordinaire, *Des candidatures officielles et de leurs conséquences* (Paris 1869), pp. 5–6, 12–13.
48 11 Nov. 1849, quoted Igersheim, *Politique*, p. 184.

conservative response to the threat of social revolution. The bureaucracy, just like the social groups from which it was recruited, continued to experience considerable difficulty in coming to terms with the transformation of the electoral system brought about by the introduction of 'universal' suffrage. Their outlook represented a particular elitist conception of society, informed by social fear. After all, manhood suffrage had deprived these classes of a privileged right to vote, which had recognised their social status.[49] The academic rector at Aix admitted in 1858 that 'universal suffrage frightens me as it frightens every honest man. It carries within it the seeds of catastrophe, of a social revolution which will break out one day, if we persist with it.'[50] 'Universal' suffrage thus continued to be seen as a 'capricious' institution. In expressing such misgivings, the procureur-général at Dijon added that 'I believe in the instability of the people's sentiments rather than in its gratitude and fear that to re-awaken too frequently its belief in its own sovereignty is likely to lead it into abuse. The masses are not incapable of reason and good sense, but they are neither sufficiently enlightened nor wise enough to intervene regularly in affairs of state.'[51] In these circumstances electoral 'abstention by the authorities would be suicidal'.[52] As in the case of a bitterly fought by-election in Seine-et-Oise in 1859, when three competing conservative candidates were tolerated, abstention might divide conservatives and moderates and encourage the republicans.[53] The rural electorate, 'easily led astray',[54] was in especial need of guidance. Even the optimists felt that if progress had been made in the political 'education' of the masses it had not gone far enough.[55] Every town and village had its 'class ... of proletarians ... brutalised by misery, morally corrupt, avid for the material pleasures displayed before its eyes ... a multitude in which every moral sentiment has been extinguished, and all respect for Divine and Human law abolished.'[56] Electoral management would survive for as long as political elites assumed it to be in their interests. The Emperor himself, in a self-justificatory letter written in exile at Camden Place in 1872, continued to insist that

in a country like ours turned upside down by so many revolutions, divided by so many political parties, given up to so many competing influences, the

[49] PG Bordeaux, 5 Sept. 1852, AN BB30/374.   [50] Aug. 1858, AN F17/2649.
[51] PG Dijon, 13 July 1857, AN BB30/377.   [52] PG Nancy, 18 Jan. 1866, AN BB30/381.
[53] PG Paris, ?Feb. 1859, AN BB30/383.   [54] PG Riom, 14 Oct. 1868, AN BB30/389.
[55] Point made by PG Paris, 5 Aug. 1863, AN BB30/384.
[56] PG? Dijon, 9 July 1855, AN BB30/377; see also e.g. Ernest du Barrail, *Histoire de la jacquerie de 1851* (Paris 1852).

election of deputies is the result of local intrigues, rather than the expression of a general ideal. To ensure that elections are sincere three things are necessary, first that Society is established on correct principles; that liberal institutions can be established in practice without threatening order and public tranquillity; finally that political customs are compatible with institutions ... Each revolution over the past eighty years, has delayed the fruitful use of liberty by half a century.[57]

The prefect's responsibilities in relation to managing the electorate were spelled out in a series of ministerial circulars in preparation for the plebiscite which followed the *coup*. The public was promised 'absolute independence, complete freedom to vote'. However, this was followed by a confidential circular which insisted that 'the Administration cannot remain impassive and inactive'. It enjoined prefects to respect 'the absolute freedom of consciences' but additionally required them to 'use ... your legitimate influence to struggle against the manoeuvres of hostile parties and to enlighten those who have been led astray'. It followed that 'the people must be in a position to discern who are the friends and who are the enemies of the government'.[58] Similar instructions were then passed down the administrative hierarchy.[59] According to a circular from Persigny in February 1852, the responsibility of the prefect was to identify the government's chosen candidates and then to support their electoral campaigns, although 'every candidate should be able to present himself without obstacle, and without constraint. The Prince-President would believe that the honour of his Government had been tarnished if the least obstacle was placed before the freedom to vote.'[60] The practice was again rather different. During his term at the Interior Ministry, Billault made the perfectly legitimate point that when, during electoral campaigns, everyone, candidates and voters, could express their preference, 'the Government alone cannot remain silent and indifferent'. In the *très confidentielle* circular, which invariably followed, he thought to add 'some special instructions'. Thus: 'I've informed you which of the candidates in your department the Government has decided to support. You will sponsor them openly and without hesitation, and combat every opposition candidate.'[61] Ideally a sense of interdependence ought to be created between the administration and local elites. According to the prefect of the Isère, notables ought to be reminded that 'they would not be able to

[57] 28 May 1872, AN 400 AP 54.
[58] Morny 8, 10 Dec. 1851, MI circular, 20 Jan. 1852 in *Documents pour servir*, pp. 33–4.
[59] See e.g. prefect, circular to mayors, 19 Feb. 1852, AN F¹ cɪɪɪ Dordogne 5.
[60] 11 Feb. 1852 in Albiot, *Les campagnes électorales*, p. 75.
[61] Circulars 30 May, 21 June 1857 in *Documents pour servir*, pp. 102–3.

survive without the administration. They constantly need it to find employment for their children, relatives, friends, and clients. The day when they appreciate that the Government is quite determined on this point, and that to obtain something from it, they will need to prove their devotion ... they will ... rally'.[62] When it came to elections to the prestigious departmental councils, notables were to be made aware again that the administration would employ all its resources against critics, although these local elections were described frequently as non-political.[63]

It was not primarily the nomination of candidates, nor even propaganda in their favour, which deformed the electoral system. These might be recognised as legitimate practices, even by opponents of the regime. Rather it was the means employed to support official candidates and to obstruct opposition that would bring the political system into disrepute. Instructions on such practices were normally marked *très confidentielle*. They required mobilisation of the entire administration. The state prosecutor at Angers pointed out to the cantonal juges de paix that 'by the nature of your functions, you will find yourselves in more direct and sustained contact with the rural population, and able to influence their choice, guide their conduct, and preserve them from all error'.[64] This, and numerous other circulars, stressed the importance of turning out the voters. Apathy and large-scale abstention could be almost as damaging to the regime's credibility as opposition,[65] although abstention might be explained away by inclement weather or even by the complete and utter confidence of the rural population in the Emperor, which, in its eyes, made voting unnecessary.[66] An internal memo, undated, but seemingly written for Rouher in 1864, estimated that (including school teachers) there were 115,770 'minor civil servants, recruited in general at local level, and whose attachment to the Government can be used not only to call upon their personal assistance but, indirectly, on their influence and that of their family and friends'.[67] Typically, the prefect of Saône-et-Loire instructed the heads of the various services in his department to 'order their subordinates to employ around them all the

---

[62] 7 March 1852, AN Fı cııı Isère 9.

[63] See MI circular, 20 July 1852 quoted Puech, *Essai*, p. 81. The principle was re-affirmed, on 15 March 1864 – quoted, E. Constant, 'Quelques observations sur l'audience et l'évolution politique d'Emile Ollivier au début de l'Empire libéral (1864-65)', *Actes du 90ᵉ CNSS Nice 1965* (Paris 1966), III, p. 307.

[64] Circular, 21 Feb. 1852, AN BB30/403.

[65] See e.g. PG Metz, circular to JP's, 12 Nov. 1852, AN BB30/406; also prefectoral circular to mayors, 21 Nov. 1852 in Puech, *Essai*, p. 75.

[66] E.g. PG Grenoble, 9 March 1852, AN BB30/403.   [67] In AN 45 AP 11.

influence derived from their positions'.[68] For the 1852 plebiscite, the academic rector at Blois warned teachers that 'it is not sufficient that you personally deposit a positive vote in the urn ... It is necessary that as the schoolmaster you prove your devotion to the new leader about to be proclaimed in France, and use your influence to persuade all the electors on whom you have any influence to vote in the same manner.'[69] Such influence was especially important in rural communes and the teachers' docility compared markedly with the radicalism of some of their number in 1848.[70] In 1863, following receipt of a circular from the Minister of Public Works, the chief engineer of the Canal du Centre observed that 'immediately I informed all those working on the canal ... of the names of the candidates adopted by the government and, conforming to your instructions, appealed to the sentiment of duty and devotion which must inform their actions'.[71] Failure to comply invited sanctions. Thus in a telegraphed dispatch on 19 February 1852 prefects were instructed to suspend and replace 'every official who opposes your actions'.[72]

If elections were 'free', those who represented the government were not. At all levels, civil servants had professional obligations. As Billault pointed out in 1857, 'the first of their duties is not to use against the Government the influence and authority derived from their official functions. That would not represent the loyal exercise of civic liberty, but would be an abuse of public power in the interests of private opinion; it would result in administrative anarchy.' He requested lists of those officials who had supported the official candidates and, more ominously, of those who had not.[73] Opposition was intolerable but neutrality or lack of enthusiasm was also unacceptable.[74] Public displays of support were required at elections and also on such occasions as the *fête de l'Empereur* on 15 August.[75] Prefects were likely to express particular irritation with those officials who, through family and social links, continued to socialise with known opponents of the regime. Transfers or early retirements might be the answer, although ministries other than Interior itself could prove obstructive, and it was often the case that replacements for politically

---

[68] 18 Nov. 1852, AN BB30/406.
[69] Quoted G. Dupeux, *Aspects de l'histoire sociale et politique du Loir-et-Cher* (Paris 1962), p. 391.
[70] Rector Ariège, report on Feb. 1852, AN F17/9279.
[71] Quoted, P. Goujon, *Le vignoble de Saône-et-Loire au 19e siècle* (Lyon 1974), p. 351.
[72] Quoted Constant, *Var*, p. 45.   [73] 1 June, 3 July 1857, in *Documents pour servir.*
[74] Prefect, 6 Sept. 1861, AN F1 cIII Orne 6.
[75] Circular, prefect Meuse to sous-préfets, 22 Aug. 1854 in M. Brion (ed.), *Le Second Empire en Meuse* (Nancy 1977), document 25.

suspect officials simply could not be found.[76] Following his appointment as prefect of the Haute-Garonne in 1852 Migneret estimated that only 53 of 985 government employees were sincerely Bonapartist. He had to content himself with requesting the transfer of some of the most senior officials including the state prosecutor, military commander, academic rector, and receiver of taxes.[77]

In general, mayors were the key electoral agents. They were in close touch with the local populations and able to make use of both official and informal influence. Prefects in 1857 were required to issue warnings to the effect that support for opposition candidates by mayors was 'incompatible with their duties as officials and that, if they persisted, the most basic demands of honour would require them to offer their resignations,' although the Minister, Billault, recommended persuasion, with recourse to dismissal only if 'absolutely necessary', in case it alienated local voters.[78] Most mayors, anxious for personal advancement or subsidies for their communes, could be depended upon. In the work of persuasion or intimidation, official candidates could rely on 'the services [in each commune] of ten civil servants, ten free and disciplined agents who put up his posters and distribute his ballot papers and his circulars'. They were the mayor, his deputy, the schoolmaster, constable, roadman, billsticker, tax collector, postman, tobacconist, and innkeeper-all of them 'appointed, approved and authorised by the prefect'.[79] Populations with limited experience of the electoral process and often with little real interest, and dependent on the goodwill of officials or landowners could be expected to do as they were told.

Indeed, given the favourable dispositions of the population towards the regime, in many places administrative pressure on voters was unnecessary and might prove counter-productive.[80] Voters should simply be encouraged to support the regime's candidates by their 'natural' superiors. Prior to every election prefects used such occasions as the *tour de revision* – the selection of conscripts in each canton, or local agricultural shows, to meet mayors, *juges de paix*, and local notables. The personal touch was greatly valued.[81] Even such an eminent representative of the regime as Achille Fould felt obliged to nurse his constituency at Tarbes.

---

[76] See e.g. prefect 7 March 1852, AN F1 cIII Isère 9; Prefect, 21 April 1866, AN F1 cIII Vendèe 8.
[77] Le Clère, and Wright, *Préfets*, p. 82.   [78] Circular 11 June 1857 in *Documents pour servir.*
[79] Quoted Zeldin, *Political System*, p. 85; see also e.g. M. Cyprien de Bellisses, *Le SUFFRAGE UNIVERSEL dans le département de l'Ariège* (Paris 1869), pp. 10–25.
[80] Point made by PG Pau, 8 Dec. 1852, AN BB30/406.
[81] MI circular, 20 Jan. 1852, in *Documents pour servir.*

He set himself up there as a country gentlemen, subsidised local newspapers, and used his influence to secure improvements to the road and
rail networks in the Pyrenees and to build up a local clientele through
appointments to a host of minor posts.[82] The ideal official candidate
was prepared to invest considerable amounts of time, effort, and money.
In an appeal, which was upheld, against the election result at Sélestat
(Bas-Rhin) in 1863, the unsuccessful candidate pointed out that 'the sous-
préfet ... in uniform, accompanied the official candidate. From morning
to night they criss-crossed all the communes in the arrondissement and
everywhere held out seductive promises concerning communal and private interests: in particular they raised hopes concerning nominations
to the offices of mayor, cantonal medical officer, juge de paix, together
with subsidies for churches, synagogues, etc.' The official candidate, in
this case the Imperial chamberlain, Zorn de Bulach, was accompanied
by a dozen mounted gendarmes and welcomed in the villages he visited
by musicians, young girls reciting poems, and men firing guns into the
air. Received by the local mayor he would be expected to address his
supporters at a private meeting, visit the priest, shake hands, and buy
drinks. His performance and promises would be discussed subsequently
in cafés and neighbourhood gatherings like the *veillées*. The rewards for
prominent supporters might include the cross of the légion d'honneur.[83]
M. Le Peintre, sous-préfet at Ambert, wrote an ecstatic letter of gratitude to Morny just before the 1852 election – 'M. le comte, I have my
cross, I have your kind letter which is just as precious. How generous you
are! How happy we are! I'm constantly congratulated and a banquet
has been organised at the mayor's house, in my honour, or, more accu-
rately, in your honour.'[84] Every little town had its *cercles* or cafés at which
such luminaries as the sous-préfet, procureur impérial, officers from the
garrison or gendarmerie, tax collector, municipal councillors, and local
notables met regularly to drink, play cards, and talk.[85] The establishment of such social networks and the distribution of patronage through
them were important means of building local alliances. Support from a
leading landowner or an employer like the Compagnie des Mines de la
Loire could also be invaluable.[86] The ability of a candidate like Adolphe
Delapalme in the Seine-et-Oise in 1852 to circulate a letter of support
from his brother-in-law, Baroche, represented the promise of influence

---

[82] Barbier, *Finance*, pp. 269–79.   [83] Quoted Igersheim, *Politique*, p. 541.
[84] Letter of 12 Feb. 1852, AN 116 AP 4.
[85] See e.g. prefect, 12 Jan. 1859, AN F i CIII Saône-et-Loire 13.
[86] PG Lyons, 8 May 1852, AN BB30/379.

with ministers.[87] Immediately before an election was always a good time to request road repairs, subsidies for public buildings or a railway line – one of the *chemins de fer électoraux* so bitterly denounced by opponents.[88] At Metz in 1857 the state prosecutor hoped that the efforts of the Est railway company, together with his personal contributions to the funds of the local friendly society, would influence the working-class vote.[89] Wherever the clergy was influential, subsidies for the renovation of churches and presbyteries was regarded as money well spent. Thus in 1852 Morny persuaded Fortoul, the Minister of Public Worship to contribute 25,000f towards the cost of restoring the cathedral at Clermont-Ferrand.[90]

Continued benevolence depended on continuous loyalty, however. The election of an opposition candidate carried with it the risk of loss of official patronage. Opposition candidates tried to compete as best they could through public benevolence, charity and the purchase of drinks, and the construction of competing social networks. Thus in September 1867, following the death of the deputy for Vendôme (Loir-et-Cher), the local mayor was summoned by the Legitimist Duc de Rochefoucault-Doudeauville to a fête at the château de la Gondinière to discuss the distribution of charity and the pressing local need for a connection to the railway line.[91] Opposition candidates were able to make particularly effective use of situations in which promised rail concessions had not materialised. The prefect of the normally reliable Hautes-Alpes anxiously requested his minister in September 1868 to put pressure on the PLM railway company at least to begin work on the promised line between Avignon and Gap.[92] If in theory anyone could become a candidate, elections were generally an expensive business, particularly for those who had to do without official support. Like the Comte de Falloux, many must have been discouraged by the expense.[93]

The complaints made about excessive pressure and illicit practices were undoubtedly only the tip of an iceberg. Even so, following the May 1863 elections serious irregularities were confirmed in 28 of the arrondissement of Sélestat's 113 communes.[94] How typical this might have been is impossible to say. Normally, the administration's response

[87] Albiot, *Les campagnes électorales*, pp. 109–10.
[88] See e.g. debate of 22-25 June 1861, reported in Darimon, *L'opposition libérale*, p. 96.
[89] PG Metz, 25 July 1857, AN BB30/380.   [90] C. Grothe, *Le duc de Morny* (Paris 1961), p. 125.
[91] PG Orleans, 8 Oct. 1867, AN BB30/ 382.
[92] Prefect, 18 Sept. 1868, AN F1 cIII Hautes-Alpes 5.
[93] Falloux to Thiers, 7 July 1866, BN naf 20619; see also unsigned report of 6 Aug. 1868 found in Conti papers, commenting on rising cost of elections – *Papiers et correspondance*, I, pp. 345–6.
[94] Igersheim, *Politique*, p. 545.

was to deny the importance of such irregularities and blame subordinates for excessive zeal, whilst pointing out that their opponents were equally guilty.[95] However, public opinion did impose limits. Even in 1852 the conduct of the prefect of the Yonne in asking mayors for lists of the names of voters who had abstained was regarded as excessive, both by the mayors to whom the request was sent and his minister.[96] So too was the action of the mayor of St-Lamine-de-Coutais, near Nantes, who simply destroyed opposition ballot papers. His behaviour was explained by 'the lack of intelligence of a rural mayor' and his inability to comprehend his instructions, and excused by his heroic military service in 1814 and obvious devotion to the Emperor.[97] In two of the communes of the arrondissement of Bressuire (Deux-Sèvres) the commissaire de police threatened innkeepers with the loss of their licences unless they supported the official candidate. He was reprimanded and posted elsewhere.[98]

As polling day approached every local official, from the mayor to the roadman, would be expected to put up the posters and distribute the brochures and ballot papers printed on the white paper which was the exclusive right of the government's candidate. They were to praise the official candidate and criticise his opponents. Typically the prefect of Ille-et-Vilaine instructed his mayors that 'No electoral poster, other than that of the official candidate, can be put up in the commune with-out the authorisation of the mayor, who is always free to refuse.' The posters and ballot papers of opposition candidates 'must be on coloured paper'.[99] In practice gendarmes and other zealous government sup-porters frequently tore down opposition posters.[100] Voting took place in the *chef-lieu* of each commune. On polling day, particularly in small communities, voters could expect to be harangued by the mayor, often in the intimidating presence of a gendarme. For those who regarded local officials and gendarmes with a mixture of fear and respect the simple fact of being presented simultaneously with a voting card and ballot paper for the official candidate often must have appeared to be an instruction.[101]

The other face of official electioneering was, of course, the treatment of opposition. Pressures clearly in breach of the May 1849 electoral law appear to have been applied frequently. This changed over time but

[95] PG Poitiers, 10 July 1863, AN BB30/382, offers all of these.
[96] PG Paris, 20 Dec. 1852, AN BB30/383.   [97] PR Nantes, 3 March 1852, AN BB30/403.
[98] PG Poitiers, 10 July 1863, AN BB30/382.   [99] Albiot, *Les campagnes électorales*, p. 97.
[100] Igersheim, *Politique*, p. 538.
[101] Numerous reports and many complaints – see e.g. PG Orleans, 31 Oct. 1863, AN BB30/382.

certainly the plebiscites and elections in 1851/2 took place in an intimidating atmosphere, especially in those areas in which the *coup d'état*
had met with resistance. In the Hérault, under martial law, election
committees, public meetings, and the distribution of electoral literature
were all forbidden. Already opposition newspapers had been closed. The
only alternative was propaganda conducted by word of mouth by the
republican candidate and his supporters, who were constantly followed
and intimidated by police agents and subject to arrest on the flimsiest
of pretexts.[102] The procureur-général at Dijon described a republican
movement, deprived of its leaders, organisation, and press, and reduced
to a few 'insignificant manifestations'.[103] Most elections were left uncontested, with an intimidated opposition largely registering its discontent
through abstention. Paris and Lyon, and other major cities, were the
exceptions. Their election results served as a warning of the surviving
threat from the left, confirming the 'audacity' and 'perversity' of its adherents, described in one, far from untypical, report as 'the corrupt,
lost in debt, noted for infamy, miscreants, debauched, vagabonds, the
lazy and drunk'.[104] The 8,000 votes for the republican Loiset in Lille
in 1857 revealed that, even without a newspaper, posters, and circulars,
informal republican organisation allowed the mobilisation of support
and ensured that voters went to the polls in groups better able to resist
intimidation.[105] Elsewhere, and in spite of a relaxation of the repressive
regime, fear of being denounced as a 'demagogue' was held to have deterred many voters from supporting the left.[106] The official response to
supposed and genuine revolutionary activity, such as the prosecution
of the secret society La Marianne in 1855 or the arrests following the
Orsini *attentat* in 1858, as well as the day-to-day brutality of the forces of
order, continued to encourage caution. Official lists of 'dangerous' individuals susceptible to surveillance and arrest were carefully updated.[107]
In 1858 these provided the information necessary to 'intimidate evil
passions and to restore ... calm and security'.[108] Subsequently, and for
the foreseeable future, there appeared to be no substantial threat unless
an unexpected calamity, like the premature death of the Emperor, be-
fell the regime.[109] However, particular care had to be taken to ensure
that opponents were not able to re-constitute their national networks.

[102] Puech, *Essai*, p. 77.   [103] 20 Feb. 1852, AN BB30/377.
[104] PG Montpellier, 5 July 1858, AN BB30/380.   [105] PG Douai, 22 July 1857, AN BB30/377.
[106] PG Aix, 28 June 1857, AN BB30/370.   [107] E.g. circular, 24 Nov. 1855, AN BB30/414.
[108] Prefect, 8 April 1858, AN F1 cIII Cher 9.
[109] See e.g. PG Orleans, 25 July 1853, AN BB30/382.

Agents of Parisian committees were to be arrested and incarcerated.[110] Every election was preceded by reminders that associations of more than twenty people were illegal. In a *très confidentielle* circular of 11 June 1857 Billault reminded prefects that 'you will no longer tolerate the organisation of election committees. The artificial efforts of electoral propaganda have no other result than to substitute the influence of a few leaders for the impartial good sense of the masses'.[111] Only 'meetings having a private character, in particular at someone's home, might be tolerated'.[112] Following the 1863 elections, the organisers of a republican committee in Paris – including the deputies Garnier-Pagès and Carnot – which had attempted to construct links with provincial groups, were found guilty under article 291 of the penal code of creating an illicit association.[113]

Republican and particularly socialist opposition, which posed a threat to the social order, was treated more harshly than that from liberals, conservatives, and clericals. Of the latter, as the state prosecutor at Besançon pointed out, 'if the Fronde continues in the salons, at least it clothes itself in mystery and limits itself to a muffled opposition'.[114] The Orleanists in Bordeaux would be described as 'a rich and fairly numerous general staff ... but completely lacking soldiers'.[115] Generally Legitimists appeared to pose more of a threat by appealing through the clergy for mass support. Thus, in 1863, in his Ascension Day sermon, the priest at Tresboeuf, near Redon, complained that France was badly ruled by corrupt hypocrites and went on to compare the Emperor with the anti-Christ, warning his congregation that 'if you don't vote for M. Duclos [a Legitimist], we will have our throats cut; there will no longer be a Pope or any religion'. He threatened to refuse communion to transgressors. However, even in this case, the Minister of the Interior concluded that a quiet warning would be more efficacious than public prosecution.[116]

Close supervision of the press was also designed to limit political debate. In a *très confidentielle* note of 12 January 1852 Morny instructed prefects to 'invite newspaper editors ... to abstain for the moment from

[110] Circular from Morny, 20 Dec. 1851, *Documents pour servir*, pp. 28–9.
[111] *Ibid.*, p. 103.
[112] Signed Dureau, Directeur du personnel at MI, 16 May 1863, in *Documents pour servir*.
[113] Cour impériale de Paris, *Affaire du Comité électoral dite des Treize, Réquisitoire et réplique de M. le Procureur Général Marnas* Paris 1864.
[114] PG Besançon, 10 May 1852, AN BB30/373.
[115] PG Bordeaux, 11 Jan. 1866, AN BB30/374.
[116] Maire Tresboeuf to sous-préfet Redon, ?July 1863; MI to prefect 24 July, AN F1 CIII Ille-et-Vilaine 13.

all discussion ... of the future elections to the Corps législatif'. On 19 February they were further instructed to suspend 'any journal which attacks the government's candidates or attempts to mislead the electors concerning the system of official candidature'.[117] In a published circular in 1857, Billault attempted to define the limits to press freedom in fairly vague terms. Whilst insisting that elections were free, he reminded prefects of their responsibilities where 'enemies of the public peace believe that this latitude offers them the occasion for seditious protest against our institutions.'[118] The expression of opposition, whether in the press or election circulars, was required to be moderate in tone.[119] Even pro-government newspapers should make every effort to avoid inflaming passions. The promotion of self-censorship was the regime's primary objective. Newspaper editors as well as the printers of opposition circulars should be concerned that prosecution or the loss of their licence might lead to bankruptcy. In justification, Billault pointed out that the free play of parties was intolerable where, unlike in Britain, not all of them accepted the constitution.[120] Electoral literature might be distributed in the twenty days preceding an election, but only with the approval of the prefect. Additionally it was subject to the normal censorship regulations.[121]

Possibly more significant than the influence and pressures exerted during elections was the constant effort made to enhance the popularity of the regime through public displays and printed propaganda. This included such events as the proclamation of the Empire on 2 December 1852 on the Place de l'Hôtel-de-Ville in Paris. It was accompanied by salvos of artillery and the ceremonial entry of the Emperor and his military household into the capital.[122] Minutely organised provincial tours, often involving the ceremonial opening of a railway line, the great symbol of modernity, which made the tours so much easier to organise, were to be a feature of the regime.[123] The prefect of the Pas-de-Calais brought the various themes of official propaganda together in reminding voters in an electoral manifesto in 1863[124] that

---

[117] *Documents pour servir.*
[118] *Ibid.*
[119] MI to prefects, 15 Feb. 1852, 30 March 1857, in *Documents pour servir.*
[120] Circular, 18 May 1863, in *Documents pour servir.*
[121] Circular Persigny, 15 Feb., re-affirmed 16 May 1863 in *Documents pour servir*; see also Fortoul, *Journal*, I, pp. 284–5.
[122] MI 2 Dec. 1852, *ibid.*
[123] See e.g. instructions from prefect Cher to mayors, 8 Sept. 1852, in Albiot, *Les campagnes*, p. 151 and also Haussmann, *Mémoires*, I, p. 547.
[124] Printed as appendix XI in Le Clère and Wright, *Préfets*, p. 353.

> In restoring the sceptre to the august heir of Napoleon I,
>   you have brought about the end of anarchy;
> The consolidation of political, religious and social order;
> The greatest expansion of work and public wealth;
> The re-establishment of French influence in the world.

Visits, in 1856, to areas in the Saône, Rhône, and Loire valleys which had experienced devastating floods as well as those to hospitals by the Empress – all carefully publicised – helped create the image of a caring ruler. When the Emperor visited Lille in 1853 the sous-préfet of the mining region of Valenciennes, assisted by major employers, ensured that workers were brought into the city to enjoy a holiday in a festive atmosphere.[125] A major tour of the Breton west in 1858 contributed to detaching the rural masses and clergy from their alliance with Legitimist landowners. These journeys, however, became shorter and less frequent as the Emperor's health deteriorated. Nevertheless, even in August 1867 and in Lille, a centre of political opposition, 200,000 to 300,000 spectators provided the Imperial couple – the hood of their coach down in spite of heavy rain – with an enthusiastic welcome. The opposition might point out that this was not entirely spontaneous, the prefect having persuaded the presidents of local organisations of old soldiers, mutual aid societies, firemen, and choral societies to mobilise their members, and certainly the enthusiasm of many of the local workers might have been ephemeral but that of the rural populations who had poured into the city was certainly sincere. Subsequently, an officially inspired article in the *Mémorial de Lille* celebrated the event:

The Empire has affirmed itself anew through the visit to Lille. The idea from which it was born, the political strength which it represents, the influence it exercises over the rural population as a result of the prestige and glory of the dynasty, all tell us that even in these solemn hours when the nation is subject to major blows ... the Empire and the People remain forever united and invincible.[126]

This was a means of pointing out to dissident notables that the strength of the regime lay in its popular support. Military parades, popular balls, fireworks, bonfires, illuminations, and religious ceremonies were also designed to reinforce dynastic sentiment. Prefects were encouraged to use the opportunities provided by events like agricultural shows, with their parades, banquets, and speeches, to praise the regime's achievements. Although the prefect of Ille-et-Vilaine had already attended twenty-three in the autumn of 1859 and still had fifteen more to go, he managed, in his

---

[125] Ménager, *Les Napoléons*, p. 147.   [126] Quoted Ménager, *Nord*, II, pp. 674–6.

official report at least, to retain some enthusiasm. This was the perfect occasion for associating the regime with rural prosperity.[127] Electoral propaganda took up the same themes – order and prosperity.[128]

There was also an outpouring of popular illustrated news-sheets and cheap pamphlets like the *Notice biographique. Principaux actes et pensées de S. M. l'Empereur Napoléon III*, compiled by Jaegle and Bigaud and published by Boucquin in 1853, or prints like those offered by Gangel of Metz representing the Emperor in his coronation robes, or those coming from the Fabrique d'Imagerie de Glémarec in Paris and most notably a lithograph portraying three horsemen, Napoleon I, his son the King of Rome and Napoleon III. A substantial market clearly existed for such products. The birth of the Prince-Imperial provided another commercial opportunity. It was celebrated in publications like the 'Details of the baptism ceremony of the Prince-Imperial followed by a description of the layette and the Imperial cradle presented by the city of Paris', published by Durand at 10 centimes. Bonapartist songs were also popular and collected in such publications as *The New Songbook of the Empire, containing Three Songs Composed for the Birth of Napoléon IV*. Theophile Gautier enriched one popular engraving of the baptismal ceremony with a poem:

> It's a Jesus with blond hair
> Who holds in his little hand
> In a blue globe the peace of the world
> And the happiness of the human race.[129]

Initially this pro-regime propaganda presented the Emperor as the man of Providence who, just like his uncle, had saved France from anarchy.[130] In 1852 the publishing house of Plon distributed an engraving of the Emperor by Janet-Lange which prefects were instructed to ensure would hang in every town hall. Also they were to support, by subsidy if necessary, the circulation of such traditional publications as the *Grand Almanach populaire pour 1852*, published by Pillet at 25 centimes, which offered practical knowledge to the rural population together with praise for Bonapartes past and present.[131] The legend accompanying the portrait of Napoleon III published by the Imagerie Wentzel of Wissembourg in

---

[127] Oct. 1859, AN F1 CIII Ille-et-Vilaine 13; see also MI circular, 1 Sept. 1866, AN F1 CIII Loiret 12.

[128] See e.g. E. Lecouteux, *L'agriculture et les élections de 1863* (Paris: Librairie agricole de la maison rustique 1863).

[129] In AN AB XIX 688. This carton and AN AB XIX 687 contain a wide range of newspapers, pamphlets, prints, etc.

[130] See e.g. anon., *Vive l'Empire* (Paris: Garnier Frères, 1852).

[131] MI circular, 2 April 1852, in *Documents pour servir*.

1853 provided a statement of the essentially moderate image the regime was anxious to convey and its repudiation of all excess. It was 'The Empire of peace, the Revolution of 1789 without revolutionary ideas, religion without intolerance, equality without egalitarian follies, love of the people without socialist charlatanism, national honour without the calamities of war.'[132] Nationalism was associated with Bonapartism in songs as well as images, on posters and in brochures like the annual *Almanach de Napoléon*, and in pamphlets celebrating military victories like that at the Malakoff in the Crimea in 1856. During the Italian campaign in 1859, low-cost publications like *Le Bellorama* and the *Bulletin de la Guerre* provided maps illustrating the progress of French arms and offered pictures of battles and portraits of the Emperor and his leading generals.[133] Triumphal and well-publicised parades – in Paris on 29 December 1856 and 15 August 1859 as well as in numerous garrison towns – associated the nation with the final victory.

To some extent the content of this official propaganda varied according to the supposed character of the audience. Whilst generally supportive of social hierarchy, in departments like Isère and Gers prefects were likely to appeal to currents of popular Bonapartism. Regular receptions and more intimate dinners, often funded out of the prefect's own pocket, were an essential means of influencing local elites[134] but, as prefects were reminded in 1865, these were not enough. Every commune ought to be visited at least once a year: 'It is important not only that you should be accessible to all, but also that you go to those who are unable to come to you. The powerful always affirm their interests, the poor are often timid. But the Empire must be seen to be extending its justice to everyone.'[135] Not surprisingly, Haussmann, prefect of the Seine, associated the popularity of the regime with the continuation of major public works projects. He pointed out that the republicans had had their opportunity and failed.[136]

Initially, at least, this system, based on the carrot and stick, appeared to function successfully. The state prosecutor at Nancy could report on 1 April 1852 that 'the administration's candidate, although little known, has secured an immense majority over former deputies who had retained widespread sympathy. This is certain proof of the confidence of the population in the regime.'[137] Republican militants were lying low; potential

[132] Quoted D. Lerch, *Imagerie et société. L'imagerie Wentzel de Wissembourg au 19ᵉ siècle* (Strasbourg 1982), pp. 251–2.

[133] AN AB xix 689.   [134] Le Clère and Wright, *Préfets*, pp. 226–32, 240–8.

[135] MI circular, 13 April 1865, in *Documents pour servir*.

[136] Circular from Haussmann to Paris voters, 19 June 1859, in Darimon, *Les cinq*, p. 38.

[137] PG Nancy, 1 April 1852, AN BB30/381.

liberal and conservative critics remained grateful for the restoration of social order. The Bonaparte legend remained vibrant, helping to create a much wider consensus of support for the new regime than its predecessors had enjoyed. However, as Haussmann pointed out in his memoirs, although under previous regimes the 'political classes' had accepted government interference in the electoral process, this new, more rigorous interventionism, particularly the system of official candidature, which attacked their own powers of initiative, aroused considerable disquiet.[138] Moreover, as an anonymous warning from a clearly well-informed secret agent, seemingly on close personal terms with ministers, pointed out: 'in accepting that the election results ... are more moderate than expected, due to the silence of the press, the banning of meetings, martial law and the impossibility of conducting a campaign, the situation is nonetheless very dangerous. The elections are not the free and reasoned expression of popular sentiment.'[139] As many reports warned, once the pressures were relaxed it could only be a matter of time before widespread opposition re-appeared.[140] Complaints about the apathy of both notables and much of the rural population were common and reinforced this feeling.[141] The regime had failed to rally important sections of the social elite and some officials were prepared to risk telling their superiors what they did not wish to hear. According to the procureur-général at Besançon, writing in July 1853:

if the spirit of opposition does not express itself in an energetic and openly hostile manner, the dispositions of the upper and middle classes are far from being favourable; they do not go so far as to express publicly their lack of sympathy for the government, but in intimate gatherings they take great pleasure in circulating a host of malignant stories and anecdotes, which pass from salon to salon, and throw discredit on those who at this moment take part in the direction of the country's affairs.[142]

The further alienation of substantial parts of the landowning nobility and clergy and of protectionist businessmen would gravely weaken a system of electoral management, which depended heavily on the co-operation, or at least passivity, of local notables. In the Nord, for example, the rise of opposition was stimulated greatly by the election of five deputies who had rejected the official label in 1863, all of them

---

[138] Haussmann, *Mémoires*, I, pp. 530–1.
[139] P.P. to MI, 9 Feb. 1852, AN 116 AP 1.   [140] See e.g. prefect, 7 March 1852, AN FI CIII Isère 9.
[141] See e.g. sous-préfet Brignoles, 27 Feb. 1852, quoted by Constant, *Var*, p. 46.
[142] 11 July 1853, AN BB30/373.

wealthy local notables with a substantial clientele and additionally enjoying the support of major industrial concerns like the Anzin mining company.[143]

There was also, certainly from 1857, a growing concern about the rise of republican opposition, particularly in the major towns. In a private letter to Billault, which includes the striking sentence 'when one is infested with vermin, one should try to get rid of them quietly and not cry out loudly that one has the plague', the Emperor revealed his bitter disappointment with the election results in Paris,[144] where republicans captured five of the ten seats. In his report to Napoleon on 8 July, Haussmann, the responsible prefect, blamed the workers of Paris for their 'blindness' and 'ingratitude,' pointing out that 'a topographical map, coloured in two shades, according to the majority vote in each quarter would reveal Paris divided into two equal parts, just like at the time of the barricades'. Like his master, he favoured greater firmness and recommended improved strategic control over the city as well as pushing industrial development and the workers out into the suburbs.[145] In similar despairing tones the procureur-général at Lyon pointed out that 'the populations of the towns have demanded equality since 1848.' Now they had voted for democratic candidates who were virtually unknown and who lacked organisational support. He concluded that 'the industrial population is ... motivated by an irremediable sense of grievance'. Accepting this, his main concern was the potential contamination of the countryside.[146] Against this background the vigorous repression which followed Orsini's attempted assassination a few months later is perhaps not surprising. However, the 1863 election results were, from the government's point of view, even worse, with the opposition vote – clerical as well as republican – rising from around 660,000 in 1857 to almost 2 million, and with a further 3 million voters abstaining. In the capital, the entire opposition list of nine candidates was successful, gaining 63 per cent of the votes cast, another major blow to the Empire's prestige, although it should be borne in mind that Darimon and Ollivier were soon to rally to the regime, and only Pelletan and Simon could be described as irreconcilable. However, as we have noted, these and subsequent elections which revealed the growing alienation of many conservatives, would encourage a process of reform and finally the abandonment of the system of official candidature.

---

[143] Ménager, *Nord*, II, pp. 556–7.
[144] Quoted Blayau, *Billault*, p. 279.   [145] Quoted *ibid.*, pp. 279–80.
[146] PG Lyons ?July 1857, AN BB30/379.

LIBERALISATION

It was evident that electoral management was becoming difficult. Complaints were increasingly frequent. Concern was expressed within the administration itself following the 1857 elections. The state prosecutor at Nîmes claimed to be dismayed by the heavy-handedness of prefects. The determination of many a mayor 'to refuse to authorise the distribution of the least offensive election manifesto', discredited the government, and seemed rather pointless given the strength of support for the regime.[147] A widespread belief developed that such abuses would disappear, 'if only the Emperor knew!' New behavioural norms were developing gradually. Criticism mounted of a system in which the mass of voters was unaware of their rights and subject to administrative pressure. As the republican deputy Jules Favre pointed out in the Corps législatif in January 1864: 'under the pretext of leading, the government commands'.[148] Edouard Ordinaire, a republican candidate in the Doubs, pointed out to voters that 'their initiative has been confiscated.' The selection of candidates by the government to support its policies meant that 'France has been delivered into the hands of a personal government which exercises absolute power over it.'[149] For such critics, official intervention was a negation both of the doctrine of separation of powers and of the freedom of the electorate, which ought to prevail in a system of manhood suffrage. The system of official candidature inevitably pushed ambitious men who failed to win selection – both former July Monarchy politicians and members of a younger generation – into an opposition role even when many of them continued to protest their loyalty to the regime.[150] This was true of the Comte de Flavigny, standing as an independent after being dropped as the official candidate at Chinon in 1863. In his electoral circular he insisted that 'you are not choosing deputies just to applaud and take note, if this was the case there would be no point in having the Corps législatif'.[151] Such candidates provided a useful focus for a protest vote. This was precisely the situation the liberal journalist Prévost-Paradol identified in 1860, where 'absolute government is able ... to contain the enemies of order for a while, but without weakening them; on the contrary it has the natural effect of providing them with unwilling allies and of increasing their number'. Reforms, like

[147] PG Nîmes, 28 Jan. and 19 Aug. 1859, AN BB30/382. [148] Quoted Puech, *Essai*, p. 136.
[149] *Des candidatures officielles et de leurs conséquences* (Paris: Le Chevalier 1869) at 25 centimes.
[150] See e.g. PG Orleans, re results of conseil général elections, AN BB30/382; Prefect, 2 Dec. 1852, AN FI CIII Ain 6.
[151] Included with report from PG Orleans, 7 April 1863, AN BB30/382.

those of 24 November 1860, which increased the powers of the Corps législatif, made free elections all the more urgent.[152] Significantly, senior officials increasingly delivered similar warnings. These contributed to changing governmental perceptions of the political situation. Already in April 1855 the prefect of the Haute-Saône wondered whether it might not be 'prudent to exercise Government influence with greater care so as to avoid misunderstandings and giving electors reasons to resist'.[153] According to the state prosecutor at Orleans, the central government's practice of ignoring local opinion and imposing its own candidates humiliated local notables and was particularly damaging.[154] Prior to the 1863 election his colleague at Nancy expressed concern about the outcome in the Epinal (Vosges) constituency where the liberal Buffet seemed likely to challenge the sitting member M. de Bourcier, an official candidate possessed of 'to say the least, doubtful ability'. Such nonentities might have been acceptable when priority needed to be given to consolidating the regime and social order, but as confidence in the future grew the electorate desired 'intelligent men, capable of exercising the control that the Emperor has himself solemnly demanded'.[155] The imposition of the Duc de Tarante, an absentee landowner living in Paris, on the arrondissement of Gien was condemned vigorously. The feeble prefectoral response that even if 'he has done nothing for us ... it is not a question of voting for M. de Tarante but for the Emperor' was not well received.[156] Local roots were becoming more important, and concessions were increasingly being made to public opinion. In 1863 in the Saône-et-Loire two of the sitting members, General Brunet-Denon, who had served in Bonaparte's Egyptian campaign, and the Comte de Chabrillan, were dropped, the one because of his age and the other due to his unreliability and unpopularity. In response to criticism by the departmental conseil général, the gerrymandering of constituency boundaries planned by a previous prefect was also abandoned. Would this be sufficient to win over disgruntled voters? The new prefect had his doubts. Previous electoral manipulation had severely weakened confidence in the administration. He even assumed – correctly – that the verification of election results by the Corps législatif would throw up enough disputes to further reinforce popular criticism.[157]

[152] *Du Gouvernement parlementaire le décret du 24 Novembre* (Paris: Levy 1860) pp. 30, 45.
[153] Prefect, 12 April 1855, AN F1 cIII Haute-Saône 12.
[154] PG Orleans, 2 April 1860, AN BB30/382.   [155] PG Nancy, 12 April 1863, AN BB30/381.
[156] PG Orleans, 26 May 1863, AN BB30/382.
[157] Prefect, 29 Jan. 1864, AN F1 cIII Saône-et-Loire 13. On resentment of gerrymandering see also PG Douai, 1 April 1863, AN BB30/377.

In many constituencies, the 1863 electoral campaign was far more agitated than had been that of 1857. The proportion of contested elections grew as fear of revolution diminished and authoritarian rule itself came to represent a burden.[158] Republican militants were beginning to re-establish themselves and create networks of sympathisers following the temporary setback resulting from the intensification of repression which had followed the Orsini affair.[159] The lesson drawn by the authorities from the elections was that the system of official candidature and the guidance offered to the electorate remained essential, but that in future candidates ought to be selected with greater 'tact' and from amongst local notables who had earned the respect of their fellow citizens, rather than outsiders.[160] Where contests occurred between supporters of the regime, increasingly it seemed wise to adopt a neutral stance,[161] although this failure to provide a lead could result in the spectacle of bribery and slander produced by the competition between Isaac Pereire and Justin Durand in the Pyrénées-Orientales in 1863. The latter had enjoyed clerical and Legitimist support against the Jewish financier, whilst republican opposition was mobilised in support of Pereire.[162] This would be one of six elections annulled by the Corps législatif. That the others all involved official candidates was taken by the press to represent a warning to the government against the excessive exercise of its influence.[163] The emphasis on the necessity of careful selection of official candidates was repeated in numerous reports from the provinces. The procureur-général at Besançon categorically stated that 'the time for imposing candidates is past.' Voters were increasingly exasperated by administrative interference. In future the views of the electors would have to be taken into 'serious consideration' and 'immoderate pressure' avoided. It was essential that 'the electors themselves become more involved in the choice of candidates as well as in the campaigns to support them.'[164] Whilst explaining the defeat of the official candidate in a by-election in the Puy-de-Dôme in terms primarily of the play of local influences, the procureur-général at Riom recognised that the result 'proves that now that the country is calm and peace reigns in the streets, even the

---

[158] See e.g. PG Paris, 5 April 1863, AN BB30/384.
[159] See also R. Huard, 'La préhistoire des partis. Le parti républicain et l'opinion républicaine dans le Gard de 1848 à 1888', Doctorat d'Etat, Université de Paris IV, 1977, p. 665.
[160] See e.g. PG Rouen, 15 Oct. 1863, AN BB30/387.
[161] See e.g. prefect, 12 April 1855, AN F1 CIII Haute-Saône 12.
[162] PG Montpellier, 9 July 1863 and 8 April 1864, AN BB30/380.
[163] See e.g. prefect, 29 Jan. 1864, AN F1 CIII Saône-et-Loire 13.
[164] PG Besançon, 13 July 1863, AN BB30/389.

most devoted populations have a marked tendency to escape from administrative tutelage and no longer accept official candidates without discussion'. More succinctly, the prefect of Saône-et-Loire noted that 'the Government could, ten years ago *impose* a candidate with impunity; today that would constitute an incitement to disaffection'.[165] The dismissal of Persigny from the Interior Ministry seemed to mark the end of an era.

Baroche, no doubt for personal as much as political reasons, given his distaste for Persigny's brutal manner and resentment of the Interior Minister's unwillingness to adopt his son as an official candidate, squarely blamed him for the disappointing results of the 1863 elections. In a letter to the Emperor he criticised 'the direction given ... to the election campaign and the violence with which he has supported some candidates and opposed others'. His own, rather optimistic, conclusion was that 'the Government of the Emperor is sufficiently strong to no longer need such activity, such a massive deployment of circulars, newspaper articles, and especially violence, to obtain the election of deputies devoted to the dynasty'.[166] Persigny would counter-attack in 1865 claiming that 'after having profoundly demoralised the administration, in disavowing the system which had ensured the triumph of the true doctrine of the Empire in the elections; after having encouraged the partisans of opposing doctrines' the government had, through the actions of Rouher and Vuitry, made two other disastrous concessions; as a result, 'on the one hand the mayors, already demoralised by the equivocal attitude of the administration, have passed ... from the hands of the government into those of the coteries which dominate the communes, on the other, through the concessions made ... on the right of association, the enemies of the Empire are able to form electoral committees in every commune. At the same time as the government's own electoral agents have been disorganised, those of the opposition have been allowed to organise.'[167] Again in March 1866 and December 1867 he warned the Emperor that the major threat was not opposition criticism but the weakness and indecision of the regime itself, the widespread perception that it was drifting aimlessly.[168]

It seems clear that major shifts in public opinion were occurring, linked both to mortality and the renewal of the electorate and the diminishing

[165] 29 Jan. 1864, AN F1 CIII Saône-et-Loire 13.
[166] Quoted Maurain, *Baroche*, pp. 276–7.   [167] Persigny to Emperor, 27 July 1865, BN naf 23066.
[168] Persigny to Emperor, 20 March 1866 in *Papiers et correspondance*, I, p. 379; letter, 15 December 1867, *ibid.*, p.13. See also Persigny, 'Note sur la situation intérieure' (Aug. 1865), AN AB XIX 175.

fear of revolution.[169] There was particular concern within the administration that it was republicans in the cities and liberals more generally that appeared to be the beneficiaries of these trends.[170] Amongst the 'political classes,' the parliamentary brilliance of Favre, Ollivier, and particularly Thiers, fully reported in the press from 1860, was clearly having an impact. Liberalism was becoming an *affaire de mode*.[171] The prefect of Saône-et-Loire observed in January 1864 that whilst the *haut bourgeois* and senior officials belonging to the *cercle* at Moulins found Jules Favre rather too extreme, they avidly read the speeches of Thiers and Ollivier and had just decided to replace their subscription to *Le Constitutionnel* with one for *Le Temps*, which was a little more critical of the regime.[172] Interest in politics was growing, with an impact even on municipal elections. The rise of opposition in Paris was judged to be the shape of things to come. If most administrative reports emphasised the continuing loyalty of the rural populations they were not prepared to guarantee this indefinitely. Indeed, they tended to describe a process of diffusion whereby liberal ideas spread from the cities out towards the smaller towns and marketing centres, and from the middle to the lower classes, particularly to the better-educated younger generations.[173] There was some comfort to be drawn from the fact that in most, especially rural, areas electors 'would certainly not vote for a candidate whose devotion was doubtful, for an utopian or an agitator, but they do want candidates they know and who inspire confidence'.[174]

The course of action increasingly favoured by many senior officials, but which would never effectively be realised, was the creation of a genuine government 'party' capable of taking the electoral initiative. The greater involvement of local notables in both the choice of candidates and campaigning seemed to be necessary to ensure greater commitment on their part, and in order to make a concession to a widespread preference for 'decentralisation'.[175] By 1868 these were the views of Pinard, then Minister of the Interior. In his instructions to prefects he insisted that 'as the role of the Corps législatif becomes more important, you must make a greater effort to constitute the government's party, to preserve its unity,

---

[169] See e.g. PG Rouen, 10 July 1865, AN BB30/385; PG Pau, 16 Jan. 1866, AN BB30/384.
[170] See e.g. PG Rouen, 11 Jan. 1866, AN BB30/385.
[171] PG Poitiers, 14 June 1864, AN BB30/382.
[172] 29 Jan. 1864, AN F1 cIII Saône-et-Loire 13.
[173] PG Orleans, 12 Jan. 1866, AN BB30/382; PG Metz, 25 July 1857 and 9 April 1864, AN BB30/380.
[174] PG Nancy, 5 Jan. 1864, AN BB30/381.
[175] PG Dijon, 12 July 1864, AN BB30/377; see also PG Nancy, 12 April 1863, AN BB30/381.

and stimulate the energy of our friends'.[176] The Emperor himself appears to have accepted that the administration might remain neutral in elections provided that candidates pledged their loyalty to the regime.[177] This shift in emphasis would have the effect additionally of reducing the dependence of deputies on the government, of further reinforcing their authority as parliamentarians, and their local status *vis-à-vis* the prefects, as providers of patronage. Not surprisingly, authoritarian Bonapartists and senior Interior Ministry officials were appalled. In relation to the relaxation of the press laws Gaston de Saint-Paul, director-general at the ministry, in a note on the political situation for the Emperor, reported that 'most of us are resigned to obeying the government's new policy, but without conviction and without confidence'. He concluded that the proposed measures would only assist critics of the regime and destroy the confidence of its supporters.[178] Significantly, liberalisation was to be obstructed deliberately by Saint-Paul, making use not only of his authority within the administration but also his contacts in the press and at court.[179] In the run up to the May 1869 elections, officials in the provinces frequently warned against just this sort of intransigence and insisted that at a time when greater press freedom ensured that administrative excesses received considerable publicity, greater caution was essential.[180] The government's own officials and particularly its mayors were often less than wholehearted in their support for official candidates, aware as they were of growing voter resentment of official 'interference'.

The various opposition parties had been able to use the existence of official candidates to justify sometimes bizarre electoral alliances.[181] Of even greater concern was the fact that so many erstwhile official candidates now sought to distance themselves from the government. Confidence in the regime appeared to be collapsing: 'France is unceasingly represented as ruined internally, isolated and humiliated externally.'[182] The typical report from the provinces continued to insist that the rural masses loved the Emperor and remained indifferent to political debate,

[176] Circular from MI Pinard, 28 May 1868, in *Documents pour servir.*
[177] Ollivier, *L'Empire libéral*, x, pp. 535–8.
[178] *Note* on political situation from M. de Saint-Paul to Emperor, 25 Nov. 1867, in Halt, *Papiers sauvés des Tuileries* (Paris 1871), p. 202.
[179] Ollivier, *L'Empire libéral*, x, pp. 535–8.
[180] See e.g. PI Nérac, report enclosed with PG Agen, 5 April 1868, AN BB30/370.
[181] See e.g. M. F. Giraudeau, 'Note sur le rôle de la presse dans les élections de 1869', 30 March 1868 in *Papiers et correspondance*, II, pp.174–5.
[182] PG Besançon, 12 Oct. 1868, AN BB30/389.

but that there was a general movement of opinion in favour of free elections and parliamentary government, which 'begins in the upper classes and has some impact even amongst the masses'. Regular elections had persuaded much of the population that they had the right to freely dispose of their votes.[183] There was a widespread sentiment that the political system, 'in submitting the government's acts to the judgement of men it has itself chosen', made a nonsense of parliamentary control.[184] Having made similar points, the state prosecutor at Aix went on to stress that 'however precious the support of the masses might be ... the educated classes are nevertheless the lever by which one acts'. It was urgently necessary to conciliate them.[185] This pessimistic appreciation of the constant *plaintes* and *critiques* from the upper classes[186] was reinforced by rural discontent caused by the prospect of an extension of conscription and tax increases, rumoured to be necessary to pay for the embellishment of Paris and high salaries for government dignitaries.[187] For the likes of Persigny and Prosper Mérimée, a close confidant of the Empress, this was all symptomatic of the regime's loss of direction and unity.[188]

The election results reflected the accelerating decline of official influence, a trajectory traced by the state prosecutor at Angers: 'in 1852, and even in 1857, voters almost everywhere relied on the authorities' chosen candidates. Nomination as an official candidate was sufficient to ensure election. In 1863 the prestige derived from this designation had, already, substantially diminished; in 1869 it had almost completely disappeared.'[189] By 1869, technology – the rapid diffusion of information – and renewed press freedom had combined to alter the conditions under which elections were fought. The opposition press more easily and rapidly influenced public opinion.[190] The period prior to the 1869 elections was extremely agitated, at least in the larger towns.[191] The context had changed dramatically; from an opposition point of view it had become far less intimidating. The new freedoms seemed to many observers to herald a return to the conditions of 1848.[192] The main issues appear to

[183] *Ibid.*, 12 Jan. 1869.
[184] *Ibid.*, 17 April 1869.
[185] PG Aix, 11 April 1869, AN BB30/389.
[186] PG Besançon, 17 April 1869, AN BB30/389.
[187] PG Paris, 30 Jan. 1866 in AN BB30/384; OC Compagnie de la Loire, 28 Nov. 1869 in AHG G8/165.
[188] *Mémoires du Duc de Persigny*, pp. 308–9.   [189] PG Angers, 12 July 1869, AN BB30/389.
[190] PG Caen, 10 Jan. 1869, AN BB30/389.
[191] On Paris see e.g. OC Cie de la Seine, 20 Feb., 27 May 1869, AHG G8/176.
[192] See e.g. PG Besançon, 12 Jan. 1869, AN BB30/389.

have been political liberty, the debate on conscription, in clerical regions the regime's Roman policy, and in industrial areas the question of tariff protection. The prefect's estimate of the local situation was to determine the course of action followed by the administration.[193] In most constituencies the system of official candidature was certainly retained, but applied with far greater moderation than in the past. Administrators and official candidates both recognised that any hint of pressure could be counter-productive.[194] Candidates were encouraged to establish their own electoral committees and to rely far more on public meetings and the press. Many of them were confused by the radical change in electoral policy.[195] They had grown used to leaving electoral organisation to the administration and were unwilling or unable to mobilise support themselves. The programmes they now presented insisted on the importance of liberty for the voter and independence for candidates. They reminded the electorate of the regime's achievements – order and prosperity. Attention was also carefully drawn to the growing 'red' menace in Paris and to the inflammatory speeches made in the political meetings in the capital. Thus voters were warned that 'the entire revolutionary army has been mobilised ... A barbarian mob is ready to strike at us.'[196] In many rural areas pressure was hardly necessary, especially where growing fear of revolution encouraged local elites and the clergy to rally to the regime. In Côtes-du-Nord, for example, the 64,000f estimated to have been spent by the liberal Glais-Bizoin on placards, brochures, tobacco, and cider were of little avail against a popular local official candidate, General de la Motte rouge.[197] In urban areas the situation was, as always, far more difficult. In forty-six constituencies official candidates were not even nominated. None of the nine Parisian seats was contested. Elsewhere, too, opponents with strong local support, like the clericals and protectionists Brame, Plichon, and Kolb-Bernard in the Nord, the republicans Grévy in the Jura, Magnin at Dijon, and Dorian at Saint-Etienne, were left unchallenged.[198]

---

[193] Barral, 'Les forces politiques sous le Second Empire dans le département de l'Isère' in *Actes du 77e CNSS Grenoble 1952* (Paris 1952), p.167.

[194] See e.g. GOC 24e Division Militaire, 31 Jan. 1870, AHG G8/176.

[195] See e.g. C. Thibon, *Pays de Sault. Les Pyrénées audoises an 19ᵉ siècle: les villes et l'Etat* (Paris 1988), p. 128.

[196] E. Malcaze, *Les agitateurs* (Paris: Dentu 1869), p. 5; see also F. de Fabj, *L'opposition dans la Seine. Aux ouvriers de Paris* (Paris: Armand Léon 1869), directed at workers; H. M. Deslignières, *Entretiens politiques du village. Le Second Empire devant l'opinion publique et le suffrage universel* (Paris: Librairie de l'agriculture), at peasants.

[197] OC cie. Côtes-du-Nord, 31 May 1869, AHG G8/182.

[198] L. Girard (ed.), *Les elections de 1869* (Paris 1960), p. vi.

Nevertheless, old habits died hard. The circular from Magne, Minister of Finance, to his subordinates, instructing them to assist local prefects, could well have been taken from the desk drawer in which it had been gathering dust since previous elections.[199] In some constituencies, official electoral practice hardly changed. Mayors continued to receive concise instructions from their prefects, sometimes even against the wishes of the official candidates. Those who had dared to support opposition candidates certainly still faced the prospect of suspension.[200] Electoral boundaries were altered in thirty-six departments although population movements in only nine justified this. In Paris the Prefect of Police, Pietri, had already described the situation as hopeless, in a personal report to the Emperor.[201] The regime's efforts were concentrated on the 2nd *circonscription*, where it was judged that the chocolate manufacturer Devinck, presenting himself as an independent liberal conservative, was the only pro-government candidate with a chance. The Louvre *quartier* with its numerous civil servants, together with some new residential areas in the west, was added to the constituency, whilst working-class parts of Belleville were subtracted, but to no avail.[202] The opposition vote in Nîmes and Toulouse was, however, more successfully drowned in a sea of pro-government rural votes.[203] In the uplands of the Ariège, mayors, supported by forest guards, gendarmes, and schoolteachers, distributed official ballot papers and ensured that voters placed the 'correct' paper in the urn.[204] In the Morvan, the mayor of Moux, Dr Monot, harangued a crowd in the village square, warning them that a vote for the republican candidate was a vote 'for revolution, for the red flag and the guillotine'. In other towns and villages, municipal employees tore down opposition posters and on election day snatched their ballot papers from voters and replaced them with those of the government's candidate.[205] At Château-Chinon the prefect of the Nièvre intervened quite forcefully with promises of railway lines and subsidies for schools and churches. Where he succeeded in mobilising the support of village mayors, the opposition vote was negligible, elsewhere their candidates were able to gain one-third to one-half of the vote.[206] What, moreover, should we

---

[199] Ollivier, *L'Empire libéral*, XI, p. 484.

[200] See e.g. prefect Côte-d'Or, 19 May; prefect Pyrénées-Orientales, 20 May 1869, AN AB XIX 173.

[201] In Sept. 1867 – Ollivier, *L'Empire libéral*, IX, pp. 601–2.   [202] Girard, *Nouvelle histoire*, p. 395.

[203] Girard, *Les élections*, pp. v–vi.   [204] Cyprien de Bellisses, *Le SUFFRAGE UNIVERSEL*, pp. 17–25.

[205] M. Vigreux, 'Des paysans républicains à la fin du second empire,' *Revue d'histoire moderne et contemporaine* (1978), pp. 466–8.

[206] Vigreux, *Paysans et notables*, p. 453.

make of the report of the gendarmarie commander in the Loire that 'the despatch of gendarmes to the most important communes allowed ... timid electors to vote freely, which they would hardly have dared to do otherwise under pressure from the *parti avancée*'.[207]

The results, involving the successful election of around 200 official candidates, were presented as a victory by the government. In reality they represented a strengthening of the republican opposition, and in particular of the supporters of further political liberalisation, whether they recognised themselves as official candidates or, as in the case of some fifty conservatives, had entirely rejected the label. It was the election of this large 'centre' made up of the liberal and conservative proponents of parliamentary government, many of them protectionists and clericals, which made further reform to bring to an end the era of personal power almost certain. The assessment prepared for the Emperor by the Interior Ministry at the end of May concluded that

in the larger towns the elections were certainly free, the government not having sufficient means of exercising pressure at its disposal ... In the small towns and the countryside, there was considerable administrative pressure; however, this has not entirely invalidated the result. In practice if the administration has inspired the results in around fifty constituencies which cannot therefore be regarded as the ... genuine expression of public opinion ... it is incontestable that by its ill-judged activities it has in many constituencies pushed a large number of voters towards the candidates of the radical opposition, doing their work for them.

The results from Paris aroused especial concern, with 234,000 opposition votes and only 77,000 for supporters of the regime. The rejection of Ollivier, together with the defeat of the moderate republican Carnot by Gambetta, signified the end of any lingering dream of reconciliation. Even before the newly elected assembly met, the advice to the Emperor was that, although the old parties were weak and the republicans hopelessly divided, the overwhelming preference of the electorate, which it would be impossible to ignore, was for further liberal reform.[208] The objective should now be the establishment of a parliamentary empire and the avoidance of a republic. This represented the eclipse of the imperialists by a reconstituted 'party of order' reminiscent of the Second Republic, but in a situation in which the Emperor might hope to recover the initiative once again. Thus, although they had secured the prospect of a return to parliamentary government, liberals were hopelessly divided

---

[207] 27 June 1869, AHG G8/165.
[208] 'Note sur les élections générales de 1869' (28 May 1869) – AN 400 AP 150.

over a further course of action.[209] The crowds celebrating republican victories on the streets of Paris – 1,600 of whom were arrested between 7 and 14 June – or at Saint-Etienne where rioters smashed convent windows, together with a series of strikes blamed on the machinations of the Workers' International, appeared to confirm the revival of the 'red menace'.[210] A conference of journalists from twenty-one conservative newspapers meeting at the Hôtel du Louvre in Paris in the second week of October agreed that this was sufficiently threatening to require active government intervention in future elections wherever it was necessary to combat 'the declared enemies of order and the established constitution'.[211] The Emperor's advisor Clément Duvernois welcomed this conservative reaction and the rallying to the regime which would inevitably result.[212] Administrative reports confirmed the strength of this development, although this did not lead them to recommend a reversal of the policy of liberalisation. According to the prefect of Loiret, the population demanded 'Neither reaction, nor dissolution' but 'the Empire and liberty', to which he added 'order and work,' in a style presaging that of Vichy.[213]

The campaign which preceded the May 1870 plebiscite was to be even more agitated. Voters were asked to respond to a statement carefully worded to appeal to liberals and even moderate republicans: 'The People approves the liberal reforms introduced into the Constitution since 1860 by the Emperor with the support of the *grands Corps de l'Etat*, and ratifies the *sénatus-consulte* of 20 April 1870.' The issue was of such crucial importance that Ollivier, the recently appointed chief minister, reversed his long-standing opposition to the use of administrative pressure. Ollivier sought to justify this on the grounds that 'in every election the Emperor himself was discussed, judged and voted on; everywhere he was the candidate, standing under a diversity of names, and each failure was his failure. It can easily be understood that every election was a matter of concern for the state.'[214] Once again subordinate officials were required to prove their loyalty through enthusiastic electioneering. A widely circulated pamphlet from *Les Ministres aux fonctionnaires de l'Empire* pointed out that 'In 1852 [the Emperor] used force to assure order; with order established, in 1870, he intends to use force to establish

[209] Point made by e.g. PG Toulouse, 7 April 1870, AHG G8/165.
[210] See e.g. OC Cie de la Seine, 27 June 1869; OC Cie de la Loire, 28 May 1869, AHG G8/165.
[211] 30 April 1870 in Poulet-Malassis, *Papiers secrets*.
[212] Letter to Emperor, 14 Nov. 1869, *ibid.*, p.134.
[213] Prefect, 21 Feb. 1870, AN F1 cIII Loiret 12.   [214] 23 Feb. 1870, quoted Puech, *Essai*, p. 32.

liberty', ending with the message: 'A *Yes* vote is a vote for liberty'.[215] Prefects were instructed to deploy 'an all-consuming activity,' whilst Ollivier himself, as Minister of Justice, ordered the state prosecutors to 'inform all the juges de paix that I would be pleased to see them join the comités plébiscitaires'.[216] One of his subordinates, the procureur-général at Pau, interpreted this to mean that 'during the campaign, the justices of the peace must twice visit every commune ... and make a special effort in places where unintelligent mayors are not likely to be able to sufficiently influence those they administer. They must establish relations with the main landowner, explain to everyone the importance of the vote, and solicit the support of all *les bons citoyens* in order to reduce the number of abstentions.'[217] Opposition billposting and meetings were to be deliberately obstructed.[218] Wherever the resources or energy of local committees appeared inadequate, prefects were encouraged to fill the gap.[219] Interior Minister Chevandier de Valdrôme's instructions to 'make every effort to avoid subordinating administration to politics, and treat with equal impartiality the honest men of every party' contrasts so markedly with the instructions given to prefects on the role of mayors in the campaign, that it is unrepresentative and thus misleading.[220]

The Emperor's own proclamation on 23 April sought to rally conservative and liberal support. Taking advantage of the unease caused by disorder, he declared that 'In voting yes, you will ward off the threat of revolution. You will establish order and liberty on firm foundations, and you will make the future transmission of the crown to my son all the easier.'[221] It was hardly surprising that in a period of political transition there was considerable confusion, with many officials reluctant to risk compromising themselves.[222] Others returned, almost instinctively, to their old practices, although the existence of a more vocal opposition probably encouraged caution. However, official circulars might be misleading. In the Nord, Prefect Masson's circular to his subordinates was certainly discreet but was supplemented by personal visits to mayors by both the prefect and sous-préfets.[223] Daumier summed the situation

---

[215] Dated 24 April 1870, AN AB xix 689.
[216] Telegrams 23 and 30 April 1870, in Poulet-Malassis, *Papiers secrets.*
[217] PG Pau, 28 April 1870, in *Papiers et correspondance*, I, pp. 477–8.
[218] Ollivier MJ to PG Besançon, 2 May 1870 and to PI Draguignan, 6 May in *Papiers et correspondance*, I, pp. 333, 336.
[219] See e.g. MI to prefect Haute-Marne, 21 April 1870, AN F7/12659.
[220] 12 April 1870 in *Documents pour servir.*   [221] Quoted Girard, *Questions politiques*, p. 133.
[222] Point made by PG Toulouse, 24 April 1870 in *Papiers et correspondance*, I, p. 473.
[223] Ménager, *Nord*, II, p. 879; see also Igersheim, *Politique*, pp. 698–9.

up effectively in a cartoon showing two brutalised peasants speaking to a mayor clearly belonging to the rural bourgeoisie. They ask: '*M. sieu l'maire* what is a *bibiscite*?' He replies: 'It's a Latin word which means *Yes*.'[224] Intimidation was not uncommon and, if less intense than before, certainly appeared threatening to strike leaders, members of the International, and radical journalists accused of provoking civil war.[225] In most areas official propaganda appears to have concentrated on the threat of revolution rather than on the positive features of liberal reform. In justifying this, the state prosecutor at Pau observed that 'there are many people who are afraid of the innovations in the system of government and their apprehensions are all the more acute since these modifications are leading to a regime which has already taken us to the edge of the abyss. They willingly close their ears to the, repeated, criticisms of personal power, and think only of the great security that it gave them.'[226] In Alsace, following an appeal by the procureur-général to Bishop Raess, an editorial in the clerical newspaper the *Elsässiche Volksbote* on 30 April declared that 'the struggle is between the Empire and the red republic, between order and revolution ... To abstain is to signify: we no longer want the Empire. But if we no longer had the Empire, the Reds would come to power and then Heaven help the honest *bourgeois* and the father of the Christian family. That is why we vote Yes'.[227] The official and conservative campaigns were much the same. For liberals a vote 'Yes' was not simply a vote for the Emperor but for 'the preservation of the sacred rights of the individual, of the family, and of property'.[228] It was a means of avoiding the excesses of either revolution or reaction. As in 1851, the choice seemed simple.[229] The result, with the regime gaining 3 million votes more than it had in the general election of 1869, would be welcomed enthusiastically, especially by the supporters of a return to an authoritarian regime. Their renewed confidence would have dangerous consequences.

[224] Reproduced in Caron-Deneuféglise, 'Le personnel', p. 548.
[225] Ollivier telegram 30 April 1870 in Poulet-Malassis, *Papiers secrets*, p. 185.
[226] 24 Jan. 1870, quoted V. Wright, *The Basses-Pyrénées from 1848 to 1870. A Study in Departmental Politics*. PhD, University of London 1965, pp. 374–5.
[227] Quoted Igersheim, *Politique*, pp. 701–2.
[228] Circular to electors, signed by deputies, departmental and arrondissement councillors of Nancy, Sarrebourg, Toul, Lunéville, etc., 25 April 1870.
[229] *Messager du Nord*, 29 April 1870, copy in AN BB30/455.

CHAPTER 5

Preserving public order

The conservative Republic and the Empire saw increasingly effective attempts to come to terms with the problems of an under-policed society undergoing complex processes of industrialisation, commercialisation, and urbanisation. If the preservation of social order is generally regarded as the primary role of government, this was particularly so in the aftermath of a period of intense political unrest, when crime and political protest were often assimilated as forms of moral deviance. In this situation winning elections and policing society must have seemed inseparable objectives, whilst the regime's legitimacy was reinforced by its claim to be defending the vital interests of *all* its citizens.

THE ORGANISATION OF POLICING

The effectiveness of political surveillance obviously depended on the workings of the police system. Substantial efforts were made to improve its efficiency. In terms of the organisation of policing, the law of 28 Pluviôse of the Year VIII (17 Feb. 1800) had provided for a co-ordinating Ministry of General Police and for prefectoral supervision of local policing. On the abolition of the ministry in 1818 its responsibilities had been transferred to the Ministry of the Interior. Its re-establishment in January 1852 represented a renewed effort to improve co-ordination and particularly the collection of political intelligence. The unscrupulousness of Maupas, the new minister, immediately provoked friction within the bureaucracy and especially bitter rivalry with Persigny, the Interior Minister.[1] As a consequence of this bureaucratic infighting and its negative impact on efficiency, the police super-ministry was again abolished in June 1852. Responsibility for policing was restored to the Interior Ministry, although effective co-ordination of the collection and

---

[1] See e.g. Emsley, *Gendarmes*, p. 126.

diffusion of political and criminal intelligence was to remain a constant problem in a society characterised by relatively small numbers of police and bureaucrats, as well as by localism, popular hostility to government officials, and a widespread unwillingness to co-operate. One interesting feature of the period was precisely the effort made to solve these problems. This involved improvement in the bureaucratic co-ordination of police activity, partly through the use of the rapidly developing rail and electric telegraph networks, and a gradual reduction in popular hostility as part of complex processes of socialisation and integration into the national society.

The communications revolution, which saw the development of an electric telegraph network, initially along the railway lines, greatly facilitated the centralisation of government. The first telegraph line was opened between Paris and Lille in July 1846. As soon as he came to power Louis-Napoleon encouraged its rapid extension as the means of 'carrying promptly the orders of the government to all parts of the territory'.[2] The new system was far more reliable and had a far greater carrying capacity than the semaphore system it replaced. News of the *coup d'état* and instructions had been transmitted to most prefectures by semaphore in a matter of hours. The confidence of local officials had been reinforced by their privileged access to information. Resistance had been discouraged. However, especially in parts of the east, its operation had been obscured by poor weather. Strasbourg only received the message ordering military action, which had been sent originally from Paris early in the morning on 2 December, by post in the evening of the 3rd. Mounted despatch riders then galloped off with instructions to lower-order administrative centres. In October 1852 all prefects were instructed to install an electric telegraph apparatus within their prefectures.[3] The last, at Mende, was linked to the network in 1855. Once the primary national, and indeed international, network, had been completed, in 1862 the decision was taken to create a secondary network incorporating the smaller towns and larger villages. Expansion of the postal service and improved deliveries had a similar impact. The importance of the development of communications for the mass media should also be borne in mind. Unlike the semaphore system, the electric telegraph was, from March 1851, open to the general public. Officials would have to deal with a rapidly growing

---

[2] Quoted C. Bertho, *Histoire des télécommunications en France* (Toulouse 1984), p. 25. See also memo from Morny as MI to Prince-President in *Moniteur*, 7 Jan. 1852.

[3] P. Reyroles, 'Les postes, télégraphes et téléphones en Côte-d'Or de 1789 à 1910', *Mémoires de l'Académie des sciences et belles lettres de Dijon*, 1961/2, p. 238.

volume of information, and face the problem of screening out useful elements from the mass flow. Obviously there would be a difficult period of transition.

Paris was the centrepiece of police reform. As Billault insisted, in a report on police reorganisation, 'the tranquillity of the city in which the Emperor resides, where the power of the government is concentrated and from which its authority radiates ... incontestably represents a concern of the first order'.[4] However, even in the capital, Napoleon's intention of creating a police force on the London model with officers patrolling beats and familiarising themselves with their neighbourhoods, could not be fully implemented. Although the number of municipal policemen in the city was increased from 750 to 2,770 in 1854, inadequate funding and insufficient personnel rendered Prefect of Police Pietri's dream of close control over the population unrealisable.[5] According to an internal Interior memo, a major part of the problem was Pietri himself, described as 'incapacity personified', together with his host of 'corrupt fellow Corsicans'.[6] By 1860, in a city enlarged through the annexation of its suburbs, there were 4,600 police, to which might be added 2,440 gendarmes. For the provinces, a decree of 28 March 1852 established 738 new cantonal police commissaires to add to the existing 630. These were to be appointed by prefects on the recommendation of mayors or, in the case of towns with populations of over 60,000, by the minister on the prefect's advice. Their responsibility would be to 'ensure more general, more active and more immediate surveillance ... to know everything, predict everything, repress everything'.[7] This extended general police supervision especially in rural areas. Even in 1860, however, there were only 1,368 commissaires for 2,850 cantons. In May 1855 police forces in seventeen cities with populations over 40,000 were expanded and re-organised, although they would remain small. For example, in 1857 Lille was policed by 44 municipal police and 16 gendarmes, Toulouse by 96 and 26, and Bordeaux by 158 and 26. Expansion continued, however. The rapidly growing industrial centre of Saint-Etienne which had a police force of twenty in 1850 increased this to seventy-six by 1861. It was claimed that this resulted in both a reduction in crime and greater political calm. Overall the 1,570 commissaires and 10,574 agents de police in post by 1870 represented a 152 per cent increase compared with

---

4 Rapport à l'Empereur du 17 Sept. 1854 in APP series DB, see also M. Bernard, 'La réorganisation de la police sous le second empire (1851–58)' in Vigier, *Maintien*, p. 124.
5 Bernard,'La réorganisation,' pp. 123, 126–7.   6 Blayau, *Billault*, p. 283.
7 Quoted Puech, *Essai*, p. 55.

1848.[8] Standards of training and supervision were also improved, as was co-ordination, with the appointment in the larger cities of commissaires centraux directly responsible to the departmental prefect and nationally, from November 1859, of the Paris Prefect of Police as Director of Public Security at the Ministry of the Interior. The prefect was expected to provide overall direction for police activity with particular responsibility for state security. This formally recognised the geographical extension of his powers, especially to Lyons and Marseilles, which had been under way for some time.[9] There were to be only four Prefects of Police during the Empire – Maupas (October 1851–January 1853); P.-M. Pietri (January 1853–March 1858); Boitelle (March 1858–February 1866); and J.-M. Pietri (younger brother of P.-M., February 1866–September 1870). The individuals appointed to this key post were all experienced administrators, capable of exercising considerable political responsibility. They reported directly to the Emperor, not only on the situation in the capital but on conditions throughout France, and engaged in a direct correspondence with prefects and state prosecutors, as well as the commanders responsible for the military divisions into which the country was divided, and for the gendarmerie. They did not hesitate to criticise ministers.[10]

The new commissaires were not particularly well paid but were often ex-army NCOs with pensions and a sense of devotion to the regime.[11] They were intensely hostile to any hint of public disorder. Some notion of the complexity of their duties can be obtained from the prefect of Bas-Rhin's instructions in 1853. These also provide an insight into his own conception of the threat to public order:

You should pay constant attention to false news, the alarming rumours spread by the malicious through the countryside and avidly listened to by the rural population. The surveillance of vagabonds, of men without fixed abode, of beggars, should never find you lacking; it is generally amongst such rootless people that are to be found the thieves, arsonists, and especially those who spread false news. Visit each commune at least once a month, speak to the mayors on all matters concerning rural policing, and avoid adopting a severe or superior attitude towards them in order to win their confidence. Inform yourself

---

[8] C. Chatelard, *Crime et criminalité dans l'arrondissement de St-Etienne au 19ᵉ siècle* (St-Etienne 1981), p. 216; C. Saurel, 'La gendarmerie dans la société de la Deuxième République et du Second Empire', Doc. d'Etat, Université de Paris-Sorbonne 1956, p. 574.

[9] Rapport à l'Empereur sur M. Collet-Meygret Directeur de la Sûreté publique, undated, in *Papiers et correspondance*, I, p. 107; circular from Rouher, Min. des Travaux publics re role of commissaires spéciaux de la police des chemins de fer created by decree 22 Feb. 1855, in Mathieu, 'Le rôle politique des commissaires spéciaux de la police des chemins de fer' in Vigier, *Maintien*, p. 152.

[10] V. Wright, Préfets de police pp. 86–7.   [11] See e.g. Constant, *Var*, III pp. 817–21.

about the political sympathies of the population, about their needs, listen with
care to their complaints. You should also pay attention ... to the intrigues which
are often hatched against the municipal authorities, try to discover the cause,
identify the authors, and especially find out who is in the wrong.[12]

Nevertheless, there were frequent complaints about the quality of recruits and their susceptibility to local influences. In Poitiers, where local
elites were clerical and Legitimist, political policing was generally ineffective. In Nîmes, bitterly divided between Protestants and Catholics,
police agents were local men, protégés of members of the town council
and hopelessly caught up in local disputes.[13] Even more subject to criticism were the gardes champêtres, the village police, grossly underpaid
and untrained, appointed by mayors, and usually controlled by them
although supposedly reporting to the cantonal commissaires and gendarmerie. The countryside and, even more seriously from the authorities'
point of view, many of the mushrooming city suburbs, were seriously
under-policed. In 1856 around three-quarters of the 36,710 rural communes had policemen – a grand total of about 67,000.[14] The prefect
of the Tarn-et-Garonne complained about their inability to suppress
poaching, their unwillingness to 'take action ... against the poor' and
tendency to 'close their eyes to the affairs of men whose influence they
fear or from whom they hope to gain something'.[15] His colleague in
Ille-et-Vilaine accepted that although improvements were under way
most rural policemen were too old and wasted their time in futilities.[16]
The prefect of Pyrénées-Orientales was very much in a minority in
recording his satisfaction.[17] Poor salaries often forced the gardes to seek
additional sources of income.[18] In Charente-Inférieure seventeen were
dismissed in 1858 for negligence or habitual drunkenness.[19] The prefects' police powers were reinforced by a decree of 5 May 1855 but effective policing and general administration remained heavily dependent on
the energy, ability, and willingness of local mayors to co-operate. Thus
the question of the selection of these key local police officials and the
reinforcement of their authority was of considerable importance to the
government.[20]

[12] Circular of 17 Feb. 1853 quoted Igersheim, *Politique*, p. 242.
[13] PG Poitiers, ?April 1860; AN BB30/385; PG Nîmes 19 Aug. 1857, AN BB30/382.
[14] C. Charle, *Histoire sociale de la France au 19ᵉ siècle* (Paris 1991), p. 82.
[15] 22 Nov. 1854, AN F1 CIII Tarn-et-Garonne 7.
[16] Monthly reports for Jan. and July 1858, AN F7/4028.
[17] Feb. 1856, AN F7/4132.   [18] E.g. prefect Marne, report on Jan. 1857, AN F7/40728.
[19] Prefect, 7 Jan. 1859, AN F7/3956.
[20] See e.g. confidential memo from La Valette, MI, 15 July 1863 in *Documents pour servir*.

Complaints about the efficiency of local mayors were only too frequent. According to one experienced observer – 'in general they keep quiet about crimes or offences they know about, whether through feebleness or ignorance, or because they are unwilling to compromise their popularity. Often it is the pressure they put on the gardes champêtres that reduces these agents to almost complete ineffectiveness'.[21] The essential responsibility for supervising *cabarets* was neglected and prefects were often poorly informed about local affairs.[22] Traditions of dealing with problems within the community itself died hard. The mayor of Verlès-Chartres in the Beauce explained his failure to report a case of rape in the following terms – 'I have come to realise, as a result of long experience, that complaints made one day are often retracted the next because facts which at first sight appeared serious, lost much of their criminality after a few hours reflection ... In addition the D ... are poor, A ... is rich, and monetary compensation would be of considerable help to the D ... As the complaint was withdrawn I believed it best to remain silent'. Subsequently the victim told gendarmes that the mayor had encouraged her to come to an 'arrangement'.[23] Given that peasants were more likely to approach their mayor than the police, his response was crucially important. The mayors themselves were likely to respond to criticism by complaining that with insufficient police support they were helpless.[24] In theory the mayor's shortcomings might be compensated for by the juges de paix or police commissaires. However, the state prosecutor at Paris concluded that in spite of their activity 'the countryside escapes all surveillance. The enemy of the government, just like the ordinary criminal, can conceal himself with impunity.'[25] Moreover, changes in established policing practices were often resented. The new commissaire de police at Morlaix (Morbihan) was treated to a *charivari* in the evening of 13 August 1866 by a crowd of 300 opposed to his efforts to regulate everything from café opening hours and the behaviour of prostitutes to weights and measures.[26]

It seems to have been generally agreed by the authorities that the only reliable force for ensuring the security of the capital and for policing the small towns and villages in which most of the population still lived was the

---

[21] M. de Goulhot de St-Germain, *Etudes sur les campagnes* (Paris 1859), p. 15.

[22] PG Douai, 2 April 1870, AN BB30/390; PG Paris, 29 Nov. 1858, AN BB30/383.

[23] J. C. Farcy, *Les paysans beaucerons au 19ᵉ siècle* (Chartres 1989), II, pp. 999–1000 and p. 1081, n. 22.

[24] E.g. report of prefect on mayors, 21 July 1852, AN F1 cIII Gironde 9.

[25] PG Paris, 18 Feb. 1854, AN BB30/383.

[26] MI internal memo, 29 Aug. 1866, AN F1 cIII Morbihan 13.

gendarmerie.[27] This was a branch of the army, recruited from amongst ex-soldiers, organised hierarchically, and under the authority of the War Minister. Its establishment was increased from 18,211 in 1848 to 788 officers and 13,798 mounted and 10,073 foot gendarmes according to the 1852 budget. The departmental gendarmerie (i.e. excluding Paris) is estimated to have represented 41.8 men per 100,000 inhabitants in 1841; 47.8 by 1851 and 51.6 by 1870.[28] Roughly speaking, there was a gendarmarie brigade of four to five men commanded by an NCO in each canton, supervised by a lieutenant or captain at arrondissement level. Prefects certainly complained about the gendarmeries' determination to obey only its own officers and the lack of co-operation between the various police agencies and with the civilian authorities. However, the gendarmerie at least was less susceptible to local influences. According to the Prefect of the Creuse 'it alone provides accurate information ... From other sources I encounter all too often partiality and passion. This is especially due to the fact that almost all the second-rank public officials originate from the department and, as a consequence, share the friendships and hatreds of their families.'[29] The procureur-général at Caen agreed, but with reservations, observing that 'one can only really count on the gendarmerie which is always zealous, which multiplies its activity, but whose personnel is insufficiently numerous for surveillance to be completely effective'.[30] They could be expected to visit each commune only once or twice a month in the conduct of regular patrols.[31] The number of gendarmes increased only slowly, although the situation was eased by the re-deployment of gendarmes from the west, where their numbers had been increased following the 1830 Revolution in case of Legitimist-inspired insurrection, and the increased mobility gained from their re-distribution to communications centres within the railway network.[32]

At least the gendarmerie could generally be relied upon to pursue criminals and provide political intelligence. In 1849 the then Minister of War, General d'Hautpoul, had conferred on the colonels commanding gendarmerie legions the 'delicate mission' of observing 'the activities and

[27] See e.g. PG Dijon, 28 Jan. 1857, AN BB30/377.
[28] Saurel, *Gendarmerie*, p. 616; Payne, *Police State*, pp. 22, 131, 235; R. Price, 'Techniques of repression: the control of popular protest in mid-19th-century France', *Historical Journal* (1982), pp. 864–5.
[29] 1 Oct. 1853, AN F1 cIII Creuse 8.   [30] 15 Jan. 1859, AN BB30/375.
[31] Saurel, *Gendarmerie*, p. 235; Price, 'Repression', pp. 865-6.
[32] Minister of War to Interior, 20 Aug. 1858, copy in AN F1 cIII Vendée 8.

political tendencies of government officials',[33] leading to such choice reports as that in November 1853 which pointed out that 'the wife of M. de Lapeyrouse, prefect of the Doubs, is more of a prefect than her husband; she absolutely dominates him'.[34]

Furthermore, they played an important role in supporting official election candidates.[35] Some officers regarded this as beneath their dignity or outside their competence but the refusal of Captain de Bouijn commanding the gendarmerie in the arrondissement of Aurillac (Cantal) to order his men to engage in electioneering, followed by his direct appeal to the Emperor, was dismissed as a serious act of indiscipline.[36]

The population seems to have regarded the gendarmerie with a mixture of fear and respect. Their limitations were outlined by the sous-préfet at Châtellerault in 1859:

the Gendarmerie, whatever its good intentions, is unable to make up for the shortcomings of the rural police. An examination of its reports proves this. Heavily equipped men, mounted on large horses entirely unsuitable for chases across fields, through vines and woods, will never prevent rural crime. Moreover, due to their distant place of residence, their uniform, and the respect they inspire in peasants, they will never be able to engage in the intimate conversations that a good *garde champêtre* knows how to encourage in order to gain the information necessary for effective policing.[37]

Moreover, neither police commissaires nor gardes champêtres could be relied upon to pass on relevant information to the gendarmerie.[38] His colleague at Pontoise (Seine-et-Oise) voiced the most common complaint in observing that

the zeal of the gendarmerie is unfortunately not supported by sufficient skill and intelligence. They proceed in a blunt military manner, which is not suitable for missions which require tact and finesse, and compromise the results by galloping around like cavalry and rendering surprise impossible. Most gendarmes have little knowledge of the private lives of the local inhabitants, are incapable of providing sensible situation reports and do not know how to bring an investigation to fruition. They are in addition much too likely to exaggerate the facts and to see delinquents everywhere.[39]

---

[33] Circular of 12 Nov. 1849, AHG MR 2003.
[34] Report of inspector-general, 9 Nov. 1853, AHG G9/5.
[35] Circular of Jan. 1854 from General A. de La Ruë, inspector-general of gendarmerie quoted Emsley, *Gendarmes*, pp. 126–7.
[36] Letters from Bouijn to Emperor, 8 Jan. and 3 Feb. 1857; response from Emperor's private secretary, 22 Jan., in *Papiers et correspondance*, II, pp. 22–6.
[37] ?April 1859, AN F1 cIII Vienne 6.
[38] See e.g. prefect Morbihan, report on Jan. 1858, AN F7/4095.
[39] 24 April 1858, quoted Saurel, *Gendarmerie*, III, p. 420.

According to the Minister of War himself, a balance needed to be established between excessive zeal on the one hand and indolence on the other.[40]

Given these various shortcomings, all too frequently policing depended on the efforts of the regular army. Large-scale demonstrations which threatened to get out of hand generally required the deployment of troops, although because they were poorly trained for crowd control and possessed unsuitable equipment this was avoided if possible. Counter-insurgency was certainly a key military function. In June 1848 and December 1851 military officers had fully committed themselves to protecting social order. Subsequently contingency plans for dealing with insurrection were updated regularly.[41] In the case of Paris the first objective would be to divide the city into two along the line of the Boulevard de Sébastopol. The capital would then be subdued as troops were deployed from barracks and central posts in each of the twenty-seven *quartiers militaires* into which the city was divided.[42] In more 'normal' times military commanders generally seem to have felt that engagement in internal security duties adversely affected the army's prestige.[43] Nevertheless, its dispersal in garrisons throughout the country suggests that the preservation of public order was conceived of as a role at least as important as national defence. Indeed, for concerned observers, this dispersal reduced the army's ability to practise large-scale manoeuvres in readiness for war.[44] Military guard posts and patrols added to the security of numerous under-policed garrison towns, large and small.[45] The civil authorities in areas threatened with subsistence disorders, disputes over access to forests, or by strikes, constantly requested a military presence, usually to the despair of local commanders who complained about the dispersal of their forces in response to frequently exaggerated fears.[46] Soldiers certainly welcomed the expansion of the civil police, which reduced their own 'demeaning' role in policing.

---

[40] Report of 24 Nov. 1855, quoted Saurel, *Gendarmerie*, III, pp.106–7.
[41] See e.g. discussion in council of ministers, 12 Jan. 1856, reported in *Journal d'Hippolyte Fortoul*, II, p. 196 and Napoleon to Randon, 27 Nov. 1861, on role of Paris gendarmerie regiment – in AN 249 AP 5.
[42] 'Notes. Défense de Paris'. Undated, AN 400 AP 42. See also 'Dispositions à prendre en cas d'émeutes et de troubles en Paris et en provinces', AHG MR 2151.
[43] See e.g. Serman, 'Le corps des officiers', p. 1371.
[44] General Trochu, *L'armée française en 1867* (Paris 1868), p. 275.
[45] See e.g. PG Orleans, 5 July 1852, AN BB30/382 re problems at Montargis (Loiret) following the withdrawal of its garrison.
[46] See e.g. Ministry of War, Direction du Personnel to MJ, 30 Aug. 1852, AN BB30/386; Price, 'Repression', pp. 869–72.

PRACTICAL POLICING

This is not the place to survey in any great detail the incidence of crime or the functioning of the police. My main concern will be with the political impact of policing, although always within the broader context of the maintenance of social order. In this sphere, policy was not devised according to objective criteria but on the basis of the authorities' perceptions of a changing situation. A particular cause of concern at mid-century was the rapid growth of cities, bringing together vast populations apparently less susceptible to the informal influences exercised in smaller communities.[47] At the same time there were rural regions, especially in the uplands, which, in the eyes of some officials, remained in 'a state of semi-barbarity', populated by 'ferocious beings [for whom] the authorities are an enemy, public order slavery, wealth an object of violent greed'.[48] Personal or collective disagreements were still all too likely to erupt into violence, frequently directed at any representative of authority who dared to intervene. This was the case when efforts were made to enforce the regulation of café opening hours or intervene in fights between rival groups of youths.[49] Serious disorders occurred in the Dreux and Chartres areas, close to Paris, in the summer of 1854, when rioters protested against a prefectoral ban on the use of thatch for roofing following serious fires. These resulted in the official's dismissal for excessive zeal.[50] In May 1859 the introduction of a toll on livestock entering the market at Tarbes resulted in a major riot involving both townspeople and peasants from the surrounding countryside. Intervention by the local gendarmerie was punished by the sacking of their barracks. Finally, order was restored by troops but at the cost of seven dead rioters.[51]

The official statistics on crime nevertheless suggested that increasing police vigilance and social change were, by the 1860s, contributing to a reduction in the rate of increase in crime, although widespread poverty and insecurity continued to impose limits on this trend.[52] At least improved communications and growing prosperity offered hope of rapid amelioration as well as the spread of *les sentiments français*.[53] Particularly notable was

---

[47] E.g. PG Aix, 28 June 1857, AN BB30/370.
[48] PG Riom, 9 Nov. 1852, AN BB30/386 re Haute-Loire.
[49] See e.g. PG Grenoble, 15 March 1852, AN BB30/378; GOC 10e DM, 1-5 and 6-10 March 1852, AHG F1/69.
[50] PG Paris, 5 July 1854, and ?Aug. 1855, AN BB30/383.
[51] Prefect Hautes-Pyrénées, report on May 1859, AN F7/4129.
[52] Chatelard, *Crime et criminalité*, pp. 28–33. For a not very reliable statistical base see MJ, *Comptes généraux de l'Administration criminelle de France*, published annually.
[53] PG Riom, 9 Nov. 1852, AN BB30/386.

the decline in all forms of popular violence, including drunken disorders and, most important for our purposes, those which might, conceivably, express social or political grievances, from folkloric protest such as the *charivari* to arson, which represented another traditional means of exercising pressure and a repeated cause of intense alarm.[54] As the economy was transformed, traditional disputes over access to forests and common land, and most significant of all, subsistence disorders rapidly declined in number. The final period of widespread popular protest concerning high food prices occurred between 1853 and 1856 and provoked the usual official concern that political agitators might take advantage of widespread popular misery.[55] Protest resulted in major problems of policing, but on nothing like the scale of 1846/7.[56] The more efficient working of markets, together with substantial counter-cyclical investment in urban renewal and rail construction, ensured that the link between agricultural crisis and industrial depression was weakened substantially. Far wider sections of the rural community appear to have shared in the profits engendered by high prices than previously. As in 1846, the government's response was the deployment of police and troops to protect markets and the lines of communication and the provision of subsidies to help fund public works employment. The onerous task of maintaining 'freedom of communication,' as late as March 1854, was defined as 'one of the principal duties of the gendarmerie'.[57] The authorities remained concerned about the threat of disorder, which previous experience had certainly led them to expect, and were surprised by its comparative rarity.[58] The procureur-général at Angers boasted in January 1854 that, for the first time in history, a year of shortage would pass without disorder.[59] His colleague at Bourges noted that 'we are experiencing something new. A slight increase in price occurs on our markets; immediately there is an influx of reserves ... and prices fall towards their previous levels'.[60] Significantly the last wave of subsistence disorders in the Limousin occurred in the year prior to the opening of the first railway lines in the region. Alain Corbin suggests that with this the *ancien régime économique* finally came to

---

[54] See e.g. rumours of 'des bandes incendiaires' around St-Brieuc and Loudéac (Côtes-du-Nord) in prefect report on June 1856, AN F7/3975.

[55] See e.g. Ministerial circular to PGs of 25 Sept. 1855 asking for lists of suspects – in AN BB30/415.

[56] R. Price, *The Modernisation of Rural France: Communications Networks and Agricultural Market Structures in 19th century France* (London 1983), ch. 6.

[57] Quoted Saurel, *Gendarmerie*, III, pp. 477–8.

[58] See e.g. PG Paris, 21 Feb. 1855 and 1 Sept. 1856, AN BB30/383.

[59] 8 Jan. 1854, AN BB30/371.

[60] 4 Oct. 1859, AN BB30/374; see also anon., 'L'approvisionnement de Paris par les chemins de fer', *Journal des chemins de fer*, 14 Oct. 1854.

an end.[61] The existence of the electric telegraph and the rapid transmission of market information was another factor promoting commercial efficiency. Due to these structural changes in the economy, the Imperial regime, which claimed to provide strong government, was also able to claim credit for improving the situation of the poor.

Disputes over wages and working conditions were other major causes of concern. The authorities' fear of the urban working class, understandable in the aftermath of 1848, if exaggerated, was nonetheless real.[62] The basic preventative tactic employed was intimidation, ideally through the maintenance of a police presence wherever workers gathered. Harassment became easier following the reinforcement, in 1854, of the existing requirement that workers should possess a *livret*, a form of internal passport.[63] Warnings and exemplary arrests, especially of supposed leaders, were likely at the merest hint of protest, organisation, or strike. Even where some sympathy for workers was evident and attempts were made to promote a more conciliatory attitude on the part of employers, it was their duty to protect the 'freedom' to work and the rights of property owners which remained foremost in the minds of responsible officials.[64] In the case of a strike involving large numbers of workers, like that by railway navvies near Montélimar (Drôme) in January 1853, military detachments were likely to be deployed to overawe workers.[65] Strikes were most likely in periods of economic difficulty, when the authorities were often conciliatory and refrained from prosecution. Statistics on strikes, which are largely based on prosecutions, thus offer a very poor representation of worker unrest.[66] The Emperor in his tract on *L'Extinction du paupérisme* had claimed to be the workers' friend. The range of legislation specifically directed at workers appeared to contradict this.[67]

From 1859, however, the police and judicial authorities were instructed to avoid prosecution save in exceptional cases. Subsequently, following strikes by Parisian printing workers in 1862, the Emperor pardoned eleven guilty participants on his own initiative, hinting at a further major policy change. Nevertheless, even if those arrested were rapidly released the prospect of fines or a short term of imprisonment, combined with the likelihood of dismissals by employers infuriated by any perceived

---

[61] Corbin, *Archaïsme*, I, p. 546.   [62] See e.g. PG Nîmes, 1 August 1855, AN BB30/382.

[63] Prothero, *Radical Artisans in England and France* (Cambridge 1997), p. 79.

[64] See e.g. PG Lyons, 5 April 1853, AN BB30/379.

[65] GOC 8e DM, 16-20 Jan. 1853, AHG G8/1.

[66] Number of strikes leading to prosecutions 1852 – 86; 1853 – 109; 1854 – 68; 1855 – 168; 1856 – 73; 1857 – 56; 1858 – 53.

[67] Point made by PG Lyons, 5 April 1853, AN BB30/379.

challenge to their authority, inevitably weakened worker resistance. The May 1864 law, which legalised strikes, thus represented a substantial concession. Comprehensible both as a political opening to the left and as part of a more general liberalisation and deregulation, this new freedom caused considerable concern amongst both officials and employers. Typically, alarmed by a strike by the cab drivers employed by the Compagnie impériale des petites voitures in July 1865, the state prosecutor at Paris demanded to know whether 'the prompt alliance of a large number of individuals reveals the existence of a mysterious association, dangerous for public order' and blamed the rapid spread and effective organisation of the strike on the existence of a network of mutual aid societies. His observation made it clear that, in practice, the impact of this legislation would be limited by the continued determination of the authorities to protect the right to work of non-strikers as well as by their almost instinctive support for employers and the cause of social order.[68] Police and troops were deployed wherever these appeared to be threatened. At the Anzin coalmines in October 1866 over 2,000 soldiers with artillery were mobilised.[69] Furthermore, although this more permissive legislation was not followed immediately by the massive wave of strikes expected by employers, a combination of factors would lead to widespread and in some cases violent worker protest as part of the general growth in tension during the regime's final years.

POLITICAL POLICE

The new Bonapartist state was distinguished by its origins. The *coup d'état* involved the declaration of martial law in 32 departments and the arrest of 26,642 people, of whom 9,581 were deported to Algeria, 239 to Cayenne and 8,000 interned or placed under surveillance in France and another 1,600 expelled from the national territory.[70] A decree of 8 December 1851 allowed prefects to transport to an overseas penal colony for five to ten years anyone guilty or simply suspected of membership of a 'secret society'. Although this draconian measure was rarely used after 1852 it survived as a hated symbol of the regime. Such intense repression certainly succeeded in its object of creating an atmosphere of terror. Morny could write, tongue in cheek, to Baroche on 9 December

---

[68] PG Paris, 4 Aug. 1865, AN BB30/384.
[69] MI to prefect Nord, 28 Oct 1866, AN F1 cɪɪɪ Nord 16.
[70] Report from de Maupas, Ministère de la police générale, n.d, in *Papiers et correspondence*, I, pp. 216–17; see also Payne, *Police State*, pp. 64–5.

1851 that 'the police at the moment are so incredibly zealous ... that I would not be surprised to be arrested myself, and I urge you to take care. *Mille amitiés!*'[71] Most state prosecutors accepted the primary need to defend social order.[72] Their membership of the social elite and dependence for professional success on the government ensured that they accepted the ruling made in a circular from the Minister of Justice on 11 January 1852 – 'the number of accused is so large that it is impossible to proceed against them by normal judicial means. The debates occurring on the application of the rules of common law are a new public danger. Measures of *sûreté générale* must be applied by administrative action.'[73] Martial law was, however, lifted on 27 March 1852 and normal legal procedures resumed.

The authorities, nevertheless, remained vigilant, with particular stress on the surveillance of suspects and of the frontiers. The activities of police spies, frequent searches of domestic premises, the opening of letters, and continued arrests of 'subversives', the scale of which was exaggerated by public opinion, all helped to sustain fear of arbitrary police action. In 'exceptional' circumstances prefects might still make use of article 10 of the *Code d'instruction criminelle* of 1800, although subsequent confirmation by the judicial authorities was required.[74] They were also regularly instructed to update lists of suspects. In Bordeaux, for example, under the direction of the prefect and the *commissaire central de police* over 300 individual dossiers were maintained between 1853 and 1860, mostly on workers, together with republican members of the lower and middle bourgeoisie.[75] These lists would be used when, following Orsini's bloody attempt to assassinate the Emperor on 14 January 1858, the government again resorted to extraordinary measures. These involved the introduction of the *loi de sûreté générale* and the appointment of a notorious hardliner, General Espinasse, as head of the renamed Ministère de l'Intérieure et de Sûreté générale. His predecessor, Billault, had rushed to see the Emperor in his box at the Opera immediately following the assassination attempt and been greeted with 'the police are doing a good job!'[76] He must have realised that his days as minister were numbered.

[71] Quoted Grothe, *Morny*, p. 90.
[72] E.g. PG Montpellier, 23 Feb. 1852, AN BB30/403; see also J.-C. Farcy, *Magistrats en majesté. Le discours de rentré aux audiences solennelles des cours d'appel* (Paris 1998), pp. 424–33; C. Charle, 'Les spécificités de la magistrature française en Europe', *Crises*, 1994, p. 68.
[73] In *Documents pour servir.*   [74] Le Clère and Wright, *Préfets*, p. 74.
[75] J.-F. Gilon, 'Surveillés et condamnés à Bordeaux entre 1850 et 1860', *Revue historique de Bordeaux* (1986/7), pp. 55–7.
[76] Quoted Blayau, *Billault*, p. 292.

In the corridors of the Corps législatif, however, there was some concern that Espinasse's political ideas 'are no better than those of a gendarmerie captain'.[77] Even the ferocious Marshal de Castellane expressed astonishment at the appointment.[78] P.-M. Pietri, the comparatively liberal Prefect of Police was also dismissed. Having chosen to ignore a warning from his agents that a plot existed, he was clearly exposed to accusations of incompetence.[79]

Napoleon's initial response to the bombing had been anxious and angry. In Espinasse's letter of appointment on 15 February the Emperor insisted that

the body of society is being eaten away by vermin which it must, whatever the cost, get rid of. There are also prefects who must be dismissed, in spite of their patrons. I count on your zeal to achieve this; do not be tempted by an untimely moderation to re-assure those who have been frightened by your appointment. It is important that you do spread fear; without that your nomination would have no purpose.[80]

This was not, after all, the first attempt to assassinate the Emperor. His life was believed to be under constant threat. In September 1854 a plot had been discovered to blow up the Imperial train en route to a meeting with the Belgian king at Tournai. Typically, the incident was used to justify a series of searches and arrests as well as a campaign to discredit republicans. Normally, official tours were preceded by searches of the homes of suspects.[81] Orsini had believed that the Emperor's death would be followed by universal revolution. As it was, the three bombs thrown at the Imperial cortège as it arrived at the Opera had injured 156 people, 8 mortally, and put the Emperor and his wife at risk. On top of poor election results in Paris the previous year, this appears to have resulted in the Emperor experiencing a major crisis of confidence. Fear of republican demonstrations at the funerals of the songwriter Béranger and of General Cavaignac in July and October 1857 had occasioned massive military deployments already. Even before the Orsini affair there had been persistent rumours of insurrectionary plots.[82] Everything achieved since 1851 appeared to be at risk. On 16 January, in a speech approved by Napoleon, Morny, now President of the Corps législatif expressed this sense of anxiety. Addressing the Emperor, he insisted that 'you have

[77] Darimon, *Les cinq*, p. 115.   [78] *Journal*, vol. V, p. 203
[79] Bernard, 'Le réorganisation', p. 134.
[80] Quoted in Espinasse's letter of resignation, June 1858, in *Papiers et correspondance...*, II, pp. 67–8.
[81] See e.g. GOC 11e DM, 6–10 Oct. 1852, AHG F1/70.
[82] See e.g. sous-préfet Montargis, 4 July 1859, AN F1 CIII Loiret 12.

only been attacked because you are the corner-stone of public order'. He demanded firm action, both internally and from those foreign governments (particularly Britain), which tolerated the presence of dangerous exiles. Morny, nevertheless, also sought to re-assure deputies that these measures were intended only to 'intimidate and disperse ... the implacable enemies of society, who detest every regime and all authority'. He ended by promising that 'the reds will realise that they will always find us blocking their way, before they can strike at the heart of France'. The speech was circulated with the official *Moniteur des communes* and posted in every commune.[83] The new legislation sought to terminate a possible republican revival through the deportation of militants.[84]

In a circular of 17 February 1858 Espinasse ordered prefects to establish lists of suspects, in consultation with state prosecutors and military commanders.[85] Those originally compiled for the Commissions mixtes established following the *coup* should have been updated regularly.[86] On 23 February they were instructed to use these lists to make a specified number of arrests in order to 'strike the troublemakers with a salutary terror'.[87] Already Espinasse felt that the measures, which had accompanied the *coup d'état*, had been inadequate. He now conceived an ambitious programme of surveillance and arrests designed to cleanse France of dangerous subversives. Officials in Paris and departments like Var or Gers which had experienced insurrection in December 1851 were, not surprisingly, hardliners in this new crisis, but Espinasse would soon be disappointed by what he felt was a lack of commitment on the part of many of his subordinates.[88] In all, perhaps 430 suspected republican leaders, mainly business and professional men, were arrested. Some were soon released but 380 appear to have been deported to Algeria.[89] According to Thourel, the state prosecutor at Nîmes, there were no legal grounds for arresting the 'suspects' taken into custody and no court would have convicted them.[90] The procedures followed in the Var might be taken as representative. There the prefect warned his sous-préfets that

---

[83] *Moniteur universelle*, 8 Feb. 1858; see also MJ circular, 18 Feb. 1858, in AN BB30/447.

[84] See Conseil d'Etat, 'Exposé des motifs d'un projet de loi relatif à des mesures de sûreté générale', 1858, AN BB30/447.

[85] AN BB30/447.   [86] MJ to PG Nîmes, 11 Jan. 1856, AN BB30/440.

[87] General Espinasse, *Mémoires* (Paris n.d.), pp. 137–9 ; see also V. Wright, 'La loi de sûreté générale de 1858', *Revue d'histoire moderne et contemporaine*, 1969, p. 420.

[88] See MI circular, 23 March 1858, AN BB30/447; also e.g. PI Auch to PG, 13 March 1858, AN BB30/447; prefect Seine, report on Feb. 1858, AN F7/4165.

[89] V. Wright, 'Loi', pp. 425–6.   [90] PG Nîmes, 7-8 March 1858, AN BB30/447.

the Republicans are planning to use the trial of Orsini and his accomplices as the occasion for disorder ... The Minister of the Interior has instructed me to make six arrests in the department, amongst dangerous men on the list of those previously pardoned. You should make ... the arrests in the greatest possible secrecy and imprison those two republicans [i.e. 2 per arrondissement], who might be considered by their contacts and activities to be the most dangerous, in the local prison.[91]

Police commissaires were invited to prepare additional lists of suspects and by early March the prefect was able to supply a further seventy-two names to the minister. By then, however, exceptional measures were already being seen as unnecessary. These arrests, combined with widespread house-to-house searches, prosecutions for possession of subversive literature, for seditious expressions and press offences had had the intimidatory effect the government desired.[92]

As a further measure of security France was divided into five military areas (decree 27 January 1858), each commanded by a marshal who was given ultimate responsibility for public order. They were instructed by Marshal Randon, the War Minister, to 'Carefully study the movement of public opinion and report on the causes of any changes, use your personal prestige and activities to enlighten it when it is blind to the truth, put it right when it goes astray, calm it when it is troubled; such is your capital role. This is why you will assume superiority over all the other local authorities.'[93] Such out-and-out reactionaries as Marshal de Castellane at Lyon were clearly thrilled by this militarisation, and by the enhancement of their power, status and, indeed, salary, which in Castellane's case would now amount to 100,000f a year plus food and lodging, together with his senatorial salary of 60,000f.[94] Castellane's initial response to the news of the assassination attempt had been to ride slowly past groups of workers on the city streets and to enjoy the feeling that even if they hated him 'they politely doffed their caps because they are afraid of me'.[95] The marshal's contingency plans for dealing with an uprising in France's second city and throughout the south-east were rigorous in the extreme, as the following order suggests: 'Soldiers must never allow themselves to be approached by a column of rioters, by women and children. Any hesitation by infantry in opening fire might compromise them and lead to them being disarmed. It is essential that

[91] Quoted Constant, *Var*, p. 925.
[92] See e.g. Correspondance au sujet de l'attentat du 14 janvier 1858, AN BB30/441.
[93] Quoted Serman, *Le corps des officiers*, p. 1325.
[94] *Journal*, v, pp. 227–8, 204.   [95] *Ibid.*, p. 202.

the rioters are instructed to halt at 200 feet; if they do not obey, once the riot act has been read ... open fire immediately.' The next sentence is particularly revealing of the kind of social hatred generated by the experience of 1848: 'Women and children are likely to attempt to murder the officers; they are the enemy's advance guard, and must be treated as such'.[96]

In practice little changed. The sense of panic and belief that the Orsini *attentat* was part of a vast republican conspiracy did not last. In June Espinasse was required to resign. He complained that his reputation for excess was unfair given that only around 300 (*sic*) of the 10,000 names included on various lists of suspects had actually been arrested.[97] His replacement by Delangle, a magistrate, was seen widely as representing the end of exceptional measures.[98] In fact, the Emperor had rapidly realised that public opinion and indeed most senior officials regarded the return to 'dictatorship' as unnecessary. Undoubtedly the assassination attempt had aroused general disgust. There was a genuine sense of affection for the Imperial couple as well as fear of the unknown were the Emperor to disappear suddenly. Nevertheless, there had been considerable opposition to the emergency legislation in the Conseil d'Etat and committees of the Corps législatif, particularly to those provisions which had broadened the definition of political crimes and enlarged administrative powers of summary arrest.[99] Not everyone appreciated Baroche's dismissal of legal scruples in the Corps législatif: 'When one faces an obvious danger, and identifies the remedy, should one be put off by the hesitations of the jurists and by procedural difficulties?'[100] In spite of effective criticism from Emile Ollivier and the Marquis d'Andelarre the legislation had been supported by 227 votes to 24, but it seems evident that many members of the majority found the proceedings distasteful.[101] The procureur-général at Nancy pointed out that, provided that legal forms had been adhered to, the energetic defence of social order would have been widely supported. The appointment of a general to the Interior Ministry had aroused fears of military rule, whilst the arrests had come too late to serve as a preventative measure and otherwise could not be justified, certainly not in terms of guilt on

---

[96] Confidential order in AHG MR 2151; see also dispositions laid down by the marshal commanding the Garde Impériale 27 April 1870 in case of disorder in Paris, *ibid.*

[97] For his long and bitter resignation letter see *Papiers et correspondance*, II, pp. 65–71.

[98] See e.g. prefect, 8 July 1858, AN F I CIII Ariège 7 and Darimon, *Les cinq*, p. 193, entry of 15 June 1858.

[99] See especially V. Wright, 'Loi', p. 419; also e.g. PG Montpellier, 5 July 1858, AN BB30/380.

[100] Quoted Maurain, *Baroche*, p. 157.   [101] Darimon, *Les cinq*, p. 108 entry, of 1 Feb. 1858.

the part of the accused.[102] His colleague in Paris summarised the views of these well-informed judicial officials: 'The law of General Security, improvised in the first moments of trouble and panic following the deplorable event, allowed the government's fears to manifest themselves, rather than providing for greater security'. Strict enforcement of existing legislation would have sufficed. As it was, the regime had suffered considerable discredit.[103] Prince Napolon warned his cousin that such extreme measures could be taken to mean that 'seven glorious years ... have counted for nothing, that we are in the same position as on the first day, and that everything has to be done again, including the *coup d'état*'.[104]

Whilst generally they were unwilling to entirely dismiss rumours of insurrectionary plots most state prosecutors refused to take them very seriously. Other than during such limited and exceptional periods as that immediately following the *coup* and the Orsini *attentat* in 1858, generally the judicial authorities insisted on respect for the rule of law and required evidence before prosecution. They were impatient with 'extraordinary' measures.[105] In spite of vigorous police activity, little of any consequence had been discovered in 1858 although, as the procureur-général at Angers pointed out, this lack of information could be taken to represent sure proof of the efficacy of secret-society activity.[106] Like any sensible bureaucrat he appears to have been covering all eventualities! Most of those deported were soon amnestied. The *loi de sûreté générale* would, nevertheless, remain in existence until 1870. Its final abrogation, together with that of the decrees of 8 to 12 December 1851, was proposed by Ollivier in a letter to the Emperor on 7 February 1870. The fundamental point made was that this extraordinary legislation had been used hardly ever in the previous eleven years and that social order was safeguarded sufficiently by articles 86 and 87 of the penal code.[107] The psychological and political impact of the law should not be underestimated, however. It had served to intimidate republican opponents of the regime. Additionally, it had increased concern amongst liberals about a regime, which could threaten to abrogate the rule of law.[108] Although

[102] PG Nancy, 9 July 1858, AN BB30/381.
[103] PG Paris, 20 Aug. 1858, AN BB30/383; see also PI Foix, 9 March 1858, AN BB30/441.
[104] Note à l'Empereur, March 1858, AN 400 AP 150.
[105] See e.g. PG Rouen, 29 Jan. 1858, AN BB30/441.
[106] PG Angers, 21 Jan. and 15 March 1858, AN BB30/419.
[107] AN BB30/447; see also Conseil d'Etat, 'Exposé des motifs d'un projet de loi portant abrogation de la loi relative à des mesures de sûreté générale', 15 Feb. 1870.
[108] For the opposing points of view compare e.g. prefect, 14 April 1858, AN F1 cIII Eure 13 with

these extraordinary powers were not used, there was also always the possibility that they might be. In a *très confidentielle* circular of 6 June 1859, the Minister of the Interior advised prefects on the measures to be taken in the event of the Emperor's sudden death. They were instructed to keep the news secret initially. Officials and troops should be gathered to take the oath of allegiance to the new ruler. Any signs of subversion should be suppressed immediately and if necessary martial law declared. On 26 September 1861 prefects were reminded again of the need to maintain an up-to-date list of dangerous subversives. Blank arrest warrants were to be prepared so that arrests could be made without delay.[109] Some tension was evident between prefects, anxious above all to suppress political subversion, and the state prosecutors who, as magistrates, resented what they saw as prefectoral contempt for legal proprieties, and for the independence of the judiciary.[110] This inevitably reduced the efficiency of the machinery of government and adversely affected the flow of information.[111] In political cases, however, particularly those involving republicans and socialists, the magistrature normally could be relied upon to play its part in political repression. Many had been unalterably marked by the events of 1848.[112]

MEASURING SUCCESS

How successful was the regime in achieving the objectives of order and stability? In the aftermath of the *coup* potential opponents undoubtedly were intimidated. They were aware that not only themselves but also their friends and families were subject to surveillance. Officials noted that suspects were desperate to avoid being compromised. They avoided former comrades and voluntarily handed over subversive literature, which had been addressed to them. Moustaches and beards once proudly worn as symbols of their political allegiance were now shaved off.[113] Subject to intimidation and, for the most part, politically inactive, former militants inevitably lost most of their influence. Betrayal was common. The anonymous author of a placard found in the rue de Noailles in Marseille in March 1868 bemoaned the fact that 'every kind of association is

PG Grenoble, 2 May 1858, AN BB30/447.

[109] See *très confidentielle* circulars from MI to prefects, 6 June 1859 and 26 Sept. 1861, in *Pièces saisies*, pp. 35, 38.

[110] See e.g. PG Riom, 10 July 1863, AN BB30/386.

[111] Le Clère and Wright, *Préfets*, pp. 98–102; Royer, Martinage, and Lecocq, *Juges et notables*, p. 249.

[112] See e.g. D. Rivet, *La vie politique dans le département de la Haute-Loire* (Le Puy 1979), pp. 204–5.

[113] See e.g. PG Aix, 16 July 1856, AN BB30/370; PG Paris, 17 March 1858, AN BB30/383.

impossible; brother suspects brother, father suspects son.'[114] Increased police activity represented the growing penetration of central political authority into daily life, and the creation at local level of new norms of behaviour. According to the procureur général at Montpellier, writing soon after the *coup*, criminality in general had declined due to 'the re-establishment of moral order, the widespread conviction that the authorities have the power and will to enforce the law.'[115] Political policing would continue, with varying intensity according to the perceived threat. In those areas in which mass uprisings had occurred in December 1851 the use of placards to anonymously express republican sentiments and to threaten revenge, as well as the singing of seditious songs, was common throughout 1852.[116] Considerable tension survived in communities long divided by social and political disputes. A placard found at Bédarrides (Vaucluse) in September illustrates the point. It was addressed 'Aux Frères et amis de Robespierre' and promised:

> Death to the Odious President of the Republic
> Death to those dressed in black [the clergy]
> Death to the Whites [the Legitimists]
> Chabut [a local politician] to the gallows
> Pillage the Rich

and concluded with an appeal: 'Stay calm, in a month France will be ours' – which cannot have done much for the nerves of local officials.[117] Police activity was especially evident in places like Clamecy (Nièvre) notorious for violence against gendarmes in December 1851 and where in 1858 a drunk's 'seditious' shouts could still earn 8 to 12 months' imprisonment.[118] Itinerants of various kinds, 'modern' commercial travellers as well as traditional peddlers, were always suspect and closely watched.[119] Railway junctions required especially careful surveillance.[120] By their very nature, private meetings aroused concern.[121] Frequently efforts were made to punish the expression of subversive ideas (*propos séditieux, propos injurieux contre l'Empereur, paroles menaçants*) by the incautious – usually drunks. These tended to take the form of simple abuse with references to Napoleon III as a 'brigand', 'thief', 'pig'; or else shouts of

[114] PG Aix, 23 March 1868, AN BB18/1766.   [115] 26 Feb. 1852, AN BB30/380.
[116] See e.g. GOC 9e DM re Vaucluse, 26–31 March 1852, AHG F1/69.
[117] Prefect, 28 Sept. 1852, AN F1 cIII Vaucluse 10.
[118] Prefect Nièvre, reports on April–May 1858, AN F7/4102.
[119] See e.g. MI circular 13 Jan. 1852 in *Documents pour servir.*
[120] See e.g. PG Grenoble, 12 Jan. 1856, AN BB30/378.
[121] Circular from Dureau, directeur du personnel at MI, to prefects, 16 May 1863 in *Documents pour servir.*

A bas Napoléon or *Vive la République*, to which might be added, as a form
of wishful thinking, such remarks as: 'if I were in Paris I'd blow out the
Emperor's brains', 'slit his throat', etc.[122] Other manifestations likely to
be prosecuted included the singing of subversive songs, the wearing of
symbolic colours like *red* ribbons and the spreading of rumours.[123] At
Châteaudouble (Var) in November 1853 an individual was sentenced to
eight days in prison for claiming, in the middle of a cholera epidemic,
that 'the government is paying men to poison the population ... the rich
don't die because they agree with the government, it's always the poor
who are the victims'.[124] The most absurd stories needed to be suppressed
in the interests of public order. During the Crimean War it was rumoured
in the Montélimar area that nobles and priests were shipping gold to the
Russian Tsar.[125] Even when, in April 1859, crowds in Lyon provided
an apparently sincere and enthusiastic patriotic send-off for troops leaving for Italy, Marshal de Castellane contemptuously observed that they
were also singing, to the tune of the *Marseillaise* (itself banned), verses
which promised to hang both himself and the Cardinal de Bonald from
the lampposts and to hammer the Prefect Vaïsse to death.[126] In other
circumstances, soldiers themselves were a favourite target for drunken
violence. At Bar-le-Duc a worker was arrested for assaulting a member
of the local garrison and telling him that he was 'a pig, a drunkard, a
thief, and a White' and adding, for good measure, the observation that
'you serve that imbecile of an Emperor'.[127] Alongside these attacks on
the regime and its agents might be set the violent and contemptuous
expressions of hatred for the 'rich'. The state prosecutor at Paris listed a
series of atrocious menaces, which he believed were representative of the
attitudes of workers in the arrondissements of Corbeil and Essonne and
concluded that they 'reveal the heinous passions and the ferocious instincts which still ferment amongst the dregs of society and demonstrate
the need for continuous surveillance'.[128] Following a period of relative
calm, liberalisation, and the sense of expectancy it created amongst republicans, would lead to a revival of political placards and seditious
shouts, particularly from 1868.[129]

[122] See offences reported in AN BB30/411.
[123] MI circular, 11 July 1852, AN F1 cIII Hérault 15.
[124] PI Draguignan, 18 Nov. 1853 quoted Constant, *Var*, p. 865; similar reports PG Grenoble, 7
Sept. and 28 Nov. 1854, AN BB30/378.
[125] PG Grenoble, 28 Nov. 1854, *ibid.*
[126] *Journal*, v, p. 246.   [127] GOC 5e DM, 21–25 May 1853, AHG G8/1.
[128] PG Paris, 29 Nov. 1858, AN BB30/383.
[129] See e.g. PG Aix, 23 March 1868, PG Bourges, 31 Oct. 1868, AN BB18/1766.

Table 4. *Convictions for political crimes, second half of 1853. Dept of Seine*[a]

Crime	Number of convictions	Crime	Number of convictions
Seditious shouts	18	Attacks (verbal) on the rights of property and the family	2
Distribution of unauthorised literature	25	Publication of printed works without prior deposit	1
Illegal workers' organisation	27	Offences against the Emperor	22
Unsigned newspaper articles	1	Exciting hatred between citizens	1
Unauthorised publication of a newspaper	7	Outrage against public morality	4
Possession of weapons	33	Publication of false news	4
Contravention of the law on bookshops	8	Illegal meetings	4
Membership of secret society	42	Display of seditious emblems	3

[a] PG Paris, 10 Feb. 1854, AN BB30/383.

The decision to prosecute in such cases was often an arbitrary one. It depended on the general circumstances of time and place. Occasionally, it was important to set an example. Thus in January 1853 sixteen men were arrested by gendarmes at St-Ambroix (Gard) for singing seditious songs at a 'socialist' banquet and were escorted to prison in Alais by 100 infantry.[130] Many of the offences were only technically 'political' as the state prosecutor at Paris admitted. In one case of 'offences against the Emperor' at Herpont (Marne) in 1853 the words used were actually judged to be so obscene that it was decided to drop the case rather than publicise them.[131] The range of offences categorised as 'political' crimes in the Seine department (including Paris) for the second half of 1853 provides some indication of the authorities' concerns (table 4). The incidents reported were, of course, only the tip of the iceberg.

[130] GOC 10e DM, 5-10 Jan. 1853, AHG G8/1.　　[131] PG Paris, 10 Feb. 1854, AN BB30/383.

In all, 202 convictions were obtained and only 17 of the accused were acquitted. Generally, prosecution had a serious basis and those brought to trial were quite likely to be convicted. At the end of the following six months the procureur-général felt able to congratulate himself on a substantial reduction in the number of cases – to 185, of which 158 resulted in convictions. This he claimed was due to 'the gradual appeasement of evil passions ... to growing confidence in the government, the spread of the ideal of order and work and increasing prosperity'.[132] In the following year prosecutions fell to 129 and convictions to 114.[133] The regime had evidently entered into a period of political repose. An internal Ministry of Justice memo insisted on the success of police surveillance and repression of secret societies in Paris.[134] There was greater concern about undetected subversive activity in the provinces where policing was far less well resourced.

Throughout 1852 police reports, often extremely detailed, continued to insist that the secret societies, which had provided the basis for resistance to the *coup d'état*, were re-organising.[135] Numerous minor incidents appeared to offer proof. However, most prefects and prosecutors received these with scepticism, dismissing them as a mere 'reflection of the fears aroused by the all too famous threat of 1852'.[136] There was also the constant irritation caused by the use of the funerals of known republicans for political demonstrations. For the police to have interfered when in July 1852, at Joigny (Yonne), around 250 'democrats' had remained in a nearby bar as a priest intoned the *office des morts* and then re-appeared to escort their dead comrade to his grave would have been counter-productive, however.[137]

A great deal of police activity focused on the cafés, which played such an important part in popular sociability. It was in the *cabaret* 'that the public opinion of the rural population is created'.[138] During the Second Republic they had provided the means by which 'oral propaganda was able to exert such a deplorable influence'.[139] Police agents were, however, only too easily detected in village cafés, or those in working-class *quartiers*, rarely frequented by strangers.[140] A decree of 29 December 1851 required prefects to license drinking places and regulate their opening hours and to close those which posed a threat to moral or political

---

[132] PG Paris, 5 July 1854, AN BB30/383.   [133] PG Paris, ?Aug. 1855, *ibid.*
[134] Undated memo, AN BB30/409.
[135] See reports from secret agents, 8 Jan. and 9 Feb. 1862, AN 116 AP 1.
[136] Prefect, 24 June 1852, AN F1 CIII Isère 9.
[137] PG Paris, 20 Aug. 1852, AN BB30/383.   [138] PG Riom, 23 July 1853, AN BB30/386.
[139] PG Orleans, 6 March 1852, AN BB30/382.   [140] See e.g. Commissaire, *Mémoires*, II p. 181.

order. In some cases the decree was rigorously enforced. In the Calvados, Prefect Tonnet was concerned that alcoholism would lead to the degeneration of the lower classes, and closed 700 cafés and bars in six years.[141] There was a widely shared perception that in the industrial centres 'husbands and fathers continue to spend a notable part of their wages on drink, and misery and idleness lead many women and girls into a state of profound demoralisation'.[142] Prostitution was one outcome, a result of 'the brutalisation of men and women, and the physical and moral cretinism of children'.[143] Shorter opening hours and higher taxes on drinks were other remedies suggested.[144] The state prosecutor at Montpellier fervently desired that the upper classes, themselves too given to drink, cards, and patronising *maisons de tolérance*, should set a better example.[145] More commonly, senior officials would continue to complain about the feeble efforts of local mayors to control café life.[146] Enforcing municipal *arrêts* on closing hours was a challenging task. It could all too easily lead to drunken assaults on the officials and police involved. Gardes champêtres were particularly susceptible to intimidation.[147] A growing concern amongst legal officials and the clergy about the increasing number of cafés and the problem of drunkenness led the Interior Minister in August 1864 to remind prefects of the need to enforce the 1851 decree but significantly with the qualification that they should 'as far as possible' ensure 'respect for the principle of commercial freedom'.[148] The number of licensed establishments, which had reached 350,424 in 1850 and been reduced to 291,244 by 1855, was allowed to rise again and reached 364,875 in 1869.[149] The existence of the decree, together with closer surveillance, however, must have forced café proprietors to police their own premises and intermittently to ban political debate.[150] In southern departments like the Var it was the *chambrées*, traditional private drinking and social associations, only some of which were even authorised, which continued to cause concern.[151] In July 1858 the state prosecutor at Toulouse confirmed that there were no secret societies in his area of

[141] Le Clère and Wright, *Préfets*, p. 123.   [142] PI Rocroi, 23 July 1854, AN BB30/380.
[143] PI Briey, 23 Jan. 1854, *ibid*.   [144] See e.g. PG Metz, 11 Jan. 1860, AN BB30/380.
[145] PG Montpellier, 8 June 1859, AN BB30/380.
[146] E.g. PI Sarreguemines, 11 Jan. 1860, AN BB30/380.
[147] See e.g. GOC 10e DM, 5–10 March 1856, AHG G8/36; prefect Côtes-du-Nord, report on Oct. 1856, AN F7/3975.
[148] MI to MJ, 16 Aug. 1864, AN BB30/380.
[149] R Forti, *The Octroi as an Index of Political, Social and Financial Controversy in France, 1871–1914*, PhD, State Univ. of New York at Buffalo, 1978, p. 123 quoting *Journal officiel*, 9 July 1892.
[150] PG Lyon, 3 Feb. 1852, AN BB30/379.   [151] Constant, *Var*, pp. 603–5.

responsibility but pointed to the existence of 'a host of working-class and artisanal associations whose ostensible goal is mutual aid, which usually pay little attention to politics but which might eventually facilitate communication and the transmission of opinions and directives'.[152] In Lille, although the police were fully aware that the clandestine republican movement was similarly based in bars in working-class districts where politics might safely be discussed, funds to support exiles collected, and Pierre Dupont's songs enjoyed, they preferred to simply watch militants rather than drive their activities underground.[153] There were, of course, limits to this tolerance and participation in regular, organised meetings was likely to result in prosecution for secret-society membership.

Following the experience of the Second Republic, the authorities remained obsessively concerned about the re-constitution of secret societies[154] and were ready to deduce their existence from the flimsiest evidence, although this did make successful prosecution difficult and only 304 convictions were recorded between the middle of 1853 and the end of 1858.[155] For the historian, as for the police authorities, evidence is fragmentary and difficult to interpret. Once again it tells us more about official mentalities than about the actual incidence of underground political activity. Were the alarming reports from small town mayors well founded? Or were they the product of exaggerated fear and local rivalries?[156] Given the secrecy involved, officials often depended on police spies or informers, some of them active on behalf of the Parisian authorities, others on the orders of local judicial and police officers. Their activities do not appear to have been coordinated very effectively.[157] Frequently, and sensibly, the authorities were suspicious of the veracity of the information these provided. After all, they had to report something to satisfy their employers. Republican electoral successes might, however, be seen as sure proof of illicit organisation. How else could the election of Hénon in Lyons in 1852 be explained: 'without preparatory meetings, without circulars, without newspaper publicity'?[158] Every rumour, seditious shout, or placard, was a sign. It was widely accepted that news of the assassination of the Emperor would provide

---

[152] Quoted R. Aminzade, 'Class Struggles and Social Change: Toulouse 1830–72', PhD, University of Michigan 1978, p. 375.
[153] Ménager, *Nord*, vol. I, pp. 386–7.
[154] See e.g. PG Aix, 9 Sept. 1852, re Marseille, AN BB30/404.   [155] Payne, *Police State*, p. 152.
[156] See e.g. letter from mayor of Nissan to sous-préfet Béziers, AN BB30/406.
[157] Prefect, 18 Sept. 1852, AN F1 cIII Isère 9; PG Lyons, 17 July 1856 and 6 Aug. 1858, AN BB30/379.
[158] PG Lyons, 8 March 1852, AN BB30/379.

the signal for an insurrection prepared by secret societies throughout France.[159]

A series of 'conspiracies' was uncovered in the early 1850s. The prefect of the Vaucluse in July 1852 discounted a police report claiming that local secret societies had recruited 600 new adherents since May, bringing the total membership to 7,200 organised in 65 companies, although he covered his own tracks by admitting that there were signs that extremists were re-organising.[160] The so-called *complot* of Saint-Jean-du-Gard was fairly typical of the outcome of police surveillance and was taken as proof of the regime's failure to dismantle fully the secret-society networks. The prefect of the Gard claimed in March 1853 that a conspiracy centred on Saint Jean, Nîmes, and Anduze, and with links to a committee in Marseille and the exiles in London, had attracted 19,000 supporters across nine departments. He demanded urgent action. Thourel, procureur-général at Aix, was convinced that the police reports had grossly exaggerated the threat.[161] In the event 25 individuals were convicted and, no doubt, local republicans were intimidated. In June the Prefect of Police claimed to have uncovered a plot in the capital. Those arrested – workers and small traders – all had political pasts which, together with their denials, was taken to imply guilt. On this occasion, fifty were arrested for belonging to an illegal society called the *Comité révolutionnaire*. Most of them were sentenced to between one and four years' imprisonment.[162] It was relatively easy to turn up incriminating evidence against men with a past, like J.-B. Beurrée a comb-maker, A. Delporte a shoemaker, his brother J.-B. a hatter, and C. Jamet employed in a bookshop. The evidence was entirely circumstantial. Certainly they met socially, and searches of their lodgings turned up all sorts of republican propaganda. Their vociferous denials were perversely taken to represent further 'proof' – and it took only a little time to 'persuade' one of the accused to confess that he had heard 'the others' plotting.[163] Meeting in the coal-mining community of Anzin (Nord) in 1856, a society called La Cocotte was similarly unravelled through a process of mutual denunciation. This began with the wife of an innkeeper called Blaize, tired of being beaten by her husband, who revealed an attempt to set up a secret society on the lines of the old charbonnerie

[159] E.g. PG Paris, 26 Nov. 1853, AN BB30/383; OC gendarmerie Côte-d'Or, 10 Oct. 1852, AHG F1/70.
[160] 18 July 1852, AN F1 CIII Vaucluse 13; see also A.Prudhomme, 'Les sociétés secrètes républicaines sous le second empire', *Mémoires sociale science Lettres Loir-et-Cher*, 1984, p. 83.
[161] PG Aix, 24 Feb. 1853, AN BB30/406.   [162] PG Paris, 5 July 1854, AN BB30/383.
[163] Paris Prefect of Police, three reports to Min. de la police générale, 9 June 1853, APP Aa 434.

with its *decuries* each led by a *decurion* who alone had contact with a *centurion*. Its leading figure appears to have been Jean Charvigne, known as 'Grand Charles', another miner-innkeeper, who was in correspondence with political prisoners imprisoned on Belle-Isle as well as with Parisian militants and exiles in Brussels and London. Members of this society appeared to have done no more than discuss the improvement of safety in the mines, the need for nationalisation, and a wage of 11 francs a day.[164]

The authorities certainly succeeded in uncovering a sufficient number of secret groups to cause continued alarm. These included Les Vengeurs in Lyon; as well as La Marianne, an organisation which had been reported since 1850 with offshoots known as La Militante in Lyon and Bordeaux.[165] The mysterious gatherings of members of La Militante, re-named les Francs-juges, in the quarries of the Buttes-Chaumont in Paris were bound to arouse suspicion.[166] Typically a secret agent employed in Lyon reported a gathering of fifteen Voraces in a bar at 5 a.m. on 3 August 1852. He claimed that they had discussed plans for an insurrection. On 9 November he reported that secret-society leaders had met in a *cabaret* outside the city to receive instructions from a Parisian *comité révolutionnaire*. Finally, on 16 May 1853 the police managed to surprise eight individuals in a grotto on the banks of the Rhône at Saint-Fonde 8 km from Lyon receiving a new member into their society and to arrest another twelve participants in a similar ceremony in the city itself. Certainly Castellane, the irascible military commander, tended to take these reports at face value.[167] In this case and another leading to the arrest in May 1854 of members of the Société des Bons-Cousins charbonniers at Fontaine-Française (Côte-d'Or) the defendants claimed to belong to a mutual aid society with no political objectives. In the second case, whilst suspecting that this traditional philanthropic organisation was being used to distribute political propaganda, the state prosecutor at Dijon nevertheless criticised the prefect for acting precipitately and on the basis of insufficient evidence. As a result the accused were acquitted and the government severely embarrassed.[168] Pastoureau, prefect of the

---

[164] L. Machu, 'Deux aspects de la répression policière dans le Nord à l'époque du Second Empire,' *Revue du Nord*, 1964, pp. 387-91.

[165] PG Paris 5 March 1856, AN BB30/383; M. Agulhon, *Marianne au combat. L'imagerie et la Symbolique républicaine* (Paris 1979) p. 165.

[166] *Gazette des Tribunaux*, 28 May 1857.

[167] Prefect 13 July, 3 and 30 Aug. 1852, AN F1 CIII Rhône 10; PG Lyon, 20 May 1853 and PI Lyon, 21 Nov. 1853, AN BB30/407; Castellane, *Journal*, IV p. 350.

[168] PG Dijon, 21 April and 5 May 1854, AN BB30/408.

Isère, in December 1865, repeated his appeals to the Minister for funds to finance secret police penetration of mutual aid societies.[169] In towns like Grenoble and Vienne masonic lodges were also suspect, dominated as they were by leading republicans.[170]

Some of the societies 'affiliated' to La Marianne – in Paris and departments like Loir-et-Cher, Deux-Sèvres, Maine-et-Loire, Nièvre, and Allier – appear to have survived the *coup* and started to recruit members once again, particularly from 1853 when militants were able to blame the government for high food prices. Activity seems to have been most intense in the west around Angers, Blois, and Tours.[171] Members were cautious, often meeting in threes, using signs and words of recognition and requiring newcomers to swear, with hand on dagger – 'I promise to be faithful to the République démocratique et sociale; I promise to sacrifice myself and abandon my family, in order to carry out any order given to me and to stab to death those pointed out to me if fate [drawing lots] chooses me.'[172] A series of arrests were made at the end of 1853 of members of what was claimed to be 'a network of secret societies which change their names from place to place, calling themselves the jeune montagne in Paris and la Marianne on the banks of the Loire.'[173] The tribunal at Tours heard the cases against sixty-four of the accused in March 1854.[174] This failed to satisfy the authorities. Aware of rising unrest, they continued to complain of the inadequacy of police resources and their reliance on vague and 'sometimes elusive' revelations.[175] In the night of 26-27 August 1855, 600 to 700 men, mostly quarry workers, gathered in the commune of Trélazé and began a march on nearby Angers. The Angers garrison was mobilised and the insurgents easily dispersed. Subsequently, 140 men were arrested and imprisoned in the château.[176] The existence of this 'bandit horde' proved to the authorities the 'incredible perversity' of these 'incorrigible enemies of civilisation', those socialists who 'want to burn and kill'.[177] Exemplary punishments were necessary. Witnesses affirmed that one of the leaders of the Trélazé movement, the slate worker François Attibert had told them that 'we'll

[169] MI internal minute, 26 Dec. 1865, copy in AN F1 CIII Isère 9.
[170] Prefect, 8 Oct. and 3 Nov. 1852 in AN F1 CIII Isère 9.
[171] PG Orleans, 28 Jan. 1854, AN BB30/382; Dupeux, *Aspects*, p. 408; Prudhomme, 'Les sociétés secrètes', pp. 83–5.
[172] Report of police commissaire at Angers to prefect Maine-et-Loire, quoted F. Simon, *La Marianne*, (Angers 1939) p. 74.
[173] PG Paris, 5 Aug. 1855, AN BB30/413.   [174] PG Orleans, 3 Aug. 1854, AN BB30/382.
[175] PG Angers, 4 Feb. 1854, AN BB30/407.
[176] GOC 15 DM, 26 Aug.–1 Sept. 1855, AHG G8/27.
[177] MJ circular, 14 Sept. 1855, quoted Simon, *Marianne*, p. 89.

take all the nobles, all the priests, all the landowners with incomes of 12,000 to 15,000 francs, and slit their throats'. Attibert was described by the police as 'dangerous ... a very good worker, thrifty, sober, a good father, good morality ... having some education ... very enterprising, prepared to sacrifice everything for his cause'. Sent to Devil's Island he would be resourceful enough to escape, before benefiting from the general amnesty in 1859 and returning to organise a mutual aid society for his fellow workers. [178]

It seems likely that the secret society to which these men belonged had members throughout the arrondissements of Bressuire and Loudun, who had also been awaiting their instructions to join in the march on Angers.[179] Already, the prefects of Cher and Nièvre had been accused of negligence for failing to report the re-constitution of secret societies further up-river, amongst the peasants around Cosne and Fourchambault.[180] Interrogations and domiciliary searches stimulated further police enquiries, leading to reports of la Marianne in areas as far afield as the Hautes-Pyrénées by a police agent described as 'more zealous than well-informed'.[181] This resulted in Paris, during the summer of 1855, in the arrest of sixty-seven members of a society calling itself L'Union.[182]

Far more dangerous to the regime appear to have been the plans of the ninety individuals arrested in Paris in June 1853 for participating in the so-called *affaire de l'Hippodrome*. It was claimed that they had planned to kidnap the Emperor during his visit to the Horticultural Society. In September 1854 a bomb was discovered set to explode under the Emperor's train en route to a meeting with the Belgian king at Tournai.[183] Further alarm was caused by the meetings, in 1855 and early 1856, of a group made up mainly of Parisian artisans at the home of a forty-year-old book-keeper called Labouret. They had discussed the course of action to be followed after the assassination of Napoleon. The two leaders were each sentenced to ten years' imprisonment.[184] The discovery of 'plots' against the Emperor alerted the authorities and was invariably followed by a rash of reports from all over the country concerning secret societies

[178] Réquisitoire de M. le PG Métivier. Affaire de l'attentat d'Angers, 12 Oct. 1855, AN BB30/413; J. Maitron (ed.), *Dictionnaire biographique du mouvement ouvrier français* (Paris 1964), entry on Attibert.
[179] PG Poitiers, 22 Aug. 1856, AN BB30/417.
[180] Directeur-général de la Sûreté publique, 1 March 1855, AN BB30/410.
[181] PG Pau, 12 Feb. 1856, AN BB30/384.
[182] PG Paris, 5 March 1856, re August 1855, AN BB30/383.
[183] Ménager, *Nord*, I, pp. 395–6.   [184] PG Paris, 30 March 1857, AN BB30/418.

and their machinations.[185] Their authors were as confused by the incidents they reported as historians have been subsequently. For example, what were the objectives of the 30 to 40 men who in the evening of 6 March 1858 disarmed the guard-post in the place de Beaune at Chalon-sur-Saône to shouts of *Vive la République* and calls for an uprising?[186] This was followed by the announcement a few days later by a shoemaker from Paris to two known 'demagogues' that an insurrection had been prepared in the capital and its outbreak would be signalled by the lighting of 1,500 fires throughout the provinces. He added that they should be ready to seize the keys of the local church and sound the *tocsin*.[187] How seriously should they take the message sent from Berne to Joseph Robin a weaver at Scey-sur-Saône which ended with the warning that 'when the mail does not arrive, don't blame the snow; arm yourselves, spread fire and blood, fall first on the police and the gendarmerie, the signal is given'.[188] The police spy Philippon in Rouen reported in 1857 that engineering workers 'are boasting of the strength of their party in the workshops, of how easy it would be to arm 2,000 men in six hours if a revolution broke out' but shrugged off this verbal violence as the day-to-day fare of the workplace.[189]

Throughout the 1850s there was considerable concern about the organisational and propaganda efforts of exiles in Britain, Belgium, Switzerland, and Piedmont. Only Belgium succumbed to French pressure to curb their activities. That Britain had harboured those involved in the Orsini affair would lead to a considerable cooling in relations.[190] The threat posed by these groups of exiles was reduced more by their own bitter rivalries and concern about the police spies in their midst. They constantly looked for symptoms of discontent in France and were as frequently disappointed and demoralised.[191] Nevertheless, police and customs officials in frontier regions were constantly on the alert.[192] There was concern also about possible links between a mysterious Comité Blanqui in Paris and secret societies in the provinces. Early in 1856

---

[185] E.g. prefect, 13 July 1852, AN F1 CIII Rhône 10.
[186] GOC 8e DM, 10 March 1858, AN G8/52; prefect Saône-et-Loire report on March 1858, AN F7/4154.
[187] *Ibid.*; see also PG Dijon, 20 March 1858, AN BB30/420.
[188] Prefect Haute-Saône report on April 1856, AN F7/4150.
[189] Quoted M. Boivin, *Le mouvement ouvrier dans la région de Rouen* (Rouen 1989), I, p. 123 n. 92.
[190] H-H. Liange, *The Rise of Modern Police and the European State System from Metternich to the Second World War* (Cambridge 1993), pp. 57–8.
[191] E.g. Rapport d'un agent secret à Bruxelles, n.d. but late 1855, AN AB XIX 173; sous-préfet Gex, 25 Nov. 1868, AN F1 CIII Ain 9.
[192] See e.g. PG Lyons, ?April 1853, AN BB30/407.

a certain Lagrange was employed as a secret agent by the Prefecture of Police. He reported on contacts between Lyon republicans, including Giraud, the former editor of the socialist newspaper *Le Peuple souverain*, and Beneto, a silk worker, with known Parisian subversives. According to a succession of police reports on meetings held in both cities in May, an insurrection was being prepared and delegates had been sent to Mâcon, Vienne, Valence, Givors, and Rive-de-Giers.[193] The procureur-général at Lyon's assessment of this information combined tact with a considerable degree of scepticism, warning that 'in general the police tend rather to exaggerate their fears'.[194] He concluded that

without, in any way, diminishing the great service rendered to us by the Paris police in unmasking the evil intentions of those miserable individuals who dream of an uprising ... I have no intention of exaggerating the importance of recent discoveries. The projects of these madmen were utterly impractical. To assassinate or imprison the authorities would have been useless and impossible. Without doubt a serious event in Paris would have had an unfortunate impact, but an insurrection in Lyon is not something one should be concerned about.

Indeed the city was calmer than it had been for forty years.[195] Nevertheless, to be on the safe side, fifty-eight arrests were ordered.[196] The *grand événement* in Paris, which would transform the political situation, and to which officials constantly referred, was assumed to be the assassination of the Emperor.[197]

The result of this repression, and the risk, undoubtedly exaggerated, of denunciation by police informers, was an effective demobilisation of organised republican opposition.[198] The movement had become 'an army of which the leaders survive, but which has no soldiers'.[199] More significant, in this situation, than the secret societies on which so much police time was lavished were the links preserved by informal gatherings in cafés and private homes.[200] Even if apparently less dangerous, these activities were sufficient to promote suspicion and alarm amongst officials and notables.[201] Indeed if information was difficult to obtain this might be taken as proof that subversives were 'working in the shadows and taking great precautions to avoid compromising themselves'.[202]

---

[193] Long, undated report from Pietri, Prefect of Police, to MI; PG Lyon, 11 Aug. 1856, both in AN BB30/417.
[194] PG Lyons, 15 June 1856, AN BB30/417.   [195] 14 June 1856, AN BB30/417.
[196] PI Lyons, 14 June 1856, *ibid.*   [197] See e.g. PG Paris, 30 March 1857, AN BB30/418.
[198] See e.g. PG Lyons, 30 July, 18 Aug. 1858, AN BB30/421.
[199] Prefect, 4 Jan. 1853, AN F1 cIII Côte-d'Or 9.
[200] See e.g. PG Douai, 27 Sept. 1855, AN BB30/415.
[201] PG Poitiers, 21 Jan. 1854, AN BB30/385 is an example to the contrary.
[202] Marshal de Castellane, GOC Lyons, 10 Jan. 1853 in AHG G8/1.

This was the conclusion of the state prosecutor at Agen when 100 domiciliary searches failed to turn up any evidence.[203] At the very least, continued surveillance was assumed to be necessary. The sous-préfet at Château-Chinon was only one of a large number of officials requesting the assistance of *un agent de la Police Secrète*,[204] for which the Interior Ministry set aside around 2 million francs a year, rising to 3,200,000 in 1858.[205] The Orsini *attentat* of course provoked intense police activity on the basis of which, not untypically, the sous-préfet at Montargis, concluded that 'secret societies no longer exist in organised form, but a variety of circumstances leads one to believe that the various elements out of which they were composed retain their links'. Thus 'during the years of subsistence crisis, on the eve of the attempts to assassinate the Emperor, meetings of individuals with known records, conversations in cafés, and the propagation of false news, seemed to reveal the existence of secret societies'. The evidence was largely circumstantial. Like so many of his colleagues, the sous-préfet insisted that there could be no certain proof because experienced revolutionaries were so adept at escaping detection.[206]

In spite of these alarms, the Emperor persisted with a series of amnesties to mark such occasions as his marriage. Prisoners were encouraged to request pardons in return for a written oath of loyalty. The authorities' response took account of behaviour since arrest, state of health, personal morality, and family circumstances, recommendations from local notables and officials, and judgements as to whether the individual concerned was genuinely repentant.[207] This policy culminated, on 16 August 1859, in a general amnesty for those convicted of political crimes, which, furthermore, restored the civil rights of those previously released. As Prince Napoleon insisted in a letter to the Emperor, the object was to 'efface the last traces of civil discord' and isolate the irreconcilable republicans associated with Barbès, Blanqui, Ledru-Rollin, and Blanc, who preferred to remain in exile rather than take the oath.[208] There were, however, frequent complaints that the Emperor's indulgence meant the return of dangerous subversives to their communities.[209] The Imperial prosecutor at Auch observed that clemency 'has only restored

[203] PG Agen, 3 July 1858, AN BB30/370.
[204] Quoted Vigreux, *Paysans et notables*, p. 361.
[205] Ministère de l'Intérieur, 'Renseignements confidentiels' 1868 in *Documents pour servir.*
[206] 4 July 1859, AN F1 cIII Loiret 12.
[207] See cases submitted for consideration in 1852–6, AN BB30/481.
[208] Prince Napoleon, Note pour l'Empereur, 18 March 1856, in Hauterive, *Napoléon III*, p. 296.
[209] E.g. PG Paris, 18 Feb. 1854, AN BB30/383.

a few to honest sentiments; most have remained just as hostile and as perverse as they were previously and ready to respond to the first appeal from their political comrades'.[210] The constant harassment of former detainees, which made it difficult to obtain work, was doubtless counter-productive.[211]

During the 1860s, as political repression grew less intense and as the younger generations, less marked by the experiences of the Second Republic, entered politics, so the necessity for secret-society activity declined.[212] The emergence in Paris of new adherents to the Blanquist putchist tradition, many of them students, would, however, cause renewed alarm. This phase was heralded by the arrests at around 11 p.m. on 7 November 1866 of forty-two people at the café de la Renaissance and subsequent domiciliary searches which turned up incriminating letters and pamphlets. It was concluded that around sixty men had been participating in regular meetings since July 1864. The leading figures were Protot and Tridon, both of whom would continue to be involved in the tortuous politics of the extreme left and finally, in 1871, in the Paris Commune. In the meantime they were given fifteen months in prison, whilst another thirteen of those arrested received sentences of from three to six months.[213] Increasingly, however, the 1864 legislation legalising strikes, together with the 1868 law on the press and meetings, encouraged the open and public expression of opposition.[214] This, too, was not without its problems for the authorities. From the autumn of 1868, and particularly prior to the May 1869 elections, extremist speeches in meetings and the celebration of opposition electoral victories in Paris and other major population centres caused considerable concern. In November 1869 the Paris procureur impérial complained that these supposedly non-political gatherings looked and sounded more and more like the clubs of 1848.[215] Increasingly, the regime appeared determined to limit the 'adverse' consequences of liberalisation. From early 1868, and with growing intensity, intermittent waves of arrests were directed at 'revolutionaries' as well as at members of the Workers' International.[216] In a deliberate effort

---

[210] PG Auch, 13 March 1858, AN BB30/447.

[211] PI Draguignan, 30 March 1853, quoted Constant, *Var* p. 85.

[212] See e.g. OC gendarmerie de la Haute-Loire, 28 July 1868, AHG G8/152.

[213] *Procès de sociétés secrètes. Etudiants et ouvriers* (Paris: Levraud 1867).

[214] A. Dalotel, A. Faure, and J.-C. Freiermuth, *Aux origines de la Commune. Le mouvement des réunions publiques à Paris 1868–70* (Paris 1980), pp. 30–1.

[215] See reports in AN BB18 1754A and 1785.

[216] E.g. OC cie. de Finistère, 28 May 1870, re arrests at Brest, and OC cie. de la Seine, 28 June 1870, AHG G8/176.

to alarm the general public, the conservative press and the government publicist Auguste Vitu, in a celebrated book on *Les réunions publiques à Paris*, were encouraged to quote copiously from speeches in favour of atheism, regicide, and the abolition of the family and private property, and to note the constant references to 1793 and 1848. As a result, under mounting pressure from anxious conservatives, the government would feel justified in enforcing restrictive legislation.[217] From the end of 1868 the proprietors of the halls in which public meetings were held were advised that they risked losing their licences. It became increasingly likely also that meetings would be brought to a premature end by the police commissaire required to be in attendance.[218] Following the May 1869 elections, an unofficial ban was placed on meetings in Paris between June and August and police harassment of speakers appears to have increased.[219] Nevertheless, an effort was made to avoid alienating moderate opinion. The police were instructed to behave with restraint and 'without employing the extreme measures that the law authorises in such circumstances'.[220] The gendarmerie commander in Lyon concurred, observing that 'it is regrettable to see the authorities alarmed so easily by reports, coming from I know not where, and taking measures which cause disquiet or bemused regret amongst sensible people, whilst amusing the frivolous or ill intentioned'.[221] In spite of restraint, in Paris, in an especially agitated week in June 1869, repeated popular demonstrations led to 1,600 arrests.[222] The disorders in the capital culminated in a demonstration by perhaps 100,000 people attending the funeral on 12 January 1870 of the journalist Victor Noir, killed by the Emperor's disreputable cousin Pierre Bonaparte. This was taken as a warning about the danger of a popular insurrection. There was growing public support for increased police severity, from moderate republicans as well as Bonapartists.[223]

Growing social fear would also lead to the stricter enforcement of the legislation on strikes during 1869 and 1870 especially in the major coal basins. Officials appear to have been certain that these strikes were politically motivated.[224] The official attitude might be represented

---

[217] See e.g. OC gendarmerie de la Seine, re meetings at Clichy and Ivry on 26 Feb. and 28 April 1869, AHG G8/165.

[218] OC cie. de la Seine, 26 Feb., 28 April 1869, AHG G8/165.

[219] OC gendarmerie de la Seine, 27 May 1869, AHG G8/165.

[220] Pietri, former Prefect of Police, evidence to Assemblée nationale, *Enquête parlementaire. Actes du Gouvernement de la défense nationale*, 7 vols. (Paris 1876), I, p. 261.

[221] OC cie. du Rhône, 28 Sept. 1868, AHG G8/152.

[222] OC gendarmerie Seine, 27 June, re week of 7–14 June in AHG G8/165.

[223] Dalotel, Faure, and Freiermuth, *Aux origines*, pp. 334, 355–60; Girard, *Nouvelle histoire*, p. 395.

[224] See e.g. PG Lyons, 10 July 1869, AN BB30/389.

by instructions from the War Minister to the general commanding the 10th Military Division in January 1869 – 'it is time to put an end to these worker revolts; I hope that the state prosecutor will prosecute this rebellion vigorously; otherwise it will be impossible to count on respect for the Law; a severe example is essential'.[225] In June, troops were deployed against strikers at Carmaux (Tarn) and at La Ricamarie (Loire). There, an attempt by crowds to force the release of arrested miners resulted in thirteen deaths when troops opened fire.[226] Four months later another fourteen fatalities resulted from clashes between strikers and troops at Aubin (Aveyron).[227] At Le Creusot (Saône-et-Loire) in the spring of 1870 the government again responded to strikes with intimidation, on this occasion in support of the ironmaster, and president of the Corps législatif, Eugène Schneider.[228] The presence of republican journalists at Le Creusot in January 1870 might have made the authorities reluctant to prosecute strikers for fear of adverse publicity but this did not protect them from subsequent dismissal.[229]

Additional alarm was aroused by the expansion of the Workers' International during 1869/70. This seemed to signify a revived socialist threat to society. Its importance was grossly exaggerated by police reports. The state prosecutor at Lyon warned that unless action was taken the result would be 'to unite all the workers in a close and powerful solidarity and to make them, as they say themselves, masters of the situation'. The outcome would be revolution.[230] M. de Laire, the senior police official in the city, complained that effective policing was becoming impossible as the number of meetings, associations, newspapers, and strikes grew, attracting 'a considerable number of unknown individuals on whose antecedents we need to be precisely informed'.[231] Reports from Marseille similarly stressed the growing fear of the propertied classes and the collapse of financial confidence.[232] In this climate, Emile Ollivier, recently appointed as chief minister of a liberal administration, was determined to safeguard social order. As Minister of Justice, he announced to state prosecutors on 30 April 1870 that 'I have, this evening, ordered the arrest of all those belonging to the International. If this organisation has

---

[225] 9 Jan. 1869, AHG G8/153.
[226] See prefect, 18 and 22 July 1869, AN F1 CIII Tarn 12; OC gendarmerie Loire, 27 June 1869, AHG G8/165.
[227] Saurel, *Gendarmerie*, III, pp. 462–3.   [228] Charle, *Histoire sociale*, pp. 132–3.
[229] Prefect telegrams, 26, 27 Jan. 1870, AN F1 CIII Saône-et-Loire 13.
[230] 10 April 1870, AN BB30/390.
[231] M. de Laire, secrétaire-général de la police politique Lyon, 21 June 1870, in *Pièces saisies*, p. 24.
[232] PG Aix, 26 June 1869, AN BB18/1785.

ramifications in your area, arrest its members'. In response to the Paris
state prosecutor's inquiry into the grounds for such arrests,[233] Ollivier
maintained that it was for membership of an 'illicit association and secret
society', and pointed out that the International 'has its members in all the
large towns: make an effort to discover them'.[234] The International was
perceived to be part of a concerted socialist plot to undermine civilised
society. On the same day he also ordered prosecution of 'those newspapers, which contain a call to civil war or outrages against the Emperor'.
In justification Ollivier pointed out that 'we cannot simply watch these
revolutionary excesses with arms crossed. Respect liberty, but provocation to assassination and to civil war is contrary to liberty.' In the days
that followed prosecutors would receive further telegrams urging them
to redouble their efforts and pointing out that the procureur-général
at Paris had decided to make use of the legislation against secret societies. The minister expressed particular concern about the situation in
Marseille, calling for examples to be made and adding 'strike especially
at the head, arrest in particular the lawyers, the gentlemen, rather than
poor devils from the people'.[235] The May 1870 plebiscite would be followed by another wave of arrests and renewed unofficial restrictions on
public meetings.[236] Since 1848 the wheel appeared to have turned full
circle. During the years of relative peace much had changed, however.
The *coup d'état* and the repression which followed had been intended to
'hold the line' and provide time for the work of *régéneration sociale*, which
alone would secure the future.[237]

---

[233] Telegram, 5.45 p.m. 1 May, in Poulet-Malassis, *Papiers secrets*, p. 134.
[234] 10.05 pm, *ibid.* p. 135.
[235] Telegrams of 30 April, 1, 2 May in *Papiers et correspondance*, I, pp. 326, 328–30.
[236] R. Wolfe, 'The Origins of the Paris Commune', PhD Harvard University, 1965, p. 80.
[237] PG Paris, 29 Nov. 1858, AN BB30/383.

CHAPTER 6

Constructing moral order

Whilst improving its capacity for repression, the regime engaged in a considerable effort to improve 'moral order' by means both of negative measures of press, literary, and theatrical censorship, and more positive attempts to develop primary instruction.

CONTROLLING THE PRESS

Social and political unrest during the Second Republic had frequently been blamed on the outpouring of cheap printed materials which had followed the February Revolution. The establishment of effective control over the press would become a major preoccupation of government. In the aftermath of the *coup d'état*, Morny (decrees of 6 and 13 December 1851) had empowered prefects to suspend or suppress newspapers, virtually at will: 'No newspaper should appear without your authorisation. You will not tolerate any discussion of the legality of recent events. Neither will you allow articles whose effect is to weaken the authority of the government'. Page proofs would have to be submitted before publication.[1] A subsequent decree, on 17 February 1852, borrowing heavily from previous legislation, required official approval for the establishment of a newspaper or for a change of ownership or editor. Newspaper proprietors were required to deposit caution money – 25,000f in towns with over 150,000 inhabitants, 50,000f in the three departments of the Paris region and in Lyon and Marseille. Higher than ever before, this was intended to guarantee the payment of fines and added to the substantial investment necessary to establish a newspaper. It was hoped that only men of means, likely to be conservative, would be able to acquire the capital. The re-imposition of stamp duty by increasing the cost of a newspaper to potential readers was intended to reduce circulation.

---

[1] *Documents pour servir*, p. 19.

Although prior censorship was abolished, each issue would have to be submitted to the authorities and every article signed. Prosecutions for press offences would no longer be subject to trial by jury. The administration, as well as being able to suppress a newspaper, would be able to issue warnings for transgressions it judged to be less serious, with a third warning followed by a two-month suspension. Editors were also forbidden to publish detailed transcripts of parliamentary debates, forcing them to rely on truncated official accounts. They frequently received warnings to avoid particular subjects. In addition prefects might require publication of official rebuttals of editorials or articles on the front page of offending newspapers.[2]

It was inevitable that, in order to avoid prosecution, the editors of those newspapers which had survived the repression of the conservative Republic would be driven into self-censorship.[3] Political caricature, the medium that had been pursued so effectively by Daumier, virtually disappeared.[4] Certainly when it came to elections it was clear that surviving opposition newspapers were expected to behave with discretion.[5] Strict controls were also imposed on printers and booksellers.[6] Nevertheless, there were always limits to the ability of the regime to control the press. Pierre Latour-Dumoulin, responsible for establishing the supervisory Direction générale de la Librairie, observed, in a report to the Emperor in 1856, that even in 1852 public opinion would not have tolerated the closure of the great liberal newspapers – *Le Siècle*, *L'Assemblée nationale*, *La Presse*, or the *Journal des Débats*. As a result he found it difficult to 'establish a happy medium', and had re-defined his role as being to 'prevent the excesses of newspapers in order not to have to repress them, temper the rigours of the law by moderating its enforcement, constantly supervise not only the pro-government press but the opposition newspapers too by moderating their contents through numerous unofficial warnings, rather than employing the double-edged weapons of official warnings and prosecution with its invariably regrettable repercussions'. The task had appeared enormous and the personnel inadequate. Therefore, he had chosen to concentrate on the Parisian press, given its especial

---

[2] Persigny, MI to Min. d'Etat, 5 Feb. 1852, AN O5/297; Directeur de la Presse to MI, 'Note sur le service de la Presse' 1868 in *Documents pour servir*; C. Bellanger, J. Godechot, P. Guiral, and F. Terrou, *Histoire générale de la presse française* (Paris 1972), II, pp. 8–10, 249–54.

[3] Darimon, *Les cinq*, pp. 90–1.

[4] A. Blum, 'La caricature politique en France sous le Second Empire', *Revue des études napoléoniennes* (1919).

[5] Circular MI to prefects, 1 June 1857, in *Documents pour servir*, p. 103.

[6] E. Bersot, *La presse dans les départements* (Paris: Dentu 1867), pp. 13–15.

importance and influence throughout the provinces, leaving the provincial newspapers to prefectoral control.[7] Formal warnings to the press were comparatively few. Suppression was rare (there were nine). Anyway, such proceedings were at first unnecessary, given that the socialist and republican press had largely been closed down already. By 1852 there were approximately 258 provincial newspapers, of which 200 supported the regime, 13 were Orleanist, 34 Legitimist, and 13 republican. In the entire period 1852 to 1860, 219 warnings were delivered to errant editors (65 in Paris, 154 in the provinces). Over half of them were concentrated into 1852/3 – in the aftermath of the *coup*, and 1859/60 – following the Orsini affair. In between, the intensity of repression was much reduced. Almost a third of the warnings were given to clerico-Legitimist organs for attacking the regime's Italian policy.[8] The ultramontane newspaper *L'Univers* was actually suppressed in January 1860 because of its 'pernicious' influence, particularly on the younger clergy.[9] Anti-religious articles, however, were always far more likely to be prosecuted. The normal tactic was for prefects first to give 'unofficial' advice and 'invite' editors to comply. The degree of tolerance varied according to local circumstances and the temperament of individual prefects. The system of official communiqués requiring newspapers to 'correct' their 'mistakes' certainly does not appear to have been applied with much consistency or purpose.[10] According to a secret agent reporting to the Interior Minister, the very fact that these communiqués were imposed ensured that no-one believed them.[11]

In addition to the repression of opposition newspapers, in a circular of 22 December 1852 Persigny called for 'an energetic intervention on the part of the administration in favour of good social principles. This intervention can best be accomplished by means of publications and pamphlets encouraged and, if need be, financed by the administration'.[12] The Division de la presse was instructed to support pro-government newspapers and 'to give direction to the newspapers which come to it every day for ideas and news'.[13] Although the funds available were always limited, small-circulation provincial papers were often heavily dependent on the local administration for legal announcements and

---

[7] Min. de l'Intérieur. Direction générale de la Sûreté publique. Presse départementale. Revue des journaux, in *Documents pour servir*, pp. 187–93.
[8] Payne, *Police State*, pp. 187–90.   [9] E.g. PG Dijon, 5 July 1859, AN BB30/377.
[10] E.g. 'Note sur le service de la presse' 1868, in *Documents pour servir*.
[11] 'P.P'. to MI, 9 Feb. 1852, AN 116 AP 1.
[12] Quoted N. Isser, *The Second Empire and the Press* (The Hague 1974), pp. 15–16.
[13] MI memo, 7 Dec. 1859, AN F18/310.

other official printing business.[14] The regime could also offer to further the careers of newspaper owners and editors. Deputies, bankers, and landowners were invited to purchase shares, and prefects and mayors to take out subscriptions.[15] Nationally, during the 1850s, the most influential pro-government dailies were the Parisian *Le Constitutionnel*, *Le Pays*, and *La Patrie*, the first two owned, from 1852, by the speculator Mirès, who thereby gained a profitable means of influencing financial markets and facilitating speculation. Officials congratulated themselves on the strengthening of the pro-government press at minimal cost.[16] A letter to Mirès from Dollinger, director of the Legitimist *Gazette de France*, in April 1856 offers a limited insight into the network of corruption, involving ministers as well as financiers, which surrounded the press. Dollinger wrote that 'knowing that every time you inaugurate a major enterprise you are in the habit of reserving some shares for the press, I take the liberty of presenting the request of the *Gazette*'.[17] In return, obviously, he would be expected to encourage investors to purchase shares in Mirès' latest enterprise. In the following decade, from his base in the financial newspaper the *Journal des chemins de fer*, Mirès would acquire an interest in a range of other journals including opposition papers like the *Journal des Débats*, *Le Siècle*, and *La Presse*. This concentration of ownership came to be regarded as a major threat by the opposition.[18] Only the collapse of Mirès' enterprises in 1861 brought this process of accumulation to an end, although some of his interests were purchased by another well-connected speculator – Morny.

More subtle efforts were also made to control the flow of information. In an age when newspapers had few means of their own for collecting information, they frequently depended on the Havas news agency, which was itself provided by the government with privileged and subsidised access to the new telegraph network and to national and international news.[19] The links between Havas and the government need to be more fully explored but certainly close relations existed between the news agency and the press division of the Interior Ministry.[20] Paradoxically,

[14] See e.g. PG Toulouse, 5 Jan. 1861 in AN BB30/388; E. Constant, 'Notes sur la presse dans le département du Var sous le Second Empire', *Provence historique*, 1960.

[15] MI circular, 18 Dec. 1852 in *Documents pour servir*.

[16] Directeur de l'Imprimerie, Rapport à l'Empereur 1856, *ibid.*, p. 193.

[17] 30 April 1856, AN AB XIX 3462.

[18] Letter to P-J. Proudhon, 2 Jan. 1861 in Darimon, *L'opposition libérale*, p. 8.

[19] P. Albert, 'La presse et le télégraphe électrique au 19e siècle' in C. Bertho-Lavenir (ed.), *L'Etat et les télécommunications en France et à l'étranger 1837–1987* (Geneva 1991), pp. 99–101.

[20] See MI, Division de la presse, 'Note sur l'organisation de la presse en vue des élections' in *Papiers et correspondance*, I, p. 26.

it was the liberal Bonapartist newspaper *Le Parlement* which in 1869 provided the clearest warning about the danger implicit in a monopoly of information: 'The Havas agency has become, by the force of circumstances, the humble servant of governments. It enjoys their protection in return for its services; it speaks or remains silent according to their needs and to inspiration from on high ... It provides the news that it is necessary to know, when it is necessary to know it; it determines what is true'.[21]

In the 1850s the Catholic press, mostly Legitimist in its sympathies, enjoyed a considerable degree of toleration. Circulations were small and their audience certainly did not constitute a threat to social order. The Parisian trio, the *Gazette de France* – intransigent in politics but Gallican in religion; *L'Assemblée nationale* – fusionist in politics; and *L'Union* – more moderate politically but ultramontane in religion, expended considerable energy quarrelling with each other and with the extreme ultramontane and initially imperialist *L'Univers*, edited by Louis Veuillot. A range of other newspapers was also tolerated including the liberal *Journal des Débats*, supported by the Rothschilds and attracting brilliant writers (circulation 8,000 in 1855), *La Presse* which appealed to businessmen (circulation 9,900 in 1859) and the republican *Siècle*[22] – so prudent that its cautious editor, Havin, was accused of selling himself to the government.[23] Available on subscription, these Parisian newspapers served as a model and provided material for the provincial press to reprint. They moulded opinion throughout France.[24] *Le Siècle* appears to have survived the *coup* only because of Morny's concern to protect its shareholders although, typically, he rationalised this objective in terms of the need for the government to acquire information about republican opinion.[25] Certainly one of the functions of the Interior Ministry's press division was to provide the Emperor, as well as ministers and prefects, with daily summaries of the news and of the state of public opinion[26] and there was an evident danger that, because of repression, public opinion would be only very imperfectly represented, increasing the regime's dependence on official reporting channels. *Le Siècle* would thus continue to appear in spite of

[21] Quoted Bellanger, *Presse*, II, p. 344.
[22] See e.g. Tulard, *Dictionnaire*; Maurain, *Politique ecclésiastique*, pp. 157–61.
[23] Darimon, *Les cinq*, p. 119, entry of 10 Feb. 1858.
[24] See e.g. PG Metz, 9 Jan. 1855, AN BB30/377.
[25] Taxile Delord, *Histoire du Second Empire* (Paris 1868), II, p. 180.
[26] MI memo 7 Dec. 1859, AN F18/310; résumés of the Paris press prepared for the Emperor, AN O5/297 Maison de l'Empereur.

repeated complaints from prefects and the police.[27] Following an initial collapse of readership, it rapidly recovered from a low of 21,325
subscribers in 1853 to 52,300 by 1861, and enjoyed a wide readership
in cafés throughout France. With the exception of the *Univers*, which
adopted an extreme stance in opposition to the regime's Italian policy
and was suppressed on 29 January 1860, it was increasingly accepted
that the closure of the other leading opposition journals would have
had too serious an impact on public opinion to be contemplated.[28] In
most departments a few small-circulation newspapers survived the *coup*.
They varied considerably in quality and influence. The department of
the Nord was exceptional, with twenty-two newspapers, including most
notably the republican *Echo du Nord* and the Legitimist *Gazette de Flandres et
d'Artois*.[29] By 1867, that is, before the substantial liberalisation of the press
laws, fifty-six opposition newspapers were being published in thirty-one
departments, especially in the south-west, west, north, and east, rather
than in the centre and south and in the Paris region.[30] Forty departments
appear to have lacked a single opposition paper. From the government's
point of view, this represented deterioration from the monopoly in 58
departments enjoyed in 1858. It still meant, however, that of 272 provincial newspapers only 50 (24 Legitimist, 8 Orleanist, 10 liberal, and 8
democratic and republican) supported opposition. In terms of circulation, government papers outran the opposition by 245,420 to 98,200.[31]

It is difficult to measure the success of press censorship. In the short
term, the voice of opposition was certainly stilled. Officials celebrated the
disappearance of the newspapers, which had often served as the bases
of republican organisation in the provinces. Once again political debate
was safely restricted to 'the serious, conscientious and enlightened',[32]
to the exclusion of that 'illiterate class unable to understand serious social questions'.[33] Censorship certainly imposed limits on journalists. It
also influenced the ways in which they were read. Thus opposition was
not entirely silenced. Writers were already versed in the techniques of
satire and subtlety. In an article on the fall of the First Empire in the
Union franc-comtoise (21 April 1853), Jacques Michel actually hazarded
the belief that 'its collapse ... must be attributed to the inability of public

[27] E.g. PG Angers, 8 July 1859, AN BB30/376.
[28] Note sur le service de la presse 1868 in *Documents pour servir*, p. 229; Bellanger, *Presse*, II, p. 259.
[29] Payne, *Police State*, pp. 201–4.   [30] Bersot, *La presse*, pp. 7–8.
[31] Bellanger, Presse, II, p. 340, re declining real cost of a newspaper for a provincial labourer:
       1910 = 100; 1795 = 821; 1834 = 576; 1851 = 288; 1871 = 224 – *ibid.*, III, p. 141.
[32] Prefect, 24 March 1852, AN FI CIII Bas-Rhin 15.
[33] PG Bordeaux, 24 Jan. 1855, AN BB30/374.

opinion, through the press or any other institution, to regulate the power of the Emperor and to restrain him when he went astray'.[34] It was safer generally, and probably just as effective, given the classical education of an audience of notables, to employ allusions to the ancient world. Estimating the influence of the press is particularly difficult. Clearly only a small proportion of the population purchased newspapers, particularly in the countryside. Even if we take account of multiple readership in reading rooms, cafés, and at work, the number of readers remained small. However, they were likely to have been influential opinion-formers. In most cases individuals would have selected a newspaper which appealed to already established political views. The role of newspapers was thus 'less to impose ideas on their readers by reasoning with them, than to formulate their confused aspirations'.[35] The state prosecutor at Besançon observed that

the time is happily past when newspapers were read out loud in the *cabarets* as if they were the catechism. People read little now but those newspapers which are read and from which those with influence in the villages draw their ideas are the *Siècle*, the *Presse*, or the *Opinion nationale*. The first is most widespread and certainly has the most influence. Peasants ... in general are not particularly interested in reading newspaper articles from beginning to end, but those individuals in the villages who pass on the news and comment on it as they wish have read the *Siècle* and gladly express those opinions which gratify their democratic instincts and satisfy the educated man's distrust of the priest.[36]

As part of the more general process of liberalisation, in a decree of 24 November 1860 the Emperor promised to relax controls over the press, a commitment implemented by a law of 2 July 1861 which stipulated that newspapers would no longer be suppressed automatically following a third warning and could in future print parliamentary debates, although only in full, and without comment. Persigny advised his prefects that they would now need to distinguish carefully between acceptable discussion of administrative actions, and attacks on the principles of the constitution, which should continue to be severely punished. In practice the distinction would frequently be lost on both officials and journalists.[37] Whilst recognising that widespread public support for liberalisation existed, prefects generally regretted that a vast area of debate had suddenly been thrown open to the press.[38] The state prosecutor at Paris had warned

---

[34] Quoted Bellanger, *Presse*, II, p. 263.   [35] PG Riom, 6 April 1870, AN BB30/390.
[36] PG Besançon, 19 Nov. 1860, AN BB30/373.
[37] See e.g. PG Douai, 3 Jan. 1861, AN BB30/377.
[38] See e.g. prefect, 15 July 1860, AN F1 CIII Somme 11.

previously that the press would be given the freedom to say that it was not free.[39] Subsequently, his colleague at Lyon would earnestly hope that there would be no further extension of political liberties, adding that: 'submission or indifference have been replaced by a revival which needs to be controlled'.[40] As he feared, the Interior Ministry would prove increasingly reluctant to invoke the press laws. There seemed little point in prosecuting papers for articles which often repeated criticisms previously voiced in the Corps législatif and which had appeared in print already. There was, as a result of this limited liberalisation, an unmistakable revival of debate in the press, and a growth in the number of titles. However, the regime received little credit for its reforms. Editors continued to complain about the irritating bureaucratic procedures they were required to observe and, following the replacement of the conciliatory Vicomte de La Guéronnière at the Bureaux de la presse in 1862, about the lack of political finesse of its remaining officials.[41] Furthermore, rising sales and advertising revenues promoted a greater sense of independence and encouraged newspaper editors to demand even greater freedom to defend the public interest.[42] In this situation prefects fought what was essentially a holding operation. Liberalisation clearly stimulated a political re-awakening particularly amongst the upper and middle classes and the more literate sections of the urban working classes.[43] Political developments in the Parisian press were soon reflected in the provinces. In the Nord, Prefect Vallon tolerated considerable clerical and protectionist criticism of the government in the *Propagateur du Nord* and, partly to offset this, allowed greater leeway to the anti-clericalism of the *Echo du Nord*. At the same time he attempted to keep the lid on the more somnolent, rural areas of his department.[44]

The danger for the regime from this changing situation was evident when the official circulation figures in 1861 revealed that it had already lost the circulation battle in the capital. Imperialist newspapers published in Paris had sold 52,832 copies and the official *Moniteur universel* a further 17,242, whilst *journaux progressistes* – including the *Siècle* (52,300) – had sold 91,292, Legitimist and clerical papers 38,285, and Orleanist and liberal 36,859.[45] The problem was spelled out by the Directeur de la presse in 1867. He recognised that the pro-government press 'no longer has much credit. In using them without restraint, without sensitivity we

---

[39] 9 Nov. 1859, AN BB30/383.   [40] PG Lyons, 30 Dec. 1863, AN BB30/379.
[41] *Documents pour servir*, pp. 225f.   [42] See e.g. PG Riom, 9 Jan. 1864, AN BB30/386.
[43] See e.g. PG Lyons, 30 Dec. 1863, AN BB30/379.   [44] Ménager, *Nord*, vol. II, pp. 514–22.
[45] AN F18/295.

have killed them'. As a result of the growth of opposition, it was becoming increasingly difficult to influence even the conservative press. In an effort to arrest the decline in circulation pro-regime newspapers like *Le Constitutionnel*, which saw its readership fall from 26,530 in 1858 to 7,600 by 1869, felt obliged to move away from an uncritical adherence to government policy and towards greater independence, without doing much to stop its decline, however. A younger generation of journalists was becoming only too aware that the road to success and fortune was no longer through Imperial favour.[46] The problem would be exacerbated as reductions in printing and distribution costs and in the *real* cost of newspapers to consumers, together with growing literacy and rising real incomes, and changes in the format and content of newspapers, contributed to the creation of a mass-circulation press.

By 1867 it had become obvious that that there was a strong case for further revision of press legislation, which was regarded widely as arbitrary and discredited, which no longer offered an adequate framework for control, and which in practice had already been largely abandoned. Nevertheless, its continued existence and occasional enforcement was enough to provoke bitter attacks on the regime.[47] An Imperial letter of 19 January 1867 promised reform of both the legislation on the press and that on public meetings, something the Emperor had only recently told Emile de Girardin he would 'never' concede.[48] Together with the lifting of the ban on the ultramontane *L'Univers*, the letter itself encouraged a further re-assertion of press independence. Finally introduced on 9 May 1868, the new legislation replaced the system of official warnings, with all its potential for arbitrariness, with the judgement of press offences by the courts and specifically the *tribunaux correctionnels*, which at least avoided trial by jury. These changes followed heated debate in government circles, which required the Emperor to overcome the forceful objections of Rouher and Baroche.[49] Gaston de Saint-Paul, the senior civil servant at the Interior Ministry, went so far as to inform Napoleon that 'most of us are resigned to obeying the government's new policy, but without conviction and without confidence'.[50] Saint-Paul's concern that liberalisation would only reinforce the 'means for attacking and overthrowing' possessed by the enemies of the regime and of social order was

[46] 'La presse et les écrivains sous l'Empire. Note remise au MI par la Directeur de la presse', 15 Sept. 1867 in *Documents pour servir*; see also D. Kulstein, 'Government Propaganda and the Press during the Second Empire', *Gazette*, 1964, pp. 128–9.

[47] Ollivier, *L'Empire libéral*, IX, p. 195.

[48] Darimon, *L'opinion libérale*, pp. 416–17, entry 19 Dec. 1863. [49] Maurain, *Baroche*, p. 379.

[50] Note of 25 Nov. 1867 in *Papiers sauvés des Tuileries*, ed. R. Holt (Paris 1871), p. 202.

shared widely within the administration and wider conservative circles.[51] No one would be satisfied. The legislation would be regarded as either insufficiently or excessively liberal. The more optimistic officials welcomed changes which might strengthen public support for the regime by exposing the 'poison' of opposition.[52] Otherwise, particular concern was expressed about the likely impact of these measures on the 1869 elections.[53] It was too late to turn back, however, and, as Ollivier had pointed out to the Emperor, the existing legal code offered numerous ways of controlling the press.[54]

Immediately before the 1869 elections a report written by one of the chefs de bureau of the press division revealed something of the political weakness of the regime, pointing out that

the Government press in the provinces is made up of numerous journals full of announcements, agricultural information and local news, performing an excellent negative role in ordinary times by satisfying the needs of the local population and obstructing the establishment of political newspapers. But they do not serve as effective auxiliaries during elections. Those newssheets, which are engaged in politics, are rarely militant. Their semi-official character, their more or less open relationship with the prefecture imposes a certain reserve on them. The editorial function is often poorly performed, sometimes even negligible, and this inadequacy becomes all the more marked in contrast with the aggressive electioneering of newspapers produced by opposition candidates and their committees.

The influence of the *Petit Journal Officiel* and the *Moniteur des Communes* was limited by their official character and unreadability. Urgent action was clearly becoming necessary. The key Havas newsagency served 307 papers, and M. Cahot, who provided news for twenty-seven, mainly liberal newspapers, was persuaded 'to introduce into his despatches ... everything which will be compatible with their political line, without revealing his relations with the government'. Articles were also placed in British, Belgian, and German papers.[55] Furthermore, a publicity group was appointed to prepare articles and letters for insertion in the provincial press during the electoral campaign and would gain access to around 150 newspapers. The Interior Ministry provided subsidies to ensure the survival of papers and to increase their print runs as well as provide for free distribution (e.g. 2,600f to the *Courrier des Gers*;

[51] See e.g. PG Orleans, 10 April 1868, AN BB30/382.
[52] E.g. PG Montpellier, 20 Oct. 1867, AN BB30/380.   [53] 11 April 1868, AN BB30/380.
[54] Ollivier, *L'Empire libéral*, IX, p. 206.
[55] 'Note sur l'organisation de la presse en vue des élections', in *Papiers et correspondance*, I, p. 12.

6,000f to the *Côte-d'Or*; 5,000f to the *Phare de Marseille*). Thirty-three journalists were sent from Paris to increase the number and improve the quality of their staff. Sympathetic owners and electoral candidates could be counted on to provide additional funds. To compete with the Parisian republican newspapers *Le Siècle* and *Le National*, which were being widely distributed in the provinces at 5 centimes a copy, it was decided to pay the owners of *Le Peuple* 60,000f to despatch 18,000 copies daily between 1 May and 1 June. These measures were expensive. The Interior Ministry press fund has been estimated at 200,000f in 1869, which although significantly higher than in previous years, still seems rather low. It was undoubtedly supplemented from secret funds and the civil list. Granier de Cassagnac of *Le Pays* alone appears to have received 176,000f.[56]

The highly influential Parisian dailies clearly represented a much greater problem than the provincial press, although things were not always what they appeared to be. For example a report to the Interior Minister in May 1866 expressed satisfaction with the services performed by the *Journal des Débats* for the government, noting that they were 'all the more precious since it is considered independent'.[57] A police report on the Lyon press in March 1869 similarly pointed out that *Le Progrès*, the organ of radical democracy, was far more useful to the administration, because 'susceptible to accommodation', than *Le Salut public* controlled by the prefecture and pretending to be independent – 'more harmful than useful and not deceiving anyone'.[58] Even Havin, editor of the leading republican newspaper, *Le Siècle*, was not entirely unsympathetic to the regime and could expect to be endorsed by the prefect when standing for election to the *conseil général* of his department.[59] Potentially more useful in terms of exercising influence was the mass-circulation *Petit Journal* with sales around 250,000. It was supposedly non-political, but its director, Millaud, had agreed to publish flattering articles on ministers and leading government supporters 'carefully written, and just bordering on the political'.[60] In addition, the Emperor's private office was to provide a novel, representing the military glories of the First Empire, for serialisation. Millaud also agreed to provide, for distribution by peddlers, lithographic portraits of official candidates at low cost. This would help

---

[56] *Ibid.*, pp. 32f, and especially Etat de la situation de la presse départementale, in *Papiers et correspondance*, II, pp. 171–2.

[57] 28 May 1866, AN F18/295.

[58] 'Rapport sur les journaux de Lyon, par le commissaire spécial de police politique', 7 March 1869, in *Pièces saisies*, p. 116.

[59] Tulard, *Dictionnaire*, p. 629.   [60] *Papiers et correspondance*, I, p. 28.

the cause, certainly, but was no substitute for the engagement of pro-
regime newspapers in high-level political debate. This would be the role
of *Le Peuple* and *La Patrie*, which would be supplied with articles and information by the Interior Ministry.[61] Copies of these newspapers were
to be sent to prefects for free distribution to influential individuals and
to cafés. Official involvement was to be disguised. Additionally, the government would enjoy the support of *La France, Le Messager de Paris, Le
Constitutionnel, Le Public, Le Pays*, and *Le Dix-Décembre*, whose editors would
be expected to receive their instructions daily at the ministry. Eminent
journalists like Cassagnac, Vitu, or La Guéronnière – the foreign policy specialist, could expect to be well rewarded for their services to the
regime.[62]

Subsequent developments, however, seemed to justify the most pessimistic assumptions of the Emperor's advisors. In the provinces, between the introduction of the new legislation and the 1869 elections
some 150 new newspapers appeared, of which 120 were hostile, thus
substantially altering the existing balance and providing the opposition,
particularly the republicans, with the essential basis for organisation as
well as propaganda.[63] In the Paris region this was seen as likely to lead
to the renewed politicisation of the lower middle and working classes.[64]
In Saône-et-Loire *Le Progrès* clearly targeted the workers of Le Creusot,
Epinac, and Montceau-les-Mines; in neighbouring Haute-Marne the
Journal de Langres appealed to the rural population.[65] In Marseille the
appearance of *Le Peuple*, edited by Gustave Nacquet, signified for the local administration 'the sudden and noisy re-appearance of the Socialist
party'.[66] In the Pyrenees *L'Indépendant de Pau* and *Le Libéral de Bayonne* were
accused of behaving with a 'total licence' reminiscent of 'the worst days
of the republic'.[67] Serious disorders in the capital in the evenings of 12 to
14 May were blamed largely on the efforts of *Le Réveil*. The contrast with
the previous silence was terrifying.[68]

According to the state prosecutor at Rouen,

the major Parisian newspapers play their part in the development of public
opinion, but the dominant factor is the little papers which every day spread
contempt and calumny concerning everything the government does, and in the
most acrimonious, denigrating and ironic tone. *Le Figaro, Le Diable à quatre*, weekly

[61] *Ibid.*, pp. 28–9.
[62] *Ibid.*, p. 30; Darimon, *Les irréconciliables*, p. 350, entry of 20 Nov. 1868; Isser, *Press*, p. 18.
[63] Zeldin, *Political System*, p. 96.   [64] PG Paris, 8 Feb. 1869, AN BB30/389.
[65] PG Dijon, 13 Jan. 1869, *ibid.*   [66] PG Aix, 4 Oct. 1868, *ibid.*
[67] PG Pau, 22 Oct. 1869, *ibid.*   [68] Prefect of Police to MI, 3 June 1869, AN 45 AP 3.

newssheets, and the opposition's illustrated newspapers, sell in large numbers and are far more widely read than the serious papers representing the same views. War is being waged on our institutions and on the men who personify them by means of ridicule and perfidious and defamatory farce. It is sad to admit that this undignified and deceitful war is enjoying success in every class.[69]

The tone of much of the press had altered as existing newspapers became more critical and with the emergence of a radical republican press amongst which Rochefort's satirical *La Lanterne* was the most notorious. In its first issue it poked fun at ministers, in its second it questioned the morality of Queen Hortense and the legitimacy of her son the Emperor. Take two examples of its humour: 'The state has ordered an equestrian statue of Napoleon III from M. Beyre: everyone knows that M. Beyre is one of our most famous sculptors of animals'. In the second, the Empress is described as a *grue couronnée*, a crowned crane or in the vernacular, I suppose, 'Queen scraggy neck'! Hardly brilliant, but its popularity, especially amongst the middle classes, reveals how low the regime had fallen in popular esteem.[70] *La Lanterne* enjoyed considerable sales in both Paris and the provinces. In Nancy 300 copies a week were being sold by July, and each of them passed rapidly from hand to hand.[71] By its eleventh number the government had had enough and Rochefort was forced into exile by the threat of fines and imprisonment. His eventual return was to be followed by his arrest when, in response to the killing of the republican journalist Victor Noir by Prince Pierre Bonaparte, Rochefort wrote a vengeful article for his new paper *La Marseillaise* (11 January 1870) – 'I was weak enough to believe that a Bonaparte could be something other than an assassin. France has been held in the bloody hands of these cutthroats for 18 years. Not content with shooting down republicans in the streets, it now ensnares them in a filthy trap to slaughter them at home. Frenchmen, have you not had enough?'

Rochefort had a number of imitators, including the future communard Lissagaray, editor of the *Avenir d'Auch*. Like most provincial papers, *L'Avenir* was forced to moderate its tone to avoid offending its readers but the tactic of denigrating the Imperial family was much the same. Its circulation had reached 1,200 by the beginning of 1869, partly through free distribution to cafés. A desperate procureur-général was afraid that prosecution would only provide it with publicity and complained that

---

[69] PG Rouen, 11 Jan. 1869, AN BB30/389.
[70] See H. Allain-Targé, *La République sous l'Empire. Lettres 1867–70* (Paris 1939), p. 179, letter to father, 21 July 1868.
[71] PG Nancy, 27 July 1868, AN BB30/381.

'the enemies it signals to the people as the authors of its misery ... are the rich, government officials and the clergy. The heroes it glorifies are the most ferocious revolutionaries of 1793'.[72] The contrast between these extremist publications and moderate republican newspapers like Ernest Picard's *L'Electeur libre* was quite marked. Benjamin Gastineau, following his dismissal from the editorship of the *Phare de la Loire* in 1869, castigated the timidity of local politicians, 'pseudo-democrats' as he saw them, and of their newspapers, in his opinion dominated by the petty interests of their shareholders.[73] The republican newspapers all agreed, however, on their condemnation of the Empire and especially of its origins, taking up the themes developed in Eugène Ténot's extremely influential books on the *coup d'état* (*Les provinces en décembre*, 1865; *Paris en décembre*, 1868). The procureur-général at Besançon represented a widespread sense of alarm: 'One cannot doubt that this incessant denigration of our institutions, this systematic criticism of the government's every act, will, in the long term, have a damaging impact'. The opposition press was making particularly effective use of fear of an eventual war with Prussia.[74] His colleague at Limoges simply reported that 'it appears that the freedom allowed to the press as a result of the Head of State's courageous initiative has placed us in genuine danger'.[75] Persigny too, from his enforced retirement, warned the Emperor that constant attacks were bringing the regime into disrepute.[76]

The administration's response to this assault had been cautious initially. Civil servants remained unsure about the Emperor's intentions, were anxious not to alienate the public, and concerned to avoid court cases, which would have allowed sharp young republican lawyers like Gambetta to renew the attack.[77] The prosecution launched against the newspapers which had supported a subscription for a statue to Baudin, the démocrate-socialiste deputy killed on the barricades in December 1851, had certainly resulted in a major propaganda victory for the republicans.[78] Nevertheless, a growing conviction was developing that there had to be limits. Napoleon warned Baroche, the Minister of Justice, on 1 July 1869 that 'if we begin by tolerating profoundly seditious articles, there'll be no justification for subsequently clamping down'.[79] Baroche's

---

[72] PG Auch, 9 Jan. 1869, AN BB30/389.
[73] *La vie politique et le journalisme en province*, little 20-centime pamphlet, n.d. but 1869.
[74] PG, 12 Oct. 1868, AN BB30/389.   [75] *Ibid.*, 13 Jan. 1869.
[76] Letter to Emperor, 27 June 1869, in Persigny, *Mémoires*, p. 498.
[77] 'Note sur le rôle de la presse dans les élections de 1869' by M. F. Giraudeau, 30 March 1868, in *Papiers et correspondance*, II, p. 176.
[78] E.g. PG Aix, 16 Jan. 1869, AN BB30/389.   [79] Maurain, *Baroche*, p. 415.

own *chef de cabinet* warned him early in August about the dangers arising from the wide circulation of *La Lanterne* (reaching 170,000) and suggested that inaction would destroy the regime's prestige at home and abroad.[80] Gendarmerie commanders, less concerned with the broader political implications, simply could not understand the hesitant manner with which ministers responded to repeated provocations by the radical press.[81] The public's response was often the same.[82] One tactic, more successful it appears in Paris than the provinces, was to bring press offences, usually that of 'exciting hatred and contempt for the government' (law of 11 August 1848) before tribunals composed of particularly reliable, and promotion-conscious, magistrates.[83] Thus Rochefort was sentenced to one year in prison and a 10,000f fine for the 6 August 1868 issue of *La Lanterne*. Editor and newspaper were driven into exile. His return to Paris to stand for election and edit the daily *Marseillaise* provoked another series of fines and his eventual arrest.[84] Other newspapers, such as the radical *Libéral du Centre* or the socialist *Rappel de la Provence*, were fined repeatedly, the former five times in June, driving it into bankruptcy.[85] The Toulouse *Emancipation* paid out a total of 26,102 francs as a result of sixteen court cases in 1869 alone.[86] Premises were subject to disruptive searches. Subscription lists were seized. Journalists intimidated. Printers faced the prospect of losing their licences. An 'incompetent' court president could, however, produce a disaster. Gambetta was able to turn the trial of Delescluze, prosecuted for organising the Baudin subscription, into the trial of the Emperor and his regime. In a long speech, reported in every paper, he described the instigators of the *coup* as 'a crowd of men lost in debt and crime'.[87]

In a letter to his wife on 15 October 1869, Napoleon appeared to regret ever beginning the process of liberalisation. He observed that 'the country is unfortunately incapable of coping with liberty ... incitement by the democratic newspapers and public meetings is bound to lead, sooner or later, to a riot, which will have the effect of a storm in purifying the atmosphere'.[88] Although the propertied classes were becoming increasingly frightened by social unrest and the verbal violence of the extreme

[80] *Ibid.*, p. 419.   [81] E.g. OC cie. de la Seine, 27 Oct. and 27 Dec. 1869, AHG G8/166.
[82] E.g. Darimon, *Les irréconciliables*, p. 299.
[83] *Les procès de presse depuis le loi du 11 mai 1868 jusqu'au 1 janvier 1869* (Paris: Bulletin de la Cour impériale 1869), p. 723.
[84] Tulard, *Dictionnaire*, p. 1126.   [85] Corbin, *Archaïsme*, II, p. 889.
[86] R. Aminzade, *Ballots and barricades. Class Formation and Republican Politics in France, 1830–71* (London 1993), p. 135.
[87] Printed in Ollivier, *L'Empire libéral*, XI, pp. 92–8.   [88] Quoted Caron, *La France*, p. 161.

left, the Emperor's advisors were divided about how to respond.[89] Some viewed the excesses of the radical press as a potential source of strength for a regime, which still represented, for most of the population, 'order and security'.[90] 'Honest men' welcomed the prosecution of Charles Hugo, editor of *Le Rappel*, and of Rochefort in January 1870.[91] A return to repression would have been 'impolitic', however, as far as the capital was concerned. There, the public meetings encouraged by liberalisation were regarded as an even greater threat than the press.[92] The obligatory presence of police commissaires and ban on political and religious discussion had done little to restrain critics of the regime. The effect of extensive reports in the conservative and moderate republican press was, however, to terrify many readers by reminding them of the clubs of 1848.[93] The journalist Auguste Vitu was instructed to prepare a cheap brochure for mass distribution which simply reproduced the proceedings of some of the most revolutionary political meetings. The tactic, according to Rouher, was to 'allow liberty to completely discredit itself through the abuses made of it'.[94]

The liberal regime established in January 1870 would find it easier to justify repressive measures. Originally, Ollivier had favoured the open debate allowed by a 'free' press and public meetings.[95] Events soon forced him to change his mind. On 30 April 1870 he instructed state prosecutors to 'no longer hesitate to prosecute newspapers ... which contain a call for civil war and insult the Emperor. We cannot simply sit back ... and watch the revolutionary flood. Respect liberty; but provocation to murder and civil war are the opposite of liberty'.[96] In demanding measures against public meetings in Marseille, which had become 'intolerably violent', he instructed the state prosecutor to 'strike at the head, arrest in particular the lawyers, the gentlemen, rather than poor devils from the people'.[97] Conservative anxiety would help to rally substantial support for a 'Yes' vote in the plebiscite on the establishment of the Liberal Empire.[98] The three nights of disorder in the faubourg du Temple

---

[89] See e.g. Duvernois to Napoleon, 8 Nov. 1869 in Poulet-Malassis, *Papiers secrets*.

[90] OC 1st Légion gendarmerie, Bulletin politique, 31 Jan. 1870, AHG G8/176.

[91] OC 1st Légion gendarmerie, 28 Jan. and 26 Feb. 1870, *ibid.*

[92] See e.g. PG Montpellier, 18 Jan. 1868, AN BB30/380.

[93] See e.g. OC gendarmerie Finistère, 29 Nov. 1869, AHG G8/166.

[94] Ollivier, *L'Empire libéral*, XI, p. 127.

[95] Letter to Emperor, 12 Nov. 1869 in Poulet-Malassis, *Papiers secrets*; report on discussion with Emperor in Ollivier, *L'Empire libéral*, IX, pp. 196–7.

[96] Circular to PGs, 30 April 1870, in Poulet-Malassis, *Papiers secrets*, p. 185.

[97] Telegram MJ to PG Aix, 1 May 1870, *ibid.*

[98] See e.g. OC gendarmerie de la Seine, 28 April 1870, AHG G8/176.

in Paris which followed the declaration of the results, and which culminated in over 500 arrests, only confirmed support for the regime. The outbreak of war would provide additional reasons for measures against those newspapers accused of 'disloyalty'.[99]

LITERARY CENSORSHIP

The regime made a considerable effort to control the press in all its forms and not only newspapers. Special *commissaires* were appointed to supervise the domestic book trade. As the Interior Minister reminded his colleague at Justice in October 1853,[100] article 8 of the law of 17 May 1819 could be employed against 'every outrage to public and religious morality'. Amongst those who fell foul of this vague catch-all article was the poet Baudelaire in 1857. According to the state prosecutor, his work was an affront to 'that great Christian morality which is in reality the only sound base for public morals'. Similarly the socialist writer Proudhon was judged to have exceeded the limits of legitimate controversy by means of such 'outrageous sarcasm' as reference to Christ as 'the putative son of God'.[101]

Efforts were also made to encourage the distribution of a moralising and 'useful' literature. Publishers sympathetic to the regime could expect to benefit from the booming market in textbooks. Plon additionally acquired the exclusive right to publish the official portrait of the Head of State which mayors were instructed to purchase.[102] Departmental councils were urged to emulate that of the Seine-et-Oise and subsidise publication of moralising versions of the traditional almanacs so popular in the countryside.[103] Commercial motives encouraged the publication of a range of periodicals, some primarily intended to appeal to popular patriotism, others to provide practical information and encourage self-improvement. The first category, including *Le Bellorama*, *Le Bulletin de la guerre*, *La Guerre d'Italie* and *Le Zouave*,[104] replete with descriptions and illustrations of heroic actions and portraits of victorious generals, appealed to latent Bonapartist sentiment. Domestic affairs such as the Emperor's marriage were also celebrated. In a typical lithograph published in Valence in January 1853, the picture and description of the ceremony was followed by a dialogue in verse, supposedly between the

---

[99] Circular in Ollivier, *L'Empire libéral*, xv, p. 67.   [100] 20 Oct. 1853, AN BB30/381.
[101] Quoted Royer, *La société judiciaire*, p. 321.
[102] Persigny to prefects, 31 Aug. 1852, *Documents pour servir*.   [103] Circular, 22 Dec. 1852, *ibid.*
[104] Examples in AN AB xix 689.

Imperial couple, in which Eugénie responds to Napoleon's declaration of love with the words:

> Just like you, Your Eugénie
> Wishes greatness for France;
> We shall ease the misery
>   of the worker, of the labourer.
> In their cottages they will bless,
> The Empress and the Emperor.[105]

The second category included publications like the Abbé Mullois' *Journal de Tout le Monde. Encyclopédie Populaire* (1856), which promised not to publish fiction, which only 'fills people's heads with chimeras and dreams'.[106] In the 1860s the establishment of popular libraries (*Bibliothèques populaires*) in local schools was encouraged. In a confidential circular in 1864 Paul Boudet, the Interior Minister, expressed his concern that some local philanthropists, 'pretended friends of the labouring classes', might seek to take advantage of this renewed drive for literacy to circulate polemical books. He recommended that only works of practical utility be made available and that library catalogues be inspected regularly.[107] Among the volumes recommended by the *Bulletin de la Société Franklin. Journal des bibliothèques populaires*, which provided lists of suitable books and offered discounts on purchases, was a translation of Samuel Smiles' *Self Help* (Plon, 3f) and Eugène Noel's *La Campagne* (Sagnier, 1f75) which sought to discourage peasant migration to the cities.[108] In a circular in 1870 the Minister insisted furthermore that prefects should be consulted on the membership of library committees, and reiterated his view that they should make available only

useful professional works, those suitable for the moralisation and instruction of the working classes. It is important to eliminate ... novels, which might create regrettable impressions; one should also take every care to exclude works of social or religious polemic and those which, under pretext of discussing political economy, serve as the means of propagating dangerous or subversive doctrines.[109]

A commission du colportage was appointed to report on urban street traders and the peddlers who distributed cheap and accessible reading materials and illustrations throughout small-town and rural France. This was a trade which would soon collapse of its own accord as the

---

[105] J.-P. Seguin, *Nouvelles à sensation. Canards du 19ᵉ siècle* (Paris 1959), pp. 37–8.
[106] AN AB xix 688.   [107] 8 April 1864 in *Documents pour servir*, p. 140.
[108] 1, 1864.   [109] *Bulletin de la Société Franklin*, no. 22, 15 April 1870.

mass-circulation press encouraged new consumer habits.[110] In the meantime the commission worked hard, particularly during the 1850s, to purify the contents of the peddlers' packs by establishing a list of approved books and prosecuting offenders.[111] It saw its objective as being to 'control publications intended for the lower classes; much more important without any doubt than the press seeking to influence the upper classes. Peddling is the instrument by which one can corrupt or moralise the popular classes ... Only those governments which understand the necessity of concerning themselves with the lower classes and know how to revive their sentiments, instincts, beliefs, and enthusiasms are likely to be stable and really conservative'.[112] Amongst books rejected in the first half of 1868 were such apparently practical manuals as *Veterinary Care in One's Home* and *Surgery for the Poor*, rightly judged to be offering dangerous self-help remedies; *Curing the Sick through Prayer and the Laying on of Hands* and *The Poor Man's Doctor*, both rejected for favouring superstitious practices, and Emile Zola's 'immoral' novel *Thérèse Raquin*.[113] However, school inspectors continued to complain that the countryside was being 'inundated' with 'immoral novels'.[114] Where peddlers were prosecuted this was most likely because they had been distributing political materials. Just to take one example, on 2 September 1854 Claude Sorbet, tramping around the villages of the Drôme, was stopped and his pack searched. It was found to contain four copies of the socialist writer Eugène Sue's *Jeanne et Louise ou les familles des transportés* and three of Victor Hugo's *Les Châtiments*. The unfortunate Sorbet lost his licence, was fined 500f, and imprisoned for a month.[115]

Such 'subversive' materials were also distributed by the new postal service, however. After its introduction in 1849 the number of postage stamps sold rapidly rose from 21,232,665 to 148,433,000 in 1855, 253,300,250 in 1860, and 438,219,000 by 1866.[116] Its sheer volume made systematic surveillance difficult although postal control appeared to be an essential part of political policing.[117] According to a confidential report to the Emperor, by 1857 letters were being opened on 'a vast

---

[110] Law 27 July 1849 and circulars of Persigny MI, 9 Feb. 1852 and Maupas, Ministère de la Police Générale, 28 July 1852 in *Documents pour servir.*

[111] See e.g. MI to MJ, 20 Oct. 1853, AN BB30/381 and especially J.-J. Darmon, *Le colportage de librairie en France sous le second empire* (Paris 1972), pp. 50–2.

[112] 14 July 1853, quoted Darmon, *Le colportage*, pp. 108–9.   [113] *Documents pour servir*, pp. 274–6.

[114] Academic rector Dijon, 14 July 1858, AN F17/2649.

[115] PG Grenoble, 7 Sept. 1854, AN BB30/378.

[116] E. Arago, *Les postes en 1848* (Paris 1867), p. 59.

[117] See Rouher's justification in Schnerb, *Rouher*, p. 167.

scale'.[118] This could be justified by the fact that domiciliary searches made it clear that republican propaganda from London and Brussels, most notably pamphlets by Victor Hugo, were bring distributed through the post.[119] Illicit materials were increasingly printed in small format, on thin paper, for ease of distribution.[120] Postal control was to be partially discredited by the activities of Collet-Meygret, who occupied the key post of directeur de la sûreté publique at the Interior Ministry. In 1857, in an effort to identify the source of information leaked to the press, he decided to open mail to and from the Imperial court in residence at Compiègne including, it was strongly suspected, though never proved, the Empress' own correspondence. In the enquiry which followed, Saintonner, the man directly responsible for postal surveillance, admitted that during the July Monarchy correspondence between the king and Guizot had routinely been intercepted.[121] Collet-Meygret was also suspected of using his privileged access to information to support a variety of speculative ventures, and to have developed close links with the financier Mirès. Further, it was claimed that he had used his role as a government representative in negotiations with the Paris Gas Company to demand 500 shares (quoted at 611f) in return for agreeing to renew its contract. When this was refused it was alleged that he had provided information to the London *Times* concerning the speculative activities of Pereire, the company's leading director. As if this was not enough, he was additionally accused of opening letters between Fould, the financier and sometime finance minister, and his mistress, and gathering information as a means of protecting himself.[122] In spite of this scandalous abuse of power, postal surveillance continued as a matter of routine. Correspondence involving known republicans and socialists was always likely to be opened.[123] M. Vandal, directeur-général des postes, offered further justification of these procedures in 1867. He pointed out that the criminal code authorised the police judiciaire to search for evidence of criminal activity and that the postal authorities only acted on instructions from magistrates and prefects, except in the case of printed materials arriving

[118] Rapport à l'Empereur sur M. Collet-Meygret, n.d., in Poulet-Malassis, *Papiers secrets*, p. 62.

[119] E.g. PG Metz, 8 Jan. 1853, AN BB30/406.

[120] E.g. *Le Bulletin français*, published in Brussels in 1852; *Lettre à Marianne* signed by members of the Comité de la Commune révolutionnaire (Pyat, Rougée, Jourdain) (London 1856), AN AB XIX 687.

[121] Rapport de M. Duvergier, ex-secrétaire-général de la Préfecture de Police, to MI, 12 Oct. 1857 in *Papiers et correspondance*, I, pp. 181f.

[122] Duvergier to MI, 12 Oct. 1857 in Poulet-Malassis, *Papiers secrets*, p. 73; undated, unsigned Rapport à l'Empereur sur M. Collet-Meygret in *Papiers et correspondance*, I, pp. 106–10.

[123] See e.g. PG Besançon, 20 June 1855, AN BB30/413.

from foreign countries, where it was itself responsible for ensuring that the press laws were respected.[124] Surveillance offered a useful means of collecting information on international attitudes towards France, and to minimise its cost it appears that foreign newspapers en route to subscribers in France were systematically read in the offices of the postal administration. Subsequently they would reach their destinations only when positive views of the regime had been expressed.[125] Official figures which claimed that in 1866 only 3,902 letters were seized, including 3,437 containing illicit foreign lottery tickets,[126] were a little disingenuous. Presumably most of the letters opened would have been re-sealed and sent on to their destinations rather than seized.

Considerable efforts were thus made by the postal and customs authorities to stem the flow of republican propaganda across the frontiers.[127] However, the Sardinian, Swiss, and especially the Belgian borders, given their length and topography, remained permeable. Residents of Lille and other northern towns continued to enjoy easy access to Belgian newspapers, frequently highly critical of the French government's policies.[128] Occasionally large-scale smuggling occurred. At Roubaix on 29 January 1853, 3,000 copies of the republican Colonel Charras' appeal to the army together with 20 copies of Hugo's *Napoléon le petit* and Schoelcher's *Histoire des crimes du 2 décembre* were seized.[129] Under considerable French pressure, the Belgian government made an effort to restrict the activities of political refugees. Increasingly London became the main centre of exile activity, the location of what senior officials appear to have believed was a *grand comité révolutionnaire* directed by Mazzini and Ledru-Rollin,[130] and then in the late 1860s of a worldwide conspiracy involving the Workers' International. This justified Ollivier's decision to reopen 'the *cabinet noir* which we closed when we came to power'.[131] It was agreed with the direction des postes that all letters arriving from Belgium and Britain should be opened.[132]

The theatre was similarly subject to constant interference again, especially during the 1850s. The papers of the Commission de censure des

[124] Extract from *Moniteur universel*, 23 Feb. 1867, AN 6 AQ 20.
[125] Rapport, in *Papiers et correspondance*, I, pp. 189–90.
[126] Direction général des postes, 'Etat indiquant le nombre des réquisitions pour saisies de lettres', n.d. in *Documents pour servir*, p. 236.
[127] See e.g. GOC 8 DM, 1–5 April 1853, re responsibilities of gendarmerie at Gex (Ain), AHG G8/1; M. Vuilleumier, 'La sous-préfecture de Gex et la surveillance politique de Genève (1848–70)', *Cahiers d'histoire*, 1964.
[128] See e.g. reports in AN BB30/405.   [129] PR Lille, 29 Jan. 1853, in AN BB30/406.
[130] See e.g. PG Dijon, 9 May 1852, AN BB30/377.   [131] Ollivier, *L'Empire libéral*, XV, p. 68.
[132] 3 May 1870, in *Papiers et correspondance*, I, p. 472.

ouvrages dramatiques reveal something of the arbitrariness with which theatre directors had to contend. A list of banned plays was prepared and the texts of proposed new productions were examined carefully.[133] The censors' role was to 'prevent representation of the antagonism between the lower and upper classes ... attacks on the principle of authority, against religion, the family, the magistrature, the army, in a word all those institutions on which society reposes; the more or less bold depiction of the depraved morals of amorous women'.[134] In December 1852 the commission refused to permit the performance of an opera entitled *La Fronde* at the Académie de Musique on the grounds that the subject was of necessity 'impregnated with a sentiment of revolt, not without inconvenience even at the Opera; in addition the presentation of riotous scenes, shouts of *To Arms* etc., would be regarded as dangerous in any theatre'.[135] Making fun of government officials was also regarded as inadmissible.[136] The comedy *Michel Perrin*, frequently performed since 1834, had to be revised for a performance at the Théâtre des Variétés in 1853 to eliminate a scene, supposedly at the Ministère de la Police, in which the minister told his subordinates that 'they would all sell themselves for next to nothing; that they were totally incompetent ... that it was time to invent a nice little conspiracy'.[137] This was clearly beyond the pale. Similarly Emile Augier's *Diane*, due to be performed at the Comédie française in 1852 was withdrawn because the central character was engaged in a plot against the life of Cardinal Richelieu, 'a man whose life is necessary to France'. Moreover, 'such a subject cannot be treated, whatever the good intentions, prudence and talent of the author, without conjuring up possible allusions'. Augier and the Comédie were again in trouble the following year because of lines like 'the insolence of the rich; the protests of the disinherited' and 'God is not just', which had to be cut, and in 1854 for the use of *argot* rather than literary French.[138] In July 1855 Augier's play *Le mariage d'Olympe* was discussed for some forty-five minutes by the Emperor and his ministers, because of the monarch's concern that yet another piece about courtesans might influence 'the idea that the lower classes, very assiduous in their attendance at the

[133] MI instructions, 18 Feb. 1852, in *Documents pour servir*.

[134] Undated, quoted O. Krakovitch, 'Mise en pièces des théâtres: la censure des spectacles au 19e siècle' in Vigier, *Maintien*, p. 297.

[135] *Papiers et correspondance*, I, p. 358.

[136] Motives for rejection of 'La Mère Moreau' at Théâtre du Palais-Royal, 30 Feb. 1852 and of 'Un regard de Ministre' at Variétés on 21 July 1854, *ibid.*, pp. 358–9.

[137] *Ibid.*, pp. 359–60.   [138] In 'Les jeunes gens' – *ibid.*, pp. 369–70.

theatre, have of the upper classes'.[139] Similarly the first performance of a melodrama entitled *Les deux dîners* planned for the Théâtre des Jeunes Elèves was postponed until the character of the rapacious *landlord* who threatened to evict poor old Vincent and his lovely daughter Pauline was replaced by that of the *usurer*.[140] The director of the Théâtre de la Porte-Saint-Martin revised a historical drama in twenty-five tableaux by Paul Meurice in 1855, against the author's wishes, so that instead of reaching its climax with scenes of revolution it ended with Napoleon I presenting eagle standards to his troops. Even in the more relaxed 1860s, Alfred de Musset's drama *Lorenzaccio*, due to be performed at the Théâtre impérial de l'Odéon in 1864, and which portrayed the debauchery and cruelty of the Medici duke, was banned because it included a discussion of regicide.[141] Anything that appeared to the censors to question the established social, moral, and political order was likely to be banned or subject to revision.

Probably of greater significance in their impact, however, were the safety regulations, introduced by Haussmann, which put pressure on managements to limit the number of places available. Together with changes in the repertoire this promoted a *bourgeoisification* of the theatre, reducing the danger of disorder and pushing the popular classes into the cafés-concerts. These were easier to supervise and to close,[142] although the popularity of illegal, revolutionary songs, posed a problem. In this respect, the grounds offered by the censors in April 1870 for the continued ban on the *Marseillaise* are revealing. They insisted that 'the patriotic *Marseillaise* no longer exists ... Party passion has travestied its meaning. The *Marseillaise* has become the symbol of revolution; it is no longer the song of national independence and liberty; it is the war song of demagogy, the hymn of the most extreme republicans'.[143]

MORAL INSTRUCTION

These repressive measures on which invariably so much of the administration's energy was concentrated were regarded, nevertheless, simply as a stopgap, a means of holding the line. The moral as well as the legal basis for the existing social and political order urgently needed to be re-affirmed. The ideal would always be to secure the 'willing' collaboration of subordinate groups and establish moral order through self-discipline

[139] Fortoul, *Journal*, II, p. 23.   [140] *Papiers et correspondance*, I, p. 369.
[141] *Ibid.*, pp. 360–1.   [142] Krakovitch, 'Mise en pièces', p. 299.
[143] *Papiers et correspondance*, I, pp. 353–4.

and respect for the established social hierarchy. One of the central questions to be addressed will be the extent to which subordinate social groups were socialised into a moral universe constructed by elites. The agents of this policy were to be the clergy and primary school teachers. Already, the key 1833 education law had established the school as 'an instrument of popular moralisation, of political stabilisation, of social conservatism and economic progress'.[144] Primary instruction was conceived of as having an essentially civilising mission. The masses were to be assimilated into a well-policed state.[145] In order to achieve these objectives the curriculum needed to be dominated by moral and religious instruction.[146] The priest, inspiring fear of Divine Retribution, would serve as a more effective guarantor of an ordered, hierarchical society and the position of its privileged elites, than the soldier.

The Falloux law in 1850 strengthened these provisions. It sought to encourage the expansion of religious education by means both of the reinforcement of its already substantial position within the curriculum and an expansion of the Catholic teaching orders. Lay teachers were to be more closely supervised and where possible replaced. It was agreed that the curriculum should be restricted to the three R's and that religious teaching should dominate everything. The views forcefully expressed to the commission charged to prepare the legislation by its chairman, Adolphe Thiers, fully revealed conservative social fear and intentions:

I formally demand something other than those detestable little lay schoolteachers; I want religious brothers, although I used once to be hostile towards them; in addition I want to render the influence of the clergy all-powerful; I demand that the parish priest's position is strengthened, made much stronger than it is, because I count on him to propagate that good philosophy which teaches that man is here to suffer and not that other philosophy which, on the contrary, tells man: enjoy yourself ... you are here below to take up your little share of happiness, and if you do not find it in your present situation, strike without fear the rich whose egotism prevents you from enjoying your share of happiness.

The eminent philosopher and educationalist Victor Cousin insisted similarly on the centrality of *l'autorité religieuse*, adding that 'It is necessary that the priest supervises every part of education, and not only the teaching of the catechism, for in learning to read, children are able to acquire bad doctrines ... The schoolmaster must learn to bend, to submit to the

---

[144] M. Gontard, *Les écoles primaires de la France bourgeoise (1833–78)* (Toulouse n.d.), p. 4.
[145] E.g. prefect Lot to Min. de l'Instruction publique, 17 Jan. 1852, AN F17/9112.
[146] Esp. *arrêt* of 25 April 1834 in Gontard, *Ecoles*, pp. 6–7.

parish priest, as well as to the mayor. Those two authorities are responsible for the supervision of the school'. The parish priest would assume responsibility for supervising the work of the schoolteacher, although the ultimate rights of the state inspectorate were preserved. With considerable cynicism, Thiers insisted on protecting the classical and secular bases of secondary education for the upper and middle classes, on the grounds that groups which were not a threat to social order had less need of religion.[147]

Teachers were in addition to be more carefully trained. Thus the new regulations for the teacher training establishments, the écoles normales, introduced in October 1852, stipulated that 'the main lessons for the students are respect for the religious and public authorities'.[148] The model regulations, circulated on 27 August 1850 by Baroche, the Minister of the Interior and of Public Instruction, insisted that 'the principal duty of the schoolteacher is to provide pupils with religious instruction, and to engrave profoundly on their souls the sentiments of their duties towards God, towards their parents, towards other people, and towards themselves' (article 1). The teacher should instruct by example as well as through his lessons, performing his religious duties (article 2) and avoiding all forms of behaviour likely to demean 'the gravity and ... dignity of his functions' (article 3). He should behave in a respectful manner towards his superiors (article 4). Primary school inspectors were instructed by the minister in 1855 to ensure that 'the truths which make Christianity the foundation of the social order are enrooted in the hearts of the children in your care'.[149] According to the academic rector in Mayenne, in a message to the cantonal delegates responsible for the daily, local supervision of schools, 'a well-directed education must have ... the effect of developing the intelligence, of forming judgement, of profoundly inscribing the sublime precepts of Christian morality, of inspiring in the pupil the love of duty, devotion to the nation, respect for authority, submission to the laws, and an attachment to the condition in which Providence has placed him'.[150]

An effort was also made to encourage the rapid expansion of the religious teaching orders. The *lettre d'obédience* (rather than the academic *brevet*) was accepted as a sufficient qualification for the female orders and communes were allowed to choose between lay and religious teachers.

---

[147] In Chennesseau, *La Commission extraparlementaire*, pp. 31–2.
[148] Quoted Maurain, *Politique ecclésiastique*, p. 142.   [149] AN F17/9373.
[150] 12 March 1854, AN F17/9280; on the ineffectiveness of supervision see e.g. PG Dijon, 12 Jan. 1866 , AN BB30/377.

The latter offered the advantages of cheapness, a sense of mission, and also cared for the sick.[151] One measure of the success of this legislation was the expansion in the numbers of boys and girls taught by members of the teaching orders from 15 per cent and 45 per cent respectively in 1850 to 22 per cent and 54 per cent by 1863.[152] During the 1850s recognition of new religious orders proceeded apace. Whereas, in 1847, 2,136 *frères* and 10,371 *soeurs* had belonged to authorised teaching orders, by 1863 the numbers had risen to 7,161 and 36,397 respectively.[153] Moreover, many lay teachers and almost all female *institutrices* were trained by the religious orders. The expansion of education for girls, always a step behind that for boys, had been another major objective of the Falloux law. Mixed instruction was seen as a threat to morality and communes with a population over 800 were required to establish a separate school for girls. The new legislation recognised the vital need to 'form good and virtuous mothers, well instructed in their duties and capable of inculcating in their children good principles and the habits of morality'.[154] Mothers who had attended school were also believed to be far more likely to educate their own children.[155]

Even at the height of their collaboration there were tensions between state and church. A substantial purge of lay teachers had already occurred during the conservative Republic and as the Falloux law took effect the administration would come to recognise increasingly the basic conservatism of the remainder. The professional objectives, personal aspirations, and hierarchical structures of the profession lent themselves to the regime's political aims. Improved salaries were intended to enhance morale and recruitment and reinforce the teachers' loyalty to the regime. It was reported from the Lozère in 1858 that 'the primary school teachers are, in general, irreproachable from the moral and religious point of view. Both male and female teachers are imbued with a sense of dignity and of the holiness of their mission. That which they know best, and practise and teach best, is the history of religion and the catechism, that is to say, morality and religion'.[156] Teachers themselves insisted on their ability to draw lessons from biblical and more recent history to persuade the masses that

[151] P. Zind, *L'enseignement religieux dans l'instruction primaire publique en France de 1850 à 1873* (Lyon 1971), p. 21; see also 'Les devoirs de l'Instituteur – extraits du règlement général des écoles primaires de Seine-et-Oise soumis à l'approbation du Conseil Impérial', 25 Nov. 1864, AN F17/9373.

[152] R. Anderson, *Education in France, 1848–70* (Oxford 1975), p. 112.

[153] Gontard, *Ecoles*, p. 135.   [154] Academic rector, Dépt. de la Creuse, Feb. 1851, AN F17/9112.

[155] E.g. Académie de Douai, *Exposé de la situation de l'enseignement* (Arras 1856), AN F17/9373.

[156] Académie de Montpellier. Département de la Lozère. Extrait du registre des délibérations du Conseil départemental de l'instruction publique. Séance du 2 août 1858, AN F17/9373.

their prosperity depended on respect for social order.[157] There had always been limits imposed on the expansion of the teaching orders. These included a shortage of personnel in spite of rapid expansion, but also resistance from within the administration. Some mayors and even academic rectors believed that increasingly lay teachers were better trained than members of the religious orders and equally committed to moral and religious instruction. Additionally, lay teachers showed more respect towards the official *Université* than did members of the religious orders, who were determined to preserve their autonomy. Government officials were also concerned about the clergy's role in supporting Legitimist political influence.[158] Above all, both state and church attached fundamental importance to achieving control over the instruction of the young. Competition between them was unavoidable. The strains were soon evident. The decree of 9 March 1852 and law of June 1854 both re-affirmed the primary supervisory role of the prefect acting through the educational inspectorate. Fortoul made it clear to academic rectors that they were to combat 'excessive' clerical influence.[159] Neither he nor his successors were opposed to the church fundamentally but they were anxious to safeguard the predominance of the state. Reports from the academic rectors in the 1850s were increasingly alarmist, criticising the standards of education offered, particularly by the female orders,[160] and accusing the church of attempting to construct an educational monopoly.[161] There was frequent resentment of the pressure placed by parish priests on municipal councillors and parents to persuade them to support the replacement of lay teachers. Ferlay, prefect of the Drôme, was concerned that 'this domineering clerical spirit will ... provoke, sooner or later, an unfortunate reaction which will be ... extremely prejudicial to religion itself'.[162] Fortoul's successor, Rouland, was even more concerned to protect the state's prerogatives, insisting upon the inspectorate's right of entry into schools staffed by the religious orders. However, any action which appeared to threaten the victory apparently gained through the *loi Falloux* was bitterly resented by a clergy obsessed with its duty to mould the minds of the young, as the means of securing eternal salvation.[163]

The alliance of convenience between throne and altar had, in spite of these problems, initially worked well. Although the local influence

---

[157] See e.g. essay by Ramel, instituteur at Marseille, AN F17 10758.
[158] E.g. PG Dijon, 18 April 1866, AN BB30/377.
[159] Circular, 12 March 1852, in Payne, *Police State*, p. 118.
[160] E.g. Rector Aix, 12 Jan. 1859, AN F17/2649. [161] E.g. Rector Rennes, 7 Jan. 1859, *ibid.*
[162] 31 Oct. 1856, AN F17/9373. [163] E.g. Maurain, *Baroche*, pp. 150-1.

of the clergy varied considerably, the church's parish organisation covered the entire country. Its bishops had thanked God for the *coup d'état*. Mgr Sibour, Archbishop of Paris, condemned those socialists who 'under the pretext of perfecting society, sought to destroy the real society established by God' and who impiously threatened property rights sanctified by the Ten Commandments.[164] The willingness of the clergy to participate in counter-revolution was hardly surprising. They remained traumatised by the anti-religious character of the first French revolution and frightened by the obvious anti-clericalism of many of the new generation of democrats. The Pope himself had been forced to leave Rome by crowds demanding political reform and his support for the war of liberation against Austria. Faced with this threat to his own authority as well as to the unity of the universal church, Pius IX had unambiguously denounced liberalism and all its works, thus enlarging the gulf between Catholic and liberal/democratic ideals. The clergy were required to demand that the faithful respect ruling monarchs and the established social hierarchy. They should teach the poor to resign themselves to their condition and to ignore the sinful advice of those who encouraged greed and envy. In return for accepting God's will during their earthly existence the poor could look forward to a Heavenly reward. There was a clear determination to mould the minds of the young.[165] If both the secular and religious authorities were anxious to secure control of the schools, the essential means of indoctrination, in this moment of extreme crisis they were also willing to co-operate.

The church received substantial subsidies, support for its educational mission, and the reinforcement of its public status, through official participation in religious ceremonies, and in return the state expected clerical support for official candidates for election, and, at the very least, a weakening of the traditionally close ties between the clergy and Legitimism.[166] The ideal bishop (appointed since the Concordat of 1802, following nomination by the Emperor and approval by the Pope) appreciated 'all the good that His Majesty has done for the church, is unreservedly devoted to the government, and moderate in character'.[167] Nevertheless, most priests responded with anger to the regime's military intervention in Italy

---

[164] Mandement ... contre les erreurs qui renversent les fondements de la Justice et de la Charité, 8 June 1851, in Mgr. Sibour *Mandements, lettres et instructions pastorales de Mgr. Sibour* (Paris 1853), pp. 23–4, 39.

[165] E.g. report on provincial council at Avignon, Dec. 1850 in B. Delpal, *Entre paroisse et commune. Les catholiques de la Drôme au milieu du 19ᵉ siècle* (Valence 1989), pp. 178–81.

[166] E.g. MI to Ministère des Cultes, 23 July 1853, AN F1 CIII Vendée 8.

[167] Prefect to Ministère de l'instruction publique et des Cultes, 3 Jan. 1856, AN F1 CIII Somme 11.

in 1859, the collapse of the temporal power of the Papacy, and the threat this appeared to pose to 'the most essential interests of Christianity'.[168] Influential Catholic laymen supported them. Ministers responded to this criticism by asking officials for detailed reports on the attitudes and actions of the clergy.[169] The archives are full of accounts of apocalyptical sermons predicting that the loss of the Papal states would be followed by a new wave of revolutions 'more terrible than that of '93'.[170] The Abbé Pourchers at Draveil (Seine-et-Oise) asked his congregation: 'Do you want to return to '93 when they fired on Christ and his priests even in the churches?'[171] Marshal Randon, the War Minister, even felt obliged to ask priests to desist from preaching at military masses.[172] Officials demanded that the bishops discipline their more extreme subordinates. Criticism of the regime, whether it came from parish priests, bishops, laymen, or the Pope himself, if published without government approval, was suppressed.

Delangle, the Minister of Justice, whilst reminding state prosecutors of the mutually beneficial relations state and church had enjoyed previously, warned them that 'poorly understood events have awakened unfortunate susceptibilities. Attacks, which were timid initially, have multiplied and become increasingly bitter. A concert is being established, publications full of hostile sentiments are being distributed, even in the schools, criticising the Emperor himself; they gleefully distort his acts and intentions; they look for every means of troubling unenlightened consciences'. He concluded that 'tolerance is no longer possible'. Whilst the government would continue to '*honour*' religion, unauthorised publications, politics in the pulpit, attacks on the person of the Emperor '*in whatever form they occur*', should be prosecuted.[173] In some areas the procureurs-généraux responded with alacrity, even ordering gendarmes to attend church services.[174] Generally they were more reserved, and avoided action which might inflame religious tension. For personal or practical reasons officials were frequently unwilling to offend influential religious leaders. The procureur at Strasbourg obeyed his minister's instructions to seize a popular pamphlet published by the bishop's printer only with

[168] Episcopal mandement of 26 June 1860 enclosed with PG Poitiers report, 25 July 1860, AN BB30/385.
[169] E.g. PG Bordeaux, 28 Feb. 1860, AN BB30/450.
[170] Sermon by curé of Allemans, reported by PI Marmande (Lot-et-Garonne), 7 March 1860, AN BB30/374.
[171] Ministère de l'instruction publique to MJ, ? March 1860, AN BB30/451.
[172] Castellane, *Journal*, V. p. 281.
[173] Confidental circular, 22 Feb. 1860 in AN BB30/450 – italics in the original.
[174] PG Riom, 26 March 1860, AN BB30/451.

considerable reluctance. Entitled *The Beer Drinker, the Blacksmith and the Pope*, the pamphlet linked 'the children of Israel' with the Protestants – who for 300 years had been trying to destroy the Papacy, as well as with bad Catholics unwilling to respect the Ten Commandments, and the English who were determined 'to set the World alight'. The procureur was not only aware that the bishop had himself corrected the proofs but appears to have shared most of the views expressed in the pamphlet and especially its all-pervading anti-semitism.[175] In the last resort, of course, state and church would continue to collaborate in the struggle against subversion. Moreover, even in areas in which the clergy retained considerable influence, it was clear that the mass of believers did not attach nearly as much importance to the Pope's temporal authority as did the clergy and Catholic elites.[176]

As relationships deteriorated over the Roman question, so the conflict over education intensified. In a memoir to the Emperor in April 1860, Rouland insisted upon the ultramontane characteristics of the church and on the inadequacy of state authority over the religious congregations. He made the telling point that 'Today, when the schoolteacher, modest and useful functionary, is devoted to the Emperor and renders notable services in the rural community, we would be gravely weakened when it came to elections if primary education were to pass into the hands of the religious congregations which depend more on Rome than on France'.[177] He would make a greater effort to protect lay teachers from the clerical pressure which the administration had encouraged previously and which teachers had often bitterly resented. Existing legislation on such matters as the authorisation of teaching congregations and the prefect's right to nominate teachers was more strictly applied.[178] The legislation on legacies and donations was interpreted in a manner less favourable to the church, reducing its ability to fund new schools.[179] Officials were coming to see the primary teachers, rather than the clergy, as the essential link between the state and the masses. Significantly, in contrast with the previous decade, prefectoral reports emphasised the construction of schools rather than the renovation of churches as their proudest achievement.[180] The implementation of decisions taken in Paris by local administrators depended a great deal on their readings of local

[175] PG Colmar, 29 Feb. and 18 March 1860, AN BB30/450.
[176] E.g. PG Rennes, 7 Jan. 1860, AN BB30/451.   [177] Quoted Zind, *L'enseignement*, p. 205.
[178] See e.g. circular of 10 April 1862, in Gontard, *Ecoles*, pp. 147–9.
[179] Maurain, *Politique ecclésiastique*, pp. 92.
[180] Point made by Huard, *La préhistoire des partis*, pp. 763–4.

situations, however. In much of the west and the Massif Central it still appeared necessary to conciliate an influential clergy although, in the longer term, the development of lay instruction was seen as a means of weaning the population away from clerical and Legitimist influence.[181] Elsewhere, as in Nancy, the academic rector Dunoyer insisted that economic prosperity, to which he linked the declining spirituality of the local population, created an urgent need to reinforce the status of the lay teacher as the moral influence of the clergy declined.[182]

Secondary education was another area of bitter controversy. In the 1850s Catholic schools had expanded rapidly and by 1865 whilst public lycées and municipal colleges attracted 46 per cent of pupils, Catholic institutions provided instruction for 24 per cent and other private schools for a further 30 per cent.[183] Ministers were concerned especially about the preference shown by members of the aristocracy and upper bourgeoisie – for religious, social, political reasons, or out of sheer snobbery – for exclusive boarding schools directed by the clergy, especially by the Jesuit, Marist, and Assumptionist orders. Both Fortoul and Rouland had come to appreciate the need to defend the secular education offered in the lycées and to curb the expansionist tendencies of the religious orders. As always, the Jesuits caused particular concern. The failure of the superior of their college at Saint-Etienne to punish pupils who had smashed and then trampled underfoot the fragments of a bust of the Emperor led to its temporary closure in December 1853.[184] The religious orders' sustained resistance to official inspection intensified suspicion that deliberate efforts were being made to suborn part of the social elite. The state prosecutor at Angers noted of the cavalry school at nearby Saumur that it 'mostly recruits officers from the private schools ... and this hostile element spreads throughout the army in a fashion which arouses concern for the future ... We are beginning to harvest the fruits of the freedom allowed to the Jesuits'.[185] Duruy, appointed Education Minister in 1863, expressed similar concern about the 1865 graduating class from the military academy at Saint Cyr, which he claimed included 76 former pupils of Jesuit schools amongst its 249 members.[186] The academic rector at Bordeaux complained of a situation in which 'a considerable portion of French youth will be educated in schools in which the spirit of the ... masters is not in general favourable to the Imperial regime, nor to the

---

[181] E.g. PG Poitiers, 11 Jan. 1866, re Vendée, AN BB30/385.
[182] 18 Jan. 1861, AN F17/2650.   [183] Anderson, *Education*, p. 113.
[184] Maurain, *Politique ecclésiastique*, pp. 144–5.   [185] 6 Feb. 1863, AN BB18/1606.
[186] Letter to Mme Cornu, 9 Feb. 1866, in Emerit, *Madame Cornu*, I, pp. 54–5.

ideas of progress and a sensible liberty on which it is based'.[187] This was regarded increasingly as a matter of crucial political importance. Nothing less than the unity of the governing classes appeared to be at stake and it was on secondary education that successive ministers focused most of their attention.

The secondary education of girls was conducted entirely in private schools largely outside the control of the state. Duruy complained to the Emperor that 'we have left this education in the hands of people who belong neither to the present world nor to this country'. In another letter, this time to the Empress, he maintained that 'the influence of the mother on the education of the sons and on the direction of ideas is too great not to worry about seeing women remain strangers to the intellectual life of the modern world'.[188] His circular of 30 October 1867 announced plans for the provision of public courses by municipal authorities to supplement the religious and moral instruction of young girls. He informed rectors (circular of 2 November 1867) that the objective was 'to ensure the disappearance of the intellectual divorce which all too frequently exists between husband and wife', adding: 'How many times is the harmony of families troubled by the differences of education, of sentiment and of ideas, which prevent husband and wife from understanding each other, and which ensure that they live in two separate and antagonistic worlds?'[189] These were to be fee-paying courses for girls from well-off families who would be expected to be accompanied by chaperones. Nevertheless, Catholic elites were quick to mobilise in opposition. The church deeply resented state interference in a sphere it believed to be particularly its own.

The appointment of Duruy, the Emperor's collaborator on his *Life of Caesar*, was widely perceived to be a direct challenge to the church. The new minister was suspect because of his reputation for anti-clericalism. The programme he presented to Napoleon on 6 August insisted upon the civilising and modernising mission of education and pointed to the humiliating contrast between the 25 per cent of illiterate conscripts entering the French army and the 5 per cent in Prussia.[190] The major enquiry ordered in 1864 revealed substantial regional and gender differences in literacy levels. According to estimates presented in the *Journal de la Société de Statistique de Paris* in 1866, 90 per cent of children of the appropriate age group attended school in the capital compared with

[187] 7 April 1859, AN F17/2649.
[188] *Notes et souvenirs*, I, pp. 198, 190; S. Horvath-Peterson, *Victor Duruy and French Education. Liberal Reform in the Second Empire* (London 1984), pp. 154–5.
[189] Quoted Maurain, *Politique ecclésiastique*, p. 840.   [190] Duruy, *Notes*, I, pp. 197–8.

76.3 per cent in the provinces. Based as they were on enrolments, these figures concealed, as senior officials realised, considerable irregularities in attendance and low levels of attainment.[191] Poverty and ignorance were closely connected. Even the official statistics in 1865 accepted that around one-third of school leavers were functionally illiterate.[192] Moreover, once they started work in field or factory, many soon forgot their earlier attainments.[193] Considerable progress had been made, however. The training of teachers and the quality of the instruction they provided had improved. The status of education was being transformed rapidly with changing public expectations and aspirations. In 1865 a teacher from Barcelonnette (Basses-Alpes) nevertheless stressed the urgent need for further progress: 'you need to have lived in the midst of the ignorant population of villages lost in the mountains to realise [that] ... between them and populations where the masses have at least some education, the difference is like that between civilised and barbaric nations. There is no restraint, and no respect ... Manners are gross, and their language has a crudeness which surprises people who have lived amongst more advanced populations'. Like his minister this humble teacher looked forward to the inevitable reduction in misery and crime, which would accompany instruction.[194]

Duruy remained especially concerned about the mediocrity of much of the teaching provided by the religious orders as well as their ultramontanism and apparent hostility to modern ideas. He insisted on the need 'to contain both the authorised and non-authorised male teaching congregations, not by harassing or persecuting them, but by forcing them to comply with the law and especially by revitalising lay education'.[195] In a letter to Etienne Conti, the Emperor's friend and secretary, Duruy expressed his concern that 'the bishops are fundamentally attached to the Pope and his policies, which are in absolute contradiction with the ideas and institutions of modern society'. He anticipated that the battle would centre on the schools. Revealing a certain anxiety about his personal situation he hoped earnestly that 'the Emperor will always understand, in spite of the honeyed words falling from certain lips, that the irreconcilable enemies of modern society will always be enemies of the Napoleons who are its representatives'.[196] He further pointed out to General Frossard,

---

[191] E.g. detailed report of PG Rouen, 11 Jan. 1866, AN BB30/387; also responses of schoolteachers in AN F17/10758.
[192] F. Furet and J. Ozouf, *Lire et écrire* (Paris 1977), I, p. 174.
[193] E.g. mayor St Jean du Gard, AN C1160.
[194] Ricame from Lons near Barcelonnette, AN F17/10758; see also Duruy, *Notes*, I, p. 55.
[195] Duruy to Napoleon, 21 April 1866, quoted Horvath-Peterson, *Victor Duruy*, p. 23.
[196] *Papiers sauvés*, ed. Holt, pp. 70-1, undated.

head of the Prince-Imperial's household, that 'the conquest of the young is indispensable ... to the establishment of a dynasty'.[197] Duruy also insisted that 'those who find themselves deprived of the national language are, at the same time, excluded from the life of the nation' and was particularly anxious to reinforce patriotism in frontier regions through the imposition of French in the schools.[198] In a letter to another of the Emperor's friends, Madame Cornu, again Duruy revealed his fundamental hostility towards the church. Equally clear, however, was the gulf between the attitudes of this essentially democratic Bonapartist and those of his more conservative colleagues. He believed that the objective of the clericals was 'to force humanity onto its knees before the Roman idol they assume to be divinely inspired. For them everything descends from on high: for us everything comes from here below, from the depths of our conscience and through reason. There is a great drama being acted out within modern society'.[199] Duruy's major objectives were the establishment of free and obligatory education. His effectiveness would be limited by the Emperor's indecision and failure to support his minister consistently against more conservative colleagues like Rouher, who described Duruy as behaving like a 'bull in a china shop'[200] and were concerned that widening access to instruction would strengthen democratic pressures, alienate clericals, and lead to increased taxation.[201] Nevertheless, even the emasculated legislation finally presented by Duruy to the Corps législatif in 1867 promised considerable improvement in the education of girls, the extension of free instruction for the poor, and better conditions for teachers, and linked both prosperity and political stability to education.[202] In spite of enthusiastic support from the parliamentary committee reporting on his proposals, and influenced by recent Prussian military successes, continued conservative criticism together with budgetary problems would present major obstacles to change. Duruy's eventual dismissal in 1869 would provide the Emperor with a useful means of facilitating reconciliation between the regime and clericals.

EASING THE BURDEN OF POVERTY

If the regime saw moral instruction as the crucially important weapon in the struggle against subversion it also appreciated the importance

---

[197] *Ibid.*, p. 69.   [198] See e.g. Igersheim, *Politique*, pp. 473–82.
[199] Letter from Duruy to Mme Cornu, 26 Sept. 1865, Emerit, *Madame Cornu*, p. 53.
[200] *Ibid.*, pp. 56–7, letter, 14 Oct. 1869.   [201] Gontard, *Ecoles*, pp. 170–1.
[202] *Le Moniteur*, 17 Sept. 1867.

of alleviating misery as a means of reinforcing social order. The Emperor prided himself on his interest in the labouring classes and appears to have been genuinely committed to improving their lot. However, if works like the *Extinction du paupérisme*, published in 1844, established his reputation as a 'socialist', they lacked precise ideas.[203] The Emperor personally supervised the work of the Société du Prince Impérial which, with limited funds, offered advances to impoverished workers to allow them to purchase tools.[204] Homes for small numbers of infirm workers were provided at Vincennes, Le Vésinet, Rouen, and Mulhouse by an 1855 decree. The subject of model housing for the poor was discussed frequently, although with very little practical effect. The *Cité Napoléon*, actually constructed in the rue Rochechouart in Paris would remain unpopular because of its moralising regulations.[205] It was generally agreed that the provision of housing should be left to the market.[206] Furthermore, if the work of urban reconstruction resulted in improvements in public hygiene, widespread indifference on the part of officials and taxpayers to the conditions of the poor continued to represent a major obstacle to improvement. A conservative regime committed to the preservation of social order would produce little specifically social legislation. The notion that governments could intervene to improve the situation of the poor was dismissed from an essentially liberal viewpoint. Thus, although there were some signs of a re-thinking in the interests of rational administration, public order, and even humanity, it was accepted generally that the main burden of assistance would continue to fall on private charity.[207] This was the conclusion of the book on *La Charité et la misère à Paris* published in 1854 by the Emperor's chaplain, the Abbé Mullois. A report from the prefect of Haute-Vienne represented the outlook of those responsible for administering relief, insisting that 'I believe neither in the possibility of curing misery, a malady inseparable from the social body, nor in the right to assistance, nor in the right to work, but I believe firmly in the power of charity to ease suffering'.[208]

If the official instinct was normally to support employers against their workers, most obviously in case of strikes, efforts were sometimes made

[203] E.g. M. Emerit, 'Les sources des idées sociales et coloniales de Napoléon III', *Revue d'Alger* (1945), pp. 429–36.
[204] P. Labracherie, *Napoléon III et son temps* (Paris 1967), p. 112.
[205] J.-P. Bebelon, 'Les cités ouvrières à Paris', *Monuments historiques*, 1977, p. 53.
[206] J. Gaillard, *Paris, la ville* (Paris 1977), p. 74.
[207] See Napoleon, 'Discours à l'ouverture de la session législative', *Le Moniteur*, 4 March 1854.
[208] 30 Sept. 1858, AN F1 cIII Haute-Vienne 11.

to protect workers against 'abuses' and to encourage employers to adopt more conciliatory attitudes. However, an unwillingness to offend the employing classes meant that little effort was made even to enforce existing legislation like that of 1841 on child labour.[209] In response to the impoverishment caused by the poor harvests of 1853/6 the most effective form of action had appeared to be the encouragement of commercial activity. However, the provision of assistance had seemed necessary both in order to alleviate misery and thus prevent disorder and as a means of stimulating public support for the regime. Subsidies were provided to local authorities to assist in the financing of public works and the distribution of charity by community bureaux de bienfaisance. During 1855, for example, the government provided 80,000f to the prefect of the Gers to supplement communal and private subscriptions amounting to 216,000f.[210] Similar assistance was provided to unemployed textile workers during the economic crisis caused by the American Civil War. In the arrondissement of Rouen at the beginning of 1863, 2,754 unemployed workers were taken on by public works projects, although at the very low wage of of75 to 1f50 an hour to encourage them to find regular employment. A further 19,028 people were assisted by the local charitable *bureaux* (around 8,000 more than normal).[211] These distributed assistance in kind and free medicine to paupers (law of 7 August 1851). However, in spite of prefectoral efforts to systematise the distribution of aid, the process remained rather indiscriminate, depending on the discretion of administrators and the resources available locally.[212] Moreover, charity provided a significant means of exercising power within communities.[213] The *bureaux* offered highly restricted access to assistance, disqualifying those with a reputation for laziness, untidiness, keeping a dog, or refusing to admit representatives of the bureaux to their homes *à toute heure*. Failure to respond positively to the 'exhortations' of officials would also lead to disqualification.[214] Those enrolled by the bureaux had no right to assistance. This would only have encouraged idleness.[215] Many rural communes did not even possess *bureaux*, further

---

[209] Prefect, 19 Feb. 1870, AN F1 cIII Nord 16; C. Heywood, *Childhood in Nineteenth Century France* (Cambridge 1988), p. 249.

[210] Prefect, 8 Jan. 1856, AN F1 cIII Gers 8.   [211] PG Rouen, 10 Jan. 1863, AN BB30/387.

[212] See Baron de Watteville, *Rapport à son excellence le Ministre de l'intérieur sur l'administration des bureaux de bienfaisance et sur la situation du paupérisme en France* (Paris 1854); also e.g. Société d'agriculture de Maine-et-Loire, in AN C3078.

[213] E.g. prefect, 20 Jan. 1861, AN F1 cIII Nièvre 9.

[214] E.g. *arrêt* prefect Moselle, 20 Aug. 1853, AN F8/210.

[215] E.g. Société d'agriculture d'Indre, AN C3079.

increasing the private and indiscriminate character of charity.[216] Assistance was far better organised and funded in the larger towns because of fear of disorder.[217] Efforts continued to be made to control bread prices. Crucially, the Caisse de la Boulangerie in Paris ensured that prices in 1853 were at levels 25 per cent below those prevailing in other major cities. These subsidies were supported by the Prefect of Police Pietri as a major contribution to the prevention of disorder but criticised as wasteful by Baroche and Rouher. It took a report by Le Play, which pointed out that bread prices were consistently lower in London and Brussels, due to the absence of regulation, finally to secure abolition of the *caisse*. Even then the government retained considerable reserve powers, reflecting the anxiety of both Haussmann as prefect of Paris and of the Emperor about the social and political impact of freedom of trade in foodstuffs.[218]

The 1852 decree on mutual aid societies offers an example of the kind of social reform likely under a regime committed to economic liberalism, anxious to encourage worker self-help, but also concerned to prevent the development of potentially autonomous institutions. Persigny, influenced by the social Catholic Vicomte Armand de Melun, persuaded the Emperor to accept legislation designed both to impose stricter controls over existing mutual aid societies and to offer them a privileged legal status together with subsidies – initially derived from the sale of the confiscated property of the Orleans family. The Emperor's aim was to encourage the voluntary devotion of the wealthier classes rather than an extension of bureaucratic activity:

mutual aid societies, as I understand them, should have the precious advantage of uniting the different classes of society, of ending the jealousies which exist between them, of neutralising, to a large degree, the results of misery, by bringing together the rich, voluntarily, through the superfluity of their wealth, and the workers through their savings, in an institution in which conscientious workers will find advice and support. This will ... reconcile the classes and moralise individuals.[219]

---

[216] See replies to questionnaire from Commission d'assistance publique dans les campagnes, established in July 1872, AN C3078.

[217] E.g. prefect Pas-de-Calais, report on Oct. 1855, AN F7/4118.

[218] Préfecture de police, *Des moyens de prévenir les fluctuations excessives du prix des blés en France. Examen préalable d'un mémoire sur le compensation des prix extrêmes du pain à Paris* (Paris 1853) and Commission des subsistances, *Taxe du pain. Rapport présenté au nom de la sous-commission par Victor Foucher* (1855) in AN AD XIX S7; Ministère de l'agriculture, *Rapport à l'Empereur sur la boulangerie* (1864), pp. 8, 27; Price, 'Poor relief', p. 444.

[219] Quoted Hatzfeld, *Du paupérisme à la sécurité sociale, 1850–1940* (Paris 1970), p. 283.

Rouher appears to have watered down the scheme originally favoured by Napoleon which involved the obligatory creation of a society in every commune, a proposal denounced by Melun, committed as he was to the voluntary principle, as 'absurd and ... dictatorial'.[220] A Commission supérieure d'encouragement et de surveillance des sociétés de secours mutuels, chaired by Melun, was established. Independent workers' societies had largely been suppressed already. The sphere of activity of newly established associations was to be restricted carefully. For example, they were not to provide unemployment relief because this would have interfered with the free working of the labour market.[221] According to the Emperor in a speech made at Lyons, 'in easing misery, in sympathising with the suffering, mutual aid societies will dismiss envy from the hearts of those afflicted by poverty or illness, they will give to those who live in comfort the means to devotedly do good. It is under this double title that they will always be the object of my warmest solicitude'.[222] Initially the role of the parish priest had been stressed[223] but this conflicted with the Emperor's determination to increase governmental influence within a sphere otherwise largely left to the church and Catholic lay associations, most notably the Société de Saint Vincent de Paul which distributed food, clothing and lessons in morality to the needy.[224] Even before relations between state and church deteriorated, concern was being expressed about the Legitimist sympathies of many of its leading members and their assumption that their social status placed them 'outside administrative control'.[225]

Traditional Christian charity was being updated to meet the needs of an industrialising society. Workers were to be encouraged to work hard and to develop the virtue of thrift in order to make provision for emergencies and old age. Between 31 December 1852 and the end of 1869 the number of 'authorised' mutual aid societies, mainly established before the decree, fell from 2,388 to 1,871 whilst the number of 'approved' societies subject to closer control, with a nominated president and 'honorary' members who would, according to Melun, 'neutralise the danger resulting from association',[226] rose from 50 to 4,398 and their membership

---

[220] B. Ménager, 'Rouher et la politique sociale du second empire' in J.-J. Becker (ed.), *Eugène Rouher* (Clermont-Ferrand 1985), p. 42.

[221] MI circular, 29 May 1852, quoted Hatzfeld, *Pauperisme*, p. 210.

[222] Watteville, *Rapport*, p. 18.   [223] *Ibid.*, p. 20.

[224] E.g. PG Metz, 19 July 1854, AN BB30/380.

[225] PG Nancy, 3 April 1857, AN BB30/381; see also Pietri, Paris Prefect of Police, 21 April 1854, in Maurain, *Baroche*, p. 123.

[226] Quoted Hatzfeld, *Paupérisme*, p. 203.

from 271,000 to 900,000.[227] These were mainly skilled craftsmen earning enough to pay their dues and enjoy greater security in case of illness or injury. Little progress was made amongst the unskilled and the rural population. In addition, and in spite of official efforts, these friendly societies often continued to provide a disguise for trades union activities.[228] Frequently workers resented the heavy-handed paternalism of the 'honorary' members, the 'do-gooders' drawn from officialdom, local elites, employers, and the clergy. It seems evident that Bonapartist social policy was only partially successful. It seems clear also that the Emperor believed that a widely shared prosperity, and the political stability that went with it, could only result from economic modernisation.

[227] Watteville, *Rapport*, p. 21.   [228] E.g. PG Nîmes, 1 Aug. 1855, AN BB30/382.

CHAPTER 7

Creating the conditions for prosperity

INTRODUCTION

Napoleon III assumed that, along with the restoration of public order and the promotion of moral order, prosperity would provide the means of ensuring social harmony. The Emperor's economic advisor, Michel Chevalier, closely reflected his master's views in a pamphlet published in 1853: 'One of the essential conditions for the stability of the state and society is growing social wealth, so that the objects and services which respond to the various human needs increase more rapidly than the population, and each individual is able to gain a better return for his work, and as a result enjoy improved nourishment, better clothing, and warmer, more brightly lit and better-furnished homes.'[1] Indeed, in establishing the level of the public works budget Rouher in 1856 insisted on the threefold objectives of satisfying the 'legitimate' demands of numerous communities, supporting entrepreneurial activity, and providing employment.[2] The Emperor also believed that economic modernisation was essential to the survival of France as a great power. He was determined to emulate Britain, the model of a modern society and a country he knew well and admired. Together with some of his closest advisors he shared a progressivist and nationalistic ideology, which ascribed a positive economic role to the state. The rapid completion of the primary rail network and the programme of urban reconstruction were the clearly defined objectives of an Emperor determined to launch and to sustain his regime on a wave of prosperity. Amongst historians a relatively positive view of the regime's economic achievements has emerged since the pioneering studies of railway construction by Marcel Blanchard in the 1930s and Louis Girard's massive volume on public works published in

---

[1] Quoted Caron, *La France*, p. 37.
[2] Ministère de l'agriculture, du commerce et des travaux publics, Rapport à Sa Majesté l'Empereur, 30 Nov. 1856, AN F14/8508A.

1951. According to Alain Plessis this was 'the first regime to have given such distinct priority to economic objectives.' It saw the 'birth of modern France'.[3]

Certainly this was an unprecedently interventionist regime. However, a distinction has been made between the 'creative' 1850s and the less dynamic decade which followed. Initially massive investment in railways and other forms of transport afforded a considerable stimulus to mining, engineering, and metallurgy, to the expansion of internal demand for both foodstuffs and manufactures, and to inter-regional competition and the development of the financial and commercial sectors. Then growth slowed, due to a combination of accidental factors like the American Civil War and the cotton crisis it caused as well as the confidence-shaking impact of changes in both the internal and international political situations. This contrast is meaningful but can be overdone. In general the Imperial years were characterised by the acceleration of structural change in the economy, as the rate of growth of the more 'modern' sectors – transport, banking, metallurgy and engineering, coal, some branches of textiles – consistently outpaced that of traditional sectors. Measuring the impact of government policy on the economy is a thankless task, given the range of variables involved. However, following the mid-century crisis, renewed political stability and the restoration of business confidence certainly facilitated recovery. International conditions were also favourable, with trade stimulated by the growth in money supply which followed gold discoveries in Australia and California. The onset of a long period of price inflation encouraged investment. The growing impact of the major market-integrating and productivity-increasing innovations associated with railway construction and factory mechanisation were powerful stimuli. The industrial economy is estimated to have shrunk by 1.83 per cent per annum between 1845 and 1850, before growing by 3.87 per cent a year between 1850 and 1855 and experiencing sustained growth thereafter – by 2.36 per cent between 1855 and 1860 and 2.19 per cent between 1860 and 1865, but with a marked deceleration in the difficult closing years of the regime when growth slowed to 1.16 per cent per annum.[4] Overall, the rate of growth does not appear to have been any more rapid than during the July Monarchy, which might suggest that market forces rather than state policy were the decisive element shaping long-term economic change. Nevertheless, the determination of the regime to promote 'industrialisation' helped shape the process. The social impact of economic

3 Plessis, *Second Empire*, pp. 62, 58.
4 T. J. Markovitch 'L'industrie française de 1789 à 1964', *Cahiers de l'ISEA* (1965–6), p. 123.

Table 5. *Net national product (millions of gold francs)*[a]

Year	1847	1872
Net agricultural product	5,153	8,267
Net industrial product	8,194	10,059
Tertiary activities	3,636	5,883
Total	16,983	24,209

[a] J. Bouvier, 'Le mouvement d'une civilisation nouvelle' in G. Duby, *Histoire de la France* (Paris 1972), III, p. 41.

change was similarly complex. New opportunities were created for many businessmen and farmers but within a rapidly changing environment. Improved communications resulted in a widespread perception that, 'the old and the new situations are incomparable: everything has changed.'[5] Change and the uncertainty it caused threatened existing relationships, and created the conditions for an ongoing *crise d'adaptation*. Therefore, the impact has to be assessed not only in statistical terms, which is difficult enough, but also by considering the psychological–behavioural effects.

Calculations of national production provide an impression of rising prosperity although they do not take into account the very unequal sharing of the wealth created (see table 5).

In volume terms, that is, correcting (roughly) for rising prices in agriculture and declining industrial prices, production probably increased by around 40 per cent and 45 per cent respectively. The substantial growth in the tertiary sector (especially transport) offers another insight into structural change in the economy. The rise in consumer demand, estimated to be of the order of 25 to 30 per cent between 1850 and 1870, provides a further indicator of rising prosperity.[6] It was certainly hoped that this would attenuate social tension and secure public order. Officials were required to provide regular and detailed assessments of the economic situation. Economic depression invariably caused grave concern.[7] The regime was anxious to claim the credit for prosperity and only too aware that it would be blamed for recession.

5 Ministère de l'agriculture, du commerce et des travaux publics *Enquête agricole 2e série. 5e circonscription Pas-de-Calais* (Paris 1867), p. 132.
6 J. Desmarest, 'L'état économique de la France à la fin du second empire', *Revue des travaux de l'Académie des sciences morales et politiques*, 1967, pp. 233–5.
7 E.g. sous-préfet Châteaubriant to Min. d'Agric, 29 Feb. 1856, AN F20/714.

Table 6. *Structure of tax receipts*

Structure of tax receipts	Percentage in 1850	Percentage in 1871
Taxes on income	30.9	21.3
Taxes on wealth	22.1	26.7
Taxes on consumption	47	52

Consideration of the policies developed to stimulate economic growth provides insights into the system of government as well as explanations of disagreement within the political and social elites. There was general agreement on the responsibility of the state for national defence and the protection of internal order. There was also a general acceptance of the need for the regulatory frameworks provided by the legal system. The expanding role of the state in the provision of education and of a modern communications infrastructure was again generally welcomed. However, the wider debate on economic policy was always likely to provoke disagreement, both within government and with the representatives of major economic interest groups. The main cause was to be tariff policy with the regime accused of sacrificing important interests by reducing protection in order to force the pace of modernisation. Nevertheless, in spite of efforts to enhance the security of the poor, this was a regime which was primarily committed to safeguarding the interests of the wealthy. Nowhere was this more evident than in the taxation system. Taxation was regarded as an unfortunate necessity, to be kept to a minimum. Most of the burden was imposed on the poorer classes through indirect taxes on consumption, whilst enlarging the tax privileges enjoyed by the wealthy (see table 6).[8]

The rates at which direct taxes were levied were low and fell disproportionately on property. Thus the system favoured those whose incomes were derived from rents and especially business profits, stocks, and shares. The more effective taxation of incomes would have required a level of intervention in individuals' private lives which contemporary opinion would have found intolerable. In this respect Duruy, who favoured replacing indirect taxes with income tax, as a matter of social justice,[9] was

---

[8] Bouvier, 'Sur l'immobilisme du système fiscal français', *Revue d'histoire économique et sociale* (1972), p. 483.
[9] Duruy letter to Mme Cornu, 14 Oct. 1869, in Emerit, *Madame Cornu*, pp. 56–7.

clearly out on a limb. This hands-off taxation policy was accompanied by deregulation with a substantial easing of the formalities necessary to establish a joint stock company, in May 1863 and July 1867. This was in marked contrast with previous restrictive legislation, which had emphasised the need to protect the public against speculative activity and fraud. The government had decided that urgent change was necessary to facilitate the accumulation of the capital necessary for industrial modernisation.[10] Ending imprisonment for debt further eased the pressures on businessmen.[11] Whilst subscribing to the ideals of economic liberalism, landowners and businessmen were anxious to secure government intervention when they judged this to be in their particular interests. In practice, policies designed to enhance prosperity and increase support for the regime frequently had the effect of stimulating the rise of opposition. For our purposes, these policies can be considered conveniently under three main headings – investment in communications and urban renewal; expansion of the financial sector; and economic liberalisation.

THE DEVELOPMENT OF COMMUNICATIONS

Introduced in 1842, the basic law on railway construction[12] provided for a sharing of the cost of construction between the state – responsible for the infrastructure, especially the track – and concessionary companies which were to provide the superstructure (stations, rolling stock, etc.). This represented a compromise between the supporters of a state railway system and those of private enterprise. To prevent the establishment of over-powerful companies the scale of the concessions was restricted initially. In the years that followed, construction was slowed by unexpectedly high costs and concern amongst investors that the concessionary period of forty-six years was insufficient to secure a reasonable return on their investments. The mid-century crisis had virtually brought construction to a halt.

Louis-Napoleon Bonaparte was clearly committed to railway construction, to engineering projects on an unprecedented scale, which seemed to offer the vital means of modernising the economy and

---

[10] D. Sherman, 'Governmental responses to economic modernisation in mid 19th century France', *Journal of European Economic History* (1977), p. 729 and 'Government policy toward joint-stock business organisation in mid 19th-century France', *Journal of European Economic History* (1974), pp. 163–5; C.Freedeman, *The Triumph of Corporate Capitalism* (London 1993), p. 130.

[11] Ménager, 'Rouher et la politique sociale', pp. 46–7.

[12] On rail construction see especially F. Caron, *Histoire des chemins de fer en France, 1740–1883* (Paris 1997); see also Price, *Modernisation*.

particularly the key coal, metallurgical, and heavy engineering industries.[13] This technocratic romanticism was at the heart of the regime's economic policy. It was not uncommon for government engineers to compare the railways and the roads leading to them with 'Prometheus' fire' through which 'the body is animated and life circulates in the newly created arteries',[14] and to claim proudly that 'the railway, with steam navigation and the electric telegraph are the most faithful expression of the massive progress achieved during this century'.[15] Immediately after the *coup d'état* a decree extended concessions to ninety-nine years.[16] The change facilitated long-term investment plans and reductions in both costs and charges. Rapid decision-making by small groups of ministers, civil servants, and railway company directors, was in marked contrast to the delays imposed, under previous regimes, by lengthy parliamentary procedures. Magne, Minister of Public Works, wrote, towards the end of 1852, that 'the immense improvements accomplished in a year ... are the most striking evidence of the confidence inspired by the Emperor, and the incredible development of the public credit which has been the happy result'.[17] The rate of construction of the railway network accelerated. From some 4,000 km in discontinuous sections, operated by seventeen companies, the length of track rose to 9,500 km by 1860 with a further 17,000 km of construction approved. By 1870 nearly 20,000 km were in use.[18] The government's role in this was substantial – approving concessions, providing a legal framework for rail operation, partially funding construction, promoting the amalgamation of small companies into larger and financially stronger regional units, and providing financial guarantees to secure extension of the network into economically less attractive areas. The engineers of the state corps des ponts et chaussées played a crucial role in the planning and technical and organisational development of technological systems of unparalleled complexity, developing rapidly, and on an unprecedented scale. It has been estimated that the railway network promoted an increase in the volume of trade of the order of 101 per cent between 1851 and 1863

---

[13] See e.g. Barbier, *Finance*, p. 179.
[14] G. Marqfoy, *De l'abaissement des tarifs de chemins de fer en France* (Paris 1863), p. 110.
[15] Conseil général du dépt. du Nord. Session de 1858. *Rapport sur la navigation intérieure par M. F. Kuhlmann*, p. 14, AN F12/6848B.
[16] F. Caron, *Histoire de l'exploitation d'un grand réseau* (Paris 1973), pp. 45–6.
[17] Quoted E. Labrousse, *Aspects de l'évolution économique et sociale de la France et du Royaume-Uni de 1815 à 1880* (Paris 1949), p. 71.
[18] F. Caron, 'L'évolution du régime français des chemins de fer' in *Les chemins de fer, l'espace et la société en France* (Paris 1989), p. 17.

and 248 per cent over the period 1851–82.[19] The reform of customs tariffs, on which historians have focused so much attention, partly because of the availability of easily accessible statistical information, was far less significant in its impact on the marketing and price of a key resource like coal, for example, than was improved transport. Thus the pithead price per quintal is estimated to have fallen by around 15 centimes due to tariff reductions and by 2 to 6f due to rail construction.[20]

It would be difficult to satisfy the rising expectations of transport users, however. Throughout the country the railway was seen as the potential source of prosperity. Demands for new lines or stations flooded into government offices. Easy access to the railway appeared to be the key to the future.[21] As the mayor of Provins pointed out, in an anguished memo, to be 9 km from the nearest station threatened total disaster for his town's grain market and flourmills.[22] Official candidates for election could do nothing better to enhance their prospects than promise a branch line or railway station.[23] Of course, priorities were always difficult to establish.[24] Particular care had to be taken with representations from powerful interest groups. For both economic and political reasons, however, the regime felt bound to respond to what was an emerging social need. The concessions agreed in 1852 and 1863 by Magne and his successor Rouher established six companies, each with a regional monopoly, in return for which each company agreed on new construction. As a further sweetener the state agreed to complex conventions negotiated between 1858 and 1863 which, in specified circumstances, would guarantee subsidies to the railway companies. In return the companies, anxious to exclude competitors from their zones of influence, agreed that their dividends should not rise above the levels prevailing in 1857, and that earnings above this level would serve to cross-subsidise the secondary networks the government was determined to see constructed. Where exploitation of these new networks had an adverse impact on company finances and dividends threatened to fall below 1857 levels state guarantees would take effect. Only in the event of earnings on the primary networks falling

---

[19] Lequin, 'La France, une et indivisible' in Lequin (ed.), *Histoire des français*, p. 115.
[20] L. Girard, *La politique des travaux publics du second empire* (Paris 1952), pp. 242–3.
[21] Point made by e.g. Prefect, 11 May 1853, AN F1 cIII Tarn 12, re Grand Central; see also e.g. petition from mayor of Wasquehal (Nord) to Emperor, 23 Sept. 1853, AN 48 AQ 3707.
[22] Chemin de fer de Paris à Mulhouse. Ville de Provins. Mémoire présenté par le Conseil municipal 1854, AN C1072.
[23] E.g. Petition from deputies of Indre, Indre-et-Loire, and Allier, 12 June 1861, AN C1072.
[24] E.g. Conseil d'Etat, Session 1868. 'Exposé des motifs d'un projet de loi relatif à l'exécution de plusieurs chemins de fer', AN cI 125.

below 1857 levels, which appeared extremely unlikely, would company dividends be allowed to fall.[25] Between 1865 and 1869 these guarantees cost the state 112 million francs, whilst the companies themselves spent 168 million francs covering the deficits of the new networks.[26]

The security these arrangements offered proved very attractive to investors, particularly when combined with the potential profitability of networks like the Nord, Est, Paris–Lyon–Marseille (PLM), and Paris–Orleans (PO). Renewed business confidence in the wake of the *coup d'état* had anyway encouraged a speculative boom. In an editorial in the *Journal des chemins de fer* (7 December 1851) Mirès welcomed the *coup*, adding that 'already important men are meeting to give firm support to the government in the development of public works'. The shares of the sixteen largest companies, which had been worth 592 million francs on 1 December 1851, rose to 809 million by 1 June 1852.[27] Financial groups easily raised capital, at least until the international financial crisis of 1857. The established *haute banque*, represented by the Rothschilds and Talabots, enjoyed considerable advantages. The proposed construction of the Grand Central, intended to unblock the natural resources of the Massif Central, offered a last opportunity for their rivals the Pereire brothers and their Crédit mobilier investment bank to fight for a share. However, this was always going to be a risky commercial venture. It appealed to investors on the basis of very optimistic assumptions about traffic, and was essentially a speculative venture, which benefited considerably from the political support of the arch-speculator Morny. The acquisition of its lines, by the other railway companies, under pressure from the government, would be a great relief for its shareholders.[28] On 5 January 1860, an Imperial letter promised further massive investment in the transport infrastructure, presenting this as the essential means of preparing the economy for the heightened competition, which would follow the treaty of commerce with Britain. The promise was generally welcomed, although it probably did little to satisfy rising expectations.[29]

During the course of their negotiations over railway concessions, increasingly close and cosy relationships developed between ministers,

[25] See F. Jacqmin, *De l'exploitation des chemins de fer. Leçons faites en 1867 à l'Ecole impériale des ponts et chaussées*, II (Paris 1868), p. 16; Girard, *Politique*, pp. 172–3, 191–200.

[26] Girard, 'Politique,' p. 293.   [27] *Ibid.*, p. 86.

[28] Barbier, *Finance*, pp. 183–4; Grothe, *Morny*, pp. 150–63; N. Ferguson, *The World's Banker. The History of the House of Rothschild* (London 1998), pp. 494–6.

[29] E.g. Comité des houillères du Pas-de-Calais, *Résumé des mémoires des cies. du bassin houiller du Pas-de-Calais en réponse au questionnaire qui leur a été adressé par le Comité central des houillères de France à Paris* (Arras 1866), p. 4.

senior civil servants like Franqueville, and financiers and entrepreneurs like Bartholony and Talabot. Although ministerial approval was required for the charges levied on freight and passengers, in practice officials tended to accept company proposals.[30] In doing so they risked provoking complaints about the monopoly powers of the railways and closed decision-making processes. In general, the increasing efficiency of railway operations, together with pressure on the companies from ministers anxious to reduce transport costs, ensured that users enjoyed considerable benefits. Rail charges fell substantially, especially in the 1850s.[31] Nevertheless, in increasingly competitive markets, some enterprises, communities, and regions were always likely to be at a disadvantage. As a result the railway companies were subject to constant criticism for their tariff policies as was the government, which accepted their charges.[32] For example, both coal-mining and agricultural interests were hostile to differential freight rates, which facilitated import penetration.[33] Other grounds for criticism included the repeated inability of companies, coping with unexpectedly rapid growth in demand, to provide a sufficient number of trains as well as adequate station facilities. The rising expectations of users in respect of speed and regularity were also difficult to satisfy.[34] To the extreme irritation of users, government engineers, such as the influential Jacqmin, could generally be relied on to appreciate fully the technical problems faced by the railway companies.[35]

Radiating from Paris, the railway substantially reinforced the economic and cultural influence of the capital, as well as the processes of political and administrative centralisation. Moreover, alongside the railway network another technological marvel took root. The electric

---

[30] E.g. Ministère des T. P., '2e note sur les transports de minerai et de houille pour la fabrication du fer par les voies navigables et les chemins de fer.' Undated but *c.* 1860, AN F12/2484.

[31] Price, *Modernization*, pp. 269–71; J. Gaillard, 'Notes sur l'opposition au monopole des compagnies de chemins de fer entre 1850 et 1860', *1848*, 1950, pp. 235–45.

[32] E.g. PG Nancy, 3 Feb. 1853, AN BB30/381 and for consideration of relatively disadvantaged regions C. Johnson, *The Life and Death of Industrial Languedoc, 1700–1920* (Oxford 1995), ch. 7; L. Wirth, *Un équilibre perdu.* (Clermont-Ferrand 1996), ch. 8; P. Cornu, *Une économie rurale dans la débâcle. Evolution démographique, économique et sociale du monde paysan dans le Cantal au 19ᵉ siècle* (Paris 1993), part II, ch. 2

[33] E.g. Comité des houillères françaises, *Note sur l'importation des houilles étrangères en France* (Paris 1859); Comité des houillères de la Loire, *Observations sur la réponse de la Cie. des chemins de fer PLM ... relative à l'amélioration des moyens de transport pour les houilles de ce basin* (Saint-Etienne 1860); on agriculture see Price, *Modernization*, ch. 9.

[34] E.g. Ministère des TP to MJ, 9 April 1853, AN BB30/381; also F. Kuhlmann on behalf of Lille Chamber of Commerce to Min. des TP, 12 Oct. 1866, AN F1 cIII Nord 16.

[35] See e.g. Jacqmin, *De l'exploitation*, II, p. 35, 117; Marqfoy, *De l'abaissement des tarifs*, pp. 71–5.

telegraph was vital to the control of the railways themselves but rapidly also became indispensable to the commercial and banking communities and to the press, none of which had previously been allowed to use the official semaphore system. The telegraph offered a high-capacity means for the rapid transmission of official and commercial information. The first trial line, Paris–Rouen, had been opened in 1844. Construction was slow initially but accelerated after 1851. During his brief occupation of the Interior Ministry in 1852 Morny had noted the low density of the French network compared with those of its neighbours and insisted that, regardless of the regime's financial situation, investment in the telegraph must be given priority.[36] By January 1855 all mainland prefectures were linked to Paris and work had begun on the establishment of a telegraph office in every canton. The length of the network grew from 2,133 km in 1851 to 40,118 by 1869 whilst, as charges fell, the number of telegrams sent rose from 9,014 to 4,754,000.[37] The far less expensive postal service also developed rapidly following the introduction of a fixed-rate 25-centime stamp in 1848. This provided another key means of state controlled communication. As the service spread to every commune the number of stamps sold increased from 21,232,665 in 1849 to 438,219,000 by 1866.[38] Improved communications meant that completion of the centuries-old process of centralisation came considerably closer.

In common with its predecessors, but now with a much greater sense of urgency, the regime also committed itself to improving the roads.[39] In particular, a considerable effort was made to open up the countryside and provide access to railway stations. These were measures greatly appreciated by rural voters, although complaints about the slowness of improvement continued to pour in.[40] Expenditure on roads and bridges varied between 33.8 million and 35.7 million in the 1850s and 39.4 and 45.2 in the 1860s,[41] but, as officials were only too aware, the resources available for road improvement would never be sufficient to

[36] Morny, letter to Prince-President, published in *Moniteur universel*, 7 Jan. 1852.
[37] A. Picard, *Les chemins de fer. Aperçus historiques* (Paris 1918), p. 236. See also E. Pélicier (sous-chef de bureau, MI), *Statistique de la télégraphie privée depuis son origine en France* (Paris 1858).
[38] Arago, *Les postes*, p. 59.
[39] See Ministère de l'agriculture, Bureau des subsistances, 'Chemins vicinaux, chemins d'intérêt commun', 31 July 1867, providing a résumé of complaints made to the 1866 agricultural enquiry. Also, undated 'Note sur l'achèvement des chemins vicinaux' – in AN 45 AP 24; Price, *Modernisation*, pp. 259–74.
[40] See e.g. *Enquête agricole*, IX (Paris 1869), p. 27, Allier. [41] Girard, *La politique*, p. 325.

satisfy perceived needs.[42] The traffic censuses of 1852 and 1857 revealed that road traffic had not declined as a result of rail competition, but was being displaced from parallel onto feeder routes.[43] Waterways were also improved, particularly to serve the coalfields of northern and central France, and as a means of ensuring some competition for the railways. According to the minutes of a meeting of the General Council of the Ponts et Chaussées on 12 July 1858, the waterways were 'the only effective restraint on the power of the railways'.[44] Expenditure rose from 18.7 million in 1853 to a peak of 28.6 million in 1862 before falling back to 14.4 in 1869. Traffic increased to a maximum of 2,225 million tonnes around 1866, by which time the railways were transporting 5,825 million tonnes.[45] Purchase of canals by the state (laws of 28 July, 1 August 1860) and their administration as a sort of public service was another means of responding to pressure-group demands for the reduction of freight charges.[46] However, outside the north and east, geography and engineering problems, as well as lack of traffic, discouraged investment and provoked frequent complaints about the neglect of waterways like the Loire, which had been so recently a major element in the transport network.[47] From 1859 substantial sums were also invested in improving the major ports, a development which, along with the configuration of the rail network, promoted a substantial concentration of seaborne trade.

URBAN RENEWAL

A further area of close collaboration between government and financial elites was the unprecedented programme of urban renewal. In spite of the piecemeal efforts of previous governments, by the middle of the century Paris was crowded and smelly, its streets cluttered with human excrement, garbage, and horse droppings. Circulation, whether on foot or by carriage, was difficult along badly paved, narrow, and ill-lit roads. The

---

[42] E.g. MI, *Rapport à S. M. l'Empereur sur le service des chemins vicinaux pendant la période quinquennale de 1852 à 1856* (Paris 1858), p. 22; Conseil général du Nord, *Rapport sur les chemins vicinaux de grande communication par M. Mailliet* (Lille 1863).

[43] M. Vallès (Ingénieur en chef des Ponts et chaussées du dépt. de l'Aisne), *Des chemins de fer et des routes impériales au point de vue de l'importance de leurs transports respectifs* (Laon 1857).

[44] Same point made in Conseil d'Etat, *Enquête sur la révision de la législation des céréales* (Paris 1859), II, p. 6, evidence of M. Darblay.

[45] Girard, *La politique*, pp. 214, 301.

[46] See Comité des houillères du Pas-de-Calais, *Pétition au sénat pour la suppression des droits de navigation* (Arras 1863).

[47] E.g. Comité des houillères françaises, *Pétition au Sénat pour l'exécution d'un canal latéral à la Loire de Châtillon à l'embouchure de la Maine* (Paris 1862).

warren of narrow streets which made up its centre – where aristocratic palaces had been abandoned by their former owners and, together with a mass of less elegant buildings, subdivided into workshops and increasingly crowded accommodation – supported a dense accumulation of artisans and casual labourers. The population of 1,234,000 within the city limits of 1846 would rise to around 1,980,000 by 1870, largely as a result of in-migration. The presence of growing numbers of desperately poor people, the visitations of cholera, as well as the threat of revolution, promoted a deep sense of insecurity amongst 'respectable' citizens as well as a growing determination that something ought to be done to improve this degraded environment, from which not even the wealthy could escape entirely. The prefect of the Rhône observed similarly that Lyons and especially its older quarters were composed largely of narrow streets bordered by tall buildings, which prevented the penetration of light and air. Many of these properties were in an advanced state of dilapidation, their sanitary facilities almost negligible. However, Lyons was no worse in these respects than other large cities and the prefect insisted that only radical action involving demolition and reconstruction on a massive scale would really improve the situation.[48] Even Rouher whose relations with Haussmann were generally tense would point out to the prefect's critics that 'it was impossible to conserve the old Paris ... in the presence of such a rapid increase in the population'.[49] In this respect urban reconstruction was a response to demographic and economic pressure as well as to social fear and fitted into a general European movement. Urban renewal and the development of industry and the services appear to have occurred on a scale sufficient to provide work for most newcomers to the city. The 'dangerous class', Marx's lumpenproletariat – that mass of un-and under-employed people, living in extreme misery and frequently resorting to crime, so characteristic of the pre-industrial city – rapidly declined in numbers. The disappearance of dearth after the mid-1850s sharply reduced insecurity. These were the developmental processes, resulting in rapid improvements in living conditions, for which the regime was able to claim credit.

Napoleon and Haussmann and their advisers were certainly able to exert a substantial influence on the timing and characteristics of urban change. Within a remarkably few years the promiscuous, febrile capital, with its seething street life, was to be transformed into a bourgeois-dominated city. Louis-Napoleon had long dreamed of re-building Paris

[48] 14 Oct. 1852 in AN F8/210; on Lyons see e.g. Robert, *Les chemins*, ch. VI.
[49] 11 April 1867 in Schnerb, *Rouher*, p. 74.

and constructing a capital suitable for a modern empire. As Persigny remembered – 'what he saw most clearly was that major works were necessary in Paris in order to improve the conditions of the popular classes, to destroy unhealthy *quartiers*, and to make the capital the most beautiful city in the world; all things he ardently desired and never ceased to recommend to us'.[50] Bonaparte's election to the presidency encouraged him to contemplate more concrete projects, beginning with completion of the rue de Rivoli that his uncle had planned to link the Louvre to the Hôtel-de-Ville. He was profoundly annoyed by the reluctance of the prefect of the Seine, Berger, to engage the city in the necessary financial commitments, and replaced him with Haussmann, an official whose air of ruthlessness certainly appealed to Persigny. Haussmann would describe himself always as the executant of the Emperor's will. In his *Memoirs* he remembered how, following his appointment to the Paris prefecture in June 1853, the Emperor had shown him a map of Paris on which he had marked the major new boulevards, which would open up the city.[51] The special nature of the relationship between the Emperor and his prefect would be emphasised in 1860 with the latter's appointment to the Council of Ministers. Above all, Haussmann contributed a systematic approach to urban renewal, which involved careful planning, and the collaboration of highly competent specialists like the engineers Belgrand and Alphand. He would devote seventeen years to overcoming the complex practical and financial obstacles to the realisation of the Emperor's dreams. As with the railways, state initiative would again be closely associated with private enterprise, an alliance celebrated by such splendid ceremonies as that for the opening of the boulevard de Sébastopol in 1858 – an opportunity to mark both the regime's civil and military achievements. The new thoroughfares, each focusing on major public buildings and monuments or on the reconstructed railway stations, together with their gas lighting, street furniture, and public gardens, conformed to a coherent urban plan. They provided for the easier circulation of traffic within the city centre, between the railway stations – 'this new symbol of a new society' – as well as with the suburbs and beyond.[52] Many contemporaries condemned the destruction of the old city's picturesque medieval streets and their replacement with broad and 'soulless' boulevards 12 to 24 metres wide, with spacious pavements and uniformly aligned buildings. If architects took advantage of the new iron

[50] Quoted Caron, *La France*, p. 39.   [51] *Mémoires*, III, pp. iv, 5.

[52] César Daly quoted H. Maneglier, *Paris impériale. La vie quotidienne sous le Second Empire* (Paris 1990), pp. 134–5.

girders for their construction, they also developed a highly ornamental and pompous neo-classical style, which fashion and bureaucratic taste would impose on city centres throughout France. Other observers accepted that the reconstruction of the capital was one of the glories of the Empire. The 1867 International Exposition provided an opportunity to reveal the glittering new city to the world.

The boulevards and new parks would allow air to flow and provide space – in the Bois de Boulogne, for example – for the fashionable to circulate. The population of the poorer *quartiers* would be encouraged to enjoy civilised family recreation in the park created amongst the quarries of the Buttes Chaumont. As part of the cleansing process, reconstruction also provided an opportunity to improve public hygiene through slum clearance, improved water supply, and the construction of a considerably enlarged sewer network, although this would take many decades to complete. This was an aspect of urban renewal which appears to have interested Haussmann far more than the Emperor. By 1870, 400 km of sewers, planned by the city engineer Dupuit, were constructed and the existing 150 km renovated. A decree-law of 26 March 1852 required that all new buildings should be linked to the sewers and, with a little wishful thinking, that this should be applied to existing buildings within ten years. In an effort to end dependence on the grossly corrupted and cholera-bearing water from wells and the Seine, 850 km of water conduits were laid. This massive increase in the supply of water allowed the cleansing of people and the flushing away of human waste and was clearly the key to improved sanitation.[53] In addition, as the city engineer responsible for water supply pointed out, 'we need to modify our habits, replace the petty-minded way in which we use water with much greater use of this element of life and domestic salubrity, and adopt those practices of bodily hygiene so important to good health.'[54]

Urban planning also sought to cleanse the city through functional and social segregation.[55] Re-development confirmed the division between the centre and the west dominated by the well-to-do and the poorer north, east, and south into which poured both new immigrants and people expelled from the centre by demolitions and rising rents. The pace of slum clearance accelerated, with 30,000 demolitions in the 1860s compared with 3,000 in the previous decade, but only 1,200 of

[53] E.g. Ville de Paris, Commission des logements insalubres, *Rapport général des travaux de la commission pendant les années 1862–5* (Paris 1866), p. 17.
[54] Quoted Maneglier, *Paris*, p. 108.
[55] See Haussmann's report on 1857 elections, in Blayau, *Billault*, pp. 397–9.

the displaced were offered some form of cheap subsidised housing.[56] For the masses Haussmann's work only intensified an already severe housing crisis. Property owners were able to take advantage of scarcity and charge high rents, substantially adding to social tension. Certainly urban renewal provided those who could afford the rents with more spacious and comfortable accommodation. The poor, who needed to live close to their work, however, were crowded into the older streets, which survived behind the boulevards. In the Marais, for example, space continued to be divided and subdivided for personal and commercial use. Artisans and workers moved into less central areas like the faubourgs du Temple, de Saint-Marceau, and Saint-Antoine, or were simply pushed out into more peripheral parts of the city. Suburban areas like Belleville experienced a largely uncontrolled in-filling of empty plots with tenements and industrial premises and little concern for public hygiene.[57] The only real effort to come to terms with these problems involved the annexation of large suburban areas by the city in 1860 in order to facilitate the extension of administrative control. In very practical terms, Haussmann had judged unacceptable 'the inconvenience resulting from the ... formation on the outskirts of major cities of independent agglomerations, parasitic accretions which live off these cities without contributing to the costs' and whose unplanned development and networks of unpaved streets obstructed routes out of the city.[58] Order had to be imposed on areas which were notoriously under-policed and suspected of harbouring criminal gangs, and in spite of the opposition of manufacturers who would subsequently be required to pay the municipal tax (*octroi*) on the entry of raw materials into the city.[59]

The twin threats of revolution and disease, so often linked in bourgeois social imagery, were thus to be destroyed. This was an 'eminently strategic programme' according to Haussmann.[60] Even if strategic concerns were of secondary importance in determining the shape of the new city centre, it would have been surprising, in the aftermath of a bloody civil war, if they had not assumed considerable importance. Buildings like the Tuileries Palace or the Hôtel-de-Ville needed to be rescued from the encroaching popular *quartiers*. The Ile de la Cité was virtually cleared of all save public buildings. Broad new boulevards, more difficult to barricade and

[56] Caron, *La France*, p. 41.
[57] E.g. M. Roncaylo, 'La production de la ville' in Agulhon (ed.), *Histoire de la France urbaine*, IV (Paris 1983), p. 119.
[58] Quoted Maneglier, *Paris*, p. 47.
[59] 'Enquête sur l'extension des limites de la ville de Paris 1859' – in AN F2 II Seine 36.
[60] Quoted Caron, *La France*, p. 268.

with barracks strategically placed at crossroads, provided for the easy movement of troops. By the end of 1860 the traditionally revolutionary faubourg Saint-Antoine had been imprisoned deliberately within a circle of avenues meeting in the Place de la Bastille at one end and the Place de la Nation at the other.[61] These massive construction projects had the added advantage of providing work on a substantial scale. Prosperity and order went together. The additional objectives were supervision, control and, if need be, repression.

A similar combination of demographic and political factors promoted urban reconstruction in the provinces, and most notably in Bordeaux, in industrial Lille where population doubled in twenty years, and in Lyon, which experienced 85 per cent growth. There, Vaïsse, a prefect with powers of initiative similar to those of Haussmann, encouraged the municipal authorities and private developers to create vast open spaces and new boulevards in the city centre and along the quays. In Marseilles, where the number of inhabitants increased by 70 per cent, the rue Impériale, largely financed by the Pereire brothers, was driven through the old city in the 1860s. Many smaller towns and villages also constructed scaled-down public buildings in the various architectural styles associated with the *fête impériale*, as well as boulevards to link their centres with the railway station. Again, reconstruction was invariably only partial, leaving large areas packed with desperately poor people living in overcrowded and unhygienic conditions.

These massive projects, which created the modern appearance of so many French towns and cities, were criticised on aesthetic but above all on financial grounds. The realisation of such ambitious projects depended on a combination of political willpower and the mobilisation of both public and private capital, with the main burden to be borne by the various municipalities. On the initiative of Persigny, the city of Paris had already been authorised to borrow 50 million francs by a law of 4 August 1851. However, opposition to tax increases required new initiatives.[62] Haussmann assumed that municipal revenues would be increased substantially by the additional values created by the growth in economic activity. The creation of the Caisse des Travaux de Paris by decree on 14 November 1858, with the right to issue short-term bonds, was intended to ensure future funding and represented, from the prefect's point of view, a great improvement on previous hand-to-mouth dependence on budget deficits and extraordinary loans. To this could be added income from the re-sale

---

[61] Gaillard, *Paris*, p. 39.   [62] See Haussmann, *Mémoires*, III, p. iv.

of properties acquired through compulsory purchase as well as direct government subsidies which covered one-third of the expense of constructing the major Paris boulevards, and even two-thirds in the case of some prestigious projects around the Tuileries and Louvre. These methods had the added advantage of reducing the possibility of interference by deputies. As late as 1865 Haussmann still felt able to float substantial loans (in this case for 270 million francs) virtually without consultation. Continued success depended, however, on stable political and economic conditions as well as the solvency of concessionary companies like the Compagnie Immobilière de Paris.[63]

Even during the 1850s there was considerable resentment of the absence of parliamentary control over such substantial public-works expenditure. Haussmann had become the symbol of authoritarian government, and was condemned even by its habitual supporters including, ominously, many deputies representing rural constituencies. Provincial taxpayers bitterly resented paying for the embellishment of the capital.[64] Haussmann's authoritarian behaviour, questionable financial methods, and doubtful accounting became the target for criticism by jealous ministers and officials of the Conseil d'Etat and Cour des Comptes, all anxious to control his initiatives. Support by the Conseil d'Etat for grossly inflated compensation claims by expropriated property owners could even be seen as a form of revenge. Haussmann's close association with the activities of groups like the Pereire brothers' Société Immobilière encouraged suspicion of illicit speculation which reached its height when, during the 1867 recession, the value of its property portfolio declined, with serious consequences for many investors in the Société itself and in its close associate the Crédit foncier. Such pillars of the orthodox financial establishment as Rothschild and Fould supported criticism in the liberal press – by Léon Say in the *Journal des Débats*, Eugène Forcade and Jules Ferry in *Le Temps* and the *Revue des Deux Mondes*. By 1869 the Paris municipal debt had risen to 1,475 million francs. Political liberalisation, the re-affirmation of parliamentary control, and abolition of the Caisse des Travaux, would require commitment of one-third of the city's income to servicing its debt. The costs of the 1867 International Exposition followed by Haussmann's assertion of the need to *dépenser des milliards* on the growing suburbs were probably the last straws. With the 1869 elections in prospect, the era of urban renewal was brought to an abrupt end.[65]

[63] Roncaylo, 'La production', pp. 106–7; Barbier, *Finance*, p. 228.
[64] See e.g. PG Grenoble, 14 April 1861, AN BB30/378.
[65] Roncaylo, 'La production', p. 107; Girard, *Napoléon III*, pp. 427–9.

FINANCIAL INSTITUTIONS

The Emperor was well aware of the need to mobilise capital for modernisation. Fiscal policy during the first post-*coup* decade was characterised by Louis Girard as *l'économie politique du 2 décembre*[66] and was designed to encourage investment. Renewed confidence amongst investors, verging on euphoria, and falling interest rates, encouraged borrowing. Persigny insisted that growing government debt could be funded out of rising tax receipts as the economy grew. Parliamentary controls on expenditure were initially negligible. The public debt rose from 6,379 million francs on 1 January 1853 to 13,865 million by the beginning of 1865,[67] a figure that did not include the sharp rise in borrowing by departments and communes and especially Paris. The inevitable result of rising and competing demands for capital, from both the public and private sectors, was a substantial rise in interest rates. As the public debt grew, so too did anxiety about tax increases. The mere suggestion by critics of the regime that an income tax might be necessary, led to virulent denunciations by the Corps législatif's budgetary commission.[68] The Emperor's *programme de la paix*, published on 15 January 1860, which promised additional infrastructure investment, followed, a week later, by the promulgation of the free-trade treaty with Britain, aroused considerable further alarm. In such circumstances, the combined opposition of representatives of high finance like Rothschild and such pillars of the regime as Magne, Baroche, Rouher, and Fould could hardly be ignored. The Emperor agreed that a balanced budget appeared to be the only means of avoiding a damaging inflation. His public acceptance of a critical assessment of financial policy by Fould, followed by the latter's appointment as Finance Minister, represented, according to the Emperor, his awareness of the 'danger' to his government.[69] Recognition of the need to restore financial confidence inaugurated major policy changes. The *sénatus-consulte* of 31 December 1861 sought to re-assure the wealthy classes by requiring future parliamentary approval for supplementary financial credits as well as closer supervision of expenditure. Eugène Forcade, writing in the *Revue des Deux Mondes*,[70] a journal partly owned by the Rothschilds, drew the further conclusion that 'effective financial administration is impossible without political liberty and the unrestrained and rigorous control provided by legislative assemblies and the vigilant polemics of a free press'. This was

[66] Girard, *La politique*, p. 396.   [67] Plessis, *Second Empire*, p. 64.
[68] Barbier, *Finance*, p. 204; A. Plessis, 'La Banque de France sous le second empire', Doctorat d'Etat, Université de Paris I, 1980, p. 939; Girard, *La politique*, p. 271.
[69] *Moniteur universel*, 29 Sept. 1861.   [70] 15 Oct. 1861, p. 1009.

precisely the kind of pressure coming from *within* the social elites, which would force the Emperor to make further concessions.

In addition to avoiding parliamentary control over expenditure, Napoleon and his closest advisors had been determined to establish their independence of existing financial institutions, controlled by financially conservative and politically Orleanist bankers. Persigny, an ardent advocate of productive expenditure, would claim later:

> I wanted an instrument which freed the new regime from the tutelage in which financiers normally hold governments; a tutelage all the more dangerous because I expected hostility from the most influential financiers towards the new government. Without doubt, in the absence of support from the Crédit mobilier, which gave them the lead and forced them to follow, the Emperor's policies, dependent on the goodwill of the *haute banque*, would not have been as bold and as free to develop.[71]

Efforts were also made to increase state influence over the privately owned Bank of France, to ensure that it served as an instrument of official policy. Thus, in the immediate aftermath of the *coup d'état* the bank's governors were persuaded to reduce interest rates and expand credit.[72] The 1850s witnessed a spectacular increase in the bank's discounting activity and profitability.[73] Increased world bullion production and the growing use and more rapid circulation of paper money would anyway have increased substantially the supply of money – from 3,900 million in 1845 to 8,600 million by 1870.[74] Nevertheless, the governors of the Bank of France, supported by such eminent members of its council as Eugène Schneider, Alphonse de Rothschild, and Alphonse Mallet, were determined to resist the threat posed by the government to the institution's 'independence'. Following a first wave of infrastructure investment encouraged by government subsidy and cheap credit, the bank sought, from 1856/7, to impose a period of anti-inflationary consolidation by increasing its discount rate from the 3 to 4 per cent prevailing since 1852 to 6 to 10 per cent.[75] Similar resistance to government policy occurred when the Emperor pushed again for cheap credit to facilitate industrial re-equipment following the commercial treaty with Britain in 1860.

[71] Quoted B. Gille, *La Banque en France au 19e siècle* (Geneva 1970), p. 127; see also letter from Persigny to Emperor, 21 June 1854, in Plessis, *Banque*, p. 1258.

[72] Plessis, *Banque*, III, pp. 908, 1205–6.

[73] *Ibid.*, pp. 1341–3, 1518; see also Ministère des Finances et Ministère de l'agriculture, *Enquête sur les principes et les faits généraux qui régissent la circulation monétaire et fiduciaire* (Paris 1867), p. 545.

[74] Point made by PG Grenoble, 13 April 1869, AN BB30/389; figures from R. Cameron, *Banking in the Early Stages of Industrialisation* (New York 1967).

[75] Girard, *La politique*, p. 362.

Growing prosperity and public works together with the increasing capital needs of business combined to encourage modernisation of the banking sector. Indeed the construction of modern communications and banking networks was closely inter-related. The mobilisation of capital was essential to the first, whilst rail and telegraph allowed the more efficient diffusion of information and effective control from the 'centre' over the financial system. The establishment of such major institutions as the Crédit mobilier investment bank (1852), together with the Crédit lyonnais (1863) and Société Générale (1864) – the pioneers of branch banking – was evidence of this revolution. The new banks offered much greater security, at lower cost, to depositors and borrowers, than the host of local banks and notaries whose ranks were depleted with every recession, and whose failures caused waves of bankruptcies.[76] In September 1852 the Pereire brothers had requested authorisation for a bank which, through the provision of cheap credit, would 'facilitate the concentration of the capital necessary for the completion of our rail network and encourage all the industries on which this depends'.[77] In establishing the Crédit mobilier they were supported by some eminent representatives of the *haute banque*, including Benoît Fould and Charles Mallet, together with the inevitable, and politically so useful, Morny. In this case the goal of economic modernisation was combined with unbridled lust for personal gain.

In the expansive 1850s the development of the Crédit mobilier as an investment bank seemed to be paying off. Its shares, which had been worth 1,000 francs in November 1852, rose in value to 1,982 in 1856.[78] However, this favourable situation was to be short lived. Here too initial success generated growing resistance. The scale of the undertaking rapidly became unacceptable in more cautious financial circles. James de Rothschild, inspired by personal as well as business rivalry, and apparently taking at face value the Pereires' dream of creating a vast holding company which would dominate the French economy, warned the Emperor about the risk of creating an uncontrollable financial force.[79] Nevertheless, the *haute banque* which he represented had participated itself, and to a substantial degree, in industrial investment and the development of new financial institutions, as well as in the battle for railway

[76] E.g. PG Metz, 14 April 1854, AN BB30/380 on impact of failure of the Leroy Bank at Sedan.
[77] Letter to MI, 10 Sept. 1852, AN F12/1791.
[78] E. Labrousse (ed.), *Aspects de la crise et de la dépression de l'économie française au milieu du 19e siècle, 1846–51* (Paris 1956), p. 61.
[79] Rouher report to the Emperor, 10 Sept. 1867 in *Papiers et correspondance*, II, pp. 233–4.

concessions. Rothschild interests had acquired stakes in the Nord, PO and PLM of far greater significance than the Pereire investment in the Midi railway company. By 1867 the Crédit mobilier had over-extended itself anyway and, in a general recession, suffered from a lack of liquidity. The Pereire were forced to surrender to their rivals unconditionally. Already, the re-appointment of Fould to the Finance Ministry at the end of 1861 had signified a return to financial orthodoxy and grudging acceptance by the Emperor of his inability to escape from dependence on established financial elites with very different conceptions of the role of the state. Fould's essential concern as Finance Minister was with short-term treasury operations, the success of which required retaining the confidence of the governors of the Bank of France and the Parisian *haute banque* – members of a social elite still influenced by memories of the inflation induced by the Law affair in the early eighteenth century and revolutionary *assignats*, and more concerned with monetary stability than economic growth.[80] In the second part of the decade the cost of borrowing rose, at a time when declining public confidence in the regime and its ability to avoid war would have reduced the incentive to invest anyway. In this deteriorating political situation, Napoleon's inability to lend support to the Crédit mobilier, an institution that for many observers had symbolised the financial creativity of the regime, signified his declining authority. This was recognised by Persigny who condemned Fould as someone who 'by his relationships, by his antecedents, by his character belongs to the category of those whose devotion is equivocal and who have not ceased to invade the Emperor's government'.[81] However, it had become clear, from the mass of administrative reports, that financial retrenchment enjoyed considerable support and that it would be politically dangerous to ignore this.[82] The growing need for financial restraint would come to affect most spheres of government activity.

THE QUESTION OF 'FREE TRADE'

The widespread disquiet aroused by the regime's 'extravagence' and particularly its expenditure on Paris and the army, was reinforced by the Emperor's evident conversion to 'free trade'. In negotiating commercial treaties the regime had two main objectives – to provide a further stimulus to economic modernisation and to offer a commitment to international peace in the aftermath of the intervention in Italy, which had

[80] Plessis, *Banque*, pp. 1385–8, 1408, 1474.   [81] Quoted *ibid.*, p. 970.
[82] E.g. PG Colmar, 9 Jan. 1862, AN BB30/376.

so alarmed the great powers. The Emperor was particularly anxious to improve relations with the British.[83] Having lived in Britain, Napoleon was convinced of the need to emulate the first industrial nation in order both to maintain France's great power status and to spread prosperity amongst its population. In 1815, after decades of war and technical isolation, protection against British exports had seemed an urgent necessity. By the 1850s this was no longer the case. Thus the Emperor was susceptible to the ideas of free traders like Michel Chevalier, Emile Pereire, and Eugène Rouher. Morny, a particularly ardent supporter of the cause, insisted that 'what French industry particularly lacks is the pressure of competition: when necessity demands, progress is rapid'.[84] As a result of his visit to the 1855 Paris International Exposition, Rouher appears to have been convinced that French industry was competitive.[85] In some respects the ground was prepared carefully. Detailed information was collected on commercial relations, particularly those with Britain. Consular officials and experts on special missions were instructed to report on the industries and transport costs of potential competitors.[86] At the same time, the likely impact of intensified competition for French industry was being assessed. From March 1856 prefects were asked to provide regular and detailed reports on industrial conditions.[87] Considerable efforts appear to have been made to gather information. The quality of the information received was very mixed, however. M. Combès, an inspecteur général des mines, complained about the difficulty of obtaining accurate information from textile entrepreneurs. He was refused access to manufacturers' financial accounts and was forced to rely on partial and often contradictory statements from industry representatives.[88] A series of official enquiries throughout the 1850s allowed interested parties to rehearse the arguments for and against protection. Ministers sympathetic to the Emperor's objectives frequently formulated the conclusions. Thus Rouher was able to insist, quite reasonably, that abolition of the

---

[83] E.g. speech by Persigny to Loire conseil général, reported by academic rector Grenoble, 28 Sept. 1858, AN F17/2649.

[84] Conseil supérieur du commerce, de l'agriculture et de l'industrie, Session 14 Nov. 1853, AN F12/2533.

[85] Undated note, AN 45 AP 1.

[86] AN F12/6445–6457; AN F12/2480; M. Moussette, inspecteur principal des chemins de fer was charged with reporting on communications in Britain – Ministère de l'agriculture, du commerce et des travaux publics, Conseil supérieur du commerce, de l'agriculture et de l'industrie, *Enquête*, I, pp. 346f.

[87] Ministère de l'agriculture, du commerce circular, 10 March 1856, AN F12/4476C.

[88] Report to minister, 24 July 1856, AN F12/2480; see also Rouher to Conseil supérieur du commerce, 17 Nov. 1853, AN F12/2533.

sliding scale of protective tariffs on cereals, already suspended following the poor harvest of 1853, would lead to increased price stability and better-supplied markets, and to a diminution in the severity of subsistence crises.[89] As improved communications appeared to have solved the problems of food supply, the debate on tariff protection increasingly focused on industrialisation. It was evident that competitiveness varied considerably between enterprises, sectors, and regions. An enquiry into the cotton and woollens industries concluded that around one-third of capacity was so archaic that it was doomed to disappear.[90] Other reports pointed to the difficult position of the charcoal iron industry with its high costs.[91] The situation of some of the modern sectors was very different. A report on French locomotive manufacturers concluded that they would remain competitive even with tariffs as low as 15 per cent. For stationary steam engine producers the figure was 10 per cent. The producers of textile machinery, manufacturing on a smaller scale, would require higher levels of protection.[92] Another, undated and unsigned, memo on the cotton industry concluded that it was essential to put an end to inertia by means of the intensification of competitive pressures.[93]

In a letter to the Emperor on 20 July 1859, Persigny, one of his closest advisors, who had been appointed to the London embassy at this crucial moment, developed the notion of 'a programme for peace intended not only to develop the wealth of France but also to convince Europe of our pacific intentions'. He divided the programme into four parts – dealing with agriculture, industry, the re-forestation of upland areas, and finally irrigation and flood control. In his reply Napoleon asked Persigny to present his ideas to the Council of Ministers. By this time the ambassador had already discussed the possibility of a commercial treaty with both Rouher, the responsible French minister, and with

---

[89] *Rapport à S. M. l'Empereur sur des questions relatives à la révision de la législation sur les céréales par le Ministère de l'agriculture, du commerce et des travaux publics*, III (Paris 1859), p. 5 – prepared on the basis of the kind of information supplied in Direction générale des Douanes et des Contributions indirectes. Rapport à Son Excellence le Ministre des Finances, 18 Sept. 1858, AN F12/2481.

[90] 'Enquête sur la situation des Etablissements qui mettent en oeuvre la laine et le coton suivie par MM. les Ingénieurs des Mines d'après les instructions contenues dans le circulaire du 8 août 1857'.

[91] AN F12/2484.

[92] Rapport sur les droits spécifiques à établir sur les produits des manufactures anglaises, en vertu du traité de commerce avec la Grande Bretagne, AN F12/2483; see also Ministère de l'agriculture, du commerce et de l'industrie, *Enquête. Traité de commerce avec l'Angleterre*, I (Paris 1860), evidence of M. Gouin, constructeur des machines.

[93] AN F12/2482; see also *Enquête*, II, p. 80, evid. of M. J. Dollfus, fabricant de toiles peintes à Mulhouse.

Lord John Russell, representing the British.[94] The intensification of competition through improved communications and the reduction of tariff protection were thus the central features of a coherent policy designed to create a new environment for entrepreneurial activity.[95] The Emperor's ideological commitment was sufficiently strong for him to accept the political risks of what he described subsequently as 'a difficult period of transition'.[96]

Certainly Napoleon can have had few illusions about the likely scale of opposition. The *sénatus-consulte* of 25 December 1852 had prepared for this very situation by reinforcing the Emperor's prerogative powers in relation to the negotiation of commercial treaties. Vainly Baroche had attempted to re-assure deputies about the Emperor's intentions by referring them to a previous statement of government policy by Fould who had insisted that 'tariff protection is necessary for our industries', but had ruined the effect by adding that this 'should not be blind, immutable or excessive.'[97] Subsequent attempts to modify tariff legislation had enjoyed mixed results. In December 1853 a reduction in the tariff on imports of iron, steel, and coal to 20 per cent was introduced. In this case the users, if not the producers, of these materials, had identified high tariffs as a major self-imposed handicap.[98] Representing the major coal producers, the Comité des houillères françaises defended its members against accusations of monopoly and speculation. The commercial policy of the Anzin mining company, the single most productive enterprise, had, nevertheless, involved restricting production to force up prices.[99] A subsequent attempt, in June 1856, to abolish the remaining prohibitions on imports met with a stormy response from the normally quiescent Corps législatif. Throughout the 1850s, official reports delivered repeated warnings about the potentially dangerous political consequences of tariff reform.[100] The civil servants of the Commission des Douanes also warned the government in 1854 that many industrialists 'assume that the principle of free trade, especially as it is professed by some of the government's closest advisers, would lead to the

[94] Letters to Emperor 20 July and 1 August 1859, BN naf 23066; see also R. Shannon, *Gladstone: 1809–65* (London 1992), pp. 395–400.

[95] E.g. *Discours de S. E. M. Fould, ministre des finances au banquet d'inauguration de service maritime de l'Indo-chine offert par la Cie. des Messageries Impériales à Marseille le 18 Oct. 1862* (Marseille 1862).

[96] Letter to Rouher, 25 Sept. 1865, AN 400 AP 44.   [97] Maurain, *Baroche*, p. 152.

[98] Ministère de l'agriculture, du commerce, et des travaux publics, Question des houilles et des fers. Note pour le Conseil supérieur, 4 Nov. 1853, AN F12/2534E.

[99] *Coup d'oeil sur la situation de l'industrie houillère* (Paris 1854), pp. 1–2.

[100] See e.g. PG Douai, 2 Oct. 1856, AN BB30/377; and on rural disquiet PG Dijon, 14 Jan. 1865, AN BB30/377.

ruin of French industry', and that theories held by 'men who have little
practical experience of business' were held in contempt. Most seriously,
constant rumours of tariff reform threatened business confidence.[101] At
the very least, businessmen demanded the postponement of change to
ensure a decent return on capital already invested as well as time to mobilise the additional investment necessary to eventually compete with the
British.[102] Nevertheless, efforts continued to prepare public opinion for
a major change in policy. An analysis of the possible objections to tariff
reductions, prepared for the Emperor by Rouher, pointed out that 'this
project has as its objective, not to provoke a dangerous competition for
French industry, but uniquely to stimulate its efforts, spur on its zeal, and
encourage useful comparisons with foreign industry'. Napoleon's anno-
tated copy of the report includes instructions, in his hand, to publish it
in the *Moniteur universel*.[103] Government officials also prepared detailed
refutations of hostile press articles.[104]

On 19 October 1859 the Emperor presented a lengthy memoir to
a meeting of ministers, which recommended a simplification of tariff
structures and a reduction of those imposed on imported raw materials.
At the same time the economist and conseiller d'état Michel Chevalier
engaged in informal discussions with Richard Cobden, the English en-
thusiast for free trade, as well as with Gladstone, the Chancellor of the
Exchequer. Accompanied by Baroche, Rouher, and Fould, Chevalier
spoke to the Emperor on 27 October and was requested to open secret
negotiations with Cobden, representing the British government. On the
basis of these, Rouher was instructed to prepare a treaty and in a letter
to Fould published on 15 January 1860 the Emperor outlined his *programme de la paix*. The treaty itself – valid for ten years – was published
in the *Moniteur* on the 22nd. In return for the removal of British tariffs
on major French exports – *articles de Paris*, silk, wine, and spirits – the
French government agreed to reduce those levied on British goods to
levels varying, according to the commodity, between 10 per cent and
30 per cent. Similar arrangements would be negotiated subsequently
with most other European states, each of them serving to renew anxiety,

---

[101] Commission des Douanes. 1er Bureau. Séance du 1er juin 1854, AN F12/2481.
[102] E.g. Conseil supérieur du commerce, de l'agriculture et de l'ind. Séance, 14 Nov. 1853 – evidence
of E. Schneider; report of commission established to examine tariffs on coal and iron, 14 Nov.
1853, AN F12/ 2533.
[103] Ministère de l'agriculture, du commerce, et des travaux publics, ?Oct. 1856, AN F12/2749.
[104] E.g. Direction du commerce extérieur, 'Observations sur un article du Constitutionnel 1 août
1859 – J. Burat relatif à notre commerce avec l'Angleterre', AN F12/2483.

particularly in frontier regions.[105] The reduction in protective tariffs was balanced by the promise of substantial investment in the transport infrastructure in order to increase the competitiveness of the French economy. This was in response to a frequently voiced complaint about the higher costs suffered by French producers[106] as well as an attempt to calm the expected storm of protest. Subsidies worth 38 million francs were also to be provided to enterprises over the next five years in an effort to ease the transition to a more open economy.[107]

Rouher publicly admitted that the treaty offered 'both advantages and inconveniences; it is a question of calculating the balance'.[108] The state prosecutor at Angers reported that, in spite of previous debate, the treaty had come as a great surprise, and warned that 'rational economic ideas are not very widespread in France' and that 'protection' was almost instinctively preferred.[109] Businessmen expressed their concern about what was bound to be a difficult period of transition.[110] The Parisian engineering entrepreneur Calla pointed out that in order to adapt he needed time, security, and guaranteed access to large markets. The state of uncertainty prevailing during the period between signature of the treaty and the final establishment of tariffs created particular difficulty.[111] As a conciliatory measure a major enquiry was conducted to give interested parties the opportunity to express their views before new tariff levels were established. An enquiry into transport was also launched[112] and an official mission despatched to gather information on British transport costs. It concluded that British industry enjoyed lower costs due to more efficient communications and more developed market integration and the specialisation and larger-scale production this made possible.[113] Clearly it would take time to construct the additional railway lines necessary to increase the density of the French transport

---

[105] E.g. PG Colmar, 10 July 1863 re Swiss textiles and 2 Oct. re watchmaking, AN BB30/376.

[106] E.g. Conseil supérieur du commerce, de l'agriculture et de l'industrie, Séance, 5 Nov. 1853, evidence of Morny and E. Schneider, AN F12/2533; Léon Talabot, Président du Comité des Forges, to Min., 20 Jan. 1860, AN F12/2484.

[107] M. Lévy-Leboyer, 'Histoire économique et histoire de l'administration' in *Histoire de l'administration française depuis 1800* (Geneva 1975), p. 66.

[108] Ministère de l'agriculture *Enquête. Traité de commerce avec l'Angleterre*, 1 (Paris 1860), p. 46.

[109] PG Angers, 1 April 1860, AN BB30/371.

[110] E.g. M. Ricote, directeur des forges et fonderies de Varigne (Haute-Saône) in evidence to *Enquête. Traité de commerce avec l'Angleterre*, pp. 398-9.

[111] Calla reporting on a meeting of engineering employers, *ibid.*, p. 401.

[112] Published as Ministère de l'agriculture, *Enquête sur l'exploitation et la construction des chemins de fer* (Paris 1863).

[113] Report of M. Moussette, inspecteur principal des chemins de fer, in *Enquête. Traité de commerce*, 1, p. 360.

network.[114] In response, Baroche insisted that French manufacturers always exaggerated the levels of concentration in British industry. He pointed out also that they enjoyed a considerable advantage due to lower labour costs. Rouher reminded businessmen that they would continue to enjoy substantial levels of tariff protection even under the new regime.[115] Subsequently he would respond to criticism from coal-mining interests by pointing out in the Corps législatif that the Anzin mining company 'which is so modest in describing its profits has increased production from 7 to 12 million metric quintaux. You can see how it is being ruined!'[117]

One thing is certain: substantial parts of the social elite and business classes, men with considerable influence, felt that their views had been ignored and that their vital interests were being sacrificed. Their confidence in the regime had been shaken badly. One official reported that 'the popularity of the Prince has been weakened profoundly; none of the errors and misfortunes of his government has resulted in such a decisive blow to his personal power'.[117] The commercial treaty represented a 'new *coup d'état*'. Indeed Napoleon admitted to Richard Cobden, the British negotiator, that parliamentary approval of tariff reform would have been impossible to secure.[118] Inevitably, established situations were threatened. Uncertainty increased. Official reports reflect this widespread unease. It did not seem possible that 'the transition from one industrial regime to another could occur without a crisis'.[119] Constant complaints were to follow, often quite aggressive in tone. They came most notably from cereals and wool producers and northern and eastern mining and metallurgical interests[120] and above all from the textile manufacturers of Normandy, the Nord, and Alsace. The commercial treaty would prove to be a major factor in the rise of opposition to the authoritarian regime. A meeting of mill owners at Les Andelys in Normandy met and 'gravely considered if they could not replace the Sovereign who took such poor care of their interests and, after recognising that ... they had no-one to put in his place, they resigned themselves to attacking his popularity'.[121] Some of the most vocal critics of 'free trade,' most notably Adolphe Thiers, the spokesman of the Anzin mining company,

---

[114] Point made by M. Barbezat, fab.de fontes moulées à Paris, *ibid.*, p. 386.
[115] *Ibid.*, pp. 454, 460, 487. [116] Quoted, Schnerb, *Rouher*, p. 94.
[117] PG Toulouse, 10 Jan. 1870, AN BB30/390.
[118] Letter from Cobden to Rouher, 10 Jan. 1860, AN F12/2482.
[119] PG Lyon, 30 Dec. 1863, AN BB30/379.
[120] E.g. Comité des houillères françaises, *Note sur la nécessité de maintenir les tarifs protecteurs* (Paris 1860), pp. 1–2.
[121] PG Rouen, 12 April 1860, AN BB30/387.

were already leading lights in the ranks of the opposition. Others like Kolb-Bernard, the sugar refiner from the Nord, Quesné, the Elbeuf mill owner, or the Marquis d'Andelarre, an innovating landowner from the Haute-Saône, had supported the regime previously. Subsequently they would tend to blame every minor economic setback on the commercial treaties. More significantly they would demand political liberalisation as the only means of preventing the Emperor from using his prerogative powers again in a manner 'contrary to the national interest'. These same interest groups had, after all, successfully used parliamentary means to oppose tariff reform during the July Monarchy. Support for 'free trade' was far from negligible and included coal users and port interests along with the producers of those luxury goods, like silk or wine, which enjoyed a competitive advantage.[122] However, protectionist groups were better organised and more vociferous. Textile manufacturers in Lille and Roubaix went so far as to reduce production and lay off workers in anticipation of a serious crisis.[123] Their prophecies of doom would prove grossly exaggerated but they would never again trust the regime. Neither would the ironmasters operating charcoal furnaces, nor the forest owners who provided their fuel and whose property rapidly depreciated, nor the peasant-workers employed in the forests, in mining ore, and in carting – all activities anyway faced with rapid technical obsolescence.[124] More productive British methods of iron and steel or textile production were often too costly to adopt, in spite of their potential advantages.[125] Another cause of considerable criticism was the government's acceptance of differential railway freight rates, which appeared designed to encourage import penetration and its apparent toleration of the railway companies' 'abuse' of their monopoly position.[126] During the 1850s, officials appear to have rejected freight-rate proposals which encouraged imports.[127] By 1864, however, coal producers in the north were complaining that even the modicum of tariff protection left to them by the 1860 Treaty was

---

[122] E.g. PG Besançon, 21 May 1860, AN BB30/373; on Lyon silk producers PG Lyon, 29 Dec. 1862, AN BB30/379; on coal users MM. Coignet père et fils, producers of phosphorus matches to Min., 15 May 1862, AN F12/6407.

[123] Ménager, *Nord*, II, pp. 470–2.

[124] E.g. Chambre consultative Joinville (Haute-Marne) to Ministère, 16 Feb. 1869, AN F12/7407.

[125] E.g. ingen.en chef des mines Haute Marne, 18 April 1860, AN F1 CIII Haute-Marne 8.

[126] E.g. Comité des houillères françaises, *Note sur l'importation des houilles prussiennes et sur la nécessité de réduire les tarifs du canal du Rhône au Rhin* (Paris 1854), p. 3; Comité des forges de Champagne, *Lettre à messieurs les députés de la Haute Marne et de la Meuse sur ... les conséquences de l'introduction en franchise des fers étrangers* (Saint–Dizier 1868), p. 9.

[127] See e.g. Ingénieur en chef des Mines. Contrôle des chemins de fer. Chemin de fer du Nord, 8 Oct. 1854, AN F14/9348.

being destroyed by the differential freight charges levied by the Nord railway company.[128]

Objective judgements concerning the impact of the commercial treaties and changing transport costs on economic change are difficult to make, even with the benefit of hindsight. The conclusions of an official *Note sur les effets du Traité de commerce* ... might well apply to the efforts of historians: 'It is not possible ... in such exceptional circumstances to determine what effect the treaty ... has had ... and all the statistics presented prove nothing.' As an article of faith, nevertheless, the author insisted that there could be no alternative to free trade.[129] Certainly economic growth remained overwhelmingly dependent on internal markets and 'it is not so much foreign production as internal competition which has represented such a blow ... for old establishments placed in defective conditions'.[130] It followed that the most important formative influence was the improvement in communications and market integration.[131] It does seem reasonable to assume, however, that in the absence of 'free trade', technical innovation and structural change in the economy would have been slower. One detailed analysis indeed concluded that 'the effect of the trade treaties has been to force our industries to ensure ... at the cost of an increase in the capital invested, a remuneration which previously they would have enjoyed from their privileged position within internal markets. They have had no choice.'[132] Those businessmen capable of adapting to new situations survived and prospered. Administrative reports frequently note the efforts of entrepreneurs to re-equip to meet expected British competition.[133] It was reported from Rouen in 1870 that although textile spinners had insisted that they faced ruin, the number of spindles they employed had increased from 1,042,520 to over 1,200,000 and their productivity by as much as one-third. Their pessimism was contradicted also by the growing opulence of their lifestyles. Yet, and although the current crisis was due to internal over-production, they would oppose violently the forthcoming renewal of the commercial treaty.[134] In terms of the analysis of the political consequences of government policy it was perceptions rather than reality which mattered.

---

[128] Comité des houillères du Pas-de-Calais, *Résumé des mémoires des compagnies du bassin houiller du Pas-de-Calais, en réponse au questionnaire qui leur a été adressé par le comité central des houillères de France à Paris* (Arras 1866), p. 8.

[129] 10 May 1868, AN F12/2515.   [130] PG Nancy, 20 Oct. 1868, AN BB30/389.

[131] M. Ricot, Directeur des forges et fonderies de Varigne (Haute-Saône) in evidence to 1860 *Enquête*.

[132] AN F1 cIII Nord 16.   [133] E.g. PG Rouen, 12 April 1860, 10 July 1865, AN BB30/387.

[134] PG Rouen, 7 Jan. 1870, AN BB30/390.

The Emperor's retention of the authority to negotiate commercial treaties, moreover, made this an issue on which a wide range of malcontents could combine. It was not simply an economic matter. The future political development of the regime was in question. The establishment of the liberal government headed by Emile Ollivier in 1870 gave protectionists new hope. Although personally in favour of 'free trade', and in spite of the Emperor's known commitment, Ollivier felt obliged to make concessions to the protectionist majority amongst his ministerial colleagues and deputies. He announced a major parliamentary enquiry into the impact of the commercial treaties. Senior officials in the provinces had recommended this as the only means of calming the widespread agitation aroused by the prospect of a renewal of the treaty with Britain. They warned that respondents to the new enquiry should not be expected to provide evidence in a calm, impartial, or even truthful manner,[135] an assessment that would be amply confirmed.[136] The government was deluged with protests as the date for renewal approached. The Chambre consultative des arts et manufactures de Tourcoing pointed out that the 'enormous sacrifices' of its mill owners had been to no avail. It admitted that, according to the official statistics, import levels were quite low but insisted that 'the problem of competition cannot be appreciated on the basis of the quantities imported. Just as it only takes a drop of water to cause a vase to overflow, so it only requires a small volume of imports ... to bring down prices and cause disaster.'[137] In similarly apocalyptical terms a petition to the Emperor from the ironmasters of eastern France announced that 'French metallurgy is exhausted and no longer capable of continuing the struggle against imports.'[138] Even if markets appeared secure at present, what of the future? Globalisation was already a menace. 'Due to the 1861 law, the world's commerce has conquered the French market. The telegraph, the press, the railways are under its orders, it is able to ... cause, through competition, the most terrible effects.'[139] Even the decline in cereal prices which inevitably followed an abundant harvest now tended to be blamed on imports.[140] A decree on 9 January 1870 which, in spite of the contrary conclusions of

[135] E.g. *ibid.*, 7 Jan. 1870.
[136] E.g. evidence of the Mulhouse textile entrepreneur, Auguste Dollfus, in *Enquête parlementaire sur le régime économique, I: Industries textiles* (Paris 1870), p. 9.
[137] 10 Jan. 1868, AN 45 AP 23.   [138] AN F12/2533.
[139] *Enquête sur le situation et les besoins de l'agriculture. Réponses faites par M. Bonnet cultivateur à Champmoron* (Dijon 1867), p. 48.
[140] Ministère de l'agriculture, Bureau des subsistances, memo on 'Question des céréales', 20 Jan. 1866, AN 45 AP 23.

Table 7. *Output 1853-69 (1890=100)*[a]

	Agriculture	Industry	Building	Exports
1853	64	51	50	25
1860	86	62	85	38
1869	114	78	105	66

[a]Based on M. Lévy-Leboyer, 'La croissance économique en France au 19e siècle', *Annales (ESC)*, 1968.

an official report presented in 1867,[141] ended the temporary, tariff-free, admission of semi-manufactured iron and textile products, was widely viewed as a symbolic first step back towards protectionism.

ECONOMY, SOCIETY, AND POLITICS

Currently, it is fashionable to stress the cultural determinants of political behaviour. This should not lead us to neglect the economic factors. Just as governments claimed credit for prosperity, so too they tended to be blamed for depression. Therefore the final section of this chapter will consider briefly the impact both of the ups and downs of the economic cycle and of the regime's interventionist economic policy on the conditions of the mass of the population and thus help to set the context for the analysis of political behaviour (see table 7).

In the countryside, in which most of the population still lived, a combination of increasing agricultural productivity and rising prices ensured the growth of all forms of rural income – rents, profits, and wages.[142] However, some regions benefited more than others. In general, these were areas enjoying optimal climatic and soil conditions, including parts of the north and north-east for cereals, of the west for dairy produce and meat, and the south for wine, and which were able to benefit from expanding markets. More marginal areas, with poor natural conditions, especially in the remoter uplands, faced growing difficulties as they were opened up, gradually, by road and rail.[143] However, even relatively 'backward' areas experienced considerable improvements in agricultural incomes, although their populations remained seriously impoverished. The secret of success was the ability to produce a commodity for which demand was expanding. The individual farmer's

[141] Ministère de l'agriculture, Comité consultatif des arts et manufactures, *Enquête sur l'application du décret du 15 février relatif à l'importation en franchise temporaire des métaux* (Paris 1867).
[142] E.g. PG Nancy, 10 April 1861, AN BB30/381.   [143] Price, *Modernisation*, pp. 314-19.

awareness of such trends and ability to respond varied according to access to both information and capital. It was, nevertheless, almost impossible to entirely escape from the reality of rapidly changing markets. The procureur-général at Grenoble illustrated the scale of change:

in every province ... one could almost say in every commune, until the last few years the inhabitants have been constrained by necessity to grow locally everything necessary to their sustenance, and this is easily understood, it was for them a question of survival because transport difficulties made it impossible to look to other parts of France for the foodstuffs they lacked ... Such facts are impossible today. Thanks to the railways and means of communication of all kinds, which criss-cross the territory of the Empire, not only has transport become easier, but also its cost has considerably diminished. The result is a complete modification in farmers' habits.

With food supply secured, a greater degree of specialisation became possible.[144] The *rapporteur* for the 1862 agricultural census insisted that 'it will be in the interests of every part of France to consecrate itself almost exclusively to the production of those foodstuffs which its climate and soil allow it to produce in the best economic conditions'.[145] This was to be the trend, pursued more rapidly than ever before, and slowly only in comparison with the post-1945 years.

Substantial social change was also under way. The poorest members of the rural community were able to take advantage of growing urban employment opportunities. Indeed, many would have little choice as the concentration of production and collapse of rural manufacture deprived them of supplementary incomes. With the disappearance of dearth, after a final crisis between 1853 and 1855 the burden of poverty was reduced perceptibly. Those who remained in the countryside found it easier to purchase or rent land or to find paid employment as agricultural labourers. Wages rose at a time when the supply of labour was declining and farming, although increasingly productive, remained labour intensive. Undoubtedly, the complaints constantly made by the employers of agricultural labour were exaggerated, but even in poor areas like the Morvan wage increases of 25 to 30 per cent appear to have been general.[146] That such increases were conceded says much about changing social relationships. Through migration, labourers were

---

[144] PG Grenoble, 10 April 1866, AN BB30/378.

[145] Ministère de l'agriculture. Statistique de la France. *Agriculture. Résultats généraux de l'enquête décennale de 1862* (Strasbourg 1868), p. 24. Same emphasis in *Enquête agricole*, VI, Seine-et-Oise (Paris 1867), p. 226.

[146] Vigreux, *Paysans et notables*, p. 395; also R. Price, 'The onset of labour shortage in French agriculture in the 19th century', *Economic History Review* (1975).

now able to escape from relationships of dependence, which previously landowners had assumed they had entered into freely.[147] Generally, by the early 1860s official reports stressed the reduction in indebtedness, improved housing conditions, better diet and clothing.[148] The Comte de Périgny, president of the Commission statistique of the canton of Contres (Loir-et-Cher) insisted that

the increase in general affluence, and the accession of a large number of families to property, has led to the creation of a mass of new farms ... The labourer, becoming the owner of a farm, spends as much time as possible caring for his property and ceases to work for others; as a result there is a shortage of farm servants, of haymakers, harvesters, of grape pickers and other rural workers. If the new landowner has acquired a farmhouse, he is no longer content, as was his father, with a single smoky room just high enough for an average man to stand, illuminated only through its door, with an uneven floor of beaten mud, constantly damp ... Now he needs more light, air and salubrity. He owns more livestock, which must be lodged better. As a result there are not enough masons, carpenters, roofers, and locksmiths. Previously many of these families were unable to keep a horse; the local roads having become passable, the number of carts has increased. Wheelwrights and blacksmiths are no longer able to cope with the work. Men no longer wear the strong and coarse clothes handed down by their fathers. They are anxious to follow fashions and dress like town-dwellers. The tailors have become over-worked ... We can continue indefinitely with this list ... Every progress creates new demands for workers ... The rise in wages ... is indicative of this increase in prosperity and more satisfying than disquieting, for those who know how to place the general above the private interest.[149]

In comparison with state expenditure on the towns, that on the countryside seemed very limited, a fact that was much resented by rural taxpayers. Government expenditure under the rubric *travaux agricoles* fluctuated widely between a low of 1 million francs in 1852 and a high of only 5 million in 1869.[150] The establishment, by private capital, of the Crédit foncier in 1852, was encouraged by the regime as a means of satisfying the demand for cheap loans, which had been such a potent political issue during the Second Republic. In practice it provided substantial long-term loans to those who could offer satisfactory security and was more accessible to urban speculators than peasant cultivators.[151] A credit of 100 million francs was provided in 1856 through loans repayable over twenty-five years, essentially to large landowners, to

[147] E.g. PG Paris, 16 Aug. 1867, AN BB30/384 re Beauce.
[148] E.g. PG Nancy, 6 July 1861, AN BB30/381.   [149] Quoted Dupeux, *Aspects*, p. 414.
[150] Girard, *La politique*, p. 316.
[151] PG Nancy, 15 Jan. 1865, AN BB30/381 – one of many referring to rural disappointment.

encourage drainage.[152] Efforts to encourage re-forestation in upland areas to prevent soil erosion and flooding, together with drainage and land improvement schemes in specific areas like the Landes and Dombes, were more successful.[153] Undoubtedly the most important and well-received measures were those promoting the improvement of rural roads and access to the rail network, although demand for what seemed to be the prerequisites for a more prosperous future proved insatiable.[154] Electoral considerations frequently influenced state investment in communications as well as the provision of subsidies for church renovation and the construction of schools.[155] Whatever the motives, the effect of road improvement was a profound transformation of agricultural markets. Most farmers were better able to market their produce and benefit from improved access to growing urban markets.

As prefects, in speeches at agricultural shows, never tired of reminding them, for most of the rural population the Second Empire was a period of rising prosperity, in marked contrast with the mid-century crisis which preceded it. There were certainly difficult years, caused by poor harvests in 1853/4 and bumper crops for both cereals and wine in 1865, which led to a collapse in prices. Some regions experienced difficulty due to increased competition. At Dijon in 1867 the *octroi* administration complained about the competition of wines from the Midi, which would have been distilled previously, but could now be transported cheaply by rail.[156] The regime benefited from an international tendency for agricultural prices to rise from 1852, although, as competitive pressures intensified, administrative reports in the late 1860s were beginning to record rising anxiety within the rural population.[157] The complaints from landowners and large farmers about the impact of rising costs on profits were certainly vociferous enough for Rouher to launch a major agricultural enquiry.[158] The responses to this came almost exclusively from rural notables who, in spite of low levels of import and their own prosperity, still looked back on a golden age of tariff protection.[159]

[152] Girard, *La politique*, p. 231.
[153] E.g. PG Grenoble, 7 April 1861, AN BB30/378 re Alps; PG Pau, 6 April 1859, AN BB30/384 re Pyrenees.
[154] E.g. 'Utilité des chemins de fer pour l'agriculture', *Journal des chemins de fer*, 15 March 1856.
[155] Girard, *La politique*, p. 320. [156] R. Laurent, *L'octroi de Dijon au 19e siècle* (Paris 1960), p. 61.
[157] E.g. Ministère de l'agriculture, Bureau des subsistances. Question des céréales. 20 Jan. 1866 records complaints from conseils généraux of Tarn, Vendée, Nord, Loiret, Cher, Vosges, Gers, Vaucluse, AN 45 AP 23.
[158] Schnerb, *Rouher*, p. 198.
[159] PG Grenoble, 10 April 1866, AN BB30/378 and marginal note by Minister to report from PG Caen, 11 Oct. 1865, AN BB30/375.

Another marked feature of the Imperial years was continued industrialisation, varying 'in form and intensity according to region'.[160] In
general terms, one can contrast the developing industrial centres of the
Paris region, Normandy, the Nord, Alsace, and the Rhône valley, with the
south, Massif Central, and Brittany. The economic upturn which would
have occurred anyway as the economy recovered from the mid-century
crisis, as a result of higher levels of international trade and the growth in
money supply and profitability, was encouraged greatly by the establishment of the authoritarian regime and apparently more secure conditions
for investment. The advent of the regime was marked by the unleashing
of a speculative boom. Reports from Rouen in June 1852 describe cotton
spinners selling in advance all they could produce and overwhelming machinery manufacturers with orders for new equipment.[161] Growth rates
during the 1850s were to be the highest achieved during the nineteenth
century. The improvement of communications represented the major
direct contribution made by the regime to the process. Furthermore,
at the same time as officials actively promoted amalgamation between
the railway companies as a means of increasing efficiency and reducing
costs, they discouraged the concentration of coal production in an effort
to promote competition and reduce the cost of fuel. This reflected an
appreciation of the importance of the development of coal and metallurgical production to the entire economy.[162]

For industry as for agriculture, improved communications and market integration both created opportunities and intensified competitive
pressures. Railway construction itself substantially increased demand
for the products of the metallurgical and engineering industries. Initially,
French producers were unable to supply rails in sufficient quantity and
they remained unable to satisfy the apparently insatiable demand for
coal.[163] These shortages encouraged demands for reductions in import
tariffs.[164] During the 1850s, however, domestic rail production increased
from 23,000 to 121,000 tonnes whilst the price per tonne fell from 302

---

[160] Plessis, *Second Empire*, p. 93.   [161] PG Rouen, 3 June 1852, AN BB30/387.
[162] See protest by Comité des houillères françaises, *Du commerce des houilles et des moyens d'abaisser leur prix de vente* (Paris 1853), p. 10.
[163] E.g. Ministère de l'agriculture .... Question des houilles et des fers. Note pour le Conseil supérieur du commerce, de l'agric. et de l'industrie, 4 Nov. 1853, AN F12 2534E; Memo. Ministère de l'agriculture .... Mines. Statistique de l'industrie minèrale. Rapport sur la situation des usines à fer et sur les voies de communication propres à faciliter le transport des minéraux et des combustibles, n.d. but *c*. 1860, AN F12/2482.
[164] E.g. letter from F. Kuhlman on behalf of Lille Chamber of Commerce to Minister, 12 Oct. 1866, complaining both of inefficiency of railway companies and inability of domestic coal producers to meet demand, AN F1 cIII Nord 16.

to 242f as a result of technical innovation, and the growing scale and concentration of production in the centre-east and north. These trends were reinforced when the 1860 treaty reduced protection by two-thirds and as improved communications intensified domestic competition. Coal production increased from 4.5 million tonnes in 1850 to 14 million by 1869, of which 4.3 million were produced in the Nord-Pas-de-Calais, 3.3 in the Loire basin, 1.3 in the Gard, and 1.3 in the Nivernais.[165] These were the areas of 'modern' industrial development. In them the mechanisation of production was promoted by a rapid growth in the number of steam engines, produced mainly in Paris and Alsace, from 5,322 in 1850 to 27,088 in 1870 and in the power generated from 71,000 HP to 305,000.[166] In terms of the numbers employed, textiles was a more significant industry. The urban mechanised sector in the east (Mulhouse), Nord (Lille), and Normandy (Rouen-Elbeuf) expanded at the expense of small-scale rural manufacture and the southern woollen industry (Nîmes etc.). The labour force rose to around 1,050,000 (of an active industrial labour force of 4.4 million) with a further 650,000 in the clothing trades.[167] Overall, a 'dualistic' industrial structure survived, not only on the basis of pockets of cheap labour but also the continued complementarity of small- and large-scale production. Geography, proximity to markets and resource endowments, ensured that, as always, some regions were better placed to engage in economic modernisation than others. The scale of production frequently remained small, particularly in clothing, construction, and the luxury trades so characteristic of Paris.

It seems clear that as a result of economic 'modernisation' living standards generally improved. Although the wealthy remained best placed to take advantage of the opportunities for enrichment, the various regional studies reveal that prosperity, especially in the countryside, was more widely shared than ever before. The real incomes of urban workers also increased, particularly during the 1860s. This did not necessarily promote positive attitudes towards the regime. Perceptions varied. Entrepreneurs found it virtually impossible to escape from an ongoing *crise d'adaptation* as communications networks were constantly improved and extended, as production techniques improved and tariff protection was reduced. They remained in a state of continuous tension about their

[165] On iron see B. Gille, *La sidérurgie française au 19e siècle* (Geneva 1968), pp. 68–9; on coal Girard, *La politique*, pp. 245–6.

[166] Gille, *Sidérurgie*, p. 70.

[167] Y. Charbit, *Du malthusianisme au populationnisme* (Paris 1981), p. 49; Price, *Social History*, pp. 28–34.

future prospects.[168] More generally, in the aftermath of a long deflation-ary period, people were frequently more aware of price inflation (at *c.* 1.5 per cent per annum) and rising prices and rents than of the gradual improvement of incomes.[169]

The ups and downs of the economic cycle also had a substantial im-pact on political attitudes. Undoubtedly, the regime had benefited from an upward turn from 1851. The restoration of public order had rein-forced business confidence. Infrastructure investment, the disappearance of dearth, and rising levels of economic activity had contributed to a level of prosperity which was in marked contrast to the misery of the middle of the century.[170] The inevitable cyclical downturns, and the fluctuations in the cost of food or rent, were easier to cope with in a context of greater prosperity. Nevertheless, the cost of living remained a potent political influence. Poor harvests might still lead to popular protest. Individuals were still likely to blame the regime for their problems.[171] Official pub-lications and newspapers thus sought to re-assure public opinion and spread the news that dearth was, in future, impossible.[172]

In practice it was the regularity rather than simply the cost of move-ment by rail, which substantially reduced regional price variations.[173] The electric telegraph provided information about markets near and far and allowed the rapid placing of orders.[174] Easier, regular provisioning of areas of deficit, the more effective organisation of public assistance, and a widespread sense of confidence in the regime combined to ensure greater price stability. Panic buying became far less common.[175] Eco-nomic mechanisms were not functioning as they had in the very recent past.[176] The government was able to impose a 50 per cent reduction on rail-freight rates for the transport of cereals, although, in order to

---

[168] E.g. PG Douai, 3 Oct. 1861, AN BB30/377; prefect, 8 Feb. 1862, AN F1 CIII Mayenne 9.

[169] See OC gendarmerie cie. du Rhône, 26 Feb. 1868, AHG8/151.

[170] Price, *Modernisation*, p. 200.

[171] E.g. Prefect of Police, 15 and 22 Sept. 1867, in *Papiers et correspondance*, II, pp. 264–9.

[172] See influential analysis by C. J. Minard, *Carte du mouvement des céréales en 1853 sur les voies d'eau et de fer de l'Empire français* (Paris 1855), pp. 1, 7; F. Jacqmin, 'Notes sur l'agriculture et les chemins de fer', *Annales des ponts et chaussées*, 4e série vol. 10, 1865, p. 324f and re-assuring articles in *Moniteur* 27 May, 14 Oct. 1854.

[173] Ministère de l'agriculture, *Enquête sur l'exploitation et la construction des chemins de fer* (Paris 1863) p. cxi; F. Jacqmin, *De l'exploitation des chemins de fer. Leçons faites en 1867 à l'Ecole impériale des ponts et chaussées* (Paris 1868), I, pp. 415, II, pp. 128–32.

[174] E.g. Jacqmin, *ibid.*, II, p. 139.

[175] Views of grain merchants in *Enquête agricole*, XXII (Paris 1867), pp. 125–6, Bouches-du-Rhône; Comice agricole canton of Pont l'Abbé (Finistère), AN C1158.

[176] PG Rouen, 12 Oct. 1861, AN BB30/387; see also résumé of reports for the Emperor on second half 1856, AN BB30/368.

assert their independence, the companies insisted that they had already, and voluntarily, made more substantial reductions than those demanded by officials.[177] In 1862 the state prosecutor at Limoges recorded popular gratitude 'to the Government of the Emperor, for making up an enormous deficit, as if by miracle'.[178] Furthermore, railway construction together with urban renewal provided major counter-cyclical inputs so that unemployment was far less serious between 1853 and 1855 than it had been in 1846–7.[179] Clearly France was emerging rapidly from the *ancien régime économique*,[180] even if in some isolated and backward areas the process took a little longer.[181]

In 1863, for the first time, a poor harvest, which previously would have resulted in marked increases in food prices, was followed instead by a fall, further indication of changes occurring in economic structures. On the initiative of Rouher, the government finally felt able to extend the deregulation of economic activity to the bakeries, by a decree of 22 June 1863, with the suspension of age-old controls. The government was determined to persuade consumers that it should not be held responsible for price rises.[182] The ending of such regulation became acceptable only with the disappearance of dearth.[183] The general crisis of 1867/8, however, was caused partly by harvest shortfalls and the impact of rising food prices on consumer demand. There were bitter complaints about the effects on the cost of living, and demands for a return to regulation.[184] The crisis was, though, short lived and would never be repeated in such a form. In future the main threat to rural prosperity would be bountiful harvests and low prices, rather than deficit and dearth.

Structural change in the economy caused uncertainty and could have damaging consequences for newly uncompetitive enterprises or regions. In more competitive markets every crisis weeded out the more archaic enterprises. In the new economy it was becoming clear also that, by making

---

[177] E.g. Réponse de la Compagnie des chemins de fer de l'Est au questionnaire sur les chemins de fer, n.d., probably 1869/70, AN 109 AQ 95; for an assessment of impact see Direction générale des chemins de fer. Chemins de fer d'Alsace to Ministère des travaux publics, 21 Jan. 1854, AN F14/9390; Ministère de l'agriculture, 'Inspection de l'exploitation commercial des chemins de fer to Ingen. en chef du contrôle des chemins de fer', 17 Sept. 1861, AN F14/9412.
[178] 20 Jan. 1862, AN BB30/378.   [179] E.g. prefect Nord, 3 April 1855, AN F12/2446.
[180] See Ministère de l'agriculture, Bureau des subsistances, 23 May 1854, AN F11/2752; discussion at meeting of Société Impériale et centrale d'agriculture, 23 March 1859, AN F11/2752.
[181] PG Nîmes, 12 July 1870, AN BB30/390.
[182] Price, *Modernisation*, p. 202; A. Plessis, 'Rouher et les grands choix économiques du Second Empire' in J. J. Becker (ed.), *Eugène Rouher*, (Clermont-Ferrand 1985) p. 35.
[183] Fortoul, *Journal*, II, p. 196.
[184] E.g. Paris Prefect of Police, 22 Sept. 1867, AN AB XIX 175.

it easier to move money as well as commodities, improved communications resulted in an increased exposure to international economic and
financial crises.[185] The financial crisis beginning in 1856 was marked by
the end of the railway boom. It was the cost of the Crimean War, and of
food imports, as well as international financial movements, which obliged
the Bank of France to increase interest rates to protect its gold reserves.[186]
Repeated changes in bank discount rates were indicative of an unstable
economic situation and, according to manufacturers, of the excessive influence of financial interests in government circles.[187] Specific events like
the cotton 'famine' caused by the American Civil War resulted in considerable misery for workers in some forty departments, but especially in
Normandy where family enterprises were unable to adjust by technical
innovation or laying in stocks. Between 70,000 and 80,000 workers and
their families were reduced to penury in 1863 when the crisis was at its
worst.[188] Recovery was rapid, resulting in a crisis in the woollen and linen
industries, which had expanded rapidly during the cotton crisis. Overproduction of textiles had become a serious problem.[189] Uncertainty, and
criticism of the regime, would again increase following poor harvests in
1866 and 1867, and particularly as part of the 'general sentiment of
malaise'[190] caused by an increasingly uncertain international situation
following the Prussian victory over Austria in 1866. The result was the
so-called *grève du milliard*, a marked preference for saving over investment
in spite of low interest rates. V. Bonnet, in an article in the *Revue des Deux
Mondes* on 15 May 1868, insisted that 'one only engages in current business and cash transactions ... capital is being withdrawn, taking shelter
as though on the eve of a tempest'. Accurate appreciation of the situation
was not easy. Nevertheless, the procureur-général at Colmar was forced
to concede, 'after taking into account the exaggerations,' that even the
relatively modern and competitive industries of Alsace were enduring
an 'extremely grave crisis,' the worst since 1848. Stocks of unsold goods

---

[185] E.g. evidence of the banker Bischoffstein, 18 Nov. 1865, to Ministère des Finances, *Enquête sur
les principes et faits généraux qui régissent la circulation monétaire et fiduciaire* (Paris 1867), p. 92; J. Wolff,
'Napoléon III face à la crise économique de 1857–8', *Souvenir napoléonien*, 1997, pp. 18–19.

[186] See Ministère de l'agriculture, to Emperor, 24 June 1854, AN F12/2481; 'Question des subsistances. Note sur la situation et sur les mesures qui pourraient être prises', n.d., prob. Sept.
1854, AN F11/2752.

[187] E.g. PG Lyon, 26 Nov. 1857, AN BB30/379.

[188] A. Lefèvre, *Sous le Second Empire: chemins de fer et politique* (Paris 1951), p. 198; on Normandy see
PG Rouen, 12 Oct. 1861, AN BB30/387; on Alsace, PG Colmar 12 Oct. 1862, 19 Jan. 1865,
AN BB30/376.

[189] PG Rouen, 10 July 1866, AN BB30/387 and 7 Jan. 1870, AN BB30/390; PG Colmar, 11 April
1865, AN BB30/376.

[190] E.g. PG Douai, 3 July 1867, AN BB30/377; PG Amiens, 9 July 1867, AN BB30/371.

were piling up and their value depreciating daily. Unemployment was growing.[191] Officials were concerned that this depressed situation would 'render the population much more accessible to the manoeuvres of the government's enemies'.[192] In 1869/70 reports from Paris insisted that economic stagnation, together with high food prices and rents and the hated *octroi*, the municipal customs tax, were the cause of considerable resentment amongst workers.[193]

Inevitably this crisis re-invigorated the protectionist cause and encouraged liberal politicians to attack a regime which had been able to introduce free trade by decree and without parliamentary debate. There appeared to be an urgent need to restrict the Emperor's personal power. Louis Buffet, a future minister in the Ollivier government, represented this position in an address to ironmasters on 19 December 1869: 'we enjoy material order, but its benefits are compromised by constant uncertainty ... Industry, commerce, agriculture ... lack the security necessary to ensure their development. All these great interests need to see a broad and certain way open up in front of them, and to be sure that its direction cannot be changed without their consent.'[194] Nothing the Emperor and his ministers could say seemed to allay public anxiety. Even senior civil servants recognised that 'the voluntary renunciation by the Head of State of his personal power is the only means of ending this discontent'.[195] Although agricultural prosperity appeared to have been restored by rising prices, businessmen and workers continued to find themselves in difficult situations and inevitably this affected their attitudes towards the regime. This question of confidence was to be of crucial importance during its final years. Economic modernisation had clearly served to accelerate the rise of political opposition.

[191] 12 Oct. 1867, AN BB30/376; see also prefect, 30 Sept. 1867, AN F1 cIII Nord 16.
[192] PG Paris, 25 April 1868, AN BB30/383.
[193] OC cie. de la Seine, 26 Feb. 1869, AHG G8/165 and 28 Jan. 1870, AHG G8/176.
[194] Quoted Girard, *La politique*, p. 388.   [195] PG Aix, 4 Oct. 1868, AN BB30/389.

Conclusion to Part II

The Second Empire was established and endured in part due to the political skills of its leading personalities. If the range of options open to politicians was inevitably constricted and the problems of a society undergoing industrialisation and urbanisation particularly complicated, Napoleon III and his ministers worked hard to enlarge the possibilities open to them. With a considerable degree of success, they had developed a policy of economic and social modernisation. Large sections of the community benefited from greater prosperity. However, the effect of this adventurous politics was to alienate powerful groups, which felt that their vital interests were under threat. As opposition increased, the regime had adapted, whether of the Emperor's free will or, increasingly, under pressure. It had gone down the extremely tortuous path of liberalisation and, as the May 1870 plebiscite suggested, again with considerable success. Napoleon III himself can be allowed to sum up the regime's achievements. In a sketch for a novel found amongst his papers,[1] a M. Benoit, who had emigrated to America in 1847, returned to France in April 1868. In America, political refugees had warned him that

> France is groaning under despotism and he could expect to find it debased and impoverished . . . Imagine his surprise!
> Amazed by universal suffrage
> Amazed by the railways, which criss-cross France;
> by the electric telegraph.
> Arrives in Paris: embellishment . . .
> He wants to purchase various objects, which are much cheaper, due to the commercial treaty.
> No riots; no political prisoners; no exiles.

---

[1] *Papiers et correspondance*, I, pp. 387–8.

Who knows what might have happened if the war of 1870 had been avoided? That it occurred and ended in a humiliating defeat, however, represented governmental failure on an unacceptable scale – a theme to which we shall return.

PART III

The rise of opposition

CHAPTER 8

The context for opposition

INTRODUCTION

The success or failure of a regime can be measured in relation to the level of opposition it arouses and also in terms of its ability to calm, institutionalise, and contain that opposition. The changing characteristics of regime and opposition were the result of a continuous dialectic – restrained by the unequal distribution of power and made possible by the inability of the regime entirely to set the terms under which the various social and political groups operated. The conditions for political activity were also established by changing socio-economic conditions, as industrialisation, urbanisation, the commercialisation of farming, and migration from the countryside gathered pace and as improved communications and rising literacy affected social relationships, the techniques of government, and the potential for organisation. The balance between continuity and change decisively shifted, presenting many with new opportunities for self-improvement but also involving much of the population in a confusing *crise d'adaptation*. These processes of social and cultural integration inevitably affected both collective identities and the mechanisms for political mobilisation.

The attempt to analyse political behaviour, in a transitional society, soon after the introduction of manhood suffrage raises all manner of analytical problems. The historian's constant efforts to explain politics in terms of ideological commitment or social allegiance are all too likely to lead to over-simplification, if only because every individual exercises a multiplicity of roles and is torn between competing loyalties. The respective weights of administrative or opposition influence on voters, the relative importance of national or local issues and personalities, the significance of the various means of informing opinion, and the perceptions and responsiveness of potential audiences all need to be taken into account. Levels of political awareness and commitment are difficult to assess, as are the relative weight of such factors as short-term economic circumstances or long-term political allegiances. Moreover, the formal exclusion of women from politics should not lead us to assume that they were entirely without influence.

To a substantial degree national politics continued to represent a struggle for power within political elites. They possessed the monetary resources, leisure, education, rhetorical skills, and network of contacts, expected of the 'political man'. Individuals were drawn into opposition from a mixture of motives, including resentment of exclusion from the ranks of the government's official candidates, established family loyalties, and principled, ideological criticism of the political system. They assumed that as well-educated men of independent means they had privileged roles to perform. Generational differences were also important as younger men, impatient to assume public roles, were turned into critics of the institutions and personalities who presented obstacles to their ambitions. Too young to have experienced the events of 1848 personally, they were also less afraid that agitation might lead to revolution.[1] In practice the candidates for election to the Corps législatif were then selected by and from narrow oligarchies. Social influence could thus be used against the regime. In the absence of organised political parties it was necessary to fund newspapers and to 'treat' voters. The leading liberal politician Adolphe Thiers depended on support from the Anzin mining company for electoral success in the Nord. Its miners were warned that their jobs were threatened by the government's tariff policy and were treated to drinks on polling day. In the Hazebrouck area of the Nord, the position of the sitting deputy, Plichon, a leading liberal and Catholic critic of the regime, was unassailable due to the support of four local landowning dynasties, closely interlinked by marriage.[2] In the woollen centre of Reims and in the silk ribbon, arms, and steel-producing city of Saint Etienne, rivalry for influence between established and emerging elites took political forms.[3] Jules Warnier, president of the Société industrielle at Reims, proud of his commitment to industrial modernisation, was exasperated by his inability to secure official recognition. According to the local sous-préfet, Warnier was 'an aristocrat by instinct, but a democrat through ambition'. By 1865 he had 'won a considerable reputation among the bourgeoisie because of his intelligence and ability, and

---

[1] See e.g. PG Paris, 5 May 1866, AN BB30/383 for an awareness of the analytical difficulties.

[2] Ménager, *Nord*, II, pp. 574–8, III, p. 1215.

[3] D. Gordon, 'Industrialization and republican politics: the bourgeoisie of Reims and Saint-Etienne under the Second Empire' in J. Merriman (ed.), *French Cities in the 19th Century* (London 1982), pp. 126–7.

in preparing himself for future political struggles through his courting of the working class.'[4]

The vote for opposition candidates, just like that for official nominees, was to a large degree determined by the fear, respect, and deference implicit in relationships of dependency. Even in opposition, notables enjoyed privileged access to government officials through both formal and informal channels. As deputies or councillors they were well placed to engage in opposition whilst collaborating with the administration in matters of day-to-day concern to themselves and their constituents. Theirs was a moderate opposition. To have attacked the bases of social order would have resulted in personal dishonour and risked social ostracism. Only amongst radical and socialist republicans, and in local elections, was a non-notable political leadership likely to emerge. Identifying influential leaders at community level is fraught with difficulty, due to the tendency of the press and official reports to focus on the more prominent figures. It is, however, essential to an understanding of the links between local, regional, and national politics. Within communities the challenge to elite dominance came essentially from middle- and lower middle-class republicans rather than the peasants and workers who, numerically at least, dominated the electorate. The procureur général at Lyon typically reminded his minister that 'it should never be forgotten that opinion is formed principally by the middle classes'.[5] The masses might have their own agendas, but oratorical skills, political and organisational experience, and social status still mattered. The complex aspirations of the poor were (re-)formulated by members of other social groups.[6] Official reports indeed emphasised the immaturity of the mass electorate. In most communities voting was rarely a matter of individual choice. The poor, susceptible to intimidation, needed to be cautious. They 'hardly dare speak, everyone is known and afraid of compromising themselves',[7] and as M. Cyprien de Bellisses, a former 'democratic' candidate in the Ariège, pointed out: 'It doesn't matter much to them whether this gentleman or that draws the deputy's salary.'[8] Nevertheless, according to the analysis of the reports of the worker delegates to the 1867 Paris International Exposition prepared for the Emperor, these skilled craftsmen, elected by their colleagues, took great pride in their ability to cast judgements on

---

[4] D. Gordon, *Merchants and Capitalists. Industrialization and Provincial Politics in Mid-19th Century France* (London 1985), p. 134.
[5] PG Lyons, 11 Dec. 1852, AN BB30/379.   [6] PG Riom, 6 April 1870, AN BB30/390.
[7] Prefect, 14 April 1858, AN F1 cIII Eure 15.
[8] *Le suffrage universel dans le département de l'Ariège*, pp. 39–40.

government policy.[9] It was claimed that amongst both Limoges porcelain workers and peasants in the surrounding countryside 'those distinguished by their political exaltation are generally those distinguished by
their intelligence and skill'.[10] Such manifestations of working-class independence and 'ingratitude' were often resented, particularly by the
middle-class politicians who aimed to provide 'democratic patronage'
(Agulhon). Nevertheless, the number of dependants they could mobilise
limited the influence of even the most powerful family of local notables.[11]

Distasteful it might be, but politicians gradually accepted the need
both to promise favours and to adopt at least the symbols and language
of participatory politics in order to win elections. Moreover, if members
of established elites looked to the popular vote to confirm their power, the
existence of manhood suffrage provided opponents or newcomers with
the means to challenge their dominance. 'Political' disputes frequently
arose out of the often bitter disagreements over communal affairs creating 'local dissidence, *les rivalités de clocher*'.[12] As the regime itself adapted
to socio-economic change, and government intervention in communities
increased through urban renewal, road works, and the construction of
schools and churches, more and more people could be persuaded that
politics was becoming relevant to their daily lives. In these circumstances
a vote for a local opposition candidate might well be compatible with
loyalty to the Emperor.[13] Political disputes were also increasingly institutionalised. The state prosecutor at Poitiers distinguished between the
eternal preoccupations of the countryside and those of the towns 'where
there is more instruction, more discussion, more readers' and where 'it is
the government itself, its forms and power, which is the principal subject
of concern, because they understand the impact of political questions on
material interests'.[14] Disputes with employers, particularly those leading
to strikes, were likely to reinforce this interest in politics.[15]

In the past, historians have concentrated often on the negative features of the Second Empire and the apparently irresistible rise of republican opposition. Frequently they have appeared to take the side
of the eventual victors. The rise of opposition has been taken to represent politicisation *per se*, as if conservative voting cannot represent a
rational choice. Monarchist and liberal opposition has been relatively
neglected in favour of this focus on republicans. A more inclusive view

  ⁹ By Devinck, dated 28 Oct. 1868, AN 45 AP 6.   ¹⁰ PG Limoges, 4 April 1864, AN BB30/378.
¹¹ PG Limoges, 13 April 1867, *ibid.*   ¹² PG Aix, 6 Jan. 1864, AN BB30/370.
¹³ E.g. PG Paris, 10 Nov. 1868, AN BB30/389 re Seine-et-Marne.
¹⁴ 20 July 1869, AN BB30/385.   ¹⁵ E.g. PG Rouen, 9 Oct. 1869, AN BB30/389.

of opposition, taking account of its variety and of 'popular' as well as 'high' politics, might reveal that the outcome was far from inevitable and that frequently decision-making by the political actors was confused and contradictory. Handy political labels obscure much of this complexity as well as the tendency of proponents of various forms of political discourse to modify their phraseology and its meaning over time. The French Revolution had established personal, familial, and group loyalty to a variety of potential regimes, each with its own ideals and symbols, images of the past, and aspirations for the future. Contemporaries described political groupings as 'parties' but it is worth remembering that, in spite of shared ideological bases and electoral objectives these were alliances between individuals with interests in common, tendencies rather than 'parties' in the twentieth-century sense. Diversity was a particularly marked feature of the political situation in the more liberal 1860s, leading to a substantial debate on political institutions and the nature of citizenship.[16]

The development of an opposition politics represented a challenge to the regime's authority. Complex processes involving the vertical and horizontal diffusion of political ideas left few communities untouched during electoral campaigns and political crises. In terms of content, the local press generally followed the lead of Parisian dailies of a similar political persuasion. Additionally, through their networks of local correspondents, provincial newspapers offered indispensable facilities for the vulgarisation of political ideas, the selection of candidates, and the subsequent diffusion of propaganda.[17] The discourse of political activists (re)-interpreted the past to construct unifying 'myths' and develop programmes for action in the present. In their diversity, ambiguity, and claims to universal relevance, most forms of political discourse sought to achieve broad appeal, although differences of emphasis did much to promote a sectionalised sense of interest, a form of 'class consciousness'. The plasticity of the language employed, with different political groups often using the same vocabulary, as well as the diverse sociological make-up of political groupings, ensured that no single discourse should be taken to represent the interests of a single 'class', however. Furthermore, historians probably tend to exaggerate the permanence and totality of political commitment. Interest in politics fluctuated according to

[16] See especially S. Hazareesingh, *From Subject to Citizen. The Second Empire and the Emergence of Modern French Democracy* (Princeton 1998).

[17] E.g. Copin, 'La presse dans l'Yonne sous le Second Empire' in L. Hamon (ed.), *Les républicains sous le Second Empire* (Paris 1993), pp. 156–7.

the political context. Fiercely fought electoral campaigns and political crises might alternate with periods of relative calm and quiet. Frequently, and especially in local elections, opposition represented little more than personal or communal rivalry, even if dressed up as some sort of Manichean struggle.[18]

THE POLITICAL CONTEXT

The re-establishment of manhood suffrage and subsequently the transition from an authoritarian towards a more liberal government were, of course, the distinctive features of the Imperial regime in comparison with previous monarchical systems. 'Universal suffrage' ensured that, at regular intervals, voters were courted by candidates for local or national office and that, gradually, a national political culture took shape although with 'strong local and regional mediations'.[19] A complex of factors informed political mobilisation. Amongst these, and contrary to the emphasis by some historians on the 'autonomy of politics', were economic and social relationships and material interests. The sheer heterogeneity of the various identifiable social 'classes'[20] should serve, nevertheless, as a warning against engaging in a simplistic Marxist deployment of 'class' as an all-embracing explanatory factor. Contemporaries, frequently employing the language of class, only rarely based this on anything like a worked-out sociological basis. In practice, individuals were faced with a range of historically constructed options and determined how to exercise their right to vote, subject to pressure from the various groups to which they belonged – family, peers, community, 'class'; from those able to exercise economic or social 'power' over them – landlords, employers, and priests; as well as from government officials. 'History', memories of past struggles and the aspirations and fears established in the past and enshrined in myths, through histories, stories, sermons, songs, and pictures, contributed to the creation of complex loyalties often cutting across those of 'class' or community. Tradition itself was constantly subject to re-interpretation and change, as part of a dialogue between past and present.

The problem faced initially by the regime was that of absorbing the masses into the political process and recognising popular sovereignty

---

[18] E.g. PG Bordeaux, 13 July 1857, AN BB30/374.
[19] J. Vernon, *Politics and the People. A Study in English Political Culture c. 1815–67* (Cambridge 1993), p. 11.
[20] Price, *Social History*, part II.

whilst achieving de-politicisation and retaining control. To a substantial extent, the forms and language of opposition were determined by the intensity of repression, which varied over time and between socio-political groups. Repression and the system of official candidature were both designed to demobilise opposition. They ensured that national organisation became impossible except at a very loose informal level – easier within elite 'parties' – and that even local activity was largely pushed underground, creating a situation in which 'prolonged silence means decomposition'.[21] Press censorship had contributed to this process of de-politicisation by depriving 'cabaret' politicians of 'the daily themes for their recriminations'.[22] 'News' should instead be provided by the *Bulletin officiel* posted outside the church or town hall on Sunday – 'an excellent means of dissipating rumour and of guiding the opinions of the rural population'.[23] The relatively few surviving opposition newspapers were tolerated for as long as they moderated their opposition and engaged in severe self-censorship.

Following the *coup* the pressing need for the authorities appeared to be the creation of a 'salutary terror' intended to ensure the failure of the 'sinister projects of the socialist horde,' and to restore confidence by destroying the influence of a 'double dissolvent, the license of the press and parliamentary agitation.'[24] The authorities universally welcomed the 'silence' of the 1850s, in such marked contrast with the agitated years of the Second Republic. The accuracy of official reporting during the authoritarian empire, when demobilisation combined with secrecy, is difficult to judge, however. A tendency to panic when anything untoward occurred was evident, especially in the early years. Even in February 1858 a five-hour delay in the arrival in Metz of official despatches from Paris could set off rumours of revolution in the capital.[25] Opposition political activity certainly survived. Something like the phrase 'the calm is more apparent than real' frequently appears in reports.[26] Of course, criticism of government policy or the failure to support official candidates did not necessarily imply rejection of the regime. Discord could result also from the selection by prefects of electoral candidates judged to be unsympathetic by local notables or some substantial part of the electorate. Thus in 1852 the failure of many peasants in the Etampes area to vote for the official candidate, the grain merchant Darblay, could be explained

---

[21] PG Riom, 7 Oct. 1858, AN BB30/386.   [22] PG Lyons, 7 Jan. 1853, AN BB30/379.
[23] PG Lyons, 3 June 1852, *ibid.*   [24] PG Montpellier, 26 Feb. 1852, AN BB30/380.
[25] Prefect Meuse, report on Feb. 1858, AN F7/4091.
[26] E.g. PG Dijon, 9 Oct 1852, AN BB30/377.

by the speculative activities in 1847 which had earned him the sobriquet 'Darblay-Famine'.[27]

Departmental (conseil général) elections generally attracted less interest than national elections or those, closer to home, in the commune. The meaning of local election results was especially difficult to assess. The administration was usually happy to accept an entente with conservative notables and to share their self-serving affirmation of the non-political character of local affairs. Even in the 1850s official control over municipal elections was far from complete. It was always difficult to distinguish between politically motivated opposition and that inspired by personal rivalry and competition for access to patronage.[28] The situation was often tense. Mayors who failed to provide sufficient support for official election candidates faced dismissal. Councils judged to be hostile were dissolved, adding to the local ferment.[29] Often, the revival of political life was evident first in municipal elections. Certainly from the mid-1860s rising levels of local participation and contestation were evident, as well as the use of political themes for debate.[30]

The existence of an authoritarian regime could not entirely prevent the expression of criticism wherever like-minded individuals happened to meet – 'in carefully chosen words' amongst the upper classes, and 'in gross and outrageous phrases' amongst the lower.[31] Informal communication networks once again became essential to the diffusion of information and development of basic forms of organisation. These varied between the traditional paternalistic networks typically employed by Legitimist nobles, supported by the clergy, to the more autonomous forms of popular sociability – in workplaces, markets, on the streets or in cafés and bars. A diffuse process of politicisation continued, reflecting the improvement of communications, the spread of literacy and awareness of a wider world, the greater prosperity and sense of security and independence prevailing amongst both peasants and urban dwellers, the sheer habit of voting and changing political circumstances. Although interest was inevitably intermittent, opposition ideas could not be eradicated entirely. In the artisanal communities of cities like Paris, Rouen, or Saint-Etienne workplace conflict helped to maintain social tension. Every little town or market centre (*bourg*) sheltered small groups of prosperous and

---

[27] PG Paris, 17 March 1852, AN BB30/383.
[28] E.g. prefect, 12 Jan. 1856, AN F1 cIII Ariège 7.
[29] E.g. dismissals of mayors of Firminy and Chambon reported by OC cie. de la Loire, 28 May 1869, AHG G8/165.
[30] E.g. PG Nîmes, 12 July 1870, AN BB30/ 390.   [31] PG Paris, 9 Nov. 1859, AN BB30/383.

educated professional men as well as successful and literate artisans and peasants. These were people who felt it necessary to adopt postures compatible with their social pretensions, those of the well-informed, newspaper-reading, opinion leader. On occasion, they would be willing to challenge established views and to assist the less fortunate and less well read to achieve an 'understanding' of political principles and practices. They might be capable of linking local problems and tensions to those of national politics, and of offering apparently simple solutions – little more perhaps than slogans or support for emblematic individuals – to otherwise intractable difficulties. This was influence based upon both individual ideological commitment and location within social networks, which allowed a role in determining the perceptions and beliefs of other people. In some rural areas, proximity to market centres or busy communications systems ensured the constant circulation of people and ideas. Lyons and the Rhône-Saône corridor are cases in point. The spread of silk weaving into the countryside intensified contact between village dwellers and the highly politicised inhabitants of the working-class *quartier* of la Croix-Rousse.[32] In contrast, the department of the Indre was reported in 1856 to be devoid of political agitation due to 'its situation, distant from the major line of communications linking Paris and Lyons to the Swiss frontier'. As a result it was sheltered from 'the circulation of socialist agents and the peddling of false news which ... constantly revives the ideas of disorder'.[33] In an area so troubled by popular protest during the mid-century crisis and where the population 'gains access to the news only by hear-say' the importance of controlling the flow of information appeared all the greater.[34] Frequently geographical isolation was associated with cultural isolation, which continued to restrict politicisation.

In the plebiscites sanctioning the *coup d'état* and re-establishment of the empire, Louis-Napoleon benefited from a broad consensus supporting the reinforcement of his personal authority. It was claimed that in the countryside most of the population adhered to 'the principle of authority, personified by a man surrounded by immense historical prestige and military pomp ... The person is everything for them, principles nothing. They are attracted by a politics which is uncomplicated, visible and strong.' Their main concerns were to acquire land and secure a good harvest and better rural roads, to avoid taxation and the conscription of

---

[32] Prefect, 14 Aug. 1866, AN Fı cııı Ain 9. [33] PG Bourges, 31 Dec. 1856, AN BB30/374.
[34] See also Prefectoral circular to mayors, Jan. 1858, AN Fı cııı Finistère 11.

their sons.[35] The concept of a limited monarchy appears to have had relatively little resonance. It followed that 'the mechanisms of parliamentary government are absolutely unknown to the rural population and do not fit in with ... the ideas of sovereignty formed by the patriarchal regime which governs the farm'.[36] The only decoration on so many walls was the lithograph illustrating the military triumphs of Napoleon I or his nephew.[37] In the 1852 general elections, however, the pro-government vote, which had reached 7.5 million in the December 1851 plebiscite, fell to around 5,100,000. Even so, opposition candidates gained only 800,000 votes; 253 official candidates and only 8 opponents were successful. More than two-thirds of the former had previously revealed Legitimist or Orleanist sympathies and were, significantly, denounced by the prefect of the Nord for displaying an attitude 'of apparent submission ... to the government in order to obtain seats in the legislature' whilst privately engaging in a 'silent, disloyal and hypocritical war.'[38] The latter included two independents, three Legitimists elected in the west, and three Republicans (Cavaignac and Carnot in Paris and Hénon in Lyons) who refused to take the oath of allegiance and were unseated. Only 183 of the 252 opposition candidates gained over 1,000 votes, but in four-fifths of constituencies opposition candidates had not dared to present themselves. Elections are always difficult to analyse. The system of official candidature, combined with pressure on voters by candidates themselves, with bribery and corruption on an unknown scale, and the lack of an effective secret ballot, combined to 'falsify' the results of voting. In this situation the most disturbing factor for the regime was the high level of abstention (c. 37 per cent).[39] Of course, abstention might represent indifference. It might indicate satisfaction with the status quo. It could also represent acceptance of the instructions of the Legitimist pretender, the Comte de Chambord, or advice from the leading republican, Victor Hugo, that abstention should represent a principled rejection of the regime and all its institutions.

By 1857, when a similar proportion of the electorate voted (62 per cent), the opposition's share had risen slightly (from 13 to 13.6 per cent) although only 148 opposition candidates managed to win over 1,000 votes and again 128 official candidates were returned unopposed.[40]

[35] PG Dijon, 9 July 1855, AN BB30/377; PG Bordeaux, 9 April 1861, AN BB30/374.
[36] PG Colmar, 24 July 1869, AN BB30/389.   [37] E.g. PG Aix, 19 April 1870, AN BB30/390.
[38] Quoted Ménager, Nord, II, p. 95.   [39] Rougerie, 'Second Empire', p. 69.
[40] P. Langoueyte, 'Candidature officielle et pratiques électorales sous le Second Empire', Doctorat d'Etat, Université de Paris I, 1990, p. 613.

These elections revealed that the various opposition groups had been weakened by defection as the fearful, ambitious, and pragmatic rallied to the new Bonapartist empire. Initially the regime's main concern had been the potential influence of Legitimist elites. It became evident rapidly that the major threat remained urban republicanism. In 1857 only between 10 and 14 of those elected could be considered to be opponents or independents. However, the refusal of Carnot and Goudchaux to take the oath of loyalty was followed by supplementary elections in April 1858. The result of the two elections was the creation of a group of five republicans willing to observe this particular formality – Ollivier, Darimon, Favre, and Picard elected in Paris and Hénon in Lyon.[41] The Parisian results provoked especial disquiet amongst the Emperor and his advisors. They certainly revealed the ability of the regime's opponents to campaign with *ardeur et vivacité* in spite of repression. Much of the urban population appeared willing to support whichever opposition candidates presented themselves.[42] These elections made it clear that in the major population centres 'anarchical fanaticism has conserved its influence'.[43] Industrialisation, urbanisation, and past agitation had had a 'durable effect', ensuring that in future 'workers will be bound together by class interests'.[44] Poverty, insecurity, hostility towards employers and the 'rich' in general as well as disappointment with the failure of the new regime to transform their situation helped to maintain discontent.[45] Probably a large part of the population remained indifferent to anything other than the politics of prosperity. Reading newspapers and discussing politics were luxuries for people who could afford neither the time nor the money and who failed to appreciate the relevance of politics to the daily struggle for survival. Often, too, they were seasonal activities. There was little spare time or energy during periods of intense agricultural work like harvest; much more during the winter months.[46]

In 1863, on a 72.8 per cent turnout, official candidates gained the support of 53 per cent of the electorate (5,308,000) whilst 19.5 per cent (1,954,000) supported the 300 opposition candidates. On this occasion only seventy-one elections were left uncontested. The appearance of an opposition candidate made it possible for the first time to vote against the regime in many constituencies. In part the increased opposition vote was

[41] W. Echard (ed.), *Historical Dictionary of the French Second Empire* (London 1985), p. 210.
[42] PG Besançon, 7 July 1857, AN BB30/373.   [43] PG Montpellier, 10 July 1857, AN BB30/380.
[44] PG Lyons, 3 June 1852, AN BB30/379.
[45] See detailed report on St-Etienne coal basin by PG Lyon, 5 April 1853, AN BB30/379.
[46] PG Lyon, 20 July 1868, AN BB30/379.

due simply to the increase in the number of candidates, and the decline in abstention from 35.5 per cent to 27 per cent of the electorate.[47] The decision to begin to vote might represent also a new level of political awareness and an appreciation of the responsibilities of citizenship. As one of the growing number of election manuals put it: abstention 'is always sterile ... He who abstains cancels himself out.'[48] In most constituencies the elections were fought in a much more relaxed atmosphere than before, with opposition candidates allowed to distribute their programmes and posters, provided that they exercised restraint. Liberalisation created a different context for political activity. There was less risk of compromising oneself. A new political 'opportunity structure' was being established. However, public meetings were still forbidden, as were election committees, although clearly these existed on an informal basis.[49] Prefects anxious not to attract negative publicity treated particularly well-known figures like Thiers, standing in both the Nord and Paris, and Odilon Barrot in Strasbourg, with circumspection.[50] Official reports commented on the growing 'ardour' displayed by the opposition.[51] Within the elites the dispute over the Papacy, as well as the commercial treaties, had reinforced a determination to protect vital interests by restricting the Emperor's personal power.

Undoubtedly, the increased number of votes for opposition candidates alarmed officials. The results from the capital caused a sensation. There, the entire opposition list of ten candidates – the republicans Ollivier, Darimon, Favre, Picard, Simon, Carnot, Guéroult, Garnier-Pagès, Pelletan, together with Thiers – was successful, gaining the support of 63 per cent of those who voted.[52] This represented a massive blow to the regime's prestige and self-confidence. Ludovic Halévy confided to his notebook on 1 June 1863 that 'Paris, this evening, has an air of insurrection and revolution ... The Republicans assure themselves that in the next elections France will follow Paris.'[53] Moreover, a similar rejection of the regime was evident in most large towns. In spite of this, the votes of the predominantly rural and small-town electorate, together with electoral manipulation, ensured an overwhelming official majority in the Corps législatif. Amongst 283 deputies there were only 32 opposition representatives – mostly elected in the Paris, Lyon,

[47] Lagoueyte, *Candidature*, p. 614.
[48] J. Clamergan *et al.*, *Manuel électoral* (Paris: Pagnerre 1863).
[49] Lagoueyte, *Candidature*, p. 668; Ménager, *Nord*, II, pp. 574–5.
[50] E.g. Igersheim, *Politique*, p. 524.   [51] E.g. PG Riom, 10 July 1863, AN BB30/386.
[52] Girard, *Questions politiques*, p. 72.   [53] Quoted Girard, *Nouvelle histoire*, p. 367.

and Marseille areas; 17 were republicans or democratic liberals, and 15 non-democratic or conservative liberals or clericals. In spite of the government's apparently overwhelming victory, the votes of the cities nevertheless encouraged the various opposition groups and substantially reduced the apathy so prevalent in the previous decade. The Emperor was fifty-five and visibly ageing. His son was only seven. The political situation appeared to have been transformed.[54] A greater independence was encouraged within the official majority as well as in the opposition. An Interior Ministry *Note pour l'Empereur* attempted to shrug off the results by reminding Napoleon that invariably Paris elected opponents of the government in power: 'Parisians are rebellious and love to give lessons to governments, even those which, like the Empire, are concerned with their well-being, and with the beauty and salubrity of the city.' Its author blamed the 'excitement generated in the *ateliers*, the *cabarets*, the secret societies, and by luxury'.[55] But what would the next elections bring? The state prosecutor at Limoges was reminded of the instability implicit in an electoral system based upon 'universal' suffrage.[56] Whilst congratulating himself on the successful outcome of two by-elections in 1865, the prefect of Basses-Pyrénées admitted that the electorate was beginning to free itself from administrative control for the first time in ten years.[57]

Moreover, these were only the first in a series of major confidence-shaking events. In particular Napoleon's obviously deteriorating health raised concern that his death might be followed by revolution.[58] Fear of war with Prussia added to the growing sense of uncertainty and contributed to 'profoundly modifying' the political situation.[59] Criticism of the incomprehensible military expedition to Mexico, of wasteful expenditure and the high taxes necessary for the embellishment of Paris, and the questionable character of Haussmann's financial methods, aroused further concern.[60] At the beginning of 1865, the procureur-général at Toulouse warned about the growing 'susceptibility' of public opinion, adding that 'the prestige which has protected the regime for the last ten years is greatly weakened; from now on the administration will not be able to make mistakes with impunity'.[61] By October 1868, according to his colleague at Besançon, 'Confidence has declined, devotion faltered;

[54] E.g. PG Aix 11 Jan. 1864, AN BB30/370.   [55] AN 45 AP 1.
[56] 6 April 1864, AN BB30/378.   [57] 5 Dec. 1865, AN F1 CIII Basses-Pyrénées 11.
[58] E.g. OC 1er Légion, 30 Sept. 1869, AHG G8/166.
[59] PG Lyons, 7 Oct. 1869, AN BB30/379.
[60] E.g. OC gendarmerie de la Loire, 28 May 1869, AHG G8/165.
[61] 7 Jan. 1865, AN BB30/388.

political parties previously without credit have regained favour and exercise an unfortunate influence.'[62] The state prosecutor at Angers summed up these feelings in warning that 'uncertainty about the future is one of the most powerful opposition arguments against the form of our government' and specifically against *le Gouvernement personnel.*[63]

In 1860 the conditions had been created for a renewal of elite politics. The promise made in a speech on 19 January 1867 and implemented by legislation in May/June 1868 significantly extended the freedoms of the press and public meeting. These measures established the conditions for a more democratic politics. There was a doubling in the number of newspapers in circulation by May 1870.[64] Increasingly, the style and content of politics was established by the 'culture of print'[65] which in reinforcing awareness of events, and the sense of immediacy, contributed to changing political perceptions. Before 1868 the opposition press had been strongest in Paris and present in thirty-one other departments largely on the circumference in the south-west, west, north, and east. Forty departments, including much of the Paris region and almost the whole of central France and the Midi, had been almost unrepresented.[66] Now the situation was to be transformed through the growing invasion of Parisian newspapers and the proliferating local press. The development of the railway network and improvement of roads made it easier for even the most isolated villages in the Haute-Saône to receive copies of such 'incendiary' newspapers as *La Cloche*, *Le Rappel*, and *La Marseillaise*.[67] Gendarmerie reports complained that no-one could ignore 'the constant criticism of the government'.[68] Everywhere a substantial increase in the political use of the printed word occurred, although this was far from excluding oral propaganda. Newspapers themselves were read aloud frequently and discussed in the workplace and café.[69] Better communications and increasing literacy improved mass access to information. 'Men who have received a certain education and who devote themselves to reading the newspapers' served as opinion leaders.[70] Certainly they had their work cut out. There appears to have been little echo of the 'subversive' meetings in Paris in 1868/9 in the surrounding countryside.[71] Nevertheless, if a sustained interest was lacking, particular issues, most notably the threat

[62] 12 Oct. 1868, AN BB30/389.　　[63] 11 Nov. 1869, *ibid.*　　[64] Tulard, *Dictionnaire*, p. 1058.

[65] Vernon, *Politics*, p. 147　　[66] Bersot, *La presse*, pp. 7–8.

[67] PG Besançon, 12 April 1870, AN BB30/390.

[68] OC compagnie de la Loire, 28 Dec. 1868, AHG G8/152.

[69] E.g. J. Hébrard, 'Les nouveaux lecteurs' in J. Martin and R. Chartier (eds.), *Histoire de l'édition française*, III (Paris 1985), p. 506.

[70] PG Nîmes, 18 Jan. 1869, AN BB30/389.　　[71] PG Paris, 8 Feb. 1869, *ibid.*

of wider conscription, could arouse intense interest in even the most iso-lated regions.[72] In such circumstances, the rapid transmission of news ensured that 'every citizen is touched at the same moment, by the same fact, regardless of where it happened', and 'the diversity of individual responses loses itself immediately in the general current which makes up public opinion'.[73]

Political debate and criticism of the regime were stimulated further by the decline of social fear, of the 'memories of a time of disorder.'[74] The desire spread for fair elections and reinforcement of the powers of the Corps législatif.[75] It was becoming evident increasingly that opposition was spreading both down the social hierarchy and from town to country, amongst those classes previously judged to be 'indifferent' to politics.[76] By 1869 the state prosecutor at Dijon was reporting that 'opinion is evidently advancing in the direction, I will not say of opposition, but towards the liberal aspirations encouraged by recent developments. The different classes which make up society, without marching in step and obeying the same instincts, take nevertheless the same direction.'[77] On the basis of the 'generally sombre pictures' drawn by his subordinates, his colleague at Toulouse concluded that 'the crisis is imminent'.[78]

The 1869 elections were quite unlike anything since 1848, especially in Paris, with crowds invading the streets and public meetings and news-papers attacking the regime in often violent terms. Opposition was becoming a normal, even a fashionable, feature of the political system. It had ceased to be risky.[79] Government warnings about the revival of the 'red spectre' do not appear to have had much impact. With the exception of a small minority of radical republicans, most opposition candidates were socially conservative notables. There were more candidates, en-joying greater freedom of expression. In most urban constituencies it was the republicans who made the running. In Paris alone over 200 electoral meetings were held and attracted tens of thousands of excited listeners.[80] The turnout for the two ballots (23–24 May, 6–7 June) was high, with 78.1 per cent of registered voters. Whilst 4,438,000 votes were cast for official candidates, opposition representatives gained 3,355,000 (32.2 per cent). They were concentrated, as before, in urban centres but

---

[72] PG Limoges, 13 Jan. 1869, *ibid.*   [73] PG Caen, 18 Jan. 1869, *ibid.*
[74] PG Paris, 5 May 1866, AN BB30/384.   [75] E.g. PG Rouen, 11 Jan. 1866, AN BB30/387.
[76] Unsigned 'Note pour l'Empereur – Faut-il avancer ou rester dans les lignes politiques actuelles', n.d., probably 1863, AN 45 AP 1.
[77] 13 Jan. 1869, AN BB30/389.   [78] 8 Jan. 1869, *ibid.*   [79] E.g. PG Pau, 24 Jan. 1870, *ibid.*
[80] Dalotel *et al.*, *Aux origines*, pp. 38–9.

there were also clear signs of growing rural support.[81] In the Gers, where government candidates successfully reminded peasants that they owed their prosperity to the Emperor, the opposition vote nevertheless rose from 19 per cent to 31 per cent of those voting.[82] In Paris, Lyons, and Saint-Etienne the authorities judged the situation to be so hopeless that opposition candidates were left unopposed.

Even before the vote, officials were warning that the new Assembly would be very different from its predecessors.[83] According to the official *Moniteur*, the government majority remained substantial, with 216 deputies compared with 74 members of the opposition (49 liberals, 19 democrats, and 6 radicals). The government was saved in many constituencies only by divisions amongst its opponents. Many of the old Legitimist and Orleanist leaders, including Falloux, Rémusat, Casimir-Périer, and Broglie, were defeated. Nevertheless, the results represented a doubling in the size of opposition, both in terms of votes and seats. In addition, ninety-eight members of the majority were 'government liberals'. It followed that if government and opposition liberals were added together, a majority of deputies was in favour of further liberal reform. The divisions amongst both government and opposition candidates suggested that major political re-alignments were likely. Eventually, many 'independents' and moderate republicans might be expected to rally to the regime, providing that it recognised the urgent need for further liberalisation and the establishment of a parliamentary regime. There was thus considerable room for compromise between politicians, the vast majority of whom were anxious to protect a social order based on the ownership of private property and to regulate and de-radicalise popular politics. More immediately there was widespread confusion and disquiet in political circles. The end of the election campaign did not mean an end to political debate and agitation, as the government had hoped.[84] A new era appeared to be opening.

Napoleon's reaction to the pressure for further reform represented by a petition signed by 116 of the newly elected deputies was relatively rapid, as we have seen. The Emperor appeared to accept that the election results proved 'the pressing need for ... liberal reforms'[85] and, on 27 December 1869, requested Emile Ollivier to form 'a homogeneous cabinet, faithfully representing the majority in the Corps législatif'.[86] The

---

[81] Langouyete, *Candidature*, p. 682.   [82] Palmade, 'Le Gers' in Girard, *Les élections*, p. 209.
[83] E.g. PG Aix, 4 Oct. 1868, AN BB30/389.   [84] E.g. PG Aix, 26 June 1869, AN BB18/1785.
[85] PG Nancy, 18 Oct. 1869, AN BB30/389.
[86] C. Nicolet, *L'idée républicaine en France* (Paris 1982), pp. 148–9.

creation of the Liberal Empire was sufficient to persuade former moderate republicans like Ollivier and leading liberals like Prévost-Paradol and E. de Laboulaye, as well as still influential figures from the past like Guizot, Rémusat, and Barrot, to accept the regime. Anxious to reinforce parliamentary controls and electoral freedom, and supported by Orleanist liberals, liberal Bonapartists had secured a major re-casting of the political system. Liberalisation appeared to have succeeded in satisfying the 'dreams of the old parties' and isolating the relatively few *irréconciliables*, that solid core of around thirty liberal and especially republican deputies permanently alienated from the regime by its violent origins. The Second Empire had been able to construct a broader consensus of support than its predecessors. With the exception of a revolutionary fringe, important enough in the major cities, most political activists seemed prepared to work within the legal and political frameworks laid down by the Emperor.[87] This is perhaps the place to consider the various forms of opposition – Legitimist, liberal, and republican – in greater detail.

[87] OC gendarmerie. compagnie de Seine-et-Marne report on Feb. 1870, AHG G8/176.

CHAPTER 9

The forms of opposition: (1) Legitimism

Legitimism was, in part, the doctrine of a social group, the nobility, struggling to retain its influence and to restore an idealised social hierarchy with the legitimate king at its pinnacle – the true Christian prince – whose inherited rights represented the application of Divine Law and historical continuity. In contrast they believed that Bonapartist and republican concepts of popular sovereignty threatened repeated upheaval and would inevitably lead, according to Louis de Ségur, writing in 1861, to 'the total destruction of divine order on earth, and the perfect reign of Satan in the world.'[1] Legitimists adopted the principles established by Bossuet at the beginning of the eighteenth century, insisting that 'God has established kings as his ministers and through them reigns over the peoples', that 'monarchical government is the best, the most durable, the strongest', and that 'royal authority is sacred, paternal, absolute'.[2] The establishment in 1848 of a political system in which the vote of the 'ignorant' counted for as much as that of the 'intelligent', made the re-establishment of hierarchical influences and, ideally, a restricted electorate, all the more urgent. As the Legitimist Pretender to the throne, the Comte de Chambord, pointed out in 1862, 'the more the democratic spirit gains ground, the greater is the urgency to regulate and organise it so as to preserve the social order from the perils to which it might be exposed'.[3] The typical Legitimist landowner must have regarded the need to stand for election and to canvass support from 'his' peasants with considerable distaste, although it was possible to adapt to the round of village fêtes and agricultural fairs.[4]

[1] Quoted by Hazareesingh, *Subject*, p. 105.
[2] Quoted Boutry, 'La légitimité et l'église en France au 19ᵉ siècle' in *Catholiques entre monarchie et république. Mgr. Freppel et son temps* (Paris n.d.), p. 165.
[3] Quoted Hazareesingh, *Subject*, p. 144.
[4] E.g. Y. Pourcher, 'Parenté et représentation politique en Lozère', *Terrain*, 1985, pp. 38–9.

In part Legitimism also represented the effort of a variety of social groups to come to terms with socio-economic change. Democratisation and secularisation, and urban, especially Parisian, influences, posed a growing threat to traditional values. Whilst 'celebrating' the opening of the railway station at Laval in 1855, the Abbé Gérault expressed his concern that 'these fast trains will serve to communicate to the people those doctrines of disorder which will precipitate the ruin of society'.[5] The rural world needed to be protected from 'the barbaric doctrines and vicious habits produced by a sensual and sceptical civilisation'.[6] The 1866 agricultural enquiry records repeatedly the alarm of landowners at growing migration to the cities, and the increasing 'insubordination' of the rural population. Together with rising wages costs, this resulted from the possibility of 'escape' from the countryside as well as from relationships of dependence which landowners assumed tenants and labourers had, previously, entered into freely.[7] In this situation the government was condemned for reducing tariff protection, for the conscription which reduced the supply of docile labour further, and above all for encouraging the growth of Paris. An incident like the collapse of the Colin de Sauvigny bank at Poitiers in July 1866, a local institution favoured by Legitimist landowners, reinforced their sense of alienation from a world perceived to be dominated by speculation and greed.[8] Legitimists were ambivalent towards existing political institutions. On the one hand, they looked to the state, in alliance with the church, to safeguard social order. On the other, they favoured greater communal and regional autonomy as a means of limiting the power of the despised prefects, who threatened their local influence, and of reducing the centralisation of government in Paris, which made it easier for revolutionaries to seize the levers of power.[9]

The language of the constant professions of loyalty to Chambord suggests that the Prince was perceived 'not only as a pretender, but as a principle',[10] a 'conception of society' rather than a 'form of government'.[11] His supporters were engaged in a social mission. More than

---

[5] Quoted M. Denis, 'Les royalistes de la Mayenne et le monde moderne', Doctorat d'Etat, Université de Paris-Sorbonne, 1977, p. 640.

[6] Comice agricole de Laval. C-R des séances, 18–21 May 1870, *ibid.* pp .632–3.

[7] Price, 'The onset of labour shortage.'   [8] PG Poitiers, 11 Nov. 1866, AN BB30/385.

[9] E.g. R. Locke, *French Legitimists and the Politics of Moral Order in the Early Third Republic* (London 1974), pp. 132–206; S. Kale, *Legitimism and the Reconstruction of French Society, 1852–83* (London 1992), pp. 135–40; Hazareesingh, *Subject*, pp. 97–110.

[10] PG Riom, 11 July 1859, AN BB30/368.

[11] R. Rémond, *Les droites en France* (Paris 1982), p. 58.

this, according to an editorial in the *Gazette de Flandres et d'Artois*, 'Legitimism ... is not an opinion, it is a living, profound and unshakeable
faith; its origins are in God's justice, it alone will earn Divine reward; it is
impossible to depart from its principles without meriting God's anger',[12]
sentiments which reveal its mystical core. Legitimists were anxious to
're-establish' a moral basis for social relationships based on the family
and religion, together with a network of associations through which hierarchical authority could be reinforced, social tensions eliminated and
the masses weaned away from 'dangerous' political ideas. In the last
resort only faith could preserve man from evil. Thus the church had a
vital educative and moralising role to play. In this task it had to be supported by the paternalistic activity of the wealthy. According to Armand
de Melun, in every village and urban neighbourhood Christian charity
would 'replace all the powers and hierarchies abolished by the Revolution, and re-establish ... those bonds, those relations of clientage, that in
the past were the prerogatives of birth and fortune'.[13] It was this dedication which, Legitimists claimed, distinguished them from a capitalist
bourgeoisie and which, with persistence, would restore their authority
over the masses. Some aspiring members of the Catholic middle classes
were attracted to the cause by an aristocratic leadership whose status
and style they admired.[14] Others reacted against aristocratic *hauteur* and
the barely concealed contempt for the 'vulgarity' of the *nouveaux riches*.[15]

In the regime's early years, with republicanism subject to intense repression, Legitimism was the form of opposition most freely expressed.
It hardly posed a threat. Although Legitimist sympathisers were present
virtually everywhere, the characteristics of Legitimism varied between
regions. In its main centres of strength in Brittany and the west its strong
rural base reflected the power of irreconcilable resident landowners.
In the almost impenetrable areas of *bocage* and dispersed habitat in
such 'counter-revolutionary' departments as the Vendée, Vienne, and
Deux-Sèvres, peasants remained bound to their 'masters' by sharecrop-
ping contracts and the distribution of charity, loans, and 'advice', and
shared a profound sense of dependence and resignation within an apparently timeless and unchanging community.[16] Their situation contrasted
markedly with that of peasants living on the more open plains, in large

[12] Quoted S. Rials, *Révolution et contre-révolution au 19ᵉ siècle* (Paris 1987), p. 218.
[13] Quoted Kale, *Legitimism*, p. 163.   [14] E.g. PG Amiens, 15 July 1862, AN BB30/371.
[15] Locke, *Legitimism*, pp. 72–5.
[16] E.g. M. Denis, 'Reconquête ou défensive' in S. Köpeczi and E. Balász (eds.), *Noblesse française.
Noblesse hongroise* (Paris 1981), p. 132.

villages with a more diverse social structure, and in which prosperous peasants and *bourgeois* were willing to compete with traditional elites for land and power.[17] Even in the west, however, the influence of Legitimist notables was threatened. During the subsistence crisis in 1854 the regime had attracted considerable praise for its efforts to assist the poor who, on occasion, even blamed the nobles and clergy for the speculation which, according to the popular perception, caused high prices.[18] Certainly noble patronage was unable to compete with that offered by the state. Even in the Vendée officials doubted the ability (or the desire) of Legitimist leaders, 'isolated in their châteaux, weakened by idleness and the shortcomings of their education, occupying their time in hunting and exchanging visits' to oppose the local administration seriously.[19] The enthusiastic welcome given to the Imperial couple on their visit to Brittany in 1858 was symptomatic of a changing situation. Peasants led by their priests flocked to Rennes to welcome the Emperor, camping out in the streets in their carts.[20] In the south-west and Languedoc Legitimism was essentially urban and dependent on the survival of traditional 'vertical' patron–client relationships and the continued ability and willingness of aristocratic and bourgeois Legitimists to commit substantial resources to 'good works' and the provision of employment. Inter-confessional rivalries and the – fading – memories of past conflict were drawn on to reinforce a shared sense of identity.[21] However, this urban Legitimism was beginning to collapse, due to the competing appeals of Bonapartism and republicanism, the decline of religious fervour, economic change, and the re-casting of the mutual aid societies and religious associations into which traditionalistic trades like the Marseille port workers had been grouped previously.[22] From Montpellier, so recently a centre of popular Legitimism, at the end of the 1850s it was reported that the majority of workers had rallied to the regime, whilst those regarded previously as the most fanatical supporters of the Bourbons had, paradoxically, turned to 'the red flag'.[23] Elsewhere, Legitimist landowners were relatively few in number and as 'chiefs without soldiers' consoled themselves at their hearth sides and in their salons with 'epigrams celebrating their lost power' and by engaging in a 'war of pinpricks' against the regime.[24]

[17] M. Faucheux, 'La Vendée' in Girard, *Elections*, pp. 149–50; Maurain, *Politique ecclésiastique*, pp. 241–6.
[18] PG Angers, 8 Jan. 1854, AN BB30/371.   [19] PG Poitiers, 10 April 1859, AN BB30/385.
[20] Academic rector Rennes, 11 Sept. 1858, AN F17/2649.
[21] E.g. G. Cholvy, *Religion et société au 19e siècle* (Lille 1973), II, p. 1033; Kale, *Legitimism*, pp. 20–1.
[22] P. Vigier, *Histoire générale politique et sociale* (Paris 1979), p. 16.
[23] PG Montpellier, 5 July 1858, AN BB30/380.   [24] PG Orleans, 25 July 1853, AN BB30/382.

They were able to retain some influence only for as long as they were moderate and avoided any hints of nostalgia for the *ancien régime*.[25] In spite of the efforts of the elites, increasingly popular Legitimism was restricted to their direct dependents.[26] This weakness would be a powerful inducement to moderation and to the temptation to rally to the Empire.[27]

Like most other conservatives Legitimists had generally welcomed Bonaparte's *coup d'état*, an act that appeared decisively to end the threat of revolution.[28] Together with the clergy, over whom they exercised considerable influence, Legitimists regarded themselves as key players in the counter-revolutionary offensive. However, in the aftermath of the *coup d'état* the Legitimist pretender the Comte de Chambord instructed them to abstain from political life. Chambord was concerned that their engagement in the political process might lead to the disintegration of support for his claims.[29] There was widespread dismay and considerable soul-searching when, in October 1852, he further instructed his supporters to resign from all public functions which required an oath of loyalty, with the notable exception of the army – the traditional means of serving France rather than the regime.[30] However, many Legitimists rejected an instruction which threatened loss of income, influence, status, and access to the patronage gained from serving as deputies, mayors, members of departmental councils, of *bureaux de bienfaisance* or the administrative councils of local hospitals.[31] Thus in 1869 Legitimists and clericals are still estimated to have made up 415 of the 957 opposition-minded members of departmental councils. Of these 69.5 per cent were nobles, most of the others officials or lawyers. They were present in most councils but especially those of the west, the Rhône valley, and to a lesser degree the Nord and Franche-Comté, and as if to confirm Chambord's fears few of them appear to have made use of their membership to express sustained political opposition.[32] Nevertheless, although many Legitimists proved willing to compromise with the Bonapartist regime, local officials would

---

[25] E.g. PG Caen,? April 1859, AN BB30/375; sous-préfet Mortain AN F1 CIII Manche 6.
[26] E.g. G. Palmade, 'Le département du Gers à la fin du Second Empire', *Bulletin de société archéologique, historique et scientifique du Gers*, 1961, p. 89.
[27] E.g. L. Girard, A. Prost, and R. Gossez, *Les conseillers généraux en 1870* (Paris 1967), pp. 140–3.
[28] E.g. Lévêque, 'La Bourgogne de la monarchie de juillet au second empire', p. 1518; Price, *Second Republic*, pp. 284–5.
[29] Zeldin, *Political System*, p. 43.
[30] PG Rennes, 10 July 1853, AN BB30/386, re arrond. Savenay.
[31] E.g. PG Orleans, 6 Jan. 1853, AN BB30/382.
[32] Girard, Prost, and Gossez, *Conseillers*, pp. 133–4, 138–40.

remind their superiors frequently that this should not be taken to imply that 'their traditional affections' had disappeared.[33] The Marquis de Calvière expressed clearly the conditional nature of the support offered by his fellow Legitimists in warning the Prefect of the Gard that

More should not be demanded from them than ... honour and conscience permits them to offer; personal devotion could not be expected, but he would offer a reasoned and sincere support for acts likely to contribute to the re-establishment of religious ideas, respect for order, the family, property and authority. To this extent, and whilst preserving the principles which in a new crisis might open the door to salvation for France, the Catholics of the Gard would serve as the most dedicated upholders of order and society.[34]

With the 1852 plebiscite sanctioning the re-establishment of the Empire, 'the question was posed clearly ... To vote for the Empire was to vote against the legitimate monarchy.' Many of those who had been willing to take the oath of allegiance to a Prince-President and thus accept a temporary transfer of power were unwilling to take this additional step.[35] Calvière, elected in 1852 as an official candidate, resigned, to avoid taking the oath of loyalty, only to be replaced by another rallied Legitimist with fewer scruples, but otherwise a similar grudging acceptance of the *status quo*.[36] Nevertheless, the Legitimist campaign for a negative vote had been surprisingly muted. Certainly, the results were disappointing. The scale of the 'Yes' vote suggests a substantial decline in the influence of Legitimist notables in former areas of strength like the south-east Massif Central, Languedoc, and parts of the west – notably Loire-Inférieure, Morbihan, and especially Ille-et-Vilaine. Undoubtedly, many Legitimists were tempted by the regime's blandishments. Others remained determined to maintain their distance. The Legitimist municipal council at Frontignon (Hérault) was suspended for refusing to celebrate the proclamation of the Empire.[37] M. Auge de Léon, the mayor of Rennes, ostentatiously refused to attend such events as the local prefect's new year reception.[38] Sermons like that preached by the priest at Xanion (Loire-Inf.), following his reading of an episcopal *mandement* praising the Emperor for saving France from revolution, pointed out that the throne really belonged to Henri V, whom God would one day restore.[39]

[33] Prefect, 15 Jan. 1859, AN F₁ cɪɪɪ Drôme 12.   [34] Prefect, 15 Jan. 1852, AN F₁ cɪɪɪ Gard 5.
[35] E.g. PG Angers, 1 Dec. 1852, AN BB30/406; PG Lyon, 11 Dec. 1852, AN BB30/379.
[36] Maurain, *Politique ecclésiatique*, p. 301; also Huard, *La préhistoire des partis*, pp. 616–17.
[37] PG Montpellier, 13 Jan. 1853, AN BB30/380.
[38] PG Rennes, 17 Jan. 1856, AN BB30/386.   [39] PG Poitiers, 31 Jan. 1854, AN BB30/385.

In some provincial cities like Orleans a distinct milieu existed, made up of genuine, and not so genuine, noble families, whose members proclaimed their undying loyalty to Henri V, whilst often pursuing the administration for favours.[40] In Poitiers, where some dozen noble families spent the winters in their town houses, exchanging visits and regularly entertaining the bishop to dinner, acceptance of an official position meant exclusion from 'society': 'an official, even if he were a Montmorency, would be regarded as a bourgeois'.[41] Typically, the state prosecutor at Angers claimed that Legitimism was nothing more than an expression of 'personal vanity' and all the more pronounced the less certain the validity of an individual's claim to nobility.[42] Boselli the prefect of the Loiret regretted that the legislation of May 1858 against the irregular use of titles remained a dead letter, obviously relishing the prospect of a close examination of the claims made and use of the *particule* (de) by some of the more pretentious local families.[43] Further south, in departments like the Var and especially Bouches-du-Rhône, Legitimist leaders were to be found amongst 'the debris of the Provençal aristocracy, in Marseille in the old families enriched by commerce, at Tarascon and Arles amongst the rich landowners'.[44] In Lyons they included nobles resident for part of the year in their town houses and 'many of the families engaged in large and small scale trade' and passionately inspired by 'this mystical Legitimism, which mixes political with religious faith.'[45] In an administrative centre with *parlementaire* traditions, like Dijon, lawyers like Edmond Boissard, Président du Chambre at the court could exert substantial influence within the local elite as well as over landowners in the surrounding countryside.[46]

The authorities took a close interest in the activities of Legitimist notables, particularly where they might be expected to exert some influence over the masses. Considerable efforts were made to win them over. Frequently, they were selected as official candidates on the recommendation of prefects claiming to be unable to find 'suitable' Bonapartists. In the 1852 elections three Legitimists were elected unopposed in the west

[40] Prefect 9 April 1859, AN F1 CIII Loiret 7.
[41] PG Poitiers, 29 Jan. 1860, AN BB30/385; see also academic rector Poitiers, 10 May 1858, AN F17/2649; A. Gough, 'The conflict in politics' in Zeldin (ed.), *Conflicts in French Society* (London 1970), pp. 128–9.
[42] PG Angers, 15 April 1859, AN BB30/385.
[43] C. Marcilhacy, *Le diocèse d'Orléans sous l'épiscopat de Mgr. Dupanloup, 1849–79* (Paris 1962), p. 392.
[44] PG Aix, 2 July 1859, AN BB30/370.   [45] PG Lyons, 11 Dec. 1852, AN BB30/379.
[46] Gonnet, 'La société dijonnaise au 19e siècle', p. 1001; see also academic rector Dijon, 17 April 1858, AN F17/2649.

(in Vendée, Maine-et-Loire, and Ille-et-Vilaine) where the administration had decided that resident nobles supported by the clergy were in an unassailable position. These were situations which bred the intransigence of families like the Charette, Cadoudal, and La Rochejacquelain, closely associated with rural communities by the still potent memories of suffering and loss during the counter-revolution of the 1790s.[47] M. La Rochejacquelain, elected to the Vendée *conseil général* in 1852, was welcomed in the villages he chose to visit by their entire populations, led by mayors and priests and young men firing guns in celebration. Elected president of the council, he refused to attend a reception for the Emperor in October 1857.[48] Whilst the state prosecutor at Aix in 1855 dismissed the local republicans as too disorganised to pose a threat, he felt that 'the partisans of the traditional monarchy ... represent a more serious danger'. They were 'from the very bottom of society to the most aristocratic heights, associated in all manner of societies and linked through the clergy' and although 'submitting to the power of the authorities, they endure the Emperor's government ... with a superb disdain'.[49] Similar situations prevailed in other southern towns like Nîmes, Alais, or Beaucaire where memories of the violent clashes with 'reds' in 1793 or 1815 helped preserve 'personal, family and party hatreds'.[50] In the absence of an organised party, Legitimist militants established diffuse local and regional links through informal social networks and kept up a correspondence with the Bureau du Roi representing Chambord in Paris. This had six members, each responsible for a particular region.[51] In the west the meeting of a learned society like the *Congrès breton* in October 1856 was one of many occasions on which Legitimist sympathisers might gather.[52]

The ambiguous position of many Legitimists was exemplified in 1855 by the prefect of the Sarthe in the person of M. de la Bouillerie, a landowner recently appointed mayor of Bazoge:

this position might lead one to believe that the family is tempted to rally; nothing of the sort. M. de la Bouillerie belongs to that fraction of intelligent Legitimists who are determined to preserve their influence and who understand that to abdicate in an absolute manner, and to isolate themselves from the population,

[47] Girard, *Problèmes Politiques*, p. 92; Kale, *Legitimists*, p. 71.
[48] PG Poitiers, 10 Oct., 10 Dec. 1852, AN BB30/385.
[49] Quoted C. Derobert-Ratel, *Les Arts et l'Amitié et le rayonnement maçonnique dans la société aixoise de 1848 à 1871* (Aix-en-Provence 1987), p. 12.
[50] Sous-préfet Béziers, Jan. 1856, AN F 1 cIII Hérault 9.   [51] Rials, *Révolution*, p. 259.
[52] PG Rennes, 17 Jan. 1857, AN BB30/386.

would represent an avoidable error. Thus [he] serves his personal interests and those of his party in accepting the function of mayor of his commune; beyond that nothing can be expected of him and the oath he has taken relates only to the municipal administration, that is, to his own interests as a large landowner.[53]

Pragmatism was allied to 'the chivalric instinct' and a romantic loyalty to Henri V.[54] As a young man, René de Belleval had planned a diplomatic career, but when the subject had been broached his father 'had proved inflexible and declared that he would not tolerate my entering the service of Napoleon III'. Within the closed circle of noble families in the Somme only a military career would have been seen as honourable.[55] According to the prefect of the Mayenne, as well as the older generation, it was the womenfolk, determined to safeguard family tradition and honour, that prevented a more thoroughgoing *ralliement*.[56]

Whilst Legitimist leaders conducted themselves with a prudent reserve, frequent minor incidents continued to alarm the authorities. Drunken shouts of 'Vive Henri V' were common as the bars closed in towns like Arles, and often led to brawls.[57] Popular protest associated the legitimate king with aspirations for a better life. A placard found on 6 February 1854 at Buis (Drôme) began: 'Long life to our true king Henri V' and went on to warn that 'bread will be expensive for as long as the perjured usurper occupies the throne'.[58] Chambord's name day in July and his birthday in September were especially potent dates. In 1858, Saint Henri's Day was celebrated on the estate of the Princess Baciocchi at Châteausaissières in Brittany by the display of four Bourbon flags and a banquet, followed by dancing, fireworks, and numerous gunshots. In September the ceremonies held at the great Breton pilgrimage centre of Sainte-Anne-d'Auray in honour of the pretender's birthday caused further concern.[59] The discovery of illicit literature was also alarming. On the eve of the 1852 plebiscite, pamphlets written by Chambord condemning the proposals[60] were distributed by militants or, in the case of those received by the officers of the 58th infantry regiment in garrison at Dijon,

---

[53] 6 Jan. 1855, quoted Maurain, *Politique ecclésiastique*, p. 30.

[54] PG Lyons, 3 June 1852, AN BB30/379.

[55] J.-M. Wiscart, *La noblesse de la Somme au 19ᵉ siècle* (Paris 1994), p. 211.

[56] 12 July 1853, AN F1 ciii Mayenne 6.

[57] GOC 9e DM, 25 Sept. 1855, AHG G8/27; prefect Bouches-du-Rhône report on September 1855, AN F7/3942.

[58] PG Grenoble, 24 Feb. 1854, AN BB30/378.

[59] Reports of prefect Morbihan on July and September 1858, AN F7/4095.

[60] 'L'événement prévu par la lettre du 27 Avril', dated 28 Oct. 1852.

through the post.[61] In October 1853 Mathieu, a carter from Napoléon-Vendée, was found to be transporting a box addressed to the Vicomte de Saint Pierre, which contained portraits of the Comte de Chambord wearing royal robes as well as a list of subscribers to the Legitimist *Chronique de Paris*, amongst them a senior government official at Poitiers.[62]

None of this, however, compensated effectively for the divisions amongst Legitimists or the lack of leadership from Chambord himself. The pretender appears to have been inspired by little more than an optimistic faith in the workings of Providence and in such outcomes as the premature death of the Emperor followed by a monarchist military *coup*.[63] The regular visits by Legitimists leaders to his place of exile in Venice or Frohsdorf provided opportunities to request instructions but were essentially moments of pilgrimage.[64] The Legitimist press remained elitist in tone and readership. Three Parisian newspapers represented the main, often bitterly conflictual strands of the movement: the *Gazette de France*, politically intransigent but Gallican in religious affairs; *L'Union*, politically more moderate but ultramontane in religion; and *L'Assemblée nationale*, in favour of fusion with the Orleanists. This appeared to make perfect sense, given that on Chambord's death the Orleanist Comte de Paris would be his legitimate successor. However, many Legitimists preferred to contemplate rallying to the Empire at that stage rather than compromise with what they perceived as bourgeois liberalism.[65] These newspapers were supported vigorously, sometimes after a brief suspension following the *coup d'état*, by provincial journals like the *Gazette de Lyon* or *Journal de Rennes*, which reprinted articles from the Parisian press and imposed a limited cohesion on the movement nationally.[66] Cautious initially, then increasingly vocal as fear both of social unrest and of government repression declined, local newspapers like the *Mémorial de l'Allier*, published in Moulins, were – certainly by the 1857 elections – more pronounced in their Legitimism. Whilst still hesitating to attack the regime directly, they featured articles on the pre-revolutionary golden age and praised the virtues of the Comte de Chambord.[67]

Officials remained divided over the most effective tactics for defeating Legitimism. In March 1852, the prefect of the Isère insisted that Legitimist sympathisers in the administration might be bound to the

---

[61] GOC 7e DM report on 11–15 and 26–30 Nov. 1852, AHG F1/70.
[62] PG Poitiers, 31 Jan. 1854, AN BB30/385.   [63] E.g. Gough, 'Conflict', pp. 134–5.
[64] E.g. PG Riom, 20 April, 11 July 1859, AN BB30/386.   [65] Rials, *Révolution*, p. 195.
[66] Bellanger, *Presse*, II, p. 270; Maurain, *Politique ecclésiastique*, pp. 157–8.
[67] PG Riom, 15 July 1857, 10 Jan. and 10 April 1859, AN BB30/386.

regime by making it clear that their careers depended on loyalty, whilst local notables should be told that access to patronage 'to place their children, their relatives, their friends, even their clients' depended on their rallying to the cause.[68] In contrast, the academic rector at Rennes advised that 'it was no longer possible to have as intermediaries between the administration and population those who use their wealth to organise charitable and agricultural societies as a means of controlling the population and isolating it from the government'. He pointed out that when the prefect of Ille-et-Vilaine had invited members of the departmental agricultural society to meet the Emperor during his tour of the west, its president had responded that he could not pass on the invitation because 'he had not received instructions from *his* king'.[69] In certain circumstances the authorities were inclined to exclude Legitimists and actively seek to reduce their influence rather than attempt to win them over. The sous-préfet at Beaune (Côte-d'Or) was easily able to dismiss them as few in number and lacking in influence.[70] In the Limousin, concessions to Legitimists were only likely to offend peasant voters who loathed the nobility.[71] The threat of an eventual re-establishment of seigneurial dues and the tithe also continued to alarm peasants in the Charentes, Dordogne, and Gironde. A Legitimist notable in Charente-Inférieure warned that if the local peasants lost their affection for the Emperor 'they would become socialists, and terrible socialists.'[72] More frequently officials assumed – as did the prefect of Loir-et-Cher – that, in the last resort, there were few completely irreconcilable Legitimists, and that in moments of crisis the vast majority could be relied on to lend assistance.[73] The wealthy nobles of the Nièvre were unwilling to rally to the regime formally, 'but are not interested in its destruction because ... it offers them security and ... they fear that a new revolution would bring back socialism'.[74] The anonymous author of a pamphlet published in Paris in 1858 insisted that it would be 'ungrateful to turn against the one who saved us and gave us tranquillity, peace at home, and the enjoyment of our fortunes', and warned that 'to try and bring down the same man, at the evident risk, if he falls, of being ruined and collectively led to catastrophe, is sheer irresponsible folly'.[75] The birth

---

[68] 7 March 1852, AN F1 cIII Isère 9.   [69] 11 Sept. 1858, AN F17/2649.

[70] 14 Aug. 1853, AN F1 cIII Côte-d'Or 7.   [71] Corbin, *Archaïsme* II, pp. 831-2.

[72] Academic rector Poitiers, 10 May 1858, AN F17/2649; see also A. Corbin, *The Village of Cannibals: Rage and Murder in France, 1870* (Oxford 1992), p. 27.

[73] 7 April 1858, quoted Dupeux, *Aspects*, p. 433.   [74] Vigreux, *Paysans et notables*, p. 368.

[75] *Comment d'après la religion et la morale doit-on comprendre la légitimité?* (Paris: Montdidier 1858), quoted Hazareesingh, *Subject*, pp. 106–7.

of the heir to the throne apparently encouraged some Legitimists to accept that they would have to come to terms with an apparently stable regime, although in noble circles wishful thinking continued to suggest that the empire would collapse eventually and provide them with their great opportunity.[76] A merchant distributing Legitimist medals in the Vendée in 1859 tried to justify this activity to the authorities by pointing out that if the Emperor were to be killed on the battlefields of Italy, and his wife and son were murdered by *les rouges*, the only way left to avoid the horrors of 1793 would be the restoration of Henri V.[77] Arguing along similar lines, Jules de Cacheleu, a landowner in the Somme and devoted Legitimist, grudgingly admitted that thanks to Napoleon 'the [wayside] crosses have been put back up, the image of the son of God has been re-established in the courts, and Catholic ceremonies have emerged from the churches in many towns to be seen by all the people'.[78] More mundanely perhaps, the prefect of the Hérault was able to congratulate himself on the attendance of aristocratic families at his New Year Ball in 1858.[79] In particular, the younger generations were growing tired of a seemingly endless and increasingly pointless opposition in anticipation of another, repeatedly postponed, restoration. They were persuaded too that participation in public life was necessary to protect the interests of the church.[80]

The growing danger in the 1850s, from the Legitimist point of view, was that the regime's efforts to win over the clergy would lead to their own isolation. Louis Veuillot, whose newspaper *L'Univers* was so popular with priests, clearly came to believe that an ultramontane church might have more to gain from Napoleon than Chambord. A song circulating in Finistère expressed the concern of local Legitimists that the clergy, following the lead of their bishops might desert the cause:

> The bishop, his crosier in his hands, like a real sergeant,
> Makes his clergy, who so respect and cherish him,
> March in step like soldiers.
> Yes! ... Just like sheep they love the wolf.[81]

---

[76] Academic rector Dijon, 17 April 1858, AN F17/2649; see also prefect, 14 April 1856, AN F1 cIII Gers 8.

[77] PG Poitiers, 2 July 1859, AN BB30/422.

[78] *L'Eglise, Napoléon III et l'Europe* (Paris: Dentu, 1861), quoted Wiscart, *Noblesse*, p. 209.

[79] Prefect, Jan. 1858, AN F1 cIII Hérault 9.

[80] PG Dijon, Jan. 1863, AN BB30/377; Cholvy, *Religion et société* II, pp. 1031–2.

[81] M. T. Cloitre, 'Aspects de la vie politique dans le département de Finistère de 1848 à 1870', *Bulletin de la société archéologique du Finistère*, 1973, p. 788.

The 1857 elections were a warning. There were fewer avowedly Legitimist candidates and they all failed. Even such eminent figures as the lawyer Berryer and the Comte de Falloux presented themselves as the defenders of 'liberty' and religion and accepted that their particular political principles were less important than the struggle for moral regeneration.[82] It took the regime's Italian policy and the threat to the temporal power of the Pope to restore the much-weakened alliance between Legitimism and the clergy.

Whilst most Legitimist sympathisers had throughout the authoritarian Empire supported the administration in its struggle against disorder, from 1859 they would represent a major element in the rise of opposition. The regime's situation was to be weakened seriously by a pronounced loss of confidence within the ranks of its own deputies and amongst Catholics within the social elite more generally. During the debate on the speech from the throne in 1861, ninety-one deputies voted against the government, delivering an unprecedented warning. Three Catholics, Cuverville, Keller, and Lemercier, elected as official candidates, wrote a joint letter warning the Emperor that his policy would 'separate every sincere Catholic from you'.[83] Pie, the bishop of Poitiers, publicly denounced the Emperor as a second Herod, forcing Persigny to instruct government officials to break off all relations with the prelate. At the same time the episcopal printer was fined 500 francs for failing to observe the censorship regulations.[84] The government would be forced, in addition, to suppress two newspapers – *L'Univers* and *La Bretagne* – which had been amongst the most enthusiastic advocates of a clerical Bonapartism previously. The *Univers* was condemned for publishing the Papal encyclical, *Nobilis certe*, which had attacked the Emperor in language almost as violent as its own.[85] However, the role of Veuillot's newspaper was taken up by the only slightly less extreme *Le Monde*. In the provinces newspapers like *L'Alsacien*, previously devoted to the regime, increasingly evinced Legitimist as well as ultramontane tendencies.[86] At the same time, in clerical areas of the west, readership of pro-government papers like *L'Union bretonne* declined as priests threatened to excommunicate its readers.[87] The cadres of the 'Party of Order' were beginning to turn against the Emperor. It was reported that amongst notables resident in

---

[82] Maurain, *Politique ecclésiastique*, pp. 222–3.   [83] Quoted *ibid.*, p. 364.
[84] *Ibid*, p. 519.   [85] Bellanger, *Presse*, II, p. 278.
[86] Presse départementale. Extraits des rapports des inspecteurs généraux, 1860–6, in *Documents pour servir*.
[87] Bellanger, *Presse*, p. 317.

Toulouse 'sincere men, who until now have devotedly and energetically supported the government are troubled profoundly and unable to conceal that, in the last resort, the interests of their faith are more important to them than political loyalty'.[88] A senior police official told the moderate republican deputy Darimon early in 1860, that although 'clerical manifestations are not much of a threat to the Empire', nevertheless it had 'broken with the conservatives and could hardly rely on the masses'. As for the clergy, 'they would never forgive the Emperor for the Italian expedition'.[89] In Brittany, seven years of efforts to secure an alliance with the clergy were compromised and, in spite of efforts by most bishops to moderate opposition, the alliance between nobles and clergy was re-established, but now with the clergy as the dominant partner. Rumours spread that the Emperor was secretly planning the separation of church and state as well as the introduction of obligatory and secular instruction.[90]

More than ever, Legitimist support for the regime was conditional, whilst the clergy would support whichever electoral candidate – official or Legitimist – committed himself most steadfastly to the Roman cause.[91] The danger to which the church appeared to be exposed by the collapse of the Pope's temporal power certainly reinforced Legitimist activity.[92] Many of those who had formerly obeyed the Comte de Chambord's instructions to abstain from politics and, like the Vicomte de Rochefoucault in the Vendômois, devoted themselves to hunting and improving agriculture, now felt that too much was at stake.[93] Many of those who had formerly rallied now changed their minds. The attendance of nobles at official functions once more declined.[94] The state prosecutor at Angers reported that 'the Legitimists ... act and speak with an audacity not seen in the last ten years. For them and for the clergy events in Italy provide a pretext for an increasingly malevolent and unjust opposition.'[95] Following a tour of his diocese by the extreme ultramontane Bishop Pie, the Prefect of Vienne complained that 'the churches have become veritable clubs which I am powerless to surveille. The pulpits have been transformed into tribunes from which many honest priests, until now inoffensive, excited, on the one hand by the bishop, and on the other by the rancour of the Legitimist party, feel obliged to clumsily protest in the

---

[88] PG Toulouse, 4 Feb. 1859, AN BB30/385.   [89] Quoted Girard, *Questions politiques*, p. 31.
[90] E.g. PG Rennes, 15 July 1865, AN BB30/386.
[91] E.g. PG Rouen, 18 Oct. 1860, AN BB30/387.   [92] PG Poitiers, 9 July 1868, AN BB30/385.
[93] PG Orleans, 7 Jan. 1862, AN BB30/382.   [94] E.g. PG Amiens, 4 July 1860, AN BB30/371.
[95] Quoted Maurain, *Politique*, p. 341.

name of the Pope, against the policies of the Emperor's government.'[96] Copies of an inflammatory pamphlet written by Pie were distributed by the clergy and members of the Société de Saint Vincent de Paul.[97] Legitimists demanded political 'liberty' in order to exert greater control over the Emperor who, by threatening the vital interests of the church, had come to 'personify ... Revolution'.[98] A campaign in favour of the embattled Papacy and political liberalisation was launched by ultramontane bishops with the support of Legitimist politicians, as well as liberals like Adolphe Thiers who had been convinced since 1848 that anything which weakened Catholicism threatened social order.

This renewed clerico-Legitimist alliance could depend on the support and influence of the clergy and on the network of charitable associations favoured by the Catholic laity.[99] In a letter to the Emperor's private secretary, Mocquard, Pietri, the Paris Prefect of Police, had already expressed his concern about the political threat from Catholic lay organisations and especially the Société de Saint Vincent de Paul.[100] Membership of these groups was an important feature of the male sociability of local social elites. It possessed 'snob' appeal and offered a refuge for those Legitimists whose loyalty to Chambord prevented them from taking an active part in politics.[101] Many senior officials were also members and mixed socially with enemies of the regime.[102] As relations with the church deteriorated the government would feel obliged to take action. It was determined to ensure that the Conseil supérieur of the Société de Saint Vincent de Paul would not be able to co-ordinate opposition. The *Conseil* was dissolved when its members refused to accept nomination of its president by the Emperor, although they would continue to meet informally. The society's local *conférences* were required by an October 1861 circular to seek official authorisation. Most (around 1,200) did, although some 300, mainly Legitimist-dominated, groups in the west preferred to cease their activities.[103]

If Catholicism was a central feature of Legitimist ideology, it remained the case that most Catholics were not Legitimists. The movement remained profoundly divided between moderates likely to rally

[96] 4 April 1860, AN F1 CIII Vienne 9.   [97] PG Poitiers, 29 Jan. 1860, AN BB30/385.
[98] PG Besançon, 21 May 1859, AN BB30/369.
[99] E.g. PG Toulouse, report on Ire semestre 1856, AN BB30/388; PG Douai, 29 July 1856, AN BB30/377.
[100] 21 April 1854, in *Papiers et correspondance*, vol. II, p. 251.
[101] Point made by sous-préfet Loudéac, 24 Sept. 1856, AN F1 CIII Côtes-du-Nord 13.
[102] PG Limoges, 27 July 1862, AN BB30/378.
[103] J.-B. Duroselle, *Les débuts du catholicisme social en France, 1822–70* (Paris 1951), p. 550.

to the regime and the irreconcilable, as well as between liberals like Berryer and Falloux, who saw Legitimism as primarily a guarantee of social order, and the ultramontane idealists, still dreaming of some kind of social monarchy and confident that Divine Providence would ensure success.[104] Even in the west, however, the efforts of nobles to rally the masses to the Papal cause met with relatively little success. The sermons and brochures denouncing as sacrilege the Emperor's failure to defend the temporal power of the Papacy had little impact. The procureur-général at Rennes observed that for the peasants, 'as long as nothing changes in the actual situation of the clergy, as long as services are celebrated with the usual pomp, then religion will not be compromised seriously'.[105] In urban centres the efforts of the clergy were even less successful. Philippon, the well-informed police spy in Rouen, sought to calm his superior's concern about the influence of the Catholic lay associations by pointing out that they provided assistance only to the small minority of regular church attenders and that most workers bitterly resented this discrimination, so that 'if ultramontanism is considered as the only party capable of causing, if not concern, at least serious embarrassment to the government, the threatening attitude of the popular classes towards it will moderate its activities and paralyse its enterprises'.[106] It would be at the electoral and parliamentary level, amongst the socio-political elites, that the Roman Question caused most difficulty. Even then extreme ultramontane doctrines would prove distasteful to many devout Catholics. Outright opposition to a regime, which continued to support the church in France, and to provide troops to protect Rome, seemed out of the question.[107] Brittany provided most of the 2,000-strong contingent of French volunteers for the Papal army – two-thirds of them young men of popular origin, following their *maîtres*.[108] In contrast, the noble residents of Paris or the Somme or the Norman department of the Orne appear to have been far less willing to make either financial or personal sacrifices.[109]

From the clerico-Legitimist viewpoint the results of the 1863 elections were mixed. In the west the government was assisted by continuing

---

[104] E.g. PG Nîmes, 9 April 1868, AN BB30/382; Huard, *Préhistoire*, pp. 1188–9.
[105] 18 Jan. 1860, AN BB18/1567.
[106] 3 June 1861, quoted Boivin, *Mouvement ouvrier*, vol. I, p. 146.
[107] E.g. PG Lyons, 1 April 1862, AN BB30/379.   [108] Rials, *Révolution*, pp. 202–3.
[109] Prefect, 13 Jan. 1865, AN FI CIII Orne 14; J. Gaillard, 'Le 7e arrondissement' in Girard, *Les élections*, p. 47; Wiscart, *Noblesse*, p. 212; J. Guenel, *La dernière guerre du pape. Les zouaves pontificaux au secours du saint-siège* 1860–70 (Rennes 1998).

Legitimist obedience to Chambord's injunction to abstain. Nevertheless, twenty-five avowed Legitimist candidates presented themselves, encouraged by their bishops to ignore Chambord's instructions.[110] Alongside them were sixteen official candidates with a fundamentally clerical outlook selected – especially in the Nord, and in the Lyon area – as a means of securing the support of the Catholic hierarchy against the republicans. At the same time, twenty-four sitting clerical deputies were deprived of their official nomination, and although six of these would secure re-election to a large degree this would be due to support from republicans, liberals, and protectionists. Even so some of the most eminent were defeated, including Montalembert, Keller, and Cuverville.[111] In the Lozère, in contrast, the Comte de Chambrun, an eminent local landowner, assisted by clerical mayors easily defeated an official candidate virtually unknown in the area.[112] In the Tarn the clergy were intensely irritated by the government's nomination of a Jew, Eugène Pereire. Similarly at Limoux in the Aude the Legitimist Guiraud, presented as the local *candidat honorable*, came close to success against Isaac Pereire. The bishop's declaration of 'neutrality' insisted that: 'Monseigneur does not doubt the profound repulsion of his clergy for the candidature of the Jew whose election would be a disgrace for ... Limoux.'[113] The *juif Isaac* was described in sermons, songs, and 'vulgar poems' as 'the foreigner', the rich man out to buy votes. In a typically anti-semitic sermon the priest at Quillan harangued the women in his congregation: 'O women without religion, who lack the courage to save those criminal husbands who stand on the edge of the precipice from which, with their heads bowed, they are about to throw themselves by voting for a Jew, the assassin of Jesus Christ.'[114] The strength of the clerical position in the Corps législatif would depend ultimately on the seventy or so successful official candidates with strong Catholic sympathies.[115]

By 1869 support for Legitimists *per se* appeared to have further declined. In southern cities like Marseille and Toulouse the popular clientele, which had traditionally supported Legitimist notables, was submerged increasingly under waves of immigrants for many of whom both Legitimism and the church were largely irrelevant. The death of the

---

[110] Marcilhacy, *Le diocèse*, p. 415; Lagoueyte, *Candidature*, p. 611; Maurain, *Politique ecclésiastique*, pp. 655–7.

[111] Zeldin, *Political System*, p. 109; Maurain, *Politique*, pp. 664–5.

[112] PG Nîmes, 13 April 1863, AN BB30/382; Jones, *Politics and Rural Society*, pp. 239–40.

[113] Maurain, *Politique*, pp. 645–53, 925.   [114] Quoted Thibon, *Pays de Sault*, pp. 130, 140.

[115] Maurain, *Politique*, pp. 665–7.

moderate Berryer and a subsequent inability to negotiate an alliance with other parties further weakened the cause in Marseille, where opposition to the regime was increasingly centred on republicanism.[116] Following the first ballot, Bishop Place advised Catholics to vote for the official candidates Lesseps and Rougement, who offered the best guarantees for 'religion, the family, property, society', and in an effort to keep out the republicans Esquiros and Gambetta.[117] In the countryside reduced incomes and the rising cost of living were beginning to affect the ability of Legitimist landowners to use charity as a means of securing support.[118] Although in *bocage* areas in the west the noble–priest alliance forged during the struggle against the revolution remained intact, it failed to prevent a renewed rallying of both Legitimists and priests to the Bonapartist regime as alarm grew concerning the growing support for republicanism. The Comte de Falloux himself was forced to withdraw his candidature following a disappointing first ballot result in the Vendée.[119] As concern about the threat to social order intensified there was increasingly little to distinguish the programmes of Legitimist candidates from those of most government supporters, save perhaps the emphasis on the importance of decentralisation as the means of reviving the authority of local elites.[120]

Legitimist divisions were revealed clearly during the 1870 plebiscite campaign. Of the major Parisian newspapers *L'Union*, inspired by Chambord, called for abstention; the *Gazette de France* for a negative response. *L'Univers* recommended abstention because of the unwillingness of the government to commit itself to the maintenance of an armed force in Rome in perpetuity. However, many Legitimists voted 'Yes' and most bishops instructed their clergy to support a government to which they might not be emotionally committed but which was certainly the least bad alternative in the circumstances.[121] Legitimists had welcomed the liberal reforms, which had provided deputies with the opportunity to control the Emperor more closely. They eagerly anticipated the report of the extra-parliamentary commission on decentralisation established by Ollivier in February, which seemed certain to promise 'greater

---

[116] A. Olivesi, 'Marseille' in Girard, *Les élections*, pp. 88–91, 104–5.
[117] Maurain, *Politique*, p. 922.
[118] E.g. OC gendarmerie Finistère, 30 May 1869, AHG G8/166.
[119] Prefect, 29 May 1869 in Holt, *Papiers sauvés*, p. 218
[120] 'Rapport sur les journaux de Lyon, par le commissaire spécial de police politique', 7 March 1869, in *Pièces saisies*, p. 4; Huard, *La naissance*, pp. 150–1.
[121] E.g. PG Caen, 11 July 1870, AN BB30/390; Constant, *Var*, pp. 1387–91.

communal liberties'.[122] The growth of support for republicanism, together with reports on the verbal violence of speakers at public meetings in Paris, also encouraged Legitimists and clericals 'to cease their regrettable hostility and lend support to a government which, better than any other, is able to protect them against the excesses of demagogy of which they have such great apprehension.'[123] Furthermore Catholics could welcome the presence in the Ollivier government of six clericals, 'who they claim are theirs', out of a total of eight ministers. They had secured the dismissal of both Duruy, the 'secularising' education minister, and of the Gallican Baroche.[124] A political realignment was well under way, within which the clericals and their Legitimist allies would form part of a broad conservative alliance dedicated to the preservation of order. The 'Party of Order' of the Second Republic was re-forming, with the Legitimists more than ever distinguished by their dedication to the interests of the church rather than by their nostalgic loyalty to the Bourbons.[125]

[122] PG Agen, April 1870, AN BB30/390.   [123] PG Amiens, 6 April 1870, *ibid.*
[124] PG Riom, 6 April 1870, *ibid.*
[125] E.g. OC cie. des Côtes-du-Nord, 30 June 1869, AHG G8/166.

CHAPTER 10

The forms of opposition: (2) Liberalism

Liberalism represented a more substantial form of opposition. Most liberals remained monarchists. They included a minority of Legitimists, with such prominent figures as Montalembert, Falloux, and Berryer, and especially the Orleanist supporters of Louis-Philippe and his sons. In general liberals accepted the principles of 1789 – equality before the law, civil liberty, the rule of law, and parliamentary monarchy – as the most effective means of securing the protection of individual freedom, private property, and social order. This was the fundamental line of demarcation between counter-revolutionary conservatism and the Orleanist/liberal tradition. Most liberals, including such eminent figures as Thiers and Charles de Rémusat, regarded democracy with distaste, afraid that it might lead to socialism. Others were more confident in the capacity of educated elites to provide leadership and were prepared to accept manhood suffrage. Increasingly, loyalty to the Orleans family took second place to a more diffuse insistence on principles which were compatible with a variety of constitutional systems. A study of the allegiances of departmental councillors in 1870 identified 157 of these local notables with Orleanism and 248 with liberalism. The former tended to be more intransigent in their opposition to the Empire. They were primarily landowners, professionals, and successful businessmen or bureaucrats who had commenced their careers under the July Monarchy. The personal or family wealth of the likes of the Duc d'Audiffret-Pasquier in the Orne, of the Perier family in the Isère, of the textile entrepreneur and ferocious protectionist Pouyer-Quertier in the Eure, provided them with opportunities for exerting influence over a dependent clientele of tenants, labourers, and factory workers. However, this influence was dispersed geographically. Orleanism lacked a powerful regional or popular base. The liberals were close in terms of origins and ideas but included a significantly higher proportion (10 per cent) of professionals. They were also generally younger men who had not participated in public life

291

during the July Monarchy and were willing to collaborate with a regime committed to reform.[1] Liberals were clearly selective in their appeals to principle. Economic liberals stressed the importance of meritocracy and the free working of the market, but only for as long as their own enterprises did not appear to need protection. More generally, even for the most principled liberal politicians, the protection of public order and the existing social system took precedence over liberty. This could be justified easily on the grounds that freedom was incompatible with anarchy.

Liberals, like Legitimists, could choose between an unreserved rallying to the Empire, resignation to its continued existence, temporary accommodation, and sustained opposition. Their decisions depended to a large degree on circumstances and a change of mind was always possible.[2] However, amongst the intransigents were such eminent and influential figures as Guizot, Thiers, Tocqueville, Rémusat, and the Duc de Broglie. According to the state prosecutor at Agen these intransigents were few in number, and could be found amongst 'the upper portion of the *bourgeoisie* ... some remaining in this party because of their formative experiences; the others men whose interests have been damaged and local importance diminished by events; or those cultivated spirits for whom political speculation has its attraction'.[3] Adolphe Thiers, who, as a historian, had done much to construct the Napoleonic legend, would remain hostile to the nephew's regime. The lesson he drew from his monumental and ongoing *Histoire du Consulat et de l'Empire* (20 vols., 1845–62) was that 'however great, however wise, however vast the genius of a man, never must the destinies of a country be delivered completely to him'.[4] However, like so many other conservative liberals, he had felt obliged to accept the *coup d'état* as the most effective means, at the time, of protecting social order. From his temporary place of exile in Brussels immediately after the *coup*, he wrote to his mother-in-law, Madame Dosne, that 'one submits, without approving ... from the need to have some sort of government' but warned that 'if this is what motivates the masses, individuals rally ... from greed for places and from ambition for honours'. As a result 'we must expect every kind of baseness'.[5] Like Thiers, Alexis de Tocqueville would never forgive Bonaparte for imprisoning him for a few days. He wrote to J.-B. Roussel shortly after his release that

---

[1] Girard, Prost, and Gossez, *Conseillers généraux*, pp. 146–52; Girard, *Les élections*, pp. v–vi.
[2] E.g. prefect, 24 June 1852, AN F1 cIII Isère 9.   [3] 9 Sept. 1853, AN BB30/370.
[4] Quoted Bury and Tombs, *Thiers*, p. 150.
[5] Letter, 18 Dec. 1851, in A. Thiers-Dosne, *Correspondances de 1841 à 1865. M. Thiers à Mme. Thiers et à Mme. Dosne: M. Dosne à M. Thiers* (Paris 1904), p. 240.

from the moment when socialism appeared, we should have been able to predict the rule of the sabre. The one engenders the other. I've been expecting
it for a long time and although I feel considerable shame and sadness for our
country and great indignation about the violence and certain base acts, I am
not surprised or very concerned. Not only do I not wish to oppose the new
government, but I sincerely hope that it will last for some time.

Only the experience of 'bureaucratic and military despotism' would re-
establish the desire for liberty. However, if he had decided not to oppose
the new regime, neither could he bring himself to adhere to it. 'I will
keep my distance until representative institutions ... are re-established.'[6]
The former Prime Minister, Guizot, echoed this, writing in a letter of 12
January 1852 that a 'perfect stranger to the existing government, I am
not at all hostile. It was inevitable and it is necessary. It has a vital mission
to accomplish.' However, like many notables he believed that the new
regime, if it were to survive, would have to adapt. He observed that 'one
can repress a riot with soldiers, one can win an election with peasants,
but soldiers and peasants are not sufficient to govern with. The support
of the upper classes that are naturally rulers is necessary. Now, they, for
the most part, are hostile to the President.'[7]

For some time, most liberals would continue to appreciate a regime
which safeguarded their social eminence and whose representatives were
anxious to protect their local political influence.[8] The Orleanist elite –
the Perier family in Grenoble, for example – thus frequently found itself deserted by the rank and file. It would remain resentful of loss of
status and influence.[9] The regime's confiscation of the property of the
Orleans family caused further heart-searching and some resignations
from official positions.[10] Duvergier de Hauranne warned the British
ambassador that this was proof of Bonaparte's 'decidedly socialist ...
tendencies'.[11] More significant, in the longer term, was the 'nostalgia'
for the parliamentary regime shared by many official deputies, officials,
and a large proportion of the mayors and departmental councillors,
which engendered a simple lack of 'devotion' to the Empire.[12] Socially
conservative but politically liberal notables who had participated in parliamentary government would find it hard to accept a diminution in their
authority, once the threat of revolution had passed.[13] There would be

[6] *Oeuvres complètes* X (Paris 1995), pp. 561–2.   [7] Quoted Girard, *Problèmes politiques*, p. 118.
[8] E.g. PG Rennes, 12 Jan. 1857, AN BB30/386.
[9] PG Grenoble, 12 Jan. 1859, AN BB30/378; Barral, 'Les forces politiques', pp. 165–6.
[10] E.g. PG Rennes, 3 Feb. 1852, AN BB30/386.
[11] Letter to Thiers, 25 Feb. 1852, BN naf 20618.   [12] PG Caen, 25 July 1854, AN BB30/375.
[13] E.g. PG Riom, 11 Jan. 1855, AN BB30/386.

growing resentment of the selection of official electoral candidates who lacked, or so it was frequently claimed, by those who felt excluded, either ability or local roots .[14] As early as 1853/4 official reports were pointing to the 'rebellious character'[15] of an urban *bourgeoisie* made up of '*rentiers*, those enriched by commerce, lawyers, doctors and some magistrates'.[16] Protestant notables in parts of the south-east (Drôme, Ardèche, Gard) were reported to be suspicious of the regime's clerical proclivities, which contrasted markedly with the favour they had enjoyed under the July Monarchy.[17] Similarly in Alsace it was the Protestant *grands industriels* who were causing concern.[18] These were groups with well-established social networks, and who were not subject to the intense repression, which had driven many republicans out of public life. In July 1858, the procureur-général at Limoges noted that 'judges who come from this milieu are devoted to order, because they fear the lower classes, but they are cold, very cold, towards the imperial dynasty ... They see the present form of government as a fatal threat to their influence and prestige.'[19] In Lyons too there were 'regrets for constitutionalism, for *bourgeois* government, for a state of things in which, through personal relationships one came close to those with power and was better able to secure favours'. According to the state prosecutor, there was an urgent need to multiply contacts with local notables.[20] It was said of M. Elie-Baille, President of the Nancy Tribunal de Commerce, that 'in the habit, under another government, of intervening with prefects over appointments and local interests, he cannot resign himself to abandoning this patronage'.[21] Furthermore, notables resented constant prefectoral interference in local affairs.[22]

During the 1850s, in spite of these misgivings, there was little sustained opposition from liberals and little sign that they exercised much influence over a mass electorate. The Comte d'Haussonville remembered how 'during these difficult early years of the Empire, the latent but determined opposition amongst those faithful to previous regimes hardly knew what to do. The country was so obviously satisfied.'[23] Those few Orleanists who stood for election in 1852 and 1857 certainly attracted little support. In Eure-et-Loir, in 1852 the Marquis de Gouvion-Saint-Cyr

[14] E.g. Goujon, *Le vignoble de Saône-et-Loire au 19ᵉ siècle* (Lyon 1974), pp. 372–3.

[15] PG Dijon, 9 Jan. 1853, AN BB30/377.   [16] PG Poitiers, 15 April 1859, AN BB30/385.

[17] PG Grenoble, 12 Jan. 1859, AN BB30/378.   [18] PG Colmar, 4 July 1858, AN BB30/376.

[19] 9 July 1858, AN BB30/378; also Corbin, *Archaïsme*, II, pp. 845–6.

[20] PG Lyons, 14 Nov. 1852, AN BB30/379.   [21] PG Nancy, 3 April 1857, AN BB30/381.

[22] E.g. prefect Saône-et-Loire, 20 Dec. 1862, quoted Goujon, *Vignoble*, p. 211.

[23] Quoted Tulard, *Dictionnaire*, p. 941.

gained 15 per cent of the vote; in 1857 a diminishing number of Orleanists was forced to support the unsuccessful moderate republican candidate.[24] The historian Mignet was greatly discouraged, complaining in a letter to Thiers that 'the prefects ... have designated unknowns [as official candidates] and everywhere they have been elected ... This represents further proof of the nature of universal suffrage and of what we might expect from it. It is from one moment to the next ... an instrument of anarchy and an instrument of servitude'.[25] The complete absence of popular support meant that there was nothing to do but wait for the regime to destroy itself.[26] In these circumstances liberal opposition might be dismissed easily as simply *frondeuse*.[27] In the privacy of their own homes, in salons and clubs, liberal politicians and intellectuals like the Duc de Broglie or Prévost-Paradol might pour scorn on the bad taste of the Imperial court and cautiously pen indirect attacks on the regime through articles praising British institutions for the *Journal des Débats* or *Revue des Deux Mondes* or provincial newspapers like *L'Ami de la Patrie* at Clermont, a newspaper which, during the Crimean war, was accused by the local prefect of 'distorting favourable news' so that 'our victories are always incomplete and our defeats always bloody'.[28] In their citadel, the Académie française, every meeting provided an opportunity for criticism. Its members ostentatiously elected known critics of the regime to their august body, sometimes instead of figures of genuine literary merit.[29] In response to all this, the prefect of the Isère suggested that government officials tempted to participate in salon society should be transferred if they failed to respond to warnings.[30] In February 1853, as one gentleman to another, Pietri, the Paris Prefect of Police, felt obliged to complain to Odilon Barrot, the leader of the dynastic opposition in the 1840s, that Barrot's wife in her salon 'not only encourages ... conversations hostile to the government, but also tolerates the spreading of false news, of untrue and calumnious rumours, the holding of the most injurious discussions about their Majesties and especially the Empress, and the repetition of ill-intentioned epigrams, and of unsuitable and dishonest pleasantries, unworthy of men of the world'. Pietri felt that things had gone too far and called upon Barrot to take his wife in hand.[31] Such warnings had little effect. The well-connected British political economist

---

[24] Farcy, *Paysans beaucerons*, II, p. 940. [25] Letter to Thiers, 7 March 1852, BN naf 20618.
[26] *Ibid.*, 20 June 1852. [27] E.g. PG Aix, 2 July 1859, AN BB30/370.
[28] Prefect, 13 July 1855, AN F1 CIII Puy-de-Dôme 10; Campbell, *Second Empire Revisited*, p. 29.
[29] Girard, *Nouvelle histoire*, p. 267. [30] 7 March 1852, AN F1 CIII Isère 9.
[31] 9 Feb. 1853, AN 271 AP 5.

Nassau William Senior reported in April 1859 that amongst the participants at a dinner at Thiers' home 'the hatred and contempt felt for Louis
Napoleon cannot be exaggerated. Every fault, moral and intellectual, is
ascribed to him without perfect consistency.'[32]

In spite of this effervescence official reports insisted that, unlike Legitimists and republicans, Orleanists lacked contact with the masses.[33]
The phrase they favoured was 'chiefs without soldiers'. Liberal politics
lacked emotional appeal. Liberals appeared devoid of 'principle' and
'conviction.'[34] A marked decline in support for an Orleanist restoration
was soon evident. Former supporters rallied to the Empire or 'are becoming simply liberal opponents, preoccupied more with the form of the
institutions than the person of the sovereign'.[35] Efforts to secure fusion
between Legitimists and Orleanists reinforced this development. Many
liberals regarded with distaste the prospect of an alliance with the proponents of Divine Right monarchy.[36] However, if a monarchist fusion
was becoming less likely it was clear that pressure for liberal reform from
both supporters and opponents of the regime was accumulating.

It would be the threat to specific vested interests which would gradually
encourage liberals to more openly express their doubts about the efficacy of authoritarian government. Thus during the 1850s the regional
monopolies conceded by the regime to the railway companies in return for further construction were criticised by Pouyer-Quertier, Dupin,
and Mimerel representing business interests. A petition from the Rouen
Chamber of Commerce to the Senate denounced the acceptance by the
administration of proposals from the companies in favour of differential freight rates.[37] Hints from the government that the prohibitions on
certain imports might be lifted resulted in complaints about a 'customs
coup d'état', which, however, were nothing compared with the storm the
1860 customs treaty with Britain would arouse. More generally deputies
expressed concern about excessive government expenditure and the lack
of effective parliamentary control over the budget. Members of municipal and departmental councils, concerned that they were not receiving a fair share of government funding, echoed this.[38] As early as the
spring of 1852 there was a widespread concern amongst businessmen and

---

[32] Letter to Sir George Lewis, 27 April 1859, NLW C.260.
[33] Résumé of reports on first six months of 1856 prepared for Emperor, AN BB30/368.
[34] E.g. PG Nancy, 3 April 1857, AN BB30/381.   [35] PG Angers, 6 Jan. 1859, AN BB30/368.
[36] E.g. PG Paris, 18 Jan. 1854, AN BB30/383; PG Grenoble, 10 Feb. 1854, AN BB30/378.
[37] Price, *Modernisation*, pp. 256f; Gaillard, 'Notes sur l'opposition au monopole', pp. 242–7.
[38] Ménager, *Nord*, I, pp. 296–8.

taxpayers that 'the government is trying to do too many things at once and abusing the credit system' and that an over-heated capital market was heading for crisis.[39] Through constant repetition these complaints would begin to weaken confidence.[40] In addition, the speculative activities of financiers closely associated with the regime and involved in urban renewal and rail construction, those symbols of the new 'monopoly' capitalism, also caused concern.[41] In July 1856 the Prefect of Police reported that many deputies were beginning to see the government's apparent indifference to their concerns as an affront to their dignity. It was this, which had resulted in a 'deplorable' parliamentary session 'in which the most direct accusations were made, in which the most offensive interruptions, the most wounding questions, might have made one believe in a return to the worst days of parliamentarism'. He was also concerned that subsequent dinner-table conversations as well as articles in the foreign press might exacerbate dissension within the social elite.[42] By the end of the decade official reports frequently pointed out that there was growing support for an extension of the opportunities for deputies to discuss government policy and for the press to print debates.[43] Few liberals wanted to replace the regime, but many wanted reform.[44] In 1859 landowners anxious that the period of temporary tariff-free import of cereals following poor harvests might be extended and manufacturers concerned that the government might be considering the permanent reduction of protection reinforced these critics.[45] Anxiety had also been aroused by the decision to intervene in Italy. The liberal deputy Plichon joined the republican Ollivier in condemning both the war and the decision-making process which had led to it. The record of the debate in the Corps législatif reveals Plichon attempting to distance himself from his embarrassing colleague, whilst accepting that they agreed on one issue, namely that 'questions of the greatest concern to the future and destiny of the country are resolved in a way that leaves the Corps législatif no longer free to take decisions'. He warned that 'it is impossible to be revolutionary in Italy and to remain conservative in France and Rome'.[46] Many liberals were convinced that France had been dragged into a risky enterprise simply to satisfy the Emperor's personal whims.[47]

---

[39] PG Besançon, 4 April 1852, AN BB30/373.
[40] E.g. Prefect of Police, 9 Oct. 1856, AN BB30/366.
[41] Letter from M. Belmont, deputy to Emperor, 14 Sept. 1855, AN AB XIX 173.
[42] 10 July 1856, AN 45 AP 5.   [43] E.g. PG Metz, 24 Jan. 1856, AN BB30/380.
[44] E.g. PG Nancy, 11 Jan. 1859, AN BB30/381.   [45] PG Agen, 4 Jan. 1859, AN BB30/370.
[46] Procès-verbaux session de 1859, séance du 27 April, quoted Grothe, *Morny*, pp. 238–9.
[47] PG Nancy, 9 April 1859, AN BB30/381; PG Dijon, 21 May 1859, AN BB30/369.

A disgruntled Persigny, sent to London as ambassador, had expressed similar misgivings in a private letter to the Emperor in June 1858.[48] Clearly, the pressures for change were accumulating. The initial concessions would do little to assuage liberal disquiet. The moderate republican deputy Darimon, in his diary entry for 27 November 1860, recorded dissatisfaction with the decree of the 24th recognising the right of deputies to discuss the address from the throne: 'the complaint is that the chamber has no means of ensuring that its opinion reaches the Emperor ... and that its action is limited to voting for *faits accomplis*'.[49]

The 1860s would be characterised by a rising tide of opposition stimulated by criticism of the Emperor's foreign policy and commercial treaties. Irreconcilable liberals led by Thiers, following his election in 1863, were able to appeal to a variety of groups anxious to defend their 'vital' interests by imposing parliamentary controls over the errant monarch. The essential liberal position was expressed by Edouard de Laboulaye in a pamphlet on *Le Parti libéral, son programme et son avenir* published in 1863. According to Laboulaye, the objective for liberals was 'above all to spread liberty throughout our institutions, because it is liberty alone which identifies the problems and which resolves them'. More resoundingly, in a brilliant speech to deputies on 11 January 1864, Adolphe Thiers called for the re-introduction of freedom of assembly, of association, and the press – for the 'necessary liberties', those essential to prevent arbitrary government. His objective was to 'ensure that public opinion, well established here in the majority, determines the progress of government'. The Empire would survive only through such concessions, and those already made had revealed that 'we are ruled by a regime with a modifiable and perfectible constitution'. Liberals would be prepared to collaborate with a regime committed to reform.[50] Thiers' speech established him as the pre-eminent parliamentary critic of the regime, a position reinforced through the publicity given to his speeches in the press and their publication in pamphlet form.[51] Liberals also assumed that ministers ought to be subject to parliamentary control and selected from amongst the parliamentary majority, and that political liberty together with administrative decentralisation would do much to promote civic virtue.[52] The publicity given to such criticism did much to restore

---

[48] Persigny to Emperor, ?June 1858, BN naf 23066.   [49] Darimon, *Les cinq*, pp. 414–15.

[50] P. Guiral, *Adolphe Thiers ou De la nécessité en politique* (Paris 1986), pp. 305–7.

[51] 'Discours de M. Thiers député de la Seine sur la politique intérieure prononcé dans la discussion de l'Adresse au Corps législatif. Séance 11 janvier 1864', AN 45 AP 8.

[52] PG Dijon, 10 April 1869, AN BB30/389.

the prestige of parliamentary institutions.[53] However, this growing desire for 'liberty' was always balanced by a waning but still intense social fear. Remembering 1848, the industrialist Pouyer-Quertier insisted that 'I want as much liberty as possible but I detest disorder and am the enemy of revolution.'[54] A deep suspicion of manhood suffrage survived, associating it both with the revolutionary tradition and the peasant support for a regime which Prévost-Paradol had described so memorably as a *campagnocratie impériale* founded upon 'rural imbecillity and provincial bestiality'.[55] The liberal ideal remained leadership by an intellectual elite. Prosperity and education offered the surest protection for social order. It followed that 'civic virtue rests in the middle classes who live off the labour of their minds and hands'. Private property was the 'fruit of liberty or, if one wishes, liberty realised'.[56] There was little space for social reform in this social and political vision defined by a wealth bourgeoisie.

Liberalism posed a threat to the regime because it represented a complex of attitudes, based on conservative cultural values, which were shared not only by those Orleanists and opposition liberals contemptuously described by one official as 'timid when they are afraid of finding themselves faced by the extreme party, ardent and irreconcilable critics once they have been reassured',[57] but additionally by many government supporters, together with some Legitimists and most moderate republicans.[58] The concessions made to liberal pressure during the 1860s reinforced the determination and ability of its proponents to secure more, stimulating 'a spirit of denigration disposed to ... criticise everything'.[59] By September 1867, Pietri, the Paris Prefect of Police, would regret that the information he had received left him with no choice but 'to present the Emperor with appreciations which might appear pessimistic'. His essential concern was that 'the active part of society, that which is most concerned about politics, which loves discussion and criticises governments, accentuates, more than ever, its opposition'. These people were concerned about foreign policy, the economic situation and 'the guarantees given to social order and conservative interests'. It was inevitable that 'incessant denigration', often directed personally at the Imperial couple, would weaken the authority of the regime. Pietri ended his report with a call for more decisive political leadership.[60] It might be tempting for the

---

[53] E.g. PG Nancy, 5 April 1862, AN BB30/381.
[54] Quoted Boivin, *Mouvement ouvrier*, vol. I, p. 293.   [55] Quoted Vigier, *Histoire générale*, pp. 44.
[56] Quoted Girard, *Libéraux*, pp. 188–9; see also J. Garrigues, *La République des hommes d'affaires, 1870–1900* (Paris 1997), pp. 36–8.
[57] PG Rouen, 20 Jan. 1861, AN BB30/387.   [58] E.g. PG Dijon, ?Jan. 1864, AN BB30/377.
[59] PG Paris, 12 Nov. 1861, AN BB30/384.   [60] 30 Sept. 1867, AN AB XIX 175.

government to dismiss parliamentary speeches and newspaper articles as so much hot air but, as one state prosecutor warned, 'there is nothing more dangerous; it is not in vain that every day ... the prerogatives of the Sovereign are questioned'.[61] In 1866, the procureur-général at Paris described a movement which was

essentially *bourgeois*. Born in Paris, it has spread throughout the rich and enlightened classes in the provinces where it is supported by sympathisers with the old parties, by a coalition of memories and expectations, ambitions and resentments. Part of the *bourgeoisie*, that which ruled during the July Monarchy and which after 1848, with a heavy heart, sacrificed its power to save the rest, today wants to regain its share.[62]

Officials frequently described a process by which criticism was diffused down the social hierarchy, from the elites to the middle classes and finally the urban and rural popular classes.[63] The development of this upper- and middle-class opposition was blamed on a number of factors. In a 'Note on the role of the press in the 1869 elections' Giraudeau, a senior Interior Ministry official, insisted on the importance of generational differences, as younger men struggled for a place in public life.[64] Thus political idealism was combined with personal ambition. There was a widespread nostalgia for the Orleanist regime, which by means of a tax qualification for enfranchisement had recognised the pre-eminence of wealth, which had safeguarded social order and through parliament subjected itself to the 'necessary' checks and balances.[65] 'Ambition, wounded pride, the need to play a role, regret for lost influence, are the main motives for this, more or less open, hostility', so prevalent amongst the 'upper classes'.[66] As fear of revolution declined, the re-assertion of an interest in politics was inevitable.[67] 'Liberalism has become fashionable.'[68] Constant denigration of the regime and its leading personalities was reported to be a feature of dinner parties, like those held by Thiers – generously supported by the Anzin mining company because of the government's 'free' trade policies – in his Parisian mansion in the rue Saint-Georges, or by Ernest Duvergier, the son of one of Louis-Philippe's ministers, in the rue de Rivoli. This was a favourite gathering place for members of the Parisian *haute bourgeoisie* and was dominated by the veteran politicians

---

[61] PG Besançon, 14 April 1866, AN BB30/373.   [62] 5 May 1866, AN BB30/384.
[63] E.g. PG Aix, 4 Oct. 1868, AN BB30/389.   [64] *Papiers et correspondance*, II, p. 176.
[65] E.g. PG Montpellier, 14 April 1867, AN BB30/380.
[66] PG Nancy, 5 April 1862, AN BB30/381.   [67] PG Agen, 7 Oct. 1864, AN BB30/370.
[68] Prefect, 29 Jan. 1864, AN F1 CIII Saône-et-Loire 13.

Thiers, Barrot, and Rémusat.[69] Similar debates occurred in salons, *cercles*, masonic lodges, and cafés all over France. The 'eloquent speeches' pronounced by liberal deputies were 'avidly read, if not by the popular classes who do not have the major newspapers at their disposal and for whom a long time spent reading is incompatible with the demands of work, at least in the *cercles* and gatherings in which they provide a daily diet for the most animated conversations'.[70]

Liberalisation of the press regime clearly accelerated this process. The government's own objectives had been mixed, including 'the reduction of the importance of the major newspapers through the creation of numerous competitors'.[71] However, the growing number and rising circulation of opposition newspapers allowed for the wider diffusion of the themes developed by liberal deputies. Particularly influential were Parisian newspapers like *Le Siècle* – 'found even on the tables of village cafés'[72] – or the more up-market *Constitutionnel* and *Journal des Débats* from which many provincial news-sheets took their lead.[73] At Saint Etienne *L'Eclaireur* was funded by the ironmaster Frédéric Dorian to represent the interests of the iron and coal industries against the more established silk-ribbon manufacturers.[74] At Nancy a group of Orleanists, Legitimists, and moderate republicans, all claiming to belong to *le parti liberal*, founded the *Journal de la Meurthe* in May 1860.[75] In the Yonne, on the death of its founder the new editor of *La Constitution* decided that there was no room for two pro-government papers and took his own into opposition.[76] At Grenoble, *L'Impartial* was regarded as the voice of the Perier family anxious to regain the influence they had possessed during the July Monarchy.[77] These newspapers stimulated and were encouraged by the critical attitudes of local elites. Following municipal elections in the south-west in 1860 'the symptoms of a spirit not evident during previous elections' were reported, *un esprit d'examen* rather than 'a genuinely hostile opposition'.[78]

Official reports stress that the liberal 'party' was a *parti des cadres* rather than a mass party. It might be capable of mobilising votes due to its resources and dependants, but not of generating popular enthusiasm.[79] However, winning votes was the object of elections. J.-B. Duvergier, a

---

[69] Ménager, *Nord*, vol. II, pp. 575–6; Garrigues, *République des hommes d'affaires*, pp. 24–5.
[70] PG Nancy, 14 April 1864, AN BB30/381.   [71] Report of 28 May 1866, AN F18/295.
[72] PG Nancy, 6 Oct. 1862, AN BB30/381.   [73] E.g. PG Paris, 15 Feb. 1864, AN BB30/384.
[74] OC gendarmerie de la Loire, 28 Aug. 1869, AHG G8/166; Gordon, *Industrialization*, pp. 133–4.
[75] PG Nancy, 6 July 1861, AN BB30/381.   [76] Copin, 'La presse dans l'Yonne', p. 147.
[77] PG Grenoble, 31 Jan. 1865, AN BB30/378.   [78] PG Agen, 6 Oct. 1860, AN BB30/370.
[79] PG Paris, 5 May 1866, *ibid.*

leading official of the Conseil d'Etat, for one, had managed to overcome his distaste for mass politics, recognising 'universal suffrage' as 'the most equitable and natural' form of suffrage in a series of articles in the *Revue des Deux Mondes* in 1868. He insisted, against those who believed that 'the organisation of parties is a monstrous abomination, the symbol of demagogy and revolutionary tyranny', that political organisation and the creation of parties was the only means of self-defence against the power of the state.[80] Through the liberal movement up-and-coming individuals competed for influence with more established notables. They were particularly resentful of the mysterious and exclusive processes by which official candidates were selected. They might prove willing to provide the financial resources necessary for an electoral challenge, for the funding for newspapers, and the paternalistic support of popular educational and mutual aid funds and respectable musical societies.[81] Opposition liberals, particularly those with monarchist loyalties, nevertheless found it difficult to secure election in the general elections of 1863 or 1869. They attempted to attract lower middle- and working-class support on particular issues like protection and political liberty, but avoided divisive issues such as wages or social conditions.[82] Workers might, as in Rouen in 1863, vote for a liberal like the incumbent protectionist Pouyer-Quertier or the virtually indistinguishable moderate republican Desseaux, but were likely to prefer candidates further to the left, where these presented themselves.[83] Ludovic Halévy, who had worked to support his cousin Prévost-Paradol's candidature in Nantes in 1869, recalled the acute sense of failure resulting from his defeat by the radical republican Dr Guépin: 'I spent the evening with the principal members of the committee that has sponsored the candidacy of Paradol. I cannot describe the pain of these honest folk. Businessmen, industrialists, wealthy landowners, they all felt crushed. The legitimate ... influence they had exercised until then ... was destroyed by universal suffrage.'[84]

Amongst businessmen nothing aroused so much anger as the *Lettre de l'Empereur* of 5 January 1860 presenting his economic programme, and the text of the commercial treaty with Britain published on the 23rd. A substantial reduction in protection was justified as the means of opening up markets and stimulating competition and economic modernisation. Businessmen thought that they had seen off 'free trade' when the

---

[80] Quoted Huard, *La naissance du parti politique en France* (Paris 1996), pp. 154–6.
[81] PG Lyons, 2 April 1863, AN BB30/379.   [82] Gordon, *Industrialization*, pp. 127–8.
[83] Boivin, *Mouvement ouvrier*, I, p. 561; Aminzade, *Ballots*, p. 198.
[84] 'Carnets' quoted Hazareesingh, *Subject*, p. 225.

possibility had previously been mooted in 1856. They received no warning of the new treaty and bitterly resented the lack of consultation and the relatively short period of transition. The prospect of additional treaties with such threatening competitors as Belgium added to their anxiety. In Rouen the strength of opinion was such that 'it is impossible to speak in favour of the treaties without rousing a tempest.'[85] Together with the Roman Question, this example of the Emperor's personal policy, this *coup d'état douanier*, would do much to reinforce demands for a return to parliamentary government. The constitution had specified that the negotiation of commercial treaties was one of the Emperor's prerogatives, precisely because intense opposition to trade liberalisation was expected.[86] Now this power was judged to be 'the most compromising and most perilous for his popularity' because it reserved to the Emperor the right to 'dispose of public property and private fortunes'.[87] Since 1815, successive governments had earned support on condition that they offered protection to *le travail national*. The real effects of the customs treaties are difficult to judge and in terms of politics hardly matter. Businessmen panicked and invariably exaggerated the negative consequences. In spite of widespread prosperity every economic difficulty, such as those caused by the American Civil War and the poor harvest of 1867, tended to be blamed on the treaties, even by habitual government supporters.[88] In Rouen in 1863, Pouyer-Quertier's electoral success was largely due to his claim that he was acting in defence of jobs.[89] The population of the Paris region similarly was judged to be 'instinctively protectionist'.[90] Efforts by the regime to justify the tariff reductions as a means of reducing the cost of living for the poor were condemned, together with the legalisation of strikes in 1864, as proof of the Emperor's 'socialist' tendencies.[91] By 1868 a protectionist group had emerged in the Corps législatif. Sixty-three deputies representing mining, metallurgical, and textile interests supported a motion sponsored by Thiers and Brame, which blamed the industrial depression on 'free trade'.[92] Certainly, three-quarters of

---

[85] PG Rouen, 7 Jan. 1870, AN BB30/390.   [86] Girard, *Problèmes politiques*, p. 99.

[87] PG Toulouse, 10 Jan. 1870, AN BB30/390.

[88] E.g. 'Rapport à la Chambre de commerce de Lille sur la situation de l'industrie de la filature de lin pendant l'année 1867', Lille 1868, AN FI CIII Nord 16; PG Rouen, 12 April 1869, AN BB30/389.

[89] Aminzade, *Ballots*, pp. 198, 201–2.

[90] OC gendarmerie de Seine-et-Marne, ?Jan. 1870, AHG G8/176.

[91] Ménager, *Nord*, II, p. 651.

[92] M. S. Smith, *Tariff Reform in France, 1860–1900: The Politics of Economic Interest* (London 1980), p. 295; Ménager, 'La vie politique dans le département du Nord de 1851 à 1877', *Revue du Nord* (1980), pp. 718–19.

deputies voted with the government. The representatives of exporting industries like silk and of the ports were in favour of tariff reductions. Agricultural interests were still enjoying the market-extending effects of rail in internal markets and, as yet, faced little international competition.[93] However, a growing sense of malaise was associated with economic stagnation, rising unemployment, and the customs treaties. In the evenings of 24 to 26 May 1869, crowds in the centre of Lille were reported to be singing the popular song 'The English will never rule in France' whilst protesting against the commercial treaty.[94] Indeed, the difficulties of the late 1860s persuaded many that the 'free trade' experiment had failed. Demands for revocation of the treaties and for the termination of the Emperor's prerogative became increasingly loud.[95]

Amongst the other issues most likely to generate heat was the conduct of foreign policy. The importance of the Roman Question has been stressed already. Whilst many liberals had been critical of the government of the Papacy, others including Thiers, rallied to the defence of the Pope's temporal power in the wider interest of protecting social order. It was Thiers' speech on 4 December 1867 which forced Rouher into an explicit and open-ended commitment to support for the Papacy against Italian nationalism, of a kind which the regime had previously avoided, earning for the minister a severe rebuke from the Emperor. Liberal Catholics like Montalembert and Falloux offered their warmest congratulations to Thiers.[96] Irrespective of attitudes towards the Papacy, the Emperor's Italian policy provided a warning of the dangers of personal rule. According to Emile Ollivier, to a large degree Morny's own support for liberalisation had been predicated on the urgent need to 'remove the conduct of foreign affairs from the solitary and omnipotent will of the Emperor'.[97] When Nassau William Senior asked Thiers whether he had approved of the Crimean War, the response was 'Yes, but not of his Italian war, or his Syrian war, or his two Chinese wars, or his Mexican war. The last four have merely wasted our money and our blood. The Italian war has given us a powerful rival ... and irrevocably weakened the power most useful to the European equilibrium – Austria.'[98] Eugène Pelletan represented this concern forcefully in a speech in the Corps législatif in January 1864 in which he pointed out

[93] Price, *Modernisation*, pp. 310–11.
[94] PG Douai, 3 July 1869, AN BB30/389 and 28 June 1869, AN BB18/1785.
[95] E.g. Prefect, 14 Oct. and 19 Dec. 1869 AN FI ciii Nord 16.
[96] Maurain, *Politique ecclésiastique*, pp. 825–31.   [97] Ollivier, *L'Empire libéral*, vol. vi, pp. 503–5.
[98] N. W. Senior, *Conversations with Distinguished Persons during the Second Empire from 1860 to 1863* (London 1878), ii, p. 176.

that 'every day the foreign press asks why our politics is revolutionary in Turin, counter-revolutionary in Rome, reactionary in Mexico, liberal in Poland, pro-slavery in America and mysterious everywhere. Do you want to end this uncertainty? Give us liberty at home!'[99] This incoherence was nowhere more apparent than in the Mexican affair, an effort to carve out a French sphere of influence in Central America, denounced as *ruineuse* by Ollivier and as a useless sacrifice of men and money by Thiers.[100] There was widespread support for these views, even if eventual withdrawal would be regarded as a national humiliation. According to the state prosecutor at Dijon, 'people remember the Imperial promises so harshly contradicted by events as well as the opposition speeches which now appear to have had the virtue of foresight'. The Emperor's claims for territorial compensation from Prussia following its victory over Austria in 1866 represented yet another humiliation.[101] The historian Mignet wrote to Thiers that 'France has not suffered so many revolutions to be ruled like this, has not transformed its social conditions to remain forever subordinate to the dangerous rule of a single will. Everyone is beginning to appreciate the consequences. After the stupid Mexican expedition comes the reprehensible aggrandisement of Prussia.'[102] The looming prospect of war with a Prussia which threatened French predominance on the Continent, represented, for many, further clear proof of disastrous incompetence. According to Thiers, in a major speech on 9 December 1867, this was the result of the abandonment of policies based upon preserving the balance of power in favour of disruptive support for the principle of the nationalities which only risked creating new and more powerful states on the frontiers.[103] Officials were concerned that Thiers' 'marvellous facility'[104] was attracting substantial support for the view that 'a parliamentary regime ... would have saved France from the perils which threaten it and the sacrifices which these will provoke'.[105]

Frequently, the preservation of peace was linked to financial questions. As early as 1852, in the privacy of parliamentary committees, deputies had expressed their desire to reinforce budgetary controls.[106] By 1861 it was being reported that 'the War on the Finances is becoming ... an auxiliary of the War on the Institutions'.[107] The Emperor felt sufficiently concerned to appoint Fould to the Finance Ministry as a means of

---

99 Quoted Grothe, *Morny*, p. 250. 100 *Ibid.*, p. 297.
101 PG Dijon, 10 Jan. 1867, AN BB30/377. 102 29 July 1866, AN AP 271 5.
103 Printed in Tulard, *Pourquoi*, pp. 146–8. 104 PG Nancy, 18 April 1866, AN BB30/381.
105 PG Rouen, 12 Jan. 1867, AN BB30/387. 106 Girard, *Problèmes politiques*, pp. 94–5.
107 PG Lyons, 27 Dec. 1861, AN BB30/379.

conciliating conservative financial opinion.[108] This seems to have done little to alleviate public concern about government prodigality.[109] Again Thiers took a lead in criticising the regime's policy. He insisted that taxes were too high, an approach which invariably attracted support and helped mould perceptions of the regime.[110] According to the state prosecutor at Paris, by August 1865, as a result of 'M. Thiers' harangues ... a substantial fraction of public opinion, growing from day to day, shows itself favourable to ideas of budgetary economy'.[111] M. Chaussé, a wealthy resident of the Place de la Concorde, was overheard, by a police spy, complaining, whilst taking the waters at Néris-les-Bains (Allier) in 1865, that 'the money the French give to the Emperor pays for his mistresses and that all the people surrounding His Majesty were scum'.[112] The reconstruction of central Paris was frequently condemned as unnecessary and in bad taste.[113] One key theme was that whilst 'Paris is bursting from abundance, the provinces grow feeble.'[114] The work in Paris was blamed for 'the desertion of the countryside', for the demoralisation of the rural population and the growing shortage of agricultural labour.[115] Even officials complained that the money spent on the capital could have been used to better effect for the construction of rural roads.[116] Parliamentary complaints concentrated on the secretive fashion in which public works concessions were made and financed and the exclusion of deputies from regular budgetary control. Haussmann, the powerful prefect of the Seine, came to personify the sort of government which liberal deputies wished to abolish. His optimistic belief that construction could be financed through borrowing which would eventually be repaid through the higher tax revenues generated by rising property values was anathema to orthodox financial opinion.[117] Moreover, often it was more effective to attack the Emperor indirectly, by means of attacks on his closest subordinates.

In January and February 1865 in a series of articles, Léon Say, a close collaborator of the Rothschilds, accused Haussmann of contracting unauthorised loans. This line of criticism was taken up in 1867 in

---

[108] Girard, *Napoléon III*, pp. 348–50.   [109] E.g. PG Agen, 3 July 1865, AN BB30/370.

[110] E.g. OC gendarmerie de Saône-et-Loire, 28 Dec. 1868, AHG G8/152.

[111] 4 Aug. 1865, AN BB30/384.   [112] PG Riom, 1 Sept. 1865, AN BB18/1707.

[113] E.g. PG Aix, 4 Oct. 1868, AN BB30/389.

[114] J.-H. Duvivier, *L'Empire en Province* (Paris: Dentu 1861), p. 9.

[115] E.g. E. Tallon, *Les intérêts des campagnes* (Paris: Librairie Internationale 1869), pp. 14, 143.

[116] E.g. OC 19e Légion gendarmerie, 30 June 1868, AHG G8/151.

[117] Girard, *La politique*, pp. 186–8, 400-1; D. Pinkney, *Napoleon III and the Rebuilding of Paris* (London 1958), pp. 190-5.

the Corps législatif by Picard, Favre, and Berryer who pointed out that whilst the Crédit foncier had placed loans worth 291 million francs on behalf of the city of Paris, the legislature had authorised only 35 million. In November Rouher as Finance Minister felt obliged to consolidate the city's various loans into a single, and far more visible, long-term debt. This did not prevent the moderate republican Jules Favre from publishing a series of critical articles in *Le Temps*, which achieved fame and made a significant contribution to discrediting the regime when they were re-published in May 1868 as *Les comptes fantastiques d'Haussmann*.[118] In 1869, responding to frequent reports of public disquiet, Rouher recognised that Haussmann had exceeded his authority and agreed to request annual parliamentary approval of borrowing.[119] Critics also called for administrative decentralisation, claiming that, as in Marseille, an elected municipal council would have called an over-powerful prefect to account.[120]

To this concern with the regime's financial stability and the disquiet caused by the deteriorating international situation were added doubts about the Emperor's health and capacity to rule. The crisis of confidence, the so-called *grève des milliards*, which ensued was a response to the speculative losses caused by the collapse of the Pereire investment bank, the Crédit mobilier and suspicion that the Emperor was planning a war against Prussia.[121] The issue of military reform brought these concerns together. To the Emperor this was the urgent means of restoring the balance of power. However, the proposals roused a storm of protest both because of their cost and the feeling that they denoted a determination to wage war. Thiers spoke in favour of the retention of a relatively small professional army and in opposition to the extension of conscription necessary for the creation of a substantial trained reserve.[122] In November 1867, the rejection of Marshal Niel's proposals was a clear sign of the growing dissolution of the government's majority.[123] Deputies were aware that the rural population regarded military service with repugnance. The traditional practice of drawing lots to choose conscripts had offered the real possibility of escape.[124] The government was warned that there appeared to be a danger that support in the countryside might

---

[118] E.g. PG Dijon, 10 April 1869, AN BB30/389.   [119] Girard, *Nouvelle histoire*, pp. 347–8.
[120] Hazareesingh, *Subject*, p. 196.
[121] E.g. Rouher to Emperor, 10 Sept. 1867 in *Papiers et correspondance*, I, p. 227 and report from Pietri, 28 Sept. *ibid.*, see also PG Lyons, 7 Oct. 1867, AN BB30/379.
[122] Guiral, *Thiers*, pp. 318–19.   [123] Point made by PG Rennes, 26 Jan. 1867, AN BB30/386.
[124] Darimon, *Le tiers parti*, p. 425, entry 16 Nov. 1866; see also M. de Benoist, *Utopies d'un paysan* (Clermont-Ferrand 1867); Tallon, *Les intérêts des campagnes*, pp. 43f.

be 'weakened fatally'.[125] Whereas in 1851 financiers, and businessmen more generally, had welcomed the *coup d'état* as the means of restoring social order, now they believed that the re-establishment of a parliamentary regime was necessary to control the Emperor.[126] As the liberal politician Buffet pointed out in a speech to the forge masters' association in December 1869: 'we have material order, but the benefits ... are compromised by constant uncertainty'.[127] Confidence needed to be restored urgently.

The decree of 24 November 1860 had allowed a debate on the Address from the Throne, the appointment of ministers without portfolio to explain and defend government policy, and the publication of debates in the press. This had done a great deal to reinforce the influence of deputies, permitting the Emperor's critics 'to prepare each year an *acte d'accusation* against him'.[128] Even so liberals had complained that not enough had been done.[129] Adolphe Thiers certainly accepted the sincerity of Napoleon's intentions. In a long letter to the Duc d'Aumale, Louis-Philippe's son, in January 1861, he recalled being told by the Emperor that a repressive regime was 'by its nature short-lived' and 'that sooner or later it would become necessary to give up something to a reborn sense of independence'. Thiers believed that Napoleon was volunteering concessions partly to ensure the succession of his son, partly because preaching liberty to the Pope whilst retaining authoritarian government in France 'touches on the *burlesque*', but that he 'lacked a clear and complete perception of what had been done', and believed that limited concessions would be sufficient. However, Thiers insisted that 'the path on which he has entered is one on which one can walk slowly, but never stop, much less go backwards'. In these circumstance the *parti libéral monarchique* should seize the opportunities offered to debate public affairs and its experienced figures, men like himself, however reluctantly, should return to public life to provide leadership to the younger generation. Thiers concluded by stressing the dangers implicit in the process – 'if the government resists when it sees that liberty is challenging its power, we will be thrown into a revolution'. Alternatively, 'if the government makes wise concessions, we will become its prisoners, obliged to loyally

[125] PG Rennes, 23 April 1867, AN BB30/386.
[126] E.g. Darimon, *Tiers parti*, pp. 407–8, entry of 7 Oct. 1866.
[127] Quoted Girard, *La politique*, p. 388.   [128] Darimon, *Tiers parti*, p. 409.
[129] E.g. M. Prévost-Paradol, *Du gouvernement parlementaire. Le décret du 24 novembre* (Paris: Lévy 1860), pp. 44–5.

surrender, not to become its ministers, but to be its supporters'.[130] These were the views Thiers presented at a meeting, early in 1863, at the Paris home of the Duc de Broglie. Liberal Catholics including Montalembert, moderate republicans like Simon, and the 'partisans of a firmly liberal monarchy', such as Guizot, attended this. The gathering decided to abandon abstention as a tactic and to contest elections, in spite of the disagreeable need to take the oath of loyalty to the regime, but in the hope of winning further concessions. Thiers claimed to have assured sceptical colleagues 'on the left', that 'the prince we have, is not like the other princes we have known. He is obstinate, without doubt, but he wants to keep his crown, and I do not believe him incapable of making concessions.'[131] In practice, the domineering behaviour of ministers like Rouher, excessive administrative centralisation and the continued subservience of many deputies would limit the impact of liberal reforms. Furthermore, the Emperor continued to resist the final step of accepting ministerial responsibility to parliament and remained determined to retain many of his prerogatives.[132] As a result, as official reports pointed out, liberalisation won few adherents to the regime, and 'agitated the country more than satisfying it'.[133] The mounting criticism this provoked in the Corps législatif, and latterly in the press, strengthened liberal opposition and broadened its social base.[134]

This was evident from election results. In 1863, although the government secured a massive majority clearly it had lost the cities and would face criticism subsequently from the more independent of the deputies elected as official candidates and a small but vocal opposition with Thiers as the leading liberal spokesman. The election had seen an attempt to bring together moderate opponents of the regime in a Union libérale. Nationally this was based on a Comité de l'Union libérale organised by the journalist Nefftzer and supported by the newspapers *Le Temps* and the *Journal des Débats*. In May, together with *Le Siècle*, *La Presse*, and *L'Opinion nationale*, they agreed to advise their readers to support the Union's candidates.[135] This revealed how close politically were those who had gathered at the home of Albert de Broglie to discuss electoral collaboration and who included liberals like his brother-in-law the

---

[130] 8 Jan. 1861, BN naf 20618; see also Bury and Tombs, *Thiers*, p. 169, whose quotation of Thiers' quip to Prince Napoleon: 'It is a confidence trick but we shall know how to profit by it' offers a different perspective.

[131] Assemblée nationale, *Enquête parlementaire*, v, pp. 1–2. [132] Darimon, *Les irréconciliables*, p. 302.

[133] PG Nancy, 17 July 1867, AN BB30/389.

[134] E.g. PG Rennes, 14 April 1868, AN BB30/386; PG Dijon, 9 July 1867, AN BB30/377.

[135] Darimon, *L'opposition libérale*, pp. 390–1.

Comte d'Haussonville, Guizot, Lanjuinais, and Glais-Bizoin, Catholics like Montalembert, and moderate republicans like Simon and Ferry.[136] In Marseille the Union enjoyed the support of three newspapers, the Legitimist *Gazette du Midi*, the Orleanist *Sémaphore*, and the republican *Phare du littoral*. This contributed to the success of the eminent Legitimist lawyer Berryer and the moderate republican Marie. Although Thiers failed, he was elected in Paris. The alliance with the republicans was particularly important in securing mass support.[137] The adherents of Union shared a commitment to parliamentary politics and an abhorrence of revolution. Jules Ferry, writing in support of the historian Edgar Quinet's denunciation of violence, agreed that 'Jacobinism is no longer an arm of war, but a threat because it evokes amongst us something even worse than the scaffold, namely support for dictatorship ... If the Revolution can do without Bonaparte, it has no need of Robespierre.'[138] Each 'party' to the Union was divided as to the wisdom of such co-operation and extremely suspicious of its allies.[139] Personality differences between leaders were a major obstacle. Ollivier recalled Morny's warning that with Thiers 'there is nothing to be done; he is amiable but incredibly presumptuous; whilst you collaborate you will find him very kind; from the moment you do not think the same, you will be nothing more than an imbecile'.[140] It was virtually impossible for clericals and anticlericals to co-operate. In Brittany, republicans frequently preferred official candidates to liberals supported by the clergy.[141] Similarly liberal Legitimists could rarely bring themselves to support even the most moderate of republicans.[142] Darimon was rather dismissive of an alliance without a programme, made up of 'veterans from all the regimes'. He felt that preaching liberty to the masses when they did not feel oppressed was futile.[143] In contrast, in his survey of *Le Parti libéral, son programme et son avenir*, published soon after the election, Edouard de Laboulaye represented the growing confidence of adherents of 'the liberal party which is gradually establishing itself little by little, but growing every day'. This was not a minor sect, he insisted, but 'an universal church where there is room for whoever believes in liberty'.[144] With growing press support, liberal deputies could realistically hope to influence public opinion.

---

[136] Assemblée nationale, *Enquête parlementaire*, V, p. 1.
[137] PG Aix, 28 Oct. 1867, AN BB30/370; see also MI, undated note on 'Succès de la coalition dans les villes' in AN 45 AP 1.
[138] Quoted Girard, *Les libéraux*, p. 196.   [139] E.g. PG Grenoble, 16 Oct. 1865, AN BB30/378.
[140] Ollivier, VI, *L'Empire libéral*, p. 503.   [141] Maurain, *Politique ecclésiastique*, pp. 662-3.
[142] E.g. PG Montpellier, 22 Jan. 1870, AN BB30/390; Igersheim, *Politique*, p. 702.
[143] Darimon, *Opposition libérale*, p. 148, entry 27 Jan. 1862.   [144] Quoted Girard, *Libéraux*, p. 188.

In the towns liberal notables also made considerable efforts to secure election to municipal councils and to enlarge the responsibilities of these bodies, in order to secure freedom from the *despotisme administratif* of the local prefect.[145] The local elections in 1865 took on an unusually political character. Prefects were criticised frequently for selecting as candidates 'personalities without value',[146] as well as for the constant infractions, by 'the numerous army of functionaries', of the laws guaranteeing electoral freedom, infractions listed by one state prosecutor as 'the refusal to allow posters, laceration of posters, arbitrary changes in the time for voting, threats, promises, letters or defamatory libels.'[147] Falloux complained that 'these really cynical procedures are profoundly wounding to all those independent men, regardless of the party to which they belong.'[148] The state prosecutor at Rouen would point out subsequently that 'the freedom left to the government to choose mayors from outside municipal councils is generally resented; there are complaints about official candidatures, as if they did not exist under every regime; people want, in politics, as well as in administration, to reduce the role of the government's agents. 1848 is no more than a dim memory.'[149] The situation in Vienne was even more serious. Twenty-three representatives of the opposition groups and only four government supporters were elected to the local council. Its rapid replacement by a municipal commission, wholly appointed by the prefect, only stirred up further opposition.[150] The same action would be taken in Toulouse where republicans, Orleanists, and Legitimists had collaborated to unseat the official candidates.[151] Such developments were to be symptomatic of the 'progress of the spirit of opposition.'[152]

The 1863 elections were followed by the gradual establishment of a Tiers parti, with a nucleus of some forty members, and two potential leaders in Thiers and Ollivier.[153] Discussing their situation in December 1865, during long walks along the Paris *quais*, the former moderate republicans Ollivier and Darimon accepted that they had burnt their bridges to the left and that in future, to avoid 'complete isolation', they would need to secure links with liberals and 'with them organise the party of the liberal Empire.' They planned to look for support for

---

[145] PG Bordeaux, 6 July 1859, AN BB30/368.   [146] PG Nancy, 12 April 1863, AN BB30/381.

[147] 5 Jan. 1864, *ibid.*   [148] Letter to Thiers, 7 July 1866, BN naf 20619.

[149] 16 July 1865, AN BB30/387.   [150] PG Grenoble, 10 April and 10 July 1866, AN BB30/378.

[151] A. Armengaud, *Les populations de l'est-Aquitain au début de l'époque contemporaine (vers 1845–vers 1871)* (Paris 1961), p. 419.

[152] PG Grenoble, 12 Jan. 1866, AN BB30/378.

[153] Assemblée nationale, *Actes*, v, p. 1, evidence of Thiers.

an amendment to the address from the throne not only from opposition liberals but from amongst *les députés de la majorité*.[154] In March 1866 forty-four deputies led by Buffet, and influenced by Thiers, signed an amendment partly drafted by Ollivier: 'France, firmly attached to the dynasty which guarantees order, is nonetheless devoted to liberty which it considers to be necessary to the accomplishment of its destiny', calling for a return to a parliamentary regime.[155] The signatories included liberals elected as official candidates, like Jules Brame and Eugène Chevandier de Valdrôme, catholics and protectionists like Kolb-Bernard and Plichon, independents with Orleanist tendencies like Buffet himself and the former republicans. They were willing to compromise with the regime, but irritated by the slowness of reform and the obstructiveness of many ministers and senior civil servants.[156] The procureur-général at Dijon expressed grave concern about this development, pointing out that public opinion 'is extremely distrustful of radical opposition' but 'doesn't always sufficiently protect itself against less obvious opponents sheltering under the flag of the regime'. He drew a parallel with the decline of the July Monarchy and concluded by reminding his minister that 'third parties sometimes end up dissolving majorities'.[157]

Efforts to re-negotiate the *Union* for the 1869 elections would founder, largely due to growing republican self-confidence.[158] Even so, in 109 of the 283 provincial constituencies there would be only one opposition candidate, forcing committed opponents of the regime to concentrate their votes.[159] The result was a substantial reinforcement of opposition in the Corps législatif. Moreover, many of those elected as official candidates were determined to distance themselves from the regime. A discouraged administration faced more confident and better-prepared critics.[160] The opposition press continued to denounce the political system. Prefects had been instructed to 'neglect nothing to prevent the election of M. Thiers'.[161] In Marseille, where the government press had denounced Thiers' protectionism and identification with northern economic interests, the liberal newspaper *Le Sémaphore* had shifted the basis of debate, apparently successfully, by insisting that 'the reconquest of free

---

[154] Darimon, *Le tiers parti*, p. 330; *ibid.*, p. 334, entry of 11 Jan. 1866.
[155] *Ibid.*, p. 360, entry of 17 March 1866.   [156] *Ibid.*, p. 330, entry of 22 Dec. 1865.
[157] PG Dijon, 11 April 1866, AN BB30/377.
[158] E.g. Olivesi, 'Marseille' in Girard, *Les élections*, p. 78.   [159] Girard, *Les élections*, p. xxviii.
[160] E.g. 'Note sur l'organisation de la presse', 15 April 1869, written by one of the chefs de bureau du Min.de l'Intérieur, division de la presse, in *Papiers et correspondance*, I, pp. 20–2.
[161] Ministerial letter, 24 May 1869, in Holt, *Papiers sauvés*, p. 222.

government and not trade is the question in this election'.[162] In a widely circulated pamphlet, Edouard Ordinaire condemned the intimidation of an ignorant electorate, as well as the continued persecution of journalists and the selection of official candidates who, 'were they the most honest men in the world, by accepting administrative support, promise in advance not to control the administration'. Although personally in favour of 'free trade' he demanded to know 'by what right ... can the fantasies of a single individual be allowed to suddenly result in ... what is the equivalent of the expropriation without compensation of industries established under a protectionist regime?'[163]

Significantly, those liberals who had consistently refused to consider a compromise with the regime, and most notably the old Orleanist and Legitimist leaders like Rémusat, Casimir-Périer, Broglie, and Falloux, were defeated.[164] The lesson drawn by Rémusat was that

we were all moderate liberals, some even conservative liberals, but at the same time we were all seen as having sentiments incompatible with the Imperial dynasty; we could be seen as moderate in our ideas, revolutionary in our intentions. We were seen as revolutionaries by conservatives, as moderates by revolutionaries and were able to win the votes of neither the wise nor of the fools.[165]

The largest group in the new Corps législatif was to be made up of liberal Bonapartists. Conscious of the regime's growing weakness and alarmed by the danger of war, 116 of these were anxious to subject the Emperor to closer parliamentary control. They signed an amendment calling for the establishment of a government responsible to parliament. These were men committed to counter-revolution as well as liberal reform. In his reply to an invitation from the Comité démocratique socialiste to address a meeting in the Avenue Montaigne in his Paris constituency, Thiers reminded voters of his contribution to the 'reconquest' of liberty and at the same time condemned the extreme left for dividing the opposition. The response when this letter was read aloud at the meeting was hissing and shouts of *A bas Thiers*.[166] Increasingly, liberals would become concerned about this apparent revival of the *spectre rouge*. The 'Party of Order' of the Second Republic was being re-constructed – clerical and

---

[162] 7 May 1869, quoted Olivesi, 'Marseille', p. 92.
[163] *Des candidatures officielles et de leurs conséquences* (Paris: Le Chevalier 1869).
[164] See e.g. letter from Louis Lecave-Laplagne to Thiers, 9 June 1869, BN naf 20619.
[165] Quoted H. Robert, 'Orléanisme' in Tulard, *Dictionnaire*, p. 942.
[166] A. Vitu, *Les réunions électorales à Paris* (Paris 1869), p. 22.

protectionist, and committed to a parliamentary system, which it was assumed would finally restore the social elites to power.

The Emperor's decision to establish a liberal regime, announced on 12 July 1869, would enlarge the powers of the Corps législatif substantially in terms of its ability to question ministers, exert budgetary control, ratify commercial treaties and hold governments responsible. Liberals were divided in their response: 'Everyone speaks ... of their devotion to liberal ideas; but beneath these elastic formulae are hidden profound differences.'[167] Suspicion of the Emperor's intentions survived. His reluctance to establish a parliamentary regime and determination to preserve important elements of his prerogative powers, in respect of the appointment of ministers, foreign policy, and control of the armed forces, was well known. A declaration by Forcade de la Roquette to the Senate that the government intended to remain faithful to its commercial treaties aroused a storm of protest. Another problem was Napoleon's determination to preserve his potentially 'antiparliamentary' right to appeal directly to the nation through plebiscites. This held out the possibility that concessions might be revoked.[168] The ambiguous status of ministers represented another problem. According to article 19 of the new constitution: 'The Emperor appoints and dismisses ministers. Ministers deliberate in council under the presidency of the Emperor. They are responsible.' The survival of an unelected Senate, even one shorn of its powers of constitutional revision, also appeared dangerous.

The Emperor's unwillingness to establish a precedent by appointing a ministry drawn from and dependent on the Tiers parti encouraged him to turn to Ollivier and ask him to form 'a homogeneous cabinet faithfully representing the majority in the Corps législatif'.[169] This would be based primarily on a centre-right made up of around 130 liberal Bonapartists who had subscribed to a text prepared at meetings on the 1, 2, and 3 December at the home of Josseau, the deputy for Seine-et-Marne. Ollivier had himself played a leading role in these deliberations. The document required from the Emperor

the loyal introduction of a parliamentary regime, the necessary form of government of the country by the country under a monarchy. A free press and elections, a responsible and homogeneous ministry, a majority organised around clearly determined principles. Decentralisation, the autonomy of the commune, canton and department, electoral reform, free elections. Jury trial for press

---

[167] PG Nancy, 17 July 1869, AN BB30/389.   [168] E.g. PG Riom, 6 April 1870, AN BB30/390.
[169] Quoted Girard, 'L'Empire libéral', p. 35.

offences, freedom for higher education, a parliamentary enquiry into the effects of the commercial treaties.[170]

At Ollivier's request, Darimon had taken soundings at the end of December amongst some 100 deputies and reported that the centre-right would support him, if only because of the strong feeling amongst them that 'the ground is shifting ... under their feet', although with strong reservations.[171] However, Persigny warned Darimon that Ollivier would be isolated and his influence in government limited.[172] The ministry eventually appointed would also include, as a symbol of *ralliement*, Buffet and the Comte Daru, both strongly influenced by Thiers, as representatives of the forty centre-left liberals-mainly clericals and protectionists – more attached to parliamentary institutions than to the dynasty. At the same time the establishment of extra-parliamentary commissions to consider reform of the administration of Paris, administrative decentralisation on a national scale, and the 'freedom' of education ardently desired by Catholics, brought such leading representatives of the liberal opposition as Guizot, Falloux, Barrot, and Prévost-Paradol into close collaboration with the administration.[173]

These developments appear to have been received with enthusiasm by most liberals, particularly those previously associated with the Tiers parti. The *Journal de Roubaix* (14 January 1870) announced that 'The Empire of 2 December no longer exists.' Those whose primary sympathies lay with Legitimism and Orleanism as well as the centre-left, however, whilst generally welcoming the constitutional changes, remained sceptical whilst hoping that additional changes would follow. The establishment of the commission on decentralisation went some way towards encouraging optimism, as did the creation, just before the outbreak of war, of a parliamentary commission of enquiry into customs tariffs which, it was widely assumed, would lead to their upward revision.[174] Alfred Mézières wrote to congratulate Ollivier claiming that 'the marriage ... of order and liberty should satisfy the French for a long time. There will no longer be a military dictatorship, but a monarchy based on the popular will, brilliant enough to please the eye, and with institutions flexible enough to evolve over time.' He concluded: 'You have proved

---

[170] Ollivier, *L'Empire libéral*, XII, p. 192.
[171] Letter to Ollivier, 29 Dec. 1869 in Darimon, *Les cent seize*, p. 220.
[172] In a conversation at a reception given by Prince Napoleon on 4 Jan. 1870 reported *ibid.*, p. 226.
[173] Campbell, *Second Empire Revisited*, pp. 85–6; P. Guiral, 'Prévost-Paradol ou L'apparent désaveu de soi-même, in Hamon, *Les républicains*, p. 138.
[174] Ménager, *Nord*, II, p. 897.

that the most important revolutions can be accomplished legally, without spilling a single drop of blood.'[175] The growing fear of social unrest also increased support for the new regime. In general, liberals warmly welcomed Ollivier's determined deployment of troops against strikers and on 12 January 1870 against demonstrators in the capital itself following the funeral of the journalist Victor Noir, shot by Prince Pierre Bonaparte. The arrests of extreme republicans like Rochefort and leading members of the International were widely applauded. Liberty – with Order – was what liberals desired. In this situation Ollivier himself had decided that to propose further reforms in the immediate future risked destabilising the regime.[176]

The plebiscite to be held in May to ratify the constitutional changes certainly aroused misgivings amongst liberals. Prominent figures like Dufaure and Thiers recommended a negative vote. An editorial in *Le Temps* warned that 'in appearance it represents a call for the definitive approval of our liberal conquests but in practice the victory would be that of the personal power'.[177] The fragility of Ollivier's position was revealed clearly when the representatives of the centre-left in his government – Buffet, Daru, and Talhouët – resigned in protest against the holding of a plebiscite, intensifying the confusion amongst rank-and-file liberals.[178] Abstention was another favoured option, although Guizot, as well as leading liberal publicists like Laboulaye and even Prévost-Paradol, would come down in favour of a positive vote. For them the creation of the Ollivier government was the penultimate step towards the establishment of a fully functional parliamentary regime. Throughout the country most liberals, including supporters of the centre-left, would vote 'Yes' out of satisfaction with the regime's reforms and due to social fear and the desire for strong government – intensified by the publicity given to the 'unhealthy doctrines of the public meetings in Paris ... and by the excesses of the demagogic press'.[179]

The plebiscite revealed that the majority of *conservateurs libéraux*, and most members of the socio-political elite, had rallied to the Liberal Empire. However, divisions amongst liberals, between personalities and factions, and over the priority to be given to liberty or order, would weaken Ollivier's authority rapidly. With the support of only the 130 members of

[175] Quoted P. Tollu, 'Démocratie et liberté' in A. Troisier de Diaz (ed.), *Regards sur Emile Ollivier* (Paris 1985), p. 138.
[176] Ollivier, *L'Empire libéral*, VII, p. 268.   [177] Quoted Igersheim, *Politique*, p. 702.
[178] E.g. OC cie. de la Seine, 28 April 1870, AHG G8/ 176.
[179] PG Nîmes, 18 Jan. 1869, AN BB30/389.

a faction-riven centre-right, in an Assembly with 292 members, Ollivier would come to depend on the group of authoritarian Bonapartists including Cassagnac, Duvernois, and Jérôme David – encouraged by the Empress and Rouher – against a left made up of unreconciled liberals and republicans. As the Emperor's health deteriorated and concern about the succession grew, it was also becoming evident that many liberal notables were indifferent to the form of the regime as long as it safeguarded their vital interests. According to the scandalised gendarmerie commander in the Seine-et-Marne, 'the egoism of the epoch has killed the parties; people want prosperity, greater wealth and don't much care which regime gives it to them'.[180]

[180] 25 June 1870, AHG G8/176.

CHAPTER 11

The forms of opposition: (3) Republicans in the aftermath of the coup d'état

INTRODUCTION

Republican opposition was the product of a founding 'myth' and of a shared political culture, language, and symbolism. Republicans shared with liberals their commitment to the central principles of 1789 – political liberty, civil equality, and the sovereignty of the nation. Additionally, they believed that the establishment of a republic based upon popular sovereignty, combined with the enlightenment resulting from universal instruction, freed from clerical obscurantism, would establish the preconditions for human happiness and indefinite progress. Republicans condemned the authoritarian and morally corrupt practices of monarchy and of an empire established by a *coup d'état*, which had been directed mainly at them. If there were important areas of agreement, republicans were also divided on both means and ends, largely as a result of the diverse traditions created between 1789 and 1799 and their subsequent re-interpretation. The heterogeneity of the 'party' was also evident in its social composition and the geography of support. Definitions of the *vraie république* differed inevitably. The main divisions, at the risk of simplification, were between 'moderates', who were virtually indistinguishable from liberals because of their economic liberalism, insistence on the sanctity of private property, and fear of the revolutionary potential of the 'people', and might be tempted to rally to a Liberal Empire; 'radicals' interested in, generally vague, measures of social reform, which would follow a change of regime; and revolutionary republicans, many of them influenced by Auguste Blanqui's conception of the leading role of a revolutionary elite, necessary in a society corrupted by twenty years of Imperial dictatorship, and willing to resort to violence in reaction to state repression, and as the means of establishing an egalitarian, socialist society. Whilst moderates and most radicals saw the extreme left as a threat to liberty, the revolutionaries themselves remained suspicious of those republicans who had supported military action against the Parisian workers in June 1848.

The *coup d'état* was accompanied by the arrest, close surveillance, or exile of republican activists. More general measures included the closure of the newspapers, which, with their networks of local correspondents, had frequently served as the basis for republican organisation. Those newspapers which were permitted to appear were subject to close censorship. Political organisation and meetings were banned. This increased the alienation of republicans from the new regime but ensured that they largely remained inactive. Terror and discouragement combined with the positive appeal of the imperial regime to demobilise most of their supporters. Republican opposition was thus generally discrete, and in many communities virtually non-existent well into the following decade.[1] In the immediate aftermath of the *coup* the state prosecutor at Lyon observed that 'in comparison with previous reports which always noted some disorder, some seditious demonstration ... and which attested to a spirit of turbulence and insurrection, I have found everywhere nothing but calm'.[2] His colleague at Dijon reported that 'disarmed by the lack of a central direction and of the resources of the press with its ingenious propaganda and incendiary predictions [republicans] are reduced to a few insignificant manifestations'.[3] These assessments appear to be confirmed by the judicial records for Paris and the Department of the Seine, which reveal a substantial, if not continuous, decline in the number of political 'crimes' throughout the decade.[4] The obsession with politics, which had been so common since 1848, was replaced frequently by a desire to concentrate on more mundane matters.[5] Nevertheless, the experience of the Second Republic had consolidated the republican 'faith' of many militants. Gradually, this would seek expression. In the meantime, republicanism survived largely as an underground movement, its existence revealed to the authorities by occasional incidents and the dubious reports of police spies.[6]

---

[1] PG Caen, 20 July 1853, AN BB30/375.   [2] 3 June 1852, AN BB30/379.

[3] 20 Feb. 1852, AN BB30/377.

[4] E.g. 219 arrests in the last quarter of 1854, 31 in that of 1858, PG Paris, 5 July 1854, ?Feb 1859, AN BB30/383.

[5] E.g. Ch. de Freycinet, *Mes souvenirs 1848–78* (Paris 1912), p. 75.

[6] I. Tchernoff, *Le parti républicain au coup d'état et sous le second empire* (Paris 1906), p. 89; also e.g. Huard, *La préhistoire des partis*, p. 659.

The immediate context was certainly anything but conducive to political opposition, particularly in its republican forms. It was republicans
who had attracted the especial attention of the authorities during the *terreur salutaire*, which had accompanied the *coup*. This had involved a settling
of accounts with the left and the spread of 'disorganisation, discouragement, and fear'.[7] According to Morny, during this phase 'the application
of the rules of common law' would have represented only 'a new public
danger'.[8] Arrests, frequent domiciliary searches, and especially the fear
they caused, largely decapitated and demobilised the left.[9] Wearing red
clothing or growing a full beard was enough to arouse suspicion. Many
democrats felt obliged to shave.[10] Known militants were subjected to
constant surveillance which, according to the prefect of Maine-et-Loire's
instructions to the gendarmerie, 'ought not to degenerate into an unjust
and intolerable harassment', although 'it would cause no inconvenience
if those subject to it are made aware that the administration is watching
them and that it would exercise its duty energetically and very severely
if their conduct were to give the least cause for complaint'.[11] The activities of police spies were magnified greatly by rumour,[12] so that, according to Proudhon, the belief spread that 'the police are organised in the
workshops as they are in the cities' and there was 'no more trust among
workers, no more communication. The walls have ears.'[13] Prosper Rossi,
a stone mason observed that, as police surveillance intensified, 'many of
the inhabitants of Toulon, known for their devotion to the socialist republic, have come to understand quickly the scale of their defeat: informers
are active, and those involved in democratic agitation are the object of
denunciations'.[14] Republicans were demoralised. Mutual denunciation
was not uncommon.[15] The contrast with the dream of electoral victory
in 1852 inaugurating a new era was only too marked. Instead, on the
occasion of the plebiscite, in an effort to curry favour the 282 political
prisoners held in the prison at Brignoles (Var) contributed 15 centimes
each towards the cost of illuminating their prison and installing three
transparencies glorifying the Emperor Napoleon.[16]

[7] PG Montpellier, 26 Feb. 1852, AN BB30/380.
[8] Circular, 11 Jan. 1852, in *Documents pour servir.*
[9] E.g. Paris Prefect of Police to Min de la police générale, 9 June 1853, APP Aa 434; GOC 9e
     DM, 25–31 Jan. 1854, re Reims, ANG G8/17.
[10] PG Paris, 17 March 1852, AN BB30/383.   [11] Quoted Simon, *La Marianne*, pp. 192–3.
[12] S. Commissaire, *Mémoires et souvenirs* (Paris 1888), II, p. 181.
[13] Quoted D. Harvey, *Consciousness and the Urban Experience* (London 1985), p. 101.
[14] Quoted Constant, *Var*, p. 24 note 140.
[15] E.g. PG Paris, 25 Feb. 1852, re arrond. Joigny (Yonne), AN BB30/383.
[16] Constant, *Var*, p. 26.

The impact of repression should be measured not only in terms of the numbers arrested. Individuals also risked other sanctions, including ostracism and dismissal by their employers, which might reduce their families to misery.[17] The Est railway company, informed by the state prosecutor at Metz of the political antecedents of its stationmaster at Forbach and workshop manager at Montigny-lès-Metz dismissed them both.[18] The efforts of the commissaire de police spéciale de chemin de fer to find evidence incriminating the 120 engine drivers and firemen employed at Montereau (Seine-et-Marne) led nowhere, however, and he was himself dismissed for incompetence.[19] The Loire mining company pursued a similar policy.[20] In Auxerre humble building workers found themselves blacklisted.[21] Militants were invariably labelled lazy, drunken, perverted – or just described as 'bad workers'.[22] The café owners who had often provided shelter and support for republicans were a prime target.[23] The threat of closure ensured that 'policing the *cabarets* is, more and more, the work of their own proprietors'.[24] Popular convivial associations like the *chambrées* of southern France or the more bourgeois *cercles* and masonic lodges, similarly were subject to closure. The Grand Orient itself, pushed by the Minister of the Interior, closed its affiliated lodges at Valence and Romans.[25]

IN THE AFTERMATH OF THE *COUP*

It was hardly surprising if, in these circumstances, most republicans remained inactive. Repression and fear massively reduced political agitation.[26] Indeed many former republicans chose to rally to the regime, whether because of disillusionment with the republic, from opportunism, or because of their appreciation of greater prosperity or support for the Emperor's foreign policy and the wars against reactionary Russia and Austria. The Bonapartist myth retained its potency. Others withdrew from political life, permanently or temporarily.[27] Just to take one example, the former minister Crémieux devoted himself, with considerable success, to his career at the Parisian bar, although he continued to meet

---

[17] V. Wright, 'The *coup d'état* of December 1851'.
[18] PG Metz, 10 March 1859, AN BB30/380.   [19] PG Paris, 13 Aug. 1857, AN BB30/383.
[20] PG Lyons, 8 March 1852, AN BB30/379.   [21] PG Paris, 26 April 1852, AN BB30/383.
[22] E.g. sous-préfet Pithiviers to prefect Loiret, 30 June 1859, AN F1 CIII Loiret 12.
[23] E.g. PG Metz, 3 Feb. 1852, AN BB30/380.   [24] PG Dijon, 6 July 1852, AN BB30/377.
[25] Derobet-Ratel, *Arts et l'Amitié*, p. 184.   [26] E.g. prefect, 24 April 1853, AN F1 CIII Var 7.
[27] E.g. prefect, 24 June 1852, AN F1 CIII Mayenne 9.

fellow republicans at informal gatherings.[28] The procureur-général at Rouen reported that 'the republicans disseminated amongst the *bourgeoisie* affect a disdainful resignation or an indifference which barely conceals the disillusionment of some and the ardent resentment of others.'[29] This widespread political demobilisation sharply reduced the contacts between the bourgeois republicans who had played the leading role in formal political organisation and the working class and peasant rank-and-file attracted by the promise of the République démocratique et sociale. The state prosecutor at Nancy pointed out that 'almost all the soldiers [the republican rank and file] voted for the Empire' whilst 'several of the most compromised leaders have left the country and others, influenced by the general situation ... have rallied to the government'. He warned, however, that 'the most tenacious, very few in number, remain discreet and expectant'.[30] If the republican movement had been weakened and fragmented, most communities retained a hard core of irreconcilables, reflecting on their experience, resenting the influence of monarchist notables supported by the administration, and still responding to the quasi-mystical appeal of La Marianne. There was always the hope of some sort of destabilising crisis caused perhaps by the sudden death of the Emperor.[31] A M.Vilfred, whose March 1852 letter to the exiled deputy Greppo was intercepted, and who seemed convinced that Napoleon's reign could not last and believed that 'regicide has a place in the republican soul', was not untypical.[32]

Signs of latent republican sympathies were reported frequently. When, in July 1852, at Barjols (Var) gendarmes cut down the last of the trees of liberty planted following the February Revolution, people were observed collecting pieces of wood and 'carrying them off like holy relics'.[33] Officials disagreed on whether what remained of the republican movement represented an army without leaders or 'an army of which the cadres survive but which has no soldiers'.[34] Together with the major industrial centres, Paris and Lyon remained the principal foci of official concern, particularly as it became evident that the efforts of the regime to win over the masses were enjoying only limited success.[35] This failure was blamed frequently on the *classe moyenne* of doctors, lawyers, notaries, vets,

[28] Aronson, *Adolphe Crémieux* (Paris 1988), pp. 291–301.   [29] 5 July 1853, AN BB30/387.
[30] 16 May 1859, AN BB30/369.   [31] E.g. PG Pau, 18 July 1856, AN BB30/384.
[32] Copy with PG Paris, 17 March 1852, AN BB30/383.
[33] PR Brignoles, 28 July 1852 quoted Constant, *Var*, p. 27.
[34] Prefect, 4 June 1853, AN F1 cIII Côte-d'Or 9.
[35] E.g. PG Lyons, 3 Feb. 1852, 6 Aug. 1858, AN BB30/379.

and small businessmen. It was claimed that these resented their subordinate social status or were hostile to the claims of the church. They were committed partisans of 'liberty' who would never forgive the Emperor for the *coup d'état* and, due to their functions, were well placed to exercise influence over a wide clientele in town and country.[36] The state prosecutor at Paris identified 'the workers in the factories and workshops and railway employees' as the major problem, along with the 'poor' who resented their expulsion from the centre of Paris as Haussmann's reconstruction got under away, as well as the 'speculation' and 'extravagance' this encouraged.[37] The Prefect of Police in October 1856 also expressed his concern about their growing 'exasperation'. The rents charged for the workers' *petits logements* were 'excessive'. Much of the population was being forced into 'miserable shacks, contrary to all the laws of morality and salubrity'. Inevitably the government attracted most of the blame.[38] In the Nord, a clear distinction was made between Lille and its suburbs – where, during the Second Republic, artisans and factory workers had been subject to sustained democratic propaganda, organised by Bianchi and his associates – and the industrial and mining villages in the surrounding countryside where republican militants were drowned in a sea of popular Bonapartism.[39] The workers of towns like Limoges, Poitiers, and Châtellerault were described as 'bowed down by energetic government' but conserving 'essentially hostile sentiments'.[40]

Republicans remained cautious but, as the state prosecutor at Orleans insisted, their 'anarchical passions are compressed rather than extinguished'. Even in little towns like Montargis, Blois, and Gien 'they hold themselves ready to take advantage of unexpected events, of public calamities which the best of governments could not prevent'.[41] It was feared that news of the death of the Emperor would relaunch 'the servile war … dreamt about in the lowest depths of our towns'.[42] The state prosecutor at Lyon reported that opposition to the government was current amongst 'not only the *déclassé* elements and the *habitués* of the *cabarets*, but in addition most of the honest workers, led astray by established traditions and the sermons of 1848. These men are convinced that Society is organised unfairly and that the workers' share is not equitable.' Although 'the newspapers are no longer carrying all the baggage of egalitarian

---

[36] E.g. prefect, 31 Oct. 1853, AN F1 cIII Loiret 7.
[37] 13 Aug. 1857, AN BB30/383.   [38] 26 Oct. 1856, AN BB30/366.
[39] Rapport trimestriel de l'état politique, moral, et religieux. Acad.de Douai, 15 April 1858, AN F17/2649.
[40] Academic rector Poitiers, 10 May 1858, AN F17/2649.   [41] 25 July 1853, AN BB30/382.
[42] PG Angers, 6 July 1855, AN BB30/371.

philosophy', this remained 'part of working-class thought and forms the basis of its political convictions'. The procureur claimed to have spoken to many artisans and been impressed by their ability to employ 'an elevated language' to develop 'a philosophical theory about social organisation'. In spite of which, he concluded that they were motivated by simple envy.[43] His colleague at Montpellier reached similar moralising conclusions, reporting that the republican movement was made up 'of all those corrupt individuals, lost in debt or noted for their infamy, heathens, the debauched, vagabonds, the lazy and drunkards; all those devoured by the need to pull down, demean, overthrow, destroy in order to finally become superior'.[44] This perception made it easy to justify repression. In Toulouse republican sentiments were reported to remain strong amongst 'the masses remembering their triumph in 1848 ... and who dream still of the transformation which will place in their hands money, property, and pleasure' and also 'amongst some small businessmen and law students'. The prefect assumed that political opposition was a sort of game for the students.[45] Support for the republican cause from professionals, small businessmen, artisans, and workers makes it clear that there are no simple sociological explanations of political allegiances, although it is impossible to ignore the very real hostility of the 'poor' towards the 'rich', against 'the class which possesses, personified', according to the procureur at Brignoles 'in every locality by those small proprietors designated by the title of *Bourgeois*'.[46]

Urban/rural distinctions were made frequently by officials, although they could not always be sustained. There was undoubtedly unrest in the countryside. The discontent of the poorest elements of the rural population, like the forestry workers of the Nièvre and Yonne, was emphasised.[47] The forestry workers of the Clamecy area, who floated logs down-river to Paris, spent their three-month winter lay-off in bars talking about the ideas picked up during their frequent visits to the city.[48] *Vignerons* continued to complain about the unfair taxes on alcohol.[49] Peasants in the Pyrenees remained obsessed with the need to abolish restrictions on rights of usage in the forests.[50] More generally peasants in debt condemned the moneylenders who remained 'the leprosy of this region and

---

[43] 20 Dec. 1853, AN BB30/379.   [44] 5 July 1858, AN BB30/380.
[45] 13 April 1859, AN F1 ciii Haute-Garonne 9.
[46] PR Brignoles, 10 June 1852, quoted Constant *Var*, p. 28.
[47] PG Paris, 29 Nov. 1858, AN BB30/383.
[48] E.g. Academic rector Dijon, 17 April 1858, AN F17/2649.
[49] E.g. PG Paris, 20 July 1852, AN BB30/383 re Bar-sur-Aube area.
[50] PG Pau, 6 April 1859, AN BB30/384.

the strength of socialism'.[51] Officials in the Var were concerned about the continued segregation evident in many communities where republicans patronised only the businesses or doctors known to be sympathetic to their cause. They were alarmed by the language of the likes of Pierre Montagne, a farm labourer at Luc who, whilst threshing in August 1853, was reported to have said: 'we should have killed all the rich in 1851. If we had slit their throats we would have their property and be much better off. We were betrayed, but we'll have our chance again; something postponed is not lost.'[52] It seemed that 'dangerous influences' survived, in even the most isolated village, sustained often by 'family traditions.'[53] Sometimes marked differences between the generations were evident. Reports from the Isère suggested that the older peasants who had experienced the Empire and Restoration were far less likely to be republican sympathisers than younger men inspired by the events of '48.[54] It was hoped that time would weaken such 'sentiments' and efface the memories of 1848 but the government was repeatedly warned that once repression became less intense 'socialism will regain its audacity and threaten civilisation'.[55]

These varied judgements were based on an awareness of a variety of symptoms of unrest and on election results. Discontent was most evident during economic crises and especially the last serious instances of dearth between 1853 and 1856. Ministers expressed concern about agitation linked to high food prices.[56] Officials in some areas were reminded of the tension which had preceded the February revolution.[57] Placards on the walls of the faubourg Saint-Antoine in Paris in the autumn of 1856 blamed the high cost of living on the regime and called for 'Death to the Emperor! Bread at 12 *sous*! Hang the landlords! ... *Vive la République*! No more Empire!'[58] The discovery of pamphlets like 'The Empire, famine and disgrace', illegally imported from Jersey, confirmed that republicans were attempting to take advantage of the situation.[59] Bread subsidies helped prevent disorder in the capital, and ensured that in some areas at least 'the government has not been blamed for the subsistence crisis, as it was in 1847; the people understand that the Emperor's government has done everything possible to ease the pain. The opening of public works

---

[51] PG Grenoble, 19 April 1859, AN BB30/378.   [52] Quoted Constant, *Var*, p. 855.

[53] PG Pau, 2 July 1859, AN BB30/384.   [54] Prefect, 24 June 1852, AN F1 CIII Isère 9.

[55] E.g. prefect Drôme, rapport du 25 au 30 juin 1854, AN F7/3989.

[56] See PG Colmar, 14 Oct. 1855, AN BB30/376; Price, *Modernisation*, ch. 6.

[57] E.g. PG Angers, 6 July 1855, AN BB30/371; PI Lyon, 8 Oct. 1853, AN BB30/379.

[58] Gaillard, *Paris*, p. 255.   [59] PG Douai, 20 Jan. 1854, AN BB30/377.

was well received'.[60] Police efforts to prevent the spread of rumours
hostile to grain 'speculators' and to the Emperor also helped.[61] Even so
in Lyon, where the silk trades were depressed in the autumn of 1853,
adding to the misery, 'false news and alarming rumours are widespread,
and avidly listened to'.[62] Although a higher proportion of the rural
population than before appears to have benefited from selling grain at
high prices, those with little or no land also experienced considerable
misery.[63]

Against this general background some republican militants attempted
to distribute pamphlets, to use funerals for demonstrations, and to employ the rich variety of voluntary associations and secret societies as
basic forms of organisation. The authorities were constantly concerned
about placards and graffiti, bar-room debate, and the shouts and yells
of drinkers as they emerged from cafés and bars at closing time. Officials complained bitterly about the government's willingness to tolerate
a few moderate republican newspapers, amongst which *Le Siècle* was the
most influential. The criticisms it printed concerning excessive bureaucratic salaries and wasteful government expenditure were read avidly in
bars, *cercles*, and masonic lodges throughout the country.[64] It survived
because of the influence of its shareholders, who included the Emperor's
half-brother Morny, as well as the moderation of its editor, Havin, who
served, in effect, as a counter-weight to the more extreme left, restricting
his contributors to eulogies of 1789, vague expressions of sympathy for
the poor, and anticlericalism. Such 'indiscretions' as the description of
the Papal States as the 'home of despotism'[65] appear to have been tolerated as a welcome alternative to the all-pervading clericalism of the
1850s. The art of allusion could also be employed to considerable effect.
The newspaper's circulation rose from 21,325 in April 1853 to 52,300
by August 1861 and its influence was extended through the reprinting of
its articles in provincial journals like the Lille *Echo du Nord*, the *Journal de
Rouen*, and *Phare de la Loire* at Nantes, although such major cities as Lyon
and Marseille lacked their own republican paper until 1859.[66]

Political exiles also had a role to play. Reports, similar to one in May
1852, according to which over 1,000 refugees in Geneva were linked to

---

[60] PG Rouen, 12 Jan. 1854 AN BB30/387; Price,'Poor relief'.
[61] E.g. GOC 21 e DM, 11–15 Nov. 1853, AHG G8/9.   [62] PI Lyons, 8 Oct. 1853, AN BB30/379.
[63] E.g. PG Paris, 18 Feb. 1854, AN BB30/383; Price, *Modernisation*, p. 199.
[64] See E.g. sous-préfet Montargis, 4 July 1859, AN F1 CIII Loiret 12; PG Nancy, 3 Feb. 1853, AN
BB30/381.
[65] *Le Siècle*, 11 Aug. 1855.   [66] Bellanger, *Presse*, p. 259.

a Comité révolutionnaire Mazzinian et Rolliniste in London, aroused concern.[67] The number of exiles had grown substantially between June 1848 and December 1851. Many had found it a struggle to make ends meet and gradually they returned to their families in France. Some, like Jean-Baptiste Audric a cabinet-maker from Montélimar, were prepared to spy on their colleagues in return for government favours.[68] Those who remained in exile, and who possessed the time and energy to participate in political activity, engaged in efforts to promote revolutionary internationalism and in often bitter doctrinal disputes and personal invective – in London especially between the supporters of Félix Pyat, advocates of regicide, and the more moderate associates of Ledru-Rollin.[69] The activities of police informers helped to maintain an atmosphere of mutual suspicion. They suffered also from the typical exiles' illusions, constantly re-affirming their belief in the imminent collapse of the Empire.

The smuggling of anti-regime literature, particularly from Belgium, Switzerland, Britain, and the Channel Islands, was another cause of official concern.[70] Substantial quantities of 'subversive' literature were seized. Thus in a fairly typical incident, innocuous in itself, three suspects were reported to have dined at Pont-de-Beauvoisin, then in Savoy, with a M. Rivière from Bourgoin, a political refugee at Chambéry. His wife was later apprehended whilst crossing the frontier carrying two copies of Victor Hugo's *Napoléon le petit*.[71] The seizure in October 1853 in the post at Portbail (Manche) of writings by Hugo and Ledru-Rollin addressed to individuals in Toul and Nancy added new names to the police lists of suspects and provided evidence of the existence of groups within France with links to the exiles.[72] Propaganda printed on fine paper and inserted into letters was especially difficult to detect. It was assumed that much more passed through the long and under-policed frontiers, smuggled under clothes or in merchandise or brought in by railwaymen.[73] In October 1852 a box containing fish addressed to a Mlle Mélanie in Lyon was found to have a concealed compartment containing 'anarchistic writings'. The addressee was arrested when she came to collect the box. Police searched her home and found incriminating letters from

[67] PG Lyon, 9 May 1852, AN BB30/379.   [68] Maitron, *Dictionnaire du mouvement ouvrier*, I.

[69] E.g. *Trois lettres au journal l'Homme* (London 1854); C. Lévy, 'Les proscrits du 2 décembre' in Hamon, *Les républicains*, p. 26; R. Gossez, 'La proscription et les origines de l'Internationale', *1848*, 1951, pp. 98–100.

[70] E.g. MI circular, 9 Feb. 1852, in *Documents pour servir*; PG Colmar, 1 July 1854, AN BB30/376.

[71] PG Grenoble, 18 Nov. 1852, AN BB30/378.

[72] GOC 16e DM, 20–25 Oct. 1853, AHG G8/9.

[73] E.g. PG Douai, 3 Sept. 1853, AN BB30/377; PG Lyon, 6 Jan. 1856, AN BB30/379.

correspondents in Lyon and Rive-de-Gier, which set off a further round of domiciliary searches.[74] Benjamin Clemenceau, the father of the future Prime Minister and resident in Nantes, had already been arrested in December 1851 and was imprisoned again, as a suspect, in March 1858. Searches of his home revealed copies of illegally imported works by the leading political exiles as well as letters from a M. Martin, living in Napoléon-Vendée, discussing the political ideas they shared and arranging to collect the illicit books and to re-distribute them. This persecution, and the nervous collapse of his sisters which followed, made the already politicised Georges all the more determined to work for the triumph of the Republic.[75] Ingeniously, copies of *Napoléon le petit* were for some time imported to Lille in busts of the Emperor.[76] The special inspectors at Pontarlier on the Swiss border reported on the seizure of works by Hugo, as well as anonymous pamphlets with titles like 'The Forty Thieves' and large numbers of popular almanacs of the type long distributed throughout France by peddlers. In January 1853, 3,000 copies of Colonel Charras' appeal to the army were seized at Roubaix.[77] The Belgian frontier appears to have been particularly permeable. In spite of French protests, Brussels would remain a major centre of republican propaganda. Its publishers distributed copies of Hugo's *Napoléon le petit* and *Châtiments* as well as a satirical *Charivari belge*, featuring Daumier's anti-Bonapartist character Ratapoil in imitation of its now much more restrained French counterpart.[78] The numerous publications left over from 1848 and 'carefully preserved by some families' also played an important part in the survival of opposition. [79]

Hugo's works certainly proved an inspiration to the regime's opponents. They set the tone also for republican historians of the Empire for generations to come. Most of this propaganda was anything but great literature. Amongst the most extreme examples were the items produced by the so-called Comité de la Commune révolutionnaire. The *Lettre au peuple*, published in London in August 1852, set out a programme which included decentralisation, direct democracy, reform of the magistrature

74 Prefect, 15 Oct. 1852, AN F₁ cɪɪɪ Rhône 10.
75 PG Poitiers, 31 Jan. 1854, AN BB30/370; G. Dallas, *At the Heart of a Tiger. Clemenceau and his World* (London 1993), p. 13.
76 A.-M. Gossez, 'Un procès pour introduction frauduleuse de livres prohibés à Lille en 1853', *Révolution de 1848*, 1907/8, pp. 257–66.
77 PG Douai, 29 Jan. 1853, AN BB30/406.
78 R. Rütten, R. Jung, and G. Schneider, *La caricature entre République et censure. L'imagerie satirique en France de 1830 à 1880* (Lyon 1996) pp. 281–3.
79 E.g. PG Lyon, 17 July 1856, AN BB30/379.

– condemned for being 'as filthy as the cassock and the uniform' – abolition of the professional army, and separation of the state from a Catholic church denounced, along with capitalism, as an accomplice in tyranny. The social programme of the démocrate-socialiste movement was retained, with its promise of the right to work, cheap credit, public ownership of transport, insurance companies, banks and mines, tax reductions for the poor, confiscation of the property of Louis-Napoleon and his 'accomplices', and obligatory, secular education. It reminded its readers that 'Insurrection' remained 'the most sacred of duties'.[80] Another letter signed by Pyat, Rougée, and Avril, published in November, called for a vote against the re-establishment of the Empire, warning voters that they could not abrogate their own sovereignty and insisting that 'the people must not go to the ballot like a flock to the abattoir, under the surveillance of the police and the gendarme's sabre'.[81] In a little pamphlet published in Brussels in 1854 Hippolyte Magen promised that for the leading figures of the imperial regime 'punishment will inexorably … reach the thrones where Perjury, Theft, Murder try in vain to conceal themselves under the diadem and tiara, the two insignia of tyranny'. Morny was described as a speculator and 'courtisan' and, like his Imperial master, one of 'Queen Hortense's numerous bastards.' Marshal Saint-Arnaud was a dissipated, failed actor.[82] In an eight-page *Lettre à Marianne*, appearing in London in February 1856, Pyat saluted the republican deity: 'You alone are our queen. We have no other sovereign but you.' She lived on in spite of the regime's efforts: 'Daughter of God, you live amongst the beggars, the humble, the poor, with the helots, the proletarians, the miserable, the oppressed, the disinherited, the devoted, the barefooted, the *sans-culottes* and the starving.'[83] Once inside France, distribution of propaganda and the ideas it contained would be ensured by militants like Alexandre Auger-Brix, an innkeeper at Poitiers, or Baritot, an *ouvrier voilier* at La Bastide near Bordeaux.[84] The oral transmission of ideas, especially by migrant workers and by mobile groups like railway workers and commercial travellers, was a further cause of concern for the authorities.[85] Another feature of this effort to keep the memory of the republic alive was the continued sale of 'plaster casts representing the dreadful heroes of our civil discord'.[86] Pipes with their bowls carved to represent Raspail

[80] Reprinted in *Les Républicains sous le Second Empire* (Paris: EDHIS, n.d.).
[81] Included with PG Lyons, 19 Nov. 1852, AN BB30/406.
[82] H. Magen, *Le pilori* (Brussels 1854).   [83] 8pp., published in London, 24 Feb. 1856.
[84] Maitron, *Dictionnaire biographique du mouvement ouvrier.*
[85] E.g. PG Amiens, 15 April 1859, AN BB30/371.   [86] PG Dijon, 8 July 1853, AN BB30/377.

or Ledru-Rollin, Phrygian caps, or nude women, were still on sale in two shops in Troyes in November 1852.[87]

Republican organisations were entirely illegal. Those that did exist were described as secret societies. Undoubtedly official reports exaggerated their numbers. Policemen were under constant pressure from their superiors to provide information.[88] In such politicised environments as Paris or Lyons any kind of gathering was likely to be described as a secret society.[89] All manner of rumours were at least half believed. The prefect of the Rhône actually suggested to Bergeret, the police commissaire spécial in June 1852, that he ought to make a greater effort to verify the voluminous information he was providing, often on the basis of anonymous denunciations, concerning the spread of such societies as the Vengeurs or Voleurs throughout the south.[90] If senior officials were not prepared to take such reports too seriously then neither presumably should the historian. Nevertheless, they should certainly not be ignored. Police reports are one amongst a number of indices of republican activity, which, more than ever, was being driven underground.

In spite of repression, small groups of militants continued to exchange visits and meet in cafés, *chambrées*, *cercles*, through friendly societies and masonic lodges, as well as on village squares and at fairs and markets. The authorities found it difficult to decide whether these amorphous gatherings represented day-to-day sociability or 'a hot-bed of political propaganda'. The prefect closed the *Cercle de commerce* at Saint Pons (Hérault) in 1856 because its members included too many 'democrats' and they had failed to participate in a 'patriotic' reception for the 35th infantry regiment.[91] The tighter regulation of café opening hours had little effect.[92] In the Nord, like-minded republicans were believed to gather in the associations typical of local popular sociability – choirs, bowls, and archery groups, as well as to play cards and enjoy illicit cock fighting. Regulation was likely to be ignored and to cause considerable irritation. In Lille, where the café Groulez was a favourite meeting place for republicans to talk and sing Pierre Dupont's songs, the police preferred to watch and listen rather than close the bar and drive these activities

[87] PG Paris, 13 Nov. 1852, AN BB30 383.
[88] E.g. MI circular to prefects, 7 Dec. 1851 in *Documents pour servir*, p. 19.
[89] E.g. Castellane, *Journal*, IV, p. 350.
[90] F. Dutacq, 'La police politique et les partis d'opposition à Lyon et dans le midi en 1852', *1848*, (1923), pp. 240–2.
[91] PG Montpellier, 16 July 1856, AN BB30/380.   [92] E.g. PG Dijon, 6 July 1852, AN BB30/377.

further underground.[93] Sylvain Carrier, a quarryman claimed by the state prosecutor at Paris to be typical of the workers of Corbeil, was convicted of singing a little ditty in a bar at Villeneuve-Saint-Georges, which included the words:

> Remember June, the Barricades,
> Blood flowed in torrents;
> Soldiers be Republicans![94]

Such songs were interspersed frequently with shouts of 'Vive la République rouge!' or 'A bas l'empereur!' The peasant J.-J.Gourdol clearly went too far, in a café near Annonay (Ardèche) in January 1858, when he sang: 'Poor France, for your suffering the people demand vengeance, the assassins of kings deserve a decoration.'[95] Parisian law students passing through the Creuse on holiday,[96] peasants or workers enjoying a drink, were all likely to break into song.[97] In September 1859 a gathering in a café in the mining town of Graissessac (Hérault), which included the mayor, sang the following song:

> The Monarchy has exhausted the patience of France,
> It is about time that the people had its turn,
> In the dark sky, on the horizon
> Rises the day of our deliverance.
> Kings need valets and Traitors,
> Courtesans and ministers.
> The People's money fattens too many masters:
> That is why I am a republican.[98]

In a report prepared by the Minister of Justice for the Emperor in 1856, mutual aid societies were described as the most dangerous form of opposition organisation.[99] In Paris and the department of the Seine by 1859 only 123 of 883, mainly trade-based, friendly societies had applied for official approval and accepted the appointed president, honorary members, and subsidies that went with this. Undoubtedly, many of the remainder were disguised trades unions. The situation was much the same in Lyon.[100] According to the police spy Philippon, in Rouen

---

[93] Ménager, *Nord*, 1 pp. 386–90. [94] Feb. 1859, AN BB30/383.
[95] GOC 8e DM, 20 March 1858, AHG G8/52.
[96] Prefect, report on September 1855, AN F7/3978.
[97] E.g. prefect Drôme, May 1855, AN F7/3989.
[98] Included with report of PG Montpellier, 29 Sept. 1859, AN BB30/422.
[99] Résumé of PG reports second half of 1856 for Emperor, AN BB30/368.
[100] F. Chavot, 'Les sociétés de secours mutuels sous le second empire', *Cahiers d'histoire de l'Institut Maurice Thorez* (1977), p. 23.

workers were extremely hostile to the authorised mutual aid societies, considering them to be 'the final stage of human degradation, where citizens are penned like beasts of burden under the searching gaze of the clergy and the other *aristos* who do not miss a single gesture, nor a single word'.[101] Many workers felt insulted by charity and were determined to retain their independence. In Lille members of dissolved associations simply gathered in a café called *L'Estaminet*.[102] The efforts of *compagnons* belonging to the various skilled trades in Chalon-sur-Saône to form a mutual aid society at a meeting attended by representatives from Lyons, Mâcon, and Tournus, and addressed by the venerable of the local masonic lodge – a known republican – as well as the meeting's failure to express gratitude to the Emperor for his support of friendly societies, was clearly cause for concern.[103] So too was the fact that the newly elected comité d'administration of the Grenoble Association for the abolition of begging was made up of well-known local republicans.[104] The members of evangelical Protestant sects – 'Methodists, Plymouthes, Momists, etc'. – in the Die and Montélimar areas were similarly suspect.[105] If the primary purpose of such gatherings was not political, they certainly facilitated the discussion and diffusion of ideas.

Traditional gatherings like the regular *veillées* at which neighbours gathered in the winter months to repair tools, sew, and talk, and share the cost of heat and light, might serve a similar purpose.[106] The workers of Marseille frequently owned or rented *cabanon* outside the city as places for rest and recreation and especially hunting and fishing. Typically, on 18 October 1852, twenty-seven men, mostly *ouvriers mouleurs*, gathered at one for a drinking session. For the occasion they wore red belts and cravats. They sang 'subversive' songs, danced the *carmagnole* and shouted 'Long live the gallows! Long live the guillotine! Down with the rich! Down with the Godly!', and listened to political 'speeches'. Twenty-five of them were arrested.[107] Possibly the two not arrested were police informants. On 12 December 1856 the young men of the commune of Cournuel (Aude) were reported to have erected an altar in front of a surviving tree of liberty and danced around it singing the Marseillaise and other republican songs.[108] The *fêtes patronales* at Besse and

---

[101] Quoted Boivin, *Mouvement ouvrier*, I, p. 77.   [102] Ménager, *Nord*, I, pp. 98–9.
[103] PG Dijon, 12 Jan. 1866, AN BB30/377.   [104] PG Grenoble, 8 July 1853, AN BB30/378.
[105] *Ibid.*, 14 Oct. 1858.
[106] E.g. L. Pinard, *Les mentalités religieuses du Morvan au 19e siècle (1830–1914)* (Dijon 1997), pp. 207–8.
[107] PR Marseille, 21 Oct. 1852, AN BB30/406.
[108] GOC 11e DM, 20–25 Dec. 1856, AHG G8/37.

Cros-de-Cagnes (Var) in the early summer of 1852 also provided opportunities to talk politics and sing the *Marseillaise* or Dupont's 'Song of the
Peasant' or '1852' – with its millenarian aspirations, and for the young
men to throw stones at the gendarmes when they intervened.[109] *Fêtes*
were also all too likely to generate brawls between rival groups.[110] The
Paris Prefect of Police insisted that 'the propaganda carried out by means
of songs is very dangerous. By this means the worst doctrines are easily
engraved on the memory of the population. These rhymed and sung
forms are introduced into all meetings, are repeated by all and constitute a real evil'. The printed forms of such notable works as *The Idiot from
Biarritz* and the former priest Constant's *Caligula*, decorated with knives,
were an obvious incitement to violence.[111]

In addition to *chansons anarchiques* police reports constantly complained
about *propos politiques* which might involve *propos séditieux*, as when a tailor at Bar-sur-Aube in November 1852 was overheard praising Barbès,
Blanqui, Nadaud, and the 'right to work,' or when M. Robert, a miner
in the Nièvre, made favourable references to the resistance to the *coup
d'état* at Clamecy.[112] *Placards* were a traditional means of expressing
grievances.[113] A shoemaker called Geoffrey, living at Cusset (Allier) was
imprisoned for three months after being caught fixing one to a wall
which began: 'Napoleon is a coward, his ministers are villains. Down
with the Emperor! *Vive la République démocratique et sociale.*'[114] A *placard*
found at La Côte-Saint-André (Isère) appealed to more distant, but still
potent, memories with a portrait of Robespierre crowned with laurels
and the legend 'The head of Robespierre is in Heaven crowned with
immortal laurels. Destroyer of Kings' and below this 'Dear compatriots, I am your protector; follow my example, and if need be give up
your life and choose death to save the nation,' and ending with the
phrase 'Honour to the great Robespierre.'[115] Another, found at Buisse
(Drôme) in the night of 14 November, conveyed a widespread sense of
disappointment with Bonaparte, appealing to the 'Republic, to which
you owe your rise, which you betrayed like a cowardly deserter of the
people's cause', promising that 'a day will come when the executioners
will fall victim to their own treachery'.[116] A *placard* found on the walls
of the town hall at Florac (Gard), immediately below an official poster

[109] Constant, *Var*, p. 28.   [110] E.g. GOC 9e DM, 11–15 Dec. 1852, AHG F1/70.
[111] Quoted Prothero, *Radical Artisans*, p. 298.
[112] PG Paris, 15 Oct. 1852, AN BB30/383; GOC 19e DM, 5–10 Feb. 1854, AHG G8/17.
[113] Price, *Modernisation*, pp.131–43.   [114] PG Riom, 29 Jan. 1856, AN BB30/386.
[115] PG Grenoble, 18 Aug. 1852, AN BB30/378.   [116] *Ibid.*, 12 Dec. 1852.

containing a speech by Louis-Napoleon, warned: 'Shameless usurper. God is our defender and in spite of the weight of your despotism the socialism which his Son implanted on earth will survive.' This was followed by drawings of a skull and knife. A law clerk called Créfeuille, who possessed a knife with a similar pattern, was arrested.[117] Republicans looked forward to the re-establishment of 'that holy Republic, whose motto is *Liberté, égalité et fraternité*' but which 'a traitor ... a hypocrite' had replaced with 'lies, hypocrisy, fanaticism, public order'.[118] There were also frequent reports of *propos injurieux contre l'Empereur* (or the Empress) and concerning the diffusion of 'false news' – rumours which spread so rapidly that this could only be due to the existence of 'secret and rapid means of communication'.[119] Forest fires in the Yonne in spring 1852 were blamed on politically motivated arson.[120] Chamard, the postilion on the Vienne–Lyon coach, was imprisoned for a month and fined 500 francs for telling his passengers, on 23 December 1853, that the Emperor had been shot and wounded, that Paris was under martial law, and the electric telegraph had been cut.[121] In March 1854 the rumour spread though the marketplace at Bourg-de-Péage (Drôme) that 100,000 workers had risen in Paris to protest against the price of bread.[122] When it was rumoured at Saint-Pons (Hérault) that beacons on the mountaintops would soon announce an uprising in Paris, all it took was a couple of accidental blazes to cause panic.[123] Similarly, the destruction of two wayside crosses near Coulommiers (Seine-et-Marne) seemed to support the rumour that revenge for the cutting of trees of liberty had been planned.[124]

All manner of seemingly trivial incidents were taken to be republican manifestations. The building labourer Robert was sentenced to two months in prison at Saintes (Charente-Inférieure) in December 1855 for telling his workmates that 'if business isn't doing well, it's Napoleon's fault; we need another Robespiere and the guillotine'.[125] A seventeen-year-old tailor at Nîmes drew another simple historical analogy on 27 February 1853 when he told his friends that Napoleon deserved the same fate as Louis XVI.[126] At Pierre (Saône-et-Loire) the bust of the Emperor

---

[117] GOC 8e DM, 16–20 April 1852, AHG F1/69.
[118] *Placard* found in square at Tarnac (Charente) on 29 May 1853, GOC 14e DM, 1–5 June 1853, AHG G8/1.
[119] PG Metz, 10 March 1859, AN BB30/380.   [120] PG Paris, 13 May 1852, AN BB30/383.
[121] PG Grenoble, 31 March 1854, AN BB30/378.   [122] *Ibid.*, 31 March 1854.
[123] PG Montpellier, 16 July 1856, AN BB30/380.   [124] PG Paris, 17 March 1852, AN BB30/383.
[125] PG Poitiers, 25 Jan. 1856, AN BB30/385.   [126] GOC 10e DM, 26–28 Feb. 1853, AHG G8/1.

normally kept in the *mairie* was found hanging by the neck nearby, with the message 'Death to Tyrants' attached to it.[127] At Pithiviers (Loiret) in January 1853 a tanner called Lecorsu was arrested for spitting on an equestrian portrait of the Emperor in a bar,[128] whilst in Bar-le-Duc (Meuse) in May a soldier was abused and told that he was 'a pig, a drunk, a thief, and a *blanc* [Legitimist], and served an imbecile of an Emperor.'[129] How seriously should the police take the utterings of Pierre Faveron, a peddler accused of telling his clients that 'Napoleon is a lazybones, a coward incapable of ruling; the Republicans are the largest party ... They are only waiting for the coronation to strike against him; and once the republicans are triumphant, it'll be time to smash and pillage the *châteaux* and the big houses.' [130]

Folkloric practices like the *farandole* and *charivari* continued to be used to express contempt for enemies. M. Lemoine, a retired civil servant living at Montluçon (Allier), was badly frightened by a crowd of women and children who pursued him though the streets on the evening of 17 July 1852 singing 'the *blancs*, we'll roast them in a cauldron'.[131] At Bourg-de-Péage, on the anniversary of the February Revolution in 1852, a group of workers in mourning dress with their faces blackened dragged a plough through the streets whilst the ploughman – well-dressed and claiming to be their 'maître' – shouted: 'Walk on, walk on, one furrow more!' and cracked his whip. Presumed to depict the slavery of the masses, this display was reported to have caused great alarm in the little town.[132] Suspected informers were a particular target. Ostracism was an effective means of indicating the community's displeasure. At Gonfaron (Var) an agricultural labourer called Muraire was reported to have been 'rejected by everyone and ... reduced to extreme misery because he can't find work in the village'. His wife was afraid to go outdoors. In September 1853, on the occasion of a baptism, a hostile crowd of around 300 people who continued to shout abuse throughout the ceremony escorted him to church.[133] An overwhelming sense of solidarity survived within many rural communities in spite of the authoritarian regime.

Republicans came together for funerals, like that, at Florensac (Hérault) in May 1852, of M. Philip, a participant in resistance to the

---

[127] GOC 8e DM, 10–15 Oct. 1853, AHG G8/9.   [128] PG Orleans, 6 Jan. 1853, AN BB30/382.
[129] GOC 5e DM, 21–25 May, 1853, AHG G8/1.
[130] PG Grenoble, 8 July 1853, AN BB30/378.   [131] PG Riom, 5 Aug. 1852, AN BB30/386.
[132] PG Grenoble, 8 March 1852, AN BB30/378.
[133] PI Brignoles, quoted Constant, *Var*, pp. 866–7; PG Aix, 24 Sept. 1853, AN BB30/407.

coup d'état, which was attended by around 400 people.[134] The burials of the wife of the socialist Raspail in Paris in 1853 or of General Cavaignac in 1857 were occasions for substantial demonstrations of strength, with which the authorities were reluctant to interfere. The prosecution of political suspects might also backfire by providing republicans with further occasions for mass gatherings, as at Blanc (Indre) in August 1858, on the occasion of the trial of a certain Bondy, defended by the eminent republican lawyer, Emile Ollivier. Only the rapid deployment of troops limited the size of the gathering.[135] The release of political prisoners provided another excuse for a demonstration. If attendance at the banquet for fifty people planned to celebrate the return to Grand-Temps (Isère) of M. Faure was sharply reduced by the intimidating presence of six gendarmes, this did not prevent the illumination of windows in the village in celebration.[136]

In the 1850s officials retained, for some time, a mind-set and anxieties created before the *coup*.[137] There were frequent rumours about secret societies, planned insurrections, and assassination plots, which were given credence by the occasional unearthing of subversive activities like those associated with La Marianne (see chapter 5). No doubt many police reports were exaggerated. They continued to record the existence of secret societies, which were mainly residual survivals from before the *coup d'état*. Efforts by republicans to be discreet could be represented easily as subversion by zealous officials.[138] Even when unable to secure hard evidence of the existence of secret societies, the authorities remained convinced that they must exist, organised in networks, linked to a *comité* in Paris or Lyon, and waiting a signal – possibly news of the death of the Emperor.

ELECTORAL ACTIVITY

The air of secrecy, which necessarily pervaded republican activity, inevitably encouraged mutual suspicion and factionalism.[139] The experience of revolutionary violence in 1848 and the threat of state repression following the *coup* had convinced many of the wisdom of moderation and

---

[134] Prefect, 2 June 1852, AN F1 CIII Herault 14.
[135] Prefect of Indre, report on August 1858, AN F7/4025.
[136] Prefect Isère, 2 August 1852, AN F7/4032.
[137] Point made by prefect, 24 June 1852, AN F1 CIII Isère 9.
[138] G. Jacquemet, *Belleville au 19e siècle. Du faubourg à la ville* (Paris 1984), pp. 502–3.
[139] E.g. PG Riom, 2 July 1859, AN BB30/386.

legalism. These moderates were hostile both to the Imperial regime and towards erstwhile allies to their left. They were themselves divided bitterly on the issue of electoral participation. The exiles were even more vociferous in maintaining a principled refusal to engage with the institutions of the Empire.[140] In February 1852, three republicans had been elected to the Corps législatif, in spite of all the obstacles. Carnot and Hénon, the philanthropic Lyons doctor, refused to take the oath of allegiance to the regime, thanking their supporters and insisting 'that our names in themselves represent a protest against the destruction of public liberty'.[141] Legrand, elected in Lille, took the oath and soon rallied to the regime. Of the 154 republicans who dared present themselves, only 27 attracted more than 1,000 votes.[142] Prefects had been instructed to prevent the distribution of candidates' *professions de foi* wherever these were thought likely to 'reawaken political passions'.[143] In the absence of candidates, many republicans could only express their opposition through abstention. The municipal elections held between 24 July and 26 September often proved more troublesome for the authorities. The prefect of the Var, where community traditions remained vibrant, described municipal councils as 'the last refuge of the government's enemies'.[144] This was also the case in towns close to Paris like Etampes and Pontoise and neighbouring communes including Persan, where the presence of a factory was a cause of social tension, and Eaubonne where the regime's difficulties were blamed on the incessant propagandising of M. Pouthier who had been mayor in 1848;[145] and in industrial villages in the Avre valley in Normandy, as well as in more populous locations like Elbeuf, Sotteville, and Orival.[146] According to the Prefect of the Hérault, 'in many communes the demagogic spirit has revealed itself again and led to deplorable results. In others internal dissension is more significant than political, and the influence of particular individuals and factions has alone influenced the electoral struggle.'[147] Republicans made use of local issues frequently – in the Var at Bandol, for example, hostility to an over-zealous police commissaire as well as to proposals to ban cesspits, unhygienic but providing fertiliser for farmers. Only time would tell whether these results were symptoms of enduring opposition or of

---

[140] E.g. Huard, *Naissance du parti politique*, pp.115–16.   [141] Albiot, *Les campagnes électorales*, p.129.
[142] Lagoueyte, *Candidature*, p. 625.
[143] Circular from MI. Persigny, 15 Feb. 1852 in *Documents pour servir*.
[144] 7 July 1854, AN F1 CIII Var 7.   [145] PG Paris, 24 Nov. 1852, AN BB30/383.
[146] Boivin, *Mouvement ouvrier*, I, p. 110.   [147] 21 Sept. 1852, quoted by Puech, *Essai*, p. 108.

the pre-eminence of local disputes over politics. New councils were often suspended and replaced with appointed commissions, an act which
probably exacerbated local animosities.[148] Discouraged by forceful official interference, the turnout for the 1855 municipal elections would be
substantially lower.

In a much less oppressive atmosphere, in the June 1857 general elections, republicans made a more determined effort, concentrating their
resources on some of the leading figures of 1848, although often as a
matter of form rather than with any genuine hope of success.[149] In a
single-sheet broadside on 'The Next Elections in France', Louis Blanc
insisted that abstention would only encourage the regime, whilst an opposition vote was a vital means of protest at a time when insurrection was
certainly unrealistic given the 'wall of bayonets [which] surrounds a disarmed Paris'. Nevertheless, he concluded that electoral success certainly
should be followed by a refusal to take the oath of allegiance.[150] Clearly
a revival was underway, even if in many areas republicans remained discouraged and inactive.[151] On this occasion, 75 of around 100 candidates
obtained more than 1,000 votes.[152] Five of the ten deputies elected in
Paris were republicans but Carnot, Goudchaux, and Cavaignac were
unseated, due to their refusal to take the oath. This left their moderate republican colleagues Ollivier and Darimon, together with Hénon,
again elected in Lyon, to carry on the parliamentary struggle against
the regime alongside a small number of opposition liberals. These representatives of the younger generation were prepared to challenge the
leadership of the *vieux*, the leaders of 1848. The ambitious lawyers Ernest
Picard and Jules Favre, as a result of by-election victories, soon joined
them. Together they would constitute *les Cinq*. All were convinced of the
futility of abstentionist tactics and were encouraged in this by Havin
the editor of the *Siècle* and Nefftzer of the *Presse*. Initially they were
largely ostracised by other deputies. However, once elected, these republican deputies possessed a much greater capacity for self-publicity,
which assured them even more prominent roles in the republican
movement.

The Parisian results, this reminder of 'the bad old days', had a substantial impact on republican morale throughout France.[153] During
the pre-election period republicans had not been permitted to form

---

[148] E.g. Constant, Var, p. 58.　　[149] E.g. Marcilhacy, *Diocèse*, p. 414.
[150] L. Blanc, *Les prochaines élections en France* (London 1857).
[151] E.g. in Seine-et-Marne – PG Paris, 20 Aug. 1858, AN BB30/383.
[152] Lagoueyte, *Candidature*, p. 627.　　[153] E.g. PG Douai, 22 July 1857, AN BB30/377.

committees, hold meetings, or distribute circulars. In spite of this, re-publican candidates had, nationally, attracted almost 500,000 votes, even though most constituencies lacked a republican challenger.[154] This rel-ative success was due to the efforts of local enthusiasts willing to brave official intimidation, who wrote out ballot papers by hand because print-ers were too afraid of losing their licences.[155] The strength of this op-position was especially evident in those communities and neighbour-hoods in which republicans, making use of informal networks based on friendship and sociability, possessed a critical mass and confidence. In the working class *quartiers* of Lille, supporters of the republican candi-date, Loiset, turned out 'street by street, almost according to their house number, keeping a watch on each other, and clearly obeying not only their inclinations, but instructions whose point of departure escapes us'. This collective act represented additionally a means of resisting official pressure.[156] In Rouen, another textile centre, republican leaders – mainly merchants and lawyers – met informally with small groups of supporters, mostly artisans, shopkeepers, and textile workers.[157] These campaigns left few written traces but were clear evidence of the survival of a solid core of militants and of a mass of voters hostile both to the regime and to its monarchist and liberal critics. This capacity for mobilisation con-vinced many officials of the existence of a vast underground republican organisation.[158] The procureur-général at Limoges could only record his pleasure that gerrymandering had ensured that the vote of the porcelain workers in the city 'has been drowned by the immense majority of rural voters.' Few workers had appeared on the first day of polling. On the second, 'they arrived in large bands, conducted by a few leaders, and orderly and quietly deposited their votes, like a well-disciplined troop. On a bench opposite the polling station, three of them took up a per-manent place in order to supervise the vote.'[159] In smaller communities, however, the defection or intimidation of an individual militant might be sufficient to demobilise the republican movement. The distance still to be travelled was all too obvious from the humiliating failure of such symbols of the republic as Lamartine at Mâcon[160] and the overwhelming success of the government.

At this national level, the elected deputies, together with journalists and the eminent lawyers involved in political trials, would increasingly

---

[154] Girard, *Questions politiques*, pp.14–16; Zeldin, *Political System*, pp. 72–4.
[155] Puech, *Essai*, pp. 36–98.   [156] PG Douai, 22 July 1857, AN BB30/377.
[157] Aminzade, *Ballots*, p. 196.   [158] E.g. prefect, 23 June 1858, AN F1 cIII Sarthe 13.
[159] 28 June 1857, AN BB30/378.   [160] Goujon, *Le vignoble*, p. 207.

provide a modicum of leadership. They were overwhelmingly moderates committed to legalistic forms of opposition. The failure of violence in 1848 and 1851 seemed to justify their moderation, and determination to distance themselves from the *rouges* and to reassure the proponents of social order.[161] The main features of their programme were political freedom, ministerial responsibility to parliament, and the separation of church and state. Social reform was mentioned rarely. The sometimes venomous distaste for socialism and all its works was evident in the correspondence between two Breton republicans, Guillaume Lejean and Charles Alexandre, and Alphonse de Lamartine. Alexandre typically condemned the extreme left for having 'killed the Republic through horror and disgust'.[162] The oratorical talents of the members of this small group and their determined opposition to such measures as the Law of General Security in 1858, together with criticism of the system of managed elections, certainly encouraged other young middle-class republicans, and particularly professionals possessing useful rhetorical and organisational skills and personal contacts, for whom an encounter with the law was less threatening than it might be for most workers or peasants.[163]

Nevertheless, the involvement of worker and peasant militants was the essential means of establishing links with a wider audience. From the bourgeois republican point of view there was a danger that repression in demobilising 'respectable' citizens and forcing the movement underground would lead to the autonomous development of informal working-class and peasant groups and to secret societies, like those of 1851, committed to revolutionary violence.[164] Social as well as political differences between moderate republican notables and more socialistically inclined workers were especially evident in industrial centres like Lille, Rouen, or Toulouse.[165]

Divisions were apparent also in relation to the regime's foreign policy. French intervention in the Crimea and war in Italy were welcomed by many republicans out of patriotism and hostility towards the reactionary empires and the Papacy.[166] Darimon spoke of a sense of crisis amongst

[161] E.g. Tollu, 'Démocratie et liberté', pp. 126–7.

[162] Letter of 10 Aug. 1852 in C. Lejean and C. Alexandre, *Correspondance (1846-69). Deux républicains bretons dans l'entourage de Lamartine et de Michelet* (Paris 1993), p. 305.

[163] See E.g. L. Girard, 'Jules Ferry et la génération des républicains du second empire' in F. Furet (ed.), *Jules Ferry fondateur de la République* (Paris 1985), p. 50.

[164] E.g. PG Nancy, 31 Dec. 1852, AN BB30/381; Ménager, *Nord*, I, p. 64.

[165] PG Douai, 29 July 1856, AN BB30/377.

[166] *Ibid.*, 9 April 1859; prefect, 5 July 1859, AN F1 c111 Var 7.

the small group of republican deputies, due to the evident popularity of the Italian war amongst the Parisian masses.[167] Ollivier warned those amongst his colleagues who favoured the war that Napoleon, 'that wretched individual, is anxious to restore the brilliance of his old blood-soaked eagle'.[168] In a letter written on 15 January 1858 he had maintained that 'Italian independence is only a pretext. In reality the Emperor is only concerned to consolidate his dynasty and silence the internal opposition which is gradually being born.'[169] Military action was also criticised for sacrificing French lives. Jules Barbotin, a shoemaker at Poitiers (Vienne), was arrested for telling an excited crowd, gazing at engravings of the Crimean battles in a shop window, that French casualties were far higher than the government claimed and that lives were being wasted 'in the interests of England'.[170] The absence of much of the army and even the possibility of its defeat might even be welcomed. According to an individual called Astieu, resident at Upic (Drôme), this offered an opportunity to shoot 'those who denounced us and all the *aristos*. We'll go to Paris, we'll get hold of Napoleon and place Ledru-Rollin at the head of the Government.'[171] Many of those republicans who had seen the war in Italy as a stage in the European revolution, in the liberation of the peoples and the creation of an universal republic, were enthusiastic for the achievements of Garibaldi rather than Napoleon III.[172] The 'premature' peace signed at Villafranca came as a great disappointment to them.[173] It 'has dissipated all their dreams and the democrats have returned to their old hostility, redoubled by anger and hatred'.[174] An anonymous letter circulating in Clermont (Puy-de-Dôme) pointed out the contradiction involved in sending French soldiers to be 'massacred' in Lombardy, 'in shouting for independence in other countries, whilst in France the people are enslaved'.[175]

The return of former political prisoners and exiles gradually strengthened local leadership but frequently at the cost of opening up new divisions. In the immediate aftermath of the *coup*, Colonel Espinasse, reporting directly to the Prince-President, had criticised the 'indulgence' of the prosecutors.[176] By the time of the general amnesty of 16 August 1859, most of those condemned in 1851/2 had benefited already from

[167] Darimon, *Les cinq*, p. 249, entry 27 April 1859.
[168] Quoted Tchernoff, *Parti républicain*, p. 273. [169] Quoted Constant, *Var*, p. 976.
[170] Maitron, *Dictionnaire biographique du mouvement ouvrier*, vol. I.
[171] PG Grenoble, 31 March 1854, AN BB30/378. [172] PG Paris, 8 June 1859, AN BB30/369.
[173] E.g. PGs Poitiers and Toulouse, 23 July 1859, AN BB30/369.
[174] PG Rouen, 20 July 1859, AN BB30/387. [175] PG Riom, 25 June 1859, AN BB30/369.
[176] Undated report in *Papiers et correspondance*, I, p. 174.

measures of clemency on such occasions as the proclamation of the Empire and the Emperor's marriage.[177] They had been required in return to sign a promise to renounce political activity, a document described by one signatory as a 'a contract with the devil' which committed neither party.[178] The state prosecutor at Lyon assumed that such sentiments were general. At the extreme, a building worker called Cochereau, imprisoned in Cayenne for his part in the June insurrection in 1848, looked forward to 'making more barricades'.[179] The privations experienced in prison or exile by political activists and the misery of the families they left behind ensured that few would feel any gratitude for their early release.[180] The procureur-général at Orleans was convinced that even if the returnees would not dare engage openly in politics, 'embittered by suffering', they would certainly contribute to the growth of opposition.[181] A political prison like Belle-Isle had served as 'a real school of socialism and demagogy', conferring on its inmates the status of republican martyrs.[182] On the issue of whether or not to accept an amnesty, the exiles were to remain bitterly divided. In an open letter published in response to the 'general' amnesty in 1859, a group led by Blanc asked: 'is it acceptable that the pardon should come from the person who committed the offence?' They rejected returning 'to live in slavery amongst slaves' and poured scorn on the ineffective republican deputies in the Corps législatif.[183] In contrast, Etienne Arago decided that it was his duty to return in order to mobilise opposition within France.[184]

The popular character of the republican movement which had increased in many localities because of the withdrawal of middle-class activists was to be challenged from around 1855/6 and particularly in the 1860s, as they regained confidence and sought to re-establish control.[185] This would take time. The failure of the Second Republic, the *coup*, and the denunciations and confessions that had followed, had left bad memories and widespread personal animosity.[186] At Angers, 'many of the democratic heroes of 1848 are treated as aristocrats and traitors by their party'. Local republican notables had either retired from

---

[177] E.g. Prudhomme, 'Les sociétés secrètes', p. 79.
[178] Letter included with PG Lyons, 6 May 1852, AN BB30/379.
[179] GOC 18e DM, 10–15 Sept. 1855, AHG G8/27.
[180] E.g. PG Nîmes, 8 June 1852, AN BB30/382; V. Wright, *'Coup d'état.'*
[181] 3 Oct. 1859, AN BB30/377.   [182] PG Angers, 6 July 1855, AN BB30/371.
[183] L. Blanc et al., *Lettres et protestations sur l'amnistie du 17 août 1859* (Lausanne 1859).
[184] M.Toulotte, *Etienne Arago* (Perpignan 1993), pp. 186–7.
[185] E.g. PG Bordeaux, 11 Jan. 1858, AN BB30/374; Huard, *La préhistoire des partis*, p. 665; Ménager, *Nord*, I, p. 409.
[186] E.g. PG Paris, 26 April 1852, AN BB30/383; PG Aix, 2 July 1859, AN BB30/370.

politics or been pushed out. Led by 'obscure' individuals the movement had 'become leveller and communist', supporting secret societies like La Marianne.[187] Similarly, from Aix it was reported that the republicans 'lack cohesion. The suspicion, which exists even between the most militant, prevents them from establishing a united group influenced by the same ideas.'[188] The risk of denunciation limited the ambitions of most republican sympathisers until well into the 1860s. The fear of prosecution and, for most workers, of blacklisting by employers, were powerful disincentives.[189] Furthermore, the improving economic situation, especially following the end of the period of inflated food prices in 1856, reduced popular discontent. Electoral activity offered additionally an important safety valve. Thus at the time of the Orsini affair many officials felt sufficiently secure to assure ministers that, because of the absence of secret societies, the security situation was very unlike that of 1851.[190] Nevertheless, the cadres of the republican 'party' were being reconstituted gradually as repression became less intense, as political prisoners were released, and exiles returned.[191]

[187] PG Angers, 8 Jan. 1854, AN BB30/371.   [188] Quoted Derobert-Ratel, *Arts et l'Amitié*, p. 12.
[189] 'Rapport de la section de Rouen', 3 Sept. 1867, to Lausanne congress of the International in Boivin, *Mouvement ouvrier*, II, p. 27.
[190] E.g. PG Montpellier, 5 July 1858, AN BB30/380.
[191] E.g. PG Paris, 20 Aug. 1858, AN BB30/383.

CHAPTER 12

The forms of opposition: (4) The republican revival

INTRODUCTION

Republicanism continued to be represented not by a party in the modern sense, but by individuals with shared values, determined to resist repression, and to establish alternative institutions. During the 1860s, in a changing political and social context, at dates which varied between places, it became easier and safer to organise and propagandise. At the same time, the regime suffered from a spreading sense of malaise linked to renewed economic difficulties, foreign policy failures which tarnished its image, the evident physical decline of the Emperor, and the unsatisfied desire for greater political freedom. A feeling that the regime might not survive provided inspiration. Who were these republicans? There are no simple sociological definitions. Perceptions of interests and their translation into political allegiance are complex matters. Class is far from being the only source of identity. Republicans could be found in all social groups. Nevertheless, artisans and urban workers were far more likely to support the republican cause than were peasants, inspired by the prosperity which appeared to confirm the promise of the Bonapartist legend. However, in certain circumstances, workers and peasants might share a hostility towards those they believed were exploiting them – bankers, merchants, employers, and both urban and rural landlords, and such old enemies as 'aristos' and priests. Moreover, anxious about competitive pressures and determined to preserve their hard-won property and social status, many small businessmen – shopkeepers and workshop owners – were sympathetic and often offered leadership at local level. Amongst the middle and professional *bourgeoisie* there was a frequent determination to grasp a share of political power. Inter-generational, confessional, and purely local rivalries were also significant. There were relatively few republicans amongst the wealthy. Yet, and although the better-off tended to express their opposition through Legitimism or liberalism, resentment of established and exclusive elites, family loyalties, and traditions, pushed some towards republicanism.[1] Socio-economic change not only brought greater prosperity but also the tensions which were part of a *crise d'adaptation*.

THE REPUBLICAN 'MOVEMENT'

Leadership of the republican movement, as the 1860s advanced, was provided again mainly by professional men – lawyers, doctors, journalists – and provincial businessmen, inspired no doubt by a variety of motives including both idealism and personal ambition.[2] The ability of these groups to contribute to the funding of newspapers, the leisure which allowed them to attend meetings, their relative freedom from police pressure, their self-confidence, and the social contacts which allowed them to dominate the selection of candidates and the transmission of information, allowed them effectively to exclude working-class and socialist competitors. A number of figures of national importance emerged. The small group of deputies, enjoying considerable status after securing election in spite of the obstacles, was to be of crucial importance in providing a sense of unity and direction. The Parisian press provided the other vital link, publicising the activities of deputies and defence lawyers. In 1863 the five republican deputies were able to present their amendments to the address from the throne as an alternative political programme.[3] They spread the message through speeches reprinted in the press as well as articles, and by means of provincial tours. That by the veteran republican Garnier-Pagès in 1863, during which he spoke at innumerable private dinners and meetings, together with the renewal of political journalism, contributed to the perception of belonging to a national 'party.'

Lawyers were especially well placed to practise eloquence and to use the courts to embarrass the regime and enhance their political careers.[4] Thus on 5 August 1864 the trial began of thirteen leading republicans, including the recently elected deputies Garnier-Pagès and Carnot, accused of belonging to an illegal organisation – in fact an electoral committee. A pleiad of illustrious republican lawyers including Favre, Grévy, and Picard as well as the Legitimist Berryer defended them. This was the ideal

[1] E.g. Huard, *La préhistoire*, pp. 120–1; J. Bouvier, 'Lyon la républicaine à la veille de la guerre de 1870', *1848* 1971, pp. 122–5.
[2] R. Magraw, *A History of the French Working Class* (Oxford 1992), I, pp. 194–5.
[3] Ollivier, *L'Empire libéral*, VI, p. 134.
[4] E.g. Nord, *The Republican Movement* (London 1995), pp. 129–30.

occasion on which to mount a protest against electoral manipulation and police harassment and to secure considerable press publicity. Appealing, even unsuccessfully, against the 500-franc fine imposed by the court provided another welcome opportunity.[5] In May 1867 it was the turn of another lawyer – Eugène Protot, less eminent and much further to the left politically. He appealed against a fifteen-month sentence for participation in a secret society and openly affirmed, in court, that his objective was 'through revolution, to destroy all the political, military, clerical, and capitalist tyrannies and create in the debris of these old iniquities eternal peace amongst nations, absolute freedom and the equal well-being of every citizen'. In spite of repeated warnings from the court president, he went on to condemn 'agricultural, industrial, commercial, and financial feudalism', the 'idle and corrupt demi-gods,' the 'prostituted newspapers', and the broken promises of a prince who had sworn to eliminate pauperism.[6] Such figures were treated as heroes and venerated as icons by the crowds who attended their trials or read about them in the press. The expanding railway network greatly facilitated their publicity campaigns. Ernest Picard, for example, was appointed to lead the defence of silk-ribbon weavers accused of threatening non-strikers at Saint-Etienne in November 1865. On his arrival at the railway station, he was met by a crowd of over 1,000 who doffed their caps silently as a mark of respect and escorted him to the residence of the moderate republican industrialist and deputy Frédéric Dorian. Following the trial (which ended with sentences of one to four months), Picard was escorted in triumph to his train by large and enthusiastic crowds.[7] He would subsequently be adopted as a republican candidate in Montpellier in 1869 following his vigorous defence of the editors of the local newspaper *La Liberté*.[8] Typically, in May 1870, Picard would arrange a visit to his constituency to coincide with a major agricultural fair in order to secure the largest possible audience. Over 1,200 people, including republican delegates from over thirty communes, similarly greeted Floquet, another well-known Parisian lawyer, at Béziers railway station on 1 May.[9] Politics was thus

5 Cour impériale de Paris, *Audiences des 24,25,30 novembre, 1,2, 6 décembre 1864. Procès des Treize. Prévention d'association non-autorisée*; Cour impériale de Paris, *Affaire du Comité électoral dite des Treize. Réquisitoire et réplique de M. le Procureur Général de Paris Donnad* (Paris 1864).

6 Cour impériale de Paris, *Chambre des Appels Correctionnels. Audience du 9 mai 1867*, AN AB XIX 3470.

7 Prefect Loire, 14, 17, 21 Nov. 1865, AN F12/4651.

8 R. Dorandeu, 'Eléments pour une étude des élites et des organisations politiques. L'Hérault à la fin du Second Empire' in *L'Hérault à la fin du Second Empire* (Paris 1989), p. 72.

9 GOC 11e DM, 6 May 1870, AHG G8/176.

personalised and dramatised and 'High' politics effectively linked to local issues.

In spite of their irreconcilable opposition to the regime, most of these well-known republican leaders were relatively moderate. This was true especially of the eminent survivors of 1848 like Carnot and Favre, who remained convinced of the power of 'truth' and the perfectibility of man by education, and who rejected class conflict. Even if they would sometimes appear to be more interested in social reform than the 'radicals' of 1869/70 their reformism was limited by their affection for private property. Their religiosity also contrasted markedly with the anticlericalism of younger men.[10] The effort to reformulate republican ideology in order to take account of the experience of the Second Republic brought other differences to the fore. During the 1857 electoral campaign, the question of the oath of allegiance had highlighted the division between the *anciens de 1848* and younger men like Ollivier, Darimon, and Hénon, who were convinced that the opposition should 'transform itself and not repeat itself', in order to be effective.[11] Subsequent by-elections had added Picard and Favre to their number, the latter a more flexible member of the older generation. Finally, in 1863/4 other *anciens* including Carnot, Marie, and Garnier-Pagès, would also take up their seats in the Corps législatif, although, because they lacked the fire of their colleagues, their prestige would soon decline.[12]

These republican notables were convinced that electoral politics combined with moderation would win over the middle classes and peasants gradually. This was certainly the contention of Jules Ferry in his pamphlet *La lutte électorale en 1863*. An economic liberal and elitist republican, he insisted that universal suffrage was 'sacred' and 'sovereign' and as such it would ensure 'honour to the multitudes, security to the disinherited, reconciliation of the classes, legality for all'.[13] However, he believed that the people were 'more accustomed to feel than to think reflectively, they are more like children than men' and thus needed an educated and civilised leadership.[14] This was a generation of republican politicians influenced by positivism, confident in the power of reason and science, in progress and in the ability of a modernising, secular education

---

[10] P. Vigier, 'Le parti républicain en 1870' in J. Viard (ed.), *L'esprit républicain* (Paris 1972), p. 17;
J.-Y. Mollier, 'Noël Parfait: une trajectoire républicaine an 19ᵉ siècle', in A. Faure, A. Plessis,
J.-C. Farcy, (eds.), *La terre et la cité* (Paris 1994), pp. 274–5.

[11] Tulard, *Dictionnaire*, p. 297.

[12] Pilbeam, *Republicanism in 19th Century France 1814–71* (London 1995), p. 250.

[13] Quoted P. Rosanvallon, *Le sacre du citoyen.Histoire du suffrage universal in France* (Paris 1992), p. 342.

[14] Quoted Huard, *Naissance du parti politique*, p. 127.

to promote reconciliation between the classes. Writing to his father in February 1867, the young republican theorist Allain-Targé maintained that 'by the diffusion of enlightenment, we will ensure the disappearance of inequality from social relationships. Everyone, taught in the same way, will engage in mutual respect and treat each other as equals.'[15] Education was central to this programme. The influential journalist Eugène Ténot insisted that the strength of the regime was 'the ignorance of the rural population'. He warned that 'most peasants do not know how to read; many have learned and forgotten; and amongst those who know how to read, how many never do! To this primordial ignorance, the mother of all the others, there is added the most profound and unbelievable political ignorance.'[16] This 'ignorance' had already brought down two republics. The aim must be to achieve 'genuine' liberty. Eugène Pelletan insisted that 'he was becoming a socialist' in demanding free and obligatory education. The exercise of popular sovereignty required political liberty and enlightenment. With political liberty, social justice was assured.[17]

Anxious to develop the loose coalition known as the Union libérale, Jules Favre was even warm in his praise of Thiers' contributions to the cause of liberty.[18] In January 1869 in Bordeaux, Jules Simon, who in 1868 had published five speeches defining *La Politique radicale*, adopted the liberal programme in calling for greater control over government policy, the avoidance of war, and reductions in expenditure.[19] Speaking before a middle-class audience in Paris in May, he denied that he was a socialist adding, however, that he recognised that 'great misery' existed and that 'I will always support those reforms which are possible and necessary to regenerate and revivify society' – above all liberty and education.[20] At a subsequent meeting he clearly felt the need to deny that he was an Orleanist, pointing out that some newspapers had actually called him a socialist, and further signalling his determination to be all things to all people with the words: 'I am called the man of the *bourgeoisie*. Yes, I am, and that of the workers as well; or rather, the man who believes that *bourgeoisie* and workers are the people, and I am the man of the people.'[21] His training as a philosopher was clearly evident! It was assumed that the threat of revolutionary violence would only frighten the population, reverse the process of political liberalisation, and reinforce

[15] Quoted P. Barral, *Les fondateurs de la 3e République* (Paris 1968), p. 49.
[16] *Le Suffrage universel et les paysans* (Paris 1865), p. 11.
[17] A. Vitu, *Les Réunions publiques à Paris*, p. 143.   [18] Letter to Thiers, 6 May 1864, BN naf 20610.
[19] PG Bordeaux, 15 Jan. 1869, AN BB30/389; J. Nordmann, *La France radicale* (Paris 1977), p. 30.
[20] Vitu, *Réunions publiques*, p. 129.   [21] *Ibid.*, p. 132.

the personal power of the Emperor.[22] The popularity of decentralisation amongst these moderate republicans can also be explained partly by this desire to counter the threat posed by Jacobin centralist ideals and revolutionary Paris.[23] At an electoral meeting in May 1869, Jules Ferry vigorously condemned 'the prefect, this pasha of Imperial France' and particularly that *préfet type: M. Haussmann*, the irregularity of whose *Comptes fantastiques* he had already so effectively condemned in a series of articles in *Le Temps* between December 1867 and May 1868.[24] Throughout the 1860s, and with increasing vigour, these republican deputies pressed for the political 'freedoms'. The concessions made by the regime and its apparently growing weakness seemed to confirm the wisdom of their legalistic opposition.

A broad liberal–democratic coalition appeared to be developing around 'core' values. Only a relatively small minority of socialists and revolutionaries were excluded entirely from this consensus. In their 1869 election campaigns in Marseille both Gambetta and Esquiros, self-proclaimed radicals, insisted on their loyalty to the Jacobin heritage, but followed the historian Edgar Quinet in rejecting the violence associated with Robespierre or else excused it in relation to the very special circumstances of 1793. Esquiros took care to distinguish democracy from anarchy and proclaimed the need for social order.[25] Following the withdrawal of Thiers, its favoured candidate, the liberal newspaper *Le Sémaphore*, conceded that if 'we have not chosen them ... if their programme is more accentuated than ours, it does not differ from our ideas and objectives on any essential points'.[26] For both Gambetta the 'radical' and the more moderate Ferry, democracy, liberty, and education would promote self-help and social equality. There was little understanding of the problems of the poor. Whilst they made vague concessions to the social aspirations of the masses they were convinced that there was no need for social intervention by the state. The message, of course, partly depended on the audience. Jules Favre speaking at Mâcon was, from a conservative perspective, 'too violent, but he pleased the workers.'[27] To a solidly *bourgeois* audience he would concede that inequality was

[22] E.g. F. Arnaud, *La Révolution de 1869* (Paris 1869), pp. ii–iv.
[23] Constant, *Var*, p. 1321; G. Marle, *Emile Combes* (Paris 1995), p. 89.
[24] Girard, 'Jules Ferry', p. 53.
[25] PG Aix, 6 July 1869, AN BB30/389; see also Jules Simon quoted Cholvy, *Religion et société*, II, p. 1025.
[26] A. Olivesi, *La Commune de 1871 à Marseille et ses origines* (Paris 1950), pp.101–2; Girard (ed.), *Les élections de 1869*.
[27] Prefect, 29 Jan. 1864, AN F1 CIII Saône-et-Loire 13.

inevitable.[28] In a rural area like the Loiret, L.-A.Cochery could promise peace, reduced taxes, and the 'necessary liberties' and re-assure peasants frightened by official attempts to associate republicans with the 'red' revolution – 'in our ranks, we count the richest landowners in the country. For us all revolution would be ruinous. Our land would lose value; our capital invested in enterprises would be swallowed up in the tempest. No! Never a revolution.'[29] In the Gard, the Comité d'initiative républicain de Vauvert insisted that 'we want progress without revolution, because revolution profits despotism more than liberty. We are the true conservatives.'[30] Considerable efforts were made to minimise the importance of potentially divisive class differences. According to the *Indépendent du Midi*, 'bourgeoisie' and 'proletariat' were not two classes but 'two different levels in the common march towards the same goal'.[31] Such embarrassing events as strikes were blamed on the regime. According to the *Progrès de Rouen*, the economic difficulties, which led to strikes, were the result of the high taxes necessary to sustain a parasitic bureaucracy, the absence of tariff protection, and the monopoly practices of the railway companies. The real enemies of both worker and employer were the regime and financial 'feudalism', the financiers and speculators closely associated with the government.[32]

The 'desertion' of Ollivier left the republicans without an obvious leading figure. In an unsigned report, dated 6 August 1868, and found amongst the papers of Conti, the Emperor's *chef de cabinet*, the author pours scorn on an opposition which, because of long years of relative inactivity, relied on candidates with 'old-fashioned and worn-out reputations' and which was attempting to 'galvanise corpses'.[33] The previous November, in a letter to his father, the young philosopher Allain-Targé had complained similarly of lack of leadership. In November 1868, however, he was able to announce that a new star had risen, and that 'Gambetta has become the leader of the great democratic party.'[34] Typically Gambetta, another lawyer, had achieved public eminence as a result of a political trial. This had involved Delescluze, editor of *Le Réveil*, who was prosecuted for opening a subscription for a statue in memory of the deputy Baudin, killed on the barricades in Paris in December 1851. The Orleanist court president allowed Gambetta sufficient latitude to turn

[28] Dalotel *et al.*, *Aux origines*, p. 65.

[29] *L'Indépendance de Montargis*, quoted Goueffon, 'Le parti républicain dans le Loiret à la fin du second empire' in Viard, *Esprit*, p. 291.

[30] Quoted Huard, *La préhistoire des partis*, p. 823.   [31] 25 Nov 1868, quoted *ibid.*, p. 826.

[32] Quoted Boivin, *Mouvement ouvrier*, I, p 334.   [33] *Papiers et correspondance*, I, p. 342.

[34] Allain-Targé, *La république*, pp. 102, 185–6.

the Baudin affair into the trial of the Emperor.[35] The regime was condemned because of its origins. Gambetta asserted that 'on 2 December, a group of previously unknown men gathered around a pretender, men without talent, honour, rank or position, the sort of men who, in every epoch, are the accomplices of brutal assaults ... A crowd of men lost in debt and crime. These are the sort of people with whose support, over the centuries, the institutions and laws have been put to the sword.' He pointed out that the regime did not even dare to celebrate its origins. The speech was reproduced widely in the press.[36]

The following year as an electoral candidate in the Paris lower middle- and working-class constituency of Belleville, selected by a Comité démocratique radicale because of his presumed radicalism, and in preference to Hippolyte Carnot, for so long the bearer of the republican flag, Gambetta invited the local electoral committees to send him their programmes so that he could respond – in a *Réponse au cahiers de mes électeurs* and the subsequent Belleville programme. In the former he called for free elections as the prelude to 'all the demolitions called for in your programme', that is, the replacement of the Empire with a republic, which would introduce a 'progressive series' of *réformes sociales*.[37] His speeches during the election campaign, in halls in the popular *quartiers* of Petite-Villette and La Chapelle, called for tax reductions, abolition of the *octroi* (the municipal tax on goods entering the city), suppression of the permanent army, and for the 'emancipation' of women through secular education, which was necessary because 'girls brought up in religious establishments are either silly things devoted to the childish practices of the Church or else prostitutes'.[38]

Whilst sharing the moderates' commitment to political democracy 'radicals' usually tended to go further in their demands for social reform. Unlike the socialists, however, they were unwilling to interfere with the fundamental rights of private property, limiting themselves to vague assaults on 'monopoly' and 'privilege' and to equally vague promises to improve the situation of the poor.[39] The revolutionary tone of speeches to working-class audiences barely concealed Gambetta's determination to create the broad social and political alliance necessary to gain power. He insisted that the real threat to social order came from government extravagance, militarism, and an adventurous foreign policy.[40]

---

[35] Ollivier, *L'Empire libéral*, vol. XI, p. 82.   [36] Rapports de police, 10 Nov. 1868, AN 61 AP 5.
[37] Vitu, *Réunions publiques*, pp. 340–1.   [38] *Ibid.* pp. 13–15.
[39] E.g. Wolfe, 'The origins of the Paris Commune', pp. 27–8.
[40] E.g. Huard, *La préhistoire des partis*, pp. 826–7.

According to Allain-Targé, Gambetta was the man who could unite the opposition, from the liberals on the right to the revolutionary republicans on the left.[41]

The liberalisation of 1868 allowed republicans, for the first time, in the 1869 elections, to mount a sustained ideological and electoral offensive against the regime and the notables who supported it. Often this was from a strong local base. In Saint-Etienne, whilst competing for influence with the previously dominant silk merchants, the ironmaster Frédéric Dorian made the most of his reputation as a 'good' employer. In May 1869 he would obtain 11,239 votes compared with 179 for the more radical Antide Martin.[42] In Lille, the older republicans – men like Alphonse Bianchi who had proved their convictions in, and after, 1848 – as well as members of the younger generation, were able to take advantage of their family name and reputation and to dominate candidate selection. They often enjoyed the status of local councillors and financed and controlled the local republican newspaper *Le Progrès du Nord* which, in spite of its circulation of only 1,000, was read widely in the city's bars.[43] Doctors and lawyers were also influential, in part due to their apparent willingness to 'do something' for the people. It was reported that the republican cadres in Paris were drawn from amongst 'doctors, industrialists, merchants', including especially 'many active and influential young men who aspire to take part in public affairs', and who were too young to have experienced and been frightened by revolution.[44] Official reports also frequently identified republican leaders as men embittered by professional failure. According to the state prosecutor at Rouen

there are very few men with a significant fortune, a good education and a position in the world who profess republican doctrine ... The exceptions, occupying a respectable place in the social hierarchy, are so rare that one can claim, without fear of contradiction, that the republican party is the refuge of the *déclassé*, of the ruined, of those who no longer enjoy position and consideration, who have fallen so low in public consideration that there no longer exists for them any hope but an upheaval.[45]

During the repressive years most middle-class republicans had largely confined their politics to the domestic sphere. Within whatever organisations survived, leadership had largely devolved on lower middle-class

---

[41] Letter to parents, 3 Aug. 1869, Allain-Targé, *La république*, p. 197.
[42] Aminzade, *Class Struggles*, p. 164; Gordon, *Merchants*, p. 152.
[43] Ménager, *Nord*, II, pp. 753–64.   [44] PG Paris, 5 May 1866, AN BB30/384.
[45] 13 April 1859, AN BB30/375.

and worker militants. However, as the focus of political activity shifted more decisively towards electoral activity, middle-class leaders felt less inhibited and better able to take advantage of the legal possibilities. They enjoyed the status that went with material prosperity, education, and profession, and were able to mobilise the resources necessary to publish newspapers and electoral propaganda. Middle-class politicians rapidly re-asserted themselves, offering the kind of 'democratic patronage' defined by Maurice Agulhon.[46] The gendarmerie commander in Paris welcomed the decline in secret-society activity. Now that 'the goal of militants is to influence public opinion, they have to act in the open'.[47] The comprehensive failure of those workers who offered themselves for election was evidence of the existence of a widely shared image of the properly qualified candidate. At an election meeting on 16 May 1869 in La Villette, one of the participants announced that he would have supported a proposed worker-candidate if only he 'had had the education necessary for the important functions he has set his sights on'.[48] In many of the public meetings in Paris in the winter of 1868/9, working-class speakers were ridiculed and shouted down because of their inferior rhetorical skills. As a certain Rouyer admitted ruefully, 'what we workers lack is the words to set out our ideas'.[49] Only gradually did men like the blacksmith Havrez gather sufficient confidence to assert that 'the workers must get accustomed to speaking ... The working class must be its own representative, so long as it chooses an element which cannot understand it, you will always be the dupes of a few ambitious men.'[50] The report of the engineering workers' delegates to the 1867 International Exposition was quite revealing. It demanded two concessions – free and obligatory education, and the right to hold meetings without restriction. Only with the enlightenment these would provide would it be possible for workers to fully exercise their political rights. The report condemned official pressure on voters, which ensured that most deputies were 'the representatives of authority rather than of the people'. Whilst accepting that 'the people has spilled enough blood in the defence of its rights', and had no desire to 'provide ... an occasion to show how wonderful was the *chassepot* rifle', nonetheless the delegates warned that they might feel obliged, unless concessions were made, to 'resort to extreme means' leading them to 'smash the following day the weapons they had manufactured the day before'.[51] In the absence of modern bureaucratic parties

---

[46] Palmade, 'Gers', p. 195.   [47] OC cie. de la Seine, 27 Dec. 1869, AHG G8/166.
[48] Vitu, *Réunions publiques*, pp. 17–18.   [49] Quoted Dalotel *et al.*, *Aux origines*, p. 127.
[50] Quoted Wolfe, *The Origins of the Paris Commune*, p. 54.   [51] AN F12/3116.

capable of offering paid employment to working-class militants, they remained absorbed by the need to make a living, painfully aware of their educational shortcomings, and largely resigned to playing a secondary, supporting role in politics. They also often enjoyed the enhanced status and sense of respectability which association with bourgeois politicians appears to have conveyed.

Similar attitudes informed the emergence of local leadership in cities like Toulouse – from amongst bourgeois professionals, intellectuals (mainly journalists), and wholesale merchants although, numerically speaking, most militants were small businessmen and artisans.[52] Again the absence of formal organisation reinforced the exclusive character of the links between local leaders and, on the one hand, the deputies who provided leadership at national level and, on the other – and through their control of the provincial press – the networks of correspondents who provided links between a regional centre and its hinterland.[53] At Vineuil, near Blois, in July 1867 the non-religious funeral of a Dr Cisset was attended by around fifty mourners representing the local republican elite and including 'doctors, merchants, M. Lesguillon the lawyer from Blois, Blazeau the editor of *la France centrale* etc.', who after listening to a panegyric by a local vine-cultivator, heard M. Ducoux, who had been Paris Prefect of Police in 1848, remind them that 'Cisset was one of those men always ready to march ... towards the triumph of the cause of humanity.'[54] In an impoverished rural area like the Morvan the republican movement around Château-Chinon was led by the lawyer Jacques Gudin, active during the Second Republic, interrogated but not arrested in December 1851, and an unsuccessful candidate for the departmental council in 1864. In the larger villages, leadership roles were assumed by men like the notary Charles Roy at Ouroux, and the wine merchants and local councillors Alexandre Enault and J.-B. Budeau at Planchez. In the smaller centres, the likes of Despiotte, proprietor of the village inn at Moux, or artisans like the shoemaker Prétat at Montsauche or the blacksmith Naudin at Goulaux, together with peasant farmers – especially those with their own land – assumed prominence.[55] In the more prosperous Beauce, a list of 38 republican notables prepared by justices of the peace in the arrondissement of Châteaudun included four landowners, four large farmers, twelve merchants, six artisans, and nine

[52] Aminzade, *Class Struggles*, p. 288.
[53] E.g. Huard, *La préhistoire des partis*, pp. 10–11; Ménager, *Nord*, II, p. 756.
[54] PG Orleans, 12 July 1867, AN BB30/382.   [55] Vigreux, *Paysans et notables*, p. 445.

members of the liberal professions. The competing republican candidates for election in 1869 were both lawyers.[56]

POLITICAL PROCESSES

The essential objective for republican political activists was to win mass electoral support. Tension built up around efforts to reconstitute the republican 'party' through the selection of candidates and the establishment of newspapers and electoral committees to lend them support. The new political context established by liberalisation inevitably led to the intensification and also the radicalisation of political activity. Regular meetings were held, at least in the major cities, from the autumn of 1868 and increased in frequency during the election campaign in May–June 1869 and the complementary elections in October. Large crowds turned out to listen to speeches by republican dignitaries.[57] According to the Interior Ministry's press division, the existing opposition press had become more critical of the regime, and forty-six new opposition newspapers had been created between January and mid-April 1869 and attracted many more readers than pro-regime papers.[58] In Marseille these included *L'Ami du Peuple* and *Le Peuple*; the latter, edited by the veteran Gustave Naquet, adopted the tone of Delescluze's Parisian newspaper *Le Réveil*. Their journalists were frequent speakers at public meetings, including those of the supposedly non-party but clearly republican education pressure group the Ligue de l'enseignement. The state prosecutor at Aix typically complained about 'the sudden and noisy re-appearance of the socialist party' in Marseille. In spite of their divisions, republicans managed to plaster the city's walls with around 6,000 posters supporting Gambetta.[59]

Newspapers remained expensive to establish. The *Progrès de Rouen* for example required 100,000 francs, provided by 101 shareholders, and a further 30,000 as caution money, supplied by three wealthy sympathisers.[60] The more radical and socialist groups found raising capital especially difficult, which obviously limited their ability to diffuse information and to organise. Many of the poorly funded newspapers, which emerged in 1868/9, existed on a hand-to-mouth basis. Some were

[56] Farcy, *Paysans beaucerons*, II, p. 943.
[57] E.g. PG Montpellier, 10 July 1869; PG Nîmes, 18 July 1869, AN BB30/389.
[58] *Papiers et correspondance*, I, pp.20–2.
[59] PG Aix, 4 Oct. 1868, AN BB30/389; Olivesi, *Marseille*, pp. 95–9.
[60] Boivin, *Mouvement ouvrier*, I, p. 286.

forced to follow the moderate opinions of potential subscribers, in order to survive.[61] Others engaged in deliberate efforts to increase circulation by arousing scandal. According to one commentator, the success of such periodicals as *Le Corsaire*, *La Lune*, and *Le Diogène* was due to 'artifices of language' which barely concealed an assault 'against all the acts of the government, against our institutions, against the imperial dynasty; a war of calumny, epigrams, jokes and odious and amusing insinuations'.[62] Constant 'ridicule' and *bouffonneries perfides*[63] contributed to the weakening of public confidence.[64] In October 1868, efforts by Delescluze to co-ordinate the activities of the republican press foundered on the political differences of its editors.[65] Nevertheless, newspaper offices offered some degree of co-ordination to the republican movement as well as providing meeting places for election committees and points of contact for the networks of local correspondents who served as their agents.

Liberalisation, improved communications, the falling cost of newspaper publication, and higher levels of literacy, ensured a more substantial circulation of pamphlets and newspapers than in 1849/51.[66] At around 15 centimes a copy, they were still relatively expensive to purchase, and too difficult to read for those with limited reading skills. Contributors to Rochefort's *Marseillaise*, Delescluze's *Réveil*, and the Hugo family's *Rappel* were reminded of the need to produce copy that was easy and interesting to read.[67] Cafés and voluntary associations with republican links – such as the Marseille Association phocéenne pour la ligue de l'enseignement, directed by anticlerical freemasons like Gaston Crémieux, which saw its membership rise from 700 to 2,000 in the early months of 1869 – together with the city's eleven masonic lodges, took out collective subscriptions.[68] Often newspapers were read aloud. During the election campaign the *chambrées* and cafés at Cuers (Var) were all reported to have received free copies of the 27 April issue of *La Sentinelle*, which contained the democratic manifesto.[69] At the very least the press offered ideas to 'opinion leaders'. In the silk workshops of Lyon, the most popular newspapers in October 1869 were reported to be *Le Réveil*, together with the local *Progrès*, which sold around 5,000 copies.[70] The expected establishment

---

[61] Copin, 'La presse dans l'Yonne', p. 148.   [62] PG Rouen, 12 Jan. 1868, AN BB30/387.

[63] *Ibid.*, 11 Jan. 1869, AN BB30/389.   [64] PG Besançon, 12 Oct. 1868, AN BB30/389.

[65] Huard, *Naissance du parti politique*, pp. 136–7.

[66] PG Besançon, 12 April 1870, AN BB30/390.

[67] E.g. PG Agen, 8 Jan. 1870 and PG Metz, 11 Jan. 1870, AN BB30/390.

[68] PG Aix, 24 Jan. 1870, AN BB30/390.   [69] Constant, *Var*, p. 1375.

[70] PG Lyon, 14 Oct. 1869, AN BB30/389; 'Rapport sur les journaux de Lyon, par le Commissaire spécial de police politique 7 March 1869' in *Pièces saisies*, pp. 4–5.

of new newspapers failed to occur in Amiens, but only due to the easy transport of papers from Paris.[71] In rural Gers, *L'Avenir*, edited in Auch by the future communard Lissagaray, was violent in tone and supported something close to the Belleville programme. It reached many communities which had not seen a newspaper since 1851.[72] Not all areas were well provided for. In the Semur and Châtillon areas of Côte-d'Or, efforts were made to pass free copies of newspapers and pamphlets from hand to hand.[73] The state prosecutor at Angers reported that it was precisely the lack of newspapers, 'to provide an impulsion', that had prevented the development of the republican 'party' in Le Mans and Saumur.[74] In many areas the administration could continue to draw some comfort from the apparent lack of interest among the rural population, although it was assumed widely that this would not be the case for much longer.[75]

In addition to snippets of news, advertisements, and political manifestos, and possibly a serialised novel, the content of most newspapers was limited. The republican press gladly took up the findings of Ténot's remarkable studies of the *coup d'état*.[76] These sought to disprove the official description of resistance to the *coup* as some sort of brutal peasant *jacquerie* and brought to the public attention the martyrdom of the republican deputy Baudin.[77] According to the procureur-général at Nancy, even though readers soon tired of the newspapers, Ténot's works, 'widely diffused and sold at low price, are to be found in all the bookshops, and sell quickly'.[78] The trial of Delescluze following the organisation of a public subscription to pay for a statue of Baudin was famously used by Gambetta, his defence lawyer, to put the regime itself on trial. The Emperor's closest collaborators were vilified in a speech re-published in virtually every newspaper.[79] Taking up his themes at a public meeting at the Salle Molière in Paris in November 1869 Jules Allix openly referred to the *crime du 2 décembre* and to a regime baptised in the blood of its people.[80] Emile Zola, in a review of Noël Blache's *Histoire de l'insurrection du Var en décembre* in *La Tribune* (29 August 1869), claimed that it proved that Louis-Napoleon Bonaparte had 'raped France'.[81] Jules Ferry's articles in *Le Temps*,

---

[71] PG Amiens, 9 Oct. 1868, AN BB30/389.
[72] PG Agen, 7 Oct. 1868, AN BB30/389; 10 Nov. 1868, AN BB18/1771; Prefect, 1 Sept. 1868, AN F1 CIII, Gers 8; Palmade, 'Gers' in Girard, *Les élections*, pp. 203–5.
[73] P. Lévêque, 'La 3e circonscription de la Côte-d'Or' in Girard, *Les élections*, p. 171.
[74] 8 April 1870, AN BB30/390.   [75] E.g. PG Rennes, 15 Oct. 1869, AN BB30/389.
[76] Girard, *Questions politiques*, p. 101; Campbell, *Second Empire Revisited*, p. 45.
[77] Mollier, 'Noël Parfait,' p. 315.   [78] 15 Jan. 1869, AN BB30/389.
[79] Ollivier, *L'Empire libéral*, vol. XI, pp. 82–98.   [80] Dalotel *et al.*, *Aux origines*, pp. 183–4.
[81] Tulard, *Dictionnaire*, p. 1342.

published in pamphlet form as *Les Comptes fantastiques d'Haussmann* and probably more discussed than read, furthermore warned about the creation of a 'financial feudalism', an *ancien régime économique*, and further discredited the regime by associating some of its proudest achievements with the greedy activities of speculators.[82] In *L'Empire industriel*, subtitled 'a critical history of the financial and industrial concessions of the Second Empire', Georges Duchêne claimed that 'the political economy of 2 December' had resulted in 'the monopolising by a coalition of banks of all the major engines of national production.' He listed 183 individuals who controlled the banks, credit institutions, railway and shipping companies, and most other large-scale enterprises. The result was the 'absorption of small-scale industry by large; suppression of the middle class, which will sink into the ranks of the prole: at the top, a few hundred criminals wasting hundreds of millions, at the bottom an entire nation exhausted by fatigue and misery, manoeuvring according to the wishes of its chiefs with the precision of a disciplined army'.[83] These were the 'facts' which fed 'the incessant attacks against the *Personal Government*'.[84]

Satire also had an impact. Rochefort's weekly *La Lanterne* achieved a circulation of 120,000, including 500 copies received by rail in a provincial town like Toulon, before being closed down.[85] Something of its tone can be gauged from its first number, in which the editor proclaimed his loyalty to Napoleon II, son of the first emperor who had died without reigning, adding that

he represents for me the ideal sovereign. No one can deny that he has occupied the throne, since his successor calls himself Napoleon III. What a reign, my friend, what a reign! Not a tax, not one useless war ... None of these distant military expeditions on which 600 millions are spent in order to re-claim 15 francs, no voracious civil lists, no ministers each performing five or six roles at 100,000 francs a part; this is the sort of monarchy I understand. Oh! yes! Napoleon II, I love you and I admire you without hesitation.[86]

The Empress was a favourite victim, with, for example, Rochefort claiming that the cholera patients she had so famously visited were people in robust health paid for playing sick. Eugénie also came to symbolise the extravagant frivolity of court life.[87]

[82] Pp. 50, 289.   [83] Paris: Librairie centrale, 1869, pp. 50–2, 232.
[84] PG Montpellier, 10 July 1869, AN BB30/389.
[85] R. Bellet, *Presse et journalisme sous le Second Empire* (Paris 1967), pp. 77–80; PG Aix, 4 Oct. 1868, AN BB30/389.
[86] Quoted P. Labracherie, *Napoléon III et son temps* (Paris 1967), p. 235.
[87] Bidegain, 'L'origine d'une réputation', pp. 61–3.

The historian's ability to penetrate the political process remains limited, however. The concerns of the procureur-général at Paris are worth noting. In relation to support for the opposition from workers and peasants, he asked:

Do they vote for opposition candidates out of a taste for parliamentary doctrine? And the candidate himself, to what sentiments does he appeal? I perfectly comprehend that he needs a banner, and that he must make a display of liberalism in his manifesto. But what do his agents say, those who are in direct contact with the voters and on whose skill the outcome of the vote often depends? They in particular exploit local passions, the divisions existing within ... communes, conflicts of interest, personal rivalry, and the desire for I know not what vague and indefinite gains which they, in the eyes of the extremely ignorant, appear to be offering.[88]

As always when political tension increased, the songs and shouts of the clients of cafés and bars took on a political tinge and police interest grew also. A typical gendarmerie report from the 19th military division (Cher, Allier, Indre) covering 6 to 10 April 1868 described the exploits of a drunken blacksmith at Clamecy, sitting on the roof of his cottage and singing the *Marseillaise* interspersed with shouts of *Vive la République*; at Saint-Pierre-le-Moutier, a cabinetmaker was arrested for singing the same republican hymn and shouting *Aux armes*; at Arquian near Saint-Amand there were five arrests at midnight on the 5th; and at Blancafort three *placards* were found bearing the words '*Vive la République* and bread at 10 centimes.'[89] Was it family or community tradition, the influence of the press or drink, which led the foundry worker Gaudin to assert as he left a bar in Agen that 'the Emperor is a dog and a thief, he is starving the people; the Republic will come soon and if I'm not killed by the first shot, I'll do my bit'.[90] More serious threats were posed following performances in the theatre at Grenoble on 26 and 30 March 1868, when a crowd largely composed of students gathered in the place Saint-André. Songs were followed by violence as the windows of the deputy-mayor's house, the bishop's palace, and the Jesuit convent were smashed.[91] At Nîmes in the night of 25–26 April, fifty drunken conscripts were joined by a couple of hundred other individuals and paraded in front of the barracks and prefecture shouting *Vive la République* and *A bas Napoléon*.[92] In midMay an attempt by the police, supported by troops, to end a 'disorder'

---

[88] 5 May 1866, AN BB30/384.   [89] GOC 19e DM, AHG G8/151.
[90] PG Agen, 12 May 1866, AN BB18/1728.
[91] GOC 22e DM, 1–5 April 1868, AHG G8/151.
[92] GOC 10e DM, 26 April and 1 May 1868, *ibid.*

at a brothel in Cette (Hérault) predictably led to a brawl and shouts of *Vive la République* together with 'Down with the Pope's soldiers' – the 87th infantry having previously served as part of the Rome garrison.[93] Carnival brought its own problems. At Bleneau (Yonne) on 6 March 1870 the traditional mannequin was stuffed with meat instead of straw and guillotined instead of burnt, with the intention, it was assumed, of frightening *les gens d'ordre*.[94] The anniversary of the foundation of the Second Republic on 24 February was celebrated noisily across France.[95]

There were signs that support for the republic was growing in the countryside. The 1866 agricultural enquiry represented an attempt to come to terms with this. It could be presented as the action of a government which cared.[96] Indeed, Republicans were impressed by the continued strength of rural support for the regime. In 1848 they had struggled to secure 'universal' suffrage and had felt betrayed by the election of Louis-Napoleon in December. Jules Ferry in his pamphlet on *Les élections de 1863* was only one of the many commentators who blamed peasant stupidity and ignorance for republican electoral failure. According to T. Marcou, a republican notable in the Aude, the obstacles were ignorance and the church – 'the population cannot read and when it has learnt the alphabet, it makes little progress ... It does not think, that is the fate of the Catholic people.'[97] Eugène Ténot also attempted to provide an explanation in terms of 'political ignorance' but his conclusions were more optimistic. The *coup d'état* had interrupted the efforts of the démocrates-socialistes to provide the rural population with political instruction. Nevertheless, every village still sheltered some democrats and Ténot called on urban republicans to make a renewed effort to re-establish contact and enlighten the peasant.[98] It would remain difficult for republicans to accept that peasant support for the regime might be due not to ignorance or intimidation but to the rational judgement that a regime which appeared to be responsible for prosperity deserved support. However, increasingly an effort was made to counter this positive image. Thus republicans criticised high taxes, and especially the indirect taxes on the consumption of wine and other produce – the *droits réunis* as well as the municipal *octroi*. They claimed that the revenue from these was wasted on extravagant courtiers, overpaid bureaucrats, the

---

[93] GOC 10e DM, 16–20 May 1868, *ibid*.
[94] Maréchal de logis commanding gendarmerie at Bleneau, 7 March 1870, AN F1 CIII Yonne 11.
[95] E.g. GOC 10e DM, 6 March 1869, AHG G8/ 165.
[96] E.g. PG Aix, 26 June 1869, AN BB18/1785.   [97] Quoted Thibon, *Pays de Sault*, p. 137.
[98] E. Ténot, *Le suffrage universel et les paysans* (Paris 1865), pp. 22–5.

embellishment of Paris, and pointless military expeditions. In a typical little pamphlet, *What They are Saying in the Village*, E. Gellion-Danglar[99] adopted the traditional form of an invented dialogue, in this case between the 69-year-old farmer Jean-Claude and a local ironmaster. The wise old peasant points out that expenditure on the army 'included a little to fight the Prussians, and a lot ... to contain the French'. Freeing women, and by implication their children, from domination by the clergy was his other main concern. Léon Montigny in his *Letters to a Rural Voter*[100] also concentrated on taxation, whilst warning voters not to take official warnings about the 'red' menace too seriously and calling on them to cease to be 'voting machines controlled by the administration ... puppets whose strings are pulled by the prefect and the mayor.' The comparative absence of the promise of cheap credit, which had been central to the démocrate-socialiste message, was a sign that the mainstream left was less radical than in 1849/51. In the Morvan, Pierre Joigneaux, whose newspaper the *Feuille du village* had made just this promise for a peasant audience during the Second Republic, now asserted that 'taxes place a heavy burden on the landowner. The little piece of land belonging to the small farmer is taxed, whilst the millionaire's wallet escapes from the tax collector's forms.'[101]

Clearly, there are no simple explanations of peasant political behaviour. Rural republicanism was a feature primarily of the small towns and market villages in which, usually, leadership was provided by professional men or resident landowners supported by artisans and merchants and the better-off and more independent peasants, and also of those areas in close and constant communication with these marketing centres.[102] This rural bourgeoisie played a crucial role in political life, with individuals choosing a 'party' to support in line with their personal principles or as a result of local faction rivalry. The results of the 1869 elections suggest that rural republicanism had retreated since the heady days of 1849/51, giving way to popular Bonapartism in areas like the Saône-et-Loire and most of the Limousin, as well as in Gers and Basses-Alpes. This was due to a mixture of motives, including hostility towards the urban bourgeoisie, by whom farmers frequently felt exploited; towards the nobles and the clergy who appeared to be enemies of the regime; as well as to Parisian agitators and 'good-for-nothing' politicians who threatened the order

---

[99] *Ce qu'on dit au village* (Paris: Degorei-Cadot 1869).
[100] *Lettres à un électeur rural* (Paris: Le Chevalier 1869).
[101] Quoted Vigreux, *Paysans et notables*, p. 434.
[102] E.g. Dupeux, *Aspects*, pp. 401–2; Farcy, *Paysans beaucerons*, II, p. 943.

and prosperity they owed to their emancipator, *l'Empereur des paysans.*[103] Nevertheless, rural republicanism remained significant especially in the east – in the east of Côte-d'Or, southern Doubs, northern Jura, north-eastern Haute-Vienne, in north-west Creuse – where migrant workers provided contact with Paris, along the Rhône-Saône corridor and on the coastal plains of Languedoc and Provence, in the Garonne valley, and to a lesser extent in northern France – in upper Normandy and the Paris basin.[104] These were mainly areas which had been politicised during the Second Republic, in which repression had often engendered a desire for revenge, in which concentrated habitat and an active so-ciability increased the population's ability to resist official pressure, and in which the clergy's influence had collapsed or was being contested.[105] The list includes areas with high and others with relatively low levels of literacy. It includes areas which were 'advanced' in economic terms, and in which migration was reducing population pressure on resources and with it dependence on traditional elites whilst, at the same time, growing prosperity increased peasant self-confidence. It also included areas, which were 'backward'. For example, in the Nièvre it was the peasants of central Morvan, living in hamlets isolated in the forests, who were won over to the republic, possibly because of the difficulties of administrative control and as the result of a long and often ferocious struggle over ownership of land, rents, and rights of usage in the forests with rich, absentee landlords like the La Rochejacquelein family.[106] The wood trade also provided regular links with Paris and with the river port at Clamecy with its notorious revolutionary tradition.[107] In broad terms, however, and in contradiction with the habitual republican assumption that the Bonapartist peasant was illiterate and ignorant it seems evident that support for the regime was more solid in the 'advanced' north, and that rural republicanism was making more progress in the less advanced areas south of the line Saint-Malo to Geneva.[108] In terms of its ability to attract support, much clearly depended on the character and energy of the republican campaign and on the links made between political principles and particular issues, as well as the effectiveness of the official riposte. Certainly, the rural population had reacted very badly to the

---

[103] E.g. Corbin, *Archaïsme*, II, p. 904; Vigier, 'Le parti républicain en 1870', pp. 20–1.
[104] Girard, *Les élections*, p. xv.
[105] E.g. PG Montpellier, 22 Jan. 1870, AN BB30/390; Cholvy, *Religion et société*, II, pp. 1035–6.
[106] Vigreux, 'Des paysans républicains', pp. 456–9.   [107] Pinard, *Morvan*, p. 222.
[108] See also F. Salmon, 'La *gauche avancée* en 1849 et en 1870: le pourquoi de la chute' in Hamon, *Les républicains*, p. 96.

government's proposed military reforms and the subsequent organisation of the Garde Mobile in what was seen by many as a prelude to war. Fairly typically, the state prosecutor at Orleans warned that 'the peasants are frightened at the thought that their sons might be taken away, that their taxes will increase, and that the labour which is already lacking in agriculture, will become even rarer'.[109] These concerns appear to have attracted much more interest in the countryside than the debate over political liberalisation. At the same time, following the poor harvest of 1867, high food prices were causing difficulties for those with insufficient land to profit. In vine-cultivating areas, discontent would be caused by the abundant crop of 1869 and the ensuing collapse of prices.[110] Political dissent might also be the result of local rivalry – *querelles de clocher* – or be caused by the 'excessive' zeal of local mayors or commissaires de police in such matters as the prevention of poaching.[111]

Mass support for republicanism, and the main effort of republican leaders remained concentrated in the urban centres. The mayor of Pau represented the views of most officials by the late 1860s in complaining that 'the towns are against us; that is to say the majority of workers in the towns'.[112] Considerable efforts were being made by republicans to appeal to 'the demagogic spirit ... always in a latent state in part of the working class'.[113] If, at local level, most of the active militants were artisans or tradesmen, many of them concerned by the growing threat from technological change and intensified competition,[114] there can be little doubt that republican ideas were commonplace within the working-class community – in songs and slogans and daily discourse – and spread through workplace and neighbourhood contacts.[115] Not untypically, in each of the nail manufactories at Laigle (Orne), influenced – it was assumed – by their foremen who had been brought from Paris, workers subscribed to *Le Siècle*, which was read aloud as they worked.[116] Insecurity, and the constant rise in food prices and rents contributed to their sense of grievance, and to the sort of irritation exemplified by a certain Perrin, a shoemaker at Neufchâteau (Vosges), who told his drinking associates how, when in

---

[109] 23 June 1866, AN BB30/382.
[110] PG Bourges 9, 16 April 1868, AN BB18/1766; Armengaud, *Est-Aquitain*, p. 420.
[111] E.g. PG Aix, 29 Jan. 1870, AN BB30/390.
[112] Letter to Rouher, 3 June 1869, AN 45 AP 3.   [113] PG Metz, 12 Jan. 1865, AN BB30/380.
[114] E.g. Prefect of Police to Rouher re 'coalitions', 26 June 1865, AN 45 AP 6.
[115] E.g. PG Nîmes, 9 April 1868, AN BB30/382; J. Lorcin, 'Le souvenir de la Révolution française dans la chanson ouvrière stéphanoise' in Société d'histoire de la Révolution de 1848, *Le 19ᵉ siécle et la Révolution française* (Paris 1992), p. 192.
[116] PG Caen, 13 April 1859, AN BB30/375.

Paris, he had seen 'the Emperor pass, asleep in his carriage like a fat, sly pig'.[117] The republican press contrasted the workers' misery with the fortunes made by speculators identified with the regime. The ending of municipal responsibility for establishing bread prices was portrayed similarly as a concession to those who wished to exploit the poor.[118] The greater press freedom, public meetings, electoral campaigns, and the publicity given to strikes in the late 1860s, and to their repression, heightened workers' interest in politics.[119] Waves of strikes in 1869/70, had affected most professions and all the major industrial centres. These provided republicans with the opportunity to condemn a regime whose soldiers shot thirteen striking miners at La Ricamarie (Loire) in June 1869 and a further fourteen at Aubin (Aveyron) in October. Dorian, the Saint-Etienne ironmaster and mine owner, organised a fund to provide support for the families of the victims.[120] If militant workers were hostile to exploitation by the 'rich', it seems clear that much of their resentment would remain focused on the imperial regime which, through its police and troops, appeared to govern in the interests of those who exploited them.[121] In these circumstances the hopes of many republicans were raised by the feeling that the regime was disintegrating, and that its liberalisation was nothing more than a symptom of weakness and represented a 'transition' towards 'a more radical transformation'.[122] They were convinced that only fratricidal divisions amongst republicans could save the Empire.[123]

REPUBLICANS DIVIDED

In spite of obvious progress, divisions between republicans were to substantially weaken opposition to the regime. The precise identification of these is not easy. There was considerable overlap between the various political groups. A certain ideological uniformity was imposed by the need they all shared to appeal for mass support. If tensions frequently existed, republicans in general drew on the 'republican memory,' on the symbolism of 1848 and 1851 as well as on that of 1789 and 1793, in order to legitimise their activity and reinforce group identity.[124] Fundamental

[117] PG Nancy, 24 April 1866, AN BB18/1728.
[118] Paris Prefect of Police, 22 Sept. 1867, *Papiers et correspondance*, I, pp. 267–8; Price, *Modernisation*, pp. 202–3.
[119] E.g. PG Riom, 10 Oct. 1867, AN BB30/386.   [120] Gordon, *Merchants*, p. 109.
[121] Point made by PG Limoges, 13 April 1867, AN BB30/378.
[122] PG Montpellier, 22 Jan. 1870, AN BB30/390.   [123] Ménager, *Nord*, II, pp. 779–80, 789.
[124] E.g sous-préfet Gex, 25 Nov. 1868, re meeting of refugees at Geneva, AN F1 cIII Ain 9.

differences were, however, apparent over the meaning of democracy and the nature of political representation. Such questions as whether deputies, as elected representatives, were to be granted discretion and held to account only at elections, or should be mandated to carry out the wishes of their constituents, were debated endlessly.[125] Differences were often apparent between generations. The *vieilles barbes de'48* were criticised by young radicals for the failure of the Second Republic and their determination to hang on to leadership roles. There were also extremely complex differences over ideology, organisation, and tactics. Any form of categorisation does less than justice to this confusion. A simple distinction might be made, as it was by the state prosecutor at Lyon in 1862, between the proponents of 'a bloody revolution' and those who followed the five republican deputies elected in 1857 and favoured 'a peaceful revolution'.[126] A more developed categorisation might identify an extreme left of revolutionary socialists, associated with the likes of Blanqui or Varlin – themselves divided on whether the objective should be communism or the egalitarian republic of small producers, and the means a violent putsch or reformist mutualism. They were distinguished from 'radicals', who were more moderate in terms both of ends and means, and whose position would come to be defined by Gambetta in his Belleville programme in 1869; and especially from moderates like Grévy, Favre, or Ferry, for whom the advent of universal suffrage had made revolution unnecessary, and who rejected violence in favour of class reconciliation.

A pamphlet on *The Electoral Struggle*, written by Jules Ferry for the 1863 elections, made the case for moderation: 'Universal suffrage is not only a sacred institution, it is the basis of all politics ... It is not only a reality, the source of Right and Justice, it is also inevitable. It is the present, it is the future ... It is in it alone that it is henceforward necessary to live, hope and believe.'[127] Moderate republicans were economic liberals, individualists anxious to condemn the Terror and to re-assure established elites through their insistence on legal forms of opposition. They were convinced that only the corruption of the electorate had prevented the establishment of the Republic, which, in the last resort, as a principle, remained above universal suffrage itself. Moderates belonged either to the 'closed left' and rejected any kind of dialogue with the regime or to an 'open left' willing, like Ollivier and Darimon, to work within the

---

[125] E.g. Aminzade, *Ballots*, pp. 15–28.   [126] 1 April 1862, AN BB30/379.
[127] Quoted Rosanvallon, *Le sacre du citoyen. Histoire du suffrage universel in France* (Paris 1992), p. 342.

constitutional structures of a liberal Empire.[128] 'Radicals' like Gambetta and Allain-Targé, horrified by Ollivier's 'treason', and blaming their elders for the failure of the Second Republic, similarly claimed for themselves allegiance to an incorruptible revolutionary tradition. The occasionally violent language of these self-proclaimed heirs of Robespierre and the Jacobin tradition should not obscure the commitment of most of them to legalism.[129] Nevertheless, they were virulently anticlerical, condemning the obscurantism of the clergy as well as the church's support for the regime. The separation of state and church and secularisation of education were central features of their various programmes. At an election meeting on 12 May 1869, the journalist Jules Vallès went further and, to great applause, maintained that 'for as long as there is a priest, a customs officer, a tax inspector, a policeman believed on oath, an irresponsible bureaucrat, a tenured magistrate; for as long as they have to be fed and paid the people will be miserable'.[130] Moderate republicans expressed concern about Gambetta's populism and anticlericalism as well as his 'fathomless ignorance'.[131] Some, like Ferry and Simon, as well as socialists influenced by Proudhon, broke with the Jacobin tradition in favouring decentralisation of government and celebrating the commune as a school for civic virtue and barrier to despotism.[132] In contrast, 'Radicals' distinguished themselves by their insistence on the need for a strong centralised state which, in the Jacobin tradition, should serve as the representative of the collective interest and popular sovereignty and which would initiate largely unspecified measures of social reform. According to Gambetta, 'once the state is organised democratically it has the duty of ensuring to the citizen the exercise of his rights and faculties ... There is no need to over-react against the administrative despotism of the old monarchies and the two Bonapartist regimes and to go as far as suppressing the idea of the state, of a social government, Initiator and Protector.'[133]

The path taken by Emile Ollivier was to serve as a warning to all 'true' republicans. Elected in Paris as one of five republican deputies, and a determined and effective critic of the regime, he appears to have started to

[128] Rials, *Révolution*, pp. 284–5.
[129] E.g. Hazareesingh, 'Defining the Republican good life: Second Empire municipalism and the emergence of the 3rd Republic,' *French History*, 1997, pp. 321–3.
[130] Vitu, *Réunions publiques*, p. 130.
[131] Quoted P. Bertocci, *Jules Simon. Republican anticlericalism and cultural polities in France, 1848–86* (London 1978), p. 149.
[132] E.g. Girard, 'Jules Ferry', p. 52.
[133] Letter to A. Lavertujon, 30 Aug. 1869 quoted Barral, *Les fondateurs*, p. 313.

have second thoughts just prior to the liberalising decree of 24 November 1860. The Italian war, the political amnesty, and the prospect of liberalisation, privately held out to him by Morny, combined to encourage a gradual rallying to the regime.[134] Carnot accused Ollivier of contemplating treason as early as March 1861 after a speech in the Corps législatif in which he had promised support to the Emperor if the monarch committed himself to political reform. Relations within the small group of republican deputies increasingly grew tense.[135] There were clear hints about Ollivier's future course of action in the 1863 election manifesto, in support of his candidacy at Toulon, Le Havre, and Paris. He claimed that his objective was to obtain *'Liberty by legal and constitutional means*, in the Emperor's own words, the crowning of the edifice'. He affirmed that since 1848 he had constantly desired 'liberty without disorder; but order without despotism.' As a deputy, since 1857, he had avoided both 'systematic approval and systematic opposition; I have pursued independence and justice, in order to conquer liberty.'[136] On 28 April 1864 he insisted that 'I never say: All or nothing ... I am grateful for what I am given.'[137] Ollivier was undoubtedly tired of the republican movement's sectarianism and ineffectiveness, as well as being personally ambitious.[138] Until early 1864, nevertheless, he saw himself still as a member of the republican opposition.[139] The final crisis in relationships occurred when Ollivier accepted the role of parliamentary *rapporteur* for the proposed legislation legalising strikes. He welcomed a 'socialist' measure likely to lead to the improvement of workers' conditions. For the likes of Jules Favre, in contrast, the legislation was unacceptable because it had been introduced by the Imperial regime.[140] Writing in his journal on 30 March, Darimon saw Ollivier's nomination for this role as having 'made the government tip towards the left', adding, rather naively perhaps, that it represented also 'good fortune for the opposition which thus is able to become a legal and constitutional party'. By the beginning of May, when finally the law was voted, Ollivier was being accused by his erstwhile colleagues of preferring expediency to principle. Darimon conceded that the left was 'irreparably' divided.[141]

---

[134] *Journal*, II, p. 204, entry 17 June 1860; see also Ollivier *L'Empire libéral*, VII, pp. 269–70, 315.
[135] E.g. Darimon, *L'opposition libérale*, pp. 296–7, entry of 29 Jan. 1863.
[136] Quoted Constant, *Var*, p. 1069.
[137] Quoted E. Constant, 'Quelques observations sur l'audience et l'évolution politique d'Emile Ollivier au début de l'Empire libéral (1864–65)', *Actes du 90e CNSS Nice 1965* (Paris 1966), p. 313.
[138] Girard, 'L'Empire libéral', p. 32; Vigier, 'Le parti républicain en 1869–70', p. 111.
[139] *Journal*, II, p. 64.   [140] Agulhon, 'L'Empire libéral' in Hamon, *Les républicains*, pp. 197–9.
[141] Entries of 25 April, 2 May in Darimon, *Le tiers parti*, pp. 142, 152.

Ollivier attempted to define his position in a widely publicised circular for the departmental council elections in the Var in June 1864, declaring that 'to strengthen itself, democracy must expand and not close in on itself, transform itself and not repeat itself ... It must prefer ideas to phrases, a realistic limited improvement to the vague hope of total reform, pursue liberty and not upheaval, progress and not revolution.'[142] The local republican 'party' split in response.[143] In a speech in the same month he insisted that 'to accept the institutions of his country, even whilst wishing they were better, then to use every legal means of improving, modifying, transforming them, that is the duty of the true patriot'.[144] By the end of the year Ollivier would be being accused of lack of 'political sense', lack of 'patriotism' and naivety.[145] Morny's efforts to secure his financial independence with a position at the Suez Company cannot have helped. Ferry and Picard joined in a campaign of personal and political denigration.[146] This was the point at which Allain-Targé, using terms like 'defection' and 'treason' in letters to his father, explained to his mother that his bitterness was due to the fact that Ollivier's 'detestable' example had 'created doubts amongst the younger generation'.[147] Certainly, Ollivier's increasingly pragmatic course helped to secure the right to strike for workers but this example of co-operation with the regime only further compromised him in the eyes of his former colleagues. The meeting, early in 1866, of some forty liberal deputies, which led to the establishment of the so-called Tiers Parti, was seen as another stage in his apostasy.[148] Ollivier's first private meeting with Napoleon on 27 June 1865, after a session of the commission on penal reform at the Tuileries Palace, had only confirmed his new sense of direction. His diary entry that evening records that 'I have been charmed by the Emperor. He was gay, open, laughed easily, and revealed an unpretentiousness which put me at ease; not very talkative certainly, but an agreeable conversationalist.' Thinking possibly of his own future role, he determined that

I do not believe that he can be taken by assault: the confused and dogmatic will have no influence over him, it appears to me that it is by slow, gentle and subtle insinuation that he can be persuaded ... I assume that, when he has confidence in someone he easily trusts their assertions, but as he has often been deceived, he must hesitate to grant that confidence. I sensed the weariness of the man of

---

[142] Quoted Constant, 'Quelques observations', p. 305.
[143] PG Aix, 6 April 1865, AN BB30/370; Constant, *Var*, p. 1127.
[144] J. Albertini, 'Le rapporteur de la loi des coalitions' in Troisier de Diaz, *Ollivier*, p. 110.
[145] E.g. Darimon, *Les cent seize*, p. 221, letter to Ollivier, 29 Dec. 1869.
[146] J. Albertini, 'Rapporteur', pp. 106–7.   [147] Allain-Targé, *République*, pp.19, 102.
[148] Tollu, 'Démocratie et liberté', pp. 131–2.

power *blasé* about men and things. He certainly will not retreat, but he will not throw himself into change; if he does advance, it will be step by step; we are not yet at the crowning of the edifice. [149]

Defending his conduct at a noisy electoral meeting in the Théâtre du Châtelet on 12 May 1869, Ollivier insisted on his continued commitment to *liberté*, which he maintained was 'an inalienable right.' It depended, however, on two preconditions, namely equality and order: 'Without equality, liberty is only a privilege for the few. Without order, it leads to the worst of despotisms.' With *liberté*, he insisted, every citizen had the right to choose his government and to 'surveil', 'control', and 'direct' it. He claimed that his disagreements with 'some democrats' were essentially over means. Should liberty be gained 'through revolution or constitutionally'? Experience had taught him that revolution led 'after many misfortunes' to 'dictatorship or despotism.' Challenged by members of the audience, he insisted that he would never have taken the oath of loyalty to the regime created by the *coup d'état* if subsequently it had not been 'instituted and confirmed' by a popular plebiscite. At this point the meeting ended abruptly with fighting in the audience and police intervention.[150] Mention of Ollivier's name, of 'the man of lies and hypocrisy' – as Lefrançais described him on 14 May – at other meetings was sufficient to cause uproar.[151] Ollivier stood for election in Paris and in Draguignan in the Var. Significantly, in both cases, the official candidate withdrew on the instructions of the Minister of the Interior.[152] The campaign in the Var was especially hard fought, with Ollivier accusing local democrats of planning a bloody revenge for the *coup d'état*, and the delegates of the *chambrées* accusing him of 'a gross insult', for which their drinking associations were closed.[153] Subsequently, speaking before the Corps législatif following the formation of his administration on 2 January 1870, Ollivier declared that his objective was to establish a durable 'national government, which will adapt with both firmness and flexibility to changing circumstances, and to the transformation of ideas, which will encourage the rise of new generations and welcome their hopes and their knowledge, which will guarantee the destiny of our great French democracy, and ensure the triumph of progress, without violence, and of liberty without revolution'. Gambetta reminded him that 'there is between us not simply a question of degree, there is a question of principle'.[154]

---

[149] Ollivier, *L'Empire libéral*, VII, pp. 406–7.   [150] Vitu, *Réunions publiques*, pp. 52–61.
[151] *Ibid.*, p. 72.   [152] Girard, *Nouvelle histoire*, p. 396; Constant, *Var*, p. 1294.
[153] Constant, *Var*, pp. 1382–3.   [154] Tollu, 'Démocratie et liberté', p. 139.

The classic socialist history of the Second Empire by Albert Thomas, together with his contribution to the Cambridge Modern History, accepted at face value alarmist contemporary official reports, as well as reflecting the essential optimism of the left of his own time, to describe an indivisible working-class and revolutionary republican movement marching towards victory. The republican 'mainstream' – moderates and most 'radicals' – had, in contrast, been increasingly concerned by what was perceived as a threat from the left posed by growing demands for working-class autonomy and the revolutionary seizure of power. The editors of *Le Réveil*, which had achieved a very respectable circulation of 16,000 by April 1869, were particularly forceful in their insistence that political reform was only the means to achieve social reform.[155] Nevertheless, Delescluze, its editor and a future leading communard, insisted that socialism meant improving the workers' lot through the full – and gradual – development of republican institutions and an alliance between the 'people' and the 'bourgeoisie', whose fears he was anxious to calm.[156] Middle-class republicans attempting to appeal to working-class audiences frequently seemed ill at ease. There was a marked contrast between the sedate *conférences* conducted, with didactic objectives, by republican deputies in middle-class Paris and popular meetings in the working-class *quartiers*. Workers were suspicious of the pretensions of the 'bourgeois' politicians who had 'betrayed' them in June 1848. They lacked interest also in the frequent hair-splitting of socialist intellectuals. The revolutionary left was inspired by an extremely heterogeneous accumulation of theory and sentiment. According to the journalist Vermorel, 'the socialists distinguish themselves from the purely political parties in that, for them, liberty is not the objective but only the means: the means of achieving universal well-being and the disappearance from the world of ignorance and misery and of substituting social harmony for the existing antagonisms'.[157] The workers' own socialism was vague and firmly linked to basic notions of justice and the coming establishment of the social republic.[158] Speaking at a meeting in Belleville in January 1870, M. Chaumière demanded to know whether it was just that 'some individuals live in immense buildings which they call palaces ... whilst others, those who produce everything ... live in infected and airless shacks'.[159]

---

[155] E.g. prospectus 15 March 1868, quoted M. Dessal, *Un révolutionnaire jacobin: Charles Delescluze 1809–71* (Paris 1952), p. 219.
[156] E.g. 27 Jan. 1870, quoted *ibid.* p. 205.   [157] *Le parti socialiste* (Paris: Chez Panis 1870), p. v.
[158] E.g. J. P. Courtheoux, 'Naissance d'une conscience de classe', *Revue économique* (1957).
[159] Vitu, *Réunions publiques*, p. 54.

On 4 February M. Bacot complained that workers were no better than slaves 'at the mercy of capital ... Never for us will bread and work be assured. And yet the landlord comes to us and says: You must pay ... The landlord, does he say: have you worked over the last three months? No, he says: give me the money or your last crust, your last bit of clothing will be mine.' He finished to *applaudissements frénétiques*.[160] One can easily imagine the discussion continuing over drinks in a neighbouring café. This apparent intellectual ferment was characterised by one official as involving, at one end of the scale 'the pretensions of economic science' and at the other simple 'envy of the bourgeois'.[161] In terms of political behaviour, the election results in both 1863 and 1869 suggest that these vague sentiments were often compatible with the reformist, patriotic, and Jacobin ideals of moderate and radical republicanism.

Outside the major cities and industrial centres, support for revolutionary socialism was extremely limited and fragmented. Even in the cities many workers believed that a socialist revolution was an unrealistic aspiration and likely to lead only to a repetition of the bloodshed of June 1848.[162] However, some working-class militants were doubtful about the commitment of an essentially *bourgeois* republican leadership to social reform. In Paris, just before the 1863 elections, worker militants from the faubourgs du Temple and Saint-Antoine were invited by the manufacturer Beslay to discuss the candidature of the moderate republican Carnot. They spelt out their response in the bronze worker Tolain's brochure 'Some truths on the 1863 elections in Paris', which criticised the dominance of the democratic movement by an exclusive group of journalists, as well as the dictatorial behaviour of Carnot. Tolain also expressed serious reservations concerning the willingness of moderate republicans to co-operate with a notorious reactionary like Thiers and insisted upon the necessity of worker candidates. This was the course of action decided upon by a group of artisans for by-elections in 1864. They selected the printing workers Blanc and Coutant and Tolain himself as candidates. Opposed by the republican leadership and without press support these three obtained 342, 11, and 500 votes respectively. Their potential supporters appear to have concluded that supporting their own meant a wasted vote and that the primary objective should be to oppose the regime in the most effective manner.[163]

---

[160] *Ibid.*, pp. 31–2.   [161] PG Dijon, 13 Jan. 1861, AN BB30/389.
[162] E.g. declaration by bronze workers of support for candidature of Garnier-Pagès – Dalotel *et al.*, *Aux origines*, p. 287.
[163] Girard, *Nouvelle histoire*, pp. 376–7.

The 'Manifesto of the Sixty', published in February 1864, aroused particular controversy. It supported proposals for worker candidates whilst denying that its signatories harboured any aspirations for 'a chimerical equality', for the redistribution of property or 'high taxes'. Instead it proposed 'freedom to work, credit, solidarity', reiterating the demands made in 1848 for producers' co-operatives as the base for the eventual abolition of class distinctions. The manifesto clearly represented the distrust felt by many artisans for bourgeois republican leaders and resentment at their exclusion from decision-making circles.[164] Moderate republicans responded with indignation, denouncing the manifesto as divisive or even as a Bonapartist plot. Probably inspired by Ollivier, another group of workers published a counter-'Manifesto of the Eighty' in *Le Siècle*, denying the existence of class divisions.[165] In 1868 in Saint-Etienne the small group of artisans who had founded a Société populaire similarly complained in their newssheet about the arrogance and disdain displayed by the rich republican oligarchy, which had selected once again the industrialist Dorian as its electoral candidate, indignantly demanding to know whether the city was 'a village peopled by ignorant serfs'.[166] An additional cause of concern for moderate republicans was the establishment of trades unions (*chambres syndicales*) – seventy in Paris alone between 1867 and 1870 – organised into local federations in Rouen early in 1869, in Paris in December, and in Lyon and Marseille in March–April 1870, and especially the popularity of the Workers' International where, as in Paris or Rouen, it provided practical support for these *chambres syndicales* and for strikes.[167] The manifesto published in 1869 by the Rouen workers belonging to the Cercle d'études économiques pointed out that only workers and *petit bourgeois* were not represented in the Corps législatif and, more explicitly, that capital was represented but labour was not and that 'the despotism of the state has no other cause than the tyranny of capitalism'. It followed that 'we need to elect workers as representatives. They alone can defend the interests of the proletarians.' The manifesto supported the notion of the *mandat impératif* – a commitment by the candidate, if elected, to support the programme voted on by his constituents or immediately resign.[168] According to the state prosecutor, the printing worker Aubry, its principal author, had claimed that local republican leaders were 'retarded bourgeois, preoccupied with vain political

---

[164] E.g. J. Bruhat, 'Le socialisme français de 1848 à 1870' in J. Droz (ed.), *Histoire générale du socialisme*, I (Paris 1972), p. 521.
[165] Tulard, *Dictionnaire*, p. 69.   [166] Quoted Gordon, *Merchants*, p. 113.
[167] Rougerie, 'Second Empire,' p. 114.   [168] Quoted Boivin, *Mouvement ouvrier*, I, pp. 295–6.

questions and as concerned as the conservatives ... to defend the interests of money and the social abuses ... which are crushing the working
class'.[169]

The moderate republican response was ferocious. For moderates and
many 'radical' republicans the revolutionary left was perceived as posing a major obstacle to the creation of the Republic. These 'mainstream'
republicans were concerned that fear of 'red' revolution might save the
Empire. The moderate *Journal de Rouen* suggested that worker candidatures were part of a government plot to divide the republican movement,
whilst, in an editorial condemning Aubry's candidature, the 'radical'
Progrès de Rouen denied that there could be 'a workers' democracy and a
bourgeois democracy', insisting that 'there is only one democracy, generously pursuing, since 1789, in spite of all the reactions, the realisation of
the social problem, the uplifting of the humble through instruction, the
material improvement of the labouring classes'.[170] Aubry's humiliating
failure provides evidence of the success of these appeals for republican
unity. He obtained only 826 of the 22,220 votes cast.[171] Following the
May election he would complain to his colleague in the International
and fellow printing worker, Varlin, that in electing bourgeois republicans,
Paris 'had again abdicated its social aspirations and made common cause
with its natural enemies.' Clearly he feared that, as in 1848, bourgeois
politicians would betray the workers' social aspirations. He would see
Varlin's decision to co-operate with Rochefort in order to gain access
to the columns of *La Marseillaise* as symptomatic of a willingness to accept a subordinate role within the bourgeois republican movement.[172]
It was to counter such suspicion that Varlin insisted in March 1870 that,
unlike in 1848, 'in order to be final, the next revolution must not stop
at a simple change in the labels attached to the government and some
minor reforms, it must radically free the worker from all capitalist exploitation and establish justice in social relationships'.[173] Reports from
the police spies who infiltrated meetings of the Workers' International
in Lyon, however, reported constant squabbling over both tactics and
the question of whether the final objective should be mutualism, with
workers' co-operatives as the basis for a new society, or collectivist and

---

[169] PG Rouen, 12 April 1869, AN BB30/389.
[170] 19 May 1869, quoted Boivin, *Mouvement ouvrier*, I, p. 292; II, pp. 150–61.
[171] J. Rougerie, 'Les sections françaises de l'Association Internationale des travailleurs' in Rougerie
et al., *La Ire Internationale, l'institution, l'implantation, le rayonnement* (Paris 1964), p. 117.
[172] Quoted Boivin, *Mouvement ouvrier*, I, p. 318.
[173] F. Jeloubovskaïa, *La chute du second empire et la naissance de la 3e République* (Moscow 1959), p. 235.

communist.[174] Most committed socialists, exercising a diffuse influence over wider groups, were still attracted to Proudhonist dreams of creating a new society through the development of producers' co-operatives and friendly societies.[175] Varlin also rejected state-centred socialism as likely to lead to a new slavery but had come to accept that 'it will be impossible for us to organise social revolution for as long as we live under a government as arbitrary as that under which we live'.[176] The bourgeois state had to be smashed, and the capitalist no longer permitted to arbitrarily dispose of his wealth, if a social system based on the principle of co-operation was ever to be created.[177] The creation in Montpellier of a new newspaper, *Les Droits de l'Homme*, in June 1870 by A. Ballu and Jules Guesde was similarly intended to combat the anti-socialist views of the republican *Liberté*.[178] The lines of division were being drawn. According to Benoît Malon, a leading member of the Workers' International who had addressed some twenty meetings in the Paris industrial suburb of Puteaux between January and April 1869, they were between 'the minority, militant, revolutionary' and 'the democratic republican majority'.[179] There might be disagreement over the value of political participation but it was impossible to ignore politics in the agitated circumstances of 1869/70, particularly where the Emperor's soldiers were killing strikers and 'preserving despotism and tyranny with the aid of *chassepots*.'[180] Tolain, the bronze engraver, warned in a speech at La Redoute in Paris in November 1869 that unless 'the abuse of property' was ended then a 'terrible social liquidation' would occur.[181]

In the cafés of the Latin Quarter in Paris, and in Lyon and Marseille, little groups of students and disaffected bourgeois, clerks and workers, considered the prospects of overthrowing the Emperor they frequently compared to Nero, discussed the contents of newspapers like *Le Réveil*, *La Marseillaise*, and *La Lanterne*, and sang revolutionary songs. Some, perhaps a few hundred, belonged to revolutionary secret societies. Young men like Tridon, Eudes, Protot, or Rigault, who had visited Blanqui in prison and, following his escape, in exile in Brussels, talked about a putsch led

[174] J. Rougerie, 'La Ire Internationale à Lyon (1865–70): Problèmes d'histoire du mouvement ouvrier français,' *Annali Istituto Giangiacomo Feltrinelli*, 1961, pp. 170–1.

[175] Exposition universelle de 1867, 'Ouvriers mécaniciens du dépt.de la Seine', AN F12/3116; Aubry's report to Lausanne Congress of International in Boivin, *Mouvement ouvrier*, II, pp. 209–11.

[176] Letter to Aubry, 6 Aug. 1869, quoted Boivin, *Mouvement ouvrier*, I, p. 340 note 45.

[177] *La Marseillaise*, 11 March 1870, quoted Rougerie, 'Les sections', pp. 126–7.

[178] Cholvy, *Religion et société*, II, p. 1043.   [179] Quoted Dalotel *et al.*, *Aux origines*, p. 40.

[180] C. Adam, April 1870, quoted *ibid.*, p. 266.   [181] Vitu, *Réunions publiques*, p. 26.

by the revolutionary elite of intellectuals and workers to seize control of Paris and thereby of France.[182] Gustave Tridon in *Les Hébertistes* (1864) had declared his faith in 'the entrails of the plebeians, the pikes of the faubourgs, the roar of the ... clubs, in those obscure and execrated men, always active, who exasperate the strong, revive the feeble, and sow everywhere hatred of tyranny'. The Blanquist activist Laballeur-Villiers revealed his venomous hatred for the social system when, speaking to the Société des Libres penseurs in Marseille, he claimed that 'what the people need is a permanent revolution. All the means are good to carry it out, the knife, poison, ambush, firearms!'[183] Blanqui himself, *le vieux*, in *Communism, the Future of Society* (1869) promised, following the seizure of power, to suppress the army which defended the regime and the magistrature which enforced class justice, to dismiss senior officials, and expel the clergy – 'the black army' which brutalised and enslaved the masses, to confiscate the property of the church, and to introduce a direct and progressive tax on inheritance. He also promised that the new regime would respect the principle of private property ownership, a commitment which would not have been very re-assuring when set besides his plans for a revolutionary dictatorship. He asserted that the new regime would need to protect itself by arming its supporters and allowing 'no freedom for the enemy'. His experience in 1848 also suggested that 'to ask the enslaved population to vote is to ask their masters ... A year of Parisian dictatorship in '48 would have spared France the quarter of a century which is coming to an end. If it takes ten years this time we will not hesitate.'[184] To militants like the students Paul Lafargue and Charles Longuet – Marx's future sons-in-law – or Albert Richard in Lyon, influenced by the Russian anarchist Bakunin, mutualism, with its idealised producers' co-operatives, was a chimera, a palliative. If realised, it would preserve inequality. They were inspired by the most radical myths of the Great Revolution.[185] A printed proclamation dated 24 June, but discovered by the police in September 1868, represented the views of these revolutionary militants. Under the title *République française. Commune révolutionnaire de Paris* its anonymous author(s) called for war to the death 'between the father of the Loan and the children of Labour', between 'the father, the son and the Holy Spirit of the *coup d'état* ... the Trinity

[182] E.g. Ier Légion de gendarmerie, Bulletin politique du chef de Legion, 31 Jan. 1870, AHG G8/176; see also OC cie. de la Seine, 28 April 1870, AHE G8/176.
[183] Quoted Olivesi, *Marseille*, p. 55.
[184] Girard, *Nouvelle histoire*, pp. 378–9; see also P. Hutton, *The Cult of the Revolutionary Tradition* (Berkeley 1981), ch. 1.
[185] Campbell, *Second Empire*, pp. 42–3; Rougerie, 'La Ire Internationale', pp 143–7.

of the squandered millions, of the false oath and the false-Jesus' and fin-ished with a call for 'insurrection against tyranny and the tyrant!'[186] It advised its readers to wait for the signal, just as the many placards found in the streets of Marseilles in March–April 1868 had called on the 'chil-dren of the Revolution' to be ready to follow the lead from Paris.[187] The Republic could be nothing more than a step towards a thoroughgoing re-organisation of society.[188] In a series of letters to Richard, the Parisian militant Malon agreed on the need to be pragmatic rather than purist and to take advantage of the wider republican campaign against the regime as a stage in the progress towards revolution.[189] Election cam-paigns, speeches, and constant agitation in the major population centres appear to have created a belief, at least within these restricted militant circles, that revolution was imminent, although their confidence might fluctuate from day to day.[190]

From the moderate republican as well as governmental viewpoint, some of the views expressed in speeches at public meetings were particu-larly threatening, as were the disorders in Paris during and after the 1869 elections. At a meeting in La Chapelle on 31 January 1869 the 'radical' journalist Louis Ulbach was denounced by a worker called Ducasses as 'belonging to that obese bourgeois democracy ... which shot the people on the 15 May, the 15 [*sic*] June and during every reaction'.[191] Those bourgeois republicans believed to be guilty of involvement in the crush-ing of the June insurrection were denounced with especial bitterness at meetings in the working-class districts of eastern Paris. In Belleville on 30 January the late General Cavaignac was condemned as the 'assassin of the people,' and 'the defender of property' as were any *cavaignaquistes* who might be present.[192] Speaking at the Théâtre Dejazet on 9 May, M. Monté reminded his listeners that '1848 led us to June, and it was not the fighters on the barricades who betrayed the Revolution, but those who ruled the Republic so badly.'[193] At an electoral meeting in the rue des Cordelières on 12 May 1869, Tolain attacked Jules Favre not only for 'not having been for an instant a socialist', but especially because he had acquiesced in the courts martial and transportations which had followed the insurrection as well as supporting the military expedition mounted by the Prince-President against the Roman Republic. He was nothing

---

[186] With report of prefect, 9 Sept. 1868, AN F1 CIII Cher 9.
[187] PG Aix, 31 March, 8 April 1868, AN BB18/1766.
[188] E.g. Millère, speaking at Folies-Belleville, Aug. 1869, quoted Dalotel, *Aux origines*, p. 262.
[189] See especially ?Nov. 1869, 26 Jan. 1870, reprinted in Rougerie, 'La Ire Internationale', p. 181.
[190] E.g. Vitu, *Réunions publiques*, p. 51; Rougerie, 'La Ire Internationale', p. 183.
[191] Vitu, *Réunions électorales*, p. 66.   [192] Speech by Civia, *ibid.*, p. 69.   [193] *Ibid.*, p. 43.

more than a duplicitous *homme politique*.[194] More emotively, M. Charlin insisted that 'the corpses of those assassinated in June are between Jules Favre and us'. Favre's own appearance at this particular venue on 14 May was brought to an end rapidly by an audience which shouted him down. M. Aubet, who took over the podium, described Favre as a traitor and 'the representative of the *bourgeoisie* and the exploiters'.[195] At another meeting he was denounced as a Girondin and the representative of 'a conspiracy of shopkeepers and journalists'.[196] Favre, 'who represents the *caste bourgeoise* and not the workers',[197] who lacked respect for 'the dignity of the sovereign people',[198] was undoubtedly a favourite target. Others included Jules Simon, denounced in a pamphlet by the journalist Vermorel, who warned his readers that the republican deputies would 'not hesitate to flatter the people's republican passions in order to exploit them for their own profit' but that 'if this revolution, imprudently provoked by them, breaks out, they will be the first to give the signal for reaction and to hurriedly associate themselves with their enemies of today to combat the revolutionary monster, just as they did in 1848'.[199] Marie was condemned for his willingness to enter into an electoral pact with the Comte de Falloux, and Carnot, Favre, and Simon for supporting measures against the people.[200] Garnier-Pagès was attacked for introducing the 45-centime tax, which had made the Republic so unpopular in 1848.[201] Facing a more sympathetic audience in one of the more prosperous districts of the capital he was able to defend himself by insisting that the tax had saved France from the shame of bankruptcy, and that 'the dissidents in June were paid by [the Legitimist pretender] Henri V and the Russians'.[202] The younger generation of moderate republicans was not spared. Picard was denounced as a 'false' democrat, as no better than an official candidate and as a friend of Favre.[203] On 17 May he even had the temerity to respond to a speech by a M. Langlois at a hall in the boulevard Magenta which had called for 'the abolition of the permanent army, suppression of the religious budget, independence for communes, reform of the magistrature, state ownership of the railways and the Bank [of France]', by denouncing socialism as 'utopian'.[204]

---

[194] *Ibid.*, p. 112.   [195] *Ibid.*, pp. 118–19.
[196] Meeting in rue du faubourg St-Jacques, 13 May, *ibid.*, pp. 114–15.
[197] M. Brisson, 11 May 1869, *ibid.*, p. 105.   [198] M. Deberle, 12 May 1869, *ibid.*, p. 111.
[199] Jeloubovskaïa, *La chute*, p. 202.   [200] Vitu, *Réunions électorales*, p. 15.
[201] Ducasse at Belleville, 1 Feb. 1869, in Vitu, *Réunions publiques*, p. 73.
[202] Electoral meeting in the 5th constituency in Vitu, *Réunions électorales*, p. 81.
[203] Anonymous heckler, 14 May 1869, *ibid.*, p. 73.   [204] *Ibid.*

These demands were the commonplaces of a 'socialist' discourse which typically demanded the right to work, more equitable taxation, equality of opportunity through free, obligatory, and secular education and an end to exploitation by means of the provision of cheap credit to peasant farmers and workers' co-operatives. Amongst Parisian artisanal militants a strong sense of injustice combined with a growing determination that workers should secure their own future. At an electoral meeting in the rue des Cordelières on 11 May, Wuillaimez prefaced these demands with an elegy to Marat, 'the greatest of the economists'.[205] Proudhon's famous phrase 'Property is theft' was repeated frequently in articles and speeches. The feminist Paule Minck agreed, adding: 'More than that, it's an assassination, it's an accumulation of shame' and drew on the history of the kings of France to illustrate her point.[206] Relatively few speakers went as far as the locksmith Garreau, who announced in March 1869 that 'I want to assassinate the bourgeoisie and the capitalists who stuff themselves with everything ... I want to take to the streets with weapons, not tomorrow but now.'[207]

In this hotbed atmosphere personality, faction, and ideological divisions amongst the revolutionaries and socialists became more intense. The more attentive observer might have noticed the quarrels between the Robespierrists and the more extreme *hébertistes* during a meeting at the Folies-Belleville on 17 January.[208] Speaking at the Salle de la Redoute, Napoleon Gaillard proclaimed himself to be 'a very advanced socialist, even a communist' and criticised the inadequacy of mutualist demands for cheap credit to fund co-operatives. He maintained that 'to raise the poor, we need to bring down the rich. We don't need to destroy interest but capital in its entirety.'[209] At a meeting held on 13 May in the Gymnase de la Sorbonne a middle-class and student audience declared its support for Henri Rochefort, the most radical of the 'radicals'.[210] The previous evening Rochefort had been denounced by Tolain as unsuitable to represent the interests of the workers because of his aristocratic social origins. Gambetta was similarly suspect.[211] Clearly there was considerable disagreement about whether or not Rochefort was a 'socialist',[212] which was hardly surprising given the varied nature and essential vagueness of the programmes advanced.

---

[205] *Ibid.*, p. 104.   [206] Quoted Dalotel *et al.*, *Aux origines*, p. 231.
[207] Quoted *ibid.*, p. 320.   [208] Vitu, *Réunions publiques*, p. 41.
[209] Quoted Dalotel *et al.*, *Aux origines*, p. 244.   [210] Vitu, *Réunions électorales*, pp. 113–14.
[211] *Ibid.*, p. 112.   [212] See also debate at meeting in the rue Monge, 14 May, *ibid.*, pp. 116–17.

GROWING ELECTORAL SUCCESS

In spite of these weaknesses, the progress of republicanism could be measured by the results of the elections held in 1863 and 1869. As a result of liberalisation and the emergence of a new generation into politics, in many areas 1863 was the first occasion on which republicans were able to mount a challenge, however tentative, to the regime.[213] Since February 1858 every candidate for election had been required to take the oath of loyalty so that those who were successful were now far more likely to take their seats. Electoral participation became more meaningful. Republican deputies were also able to make full use of the new parliamentary procedures and present vigorous amendments to the address from the throne as a means of offering an alternative political programme to the electorate.[214] Opposition candidates attracted 37 per cent of the votes cast. Thirty-two were elected, eighteen of them moderate republicans. Paris and its suburbs had decisively abandoned the regime with the election of nine republicans – Favre, Picard, Ollivier, Darimon, Guéroult, Pelletan, Simon, and Havin, together with Thiers. Of the 235,000 votes cast in the capital, official candidates had gained only 82,600. The number of abstentions had fallen from 143,000 to 86,000.[215] The successful opposition list of candidates had been selected and supported by a self-appointed committee chaired by Carnot and including the editors and leading journalists of *Le Siècle, La Presse,* and *L'Opinion nationale.*[216] They published a *Manuel électoral* with advice on registration procedures, and made a considerable effort to encourage registration, which clearly paid off.[217] However, their efforts also had the effect of intensifying personal differences between republican leaders. The reduction in the number of constituencies from ten to nine caused problems. Darimon, for one, resented Carnot's pretensions and particularly the suggestion that he should be dropped from the republican list because of his friendship with Prince Napoleon and poor oratorical skills. Darimon claimed that the proceedings 'well reflected the petty passions, which agitate the envious, stupid, and wicked world ... It's a democratic jesuitism, cleverly disguised under a scaffolding of grand phrases and great principles.'[218]

---

[213] E.g. Armengaud, *Est-Aquitain*, p. 413; Ménager, *Nord*, II, p. 493.
[214] Ollivier, *L'Empire libéral*, vol. VI, p. 134.   [215] Girard, *Nouvelle histoire*, p. 370.
[216] Darimon, *L'opposition libérale*, pp. 390–1, entries 8, 11 May 1863; Ollivier, *L'Empire libéral*, VI, pp. 232–8.
[217] Darimon, *L'opposition libérale*, p. 145, entry 18 Jan. 1862; see also PG Lyons, 1 April 1862, AN BB30/379.
[218] Darimon, *L'opposition libérale*, p. 349, entry 26 March 1863.

Support for republican candidates was evident especially in the popular *quartiers* of the north and east, in areas like Arts et Métiers and the faubourg Saint-Antoine. The destructive impact of Haussmann's reconstruction on lower middle and working-class communities undoubtedly had reinforced hostility towards the regime.[219] Ludovic Halévy noted the general sense of elation following the declaration of results, writing in his diary on 1 June that 'this evening Paris has an air of riot and revolution ... The government has been routed totally ... On the boulevards people are snapping up the evening newspapers which contain the results ...This is the first serious political agitation to move Paris since the *coup d'état*. The republicans are confident that in the next elections France will follow Paris.'[220]

In addition to this triumph in the capital, Favre and Hénon were successful in Lyon – where officials noted the efforts of local committees and their canvassers to identify supporters, to ensure that they were registered and that they voted.[221] Marie was elected in Marseille, Dorian in Saint-Etienne, Magnin in the Côte-d'Or, and Glais-Bizoin in the Côtes-du-Nord. Even where republican candidates were not successful clearly support was growing. In a number of cases victory had been prevented only by zealous official gerrymandering of constituency boundaries. This was the case in Rouen where L.-P. Desseaux, a moderate republican who had served as a repressive state prosecutor during the Second Republic, had been selected as candidate. His manifesto proclaimed his loyalty 'to the ideas of a sensible liberty and deplores anything that is the result of brutal Force'. His only concession to his predominantly worker constituency was to observe that it was necessary to 'study the means of supplementing the lack of work by a sufficiently remunerative equivalent not imprinted with the stamp of charity'.[222] The *Journal de Rouen* adopted a similar approach, insisting on the need to reduce military expenditure and the burden of taxation. It was the violence of the oral propaganda in the bars and workshops, the tirades against employers, the demands for higher wages, which concerned the authorities.[223] In the Var, a centre of démocrate-socialiste strength in 1851, the cohesion of republican support in towns like La Seyne and Toulon once again impressed officials.[224] In Pyrénées-Orientales where the obvious candidate, the eminent local republican Emmanuel Arago, refused to take the oath of loyalty, the regime adopted a neutral stance between two

---

[219] E.g. Girard, *Questions politiques*, p. 80.
[220] 'Carnet', I, 1934, p. 36, quoted Girard, *Nouvelle histoire*, p. 367.
[221] PG Lyon, 3 July 1864, AN BB30/379.   [222] Quoted Boivin, *Mouvement ouvrier*, I, p. 148.
[223] PG Rouen, 10 April 1863, AN BB30/387.   [224] Constant, *Var*, pp. 1077–8.

pro-government candidates. Republicans chose to support Isaac Pereire who was judged to have brought work to the region, and in spite of his reputation as a speculator, in preference to Justin Durand, the candidate supported by the Legitimists, clericals, and anti-semites.[225]

Their victory in Paris substantially increased the optimism of republicans throughout the country.[226] The state prosecutor at Lyon complained that 'along the railway lines and the banks of the Saône and Rhône it is possible to follow, with the results, the progress of this contagious ill'.[227] There were frequent complaints about the growing number of subscriptions to Parisian newspapers, especially *Le Siècle*.[228] Following the election, the enlarged group of republican deputies, although riven by disputes, began to meet as a caucus at Marie's home in the rue Neuve-des-Petits-Champs to prepare for future contests and provide assistance to republicans in the provinces.[229] Garnier-Pagès, for one, made use of the expanding rail network to visit more than sixty towns.[230] In Montpellier he advised an audience of republicans from throughout the region to avoid candidates with 'names too compromised by advanced opinions'.[231] Contesting municipal elections was another means of advancing the cause and in many communities represented a key stage in the democratic struggle against the regime. As early as 1860 officials were complaining about the rise of an apolitical 'questioning attitude' as well as a much rarer 'spirit of disorder' or even 'vague aspirations towards greater freedom', especially in areas with republican traditions.[232] The suspension of uncooperative or factionalised councils was becoming increasingly common.[233] In Lyons the candidature of the former deputy and political detainee Sébastien Commissaire for the departmental council elections in 1864, with the support of a committee made up mostly of workers, was opposed by middle-class republicans and liberals, by shopkeepers and the workshop *patronat*, as well as by the préfecture.[234] In part at least, this revival of local politics – seen in a rising participation rate (20 per cent in 1855, 33 per cent in 1860 and 70 per cent in 1865)[235] – reflected the revival

---

[225] PG Montpellier, 9 July 1863, 8 April 1864, AN BB30/380.
[226] E.g. PG Rouen, 10 April 1864, AN BB30/387.
[227] PG Lyons, 27 June 1863, AN BB30/379.
[228] E.g. PG, Pau 15 April 1865, AN BB30/384.   [229] Ollivier, *L'Empire libéral*, VI, p. 405.
[230] Pilbeam, *Republicanism*, p. 249.   [231] PG Montpellier, 8 Oct. 1862, AN BB30/380.
[232] PG Agen, 6 Oct. 1860, AN BB30/370.   [233] E.g. Goujon, *Le vignoble*, pp. 150–3.
[234] Commissaire, *Mémoires*, II, pp. 191–9.
[235] E. Lavoie, 'Les élections municipales sous le second empire' in *Europe et Etat* (Aix-en-Provence 1993), p. 640.

of republican militancy and further encouraged the politicisation of popular sociability.[236]

The liberalisation of the regime's policy towards municipal administration from 1865 was another important factor. Subsequently, republican municipalities were much less likely to be dissolved. From that year local elections became far more political, often on the basis of alliances between liberal and moderate republican notables determined to unseat pro-government councillors.[237] Although official reports, whilst recording republican successes, generally stressed that most results remained satisfactory,[238] the election of republican-controlled councils in Marseille, Toulouse, and Bordeaux caused serious difficulties. Incidents like the replacement of the council at Toulouse in 1866 with a commission appointed by the prefect, encouraged demands for the recognition of local liberties and decentralisation of government.[239] Frequently, however, the determination of republican councillors to prove their competence led to growing day-to-day collaboration with the prefectoral administration and to a process by which republican notables were integrated into the machinery of government.[240] As at Saint-Etienne, the capture of local power could also lead to bitter disputes between middle-class republican councillors and socialists, especially workers, who still felt excluded.[241] In these circumstances, the government was not prepared to allow the election of mayors, those key figures in the Imperial administration responsible for policing local communities and organising elections. Indeed, Paris and Lyon remained deprived of the right to elect their own councils, leaving executive power firmly in the hands of their prefects.[242] By the early summer of 1870, when municipal elections were once again due, official anxiety concerning the results had become considerably more intense.[243] In the meantime, of course, another general election had been fought.

By 1869 foreign policy reverses and a difficult economic situation had undermined the regime's prestige. The liberalisation of the legislation on meetings and the press had changed the political situation profoundly and ensured that the elections were by far the most agitated of the regime. The results revealed an increase of around one million in the opposition vote, to 3,300,000 – and made it clear that the regime

---

[236] E.g. Constant, *Var*, pp. 609–13.   [237] Lavoie, 'Elections municipales', pp. 634–5.
[238] E.g. Palmade, 'Gers', p. 93; Lavoie, 'Elections municipales', pp. 630–41.
[239] Aminzade, *Class Struggles*, p. 382.   [240] Constant, *Var*, pp. 1162–3, 1589.
[241] PG Lyons, 3 July 1864, AN BB30 379; Aminzade, *Class Struggles*, p. 165.
[242] Hazareesingh, *Subject*, pp. 265–71.
[243] E.g. OC gendarmerie de la Seine, 28 June 1870, AHG G8/176.

had lost the support of the electorate in most towns and cities. Support for the republican cause appeared to be increasing everywhere. There were more candidates – 110 in 71 departments compared with 70 in 1863 – making them the largest opposition group. In an effort to make the best use of their 'big' names they took full advantage of the possibility of multiple candidatures. For example, Favre appears to have stood for election in eleven provincial constituencies and Simon in eight.[244] In Paris, 234,000 voters supported opposition candidates, 82,500 governmental candidates, and 76,500 abstained. Amongst the candidates, the moderate republican proponents of a liberal democracy had been joined by more radical figures totally opposed to any sort of accommodation with the regime, and most notably by Gambetta, d'Alton-Shée, Raspail, Rochefort, and Bancel, the former démocrate-socialiste deputy and exile who took 63 per cent of the vote against Ollivier after a stormy campaign.[245] The organisers of a meeting in the Châtelet theatre designed to support Ollivier provoked a major riot when they attempted to exclude hostile groups. These clashed with police in the square in front of the theatre and for the next three evenings there were disturbances in the Latin Quarter and along the boulevard Saint Michel, involving possibly as many as 15,000 people. Amongst the 149 arrested were 93 manual workers, mostly in their teens or early twenties, together with 56 students and clerks. Clearly, the Paris Prefect of Police, Pietri, was concerned that some agitators were attempting to turn these disorders into an insurrection.[246] This re-appearance of 'revolutionaries' on the streets of the capital undoubtedly caused considerable alarm. Darimon, the former republican, recorded his concern at 'the indifference of the population in the presence of rioting', comforting himself with the observation that if Paris was 'completely disaffected' at least the republicans remained divided and the city 'is probably not yet ripe for revolution'.[247]

In the absence of official candidates, the real struggle in the capital was between republicans. In the 3rd *circonscription*, which included the faubourgs du Temple and Saint-Antoine, Garnier-Pagès, who as finance minister in 1848 had played a leading role in the closure of the National Workshops and the suppression of the June insurrection, endured nightmare election meetings to defeat the 'socialist' Raspail, another eminent survivor of 1848.[248] In working-class Belleville, the contest was between Carnot and Gambetta, the rising star, who triumphed with 21,744 votes

[244] Lagoueyte, *Candidature*, pp. 631–2, 636.   [245] Girard, *Nouvelle histoire*, p. 397.
[246] Prefect of Police to MI, 3 June 1869, AN 45 AP 3.
[247] Darimon, *Les cent seize*, pp. 13–14, entry 13 June 1869.   [248] Dalotel *et al.*, *Aux origines*, p. 221.

to 11,604. According to the city's gendarmerie commander this was because 'the working class had been canvassed without stop for a long time ... and voted *en masse*' for Gambetta whilst much of the middle class had opted for abstention.[249] Afraid of being outflanked on the left, Gambetta had accepted the *cahiers des doléances* prepared by local election committees and presented their political programme with its aspirations for social reform, laying ringing claim to the revolutionary heritage. In contrast, his personal address to the voters, insisted on the primacy of politics. In his address to a more middle-class right-bank constituency Favre concentrated on administrative decentralisation and the disestablishment of the church. He and Garnier-Pagès would be elected only on the second ballot and with the support of voters who had supported pro-regime candidates on the first ballot.[250] Nevertheless, the call for republican unity made by Bancel before an audience at the Salle Molière still had considerable popular appeal. He proclaimed that 'all those who recognise the sovereignty of the people and wish to reconquer the freedom and independence of the nation are united. We will arrive all the more promptly at the realisation of social reform ... if this is not contrary to the principles of property and liberty which were inscribed in '89 in the Declaration of the Rights of Man.'[251] There was so much overlap between their programmes that few republicans could dissent and many socialists would doubtless share a perhaps naive confidence in 'universal' suffrage.[252] Cross-class solidarities remained strong, reflecting a determination not to weaken the common struggle for the Republic, one and indivisible. In his campaign in Marseille, Gambetta's emphasis on the importance of preserving social order was sufficiently convincing to win the endorsement of Thiers.[253] When he opted eventually for the port city, Rochefort, who had failed against Favre in May, was again able to defeat Carnot in Belleville by 17,978 votes to 13,445.[254]

Similar divisions were evident in Lyon, where there were bitter disputes over the selection of candidates, between the supporters of the sitting deputies, Hénon and Favre, and 'radicals' determined to make a point by selecting the former political prisoners Raspail and Bancel.[255] The 'radicals' were well placed to appeal to a broad lower middle- and working-class audience. Socialist and working-class candidates invariably

[249] OC compagnie de la Seine, 27 May 1869, AHG G8/165.
[250] *Ibid.*, 24 Nov. 1869; Girard, *Nouvelle histoire*, p. 398.   [251] Vitu, *Réunions électorales*, p. 40.
[252] E.g. Aubry to Varlin, 26 May 1868 in Boivin, *Mouvement ouvrier*, II, p. 48.
[253] PG Aix, 26 June 1869, AN BB18/1785 and 6 July 1869, AN BB30/389.
[254] Rougerie, 'Belleville' in Girard, *Les élections*, pp. 9, 18.
[255] PG Lyon, 16 April 1869, AN BB30/389.

failed. At Saint-Etienne most workers supported the moderate republican ironmaster Dorian, who received 11,239 votes against the Legitimist Rochetaillée, who gained 4,908, and the socialist Martin, the failure of whose attempt to challenge the republican notables was evident from his 1,791 votes. Crowds celebrated Dorian's victory by singing the *Marseillaise* in front of the Prefecture but then gave Dorian a fright by smashing the windows and interiors of the Jesuit and Capuchin convents.[256] In the first ballot at Rouen, the moderate republican Desseaux came second to the liberal Pouyer-Quertier but nevertheless destroyed the credibility of the socialist worker Aubry who attracted only 826 votes. In spite of this Aubry refused to stand down for the second ballot arguing that, from the working-class point of view, there was little to distinguish the other candidates. He was condemned, by workers as well as Desseaux's supporters, for weakening the republican cause.[257] In the neighbouring port of Le Havre the 'radical' republican millionaire Le Cesne was condemned by the Bonapartist press as a subversive and by Delescluze as 'the fine flower of reaction'.[258] In Lille, moderate republican notables decided to support the liberals Thiers and Kolb-Bernard and were roundly denounced by Delescluze in *Le Réveil*. The frustration and anger of many rank-and-file republicans surfaced in disorder when the results were declared.[259] Jules Simon at Montpellier was also desperately anxious to re-assure 'respectable' members of the electorate, insisting that 'we also want order. There is no need for violence or disorder.'[260] In his native Jura, Grévy was elected unopposed and with conservative support due to his moderation.[261]

Republicans were certainly increasingly well organised. At Nîmes in February 1869, 160 delegates of the local *cercles* established an electoral committee and similar bodies were created in small towns and market villages throughout the Gard.[262] The procureur impérial at Draguignan explained that the 3,000 republican votes cast there reflected the lack of intelligence of much of the electorate, together with the fact that 'no effort has been spared by the supporters of M. Laurier, neither pressing solicitations, nor absurd promises'. He warned that the campaign against the proposed new military law, with its presumed effects on conscription and taxation, had weakened peasant support for the regime

---

[256] PI Saint Etienne, 25 May 1869, AN BB18/1785; Gordon, *Merchants*, p. 152.

[257] Boivin, *Mouvement ouvrier*, I, pp. 303–4, 307 n. 53, and II, p. 297.

[258] C. Malon, *Jules Le Cesne. Député du Havre* (Luneray 1995), pp. 61–7; P. Ardaillou, *Les républicains du Havre au 19ᵉ siécle* (Rouen 1999), pp. 154–8.

[259] Ménager, *Nord*, II, pp. 815–7.   [260] Quoted Cholvy, *Religion et société*, II, p. 1025.

[261] PG Besançon, 12 Oct. 1868, AN BB30/389.   [262] Huard, *La préhistoire des partis*, p. 813.

significantly.[263] In Dijon, a well-established group of moderate republicans attracted middle-class support in the city and the small market towns in the region, and the support of shopkeepers, artisans, and the better-off peasants determined to secure greater communal autonomy.[264] In the Loire, republican activity in support of Jules Favre was directed by a committee of manufacturers in the industrial town of Roanne, whose agents distributed propaganda in the countryside.[265] The manifesto published in the Aisne – again in support of Favre – by the professionals, businessmen, and *cultivateurs* of the Comité démocratique de l'arrondissement de Vervins, concentrated almost entirely on the need to free universal suffrage from the tyranny of official candidature, whilst pointing out that the regime's efforts to buy peasant support through improved rural roads was paid for by their taxes.[266] Ambitious candidates had to be prepared to invest time and money. In the Côtes-du-Nord Glais-Bizoin was unsuccessful in competition with General de la Motterouge, in spite of spending an estimated 64,000 francs on pamphlets, placards, and treating voters to cider and tobacco in village bars.[267] In Nantes the ageing philanthropist Dr Guépin, however, was rewarded for decades of devotion to the poor.[268]

Overall, the republican share of the vote, which had been 10.4 per cent in 1863, rose to 31.2 per cent in 1869 – still well below the 40 per cent of the Second Republic, although given official pressure it seems likely that *potential* republican support was higher than the final vote indicated.[269] Many republicans were greatly encouraged by the results. According to official reports, a process of politicisation, similar to that during the Second Republic, was well under way. Organisation and agitation continued. In Marseille, 1,500 to 2,000 people described as 'the active army of disorder, permanent, organised, disciplined', regularly attended political meetings after the elections.[270] The appearance of the prefect in proximity to one of these encouraged the crowd to chant the *Miserere* and *De profondis*, presumably to celebrate the coming death of the regime.[271] In Paris and Lyon, where the election campaigns had been

[263] Quoted Constant, *Var*, p. 1321.

[264] Lévêque, 'Conservatisme sans cléricalisme. L'évolution politique du Châtillonnais aux 19ᵉ et 20ᵉ siécles' in Faure *et al.*, *La terre*, p. 338.

[265] OC 19e Légion gendarmerie, 27 April 1869, AHG G8/165.

[266] *Manifeste électoral du Comité démocratique de l'arrondissement de Vervins et des cantons de Rozoy et Marle, 13e circonscription de l'Aisne, 3 avril 1869.*

[267] OC gendarmerie Côtes-du-Nord, 31 May 1869, AHG G8/165.

[268] PG Rennes, 26 June 1869, AN BB18/1785.   [269] Huard, *La préhistoire des partis*, pp. 839–40.

[270] PG Aix, 24 Dec. 1869, AN BB30/390.

[271] PG Aix, 2nd report of 26 June 1869, AN BB18/1785.

extremely agitated and republican success overwhelming, crowds celebrated victory and protested at the same time. They celebrated because, as Jules Claretie pointed out in a hastily written pamphlet, Paris had voted for freedom.[272] They protested because of the success of moderates like Garnier-Pagès and Favre and the failure of Rochefort, the darling of the extreme left. The rejection of the Republic in the provinces greatly intensified the sense of frustration. There were serious disorders along the boulevard Montmartre, in Belleville and the faubourg du Temple between 7 and 11 June. Every evening crowds gathered, estimated at their peak, on 10 June, to number around 20,000. Newspaper kiosks were set on fire and windows and street lights smashed. Police, and eventually cavalry, brutally dispersed the demonstrators. Of the 1,600 arrested, however, most were judged to have been merely spectators and only 160 were sent for trial as active participants. The editors of *Le Rappel* and *Le Réveil* were additionally arrested on a charge of incitement.[273] Disappointment also provoked less serious disorders in a number of provincial towns,[274] particularly where, as in Nantes, an urban republican majority appeared to have been reversed by the rural vote.[275] In Toulouse, where serious rioting had occurred previously in March 1868 in protest against the new conscription law, the overwhelming success of the republican candidate Duportal in the city itself was also cancelled out by the rural vote, provoking three days of rioting by workers.[276]

In the succeeding months agitation was kept alive by strikes and the by-elections necessary because of multiple candidatures. Disorder reached a climax in January 1870, when Pierre Bonaparte, a notoriously violent relative kept at arm's length by the Emperor, was challenged to a duel by the equally disreputable Corsican journalist Pascal Grousset, and shot and killed Victor Noir, one of his antagonist's seconds. Subsequently Bonaparte would be tried and acquitted, probably legitimately, on the grounds of self-defence. In the meantime, however, in *La Marseillaise*, Rochefort seized the opportunity to attack this regime of 'cut-throats.' He appears to have considered turning Noir's funeral into an insurrection but backed down when Favre, Picard, and Gambetta refused to

[272] *La volonté du peuple*, pp. 23–4.
[273] OC cie. de la Seine, 27 June 1869, AHG G8/165; Girard, *Nouvelle histoire*, pp. 398–9; Jacquemet, *Belleville*, pp. 527–9.
[274] Ministère de Justice, undated 'Note sur la répression des troubles qui ont eu lieu dans plusieurs villes à l'occasion des élections', AN BB18/1785.
[275] Prefect Loire-Inf. telegram 6.20 p.m., 8 June 1869, re Nantes, in Holt, *Papiers sauvés*, p. 225.
[276] Aminzade, *Ballots*, pp. 132–3.

support him.[277] Nonetheless, probably around 100,000 people attended the funeral, including most of the future leaders of the Paris Commune. The efforts of Flourens and other Blanquists to lead a march into the centre of Paris had little effect, although during the following night there were repeated clashes between police and demonstrators.[278] Rochefort's own arrest and trial on 7 February provoked further demonstrations in the capital and Marseille.[279] Rochefort was actually arrested at a public meeting. Theatrically, the response of Flourens, its president, was to brandish a revolver, wave a sword, and declare 'the government deposed and the revolution in permanence', before leading a group of about sixty people to Belleville. There they constructed a barricade in an attempt to stimulate an uprising, before melting away as the police arrived. In the rue Saint-Maur an omnibus was turned over to block the street. Most republicans were determined to disassociate themselves from these incidents. *Le Rappel* put the blame on ruffians employed by the Prefecture of Police. Benoît Malon and other worker militants signed a manifesto warning against impatience and the danger of provoking the authorities into repressive measures.[280]

The renewed campaign of repression inaugurated by the authorities in 1869/70 again had a demobilising effect on some parts of the republican movement, although it does need to be borne in mind that it was far less intense than that of the 1850s. The secrétaire-général of the Lyons police indeed complained that the changed circumstances meant that there were insufficient police to cope with the growing number of meetings, newspapers, and strikes.[281] The authorities also appreciated the potential value of extremist speeches and articles in the meetings and press. A civil servant, Auguste Vitu, was instructed to publish selected examples in a book, which was distributed to every commune with the object, according to Rouher, of 'allowing liberty to completely discredit itself, through the use made of it'.[282] Widespread social fear would have a substantial impact on the plebiscite results in May 1870, as well as reinforcing the divisions between the more moderate, legalistic republicans and those willing to contemplate violence.[283]

---

[277] OC compagnie de la Seine, 28 Jan. 1870, AHG G8/176; R. Williams, *Manners and Murders in the World of Louis-Napoleon* (Seattle 1975), pp. 127f.
[278] Girard, *Nouvelle histoire*, p. 405.
[279] OC compagnie de la Seine, 26 Feb. 1870, AHG G8/176; Constant, *Var*, p. 1368.
[280] Jacquemet, *Belleville*, p. 527; Dalotel *et al.*, *Aux origines*, pp. 346–9.
[281] 21 June 1870 in *Pièces saisies*.   [282] Ollivier, *L'Empire libéral*, XI, p. 127.
[283] E.g. Girard, *Nouvelle histoire*, pp. 486–7.

THE PLEBISCITE OF MAY 1870

The results of the plebiscite appeared to confirm the worst fears of republicans. The ballot was preceded by a hard-fought campaign in which the irreconcilable opponents of the regime opposed the defenders of social order and of the 'progress' made during the Empire. The former were mainly republicans, together with some Legitimists and liberals hostile to the regime's retention of the 'anti-parliamentary' practice of holding referenda.[284] The plebiscite question was worded carefully in order to maximise support. 'The liberal reforms introduced into the constitution since 1860' were approved by 7,300,000 to 1,600,000. There were 1,900,000 abstentions. Only the departments of the Seine and Bouches-du-Rhône provided a 'No' majority. The Parisian vote – 184,000 *non* and 138,000 *oui*–was much less hostile to the regime than the 1869 election results, as middle-class voters, disturbed by the extremism of the public meetings and by disorder in the streets, opted for the liberal Empire.[285] Overall, 59 per cent of Parisian voters submitted *non* ballots but with the proportion rising to 72 to 77 per cent in the working-class strongholds of Montmartre, La Chapelle, La Villette, Belleville, and Ménilmontant and 57 to 71 per cent in the suburbs of the left bank and the old revolutionary faubourgs of the right.[286] Once again, opposition would be urban rather than rural. In Haute-Vienne, 49 per cent of the voters in industrial Limoges rejected the government's proposals; in smaller manufacturing centres the proportion was 26.3 per cent; and in rural communes a minute 2.7 per cent. Similarly, in the rural communes of the Corrèze and Creuse the 'no' votes represented only 1.1 per cent and 3.9 per cent of those cast.[287] The national average of 17.6 per cent represented a loss of half the votes gained by the opposition the previous year. In comparison with the results of the 1852 plebiscite on the establishment of the Empire, support for the regime had grown in the west, remained at least stable in the north and north-east, stagnated in the south and much of the centre and south-west, and declined only in Paris and the east. The particular weakness of the regime's position was the hostility of substantial portions of the populations of the major cities.[288]

Even before the plebiscite there had been signs that republicans were divided over their response to the Liberal Empire. Jules Favre had conceded in the Corps législatif on 22 February that 'it is perfectly correct to

[284] Tollu, 'Démocratie et liberté', pp. 148–9; Ménager, *Nord*, II, p. 876.
[285] Wolfe, *Origins*, pp. 76–7; Dalotel *et al., Aux origines*, pp. 302–3.
[286] Girard, *Nouvelle histoire*, pp. 486–7.   [287] Corbin, *Archaïsme*, II, pp. 905–6.
[288] Ménager, *Napoléons*, pp. 222–57.

make use of the phrase *new regime*: the advent of the existing cabinet is not a change of personnel but a change of system; it involves the substitution of one political ideal for another. The parliamentary regime, that is to say government ... by an assembly is a considerable fact which I am far from wishing to diminish.'[289] At Toulon, a group of well-known local republicans had gone further and announced that in spite of its imperfections the new constitution 'promises sufficient liberty ... assures a serious control over the acts of the Government, and finally renders universal suffrage master of itself'.[290] However, more representative of republican opinion was the declaration of the Comité radical d'Alès published in *La Liberté de l'Hérault* on 4 May which warned that 'the December government, outdated, worn out, at the end of its resources, is making a last effort to retain the power which it, 18 years ago, snatched from the sovereign people'.[291] Republicans stressed the illegitimacy of the regime and thus of its plebiscite. There could be no compromise given 'the crime of its origin'.[292] Speaking at the Folies-Bergère in Paris, M. Guyot made the point more dramatically, challenging his audience: 'if you accept that a man can take a nation by theft, by means of an assassination in the night, just like a brigand stops and pillages a coach on the highway, then vote Yes. If not vote No.'[293] Jules Grévy was hardly more restrained. In an open letter to his constituents in the Jura he insisted that 'France remains bowed down under the hand of a man, and in the future, the *coup d'état* will remain suspended like a sword above its head ... The Empire is despotism behind the mask of democracy.'[294]

Speakers in the public meetings in Paris were divided on how to vote. Those from the 'popular' classes and particularly 'socialists' appear to have favoured abstention or else spoiling their ballot papers by writing on them such slogans as *Vive la République démocratique et sociale* or *Vive la Constitution de '93*. They frequently quoted Rochefort to the effect that a 'yes' vote meant supporting the regime but a 'no' vote meant supporting an equally reactionary *République bourgeoise*. The joint manifesto of the Parisian sections of the International and the Chambre fédérale des sociétés ouvrières declared *insensé* anyone who could believe that the new constitution would lead to social reform and reminded workers of the massacres of strikers along with their women and children at Aubin

---

[289] Quoted Tollu, 'Démocratie et liberté', p. 141.   [290] Quoted Constant, *Var*, pp. 1389–90.
[291] Quoted Huard, *La préhistoire des partis*, p. 821; see also PG Montpellier, 22 Jan. 1870, AN BB30/390.
[292] G. Chaudey, *L'Empire parlementaire est-il possible?* (Paris: Le Chevalier 1870), p. 70.
[293] Quoted Delotel *et al.*, *Aux origines*, p. 186.
[294] Quoted P. Jeanbrun, *Jules Grévy* (Paris 1991), p. 125.

and Ricamarie.[295] The Rouen Fédération ouvrière also recommended returning blank ballot papers, insisting that 'we are completely indifferent to the subject posed because it is deprived of all economic interest, because it contains ... no proposals likely to prove to the masses that their interests occupy a place in the Edifice of government'. The new constitution, like that of 1852, 'leaves to a single man or to the privileged class the direction of affairs which ought to belong to the people who work for ALL'.[296] The injunction to abstain appears to have been ignored by most workers. In both Paris and the provinces they preferred to express their opposition to the regime with a negative vote.

The opposition, especially republican, was even better organised than it had been the previous year.[297] A Parisian committee headed by Favre, Picard, and Gambetta prepared a 'Manifesto of the left and the democratic press', whilst Delescluze and *Le Réveil* organised a more radical Comité central antiplébiscitaire, made up of journalists, representatives of election committees which had continued to meet, and workers nominated by public meetings and sections of the International. Gambetta and Delescluze were both, however, along with such moderate republicans as Garnier-Pagès and Dorian, co-signatories of a *Manifeste de la Gauche* published on 20 April, which insisted that 'personal government is not destroyed, it conserves intact its most redoubtable prerogatives', and warned that by means of the plebiscite the Emperor was demanding again 'a free hand' and 'the alienation of your sovereignty'. Only a 'no' vote would secure the sovereignty of the people and promote the reconciliation of the classes 'in the name of order and social peace'.[298] An appeal to the army called on soldiers, tired of serving as the 'ramparts' of the regime and of suffering in 'impious or sterile wars', to support the campaign.[299] Paris remained extremely agitated, with large crowds attending anti-plebiscite meetings – 3,000 at the Folies-Bergère on 29 April, 4,000 in Puteaux on 1 May. Even so, the situation was less tense than in the autumn, as a result of the arrest or exile of many militants.[300]

---

[295] *Manifeste antiplébiscitaire des sections parisiennes fédérées de l'Internationale et de la Chambre fédérale des sociétés ouvrières* (Paris 1870).

[296] Quoted Boivin, *Mouvement ouvrier*, II, p. 248.

[297] E.g. PG Bourges, 4 July 1870, AN BB30/390; Huard, *Naissance du parti politique*, p. 132.

[298] *Manifeste de la Gauche 20 avril 1870* (Paris 1870), signed by Arago, Bancel, Crémieux, Dorian, Esquiros, Ferry, Gambetta, Garnier-Pagès, Pelletan, Simon, etc., as well as delegates of *la presse démocratique*, including Delescluze.

[299] *Le Comité des députés de la Gauche et des délégues de la presse démocratique A L'ARMÉE* (Paris 1870), signed by Gambetta and Delescluze.

[300] Jacquemet, *Belleville*, p. 527; Dalotel *et al.*, *Aux origines*, p. 126.

In the industrial Nord, the anti-plebiscite committees formed at Lille, Douai, Cambrai, and Valenciennes organised a large number of public meetings. Even in Lille, however, they would only attract 51 per cent of the votes cast.[301] In Rouen, moderate and 'radical' republicans managed to establish a joint Comité antiplébiscitaire which organised two public meetings attended by 4,000 to 5,000 people at the beginning of May. The moderate republican deputy Desseaux warned his audience that the regime's objectives were to 'wash away the original sin of 1851: to consolidate the hereditary power of the Bonaparte family; to re-affirm the personal power'.[302] In Alsace most of the Protestant manufacturing elite declared their support for the anti-plebiscite cause. The democratic manifesto was published in the newspapers they subsidised on 24 April. The Colmar *Courrier du Haut Rhin* announced the formation at its offices of a Comité central antiplébiscitaire départemental and invited local committees to collaborate. It also printed in its margins six *non* ballots for its readers to use. The Mulhouse *Electeur Souverain*, written for a popular audience, appealed to the peasants to vote against the conscription of their sons and high taxes. It also felt it necessary to deny that urban workers were in favour of revolution. The campaign in the province was orderly, with only minor disorders, most notably at Ribeauvillé on 2 May, where factory workers demonstrated in front of the town hall shouting *Vive la République* and 'Shit for the Emperor' and beating up local policemen when they attempted to interfere.[303] In towns like Dijon the existence of a republican-dominated municipal council offered both verbal and practical support, including the provision of rooms for meetings.[304] In Toulouse the offices of *L'Emancipation* served as the meeting place for a committee made up of the newspaper's editors, delegates of 'workers' meetings' and the election committees established in 1869. It called for donations to the campaign fund and for local groups to request copies of an issue which reprinted a speech by Gambetta together with *non* ballot slips for distribution – and all for 10 centimes. *Le Progrès libéral* (5 May) warned against government efforts to frighten the rural population with rumours of revolutionary plots. *Le Jura. Journal démocratique de l'Est* (8 May) similarly offered advice on registration and voting procedures, together with copies of an 'Elementary Catechism for the use of the Voter' which

[301] Ménager, *Nord*, II, pp. 880, 890.   [302] Boivin, *Mouvement ouvrier*, I, p. 382.

[303] Strauss, 'Opinion publique et forces politiques en Alsace à la fin du second empire' in L'Huillier (ed.), *L'Alsace en 1870-71* (Strasbourg 1971), pp. 150–73.

[304] P. Crapo, 'Art and politics in the Côte-d'Or: Gustave Courbet's Dijon exhibition of May 1870', *French History*, 1995, p. 327.

pointed out that, whenever it wished, the government would be able to make use of the plebiscite to withdraw its liberal reforms. To reinforce this point, the *Reveil de l'Ouest* published the Emperor's oath of loyalty to the Republic in 1848. This was not a man who could be trusted.[305]

The manifesto of the Comité démocratique du Var was one of many seeking to disassociate the republican movement from revolution. It reminded voters that 'Universal suffrage will render you masters of your destinies. Know how to use it and you will arrive, without upheaval, without disorder, at that fraternal Republic, so desperately desired, which will unite all the peoples under the same banner, LIBERTY.'[306] This was accompanied by the usual promises to reduce the size of the army and taxes, found also in the manifesto directed at the rural population by a committee at Ussel in the Corrèze. This linked the victory of the 'no' vote to the establishment of the Republic and enjoined its readers to

'Vote *no* and you will see taxes fall, the army become pointless and disappear; your sons will have no other interests than those of honest work; no longer will a single man devour 38 millions annually; no longer will palaces be constructed to lodge prefects, sous-préfets and all the functionaries who only live off the coppers you have struggled to earn; no longer will they treat you with arrogance, they will become instead what they ought to be, your servants; the *coup d'état* will no longer be in permanence.[307]

The results of the plebiscite came as a considerable shock to those republicans, the majority, who had determined to work legally to transform and then replace the regime. They emphasised the gulf between urban and especially Parisian republicanism, and the willingness of most voters to accept the liberalised Empire. The regime had transformed itself. There appeared to be no prospect of the establishment of a republic in the foreseeable future. Gambetta confessed as much in telling a journalist that 'the Empire is stronger than ever', whilst a depressed Favre concluded that there was 'nothing more to do in politics'.[308] A poor showing in the departmental council elections in June seemed to confirm these pessimistic assumptions. Disappointment was expressed also by violent protest, with three nights of disorder in Paris, centred once again on the faubourg du Temple and which resulted in 'several' deaths and over 500 arrests.[309] Frightened by this response, Picard helped to form a 'constitu-

[305] Copies in AN BB30/455.
[306] Quoted Constant, 'Image du républicain varois à la fin du second empire' in Viard, *L'esprit républicain*, p. 285.
[307] Quoted Corbin, *Archaïsme*, II, p. 903.
[308] Quoted C. Seignebos, *La Révolution de 1848 – Le Second Empire* (Paris 1921), p. 94.
[309] OC compagnie la Seine, 28 May 1870, AHG G8/176.

tional left' in close association with liberals linked to Thiers and seemed quite likely to follow most of them and rally to the liberal Empire.[310] Similarly Gambetta appreciated the need to clearly disassociate himself from the 'reds'. He wrote to his friend Juliette Adam that 'we have no interest in seeing the Revolution triumph through an insurrection, which would have as its representatives Delescluze, Flourens...'[311] There was concern also that the regime would be sufficiently encouraged by the results to return to a more authoritarian politics.

The weaknesses of the republican movement had been highlighted. Certainly there had been progress in terms of organisation and support. The process of political 'modernisation' and the institutionalisation of conflict, beginning in 1848, had soon been interrupted. Following the 'perversion' of popular sovereignty by the 'political system of Napoleon III', it had been resumed during the 1860s. Elections had encouraged a polarisation – for or against the republic. Republicanism remained strong amongst the professional classes, the lower middle class, artisans and workers and particularly in the major cities and industrial centres. It was relatively weak amongst the propertied classes, in the countryside, and wherever the clergy were influential. Moreover republicans remained divided, often bitterly, over both ends and means. It is difficult to dispute the conclusion of Georges Weill's classic *Histoire du parti républicain* that 'the divisions amongst republicans had never been as strong as at the end of the Empire'.

---

[310] Girard, *Les libéraux français*, p. 211.   [311] Quoted Constant, *Var*, p. 1419.

Conclusion to Part III

Prior to the 1869 election, the state prosecutor at Toulouse typically complained that government supporters were 'irresolute, divided and profoundly alarmed: its enemies have never been so confident and so assured of their coming success'. He added plaintively that 'things cannot continue this way ... but what is to be done?'[1] His colleague at Aix warned that, however firm peasant support might appear to be, it was impossible 'to ignore the wishes of the enlightened part of the nation ... the lever with which one takes action'.[2] There was a real danger that the electorate would emancipate itself from official control. Not all reports were as blunt, but most shared this essential pessimism. The results of the election appeared to confirm the urgent need to make concessions to liberal opinion, to reconstruct a conservative alliance, and to isolate the irreconcilable republicans.[3]

For liberals, particularly those of the younger generation influenced by American and British constitutional theories and lacking any personal ties to the Orleanist princes, what mattered was the restoration of the political influence of the social elites. This might be achieved by means of the Emperor's recognition of the 'necessary liberties' defined by Thiers in 1864. An alliance with the moderate republicans around the notion of 'the best of republics' was the only alternative.[4] The reform of existing institutions remained, however, the preferred, and certainly the least disruptive, option.[5] The liberal Bonapartist Chesnelong, deputy from the Basses-Pyrénées, declared that 'in spite of its faults, the Empire is still the pivot of order in France and in Europe. We need to know how to maintain it in resisting it, in developing within it if possible, and I believe it to be possible, the spirit of purified conservatism represented

---

[1] 8 Jan. 1869, AN BB30/389.   [2] 11 April 1869, AN BB30/389.
[3] E.g. PG Colmar, 18 Jan. 1870, AN BB30/390.
[4] E.g. PG Rouen, 12 Jan. 1867, AN BB30/387.
[5] E.g. L. Prévost-Paradol, *La France nouvelle* (Paris 1868), p. 133.

by a sincere and prudent liberalism.'[6] These were the views expressed in the *interpellation* signed by 116 deputies in July 1869 which called on the government to 'give satisfaction to the sentiments of the country, in associating it in a more effective manner in the direction of affairs' and for the formation of a government responsible to both the Emperor and the Corps législatif.

The Liberal Empire was a concession, not to republicans, but to socially conservative liberals. It represented a concession to the social vision of the *grande bourgeoisie* and would be marked by the rallying of such previously irreconcilable figures as Prévost-Paradol, who accepted the Washington embassy, as well as by Guizot and Odilon Barrot, who agreed to preside over extra-parliamentary commissions of enquiry into administrative decentralisation and the reform of higher education. They would not have accepted ministerial office but had concluded that the Emperor deserved the support and encouragement necessary to take the last few steps.[7] Nevertheless, the constitutional changes emerging from the *sénatus-consulte* of 8 September 1869 failed to satisfy liberals entirely. The powers of the Corps législatif were certainly to be increased substantially. It would gain the right to initiate legislation, previously reserved to the Emperor. Budgetary controls were to be reinforced and the approval of deputies required on such contentious matters as customs treaties. The impact of this last concession was reinforced by the announcement of an enquiry, which it was assumed widely would lead to the re-establishment of tariff protection.[8] In theory, ministers would remain responsible to the Emperor alone, but in future the assembly's approval would be essential to the functioning of government. The Emperor explicitly conceded this in his invitation to Ollivier on 28 December: 'I request you to designate the individuals who might form with you a homogeneous cabinet, faithfully representing the majority in the Corps législatif.'[9] Napoleon, however, retained considerable executive power including control over the bureaucracy and military and the right to declare war. Administrative centralisation remained a powerful tool in the Emperor's hands.[10] Considerable concern was caused by article 13 of the new constitution, which provided for the plebiscites by means of which, if he chose, the Emperor could appeal directly to the people without consulting his

[6] Quoted Girard, *Questions politiques*, p. 108.
[7] Evidence of Thiers in Assemblée nationale, *Enquête parlementaire*, V, p. 2.
[8] E.g. PG Amiens, 6 April 1870, AN BB30/390.   [9] Rougerie, 'Second Empire', p. 103.
[10] Ménager, 'Le bonapartisme pouvait-il être parlementaire?' in J. Tulard (ed.), *Pourquoi réhabiliter le second empire?* (Paris 1997), pp. 126–7.

parliament: 'The Emperor is responsible to the French people to whom he always has the right of appeal.' Ministerial resignations on this issue reflected continued doubt concerning the Emperor's willingness to accept the role of a constitutional monarch fuelled by his known determination to defend the *bases fondamentales* of his regime.[11] On the other hand, there was considerable sympathy for the approach to government signalled by Napoleon on 29 November in a speech at the opening of the parliamentary session – 'France wants liberty with order; I answer for Order; help me, gentlemen, to save liberty.'[12] As in 1848, most liberals were coming to assume that the main threat to both order and liberty came from the left.

Some republicans were also willing to consider a compromise. The majority of moderates remained committed to legal opposition, encouraged, according to Jules Favre, speaking in a debate in February 1870, by the establishment of a 'new regime', a 'parliamentary regime'. Significantly the debate was followed by a vote of confidence in the Ollivier government supported by 232 deputies and opposed by only 18.[13] However, there was still considerable uncertainty about the future. A report from Toulouse noted that 'in the upper classes the ministry has more numerous supporters than the dynasty'.[14] Ollivier himself had been anxious about the likely strength of support for his ministry amongst liberal deputies and would hardly have been re-assured when, asked to make soundings, Darimon reported that 'at the moment when the government decided to abdicate in favour of the majority, it found itself without a majority'.[15]

Nevertheless, the plebiscite results suggested a widespread rallying to the Liberal Empire. Most liberals with monarchist sympathies, as well as a significant minority of moderate republicans, found it impossible to reject the reforms. The Emperor's proclamation on 23 April promised that a positive vote would not only sanction the reforms introduced since 1860 but 'banish the threat of revolution', and establish 'order and liberty on a solid base'. He sought to eliminate another common cause for concern by pointing out that a parliamentary system would make easier 'the transmission of the crown to my son'.[16] The official plebiscite campaign appealed to the social fear created by a carefully manipulated 'red' scare. Maximum publicity was given in the conservative press and through

[11] W. Smith, 'La constitution de 1870 et la crise Hohenzollern' in Troisier de Diaz, *Ollivier*, p. 209.
[12] Quoted Girard, *Empire libéral*, p. 35.   [13] Tollu, 'Démocratie et liberté,' pp. 141–2.
[14] PG Toulouse, 7 April 1870, AN BB30/390.
[15] Darimon, *Les cent seize*, p. 153, entry 31 Oct. 1869.   [16] Girard, *Questions politiques*, p. 133.

official action, to the extremist speeches made in Parisian meetings.[17] The prosecution of radical and socialist newspapers was postponed, on the assumption that 'the excesses of the press are more profitable than dangerous to the government'.[18] The semi-official manifesto emanating from the committee chaired by the Duc d'Albufera warned against the machinations of a 'decidedly irreconcilable minority' willing to resort to 'any means, any weapon: abuse, calumny, riots, clubs, plots, assassination, *bombes infernales*'.[19] Comparisons were drawn in the press with the pre-revolutionary situation in 1847.[20] A major political re-alignment was under way, a process of polarisation described by the state prosecutor at Bordeaux who drew the obvious analogy with the situation in 1849/51, 'when all shades of the conservative party became one, to form what was then called the great Party of Order'.[21] For most liberals, 'liberty' depended both on the curbing of the personal power of the Emperor and on the preservation of order.[22] 'Mutual concessions' appeared necessary between *les classes intelligentes* and the government, in the interests of *conservation sociale*. Once again, liberal monarchists appreciated that 'the Napoleonic Dynasty alone is capable of holding aloft the Banner of Monarchy' and of protecting them from the 'urban proletariat'.[23] Catholic critics of the regime similarly rallied, re-assured by the reinforcement of their parliamentary influence, and once again willing to associate the Emperor with the Pope as the primary defenders of moral order. The virulent anticlericalism of the public meetings suggested that Christian civilisation was again menaced.[24]

Certainly, government officials welcomed this 'rapprochement' between 'conservatives of diverse nuances', of the 'immense majority' who accepted the consolidation of the regime around liberal institutions as the only alternative to 'a social revolution'.[25] With strikes, and repeated disorders in the capital, widespread agitation seemed to prove the existence of an internal *armée révolutionnaire*, whilst the Workers' International represented the universal threat of revolution.[26] The influential journalist Gustave de Molinari warned in the *Journal des Economistes* that illusions about the masses were no longer possible – 'of every ten workers interested in more besides eating and drinking, nine are socialists'.[27]

---

[17] Vitu, *Réunions publiques*, p. 96; *Réunions électorales*, p. 158.
[18] PG Nancy, 20 Jan. 1870, AN BB30/390.   [19] Quoted Malon, *Jules Le Cesne*, p. 91.
[20] E.g. Ménager, *Nord*, II, p. 790.   [21] 8 April 1870, AN BB30/390.
[22] E.g. PG Aix, 24 Jan. 1870, AN BB30/390; Garrigues, *République des hommes d'affaires*, pp. 37–8.
[23] PG Dijon, 14 Jan. 1870, AN BB30/390.   [24] PG Amiens, 6 April 1870, AN BB30/390.
[25] PG Aix, 22 Jan. 1870; PG Bordeaux, 8 April 1870, AN BB30/390.
[26] E.g. PG Lyon, 9 July 1870, AN BB30/390.   [27] Quoted Jeloubovskaïa, *La chute*, p. 21.

As economic change and urbanisation created a larger and apparently more aggressive working class, liberals and all those who wanted stability looked to the government for protection. This was certainly the case in Paris where the 'honest classes,' whilst welcoming the implementation of liberal reforms, evinced a growing 'disgust' for the elements of disorder.[28] At nearby Melun a liberal committee pressed for a 'yes' vote on the grounds that 'a negative vote or abstention would lead us into the unknown, that is to say, fatally, inevitably, to revolution or reaction. We want neither one nor the other.' A 'yes' vote would guarantee order and liberty and prevent a return to the misery of 1848.[29]

In the provinces there was a growing resentment of Paris and its politics, and a diffuse fear of social revolution, which partly explains both the vogue for decentralisation and the ferocity of the repression of the Paris Commune in 1871. In Rouen, liberal and moderate republican opposition was reported to have been considerably weakened by 'the angry tone of the radical press and the terroristic socialism preached in the public meetings in Paris.'[30] The Legitimist *Journal de Loir-et-Cher* (29 April) insisted that the constitutional question 'of more or less institutional liberty does not present itself with as much clarity to most minds as the choice between the Empire, with its reforms, and the revolution and republic, these two terms are identical, since the one is impossible ... without the other'.[31] The liberal *La Constitution*, published in the Yonne, similarly declared that 'the vote in 1870 is not one in favour of the Empire ... but simply a vote against revolution ... which the country does not want at any price'.[32] On 19 May, welcoming the results of the plebiscite, the Emperor himself insisted that the real issue had not been constitutional reform but a choice 'between revolution and the Empire'.[33]

Political polarisation had left the republicans as virtually the only 'serious adversaries' of the regime.[34] Writing in the *Indépendant du Tarn* on 2 June, B. Lavergne attempted to explain their recent defeat. If support for the republican cause had held up in the towns and amongst workers, 'fear of socialism drives the liberal *bourgeoisie* away from us'. Amongst the rural

---

[28] Bull. politique du chef de Ier Légion de gendarmerie, 31 Jan. and 28 Feb. 1870, AHG G8/176; also OC compagnie de la Seine, 28 April 1870, AHG G8/176.

[29] *Aux électeurs* – signed by members of a committee of local notables. Similar manifesto to the 'Electeurs du 6e arrond. de Paris' signed by E. de Royer and a long list of notables; see also that from a 'Comité de la Ligue de l'Ordre'.

[30] PG Rouen, 12 April 1869, AN BB30/389.   [31] Quoted Dupeux, *Aspects*, p. 400.

[32] Quoted L. Strauss, 'Opinion publique, et forces politiques en Alsace à la fin du Second Empire. Le plébiscite du 8 mai 1870 dans le Haut-Rhin' in F. L'Huillier, *L'Alsace en 1870–71* (Gap 1971), p. 46.

[33] Girard, *Questions politiques*, p. 135.   [34] PG Limoges, 14 July 1869, AN BB30/389.

population, prosperity and the peasants' belief that the regime protected
them against the restoration of the *ancien régime*, together with their hostility towards an urban bourgeoisie, which they believed exploited them,
ensured that they remained overwhelmingly loyal to 'their Emperor', the
elect of December 1848.[35] Even if their decision was not based on a detailed and informed analysis of the new constitution, nevertheless it could
be seen as representing a rational choice, rather than, as Republicans
so often claimed, resulting from ignorance and intimidation. Whatever
the cause, republicans were disheartened. In an article in the *Courrier
du Haut-Rhin*, A. Maudit explained their poor showing as the result of
their own internal divisions and lack of 'credibility'. France lacked 'a
strongly constituted democratic party ... sufficiently rich in capable men,
providing ... the elements of a government ready to function, in favour
of which the country – which above all takes account of the conditions
of security which allow it to live – might be able to decide to reject ...
the existing government'. Gaining public confidence would require a
considerable effort over a long period.[36] Instead there was every prospect
of further divisions emerging between a group led by Gambetta, Grévy,
and Glais-Bizoin, editor of *La Tribune* – a 'closed left' which would
remain irreconcilable; and an 'open left' led by Picard, which through
its newspaper *L'Electeur libre* invited the support of all those in favour of
further democratic reform of the regime.[37] The apparently successful
renewal of the Empire encouraged a renewed process of *ralliement*.[38]

As late as the early summer of 1870 there thus appeared to be no
real threat to the survival of the regime. The establishment of a Liberal Empire, with a strong executive power held in check by rejuvenated
parliamentary institutions, seemed to herald a long period of political
stability during which the regime's founder, the rapidly ageing Emperor,
would undoubtedly be replaced by his young son. Even this prospect
was now regarded by officials with equanimity. The administrative–
military plans for such an eventuality had long been prepared.[39] The
'notables' who largely provided the nation's political personnel had been
re-assured; their right to a share in political power commensurate with
their wealth and status had been recognised. At the same time the popular support necessary to legitimise the regime had survived. The Empire
appeared to have weathered the storm which had threatened its existence

---

35 Ménager, 'La vie politique,' p. 722; Armengaud, *Est-Aquitain*, pp. 442–3.
36 Quoted Strauss, 'Opinion publique', p. 182.   37 Tulard, *Dictionnaire*, p. 554.
38 E.g. PG Besançon, 8 July 1870, AN BB30/390.
39 MI *très-confidentielle* circulars 6 June 1859, 26 Sept 1861, in *Pièces saisies*.

and, almost uniquely, to have achieved the very difficult transition from its authoritarian origins to institutional stability. As Darimon, the former republican, reported enthusiastically in his diary: 'these events have no analogy in our history ... This is a reign which has transformed itself to form a barrier to the threat of revolution.'[40] It even appeared that the prospect of war, so frequently predicted after the Prussian defeat of the Austrians at Sadowa in 1866, had receded. Indeed, one of the earliest measures of the Ollivier government, was the decision to reduce the 1870 contingent of conscripts by 10,000.[41] However, there was still one danger. Ludovic Halévy, the librettist, who thanks to Morny had been appointed secretary to the Corps législatif and was responsible for preparing its minutes, perceptively wrote in his notebook: 'Too many Yes votes. The Emperor will believe that this is still the France of 1852 and do something stupid.'[42] It would be defeat in war, and not political opposition, which would destroy the Second Empire.

[40] Darimon, *Les cent seize*, p. 221, entry of 29 Dec. 1869.
[41] On public reaction see e.g. OC gendarmerie de la Seine, 28 April 1870, AHG G8/176.
[42] Quoted Girard, *Questions politiques*, p. 138.

PART IV

War and revolution

CHAPTER 13

War and revolution

In July 1870 France again went to war. Defeat led to the collapse of the regime. The report of the subsequent commission of enquiry began the construction of a myth, which blamed the disaster entirely on the Emperor and a small number of generals. Napoleon, Marshal Bazaine, and the military intendancy were the most convenient scapegoats. The official history of the war, which followed, obeyed ministerial instructions to present only such facts as enhanced the army's reputation. Napoleon III, so despised by republicans as 'the man of 2 December', had now achieved infamy as 'the man of Sedan.'[1] The purpose of this chapter might be defined, reversing the order of Marx's words, as to 'demonstrate how the *class struggle* in France created circumstances and relationships that made it possible for a *hero* to play a *grotesque mediocrity's* part'.[2] Rather than apportioning blame, however, the historian's task is to achieve understanding. The questions seem clear enough. What were the regime's foreign policy objectives? To what extent were they achieved and with what consequences both for France and international relations? What were the inter-relationships between internal and external politics? Given a predilection for high-risk strategies, which had already led to war on two occasions, how well prepared was the French army? Why was the decision to go to war taken in 1870? Why were the French defeated and why did the regime collapse?

FOREIGN POLICY

In a famous speech at Bordeaux on 9 October 1852 Napoleon had sought to re-assure both his compatriots and the European powers by insisting that 'The Empire means peace.' Subsequently, in a memoir

[1] Assemblée nationale, *Enquête parlementaire*; Holmes, *The Road to Sedan* (London 1984), p. 2; Agulhon, 'Les républicains dans la guerre de 1870–1' in Tulard (ed.), *Pourquoi réhabiliter?*, p. 18.
[2] Cf. *Marx–Engels Selected Works*, p. 244.

dated 22 January 1859 and addressed to Comte Walewski, the current
Foreign Minister and illegitimate son of Napoleon I, he would maintain
that 'No-one has been able to appreciate that in using these words the
Emperor did not commit himself to never going to war ... The real
meaning of the speech then is this: I will only go to war when forced to
defend the national honour and to achieve a great and lofty objective
determined by the genuine interests of the country.' He proceeded to
weigh up the possibilities of internal and international opposition to
the projected war against Austria and concluded that the risks were
small, particularly if public opinion was prepared carefully. Referring
to his uncle's commentaries on Julius Caesar he pointed out that in the
aftermath of revolution an external war was 'necessary ... to amalgamate
the remains of all the parties'.[3] Military greatness and martial display
were essential features of Bonapartism. Napoleon's particular objectives
appear to have been to 'restore France to its proper rank' as the pre-
eminent European power, by destroying the 1815 peace treaties and
securing the natural frontiers on the Alps and Rhine, and to ensure the
pacification of Europe by means of its reconstruction on the basis of
its major nationalities. These should be assembled in loose (con)-federal
structures, too weak to challenge French predominance, rather than as
unitary states. The regenerated continent would be given a greater sense
of mutual dependence through the encouragement of free trade.[4] There
was an additional element of pragmatism in his recognition that 'the
nationalities do not define themselves solely in terms of language and
race: they depend especially on the configuration and conformity of ideas
born of common interests and a shared history'. From this it followed
that 'German nationality, no more than French would not include all
those speaking the same language. Alsace is French although German
by race.'[5]

Napoleon's vision of the unrealised greatness of France was a widely
shared feature of the general political culture, reinforced in his case of
course by his Bonapartist inheritance. His sense of destiny inspired him
to develop personal foreign policy objectives, often employing secret
diplomacy.[6] The foreign ministers he appointed were mainly dependent
career diplomats, frequently replaced. Thouvenel made clear both his
frustration and the dangers inherent in this process, in asking: 'What

---

[3] T. Edelston, *Napoleon III. Speeches from the Throne* (Paris 1931), pp. 161–6.
[4] 'Discours à l'ouverture de la session législative', 7 Feb. 1859 – *ibid.*, p. 167.
[5] Letter to Ollivier, 7 Nov. 1867 in Ollivier, *L'Empire libéral*, XII, pp. 146–7.
[6] Schnerb, *Rouher*, p. 177.

am I doing here? I am ignorant of the Emperor's political plans. I work in the dark, without objectives, without plans, advancing, retreating, playing a double game which is never explained.'[7] Drouyn de Lhuys, twice foreign minister, complained to the Austrian diplomat Hübner that 'the Emperor has immense desires and limited abilities. He wants to do extraordinary things but is only capable of extravagances.'[8] Together with Morny he pressed for alliances with the conservative powers, and especially Austria, as the most effective means of securing peace and economic prosperity.[9] However, although there were substantial continuities with the policies pursued by previous regimes, the Emperor preferred to adopt the more adventurous options favoured by many republicans. Whilst it seems clear that he would have preferred to solve disputes through the workings of an international congress system rather than by recourse to war, he was clearly prepared to contemplate resorting to force.[10]

With British support, the objective of the Crimean War (1854–6) was to destroy the 1815 peace settlement and to restore French pre-eminence at the expense of Russia. At first the war was not particularly popular, except amongst those democrats who welcomed a campaign against the most reactionary power in Europe and, at the other political extreme, the Catholics who saw the war as a crusade against Orthodox heresy.[11] The news of military victory and the returning army, as it paraded through the capital, was received with enthusiasm, nevertheless. The proclamation of 3 May 1859, which sought to justify military intervention in Italy against Austria, subsequently revealed many of the contradictions of Imperial policy. The Emperor declared that

France has proved its hatred of anarchy. It has given me sufficient power to reduce the fomenters of disorder and the incorrigible representatives of the old parties, those who ceaselessly treat with our enemies, to impotence. But it has not abdicated its civilising role. Its natural allies have always been those who desire the improvement of humanity. When it draws it sword, it is not to dominate, but to free ... The objective of this war then is to give Italy back to itself, and not to make it change master. As a result we will have, on our frontier, a people, which owes its independence to us.

---

[7] Quoted A. Wahl, *Les françaises et la France* (Paris 1986), p. 6.

[8] Count Hübner, *Neuf ans de souvenirs*, II (Paris 1905), p. 146

[9] L. Case, *French Opinion on War and Diplomacy during the Second Empire* (Philadelphia 1954), p. 234.

[10] W. Echard, *Napoleon III and the Concert of Europe* (London 1983), pp. 31–2.

[11] R. Marlin, 'L'opinion franc-comtoise devant la guerre de Crimée', *Annales littéraires de l'Université de Besançon* (1957), pp. 18, 24–5.

In an effort to re-assure Catholics, he added: 'we are not going to Italy to cause disorder, nor to threaten the power of the Holy Father whom we restored to his throne, but to remove the foreign pressure which imposes itself throughout the peninsula'.[12] The British ambassador, Lord Cowley, reported that Walewski had told him that the Emperor 'in reality did not care one farthing for His Holiness, but he is afraid of offending the French clergy and thereby weakening his own position at home'.[13] However, a policy of liberation which insisted upon the defence of the reactionary Papal States was likely to offend many Italian nationalists as well as the more democratic liberals and republicans in France and without conciliating the Catholic elites. It was bound to arouse suspicion and alarm amongst the other European powers. Napoleon had hoped to exclude the Austrians from Italy, and to create a situation with some similarities to that which had prevailed during the first Empire, with Piedmont as the kingdom of upper Italy, together with an enlarged Tuscany, to add to the Papal States in central Italy and the Bourbon kingdom of Naples in the south.[14] He had certainly not planned to assist in the creation of a powerful unitary kingdom as a neighbour. Garibaldi's invasion of the kingdom of Naples would transform the situation, however. This outcome should have served as a warning about the unexpected consequences of an adventurous foreign policy.

Napoleon was always very concerned about the impact of foreign policy on public opinion. The government required frequent reports from officials and made efforts, through the press, to stimulate positive attitudes.[15] However, for most conservatives the guiding principle was stability. There was little support for the principle of the nationalities to which the Emperor claimed allegiance. According to Nassau William Senior, fellow guests at dinner in Guizot's residence, discussing the prospect of war, had little sympathy for the Italian cause. His soundings revealed that 'the only war that would be popular would be one with England ... a war to liberate the oppressed nationality of Ireland'.[16] As we have seen, war against Austria would prove to be a major stimulus to the emergence of liberal-conservative opposition. The liberal Catholic deputy Plichon condemned both the war and the decision-making process which had led to it as *intolérable*. As a result, 'questions of the greatest importance for the future ... of the country are discussed and settled in a way that does not involve the Corps législatif'. He had voted for war credits only

---

[12] Quoted Girard, *Questions politiques*, p. 29. [13] Quoted Case, *French Opinion*, p. 86.
[14] E.g. Rougerie, 'Second Empire', p. 85. [15] E.g. Marlin, 'Opinion', pp. 19–20.
[16] 27 April 1859, NLW C.260.

because French soldiers were already engaged in battle, but if given the opportunity certainly would have opposed the war. More generally, he condemned military adventures with inevitably uncertain outcomes, pointing out that 'it is not only the external security of the country which might be compromised, but also its internal peace. We cannot be revolutionary in Italy and remain conservative in France and Rome. We cannot arouse the revolutionary spirit in one place without reviving it in all the others.'[17] In contrast, Ollivier, like most republicans, was an enthusiastic supporter of the Italian cause and of the war against Austria, 'the most odious incarnation of temporal despotism'. However, he was also suspicious of the Emperor's motives, fearing that 'Italian independence is only a pretext ... Basically the Emperor is only concerned to strengthen his dynasty and silence the slowly emerging internal opposition.'[18] Typically, reports on a wider public opinion advised that the war would remain popular 'for as long as taxes are not increased and the cost of exoneration from military service remains the same, and for as long as trade and agriculture are not affected profoundly', and only for as long, it was stressed, as the population was free of 'heavy sacrifices'.[19]

In the following decade, probably nothing better symbolised the dangers of the Emperor's personal power and military adventurism than the disastrous Mexican expedition. Over-optimistic reports from Dubois de Saligny, the French representative in Mexico, had encouraged Napoleon in his dreams of creating a client state in the Americas.[20] Eventually 30,000 troops had to be committed, and to very little effect. Even amongst the Emperor's close associates there was an unwillingness to accept that any possible gains could outweigh the possible complications.[21] Italian affairs also continued to cause difficulties with conservatives, although a French garrison remained in Rome to protect the Papacy and assist in the re-organisation of the Papal army. In November 1867, the two forces combined at Mentana, to defeat Garibaldi's attack on the city. Nevertheless, in a major speech on 4 December, whilst insisting on the necessity of guaranteeing the Pope's temporal power, Thiers returned to the attack on the principle of the nationalities. He poured scorn on a policy which had created a united Italy and which threatened to unify Germany, and pose an even greater threat to French interests.

[17] Quoted Grothe, *Morny*, pp. 238–9.
[18] Letter to Emile Guiter, 15 Jan. 1859 in P. Guiral, 'Emile Ollivier et la politique extérieure' in Troisier de Diaz, *Ollivier*, p. 194.
[19] E.g. PG Paris, 9 Nov. 1859, AN BB30/384.   [20] Tulard, *Dictionnaire*, p. 59.
[21] E.g. letter Fould to Baroche, 19 Sept. 1862 in Maurain, *Baroche*, p. 302.

The government's spokesman in the Corps législatif, Rouher responded
with an apparently open-ended commitment to the Papacy in which he
promised that 'Italy will never gain possession of Rome, never! France
will never tolerate such a violent attack on its honour and on the Catholic
faith.'[22] He thus succeeded in destroying any latent Italian gratitude for
former French support and contributed to the country's growing diplomatic isolation. Napoleon reprimanded his minister severely, reminding
him that 'in politics one should never say: Never.'[23] In contrast, liberal and clerical deputies were delighted. The leading liberal Catholic
Montalembert wrote to congratulate Thiers on the success of his parliamentary tactics. The concession obtained from Rouher signified that
'parliamentary government has been re-established thanks to you. The
Pope has been ... saved by you and by the influence of parliamentary
debate and free discussion ... which Catholics so blindly and cowardly
renounced in 1852.'[24]

The main result of Napoleon's foreign policy and his determination to
re-make the map of Europe was to ensure growing international distrust
of French intentions and effective diplomatic isolation. The Crimean
War and subsequent expressions of sympathy for Polish independence
alienated Russia; the Italians resented French annexation of Nice and
Savoy as the price for support in 1859 and especially the obstacle to further progress to unity represented by the garrison in Rome; the Austrians,
defeated in 1859 and then even more humiliatingly by Prussia in 1866,
added the absence of French support against their northern enemy to
their existing list of grievances; British suspicion was aroused by the
Italian campaign and the Emperor's evident determination to turn the
Mediterranean into a French lake. When, following the Prussian victory
at Sadowa, and in an effort to defend the *status quo* and French security,
Napoleon proposed alliances to both Austria and Italy, it was probably
too late. Gramont, then ambassador in Vienna, was warned in 1867, by
the Austrian ministers Beust and Andrassy, not to expect Austrian support, although negotiations continued through the spring and summer of
1869 and July–August 1870. It seems unlikely that Franz-Joseph would
have been prepared to risk another war with Prussia and her German
allies unless they were already on the verge of defeat.[25]

Sadowa substantially upset the European balance of power. On the
advice of most military experts, Napoleon had expected a prolonged

[22] *Ibid.*, p. 394; Schnerb, *Rouher*, pp. 219–20.
[23] Quoted Maurain, *Politique ecclésiastique*, pp. 829–30.   [24] Quoted *ibid.*, p. 830.
[25] E.g. Assemblée nationale, *Enquête parlementaire*, v, p. 3, evidence of Thiers.

and indecisive war.[26] This would have created opportunities for French mediation whilst the threat of intervention might have restored the nation's international status and secured tangible territorial gains – the west bank of the Rhine and the frontiers of 1814 – as well as greater influence over the states of southern Germany. Later, the eminent military writer General Trochu would claim, as foreign minister Drouyn de Lhuys had advised, that France should have mobilised a *corps d'observation* on the German frontier.[27] This would have drawn Prussian forces away from the Austrian front and possibly altered the course of the war, and secured Austrian support in 1870.[28] According to another influential officer, General du Barail, it was the Emperor's hesitation which 'created Germany'.[29] That military intervention did not occur was due to Napoleon's belief that the army was not ready,[30] to the speed with which Austria was defeated, and to the numerous reports from the provinces insisting that public opinion was opposed to war.[31] For all these reasons, the Foreign Minister was instructed to insist upon the government's pacific intentions.[32] The Emperor had decided that it was essential to avoid posing a threat which might push the south German states into the arms of Prussia. He was determined to work towards closer ties with both these states and Austria.[33]

The clear emergence of Prussian dominance in Germany, based on considerable military strength, was perceived as a threat to the status and security of France. Napoleon's efforts to persuade the public that the development of greater unity in Italy and then Germany was part of his grand design carried little conviction.[34] Informed opinion reacted with alarm to the Emperor's unrealistic demand for compensation – in the form of Belgium or at least Luxembourg – for accepting the outcome of the Austro-Prussian War.[35] Bismarck's very public rejection of these proposals considerably added to the sense of humiliation.[36] Marshal Randon, the war minister, clearly irritated by the rejection of his advice in favour of military intervention, would subsequently affirm that 'it is we

[26] Schnerb, *Rouher*, pp. 185–6.   [27] *Mémoires du Maréchal Randon*, II (Paris 1877), p. 146.
[28] Assemblée nationale, *Enquête parlementaire*, V pp. 123–4.
[29] Barail, *Mes souvenirs* (Paris 1896), III, pp. 106–7.
[30] 'Note dictée à M.Pietri', n.d., AN 400 AP 67; Schnerb, *Rouher*, p. 194, re advice of Marshal Niel.
[31] E.g. Ménager, *Napoléons*, pp. 213–14.
[32] Emperor to Drouyn de Lhuys, 11 June 1866, AN 400 AP 42.
[33] 'Note dictée à M.Pietri', n.d., AN 400 AP 67.
[34] See circular from foreign minister La Valette to ambassadors in Wahl, *Les françaises*, p. 21.
[35] E.g. report of M. Magne to Emperor, 20 July 1866, in *Papiers et correspondance*, I, pp. 239–42.
[36] E.g. Schnerb, *Rouher*, pp. 189–90; Case, *French Opinion*, pp. 219–20.

who were beaten at Sadowa' and claim that he had prepared contingency plans for the mobilisation of 250,000 men in twenty days. Instead the result was 'Austria crushed and ... Prussia triumphant, mistress of Germany, France humiliated and seeing at its gates a formidable neighbour.'[37] Divisions amongst the Emperor's closest advisers would add to the burden of decision-making. The Empress, another advocate of action in 1866, blamed the outcome on Rouher's influence over her husband, bitterly informing the Austrian ambassador, Richard Metternich, that the minister 'is the cause of our moral decline', and adding that 'if we let him go on, [he] will have us dethroned'. The growing fragility of the Emperor's health increased her anxiety and her determination to safeguard the succession of her son by playing a more active political role.[38]

French perceptions of Prussia became increasingly negative. The slogan 'Revenge for Sadowa' was popular in some sections of the press.[39] The assumption that war was inevitable would become a major cause of economic stagnation. The belief that a successful war was necessary to end this uncertainty appears to have been widespread, particularly amongst committed Bonapartists.[40] Typically, whilst criticising the regime's policy and presenting himself as committed to peace, Thiers appears to have done his best to whip up this war fever.[41] From 1868, however, tension declined. The establishment of a government led by the Germanophile Ollivier would, briefly, make war seem even more unlikely.[42] On 30 June 1870, proposing a reduction in the size of the military contingent for 1870 Ollivier declared that 'the Government has no concerns, never has the preservation of peace been more assured'.[43] He repeated this message in response to a question from Favre on 6 July, adding that: 'Since you speak to us of Prussian Sadowa, I will reply that we have won a French Sadowa, the plebiscite.'[44]

MILITARY READINESS

Clearly the Prussian victory had rung alarm bells about the state of readiness of the French army. This needs to be considered in relation to four

---

[37] *Mémoires*, II, pp. 145–9, 169.   [38] Quoted Case, *French Opinion*, p. 218.

[39] Koch, 'Du printemps des peuples à la guerre franco-allemande' in Rütten, *La caricature*, p. 373.

[40] E.g. Paris Prefect of Police, 28 and 30 Sept. 1867, in *Papiers et correspondance*, II, pp. 271, 274; Igersheim, *Politique*, p. 641.

[41] Guiral, *Thiers*, pp. 329, 334–5 and 'Emile Ollivier et la politique extérieure,' pp. 196–7.

[42] E.g. OC cie de l'Oise, Feb. 1870, AHG G8/176; S. Audoin-Rouzeau, *1870. La France dans la guerre* (Paris 1989), p. 30.

[43] Assemblée nationale, *Enquête parlementaire*, V, p. 2, evidence of Ollivier.   [44] *Ibid.*, p. 473.

areas of activity – political, strategic, operational, and tactical.[45] At the political level, in many eyes, the army was the primary representative of the regime and the symbol of the nation's glorious past. It defended the nation against its external enemies. It was also the institution of the *coup d'état* and since 1848 had served as 'the rampart of society'.[46] The army was frequently on public display at ceremonies in the many garrison towns throughout the country. Although the Second Empire was far from being a military dictatorship and, indeed, many senior officers were sentimentally attached to the monarchist pretenders,[47] there can be no doubt about the army's growing loyalty to the regime or about its central institutional importance. Officers welcomed the restoration of social order, their careers benefited from the regime's wars, and their status was reinforced through parades, the distribution of decorations, and the Emperor's adoption of the traditional monarchical panoply of the military household. In public processions généraux de division symbolically assumed a place ahead of bishops, prefects, and procureur-généraux. Furthermore, these senior commanders were well rewarded through salaries and indemnities and, for those most in favour, by means of ennoblement and appointment to the senate.[48] The social origins, career ambitions, and professional disposition of members of the officer corps thus ensured – whatever their individual political sympathies – that they constituted a disciplined and conservative force, obedient to the government of the day, provided that it was itself committed to the defence of social order. The experience of 1848 had instilled in officers a deep suspicion of and often contempt for politicians. They had welcomed the re-establishment of strong government with an Emperor who had a considerable personal interest in the organisation and equipment of the army and in improving soldiers' conditions.[49] The Emperor's role in the Italian campaign furthermore showed how seriously he took his position as commander-in-chief.

To be effective, the army depended on the support of the political leadership and the wider political elite in order to secure an adequate share of manpower and financial resources. The definition of its objectives also depended closely on politicians although, of course, military assessments of potential threats and recommended responses played their

[45] A. Millett and W. M. Murray, 'The effectiveness of military organization' in A. Millett and W. M. Murray (eds.), *Military Effectiveness*, I (London 1988), p. 3.

[46] J. Delmas, A. Blanchard, G. Bodinier, *et al.*, *Histoire militaire de la France* (Paris 1992), II, p. 466.

[47] Serman, *Le corps des officiers*, pp. 1235, 1309.   [48] *Ibid.*, p. 1318.

[49] E.g. J. Vidalenc, 'Quelques remarques sur les rapports entre officiers et soldats dans l'armée française de la Révolution à 1914', *Revue internationale d'histoire militaire* (1955), p. 513.

part in the decision-making process. The shortcomings of the army thus reflected both its own failings and those of the regime it served. Military effectiveness also depends on the competence of an army's officers. Officer recruitment was the most democratic in Europe with, in February 1848, 69 per cent of officers on active service being former NCOs and only 31 per cent products of the military schools. By 1869 the latter had risen to 39 per cent.[50] This ceased to be the case for the higher ranks where patronage clearly mattered at least as much as the technical skills acquired through the military schools and experience of command. Wealth, family traditions of service, connections, and possession of the social graces necessary to mix in 'society' and circulate at official receptions all mattered. As a result, 39 per cent of généraux de division were, by origin, nobles and most of the remainder came from well-off families of local notables. Whilst only 25 per cent of captains had attended the military schools, this rose to 80 per cent of generals.[51] Their professional training was rather limited, however. The military schools, particularly Saint-Cyr, concentrated above all on the formation of character and knowledge of regulations rather than strategic studies. They produced conformists. The report of a commission of enquiry in 1860 revealed that students at Saint-Cyr took little interest in their studies and that 'the consequence of this state of affairs menaces the army in the future'. Its recommendations were ignored.[52] Significantly it was the sons of serving officers rather than the intellectually deserving who received free places.[53] Besides patronage, subsequent promotion depended on seniority or the display of physical courage, for which the continuing colonial war in Algeria, fought with scant concern for the treatment of 'natives', provided the opportunities. Obedience was considered to be a more important virtue than intelligence, and a reputation for cleverness could be damaging professionally.[54] The inspection system was concerned essentially with the ability of senior officers to maintain discipline and turn out well-drilled units.

According to William Serman, senior officers owing their rank more to their social origins and contacts than ability, were characterised by 'an archaic mentality, inspired by the *ancien régime*, according to which chivalric valour was a general's virtue, whereas intellectual effort, strategic

[50] Serman, *Le corps des officiers*, pp. 221, 234.   [51] *Ibid.*, pp. 1323–5.

[52] T. Adriance, *The Last Gaiter Button. A Study of the Mobilization and Concentration of the French Army in the War of 1870* (London 1987), p. 26.

[53] Serman, *Le corps des officiers*, p. 536; Delmas *et al.*, *Histoire militaire*, p. 451.

[54] Serman, *Le corps des officiers*, p. 1321; R. Holmes, *The Road to Sedan: The French Army 1866–70* (London 1984), p. 114

thought, imaginative tactics and a talent for organisation were disdained ... If the lessons of Sadowa were not drawn by our generals, this was not because they did not wish to, but because their mentality made them incapable of doing so.'[55] This mentality was reinforced by the sense of social superiority and the snobbery characteristic of the *relatively* homogeneous products of the military schools. An ethos – almost of amateurism – prevailed throughout the officer corps.[56] For many young gentlemen the army offered a means to 'usefully occupy their youth'.[57] It represented a temporary phase in their lives, in the absence of anything better to do and whilst waiting for marriage or an inheritance. Gustave de Beaumont observed to his friend Tocqueville that the alternatives for his son had been to enter Saint-Cyr and 'become an officer or do nothing more than fish for trout and chase hares'.[58] Although the Second Empire enjoyed substantial success in attracting members of the social elite into its service and in promoting a renewal of traditions of service to the state and, indeed, a remilitarisation of the nobility, only around 8 per cent of officers on active service between 1848 and 1870 were nobles, compared with 51 per cent in Prussia in 1865.[59] Even the cavalry, where perhaps 25 per cent of officers were nobles, owed its aristocratic reputation to the lifestyle of its officers, rather than their social origins. Yet the officers' professional success depended on their ability to adopt the style and attitudes of this relatively small group and accept the rituals associated with the British officers' mess.[60] As Beaumont wrote to Tocqueville, a military career 'besides being risky, is not suitable for an independent character'.[61]

In spite of such pressure to conform, the officer corps was riven by social and cultural divisions, as well as those between the clienteles of various senior officers, and by rivalry between its different arms. One extremely well-connected officer, an aide to the Emperor, recruited as a spy by the Russian military *attaché*, condemned the personal ambition and rivalries between senior generals and the utter arrogance of marshals like Castellane, Pélissier, and Magnan.[62] If a substantial proportion of officers were promoted from the ranks, their presence was often regretted

[55] Serman, *ibid.*, p. 1330.

[56] *Ibid.*, pp. 492–3 and 'La noblesse dans l'armée française' in G. Delille (ed.), *Les noblesses européennes au 19ᵉ siècle* (Rome 1988), p. 557.

[57] H. Taine, *Carnets de voyage. Note sur la province (1863–65)* (Paris 1897), p. 89.

[58] 5 Nov. 1857 in *Correspondance*, II, p. 509.   [59] Serman, *Le corps des officiers*, p. 635.

[60] *Ibid.*, pp. 611, 635.   [61] Quoted *ibid.*, p. 687.

[62] Report of M. Tonnelier, a counter-espionage agent, on intercepted correspondance, 12 March 1858, in *Papiers et correspondance*, I, p. 114.

by senior officers, concerned that this threatened to diminish the social status of the entire officer corps.[63] There was no special school for former NCOs, so their theoretical knowledge was limited in the extreme. General Ducrot described such officers as 'remarkable by ... the intelligent practice of all the secondary aspects of their profession'.[64] Promoted relatively late in life, close to their men in terms of social origin and culture, they provided the basis for military routine and regimental *esprit de corps*. Often unfit (the average age of infantry captains in 1869 was forty-three)[65] and poorly educated, they would find it particularly difficult to adapt to new technology and rapidly changing battlefield conditions.

The size of the army was determined by legislation which ensured that the relatively well off could avoid military service and even the poor had a reasonable chance of escape. Each year twenty-year-olds drew lots to determine whether they were liable for military service. If they were unlucky enough to draw a *mauvais numéro* there was still the option, for those who could afford the fee, of hiring a substitute, or from 1855 of purchasing exoneration, which provided a bonus to encourage the re-enlistment of experienced soldiers. The number needed (the contingent) was established according to military assessments of need and the government's financial circumstances. It was usually between 80,000 and 100,000, providing for an army of 370,000 in 1870, made up of one-quarter conscripts, one-quarter replacements and one-half volunteers, most of them re-enlistees.[66] Thus the rank-and-file were initially recruited mainly by conscription and then turned by long service, strict discipline, frequent garrison changes, and isolation from civilian society, into professional soldiers. Conscripts who had completed their seven years' service (although many were released sooner for budgetary reasons) frequently re-enlisted and provided the bulk of NCOs. The latter were an ageing and often disillusioned group. They dominated the basic training of new recruits and directed the constant and, from the point of view of military effectiveness, pointless drilling.[67]

This was the army which had acquired an enviable reputation through its victories in the Crimea and Italy, successes that gave its senior officers a false confidence both in their own abilities and in the efficiency of the military organisation. The institutional culture and military doctrine of the French army would be slow to change in a period when the

[63] Castellane, *Journal*, vol. IV, p. 155.
[64] Quoted P. Duffour, 'Le soldat français de 1870', *Revue historique de l'armée*, 1971, p. 35.
[65] *Ibid.*, p. 38; Holmes, *Sedan*, p. 43.   [66] Echard, *Dictionary*, p. 20.
[67] Duffour, 'Le soldat français', p. 33.

technology for waging war was being transformed. Successive mobilisations – in 1854 and 1859 – had been chaotic. Nevertheless, officers took pride in improvising, in 'always muddling through,' as they had repeatedly during campaigns in Algeria.[68] In 1859 the peacetime structure of the army had proved entirely unsuitable for its wartime organisation, and both men and supplies had been slow to arrive at the front. The only bright spot had been the successful use of the railways.[69] However, little effort seems to have been made to learn from these experiences, and this in spite of the Emperor's own forceful condemnation of the military system. In a letter to Marshal Randon, written in the middle of the Italian campaign, Napoleon complained about the disorganisation of the supply train and medical services as well as the general lack of preparedness.[70] All that these campaigns had revealed was that the French army, in terms of organisation and training, was somewhat less of a shambles than that of Austria, Britain, and Russia.[71] The Emperor's cousin, the Prince Napoleon, insisted on the urgent need for adequate contingency planning and the creation of a substantial reserve of manpower, warning that 'more terrible and more threatening events than those of which Italy is the theatre are preparing themselves' and, in particular, drawing attention to the Prussian ability to concentrate large forces rapidly by rail.[72] Left behind in Lyons, and irritated by his lack of an active command, Marshal de Castellane also expressed his concern that 'these victories will be regarded by the numerous lovers of sloppiness as proof of the excellence of their methods. In the first lengthy campaign it will be fatal.'[73]

Without a properly constituted general staff to identify and correct shortcomings, little was likely to be achieved. Strategic planning and the organisation of mobilisation were both neglected. Decision-making was too centralised. During the Crimean War Napoleon had even attempted to command the army from Paris through the newly laid telegraph line. Pélissier, the French commander, had threatened to resign 'a command impossible to exercise at the sometimes paralysing extremity of an electric wire'.[74] Although recruited from amongst the elite graduates of the military schools, and often destined for high command, staff officers performed little more than routine administrative duties. Intelligence

---

[68] Adriance, *Gaiter Button*, p. 29.
[69] M. Charté-Marsaines, 'Mémoire sur les chemins de fer considérés au point de vue militaire', *Annales des ponts et chaussées*, 4e série, IV, pp. 13f.
[70] 26 May 1859, AN 249 AP 5.
[71] See also M. Howard, *The Franco-Prussian War* (London 1967), pp. 17–18.
[72] Prince Napoleon, 'Défense de la France. Note à l'Empereur', 1 May 1859, AN 400 AP 150.
[73] 9 Aug. 1860 in *Journal*, V, p. 259.   [74] Bertho, *Histoire des télécommunications en France*, p. 44.

was collected but rarely collated or its findings disseminated. The various divisions of the War Ministry were prolific with bureaucratic circulars but their activities largely went uncoordinated. Much depended on the personality and ability of the minister. However, his status suffered from an obvious subordination to the Emperor who, whilst being extremely interested in military matters, relied more on the advice of his aides-de-camp and other well-placed officers.[75] Several sets of contingency plans were prepared. Most emphasised the value of fortresses as a means of delaying the enemy whilst mobilisation occurred and additionally as pivots around which the field army could manoeuvre. In contrast, the plan prepared in 1864 predicated the possibility of war with the German states, and insisted on the need for a rapid offensive. It defined concentration areas for three armies and allocated units and commanders to each of them. The most serious attempt to draw on the lessons of Sadowa, by the Emperor's aide, General Frossard, ominously assumed that the firepower derived from new weaponry would give a decisive advantage to the defence. Nevertheless, the new strategic plan introduced in spring 1870 was based on an even more offensive strategy designed to encourage Austrian intervention against Prussia. Even then there was still no agreed, overall plan, which might have served as the basis for discussion by senior commanders.[76]

The peacetime organisation of the army into military divisions reflected a primary concern with the preservation of internal order rather than preparation for war. Not surprisingly, after the events of 1848, detailed contingency plans existed for combating insurrection in the capital and other major cities.[77] The Emperor himself saw the 1,400-strong gendarmerie regiment, which formed part of the Imperial Guard, as 'the linchpin of resistance' to any uprising in Paris.[78] As a result, the army remained little more than 'a conglomeration of regiments'.[79] Generals, who certainly displayed considerable personal courage in colonial skirmishes, had little experience of commanding larger forces. In this situation, tactical doctrine was slow to change. The infantry regulations, originally drafted in 1839, were revised in 1869 but had not been implemented fully by 1870 so that regiments would often preserve excessively tight formations in the face of artillery fire. As a result of Algerian

75 Holmes, *Sedan*, pp. 16–19; Adriance, *Gaiter Button*, p. 28.   76 Audoin-Rouzeau, *1870*, p. 82.

77 Marshal Vaillant, 'Dispositions arrêtées pour la défense de Paris en cas d'émeute', AHG MR 2151; see also Castellane, *Journal*, IV, p. 121.

78 Napoleon to Marshal Randon, 27 Nov. 1861, AN 249 AP 5.

79 H. Dutailly, 'L'armée du Second Empire' in J. Perot *et al.*, *Une visite au camp de Châlons sous le second empire* (Paris 1996), p. 10.

conditions, troops were burdened with over 30 kilos of equipment at a time when over 80 per cent of conscripts were under 1 m 70 tall.[80] The advisory Comité de cavalerie in 1869 recommended the revision of the 1829 regulations still in force. Regiments, which trained solely for charges, had revealed in Italy their utter incompetence for reconnaissance. Certainly, the Emperor doubted the value of 'large masses of cavalry' against infantry equipped with repeating rifles.[81] The artillery regulations were virtually non-existent, providing instructions for the bombardment of infantry but not for counter-battery work.[82] The large number of fortresses – 199 in 1848 – reflecting an engineer's view of strategy, absorbed considerable resources, but were susceptible to artillery.[83] According to the Emperor, the result was that 'there are walls everywhere without the soldiers to defend them. We spend immense amounts for very slender results.'[84] Although the training camp at Châlons was established by the Emperor in 1856 with serious intent, the text-book manoeuvres practised there, with the parades and ceremonial which accompanied them, contributed little to the development of co-ordination between the various arms. They were part of the *fête Impériale*, theatre rather than a serious preparation for war. Trochu insisted on the urgent need both to concentrate troops in larger units during peacetime and to multiply the frequency and increase the realism of manoeuvres.[85] Military thinking, however, continued to be based on a faith in the offensive spirit and the superior fighting ability of the French soldier, and on the Napoleonic practice of deploying dense columns preceded by sharpshooters, with the attack culminating in a charge with fixed bayonets. Discussion of the impact of technological change and increased firepower was very limited.[86]

Industrial development had affected military technology profoundly. The technical experts in 1858 had rejected the *chassepot*, a breach-loading rifle. It was only accepted finally at the Emperor's insistence and in the light of the overwhelming superiority in terms of the range and rapidity of fire enjoyed by Prussian troops using a similar, but inferior, weapon at Sadowa.[87] The introduction of rifled, breach-loading steel artillery

---

[80] Audoin-Rouzeau, *1870*, p. 80.

[81] Napoleon to Marshal Niel, 28 Sept. 1867, AN 400 AP 42.

[82] Regnault, 'Le haut commandement et les généraux français en 1870', *Revue historique de l'armée* (1971), p. 12.

[83] Delmas *et al.*, *Histoire militaire*, II, p. 479.

[84] Napoleon to Marshal Randon, 27 Nov. 1861, AN 249 AP 5.

[85] Trochu, *L'armée française en 1867* (Paris 1868), pp. 275–6; Dutailly, 'L'armée', pp. 10, 13–24.

[86] Holmes, *Sedan*, pp. 208–13.   [87] Serman, *Le corps des officiers*, pp. 1428–9.

was to be even slower because of both technical conservatism and financial constraints, at a time when priority was being given to re-equipping the army with its new rifle. Certainly Napoleon, personally informed by Colonel Stoffel, the military attaché in Berlin, was aware of the danger which might be posed by weapons with a range far superior to that of French artillery.[88] Insufficient consideration was also given by the military authorities to the potential advantages of rail transport for both initial mobilisation and subsequent supply of the army. Transport from rail-heads depended on the ability to requisition large numbers of peasant carts, but little thought was given to the procedures or to subsequent route selection.[89]   Logistics appears to have been regarded as almost on a par with shopkeeping and as something with which a gentleman did not concern himself. Thus the munitions needs of troops equipped with the new breach-loading rifles were not really assessed. Appointment to the understaffed corps de l'intendance was regarded as a sign of failure. Generally its senior officers lacked relevant experience.[90] The transport *train des équipages* similarly had no attraction for graduates of the military schools.[91]   The lack of a peacetime organisation to which logistical (and medical) units might be attached further limited the potential for planning. In addition, the direct control normally exercised over the logistical services by the Ministry of War ensured that their officers developed an obsessive concern with bureaucratic niceties and, in wartime, an excessive degree of independence from army commanders.[92] Certainly, the absence of forward planning had caused massive administrative and practical problems during the Crimean and Italian campaigns. Rather than the system, these were blamed on the incompetence of supply officers. General Bosquet's simple solution would have been to erect a gallows with a military *intendant* hanging from it as a warning to the rest.[93] Themselves the product of essentially agrarian societies, senior officers would find it difficult to come to terms with industrial warfare and to translate technical change into tactics. Due to the war of 1866, the Prussians had the benefit of more relevant experience, as well as a general staff capable of analysing the events and drawing lessons.

Drawing on his personal experience of the Italian campaign, the Emperor had expressed concern about a number of deficiencies in the process of mobilisation and subsequent concentration and particularly

[88] Napoleon to Marshal Niel, 28 Sept. 1867, AN 400 AP 42.   [89] Holmes, *Sedan*, pp. 79–82.
[90] Trochu, *L'armée française*, p. 141.   [91] Serman, *Le corps des officiers*, p. 1801.
[92] Adriance, *Gaiter Button*, pp. 24–5; Dutailly, 'L'armée', p. 12.
[93] P. Chalmin, *L'officier français de 1815 à 1870* (Paris 1957), p. 282.

concerning the lack of trained reserves.[94] Sadowa increased his anxiety. Clearly, there was a need to plan for a war in which Prussia would be the likely enemy. The Prussians in 1866 had been able to mobilise 730,000 trained soldiers, of whom 356,000 had been deployed in military operations. Marshal Randon had claimed to be able to dispose of 655,000 men, but this figure included 270,000 untrained 'reservists' and troops already committed in Algeria, Mexico, and Rome. His successor at the War Ministry, Marshal Niel, estimated that once these were taken into account only an obviously inadequate 200,000 men would have been available to form an army of the Rhine.[95] The weaknesses of the French army were becoming only too evident, at least to those who wished to see. In a meeting with the Emperor at Saint-Cloud in February 1860, attended by his marshals, Castellane had poured scorn on those like MacMahon, 'instructed in the African school', and insisted that 'if we are involved in a long war, something more than *élan* will be needed'.[96] Nevertheless, there were many senior officers who resisted change which might disrupt an institution which had enjoyed a succession of victories. They continued to assume that the superiority of the French national character and the *esprit militaire* displayed by its soldiers provided a considerable advantage over any enemy. Marshal Randon insisted that when it came to war the initial presence of trained soldiers mattered more than reserves. In successive reports to the Emperor he sought to minimise the army's shortcomings.[97] The reformers themselves were divided over priorities and only too aware of the financial constraints.[98]

After decades of neglect, in the aftermath of Sadowa, the Emperor made a considerable effort to introduce change. Foreign Minister La Valette reminded his colleagues that 'the greatness of a country does not depend on the weakness of its neighbours. France must perfect its military organisation.'[99] On 7 September 1866 Napoleon wrote to Randon ordering a study of the measures needed to increase the size of the reserves, and on 6 November a recently appointed military commission made his successor as war minister, Marshal Niel, responsible for the preparation of legislation. With Prussia as the most likely enemy, it seemed logical to introduce reforms along the lines of those already successfully introduced in the German state. These provided for shorter periods of service, for

[94] Napoleon to Marshal Randon, 27 Nov. 1861, AN 249 AP 5.
[95] Delmas *et al.*, *Histoire militaire*, pp. 419–20.   [96] *Journal*, V, p. 328.
[97] Randon, 'Note sur la situation de l'armée en 1866'; 'Note sur la situation de l'armée en 1867'; Randon report to Emperor 10 Dec. 1866, AN 400 AP 42; letter to Emperor, 28 Sept. 1866, in Randon, *Mémoires*, II, p. 170.
[98] Barail, *Mes souvenirs*, II.   [99] Quoted Maurain, *Baroche*, p. 313.

the conscription of much larger proportions of the relevant age group and, by this means, the creation of a large trained reserve.[100] Seventeen months would elapse between the Emperor's letter of 7 September and the voting of a new military law. Even then the weight of opposition from senior generals and politicians, as well as from 'public opinion', was such that only a mediocre compromise was finally agreed on and many of the proposals it contained would not fully be implemented. Trochu insisted on the urgent necessity of defining a clear strategic doctrine and regretted the lack of a greater sense of unity and respect for hierarchy and discipline amongst the senior officers who obstructed change.[101] This inability of the regime to impose reforms, which the Emperor himself had insisted were a vital necessity, was an obvious sign of the decline in his authority.

The generals were not alone in their reluctance to countenance radical reform. Leading ministers, like Rouher, anxious about the electoral impact of new legislation, were less than whole-hearted in their support, as were the members of the Conseil d'Etat and official deputies in the Corps législatif.[102] With Thiers as their mouthpiece, liberal deputies insisted on the need to preserve a quasi-professional army, isolated from the masses, dedicated to preservation of social order and trained to perfection. Thiers spelled out the danger, which could be expected from a mass conscript force, the 'people in arms'.[103] The link between social fear and opposition to reform was also evident when the Paris state prosecutor asked whether 'this system would not pose a serious threat to the stability of our institutions in introducing to the use of weapons and military manoeuvres a section of the population which would not be restrained by a sense of duty and which, during a day of protest, might turn against society the knowledge and experience acquired for its defence'.[104] Reports from the provinces warned that the extension of military service to larger numbers would threaten the loyalty even of the rural population which favoured the existing system in which most young men were able to escape military service through the drawing of lots.[105] Ollivier believed that the proposals could be 'fatal' for the regime. General Palikao warned the

---

[100] E.g. Crepin, *La conscription en débat ou le triple apprentissage de la nation, de la citoyenneté, de la république (1798–1889)*(Arras 1998), pp. 96–7.

[101] *Ibid.*, p. 274.

[102] Schnerb, *Rouher*, pp. 221–2; W. Smith, 'Le rôle politique de Rouher sous le Second Empire' in Becker, *Rouher*, pp. 54–7.

[103] Crepin, *Conscription*, p. 100.   [104] 16 Nov. 1866, AHG G8 185.

[105] E.g. PG Caen, 15 April 1867, AHG G8/186; G. Wright, 'Public opinion and conscription in France, 1866–70', *Journal of Modern History* (1942), pp. 26–45; Ménager, *Napoléons*, pp. 214–19.

Emperor himself that 'Your Majesty's government has already lost the towns; this law will lose it the countryside.'[106] Rumour exaggerated the likely impact of the reforms, as well as intensifying concern that war was possible in the near future.[107]

A system, which through replacement allowed the sons of the propertied classes to avoid military service, had its attractions. It ensured their opposition to the creation of a socially more inclusive army. The state prosecutor at Nancy maintained that such proposals would 'violate the law of equality more than they apply it ... because, in general, a labourer, a worker, a peasant, has more to gain than to lose from passing six years with a regiment, whereas those who, by the chance of birth or the often excessive sacrifices of their families, have been able to devote themselves to serious and special studies will see their futures entirely shattered by their untimely enrolment in the army'.[108] Landowners were anxious that the labour shortages they constantly complained about as migration to the towns intensified would be exacerbated.[109] The problem for the government was that many of its habitual supporters were hostile to the extension of conscription.[110] Opponents of change could even draw on the support of most military 'experts', who assumed that only long service could ensure adequate training. In his influential study *L'armée française en 1867* (1868), General Trochu claimed that changes in tactics and organisation were necessary rather than an increase in numbers. Marshal Niel himself, clearly shaken by the strength of opposition expressed at a meeting with members of the Corps législatif's budgetary committee, reported to the Emperor – 'so much bitterness, so many disobliging expressions for ministers!' On this occasion the Imperial Guard, which Niel viewed as the essential reserve in case of war, had been targeted by the supporters of budgetary economy.[111] There was already considerable concern about the cost of new weapons.[112] Republicans like Jules Favre had their own reasons for rejecting reform. They were anxious that universal service would militarise the young and viewed the regular army – the army of the *coup d'état* – as a 'praetorian' force. In a romantic mythification of the revolutionary past they insisted that, in case of war, young men would accept their patriotic duty and save the nation, as in

[106] Quoted Schnerb, *Rouher*, pp. 200–1.
[107] E.g. J. Casewitz, *Une loi manquée, la loi Niel, 1866–68. L'Armée française à la veille de la guerre de 1870* (Paris 1960), p. 67.
[108] 14 Jan. 1867, AHG G8/166.   [109] Price, 'Onset of labour shortage', p. 266.
[110] See also Crepin, *Conscription*, pp. 274–5.   [111] Niel to Emperor, 13 July 1868, AN 400 AP 42.
[112] E.g. Fould to Baroche, quoted Maurain, *Baroche*, p. 313; Barbier, *Finance*, p. 240.

1792, through the *levée en masse*.[113] According to Jules Simon, 'since we repulsed the invader with an improvised army, what need is there for an expensive and undemocratic permanent army?' Their favoured option was a militia to replace the regular army.[114]

An open admission of military inferiority, which might have rallied support for reform, would have been too damaging politically for the regime to contemplate. The new military law thus fell far short of the Emperor's intentions, and even then was supported by many official deputies only with extreme reluctance. It reduced the period of military service from seven to five years, with a further four in the reserve but without additional training. Those exempted from service after drawing a *bon numéro* in the ballot or paying for exemption – around two-thirds of the age group – were to serve in a Garde Nationale Mobile and undergo two weeks' annual training, with each session not to exceed twenty-four hours, for a period of five years.[115] The proposals and their implementation aroused considerable popular opposition, culminating in serious riots in Bordeaux and Toulouse in March – April 1868 involving young men called up for training in the Garde Mobile.[116] Marshal Le Boeuf, who succeeded Niel after his death in 1869, was far less committed to reform than his predecessor and ensured that little was done to increase the strength of the army. It was widely assumed in Paris by the beginning of 1870 that because of the strength of public hostility the authorities had abandoned its plans for the Garde Mobile.[117] The failure to train the Garde and to plan its mobilisation would severely limit its potential as a reserve when war broke out. Niel had also been concerned to improve mobilisation procedures through the creation of the framework for a field army and the establishment of a commission to plan for the military use of the railways. Again, little was achieved before his premature death.[118] This was in marked contrast with the high level of responsibility accorded to the Prussian general staff and its meticulous planning for mobilisation of an army which, in peacetime, already had an organisation which would serve as the basis for wartime mobilisation and which could also rely on substantial trained reserves. In spite of the French reforms the organisational gulf continued to widen as the Prussians learnt from their mistakes in 1866.[119]

---

[113] J.-J. Becker and S. Audoin-Rouzeau, *La France, la nation, la guerre, 1850-1920* (Paris 1995), p. 47.
[114] Quoted Audoin-Rouzeau, *1870*, p. 78.   [115] Duffour, 'Le soldat français', pp. 24f.
[116] Casewitz, *La loi manquée*, pp. 127–30.   [117] OC cie. de la Seine, 26 Feb. 1870, AHG G8/176.
[118] Adriance, *Gaiter Button*, pp. 34–5.
[119] G. Wawro, *The Austro-Prussian War* (Cambridge 1996), p. 283.

THE ROAD TO WAR

In spite of liberalisation, the political system had left considerable prerogative power in the hands of the Emperor. He had been especially determined to reserve to himself the spheres of military and foreign policy and was anxious to exercise his rights.[120] In spite of his misgivings, he had felt obliged to give priority to domestic political stability over preparation for a war which might never happen. His objective, or so he informed the Prussian ambassador, the Count von der Goltz, was 'to organise my army, not on a war footing, but on that of a respectable peace'.[121] It seems all the more surprising then that in 1870, following the brilliant success of the plebiscite, he would be prepared to risk war, particularly in the light of his own awareness of the weaknesses of the French army. Perhaps his dangerous frame of mind was evident in a short note written to Rouher on 11 June 1869 in which he announced that 'what is missing ... is the occasion to strike a major blow which will rouse the public's spirits'.[122] Foreign policy decisions were also subject to the interplay of competing influences amongst courtiers, politicians, diplomats, and soldiers, members of a narrow social circle who saw themselves, nevertheless, as personifying the national interest. They were influenced by perceptions of the likely internal and international impact, as well as by the diffuse responses of a 'public opinion', itself subject to political manipulation.

The international situation had remained tense since July 1866 when the crushing defeat of the Austrian army at Sadowa had kindled a widely held assumption that a showdown between France and Prussia was inevitable in the not too distant future. Although subsequently tension had eased, the Emperor continued to be provided with regular reports on military readiness for war. That dated 11 February 1869 still assumed that 'the two nations will be fatally led to an armed struggle', and significantly warned that 'the objective of French policy must then be to avoid war save in the best conditions and with allies [Austria and the south German states] with defeats to repair and a powerful interest in uniting their efforts to our own'.[123] Napoleon himself appears to have become increasingly cautious. A lengthy note from Prince Napoleon following the disastrous 1869 elections, and carrying the annotation *très important* in the Emperor's handwriting, included three recommendations on foreign policy: 'Relative disarmament; a policy of peace especially towards

---

[120] E.g. Ollivier, xv, p. 84.
[121] Napoleon to Marquis de Moustier, 7 May 1867, AN 400 AP 42. [122] *Ibid.*
[123] Ministère de la Guerre, 'Note pour l'Empereur', 11 Feb. 1869, AN 400 AP 42.

Germany; evacuation of the Papal States.'[124] In a circular to ambassadors during his brief sojourn at the Foreign Ministry, Daru spelt out
the implications: 'I want peace, France desires it. Great changes have
been accomplished in Europe in the last twenty years; we have not made
them, but our policy is to preserve the *status quo*. For this, avoid agitating
Europe; do not raise questions, and if they are born smother them as
soon as possible ... Every European country has enough to do at home
without whipping up external quarrels.'[125] Ollivier would be even more
determined to improve relations with Prussia. In a letter to Clément
Duvernois, the Emperor's intermediary, in October 1869 he insisted
that 'the moment to stop Prussia has passed, irrevocably passed, and the
safety and greatness of the Empire can only be looked for in respect for
the principle of the nationalities ... Far from resolving anything [war]
will confuse and compromise everything.'[126] On 30 June 1870 Ollivier
would take obvious delight in announcing that the number of conscripts
to be called up in 1870 would be reduced from 100,000 to 90,000.[127]
On the following day, the first reports were received of the Hohenzollern
candidature. Even then, and as late as 6 July, Ollivier was able to assure
deputies that 'the Government is not concerned, in no period has the
preservation of peace in Europe appeared more certain'.[128]

The candidature of Prince Leopold of Hohenzollern-Sigmaringen, a
member of a junior branch of the Prussian ruling family, for the Spanish
throne appeared to 'informed' opinion to represent a deliberate provocation and to threaten France with encirclement and a further decisive shift
in the balance of power. There was considerable pressure from deputies
and in the press for a firm response. On 6 July, in response to criticism
of government weakness by the centre-left deputy Cochery, the Duc de
Gramont, foreign minister since mid-May and previously ambassador
in Vienna, felt obliged to agree that it was impossible for France to 'accept that a foreign power, by placing one of its princes on the throne of
Charles V should be able to upset ... the existing equilibrium of forces in
Europe, and threaten the interests and honour of France'. He warned
that 'the government ... offers to the Spanish and Prussian governments
the alternative of either backing down or taking up arms'.[129] Ollivier's
efforts to calm the debate and to insist that war was far from inevitable,

---

[124] AN 400 AP 150.　　[125] Quoted P. de la Gorce, *Histoire du Second Empire* (Paris 1909), VII, p. 175.
[126] *Papiers et correspondance*, I, p. 258.
[127] Assemblée nationale, *Enquête parlementaire*, I, p. 470, evidence of Marshal Le Boeuf; Guiral, 'Emile
Ollivier et la politique extérieure', p. 199.
[128] *Enquête parlementaire*, I, p. 470.
[129] Gramont, *La France et la Prusse avant la guerre* (Paris 1872), pp. 40–1.

largely fell on deaf ears.[130] The Emperor still hoped for a diplomatic victory. However, the determination of some of his closest advisors to turn the affair into a public humiliation of Prussia, as a means of enhancing the regime's status both internally and externally, was leading the regime into a dangerous, and ultimately fatal, game of brinkmanship. Even Ollivier warned Lord Lyons, the British ambassador, that his new liberal government, in response to any future provocation by Prussia, 'must show firmness and spirit or we shall not be able to cope with Revolution and Socialism at home.'[131] Feeling threatened by Rouher, he appears to have been determined to be seen to be responding to the Prussian challenge with greater firmness than his predecessor.[132] The withdrawal of Prince Leopold's candidature on 12 July in response to French concern should have been sufficient. Ollivier, who had been excluded from the discussions between the Emperor and his advisors, was delighted. According to Guizot this was 'the finest diplomatic success I have seen in my life'.[133] However, the following day Gramont insisted to Lord Lyons that 'the government will not survive in the Chamber tomorrow unless it is able to present definite Prussian concessions'.[134] Anticipating the demands of 'public opinion' would remain one of the regime's essential, unstated objectives.

Pressure for tough action was evident, particularly in the conservative press. The catholic newspaper *L'Univers* insisted that 'Patriotic sentiment in France was immediately excited by the news. The phrase: *a Prussian king in Madrid* raced through the public like a rumour presaging war' (7 July 1870). The authoritarian Bonapartist Granier de Cassagnac, writing in *Le Pays* on 10 July, expressed his contempt for the government's hesitation: 'It isn't important that this matter should be settled. Profit from the occasion, clear the account from the past, and guarantee the future whilst we can ... We can no longer live in this manner. Lawyers rule us.' In an editorial the following day he affirmed that 'there is only one cry coming from the ranks of the majority: finish with it.' He had sufficient confidence to add that 'France has never been as well prepared as at this moment. It would be an error ... a crime, not to profit from the present situation, and provide a solid and definitive basis for order and peace in Europe.' Marshal Vaillant agreed. In discussion with the Emperor on 7 July, he insisted, that 'at last the shroud of Sadowa which

---

[130] E.g. Tollu, 'Démocratie et liberté', pp. 154–5.   [131] Quoted Tombs and Bury, *Thiers*, p. 177.
[132] Schnerb, *Rouher*, pp. 372–3.
[133] W. Carr, *The Origins of the Wars of German Unification* (London 1991), p. 155.
[134] Quoted Smith, 'La constitution de 1870', p. 220.

has smothered us for four years is being lifted. You will never be able to find a better occasion. You must profit from it, Sire, the nation will follow you.'[135]

The evidence concerning the decision-making process is confused. It was produced at different times and for different audiences, to justify rather than to explain. Thus Ollivier would later condemn the tone of the letter in which Gramont demanded further guarantees from the Prussian king.[136] The Foreign Minister in turn would insist that this demand 'was imposed by public opinion, by national sentiment and by the unequivocal demonstration of opinion in the Chambers'. He maintained that his request had not constituted an ultimatum and that, if Prussia had not already determined on war, it would have served as the basis for further negotiation.[137] In any case Benedetti, the French ambassador, requested a meeting to discuss additional guarantees. The Prussian king courteously refused, during a brief discussion at the spa resort of Ems where he was taking the waters.[138] A report on this encounter was, routinely, forwarded to Bismarck in Berlin. It was the chancellor's doctoring of this telegram in order to make the king's refusal sound insulting, and the use of the electric telegraph to rapidly diffuse news of the 'insult' throughout Europe in order to 'humiliate' the French government, which brought the crisis to a head and pushed the Emperor into a declaration of war on 19 July.[139] Assessing the impact of the telegram, an extremely angry Ollivier concluded that 'if we take it to the Chamber they'll throw mud at our carriages and shout us down'.[140] Bismarck's intention, as the Emperor appears to have realised, had been to engineer a crisis. It had probably not been the Prussian chancellor's intention from the outset but the French demand for guarantees provided a heaven-sent opportunity to provoke Napoleon into a declaration of war. It was assumed that the outcome would significantly reinforce Prussian hegemony within Germany. The 'Ems telegram', prepared by the Chancellor in accord with the War Minister von Roon and the army chief of staff von Moltke, was to be the means.[141] Moreover, Bismarck's assessments of the respective military and diplomatic strengths of the two powers were to prove far more accurate than those of the French decision-makers.

[135] Vaillant, 'Carnets' quoted Ollivier, *L'Empire libéral*, XIV, p. 117.
[136] Ollivier, *L'Empire libéral*, XIV, p. 246.
[137] *Enquête parlementaire*, V, pp. 46–8, evidence of Gramont.
[138] *Ibid.*, p. 373, evidence of Benedetti.   [139] V, pp. 46–8 evidence of Ollivier.
[140] Ollivier, *L'Empire libéral*, XIV, p. 373.
[141] Carr, *Wars*, pp. 180–5; F. Roth, 'Napoléon III et la déclaration de la guerre en 1870' in Tulard, *Pourquoi réhabiliter*, p. 155.

Ultimate responsibility for the French decision to go to war, as well as for the inadequate assessment of the risks involved, nevertheless rested with the Emperor. This was certainly Ollivier's view, expressed in his vast justificatory work, *L'Empire libéral*. Implicitly admitting his own weaknesses, constitutional, political, and personal, he claimed that the war represented the final affirmation of the Emperor's personal power. However, the continuing deterioration in the monarch's health was having a negative impact on his ability to exercise this power. Constant pain is likely to have affected his concentration and decision-making abilities. Certainly, contemporaries were struck by the rapidity with which the Emperor, now aged sixty-two, seemed to be ageing and by his generally unhealthy appearance. Thiers was not alone in reporting that 'he had ... lost much of his willpower ... he was uncertain in his opinion and unable to take decisions without considerable hesitation'.[142] The decision on 12 July to demand further guarantees was undeniably taken by Napoleon and Gramont without consultation. According to Ollivier,

it appeared that he [Napoleon] was in favour of war and as he was certain that he would not obtain my support, nor that of the cabinet for this policy, he imposed it by an act of personal power. Only one minister felt able to support this, only one forgot the protective rules of the parliamentary regime. Gramont was not imbued with the requirements of this regime, he remained an ambassador used to obeying all the orders of his sovereign.[143]

The Emperor failed to avoid Bismarck's trap to a large extent because of pressure from the close circle of courtiers and politicians identified with authoritarian Bonapartism, like Jérôme David and Cassagnac. They were marginalised in the new Corps législatif, with only around eighty representatives, but had been encouraged to re-assert themselves by the plebiscite. These deputies, supported by newspapers like Cassagnac's *Le Pays* and Girardin's *La Liberté*, claimed to represent 'public opinion' and acted as a war party, whipping up enthusiasm for a campaign to teach the Prussians a lesson.[144] They were convinced that a successful war would lend weight to their counter-attack against the liberal regime.[145] Although excluded from the decision-making process, Ollivier would feel obliged to accept his share of the responsibility, out of a sense of personal loyalty. Furthermore, as he was only too aware, he lacked a parliamentary majority, ministers were divided, and criticism of him personally was

---

[142] *Enquête parlementaire*, V, p. 3; see also Roth, *ibid.*, pp. 153–4.   [143] Ollivier, XIV, p. 262.
[144] E.g. *Le Pays*, 8 July 1870.
[145] See e.g. Thiers to Rémusat, 21 July 1870, BN naf 20620; Ollivier, *L'Empire libéral*, XIV, pp. 261–2; Maurain, *Baroche*, p. 488.

prevalent amongst authoritarian Bonapartists and in court circles. These pressures reinforced his sense of dependence on the Emperor and his concern that if he did resign the political liberalisation to which he was so committed might be compromised by the appointment of Rouher as his successor.[146]

At meetings of ministers convened to discuss the Ems telegram on 14 July, Gramont, supported by the confident War Minister Marshal Le Boeuf, energetically affirmed that the army was ready and the moment opportune for finally settling differences with Prussia. The decision to proceed with military mobilisation was finally taken. Reported Prussian preparations created a sense of urgency. The Emperor had the constitutional right to declare war. Nevertheless, and in order to rally support, it was decided that the Corps législatif should be given time to discuss the situation.[147] In spite of his own misgivings, Ollivier stood before deputies and in an extremely tendentious description of the course of the crisis placed the blame entirely on Prussia. He contemptuously brushed aside comments like those of Jules Favre who likened the proceedings to 'the personal rule of Louis XIV'.[148] Then, in a phrase which would haunt him for the rest of his life, and for which he would never be forgiven, he accepted war with 'a light heart, because this war which we are going to wage has been forced on us ... because our cause is just ...'.[149] In response to Thiers, Ollivier insisted that 'we have found ourselves faced with an insupportable affront, in the presence of a threat which, if we had allowed it to realise itself, would have reduced us to the last rank amongst states'.[150] Throughout his long life, he would continue to insist that Bismarck's determination to aggrandise Prussia had made war unavoidable.[151] There was certainly bellicose pressure on ministers from the right. Rouher, president of the Senate, later admitted that 'we had not wanted war ... Neither did we fear it. Our army appeared ready. We had to take up the challenge. We no longer had any choice but between war and dishonour.'[152] In the Corps législatif, Cassagnac, supported by Clément Duvernois and Jérôme David, bitterly opposed compromise, promising that 'France, once launched against the enemy will be unstoppable and if you, the ministers of 2 January, persist in obstructing her passage, she will pass over your bodies.'[153] Supported by a substantial

[146] Assemblée nationale, *Enquête parlementaire*, V, pp. 2–3, evidence of Ollivier; Ollivier to Duvernois, 5 Oct. 1869, in *Papiers et correspondance*, I, p. 262, reveals his insecurity.
[147] Ollivier, *L'Empire libéral*, XIV, pp. 390–5; *Enquête parlementaire*, V, p. 48, evidence of Gramont.
[148] *Enquête parlementaire*, I, p. 477.   [149] *Ibid.*, p. 478.
[150] Ollivier, *L'Empire libéral*, XIV, p. 415.   [151] E.g. Ollivier, XV, p. 160.
[152] Quoted Roth, 'Napoléon III', p. 16.   [153] Quoted Girard, *Napoléon III*, p. 465.

part of the Parisian press as well as by nightly demonstrations on the streets of the capital between 6 and 15 July, this sort of intransigence appears to have impressed ministers, and particularly Gramont.[154] Pietri, the Prefect of Police, would later insist that, although anxious to preserve peace, the Emperor himself had succumbed to the 'popular' enthusiasm for war.[155]

At the decisive meeting of the council of ministers, attended by the Empress, at Saint Cloud in the evening of 14 July, Napoleon appears to have almost fatalistically accepted the views of those who insisted that further humiliation by Prussia was unacceptable and would threaten the future of the regime.[156] In spite of some misgivings, he gave way to a combination of these pressures and his own determination to restore French predominance in Europe. In the aftermath of liberalisation he might also have wanted to re-assert Imperial authority, especially in the reserved areas of prerogative power. In a political system in which the Emperor ultimately took foreign policy decisions more needs to be known about the influence of his personal entourage – people with power but not responsibility – as well as the views of those whose official positions gave them formal authority. According to Thiers, admittedly not the most reliable of witnesses, the war party was led by the Empress, anxious to safeguard her son's future, particularly in view of the decline of her husband's health. Her influence over her husband has been condemned frequently.[157] Her supporters were mainly authoritarian Bonapartists determined to impose a check not only on Bismarck but also on liberal aspirations within France.[158] To this extent the war would represent a displacement of internal into external politics. Certainly, Eugénie was more than willing to listen to the confident advice offered by Marshal Le Boeuf, 'drunk with ambition', and of Gramont, 'that ambitious and incapable idiot', as Thiers so delicately put it.[159] On the influence, as well as the abilities, of the Duc de Gramont there appears to be little dissent. The initial appointment, immediately following the plebiscite, of this former ambassador to Vienna, notorious for his abrasive character and hostility to Prussia, must have sent dangerous signals to Berlin.[160] His subsequent behaviour was hardly conducive to effective crisis management. His

[154] See Gramont despatches to Benedetti in Audoin-Rouzeau, *1870*, p. 328 n. 29.
[155] *Enquête parlementaire*, V, p. 113.   [156] Roth, 'Napoléon III', p. 165.
[157] For a more balanced judgement see W. Smith, *Eugénie, impératrice et femme* (Paris 1989).
[158] Barail, *Mes souvenirs*, III, pp. 108, 121, 143; Schnerb, *Rouher*, pp. 186–7; Case, *French Opinion*, p. 218.
[159] Letter to Rémusat, 21 July 1870, BN naf 20620.
[160] E.g. Guiral, 'Ollivier et la politique extérieure', p. 201.

forceful declaration to the Corps législatif on 6 July influenced by a determination to be seen to be protecting the 'honour' of France, inflamed rather than followed public opinion.[161] Perhaps most damning of all was his own admission that, in spite of the high-risk strategy being followed, 'we had not adequately analysed and studied the military situation from the point of view of mobilisation and the strength of the reserves'.[162] The diplomatic situation was another vital area, which the foreign minister had failed to consider adequately. In the absence of formal alliances it was simply assumed that, following the expected early French victories, sympathetic powers, and most notably Austria, would join in the fray.[163] This was in spite of the formal Austrian response to Cazaux, the French minister in Vienna, that 'Neither the government, nor the Emperor, are disposed to suddenly engage themselves in an affair ... on which we have never been consulted and which has been further aggravated by the language of the Tuileries.'[164] Gramont's weak excuse that alliances would have been inappropriate 'in the middle of the pacific situation prevailing in Europe over the past few years' and that the crisis had come as a great surprise[165] ignored the international tension prevailing since 1866.

Subsequently it would prove very convenient for the likes of Marshal Le Boeuf to escape from their own responsibility by blaming the decision to go to war on the pressure of public opinion.[166] In his memoirs, Haussmann would go a step further and blame 'the adventurous foreign policy' on the new liberal institutions, on the susceptibility of 'constitutional ministers' to 'an overexcited Public Opinion. Instead of directing it and containing it, undoubtedly they hoped to use it to consolidate their threatened power', adding that in these circumstances 'the Sovereign felt morally obliged to accept the perilous consequences'.[167] Yet in reality the press had been divided, with the republican *Siècle* and liberal *Temps* urging restraint, and, although undoubtedly substantial anti-Prussian feeling had developed since 1866, only a very small part of the population had actually taken to the streets in support of war. Patriotic demonstrations by an enthusiastic minority were taken to be representative of the entire Parisian population, and, indeed, by diplomats, of the whole of France. It was not so much 'public opinion' which influenced decisions as the determination of those politicians who wanted war to hear a particular message, which coincided with their own previous predilections.

---

[161] See Audoin-Rouzeau, *1870*, p. 44.   [162] Gramont, *La France et la Prusse*, p. 318.
[163] E.g. Girard, *Napoléon III*, p. 459.   [164] Quoted Wahl, *Les françaises*, p. 54.
[165] *Enquête parlementaire*, v, pp. 48–50, evidence of Gramont.
[166] *Ibid.*, p. 23.   [167] *Mémoires*, II, p. 568.

Especially in the sphere of foreign policy, decision-making remained the preserve of a tiny minority, influenced by little more than the views of members of the social networks to which they belonged. Similarly, in canvassing provincial opinion, prefects tended to take particular account of the views of narrow local elites. Ministers again read these as confirmation of the 'unanimous' support for war.[168] During a rapidly developing crisis, 'public opinion' could thus be constructed with relative ease.

Indeed, the situation had developed so rapidly that even in Paris there were only ten days between the public becoming aware of the crisis and the voting of war credits. Initially, outside the ranks of the habitual readers of the 'quality' press, there was little public interest in the Hohenzollern candidacy.[169] In the capital, news of the 'threat' subsequently spread rapidly and was then diffused more gradually in the provinces. The rural population appeared initially more concerned about the threat posed to the harvest by drought.[170] Gramont's speech on 6 July was reported to have aroused a 'real patriotic enthusiasm' in Paris, especially amongst the working classes.[171] One police informer reported that 'although the war is considered by the workers to be a calamity, Prussian arrogance has wounded our patriotism and the people of Paris will certainly repeat the demonstrations of 1859'.[172] Patriotic songs could be heard in working-class bars in cities throughout France.[173] These bellicose attitudes were reinforced by the general confidence in the ability of the French army to emerge victorious. This assumption was fundamental to the decision to go to war. Gramont's statement to the post-war commission of enquiry is revealing on a number of counts: 'When one goes to war, the assumption is that one is the strongest; if one goes to war and is defeated, it is evident that one has deceived oneself about the state of one's forces, and that is a mistake.' He had firmly believed in the 'moral' and 'scientific' superiority of French arms but, as he now insisted, whilst transferring blame, 'I was not a soldier.'[174] He had come to regret his previous acceptance of assurances from military commanders based essentially, as we have noted, on their arrogant and complacent self-esteem and unwillingness

---

[168] See e.g. *Actes*, V, p. 113.

[169] S. Audoin-Rouzeau, 'French public opinion in 1870–1 and the emergence of total war' in S. Förster and J. Nagler (eds.), *On the Road to Total War. The American Civil War and the German Wars of Unification* (Cambridge 1997), pp. 394–9.

[170] E.g. prefect Ardèche, 10 July 1870, *Enquête Parlementaire*, I, p. 464; prefect Ille-et-Vilaine, 9 July 1870, *ibid.*, p. 467.

[171] E.g. evidence of Pietri, Prefect of Police, *ibid.*, V, p. 113; Ollivier, *L'Empire libéral*, XIV, pp. 116–17, quoting police reports.

[172] Ollivier, *L'Empire libéral*, XIV, p. 495.

[173] E.g. Lorcin, 'Souvenir', pp. 193–4.   [174] *Enquête parlementaire*, V, p. 50.

to admit to the shortcomings of an institution they tended to worship rather than serve. The dangers of excessive civilian confidence in military 'professionalism' are evident in Le Boeuf's erroneous assumption that Prussian mobilisation was already under way by 14 July. This enabled him to persuade the Emperor and ministers who had previously remained reluctant to order French mobilisation, in case it precipitated conflict, to issue the order that very day.[175] Napoleon was probably one of the few who did not share this confidence in the superiority of French arms. Walking in the park at Saint Cloud with his *confidante* Princess Mathilde, the Emperor was reported to have responded to her observation that war was surely necessary to reinforce the triumphant impact of the plebiscite, with a sceptical 'Ah! you don't know everything. There are so many difficulties; war would be a happy diversion. And what strength if we succeed!' Asked what would be the consequence of failure, he remained silent, provoking the princess into teasing him: 'you see, look at yourself, do you have a warlike appearance?' The Emperor's response, 'It's true, I am in a sorry state' was followed by the revealing admission: 'And then, I don't have great confidence.'[176]

Ollivier's request to the Corps législatif to vote war credits, made in the early afternoon of 15 July, was certainly received with enthusiasm. Opposition came only from a small minority of deputies, including the liberals Brame and Thiers and the republicans Favre and Gambetta. The liberal opposition had criticised the government for accepting humiliation in 1866. It was difficult to condemn its more forceful response in 1870.[177] With considerable courage, given the constant interruptions and insults thrown at him, Thiers demanded to know from Gramont,

is it true that on the essentials, that is to say the candidature of the Hohenzollern prince, your complaints have been heard and accepted? Is it true that you are breaking off [negotiations] over a question of susceptibility? Well, gentlemen, do you want the rest of Europe to say that the fundamentals having been accorded, you have decided to shed torrents of blood over a question of form?[178]

Thiers was certainly not opposed to war with Prussia on principle and favoured *revanche* for 1866. However, on this occasion, he felt both that the moment had been badly chosen and correctly assumed that the authoritarian Bonapartists would seek to use war as an opportunity to re-establish their dominance. Thiers thus feared both defeat and the prospect of a victory, which might 'take our liberty away'.[179] The

[175] *Ibid.*, V, pp. 22–31, evidence of Le Boeuf.   [176] Ollivier, *L'Empire libéral*, XV, p. 157.
[177] Point made by Pietri, *Enquête parlementaire*, V, p. 113.   [178] Speech in *ibid.*, I, pp. 475–6.
[179] Letter to Rémusat, 21 July 1870, BN naf 20620.

appropriations were voted finally around midnight by 245 votes to 10. At the last moment Thiers, together with some republicans including Gambetta, Ferry, and Picard, accepted that the argument had been lost, and that their patriotic duty was to rally to the war effort.[180] On the evening of 16 July 1870, crowds on the boulevards demonstrated with flags, shouts of *Vive l'Empereur, Vive l'armée, Vive la France*, and by singing the *Marseillaise*.

Napoleon, in exile, would insist that 'responsibility ... must be divided evenly between the government, Chamber and myself; if I had not wanted war, I would have dismissed my ministers, if they had opposed it they should have resigned, finally if the Chamber was opposed to the enterprise it could have voted against it.'[181] However, his personal responsibility was much greater than this statement suggests. Certainly war had been declared largely in response to a deliberate provocation inducing an accumulation of pressure from deputies, sections of the press, and 'public opinion'. Nevertheless, the crucial decisions were taken by the Emperor and his Foreign Minister, with the Council of Ministers and deputies convened to ratify them subsequently. The essential objective was victory as the means of securing the position of the regime within France and of restoring French dominance in Europe. However, the Emperor and his advisors had fallen into a trap, because of their overwhelmingly emotional response to Bismarck's provocation and failure to calmly assess the risks. The responsible professional experts, the foreign minister Gramont and war minister Le Boeuf, moreover, provided inaccurate information and misconceived assessments of the diplomatic and military situations. The individuals best placed to resist the pressures in favour of war, the Emperor himself and Ollivier, were on the one hand too physically and mentally exhausted to provide effective leadership, and on the other, too aware of his political isolation. Baroche, who as a member of a Senate commission chaired by Rouher, had signed a report unanimously approving the government's conduct of affairs, expressed his private concern about the readiness of the army in a letter to his son on 17 July. The commission had certainly not been impressed by Gramont's 'long and diffuse explanations' or by a diplomacy, which had made it 'impossible to honourably avoid war'. Its members had concluded reluctantly that, in the circumstances, there was nothing to do except express public support and make the best of the situation.[182] On 28 July, accompanied by the Prince-Imperial, Napoleon left Saint Cloud to

---

[180] Audoin-Rouzeau, *1870*, pp. 63–4.
[181] Reported by Prince Napoleon in letter to Ollivier, quoted Tulard, *Dictionnaire*, p. 937.
[182] Maurain, *Baroche*, pp. 489–90.

assume command of the armies. This was another error of judgement, compounded by the appointment of the still politically inexperienced Eugènie as Empress-Regent.[183]

THE PUBLIC RESPONSE TO WAR

Public reaction to the prospect of war was mixed. In the most recent study of public opinion, Audoin-Rouzeau insists on the difficulty of identifying countless individual, social, and geographical nuances and tracing change over time.[184] Much would depend on how the news was constructed and presented by the government, by the semi-official Havas news agency, and a newspaper press which represented a variety of political persuasions. The 'deforming' impact of rumour would play a role also, especially once conflict began. In assessing the relative value of the various sources of information on opinion, Audoin-Rouzeau joins L. M. Case in stressing the value of reports from procureurs-généraux and prefects to ministers and an Emperor obsessed by the need for accurate assessments of public opinion.[185] However, the historian should take heed of Saint-Marc-Girardin's warning to the official enquiry that in asking for reports on public opinion the government 'asked the question after having given the answer'.[186] At any rate, on 7 July officials were instructed to provide assessments of public attitudes to the prospect of war.[187] Unfortunately, whilst these provide a considerable amount of information on the provinces, most of the reports dealing with Paris were destroyed during the Commune.[188]

The democratic press was certainly hostile, with *Le Rappel* warning on 1 August that the war would probably end with a triumphal parade through Paris led by the Emperor and the Prince-Imperial and behind them, 'bound and bloody, two people, one of them Prussia, the other Liberty'. Initially at least, some liberal Bonapartist papers shared these concerns. The authorities were particularly concerned about Paris and the major industrial centres, although the revolutionary left had already been weakened by a wave of arrests.[189] The Paris sections of the Workers' International published a manifesto in Delescluze's *Le Réveil* on 12 July denouncing the imminent war. Addressed 'To the workers of all countries' it asserted that 'war over a question of predominance or

---

[183] Smith, *Napoleon III* (London 1995), pp. 102–3.   [184] Audoin-Rouzeau, *1870*, p. 43.

[185] Case, *Opinion*, p. 6; Audoin-Rouzeau, *1870*, p. 330 n. 30.   [186] *Enquête parlementaire*, I, p. 463.

[187] J. Pointu, *Histoire de la chute de l'Empire* (Paris 1874), p. 61.   [188] E.g. Case, *Opinion*, pp. 11–12.

[189] MJ to PG Blois, 3 Aug. 1870 in *Papiers et correspondance*, I, p. 457.

dynasty can only appear, in the workers' eyes, as a criminal absurdity'. Martial law was declared throughout the Saône-et-Loire on 9 August, following the distribution of similarly worded leaflets in Le Creusot.[190] The Rouen section similarly denounced the war and called for international opposition.[191] In private Aubry, its leading light, was more fatalistic, concluding that only social revolution and the elimination of kings and permanent armies would bring wars between nations to an end.[192] Substantial protest demonstrations were organised in Paris and Marseilles, but were easily dispersed by the police. 'Seditious' shouts were reported from all over the country.[193] At a more 'refined' level, and in private, the novelist George Sand, writing to her dear friend Gustave Flaubert on 26 July, expressed her concern about patriotic songs and emotions likely to turn men into 'ferocious and vain brutes'.[194] Flaubert himself complained bitterly about 'the irremediable barbarism of humanity' and the *vertige* to which individuals gave themselves, pouring scorn on 'the *bourgeois* (yes! The odious Rouen *bourgeois*, the cotton mill owner)', whose 'ferocity [was] *impossible to describe*. He believes that ... Bismarck has been insolent to him.'[195] The Legitimist businessman Denis Benoist d'Azy, writing from Paris on 15 July, reported to his brother that 'Here everyone wants war. The day-before-yesterday peace, yesterday war, today God knows what. There has never been such a mess and such mad leadership in a crisis.'[196] A few days later and closer to the frontier, the letters of the Mulhouse industrialist Charles Mertzdorff on 20 July, written whilst he helped organise a collection for wounded soldiers, reveal mounting anxiety.[197]

Many potential critics must have been discouraged by the evidence of patriotic fervour and the growing sense of isolation as press censorship silenced dissident voices. From the Côte-d'Or it was reported that 'the advanced party has not ceased to exist but it offers only very rare signs of life; it feels obliged to be prudent; those of its members who

---

[190] Tulard, *Dictionnaire*, p. 656; see also Ponsot, *Les grèves de 1870 et la Commune de 1871 au Creusot* (Paris 1957), p. 39.
[191] 'Appel de la Fédération ouvrière rouennaise aux travailleurs de Prusse et d'Espagne,' published in *La Réforme sociale*, 31 July 1870, printed in Boivin, *Mouvement ouvrier*, II, pp. 286–7.
[192] Boivin, *ibid.*, I, p. 410.   [193] Audoin-Rouzeau, *1870*, pp. 69–70.
[194] Flaubert, *Correspondance*, IV.
[195] Letter to Edma Roger des Genettes, 31 July 1870, *ibid.*, pp. 215–16.
[196] Quoted Locke, *Fonderies*, p. 270.
[197] C. Dauphin, P. Lebrun-Pézerat, and D. Poublas, *Ces bonnes lettres. Une correspondance familiale au 19e siècle* (Paris 1995) pp. 288–9.

speak against the war would be described immediately as Prussians'.[198]
Police reports commented on the growing moderation of press criticism
– with *Le Siècle*, for example, insisting on 16 July that it would in future
support the war effort – and the decline of revolutionary agitation in
the working-class *quartiers* of the capital where 'preoccupation with the
war and general enthusiasm have paralysed action, for the moment at
least'.[199] Generally, and especially in rural areas, initial surprise caused
by the rapid development of the crisis, was followed by a rallying to
the national cause.[200] In rural communities in Seine-et-Marne where
peasants had favoured peace at first, it soon became evident that this
would be the most popular of the regime's wars.[201] A sort of *union sacrée*
developed, presaging that of 1914, and especially evident in the eastern
departments most threatened by invasion and in which memories of the
brutal Prussian occupation in 1814–15 survived. The state prosecutor
at Colmar in Alsace insisted that 'the war has cut short all the preoccupations of internal politics' and has 'united all the parties and all classes
in the same patriotic enthusiasm'.[202] These were also the areas in which
'informed' opinion at least was anxious already about the threat posed by
the extension of Prussian hegemony over the south German states. In the
frontier city of Strasbourg on 16 July, patriotic crowds revived the songs
which had encouraged earlier generations of soldiers and especially the
previously banned *Marseillaise*.[203] The Emperor himself had authorised
Marie Sass to sing the revolutionary hymn, which she did, to hysterical
applause, draped in a tricolour at the Opera on 14 July. Conservatives
can hardly have found this constant singing very re-assuring. The Legitimist *Union* complained on 16 July that 'the *Marseillaise* was the hymn of
the guillotine' and threatened to dishonour the military campaign.[204]

Such manifestations were regarded with distaste by many of the
clerical and Legitimist critics of the regime. Nevertheless, the authorities
were impressed by their willingness to rally to the national cause and by
the fervent prayers for victory intoned by parish priests.[205] Mgr Plantier,
Bishop of Nîmes, who, privately, saw the war as Divine punishment for

---

[198] 31 July 1870, quoted Audoin-Rouzeau, *1870*, p. 72.
[199] OC cie. de la Seine, 30 July 1870, AHG G8/176.
[200] MJ to Emperor at Metz, 7 Aug. 1870 in *Papiers et correspondance*, I, p. 458.
[201] OC gendarmerie Seine-et-Marne, ?July 1870, AHG G8/176.
[202] 21 July 1870, AN BB 30/390.
[203] G. Foessel, 'La vie quotidienne à Strasbourg à la veille de la guerre de 1870' in F. L'Huillier, *L'Alsace en 1870–71* (Gap 1971), pp. 41–2.
[204] See also J.-P. Chaline, *Deux bourgeois en leur temps: documents sur la société rouennaise du 19ᵉ siècle* (Rouen 1977) – letter of 22 July.
[205] E.g. prefect, 10 Aug. 1870, AN F1 CIII Lot 7; prefect, 2 Aug. 1870, AN F1 CIII Tarn-et-Garonne 5.

the Emperor's Italian policy, nevertheless, prayed for victory.[206] Mgr Dupanloup asked God to 'Make justice triumph ... by the hands of France.'[207] Liberals and the vast majority of republicans were also prepared to commit themselves to the war effort.[208] Most were persuaded easily that this was a 'just' war. According to the *Journal de la Haute-Saône* (19 July 1870) – 'the hour of vengeance has sounded. It is the duty of our valiant army to humble Prussian pride, and to put in its place this power which presumes to dominate Europe ... Our soldiers will serve the interests of Europe, the cause of right, justice and the liberty of the peoples.' An editorial on 27 July insisted that the Hohenzollern candidature was merely the occasion for and not the cause of war.[209] Broad sections of the press, especially on the authoritarian right, similarly demanded revenge for Sadowa.[210] Most of the press stressed the readiness of the army, helping to encourage a boundless spirit of optimism.[211]

The departure of military reservists and the mobilisation of 450,000 men of the Garde Nationale Mobile from 17 July brought home the reality of war to many families. Nevertheless, prefects reported that, even if there was little enthusiasm and peace would have been preferred, there was still a widespread belief that war had become inevitable and a quiet confidence that it would result in a complete victory.[212] This helped to promote a resigned acceptance of the situation, reinforced by the government's publication of, and commentary on, the Ems telegram. Gradually resignation turned into enthusiasm. Groups like businessmen, concerned about the disruptive impact of war on the economy, rationalised their situation by looking forward to the victory, which would end the persistent malaise which had affected confidence since 1866.[213] Regiments marching to railway stations *en route* to the front, their bands playing, were sent off by large and enthusiastic crowds singing patriotic songs.[214] A widespread sense of patriotic commitment appears to have existed by 1870, due to the efforts of the schools, media, and to community processes

[206] Huard, *La préhistoire des partis*, p. 873.
[207] 25 July 1870, quoted Ollivier, *L'Empire libéral*, xv, p. 61.
[208] E.g. *Enquête parlementaire*, I, p. 453, evidence of Henri Martin; p. 479 Jules Simon.
[209] Quoted H. Carel, 'Le département de la Haute-Saône de 1850 à 1914', Doctorat ès lettres, Université de Paris-Sorbonne, 1970, p. 437.
[210] E.g. *Mémorial de Lille* 13 July 1870, quoted Ménager, *Nord*, p. 901.
[211] E.g. *Le Constitutionnel*, 29–30 July 1870.
[212] E.g. prefect Loire, 9 July 1870, *Actes*, I, p. 467; Audoin-Rouzeau, *1870*, pp. 48–90.
[213] Prefect Bouches-du-Rhône, 9 July 1870, *Actes*, I, p. 465; OC gendarmerie de la Seine, 30 July 1870, AHG G8/176.
[214] E.g. PG Limoges, 26 July 1870, AN BB30/390; OG gendarmerie Finistère, 28 July, AHG G8/176; prefect, 1 Aug. 1870, AN F1 CIII Orne 9.

of socialisation. This was sufficient to turn a dynastic into a national war. Peasants already appear to have been turned into Frenchmen before the advent of the Third Republic. However, this initial sense of unity was to be short-lived. It reached its apogee with news of the French 'invasion' of Germany and the insubstantial victory at Sarrebrücken on 2 August. The public reactions to this minor affair were as exaggerated as the press reports describing it. Buildings were illuminated and crowds celebrated in the streets.[215] News of the first defeat, at Wissembourg on the 4th was received by telegram in the night of 4–5 August and announced publicly in the afternoon. The situation was to get worse rapidly.

MILITARY DEFEAT

The shortcomings of the French army have been rehearsed already. As a result of the failure to introduce substantial reforms, it was neither as large nor as well trained as it might have been. Its officer corps was seriously deficient, particularly at senior levels, and the absence of a general staff on the Prussian model meant a lack of adequate contingency planning and inadequate co-ordination of its movements in case of war. Such resources as it had were to be tragically wasted.[216] The army was rooted in the Restoration era. It was organised to engage in limited wars and to preserve internal order. Nevertheless, inspired by past success, and encouraged by the effectiveness of the new *chassepot* rifle, Marshal Le Boeuf appears to have been genuinely confident.[217] It was further assumed, with supreme optimism, that early French victories would bring Austria into the war. The decision by the Emperor to take command of the armies was to be disastrous, however. Contingency plans were largely made redundant when, at the last minute, Napoleon, over-riding Le Boeuf's protests, determined on a broad movement into German territory in the hope of detaching the southern German states from their alliance with Prussia and linking with Austria. This resulted in the replacement of the three armies originally provided for with one much larger force strung out along the German frontier. It would be particularly difficult to co-ordinate its activities, whilst the commanders of the eight army corps involved had neither the experience nor the confidence necessary to take independent decisions.[218]

[215] Audoin-Rouzeau, *1870*, pp. 93–5.
[216] See e.g. C. de Freycinet, *La guerre en province* (Paris 1871), pp. 332–5.
[217] *Enquête parlementaire*, V, p. 24, evidence of Le Boeuf.
[218] Ollivier, *L'Empire libéral*, XV, pp. 105–6; Adriance, *Gaiter Button*, pp. 55–62; Holmes, *Sedan*, pp. 174–5.

The process of mobilisation highlighted many of the weaknesses of both the political and the military systems. The pre-war military divisions had been essentially administrative units, with troops within them dispersed to assist in the protection of social order. The formations, which composed the new divisions, had no experience of working together. It was assumed that active wartime divisions, with all their component elements – that is, artillery, engineers, transport – would be formed in their concentration areas close to the frontier. The railway was to be the decisive element in the process. However, rail transport and subsequent movement by road away from railheads called for careful and detailed planning. Unfortunately, the military railway commission, which had been established to assess the capacity of railway lines, stations, and goods depots and to lay down timetables to prevent congestion, had rarely met. The considerable efforts made by the railway companies, especially the Est, could not compensate for the absence of military plans.[219] The movement of men, guns, horses, wagons, munitions, food, and sundry supplies soon congested the railways. The key railway yards at Metz rapidly filled with wagons containing badly needed food and munitions, most of which could not be unloaded because of confused instructions, and a lack of the labour, horses, and carts which should have been provided by the Train des Equipages militaires.[220] Telegrams from officials at the War Ministry, which attempted to impose order, only added to the confusion. There were constant complaints about the lack of ovens with which to bake bread, of maps, guns without cannonballs, and horses without harness.[221]

'Fighting' soldiers invariably blamed the intendancy for all these problems rather than a lack of planning. However blame is apportioned, the end result remained a substantial reduction in the mobility and fighting ability of the French army. The advantages which the French might have gained from the superior carrying capacity of their railway network were thus thrown away.[222] The much more effective use made by the Prussians of this new technology illustrates the general superiority of the process of mobilisation east of the Rhine. Significantly, as a junior staff officer, Moltke, the chief of the Prussian General Staff, had published a study of the value of the railways for the military as far back as 1843.

---

[219] Ollivier, *L'Empire libéral*, XV, p. 202; Serman, *Le corps*, p. 1442; A. Mitchell, *The Great Train Race. Railways and the Franco-German Rivalry* (Oxford 2000), pp. 32–6.

[220] Intendant 3e Corps, 24 July in *Papiers et correspondance*, I, p. 442.

[221] Senior Intendant Metz to colonel commanding artillery 3rd Corps, *ibid.*, pp. 439–46.

[222] F. Jacqmin, *Les chemins de fer pendant la guerre de 1870–71* (Paris 1874); M. van Crefeld, *Supplying War* (Cambridge 1977), p. 86.

Subsequently he had ensured, both in the Danish war in 1864 and against Austria in 1866, that the rail network was put to the best possible use and, in the aftermath of these wars, that the experience gained was analysed carefully.[223] The slowness and chaos of their mobilisation would prevent the French armies from launching the rapid offensive, which Napoleon had intended should occur before the completion of Prussian mobilisation. Superior planning and preparation would ensure that the mobilisation of the Prussian and other German armies was achieved more rapidly and completely.

Marshal Le Boeuf had assumed that two weeks would be necessary, from 14 July, to complete mobilisation. However, even on 1 August the Army of the Rhine was composed of at most 280,000 men instead of the 330,000 he had promised and many of its formations were either not complete or in the wrong place. The shortage of manpower and supplies forced the Emperor to abandon his offensive.[224] The dispositions already taken up for offensive action would prove to be unsuitable for a defensive campaign, however.[225] Moreover, concentration had still not been completed in time to meet the Prussian offensive on 6 August. Many units would remain too distant from each other to provide mutual support. Defeats at Wissembourg, Froeschwiller, and the Spicheren Heights on the 4 and 6 August revealed the danger both from dispersal and the lack of accurate information concerning the enemy's dispositions. The effect was to divide the French forces and open up France to invasion. There can be little doubt about the courage of individual soldiers. Casualties were extremely heavy in these frontier battles. Frontal assaults proved very costly for both sides. The use of cavalry, launched across unsuitable terrain, and against an unprecedented level of defensive firepower, led to pointless slaughter. The superiority of the French *chassepot* rifle was more than cancelled out by the greater range, murderous accuracy, and more effective deployment of Prussian artillery. The potential of the primitive machine gun, the *mitrailleuse*, was wasted because of lack of training in its use.[226]

The chaos resulting from the haphazard process of concentration was compounded by the shortcomings of the command structure of the Army of the Rhine. As supreme commander, the Emperor proved to be hesitant

---

[223] M. Messerschmidt, 'The Prussian army from reform to war' in Förster and Nagler, *Total War*, p. 272; A. Bucholz, *Moltke, Schlieffen and Prussian War Planning* (Oxford 1991), pp. 41–2.

[224] Serman, 'French mobilization in 1870' in Förster and Nagler, *Total War*, pp. 284–6; Adriance, *Gaiter Buttons*, pp. 70–80.

[225] *Enquête parlementaire*, V, p. 25, evidence of Le Boeuf.

[226] Audoin-Rouzeau, *1870*, pp. 96, 99–101; Holmes, *Sedan*, pp. 227–32.

and indecisive and burdened by the extremely poor state of his health – in a word, incompetent. His frame of mind can be judged from a letter he wrote to the Empress soon after his arrival in Metz: 'Nothing is ready. We haven't enough troops. I believe we are already lost.'[227] It was clear that subordinates had little confidence in his judgement.[228] This was a considerable shortcoming for a command system based on 'charismatic leadership'.[229] Furthermore, the absence of a permanent chief of staff meant that there was no one with the experience and authority to take control in place of the Emperor. Le Boeuf, who was certainly no Moltke, had relinquished the War Ministry to become major-general of the army. He seems to have expected to assume effective command but was rapidly disabused. The Emperor had no intention of allowing his generals to take initiatives. The telegraph instead transmitted a confusing flow of orders and counter-orders.[230] Only a commander of exceptional ability might have compensated for the lack of a worked-out strategic plan and of a proper general staff, for the defective training of officers at every level, and numerical inferiority. Clearly neither Napoleon who, initially at least, assumed complete responsibility, nor the Marshals MacMahon and Bazaine when they took over, would be up to the task. Indecision was to be characteristic of all three.[231] When, on 5 August, Napoleon finally decided to relinquish command, his failure to appoint a clear successor and continued interference irretrievably blurred the chain of command.

The senior generals, with few exceptions, appear to have learnt little from their experiences in the Crimea and Italy and proved to be insufficiently intelligent or flexible to adapt to confused and rapidly changing battlefield conditions. Even if selected from within a narrow social circle, senior Prussian officers exhibited a far more developed sense of professionalism. They were better trained to command large units and to cope with unexpected difficulties, whilst an efficient staff system ensured that their objectives were defined more clearly and that they enjoyed greater freedom from political interference.[232] Faulty command mechanisms, the failure of the French cavalry to engage in effective reconnaissance which might have provided commanders with some awareness of the location of the enemy, uncertainty about the intentions of their

---

[227] Quoted W. Smith, 'La politique extérieure de Napoléon III: une politique des nationalités' in Tulard, *Pourquoi réhabiliter*, p. 103.

[228] *Enquête parlementaire*, v, p. 406, evidence of General Ladmirault.   [229] Holmes, *Sedan*, p. 179.

[230] Ollivier, *L'Empire libéral*, xv, pp. 173, 319–20; xiv, p. 386.

[231] *Ibid.*, xv, p. 173; see also evidence of MacMahon in AN 400 AP 69.

[232] Wawro, *Austro-Prussian War*, p. 287.

commander-in-chief and the inability of the two marshals to make rapid
and clear decisions, all contributed to a failure to concentrate their forces
in order to compensate for numerical inferiority. As a result, the French
were unable to achieve even the local superiority which might have
allowed them to take advantage of Prussian mistakes. At Froeschwiller
on 6 August they lost whatever slight hope there might have been of
gaining the initiative.[233] The disorganised retreat which followed, with
its marching and counter-marching, during which exhausted troops from
various units became entangled and their movement slowed to a crawl,
was due to a failure to assign marching routes. Chaos multiplied as units
attempted to redeploy. The breakdown of supply and of discipline, as
soldiers took to foraging and looting, provided a mere foretaste of what
was to come.[234] General Schmitz was appalled by the state of the retreating troops, many of whom had abandoned their equipment. He
later admitted that 'I was overwhelmed by a very profound sadness and
apprehension for the future.'[235] In a letter to his wife, Adolphe Clary, an
aide-de-camp to the Emperor, wrote on 7 August that 'I very much hope
that we will make use of this day of respite to concentrate our forces and
no longer remain strung out ... in small units ... It is a real war we are
involved in and not an African campaign.'[236] The Education Minister,
Maurice Richard, sent on a fact-finding mission from Paris, was another
witness to the accumulating chaos as well as to the Emperor's inability to
sit on a horse, his disabling headaches and growing sense of despair.[237]

Indeed, Napoleon appears to have sunk ever further into a mood
of total depression.[238] In this situation, and especially once the Emperor had relinquished command on 12 August to Bazaine, it seemed
to Ollivier, Rouher, and Pietri that he should return to his capital city,
bring the regency to an end, assert his own authority, and rally support.[239]
According to Marshal MacMahon, Napoleon accepted this in the morning of 17 August.[240] However, the Empress, supported by Persigny, was
determined that her husband should not be accused of having abandoned the army. She was reported to have angrily told Richard on his
return to Paris that 'To leave the army on the eve of a battle would be
dishonourable!'[241] In accepting her advice, the demoralised Emperor

---

[233] *Enquête parlementaire*, VI, pp. 352–3, evidence of Bazaine.
[234] Adriance, *Gaiter Button*, pp. 128–9; Audoin-Rouzeau, *1870*, p. 103.
[235] *Enquête parlementaire*, V, p. 433.   [236] Tulard, *Dictionnaire*, p. 298.
[237] Ollivier, *L'Empire libéral*, XVI, pp. 385–6.   [238] *Ibid.*, pp. 385–8, quoting Maurice Richard.
[239] Ollivier, *L'Empire libéral*, XVI, pp. 283–4, 333, 371.
[240] *Enquête parlementaire*, V, p. 14; see also pp. 434–5, evidence of General Schmitz.
[241] Ollivier, *L'Empire libéral*, XVI, pp. 388, 390–2.

was clearly conceding considerable political authority. There was growing interference also in military matters. The original plan, agreed on 18 August, was for a retreat by the Emperor and troops commanded by MacMahon towards the training camp at Châlons in order to reorganise, reinforce, and replenish his battered forces, to be followed by their deployment in defence of Paris.[242] This was abandoned following warnings to the Emperor from both the Empress and the newly appointed Prime Minister, General Comte Palikao, on 22 August, that public opinion would condemn such a move which meant abandoning Bazaine's army to its fate.[243] Bazaine had fought a breakout battle at Gravelotte-Saint-Privat on 18 August in an effort to avoid encirclement at Metz. Heavy casualties had been inflicted on the Prussians but the usual lack of planning and slowness of movement had turned tactical success into strategic disaster. The 180,000 men of the Army of the Rhine would remain blockaded in the city until it finally surrendered in October. According to MacMahon, however, the decision to move east again was taken, without interference by the Emperor, in response to orders from Bazaine received at 4 a.m. on the 22nd and on the assumption that Bazaine's army would attempt to break out again from its positions around Metz.[244]

The attempt to relieve Bazaine's encircled army was to prove fatal. Success depended on rapid movement in the hope of avoiding encounters with major German forces. On 23 August the Emperor and MacMahon set out from Reims with a poorly supplied and badly organised force made up of disparate elements, including remnants of the Army of the Rhine, troops from the Spanish frontier, and virtually untrained Gardes Mobiles. Moving slowly – 60 km in five days – because of congested roads and a lack of supplies, increasingly exhausted and demoralised, the new army marched east. By 25 August Moltke was already aware of its destination through the indiscretion of the Paris press. MacMahon informed Rouher on the 26th that Bazaine's position was irretrievable and the following day, clearly in despair of ever reaching his goal, he decided to take the road to Paris, only for the Emperor to receive another forcefully worded message from Palikao, warning him that 'if you abandon Bazaine, there will be a revolution in Paris, and you will yourself be

---

[242] *Ibid.*, XVI, p. 283; *Enquête parlementaire*, V, pp. 15–16, evidence of Marshal MacMahon. See also deposition of MacMahon in AN 40 AP 69; report of discussion between MacMahon and Rouher, 21 Aug., in Schnerb, *Rouher*, pp. 280–1.

[243] Telegram from Palikao to Emperor, 22 August 1870, in *Papiers et correspondance*, I, pp. 429–30.

[244] *Enquête parlementaire*, V, p. 15.

attacked by the entire enemy force'. Anyway, Paris was secure behind its fortifications.[245] On 31 August the army was forced by the approaching Prussians to seek refuge in the fortress town of Sedan. Typically, the French failed to occupy the heights south of the town, from which on 1 September Prussian artillery began to pour shells into the entangled mass of troops, horses, and wagons below. At 11 a.m. on 2 September, concluding, on the advice of his generals, that escape was impossible and further slaughter useless, Napoleon surrendered with over 100,000 men and 400 guns.[246] The Emperor's state of mind might be judged from a note to his wife on 2 September, in which he wrote that 'I cannot say how much I have suffered and am suffering ... I would have preferred death to witnessing such a disastrous capitulation.'[247]

THE HOME FRONT

Throughout the war the military authorities had attempted to control the diffusion and interpretation of news. Marshal Le Boeuf was rightly concerned that the newspapers might provide the Prussians with information on troop movements and had initially forbidden journalists to accompany the army. Even the Empress had felt this to be rather excessive, but little provision was made for journalists except for the creation of a press office at the Ministry of the Interior.[248] However, that ministry's main concern was to dictate the official press releases prepared by the Havas news agency. The press was simply forbidden to publish non-official information.[249] In practice this meant that 'good' news spread rapidly and the diffusion of 'bad' news was delayed. Along with the 'news', transmitted to prefects and sous-préfets for publication, came proclamations from the Empress-Regent and government, calling on the population to perform its patriotic duty.[250] Anxious crowds gathered regularly in front of government buildings on whose doors official posters presented the latest information.[251] However, the government itself was ill informed by the vague despatches it received from the front. Ollivier

---

[245] Palikao to Emperor, 27 Aug. 1870, AN 400 AP 67; evidence of Rouher in *Enquête parlementaire*, V, p. 107.

[246] See letter from Napoleon to MacMahon, 25 Sept. 1870, responding to the Marshal's self-exculpatory report on Sedan, and 'Note' written by the Emperor on 3 Oct., AN 400 AP 42.

[247] AN 400 AP 69.   [248] Ollivier, *L'Empire libéral*, XV, pp. 75–8.

[249] AN F7/12680 contains press releases; see also A. Dupuy, *1870–1871. La guerre, la Commune et la presse* (Paris 1959), p. 58.

[250] P. Charbon, 'Comment les français furent informés des événements guerriers de juillet à septembre 1870', *Relais. Revue des amis du musée du la poste*, 1994, pp. 19–21.

[251] See e.g. PG Bordeaux, 10 August 1870, AN F7/12660.

felt obliged to appeal directly to the Emperor on 7 August, 'in heaven's name, details immediately', in order to calm the Paris population.[252] The Prefect of Police shared his concern, partly because of the activities of stock exchange speculators who were spreading news of fictitious victories in order to drive up share prices.[253]

The silence of the press only increased public anxiety and encouraged the spread of rumour. Crowds gathering on the boulevards greeted the false news of a victory, which spread in Paris on the afternoon of 6 August, with great enthusiasm. According to Ollivier, the reaction of the Parisian public to the news of defeats at Forbach and Froeschwiller was 'stupor, the oppressive sense of devastation which follows on from great hopes deceived'.[254] This led to demonstrations in the afternoon of the 7th in support of the general arming of the population and a *levée en masse* along the lines of that of 1792. In this case patriotic appeals were being used by a relatively small number of militants to revive essentially republican demands. More immediately threatening to the authorities was the group of 700 to 800, which attempted to pillage gunsmith's premises.[255] Anxiety spread and became more intense. There were constant rumours about spies. Many towns experienced a run on their banks as people began to hoard gold coins.[256] Panic threatened, especially in those regions closest to the frontier, but by 18 August, even in the Breton community of Nort-sur-Erdre rumours of defeats had 'filled with consternation, frightened, and shattered the people'. The juge de paix reported that 'many already believe that, as in 1815, the Prussians will come to Nort, and talk about their exactions, their violence, their insolence. I try in vain to make them see sense. What can I do against brute fear and stupidity combined? The most absurd rumours circulate, spread by the bad press and depraved spirits.'[257] In Normandy, the novelist Gustave Flaubert was easily discouraged. He complained to George Sand, as early as 3 August, that 'we are entering into the *darkness.*' Clearly depressed, he wanted to know whether 'the wars between the races are perhaps recommencing?' predicting that 'we shall see, within a century several million men slaughter each other in a single meeting.'[258] At Nohant in the depths of rural Berry, and only apprised of the defeats on the 7th, Sand agreed on the futility of it all.[259] Increasingly, too, workers

---

[252] Ollivier to Emperor in AN F7/12660.
[253] Prefect of Police to MI, 6 Aug. 1870, AN F7/12660.   [254] Ollivier, *L'Empire libéral*, XVI, p. 335.
[255] Audoin-Rouzeau, *1870*, pp. 125–7.   [256] Prefect Nord, 18 Aug. 1870, AN F7/12660.
[257] Quoted M. Launay, *Le diocèse de Nantes sous le Second Empire* (Nantes 1983), II, p. 868 n. 4.
[258] Letter of 3 Aug. 1870 in Flaubert, *Correspondance*, IV, pp. 219–20.   [259] *Ibid.*, pp. 219–20.

were becoming anxious about the impact of declining business activity on their employment prospects.[260] The industrialist Charles Benoist d'Azy claimed on 11 August that rising social tension reminded him of 1848.[261] Attendance at church services increased substantially as anxiety spread.[262] By 25 August it was being reported from Toulon on the Mediterranean coast that 'the defeats suffered by our army have demoralised the population completely'. No one any longer believed the official despatches. Yet people were still hanging on to something positive, in this case the belief that Marshal Bazaine, in spite of his encirclement at Metz, would somehow impose a crushing defeat on the enemy.[263]

The prospect of disorder grew. In Marseille on 8 August news of the defeat at Forbach led to a gathering, organised by republicans and socialists, of perhaps 40,000 people in front of the prefecture and the installation of a revolutionary committee in the city hall. The crowd was easily dispersed and the members of the committee arrested but this was a warning.[264] Minor disorders were also reported from Toulon, Montpellier, Nîmes, Mâcon, Le Creusot, Beaune, and Limoges. Conscripts from the Avignon area were reported to have substituted for the first couplet of the *Marseillaise* the words 'The Republic calls us.'[265] Soldiers leaving for the front were advised by republicans at the railway station in Cordes (Tarn) to fire on the Emperor rather than the Prussians.[266] In Périgueux and Angoulême the seminaries were attacked.[267] In Paris itself on the 9th there was a demonstration in front of the Palais Bourbon, the meeting place of the Corps législatif, involving anywhere between 10,000 and 30,000 according to the source consulted, in support of the establishment of a Comité de défense nationale and which greeted deputies with shouts of *A bas l'Empire*. Firm military action was taken to disperse the crowd.[268] These disorders were followed by a period of relative calm, in part due to the authorities' firmness. The introduction of martial law in Paris, the Var, and Bouches-du-Rhône,[269] was followed by a series of arrests and the closure of newspapers including *Le Réveil* and

---

[260] E.g. prefect, 27 July 1870, AN F1 CIII Nord 16. For economic impact see AN C.2875.

[261] Letter in Locke, *Fonderies*, p. 271.

[262] Letter of 21 Aug. 1870 in Chaline, *Deux bourgeois*, p. 194.   [263] Constant, *Var*, p. 1481.

[264] Olivesi, *Marseille*, pp. 69–73.

[265] Baron de Rivière to Thiers, 12 Aug. 1870, BN naf 206207.

[266] Faury, *Cléricalisme*, pp. 87–8.   [267] Reports in AN F7/12660.

[268] *Enquête parlementaire*, V, p. 113, evidence of Pietri, Prefect of Police; Carrot, *Le maintien de l'ordre*, p. 573; Gossez, 'Le 4 Sept. 1870 initiatives et spontanéité,' *Actes du 77ᵉ CNSS* (Paris 1952), p. 508.

[269] On the necessity of this see e.g. Commissaire spécial du chemin de fer to Prefect of Police, 10 Aug. 1870, AN F7/12660.

Le Rappel.[270] Emile Zola, editor of *La Cloche* was prosecuted for writing that, once France had been delivered from the Prussians, it should be saved from the Empire (5 August) and laying exclusive claim on behalf of republicans to the patriotism of *La Marseillaise*.[271] Then, on 14 August, 200 to 300 Blanquists, led in person by *le vieux*, launched a feeble attack on the fire brigade barracks at La Valette in an attempt to seize arms.[272] Still anxious to distance himself from revolutionary violence Gambetta blamed *provocateurs*.[273]

There were also some attacks on supposed 'enemies' of the regime, which revealed very different perceptions of the situation, especially in the countryside. There, 'news' was especially slow to arrive. Popular attitudes were determined by rumours of the imminent arrival of Prussian forces as well as by existing social tensions, and by memories of the murder and pillage committed by the victorious allies in 1815. In an exceptional case, on market day at Hautfaye in the Dordogne on 16 August, a local noble, unfairly accused of displaying sympathies for the republicans and by implication for the Prussians, was tortured and murdered. According to the state prosecutor at Bordeaux,

the cause of the crime appears to have been less a project planned in advance than the general sentiment of hostility of the peasants against the nobles and priests who are accused here of sending money to the Prussians. An unfortunate incident, coinciding with the emotion caused by the general unrest, appears to have led to the catastrophe. These appalling scenes were accompanied by shouts of *Vive l'Empereur!*[274]

This kind of social tension and the hostility it produced towards all the Emperor's enemies – nobles, priests, and republicans – was common throughout the south-west.[275] Additionally, the textile workers of Armentières (Nord) and some other industrial centres expressed their preference for the regime over a republic likely to be dominated by the 'bourgeois' republicans they identified with their employers.[276] Peasants in areas as diverse as Brittany and the Midi were reported to be as afraid of the 'reds' in the cities as of the Prussians.[277]

As the military situation deteriorated, criticism of the regime mounted amongst deputies and in the press. Supported by Pietri, Ollivier tried to

---

[270] Ollivier, *L'Empire libéral*, XVI, pp. 330, 347.   [271] Dupuy, *Guerre*, p. 61.
[272] OC 1er Légion, 1 Sept. 1870, AHG G8/176; Carrot, *Maintien*, p. 574.
[273] Pointu, *Histoire de la chute*, p. 134.
[274] Quoted Audoin-Rouzeau, *1870*, p. 130; see especially Corbin, *Cannibals*, pp. 55–66.
[275] E.g. PG Toulouse, 31 Aug. 1870, AN BB30/390.   [276] Ménager, *Nord*, II, pp. 912–13.
[277] E.g. Commissaire spécial du chemin de fer to Paris Prefect of Police, 10 Aug. 1870, quoted Launay, *Le diocèse de Nantes*, vol. II, pp. 867–8.

insist on the return of the Emperor to Paris to bolster morale and reinforce the government's authority but was opposed by the Empress, determined that her husband should not return to his capital discredited by defeat.[278] Nevertheless, Eugénie felt obliged to receive a deputation of six deputies, led by Brame, at 10 p.m. on 8 August. These represented a broad swathe of liberal and conservative opinion. Amongst their demands were the dismissal of Ollivier, widely blamed for the disastrous conduct of the war, the appointment of the popular General Trochu as War Minister and of the ageing but energetic General Cousin-Montauban, created Comte Palikao for his exploits in China in 1860, as commander of the Army of Paris. Furthermore, they demanded the addition of representatives of the Corps législatif to the government's Conseil de défense.[279] Ollivier was abandoned easily as a useful scapegoat. He came under attack from all quarters in a tense session of the Corps législatif on 9 August and felt obliged to resign, following an overwhelming vote in favour of a motion demanding a new 'cabinet capable of organising the nation's defence' presented by the authoritarian Bonapartist Clément Duvernois.[280] Given the complete lack of confidence between the Empress and Ollivier and his suspicion of her closest confidants, this was probably essential to the effective conduct of government.[281] In the meantime, and without consulting her husband, the Empress replaced Ollivier and his colleagues with Palikao and ministers who, with the exception of the clerical Brame at Education, were drawn exclusively from amongst the proponents of the authoritarian Empire. The government was certainly no longer representative of the majority in the Corps législatif. The impression that the authoritarian Bonapartists had recovered power was reinforced by the Empress-Regent's decision that members of the Conseil privé, including Persigny and Rouher, should attend ministerial meetings.[282] Most politicians patriotically accepted the change, though with some reluctance, and partly because of the popular appointments of Marshal Bazaine to command the Army of the Rhine and on 17 August of the egotistical General Trochu as governor of Paris. On 27 August, Thiers, the most eminent member of the liberal opposition, would be added to the Conseil de défense. These were confidence-building measures. At the same

---

[278] Ollivier, *L'Empire libéral*, XVI, pp. 388–96.

[279] *Enquête parlementaire*, V, pp. 6–8, evidence of Thiers; pp. 65–6, evidence of Baron Jérôme David.

[280] Ollivier, *L'Empire libéral*, XVI, pp. 398–401, 412–30.

[281] See *ibid.*, XVI, pp. 377–8, 412–31; *Enquête parlementaire*, VI, pp. 422–4, evidence of M. Josseau; V, p. 83, evidence of Jules Brame; see also 'Résumé des événements du 28 juillet au septembre 1870', AN 400 AP 69.

[282] Maurain, *Baroche*, p. 491.

time efforts were made to strengthen the military position. The civilian Garde Mobile had been mobilised already on 26 July. On 8 August a decision was taken to enrol all men aged between thirty and forty in a mass National Guard, although fear of the political consequences of mass armament – the 'right to a gun' had been one of the democratic demands of 1848 – together with shortages of equipment ensured that this occurred only slowly. The entire military class liable for military service from 1870 was called up a year in advance and from 27 August the Garde Mobile was made fully liable for active service.[283]

Popular reactions to these measures were mixed. The successful floating of a war loan suggests that, however briefly, they enjoyed some success. However, significant numbers of men failed to report for duty. It was noted, in particular, that at the moment when a substantial effort was being made to ready Paris for a siege, many able-bodied men from the better-off classes were leaving for healthier climes. Widespread indiscipline was also reported, especially amongst the Gardes Mobiles.[284] Republicans remained divided. In the short term, any threat from the revolutionary left was limited by its own weakness. Rochefort had been arrested; Delescluze and Blanqui had escaped to Belgium. When, on the evening of 14 August, delegates from the International's *Fédération ouvrière parisienne* had demanded leadership from a group of republican politicians, including Pelletan, Emmanuel Arago, and Glais-Bizoin, they were spitefully reminded of the failure of the workers to support resistance to the *coup d'état* in December 1851. However, successive defeats were leading to the crumbling of loyalty to the regime. Increasingly, in the provinces at least, the elected Assembly rather than the Emperor was becoming the primary source of legitimacy in the state. In Paris there was much less sympathy for an institution perceived as overwhelmingly representative of a narrow social elite. Instead, attention focused on its thirty republican members. With their hopes for major political changes increasingly aroused, these did not want to help save the Empire, but neither did they want to take the risk of unleashing a potentially revolutionary movement. The message from both Ferry and Gambetta was one of restraint.[285] For many republicans the question of the dynasty had to be postponed, anyway, until the end of the military crisis.

[283] Gossez, '4 Sept. 1870', p. 511; Audoin-Rouzeau, *1870*, pp. 112–14.
[284] Reports in AN F7/12660; see also OC cie. de la Seine, 30 Aug. 1870 and of Seine-et-Oise, 28 Aug. 1870, AHG G8/176.
[285] Gossez, '4 Sept. 1870', pp. 508–10; Girard, *Nouvelle histoire*, pp. 411–12.

By the end of August police reports on Paris were delivering ominous warnings. According to the city's gendarmerie commander, 'all social classes share a great dissatisfaction with those who launched the country into war, without having prepared the means to support the struggle'. He still hoped that 'some victories will calm this irritation against the Emperor's rule', but clearly was giving way to despair. He was concerned seriously about the activities of secret societies and especially about 'the political parties [which] have put aside for the moment, their diverse and contrary aspirations; but it is clear that they are impatiently waiting for the moment when they will be able to express their recriminations, and attempt to make their opinions prevail'. He added that 'many people consider that the Emperor's abdication is essential to save his dynasty.' Similar observations were being made in police reports from throughout the Paris region.[286] News of the defeat and capitulation of the army led by Napoleon and MacMahon at Sedan, and the widespread sense of national humiliation which this engendered, rendered the collapse of the regime almost inevitable. Its legitimacy, and even the potency of the Napoleonic legend, had been destroyed. The Empress clearly realised this, angrily responding to the news: 'A Napoleon does not capitulate. Why did he not get himself killed? He has not realised that he has dishonoured himself.'[287] Already demoralised by the succession of defeats, ministers were stunned by the gravity of this news.[288] They would subsequently prove unable to offer effective leadership.[289]

REVOLUTION

Little news was received from the armies between 29 and 31 August, even by the government.[290] On 2 and 3 September rumours were widespread. Most deputies would have been made aware of the coming disaster through the Belgian press. Chevreau, Minister of the Interior, who later claimed to have received official news of Sedan between 4 p.m. and 5 p.m. on the 3rd, added that he had been extremely apprehensive for the previous forty-eight hours, due to the complete loss of communication with the Emperor and his army and the receipt at his ministry of telegrams from local officials reporting the passage of 'soldiers fleeing in

---

[286] OC cie. de la Seine-et-Oise and Seine-et-Marne, 28 Aug. 1870; cie. de la Seine, 30 Aug. 1870, AHG G8/176.
[287] Quoted A. Dansette, *Deuxième république et second empire* (Paris 1942), p. 412.
[288] *Enquête parlementaire*, V, p. 92, evidence of M. Callet.
[289] Complaint by M. Dréolle, deputy, *ibid.*, p. 104.   [290] See press releases in AN F7/12680.

disarray'.[291] The government finally received a despatch from the Emperor announcing the surrender at Sedan in the middle of the afternoon and confirmed the news to deputies around midnight. A circular was sent to the provincial authorities around 10.30 p.m. for publication the following morning. A revolutionary situation began to develop rapidly in the capital. Napoleon had expected this. In a telegram sent on 2 September to the Empress he wrote: 'after the irreparable misfortunes I have witnessed I think of the dangers you are facing and am very anxious about the news I receive from Paris'.[292] As we have seen, agitation had been growing since the first defeats. Ollivier had been dismissed, partly as a means of responding to public criticism. In private meetings on 31 August and 1 September Thiers, Favre, Ferry, and Gambetta had already discussed the possibility of replacing the government with one entirely dependent on the Corps législatif, but from which the republicans, unacceptable to the majority, would have been excluded.[293]

An effort would still be made to save the regime. Following the receipt at 4 a.m. on the 3rd of a telegram from her husband announcing his captivity, the Empress convoked a meeting of her ministers at the Tuileries together with the presidents of the Corps législatif and Senate (Schneider and Rouher), the members of the Conseil privé, and Pietri, the Prefect of Police.[294] Some Bonapartist deputies suggested that Palikao should assume the role of military dictator.[295] Jérôme David, the Minister of Public Works, and Prosper Mérimée, both of them close to the Empress, tried to persuade Thiers to head a government of national defence.[296] Afraid of popular revolution, republican deputies proposed the setting up of an executive commission to include Thiers, Trochu, the military governor, and, to represent continuity, Schneider. According to Picard, their objective was to 'head off the popular movement expected the following day, to remove all pretext for its involving itself in government and especially of degenerating into an insurrection'.[297] Favre was prepared to go further, insisting that 'the government has in fact ceased to exist', but even he did not want to risk civil war by calling for the establishment of the Republic. Instead he declared that it was 'necessary for all parties to efface themselves before a general [Trochu] who will take responsibility for the defence of the nation'.[298] There appears to have been a general

[291] *Enquête parlementaire*, v, p. 119.   [292] AN 400 AP 43.
[293] *Enquête parlementaire*, v, pp. 172–3, evidence of Jules Ferry.
[294] *Ibid.*, i, p. 177, report of Comte Daru.   [295] *Ibid.*, v, p. 73, evidence of Palikao.
[296] Rials, *Révolution*, p. 302.   [297] Gossez, '4 Sept. 1870', pp. 515–16.
[298] Pointu, *Histoire de la chute*, p. 162.

unwillingness to accept responsibility in this dire situation.[299] In the evening of 3 September, as crowds gathered on the boulevards, in a last desperate effort to save the regime, Schneider unsuccessfully attempted to persuade the Empress to transfer her powers as regent to the Corps législatif. Events gathered pace. At a short session beginning at 1 a.m. on the 4th, Favre introduced a motion signed by twenty-seven republican deputies which proposed that 'Louis-Napoleon Bonaparte and his dynasty are declared to be deprived of the powers conferred on them by the constitution' and that the Corps législatif (with its Bonapartist majority) should elect a commission 'which will be invested with the power of government' with, as its essential mission, 'to chase the enemy from our territory'. There were few protests. Ministers remained silent.[300] At a meeting with the Empress at 7 a.m., a Conseil de régence was proposed, with Palikao as *Lieutenant de ce conseil*. This would have assumed the powers held by the Empress. She does not appear to have objected.[301] In the day that followed, the question of 'deposition' was taken up more forcefully by Gambetta, Favre, Picard, and Ferry.[302] Concerned by news of revolution in Lyon, most deputies appear to have favoured Thiers' proposal for the creation of a Comité de gouvernement et de défense nationale.[303] The search for a compromise continued. Palikao agreed on the need to drop all mention of regency but continued to insist on a form of words – 'Conseil *du* gouvernement' rather than *de* – that, at least formally, preserved the regime. Thiers' original proposal, which had contained the phrase 'considering the vacancy of power', was revised by its author to 'given the circumstances' to attract Bonapartist support.[304] The authoritarian Bonapartist minister Duvernois complained that these proposals would establish a provisional government and represented a means of 'eliminating' the regime, but conceded that they were at least compatible with 'the preservation of order'.[305] Thus by the morning of the 4th no one appeared willing to defend the regime.[306] Regardless of party, deputies assumed now that 'it was essential for the Chamber to take power if it does not want it to fall into the street'. Their great fear was that

[299] E.g. *Enquête parlementaire*, v, p. 8, evidence of Thiers.
[300] See e.g. *ibid.*, v, p. 400, evidence of M. Guyot-Montpayroux; vi, pp. 424–5, evidence of Josseau, deputy.
[301] *Ibid.*, v, p. 94, Comte Daru resuming evidence of Brame, Buffet, and Kolb-Bernard; p. 378, evidence of Buffet.
[302] P. Antonmattei, *Gambetta* (Paris, 1999), p. 88.
[303] Tulard, *Dictionnaire*, pp. 1094–6; Schnerb, *Rouher*, pp. 282–3.
[304] *Enquête parlementaire*, vi, pp. 424–5, evidence of Josseau; v, p. 74, evidence of Palikao; p. 100, evidence of Brame.
[305] *Ibid.*, v, p. 100,, evidence of Duvernois.　　　[306] *Ibid.*, v, p. 400, evidence of Guyot-Montpayroux.

not only the Emperor, but they too, would be thrust aside by a popular revolution.[307]

A rapid decision might have allowed the Corps législatif to assume power and issue a patriotic appeal to the nation. However, by the time the parliamentary committee appointed to prepare legislation implementing Thiers' proposals had completed its deliberations, it would be too late. The *projet de loi* finally presented at 2.30 p.m. proposed that 'Considering the circumstances the Chamber will elect a commission of five members chosen by the Corps législatif' which would appoint ministers, and that 'a Constituent Assembly will be elected as soon as the circumstances permit' which would 'pronounce on the form of government'.[308] It was at this point that the crowd intervened. The deputies' worst fears of an 'appalling cataclysm'[309] appeared about to be realised. The republican writer Juliette Adam described the developing situation in central Paris in the evening of the 3 September, as the population responded to the spreading news of the military catastrophe:

towards seven in the evening the boulevards became crowded, everybody spoke at the same time, groaned, expressed outrage, and held forth; many cried with rage. In the enormous noise made by the crowd I distinguished two things: complaints and threats ... Around ten, the boulevards from the rue Montmartre to the new Opera, resembled an immense forum ... Hatred, violence overwhelmed every heart; threats, abuse, recriminations, piled up on Bonaparte ... Soon an immense, interminable column came together covering the highway and the pavements, chanting the word deposition to the air of des *Lampions*, gathering together all those it met on its passage, marching towards the Bastille ... arousing the faubourg Saint-Antoine, from its slumbers of the past twenty years. When we returned from the place de la Bastille towards the boulevard Montmartre we formed a vast, dense, serried mass.'[310]

The symbolism of songs, slogans, and destinations is obvious.

At 9.40 p.m. on 3 September Pietri, the Prefect of Police, had telegraphed the Empress, the Ministers of War and the Interior, as well as Trochu, the military governor of Paris, to warn them that 'there is considerable agitation in Paris. Groups criss-cross the boulevards and main roads shouting seditious slogans. At nine, several hundred people attacked the police post on the boulevard Bonne-Nouvelle. After a vigorous struggle, the attackers were repulsed.'[311] Blanquist activists like Pilhes and Granger played a significant role in this agitation, shouting

---

[307] See e.g. *ibid.*, VI, pp. 424–5, evidence of Josseau.
[308] 'Résumé des événements du 28 juillet au 4 septembre 1870', AN 400 AP 69.
[309] *Enquête parlementaire*, V, p. 93 evidence of Brame.   [310] Quoted Rials, *Révolution*, p. 303.
[311] *Enquête parlementaire*, V, p. 114, evidence of Pietri.

Vive la République and *Déchéance* and helping to spread the news that a demonstration would occur the following day. Although Blanqui himself, along with Delescluze and other revolutionaries (some of them police informers) met throughout the night in a house in the rue de la Sourdière, they do not appear to have agreed on a course of action. However, the situation must have seemed ripe for revolution.[312] Similar thoughts must have crossed the minds of the moderate republican deputies meeting at Jules Simon's home and the nearby Café de Londres in the boulevard de la Madeleine.[313] Certainly there was general agreement that 'after Sedan the Empire will no longer be able to preserve itself'.[314]

On the following day, a Sunday, the crowds were slow to gather. The Place de la Concorde was half empty at midday, although a crowd of 500 to 600 people at the head of the bridge across to the Palais Bourbon were already putting the military guard under some pressure. In the afternoon, as rumours of police brutality spread, the crowd, drawn from all social classes, grew to include large numbers of uniformed and armed National Guards, together with many women and children. Whether because they were guardsmen claiming to be reporting for service at the Palais Bourbon, or through incompetence, members of the crowd were allowed to cross the bridge and push their way, by about 2 p.m., to the railings surrounding the Palais and soon after into the building itself.[315] The parliamentary enquiry held in the aftermath of the Commune attached considerable importance to the failure of the responsible police and military authorities to ensure the security of the parliament building and to prevent the interruption of debates, which would have resulted in an orderly and legal transfer of power. The president of the Commission of Enquiry, the Comte Daru would also blame deputies for unnecessarily prolonging their debates and thus allowing a revolutionary situation to develop.[316] The military contingency plans for dealing with insurrection in the capital had been revised as recently as 27 April.[317] However, the war had considerably depleted the Paris garrison. Schneider, the presiding officer of the Corps législatif had already expressed concern about its security.[318] Palikao on 2 September ordered 1,000 troops, 2,000 gendarmes, 1,000 municipal police, and 1,000 National Guards to protect the Assembly and its approaches. According to Duvernois it was

---

[312] *Ibid.*, III, p. 98, evidence of Pietri.　　[313] *Ibid.*, p. 98, evidence of Renault.

[314] *Ibid.*, p. 211, evidence of Pelletan; p. 249, evidence of Gambetta.

[315] Rials, *Révolution*, pp. 304–6.　　[316] *Enquête parlementaire*, V, p. 10.

[317] 'Dispositions à prendre en cas d'émeutes et de troubles en Paris et en provinces.' Also circular from marshal commanding Garde Impériale, 27 April 1870, AHG MR 2151.

[318] *Enquête parlementaire*, V, p. 374, evidence of Schneider.

intended that troops would intervene only as a very last resort.[319] They had little time to prepare for their responsibilities.[320] Moreover, Pietri was alarmed by the open manifestation of 'hostile sentiments' by the National Guards.[321] Once again senior military officers were to prove themselves 'divided and indecisive'.[322]

The decision taken by the Emperor to appoint Trochu as military governor of Paris, taken because of his popularity and reputation as a military 'expert', had had the effect of diminishing the authority of Palikao, the Minister of War and head of government.[323] Furthermore, because of his numerous responsibilities, Palikao had handed responsibility for the security of the Corps législatif to General Saumain, commander of the Paris military division, who appeared not to know whether he was responsible to Palikao or Trochu. In turn, Saumain handed operational control over the forces guarding the Palais Bourbon to General Caussade, who would later be described by Palikao as 'feeble', 'a very old, very fat man' and certainly not his choice for the post. Caussade would die, apparently of an apoplectic fit, whilst commanding a division during the siege of Paris by the Prussians. In an attempt to defend his memory, his nephew claimed that the general had had to contend with inadequate resources and contradictory orders from Palikao and Trochu.[324] Recently brought out of retirement and in poor health, Saumain, his immediate superior, would admit later that he had not realised the seriousness of the situation. After being stationed in Paris for fifteen years, he had long ago learned to discount the exaggerations of police reports. Only the request of Ferdinand Barrot at midnight for troops to protect the Senate had given him second thoughts and, following instructions from Palikao the next morning, he had sent twice as many men as he had originally intended to protect the Palais Bourbon. Even then it was only around 2 p.m. when the supposedly reliable, *bon*, battalion of National Guards protecting the Palais joined in the shouts of *Vive la République*, that he finally appears to have realised the danger of the situation. He later admitted that he had become 'very frightened'. There were no orders, 'no

---

[319] *Ibid.*, V, p. 100, evidence of Duvernois.
[320] *Ibid.*, VI, p. 131, evidence of Motterouge; III, p. 70, letter from Captain Poupart of 116e regiment to General Frémont, 8 Oct. 1873; Carrot, *Maintien*, p. 579.
[321] Telegram 2 p.m., 4 Sept. 1870 to Empress, Ministers of War and the Interior, and to General Soumain in *Enquête parlementaire*, II, p. 2.
[322] Holmes, *Sedan*, p. 136; *Enquête parlementaire*, V, p. 376, evidence of Schneider.
[323] *Enquête parlementaire*, VI, p. 118, evidence of Henri Chevreau, Minister of the Interior.
[324] *Ibid.*, V, p. 79, evidence of Palikao; p. 381, evidence of General Lebreton; III, p. 98, letter from F. de Caussade to Comte Daru, 13 Aug. 1873.

direction.' His anxiety was considerably increased when, at 2.30 p.m. M. Duvergier, the secretary-general at the Prefecture of Police, announced that he was leaving, and believed that the prefect was already on his way to Belgium. Duvergier had added: 'I'm leaving you in a fix; do whatever you can.' Addressing his brother, who stood at his side, Soumain admitted that 'We are lost! This is the end!'[325] Throughout this, Trochu, a difficult personality at best, refused to involve himself in the defence of the regime. Pietri and Brame both placed most of the blame for the course of events on the military governor.[326] Napoleon would also condemn Trochu for his failure to support the Empress.[327] Henri Chevreau, the Interior Minister, was convinced that if Trochu, popular with the crowds, had placed himself at the head of his troops, the security of the Palais Bourbon would have been assured.[328] General Lebreton, who asked Trochu to do precisely this, claimed that his only response had been to criticise Palikao, as he would again before the commission of enquiry.[329]

This sense of uncertainty and confusion, and the unwillingness to accept responsibility so characteristic of senior officers, unsurprisingly spread to their subordinates. In such uncertain circumstances junior officers were unwilling to order their men to fire on the crowds. The news that the Republic had been proclaimed in Lyon increased their reluctance.[330] The rank and file were equally agitated and demoralised by the news of defeat and their own difficult situation.[331] Neither the police nor members of the military cordons were willing to use the force necessary to prevent guardsmen, claiming to be reporting for duty at the Palais or asking to see their deputies, from infiltrating into its precincts.[332] The small force of loyalist National Guards that had been permitted to exist since the *coup d'etat* had been greatly expanded in response to popular pressure, since the outbreak of war. It was now made up mostly of men hostile to the regime, which further increased the threat of civil war.[333] M. Jacob, a police commissaire, complained about an order to replace the unpopular uniformed police with unreliable National Guards on the approaches to the assembly.[334] Colonel Allavère, commanding three

[325] *Enquête parlementaire*, V, pp. 104, 406–7, evidence of General Saumain.
[326] *Ibid.*, V, pp. 90, 95 evidence of Brame; p. 414, evidence of Pietri.   [327] AN 400 AP 69.
[328] *Enquête parlementaire*, V, p. 120.
[329] *Ibid.*, V, pp. 381–2; see also p. 125, evidence of Trochu.
[330] *Ibid.*, III, pp. 70–2, evidence of Captain Poupart of 116e ligne.
[331] *Ibid.*, V, p. 140 deposition of General de Maupeou; Gossez, '4 Sept. 1870', pp. 522–3.
[332] *Ibid.*, III, pp. 70–1, evidence of Captain Poupart; V, p. 115, evidence of Pietri.
[333] Girard, *Nouvelle histoire*, pp. 411–12; Carrot, *Maintien*, pp. 575–6.
[334] *Enquête parlementaire*, V, p. 395.

squadrons of mounted gendarmerie, condemned General Caussade's unwillingness to allow him to push the guardsmen out of this supposedly secure area around the parliament building.[335] As the situation continued to deteriorate, deputies who went to the Prefecture of Police to ask for assistance found senior officials unwilling to commit themselves and more concerned with burning compromising papers.[336] A senior police officer, M. Claude, remembered 'police commissaires and policemen running up anxiously and looking for instructions which they were not given ... As the final defeat approached the prefect was more and more busy, the chief of the municipal police unable to receive visitors, the chief of the political police unable to be disturbed.'[337] Around 2.30 p.m. the grilles erected to protect the entrance to the Palais Bourbon were opened to admit a delegation of National Guards and the crowd, meeting no opposition from troops, broke through finally. General Lebreton, the *questor* responsible to the Corps législatif for its security, refused to allow a police commissaire to read the riot act.[338] Troops were simply ordered to prevent National Guards entering the debating chamber with their weapons.[339] Around 3.15 p.m. an agitated Pietri announced to the Empress that 'We have been betrayed. Further resistance is impossible: the forces on which I believed we could count have abandoned us.' The Tuileries Palace itself was virtually undefended. The Empress herself does not appear to have been willing to contemplate the bloodshed, which a vigorous defence of the regime would have required.[340] By this time, anyway, troops at the Caserne Napoléon, many of them recently conscripted, were shouting *Vive la République* from their barrack windows and those sent to disperse crowds in the nearby place de l'Hôtel-de-Ville (*c.* 2.30 p.m.) had instead joined them.[341]

In the Assembly, republican deputies tried to persuade the demonstrators to leave its members to their deliberations. Marchand, the editor of *Le Candide*, climbed into the presidential podium and demanded instead that deputies proclaim the Republic. Moderate republicans were reluctant to go so far. Ferry refused. As the crowds poured in, Grévy admitted to the Bonapartist minister Jérôme David that 'I would have wished to see the Republic arrive in a legal manner and not by revolution.' Favre admitted later that without the intervention of the crowd he would have

---

[335] *Ibid.*, p. 387.
[336] *Ibid.*, II, p. 257, evidence of M. Carré-Kérisouët, deputy; VI, p. 425, evidence of Josseau.
[337] Quoted V. Wright, 'Les préfets de police,' p. 88.   [338] Carrot, *Maintien*, p. 581.
[339] *Enquête parlementaire*, III, p. 72, evidence of Captain Poupart.
[340] *Ibid.*, V, pp. 164, 120–2, evidence of Chevreau.
[341] *Ibid.*, V, pp. 404–6, evidence of General Soumain.

accepted the transfer of power to a majority within the Imperial Corps
législatif which, in spite of electoral manipulation had, he recognised,
been elected by means of universal suffrage. His experience of the invasion of a previous assembly by crowds on 15 May 1848 – this *profanation
de l'Assemblée* – had left him profoundly afraid of *la multitude*.[342] Gambetta
also regretted later the slowness with which deputies had deliberated,
ignoring the threat from the crowds outside. Now, in an effort to calm
the crowd, he read out a motion of *déchéance*.[343] Recognising that there
was no chance of controlling the crowd, Favre acceded to demands that
the Republic be proclaimed, as in 1848, from the Hôtel-de-Ville and led
the demonstrators there.[344] Together with Ferry and Kératry, he succeeded in securing, by acclamation, the establishment of a Government
of National Defence made up of, and legitimised as, *les députés de Paris* –
Arago, Favre, Crémieux, Garnier-Pagès, Gambetta, Ferry, Glais-Bizoin,
Pelletan, Picard, Simon, and Rochefort. This was overwhelmingly a government of moderates, opposed to violence and committed to social order. Favre, Simon, Ferry, and Gambetta would all insist that they had
agreed to take power only to head off the threat of revolution and to
prevent a repetition of 1848.[345] Kératry assumed control immediately of
the nearby Prefecture of Police and Etienne Arago of the Paris city administration. The leaders of the revolutionary left like Blanqui, Millière,
and Pyat and the future leaders of the Paris Commune like Delescluze
and Flourens had been out-manoeuvred.[346] As requested by the new
ministers, at around 5.30 p.m. the military governor General Trochu
arrived, having announced to his aides that 'I am going there to do a
Lamartine.' He was assured that the new government was committed to
the protection of property, religion, and the family and would accept his
demand to be made its president.[347]   Favre told Adolphe Thiers that,
whilst being technically illegal, the government represented 'as much order as the revolution just unleashed could support'.[348] He subsequently
presided over a rump of the Chamber in the evening and advised the
deputies present that opposition would be 'unpatriotic ... In the presence of the enemy ... I think that there is only one thing for us to do:
to retire with dignity.'[349] Isolated, and almost ignored in the Tuileries,
and following the advice of General Mellinet and Pietri that the situation

[342] *Ibid.*, V, p. 89, evidence of David; pp. 149–50, evidence of Favre.
[343] *Ibid.*, V, pp. 248–9; I, p. 182, report of Comte Daru.
[344] *Ibid.*, VI, pp. 425–6, evidence of Josseau.
[345] *Ibid.*, I, p. 184; see also V, p. 199, evidence of Jules Ferry.
[346] See e.g. Pointu, *Histoire de la chute*, p. 169.   [347] Carrot, *Maintien*, p. 583.
[348] Quoted *ibid.*, p. 584.   [349] Quoted Bury and Tombs, *Thiers*, p. 183.

was hopeless, the Empress had quietly left the palace around the time, *c.* 3.30 p.m., when the crowds were entering the Hôtel-de-Ville. Palikao, arriving to request instructions found the gates closed – and went home.[350] Throughout the city crowds were tearing down the Imperial arms from buildings.[351] A revolution had been accomplished without a single casualty and in a carnival atmosphere.

At 6 p.m. a *très urgente* telegram was sent from the Interior Ministry to prefects, sous-préfets, generals, and *all* telegraph stations – signed by Gambetta.[352] He announced that 'Deposition has been pronounced by the Corps législatif' and that 'The Republic has been proclaimed at the Hôtel-de-Ville. A gouvernement de défense nationale, with eleven members, all Parisian deputies, has been established and ratified by popular acclamation.' In a telegraphed circular sent at 8 p.m., Kératry announced that Paris was calm and that 'the population is happy to acclaim the Republic'.[353] Gambetta's telegram must have caused consternation, although its contents cannot have come as a total surprise. Earlier in the day – around 4 p.m. – prefects had already reported receipt of telegrams announcing the establishment of the Republic in Lyon and had hastily sent messages to the Minister asking for news concerning the state of affairs in the capital.[354] Posters announcing the news of Sedan had appeared in Lyon from around 7 a.m. and crowds had gathered on the Place des Terreaux in front of the Prefecture. Statues of the Emperor and Empress and emblems of the Empire had been smashed. Unsure of the loyalty of his troops, the local military commander ordered them to return to barracks. Between 8 and 9 a.m., 100 people pushed their way into the building and the Republic was proclaimed, on one floor by the 'radicals' Dr Durand and Désiré Barodet, together with the former moderate republican deputy, Dr Hénon, on the other by Charles Beauvoir a member of the International, along with two workers. Soon afterwards the names of members of a 67-strong Committee of Public Safety, made up of professionals, tradesmen, and about twenty silk weavers, were read out to and acclaimed by the crowds below. Moderate Republicans, joined by Béranger the Imperial *avocat-général*, had been meeting for weeks to plan an orderly transition of power when the moment came.[355] The

---

[350] *Enquête parlementaire*, V, p. 75, evidence of Palikao; see also 'Résumé des événements du 28 juillet au 4 septembre 1870' in AN 400 AP 69.

[351] Pointu, *Histoire de la chute*, p. 170.   [352] *Enquête parlementaire*, III, p. 157.

[353] AN F7/12661.

[354] E.g. prefect Côte-d'Or, 4 p.m., 4 Sept; prefect Jura 4.35 p.m., AN F7/12666.

[355] Based on *Enquête parlementaire*, V, pp. 501–4; J. Archer, 'La naissance de la 3e République à Lyon,' *Cahiers d'histoire*, 1971, p. 5f; Robert, *Les chemins*, pp. 170–2; Le Clère and Wright, *Préfets*, p. 289.

poster announcing this action, which began to appear from around 10 a.m. declared that 'the misfortunes of the nation dictate our duty. We decree the immediate deposition of the Emperor and the proclamation of the Republic.'[356]

In Marseilles, although the authorities had appeared confident of their ability to retain control on the morning of 4 September, a moderate republican municipality assumed power, with mixed emotions – welcoming the new republican era and hoping for the more effective waging of the war, but frightened by the arming of the masses.[357] In Bordeaux, in the afternoon of the 4th, the National Guard refused to take action against demonstrators and joined them in destroying a statue of the Emperor.[358] In the Nord, news of the military disaster had filtered through from Belgium from the evening of 1 September. Its impact had been reinforced by the appearance of large numbers of demoralised and wounded soldiers. The prefect Masson's proclamation on the 3rd simply added to the panic. He warned that 'the war is coming closer to us. The bravery of our army has not been enough to keep them from our hearths.' He issued a call to arms, which might have been amusing if the situation had not been so serious. 'Everyone arm themselves: hunting rifles, arquebusiers, scythes and forks, lances, halberds, bows and arrows, crossbows, one- and two-handed swords, spades, hoes, fire shovels, spits, fire-tongs, broken glass, everything is a weapon in the hands of the sons of 1792.'[359] The response of many villagers was to pack their belongings onto their carts and head for Lille, in the hope of escaping the dreaded Prussians. Masson delayed his announcement of the change of regime so that it was the arrival, at 10 p.m., of a train from Paris that spread the news. A crowd of 3,000 to 4,000 which gathered in front of the prefecture was persuaded by the republican leader Testelin to disperse and power was handed over without violence.[360] Typically, the following day the conservative *Mémorial de Lille* called for patriotic unity, declaring that 'all opposition on our part would be a crime, a betrayal of the nation'.[361]

In most places the news of Sedan was rapidly followed by that of the proclamation of the Republic in Paris.[362] The sense of shock was such that the Imperial authorities generally accepted the situation. They informed Gambetta that they would remain at their posts until replaced,

---

[356] *Enquête parlementaire*, II, p. 30.
[357] *Ibid.*, V, p. 548, evidence of Thourel; Olivesi, *Marseille*, pp. 75–81.
[358] Audoin-Rouzeau, *1870*, p. 141.   [359] Quoted Ménager, *Nord*, II, pp. 913–14.
[360] *Ibid.*, pp. 914–15.   [361] Quoted Ménager, *Les Napoléons*, p. 269.
[362] E.g. Constant, *Var*, p. 1481, re Toulon.

although some were soon forced to withdraw by hostile crowds.[363] Moderate republicans were anxious to secure an orderly transfer of power. In Toulouse and Saint-Etienne, republican councillors elected in August assumed control of the administration and set about arming the National Guard. The 'radical' leader in Saint-Etienne, César Bertholon, ordered the red flag, initially hoisted over the town hall, to be replaced by the tricolour, a more palatable symbol.[364] In the circumstances, in cities like Limoges, the cause of national defence was widely assumed to take precedence over calls for social reform. This reduced the divisions amongst republicans. Many Catholics followed Bishop Pie in seeing Sedan as an 'act of Divine Retribution', and rallied to the new regime,[365] although the anticlericalism of some of the newly appointed republican prefects, like Martin Nadaud in the Creuse, would cause considerable concern.[366]

Not all was sweetness and light. The Bonapartist press generally remained quiet, although three Parisian newspapers – and most notably Cassagnac's *Le Pays* – protested about the overthrow of the regime.[367] In the Nord, the municipal authorities in Cambrai and Roubaix refused to proclaim the Republic; at Dunkirk the *Messager du Nord* condemned the dissolution of the Corps législatif and the usurpation of power by the Parisian deputies; at Tourcoing, workers hostile to their republican employers demonstrated in support of the Emperor.[368] In many of the more isolated rural areas the news of Sedan and of the establishment of the new regime came as a great surprise.[369] Tesselin, the republican prefect of the Nord reported on 17 September that 'the peasants say that the Emperor has been betrayed by the rich and the republicans'.[370] The substantial purge of local mayors by the newly appointed prefects caused widespread irritation.[371] Charles Benoist d'Azy, writing from Marseille on 4 September represented widespread conservative concern: 'the word republic resonates in such a terrible fashion in the ears of many people. Will we be victorious over our enemies; will we be defeated from two sides? Terrible calamities are revealing themselves ... God help us.'[372] Social fear, so intense in 1848, rapidly revived. The proclamation of the Republic was the outcome of an unexpected series of events. Occupying the key office of Minister of the Interior, Gambetta was determined to

[363] E.g. sous-préfet Château-Thierry, 5 Sept. 1870, AN F7/12661; Le Clère and Wright, *Préfets*, pp. 289–90.
[364] Aminzade, *Ballots*, pp. 221–3.   [365] Gough, 'Conflict,' p. 167.
[366] E.g. Corbin, *Archaïsme*, II, pp. 909–10, 917.   [367] Ménager, *Les Napoléons*, p. 269.
[368] *Ibid.*, p. 270 and *Nord*, II, p. 917.   [369] E.g. Carel, *Le département de la Haute-Saône*, p. 441.
[370] Quoted Ménager, *Nord*, II, p. 919.   [371] Ménager, *Les Napoléons*, p. 277.
[372] Quoted Locke, *Fonderies*, pp. 272–3.

use his authority and the appointment of republican officials throughout France to impose the new political order, as well as a more effective military mobilisation on a country which had not wanted the Republic. At best, the new regime could hope for conditional support. As the newly appointed prefect of the Cher admitted, 'without being acclaimed with great enthusiasm, the Republic has been received with satisfaction, less because of its republican form than because it constitutes a new Government from which we can expect a new and different direction.'[373] A second short-lived *union sacrée* was being constructed. As the formerly Imperialist newspaper the *Moniteur du Puy-de-Dôme* put it: 'Let the Republic save the nation, and it will have our loyal support, and that of all good French citizens.'[374]

[373] 8 Sept. 1870, AN F1 cIII Cher 9.
[374] Quoted Audoin-Rouzeau, 'French public opinion', p. 402.

General conclusion

After Sedan, Napoleon remained a prisoner in Germany for over six months, until his release in March 1871. Subsequently he established his family in England, in a mansion at Camden Place, Chiselhurst. There he began to plan another *coup d'état*, but the continued deterioration of his health made this an unrealistic prospect. He died on 9 January 1873, following an operation to remove a stone from his bladder. This was not, however, the end of Bonapartism. The outbreak of the Paris Commune, within days of the deposed monarch's arrival in Britain, culminating in the slaughter of 20,000 men and women by the former Imperial army, released from its German prisoner-of-war camps for the purpose, revealed once more the intensity of social fear and the potential for conflict in French society. The death of the discredited Emperor left Bonapartists with an attractive candidate for the throne in the person of his son, born in 1856. By 1874, a propaganda campaign in favour of the Prince-Imperial supported by over seventy newspapers and an outpouring of pamphlets and prints was being organised by former pillars of the empire such as Rouher and Pietri. In the 1876 general election, some seventy-five Bonapartists were elected, notably in the south-west. At its peak in October 1877, there were 104 Bonapartist deputies. They were overwhelmingly conservative and clerical, wealthy and paternalistic, and enjoying solid local political bases – men like Granier de Cassagnac in the Gers, Echassériaux in Charente, and the Baron de Bourgoing in the Nièvre. Elsewhere, although much of the previous support for a democratic Bonapartism was draining away to the republicans, a latent sympathy survived. This continued to associate the Empire with prosperity and attracted support in regions as diverse as the cereal-cultivating plains of the Beauce in the Paris basin and the vineyards of the Hérault. There were also many sympathisers in the bureaucracy and the army. However, with the futile death of the Prince-Imperial in Africa, fighting the Zulus with the British army, the movement largely expired.

How should we conclude? Previous assessments have very much reflected historians' personalities and contemporaneous public concerns. These have ranged from the efforts to establish the Third Republic, to the need to promote economic development during the inter-war depression and period of post-war reconstruction, and the emergence of General de Gaulle at the head of another 'Bonapartist' regime. The label has been used as an explanatory category by both historians and political sociologists, and as a term of abuse by politicians and journalists. Given the intensity of their social fear, the preference of elites for strong authoritarian government, in the aftermath of the 1848 Revolution, was not surprising. They would probably have made a pact with the devil in order to safeguard their property and privileges. Indeed, much wider sections of the population desperately desired a return to order and prosperity, to 'normality' as they conceived it. In this respect, the parallels with Germany in 1933 and the rise of Hitler are striking. The authoritarian option carried substantial risks, however. It involved granting considerable power to a single individual, an opportunist with his own agenda, his own strengths and weaknesses. Moreover, effective government would depend on the ruler's physical and mental well-being, and persistent ill health and premature ageing soon reduced Napoleon III's capacity to rule. The dangers of personal rule would become increasingly apparent to many erstwhile supporters of the regime, through a series of policy decisions which appeared contrary to the interests of powerful interest groups.

From personal inclination and under pressure, Napoleon was at least prepared to adapt and to engage in the difficult process of transition from authoritarianism towards a more liberal political system. What started as a series of voluntary concessions, made possible by the regime's triumph against the revolutionary menace, rapidly turned into unwilling concessions to pressure from the socio-political elites upon whose collaboration the Empire depended. A sense of expectancy built up which was difficult to satisfy. Latent tensions were once again openly displayed as pressure from above eased and the various social and political groups felt able to compete for power. Unable to win over the urban masses and faced with a gradual weakening of the loyalty of the rural population, the Emperor finally conceded a 'liberal' constitution which, whilst allowing him to retain substantial personal power, especially in matters of defence and foreign policy, substantially reinforced the potential for parliamentary control. The plebiscite in May 1870 seemed to herald a new beginning. The institutions created as part of a violent counter-revolution had been adapted to meet the needs of a changing society with different political aspirations. The new regime, seen as a process rather than an end, and bearing many similarities to the presidential system of the Fifth Republic established by de Gaulle, would probably have been viable. This, however, is mere speculation. The liberal experiment was cut short by catastrophic military defeat, which destroyed the regime's legitimacy and the strength of the army, in the circumstances the only force capable of protecting it against revolution.

According to Robert Tombs, Napoleon III's particular political achievement and major contribution to the European political tradition was to reveal that 'democracy did not necessarily mean revolution, but that it could be made a tool of government'.[1] This required a populist appeal, drawing on the various strands of the Napoleonic tradition to offer strong government, which guaranteed the gains of 1789, as well as protecting a hierarchical social order and the conservative trinity of property, family, and religion. The Emperor considered himself to be the embodiment of the will of the people; Parliament or party, in comparison, represented only particular, 'selfish' interests. Through the plebiscite, the people confirmed the legitimacy of his rule. A movement essentially of the right, given its determination to protect the established social order, Bonapartism succeeded in creating a much wider consensus. Strong government combined with democratic procedures and the promise of prosperity and national glory. State building and economic modernisation continued apace. In spite of manipulation, elections were increasingly perceived as providing opportunities for voters to make representations to government, seek to influence policy and even issue a challenge. By 1870, and in contrast with 1851, it was not democracy but authoritarian government which appeared condemned.

Following Max Weber a three-fold distinction can be maintained between political power based on traditional, on 'charismatic', and on legal–rational authority. Charisma, in this sense, is an attribute of an individual with a sense of mission, capable of advancing a personal vision. The seizure of power through a *coup d'état*, however, implied a compromise with existing power-holders within the civil and military bureaucracies as well as the social milieu from within which they were recruited. In the absence of the 'totalitarian' party so characteristic of twentieth-century dictatorship, the regime also remained susceptible to challenges from loosely organised 'parties' determined to articulate alternative

---

[1] 'Inventing politics: from Bourbon Restoration to republican monarchy' in M. Alexander (ed.), *French History since Napoleon* (London, 1999), p. 67.

political conceptions (Legitimist, Orleanist/liberal, republican, and socialist) and to protect particular interests. The organisation of 'parties' crucially influenced the distribution of power, structuring the relationship between the state and the electorate, influencing the potential for either consensus or conflict, and defining the characteristics of an evolving political culture. In these circumstances the Emperor felt obliged to seek an accommodation with social elites and finally, through the Liberal Empire, to negotiate a substantial redistribution of power. This involved a significant shift from charismatic towards legal–rational authority by means of the establishment of a parliamentary regime, which would be offered guidance by a strong executive power – the Gaullist as well as the Bonapartist synthesis. Success depended a great deal on the quality of the leadership on offer and on the avoidance of a risky war. The regime would be brought down not by internal opposition but by an inability to manage foreign policy effectively. Even in democratic polities, the conduct of foreign affairs is frequently assumed to be a reserved area, with the head of state all too easily led into hasty action by professional advisors and media pressure, as well as an arrogant determination to avoid loss of face. The propensity for military adventure, however, remained an integral part of Bonapartism as defined by Napoleon III. Yet, whilst he possessed many qualities as a politician committed to economic and political modernisation and to the establishment of a stable political system, the Emperor most certainly lacked his uncle's military genius. Personal failings and the continued shortcomings of the political system combined with unexpected external events to destroy the Second Empire.

Select bibliography

UNPUBLISHED PRIMARY SOURCES

1. ARCHIVES NATIONALES

Series BB: Justice

BB II 1118 Results of plebiscite of 21–22 December, 1851

BB 18: correspondance générale

1460 Dévastations commises dans les forêts après la Révolution de février

1461 Diverse disorders

1462 Poursuites contre les auteurs des rébellions survenues à la suite de la perception des 45 centimes (1848–9)

1463 Complot du 15 mai 1848

1464 Diverse

1465 Insurrection de juin 1848: répercussions dans les départements

1469 Dossiers sur les clubs

1471–3 Dossiers sur les sociétés secrètes

1475–9 Dossiers concerning strikes and workers organisations

Information on popular protest: 1186, 1188–93, 1319–20, 1436, 1438, 1440, 1444, 1447–8, 1448B, 1449, 1451–2, 1454, 1460–1, 1475–9, 1484, 1517, 1537, 1545, 1553, 1558, 1563, 1581, 1618, 1633, 1639, 1644, 1707, 1715, 1728, 1754A, 1757, 1765–7, 1769, 1772, 1785

1717 municipal elections 1865

BB19: 37–42 Procureurs-généraux: reports on subsistence disorders 1846–7

BB20: 141, 157, 193 Reports on assizes, 1846–56

BB24: Requests for pardons

286–347, 500–6 For involvement in subsistence disorders

348–68 during 1848–9

385 during 1850

401–4 during 1851–2

448 General amnesty 1859

448–56 during 1854

478–83 during 1855

484–8 during 1856
494–9 during 1857
BB30: Rapports des procureurs-généraux
  332 Affaires politiques: correspondance 1848–9
  334 Affaires politiques: correspondance 1850–June 1851
  335 Affaires politiques: correspondance July 1851–2
  358–61 Troubles postérieurs à la Révolution de février 1848: correspondance
    et rapports
  366 Supplementary reports
  369–90 General reports, 1849–70
  389–402 Commissions mixtes 1851
  391 Affaires politiques November 1850–April 1851
  392A Affaires politiques March–April 1851
  392B Affaires politiques May 1851
  393 Affaires politiques June–July 1851
  394 Affaires politiques August–November 1851
  395 Evénéments de décembre 1851
  396 Affaires politiques December 1851
  397 Affaires politiques December 1851–January 1852
  403–4, 409–18 Political situation 1852
  405 Seditious literature
  406–7 Political situation 1852–4
  408–10 Political situation 1854
  411–12 Offenses contre l'Empereur
  413–14, 418, 421, 481 Secret societies
  415–17 Political situation 1855–6
  419, 440–1 Orsini affair
  420 Political situation 1857–8
  422, 442, 444, 450–1 Reactions to war 1859
  423 Official response to Ténot's publications on *coup d'état*
  426–31 Elections
  432–3 Subsistence disorders, 1853–6
  434–5 False news, 1853–6
  455 Opposition press 1870

Series C: Assemblée nationale

C930, 934–42 Enquiry into the events of May and June 1848: evidence
C943–69 Enquête sur le travail agricole et industriel. Décret du 25 mai
    1848
C987 Relations with railway companies
C1072, 1125 Petitions requesting railways
C1157–61 Agricultural enquiry 1870
C2854 Complaints from chambers of commerce about railway companies
C2874 Commission d'enquête sur les forces militaires

C3007 *Commission d'enquête sur les forces militaires*
C3078–81 Public assistance

Series F: Administration

F1a 10: Proclamations et actes publics des préfets à l'occasion des événements de décembre 1851 et janvier 1852

F1cIII: Correspondance des préfets

Ain 3, 9; Allier 10; Alpes, Basses- 4; Alpes, Hautes- 5; Ardèche 5; Ariège 7; Aube 9; Bouches-du-Rhône 12–13; Calvados 14; Charente-Inférieure 9, 13; Cher 9; Côtes-du-Nord 11, 13; Dordogne 5; Doubs 12; Drôme 12; Eure 13; Finistère 11; Gard 14; Gers 8; Gironde 10; Hérault 15; Ille-et-Vilaine 13; Indre 8; Indre-et-Loire 10–1; Isère 9–10; Jura 14; Loire 8–9; Loire-Inférieure 12; Loiret 12; Lot-et-Garonne 13; Lozère 9; Maine-et-Loire 12; Manche 6; Marne 9; Marne-Haute 8; Mayenne 9; Meurthe 17; Meuse 11; Morbihan 13; Nièvre 9; Nord 8, 14–16; Oise 11; Orne 14; Pas-de-Calais 17; Puy-de-Drôme 10; Pyrénées, Basses- 11; Pyrénées-Orientales 8; Rhin, Bas- 15; Rhin, Haut- 14; Rhône 10; Saône, Haute- 9, 12; Saône-et-Loire 8, 13; Sarthe 13; Seine 12, 30–2; Seine-Inférieure 16–17; Seine-et-Marne 7, 11; Sèvres, Deux- 11; Somme 10–11; Tarn 12; Tarn-et-Garonne 7; Vaucluse 10; Vendée 8; Vienne 9; Yonne 11

Police générale

F7: rapports et correspondance reçus par le ministère de l'Intérieure

2585 Insurrection de juin 1848: liste générale des inculpés
2595 Evénéments de 1851: decisions des Commissions mixtes

3909 Ain, 3913 Aisne, 3916 Allier, 3919 Alpes, Basses-3922 Alpes, Hautes-3925 Ardèche, 3928 Ardennes, 3930 Ariège, 3933 Aube, 3935 Aude, 3938 Aveyron, 3942 Bouches-du-Rhône, 3946 Calvados, 3949 Cantal, 3952 Charente, 3956 Charente-Inférieure, 3959 Cher, 3962 Corrèze, 3971 Côte-d'Or, 3975 Côtes-du-Nord, 3978 Creuse, 3981 Dordogne, 3985 Doubs, 3989 Drôme, 3992 Eure, 3996 Eure-et-Loir, 4002 Finistère, 4005 Gard, 4008 Garonne-Haute, 4011 Gers, 4015 Gironde, 4018 Hérault, 4022 Ille-et-Vilaine, 4025 Indre, 4028 Indre-et-Loire, 4032 Isère, 4036 Jura, 4039 Landes, 4042 Loir-et-Cher, 4046 Loire, 4050 Loire, Haute-, 4058 Loiret, 4061 Lot, 4064 Lot-et-Garonne, 4067 Lozère, 4071 Maine-et-Loire, 4075 Manche, 4078 Marne, 4081 Marne, Haute-, 4084 Mayenne, 4088 Meurthe, 4091 Meuse, 4095 Morbihan, 4099 Moselle, 4102 Nièvre, 4106 Nord, 4110 Oise, 4114 Orne, 4118 Pas-de-Calais, 4122 Puy-de-Dôme, 4126 Pyrénées, Basses-, 4129 Pyrénées, Hautes-, 4132 Pyrénées-Orientales, 4137 Rhin, Bas-, 4142 Rhin, Haut-, 4146 Rhône, 4158 Sarthe, 4165 Seine, 4191 Seine-et-Marne, 4197 Seine-et-Oise, 4150 Saône-Haute, 4154 Saône-et-Loire, 4200 Sèvres, Deux-, 4204 Somme, 4207 Tarn, 4210 Tarn-et-Garonne.

1 2654–61 Dépêches des préfets 1 870
1 2680 Franco-Prussian War: official press releases
1 2710–1 3 Correspondence concerning individuals condemned following the events of December 1 851

Series F8: Public hygiene

210–1 1   Commissions des Logements insalubres

Series F9: Affaires militaires

1 072 Reports concerning the Garde Mobile

Series F1 1 : Subsistence

2680 Correspondence with cantonal statistical commissions, 1 862
2682–4 Correspondence with cantonal statistical commissions, 1 853–60
2689 Correspondence with cantonal statistical commissions, 1 864–5
2690, 2694 Subsistence 1 867
2734 Enquête agricole 1 866
2752 Trade in cereals and flour
2755–6 Subsistence 1 850–1
2758 Subsistence, 1 846–7
2760–6, 2780, 2786, 2790 Bread prices and effects of ending restrictions on bakers, 1 863
2801 –2 Provisioning of Paris

Series F1 2 : Commerce and industry

2370–4 Wages, living standards
2337–8, 2446, 7600 Economic effects of 1 848 Revolution
2481 –2 Commission des douanes, treaty of commerce
2483 Assessments of competitiveness of French industry
2495–6 Economic situation 1 849–51
2515 Note sur les effets du Traité de commerce
2522A Price of grain
2533 Economic situation 1 853
2715B Chamber of commerce reports
3109–21 Reports of worker delegates to Exposition universelle 1 867
4476C Industrial situation 1 849–50
4651 –2 Strikes: Second Empire
4841 Customs tariffs
4854 Petitions concerning tariffs
6407 Effects of 1 860 commercial treaty
6445 Assessment of commercial relations with Britain prior to 1 860 treaty

Series F14: Public works

8508A Rouher, Rapport à S. M. l'Empereur 1856
9066 Requests for railway lines, stations; complaints about rail tariffs
9279 Chemins de fer: Etudes
9412 Transport of foodstuffs

Series F17: Education

2649 Rapports trimestriels de l'état politique, moral et religieux, 1858–9
9109–14 Preparation and implementation of 1833 and 1850 laws
9146 Popular literature
9279–80, 9312–13, 9373–4 Reports of academic rectors and school inspectors
10758–85 Teachers' *mémoires* on needs of primary education in rural communes

Series F18: Press

294 Situation de la presse départementale, 1868
297 Inspection générale de l'imprimerie, de la librairie et du colportage

Series F19: Police des cultes

5604 Seconde République

Series F20

714 Prix et Salaires

Series F70

252–3 Exposé de la situation de l'Empire présenté au Sénat et au Corps législatif
422 Voyages de l'Empereur

Series O: Maison de l'Empereur

297, 305 Presse parisienne

Series AB

AB XIX
173–5 Papers confiscated from the Tuileries Palace in 1870
687–9 Collection Duménil: popular newspapers, almanacs, etc.
1707–8 Telegrams, 18–20 June 1870
3321 Diverse, including letters from Blanc, Thiers, Veuillot, etc.

Series AD

AD XIX
S 1–7 Paris Prefecture of Police: administration; subsistence 1858–60

AD xix

H 48 Rapport à S. M. l'Empereur sur l'état de l'enseignement primaire ... , 1863

Series AP (private papers)

43 AP Faucher
44 AP 1 Persigny
45 AP 2–3, 6–11, 23–4 Rouher
116 AP 1 Maurin
249 AP 5 Randon
270 AP 1 Chanzy
271 AP 4–5 Barrot
400 AP 41–4, 54, 67, 69, 93, 129, 139, 144, 150 Fonds Bonaparte
639 AP 1 Crémieux

Series AQ: Archives d'entreprises

6 AQ 2, 5, 20 Maurin papers re postal services
48 AQ 3659, 3707 Nord railway company, requests for railway stations
60 AQ 336 Paris–Orleans railway company, Evénéments politiques 1848

2 . ARCHIVES DE LA PRÉFECTURE DE POLICE

Aa 427–429 Evénéments divers 1848
432 Workers' associations and secret societies
433 Events of December 1851
434 Attentats et complots Second Empire

3 . ARCHIVES DU SERVICE HISTORIQUE DE L'ARMÉE DE TERRE

E5 153–9 Correspondance générale, 1846–7
F1 Correspondance militaire générale: République de 1848
 9 Correspondance générale 16–30 juin 1848
 16–17 Rapports des 5 jours (1848–9)
 51–4 Correspondance générale, 2 December 1851–January 1852
G8 Correspondance générale Second Empire
 1–176 Correspondance générale, 1852–70
 194–6 Records of the military and mixed commissions established in December 1851
MR 2151 Dispositions à prendre en cas d'émeutes et de troubles en Paris et en provinces
 2259 Reconnaissance. Mémoires topographiques (Paris region)

4 . BIBLIOTHÈQUE NATIONALE

naf 20617–19 Thiers papers
naf 23064–6 Persigny papers

Vp 9237f Chamber of Commerce requests for improved communications
Vp 927of Chamber of Commerce requests for improved communications, re customs tariffs

5 . NATIONAL LIBRARY OF WALES, ABERYSTWYTH

Nassau William Senior papers A36, 39–40; C75, 83–4, 132, 214, 249, 260, 267, 332–3, 356, 367, 445, 450–1, 479, 707, 745, 817

PUBLISHED PRIMARY SOURCES

1 . OFFICIAL PUBLICATIONS, COLLECTIONS OF DOCUMENTS

Assemblée nationale, *Rapport de la commission d'enquête sur l'insurrection qui a éclaté dans la journée du 23 juin et sur les événements du 15 mai*, 2 vols., 1848
Assemblée nationale, *Enquête parlementaire sur les actes du Gouvernement de la Défense nationale*, 7 vols. 1876
Chesseneau, G. (ed.), *La Commission extra-parlementaire de 1849*, Orleans 1937
Conseil d'Etat, *Enquête sur l'application des tarifs des chemins de fer*, 1850
Conseil d'Etat, *Enquête sur la boulangerie du département de la Seine*, 1859
Conseil d'Etat, *Enquête sur la révision de la législation des céréales*, 3 vols., 1859
Cour d'assises de l'Indre, *Affaire des troubles de Buzançais*, Châteauroux 1847
Cour impériale de Paris, *Affaire du Comité électoral dite des Treize. Réquisitoire et réplique de M. le Procureur Général Marnas*, 1864
Cour impériale de Paris, *Les procès de presse depuis la loi du 11 mai 1868 jusqu'à 1 janvier 1869*, 1869
Documents pour servir à l'histoire du Second Empire: circulaires, rapports, notes et instructions confidentielles, 1872
Enquête parlementaire sur le régime économique, 2 vols. 1870
Ministère de l'agriculture, du commerce et des travaux publics, *Enquête. Traité de commerce avec l'Angleterre*, 8 vols., 1860
Ministère de l'agriculture, du commerce et des travaux publics, *Documents statistiques et administratifs concernant l'épidémie de choléra de 1854*, 1862
Ministère de l'agriculture, du commerce et des travaux publics, *Enquête sur l'exploitation et la construction des chemins de fer*, 1863
Ministère de l'agriculture, du commerce et des travaux publics, *Rapport à l'Empereur sur la boulangerie*, 1864
Ministère de l'agriculture, du commerce et des travaux publics, Commission de l'enseignement professionnel. *Enquête*, I 1864
Ministère de l'agriculture, du commerce et des travaux publics, *Enquête agricole*, 37 vols. 1867–72
Ministère de l'agriculture, du commerce et des travaux publics, Bureau des subsistances, *Récoltes des céréales et des pommes de terre de 1815 à 1876*, 1878
Ministère des finances, *Enquête sur les principes et faits généraux qui régissent la circulation monétaire et fiduciaire*, 1867

Ministère de l'instruction publique, *État de l'instruction primaire en 1864 après les rapports des Inspecteurs d'Académie*, 2 vols., 1866

Papiers et correspondance de la famille impériale, 2 vols., 1871

Papiers sauvés des Tuileries, ed. R. Holt, 1871

Papiers secrets et correspondance du Second Empire, ed. P. Poulet-Malassis, 1873 (2nd edn)

Pièces saisies aux archives de la police politique de Lyon. Publiée par ordre du Conseil municipal, Lyons 1870

Préfecture de Police, *Des moyens de prévenir les fluctuations excessives du prix des blés en France*, 1853

Préfecture de Police, *Commission des subsistances. Taxe du pain. Rapport*, 1855

Procès-verbaux du Gouvernement provisoire et de la Commission du pouvoir exécutif 1950

Statistique de l'assistance publique de 1842 à 1853, Strasbourg 1858

Statistique de l'industrie à Paris résultant de l'enquête faite par la Chambre de commerce pour les années 1847–48, 2 vols., 1851

Statistique de l'industrie à Paris résultant de l'enquête faite par la Chambre de commerce pour l'année 1860, 1864

Ville de Paris, Commission des logements insalubres, *Rapport général*, 1866

Watteville, Baron de, *Rapport à son excellence le Ministre de l'Intérieur sur l'administration des bureaux de bienfaisance et sur la situation du paupérisme en France*, 1854

2 . NEWSPAPERS AND PERIODICALS

L'Ami du peuple, Annales de l'agriculture française, Annales des ponts et chaussées, Bulletin de la Société Franklin, Le Constitutionnel, La Gazette de France, La Gazette des Tribunaux, Journal d'agriculture pratique, Journal des chemins de fer, Journal des Economistes, La Liberté (Rouen), La Mutualité, Le National, Le Peuple, La Presse, La Réforme, Le Représentant du Peuple, La Révolution démocratique et sociale, Le Revue des Deux Mondes, Le Siècle, L'Union, L'Univers, La Voix du Peuple, La Vraie République

3 . CONTEMPORARY BOOKS AND PAMPHLETS

(Place of publication Paris unless otherwise stated)

Albiot, J., *Les campagnes électorales 1851–69*, 1869

Allain-Targé, H., *La république sous l'Empire. Lettres 1867–70*, 1939

Anon., *L'Armée et le socialisme, simples réflexions sur la question du moment, par un paysan qui a été soldat*, 1849

Le Socialisme c'est la famine, Bordeaux 1849

La solution donnée par le Président de la République aux sinistres complications politiques qui pressaient la France avant le 2 décembre 1851, peut-elle être considérée comme définitive?, 1852

Vive l'Empire, 1852

Des moyens de prévenir les fluctuations excessives du prix des blés en France, 1853

De l'enquête agricole par un médecin de campagne, Châteauroux 1866

De la nécessité d'un Nouveau coup d'état avant le couronnement de l'édifice, 1869

Apponyi, R., *De la révolution au coup d'état*, Geneva 1948

Arago, E., *Les postes en 1848*, 1867

Arnaud, F., *La révolution de 1869*, 1869

Audiganne, A., *Les populations ouvrières et les industries de la France dans le mouvement social du 19ᵉ siècle*, 2 vols. 1854

 'L'industrie française depuis la révolution de février', *Revue des deux mondes* 2 (1849)

Barail, General du, *Mes souvenirs*, 3 vols., 1894–6

Barbier, P. and Vernillet, F., *Histoire de la France par les chansons*, vol. VII: *La République de 1848 et le Second Empire*, 1959

Barrail, E. du, *Histoire de la jacquerie de 1851*, 1852

Barrot, O., *Mémoires posthumes*, vols. II, IV, 1875–6

Bastelica, A., *Avertissement aux travailleurs électeurs de Marseille. Le suffrage universel et la révolution*, Marseilles 1869

Baudry, E., *Les paysans aux élections de 1869*, 1869

Benoist, J. *Confessions d'un prolétaire*, 1968

Benoist, M. de, *Utopies d'un paysan*, Clermont-Ferrand 1867

Bergier, J. *Le journal d'un bourgeois de Lyon en 1848*, n.d.

Bersot, E, *La presse dans les départements*, 1867

Blanc, L. *Révélations historiques*, Leipzig 1859

 Les prochaines élections en France, London 1857

Blanc, L. et al., *Lettres et protestations sur l'amnistie du 17 août 1859*, Lausanne 1859

Blanqui, Auguste, *Textes choisis*, 1955

Blanqui, Adolphe, 'Les populations rurales de la France en 1850,' *Annales provençales d'agriculture*, 1851

Bonaparte, L.-N., *Des idées napoléoniennes*, 1860

Bonnet, A., *Enquête sur la situation et les besoins de l'agriculture*, Dijon 1867

Bonsens, M., *Dialogues électoraux. L'ouvrier, le bourgeois, le paysan*, 1869

Boucher de Perthes, J., *Misère, émeute, choléra*, Abbeville 1849

Brame, J., *De l'émigration des campagnes*, Lille 1859

Bugeaud, Maréchal, *Veillées d'une chaumière de la Vendée*, Lyons 1849

 La guerre des rues et des maisons, 1997

Camp, M. du, *Souvenirs d'un demi-siècle*, 2 vols., 1949

Castellane, Maréchal de, *Journal*, vols. III, IV, V, 1897

Caussidière, L.-M., *Memoirs*, 2 vols., London 1848

Chaline, J.-P. (ed.), *Deux bourgeois en leur temps: documents sur la société rouennaise du 19ᵉ siècle*, Rouen 1977

Charté-Marsaines, M., 'Mémoire sur les chemins de fer considérés au point de vue militaire', *Annales des ponts et chaussées*, 4th series, vol. IV, 1862

Chaudey, G., *L'Empire parlementaire est-il possible?*, 1870

Chevalier, M., *Des forces alimentaires des états et des devoirs du gouvernement dans la crise actuelle*, 1847

Claretie, J., *La volonté du peuple*, 1869

Cochet de Savigny, Baron (editor of *Journal de la gendarmerie*), *Notice historique sur la révolution du mois de décembre 1851*, 1852

Comité électoral de la rue de Poitiers, *Simples réflexions morales et politiques*, 1849

Comité des houillères, *Pétitions au Sénat*, Arras 1863

Comité des houillères du Nord et du Pas-de-Calais, *Réponse au questionnaire adressée aux compagnies houillère par la commission d'enquête parlementaire sur le régime économique*, Douai 1870

Commissaire, S., *Mémoires et souvenirs*, 2 vols., 1888

Commune révolutionnaire, *Lettre au Peuple*, London 1852

Cottin, P., *De l'enseignement primaire dans les campagnes et de son influence sur la vie politique des populations*, 1868

Cyprien de Bellisses, M., *Le SUFFRAGE UNIVERSEL dans le département de l'Ariège*, 1869

Darimon, A., *A travers une révolution (1847–55)*, 1884
    Histoire d'un parti. Les cinq sous l'empire (1857–60), 1888
    L'opposition libérale sous l'Empire (1861–63), 1886
    Le tiers parti sous l'Empire (1863–66), 1887
    Les irréconciliables sous l'Empire (1867–69), 1888
    Les cent seize et le ministère du 2 janvier (1869–70), 1889

Deslignières, H. M., *Entretiens politiques du village. Le Second Empire devant l'opinion publique et le suffrage universel*, 1869
    Deuxième procès des ouvriers typographes en 1ʳᵉ instance et en appel juillet 1862, 1862

Duchêne, G., *L'empire industriel. Histoire critique des concessions financières et industrielles du Second Empire*, 1869

Dumay, J., *Mémoires d'un militant ouvrier du Creusot (1841–1905)*, Grenoble 1976

Dumon, A., *Révélations sur le plébiscite et le comité central*, 1870

Dupanloup, Mgr, *L'athéisme et le péril social*, 1866

Dupont, P., Sue, E., and Schoelcher, V., *Le républicain des campagnes*, 1849

Duruy, V., *Notes et souvenirs*, 2 vols., 1901

Duvivier, J.-H., *L'Empire en province*, 1861

EDHIS, *Les républicains sous le Second Empire*, n.d. (major collection of pamphlets, manifestos, etc.)

Edleston, T., *Napoleon III. Speeches from the Throne*, 1931

Emerit, M. (ed.), *Lettres de Napoléon III à Madame Cornu*, 1937

Espinasse, General, *Mémoires*, n.d.

Faucher, L., *Correspondance*, 2 vols., 1867

Falloux, Comte de, *Memoirs* 2 vols., London 1888

Filippi de Fabj, F., *L'opposition dans la Seine. Aux ouvriers de Paris*, 1869

Flaubert, G., *Correspondance* IV: *Janvier 1869–décembre 1875*, 1998

Fleury, General Comte, *Souvenirs*, 2 vols., 1897

Fortoul, H., *Journal*, 2 vols., ed. G. Massa-Gille, Geneva 1989

Freycinet, C. de, *La guerre en province*, 1871
    Mes Souvenirs 1848–78, 1912

Gambetta, L. and Delescluze, C., *Le comité des députés de la Gauche et des délégués de la presse démocratique à l'armée*, 1870

Garnier, J., *Le droit au travail à l'Assemblée nationale, recueil complet de tous les discours prononcés dans cette mémorable discussion*, 1848

Garnier-Pagès, L. A., *Histoire de la Révolution de 1848*, 1872

Gastineau, B., *La vie politique et le journalisme en province*, 1869

Gellion, Danglar, *Ce qu'on dit au village*, 1869

Goulhot de Saint-Germain, M. de, *Etudes sur les campagnes*, 1859

Gramont, Duc de, *La France et la Prusse avant la guerre*, 1872

Granier de Cassagnac, A., *Récit complet et authentique des événements de décembre 1851*, 1852

Guéronnière, Comte A. de la, *Enquête parlementaire. La voix de la France*, 1869

Guillaume, H., *La vie d'un simple*, 1904

Guiral, P. and Brunon, R. (eds.), *Aspects de la vie politique et militaire en France au milieu du 19e siècle à travers la correspondance reçue par le Maréchal Pelissier (1828–64)*, 1968

Guizot, M., *Mémoires pour servir à l'histoire de mon temps*, vol. VIII, 1867

Haussmann, G. E. *Mémoires*, 3 vols. 1890–3

Hauterive, E. d,' *Napoléon III et le prince Napoléon. Correspondance inédite*, 1925

Hautpoul, Général Marquis de, *Mémoires* 1906

Instruction pastorale de Mgr. l'Evêque d'Amiens sur le Pouvoir à l'occasion du rétablissement de l'Empire, Amiens 1853

Hennequin, P., *Relation des événements survenus dans l'Allier en 1851*, Moulins 1852

Hodde, L. de la, *Histoire des sociétés secrètes et du parti républicain de 1830 à 1848*, 1850

Hubner, *Neuf ans de souvenirs*, 2 vols., 1904

Hugo, V. *Napoleon the Little*, London 1852

Jacqmin, F., *De l'exploitation des chemins de fer. Leçons faites en 1867 à l'Ecole impériale des ponts et chaussées*, 2 vols., 1868

Les chemins de fer pendant la guerre de 1870–71, 1874

Jaegler, E. and Bigaud, N., *Notice biographique. Principaux actes et pensées de S.M. l'Empereur Napoléon III*, 1853

Kerry, Earl of (ed.), *The Secret of the Coup d'État*, London 1924

Lacombe, C. de, *Les préfets et les maires*, 1869

Lamartine, A. de, *Histoire de la Révolution de 1848*, 2 vols., 1852

Laurent de Villedeuil, P., *Oeuvres de Emile et Isaac Pereire*, 4 vols., 1919–20

Laurier, C., *Simple entretien avec un préfet de l'Empire*, 1867

Lavialle de Lameillène, *Documents législatifs sur le télégraphe électrique en France*, 1865

Lavollée, C., 'Statistique industrielle de Paris', *Revue des deux mondes*, 1865

Lecanu, A., *La révolution par le suffrage universel*, 1869

Lecouteux, E., *L'agriculture et les élections de 1863*, 1863

Ledru-Rollin, *Le 3 juin*, Brussels 1850

Lejean, C. and Alexandre, C., *Correspondance (1846–69). Deux républicains bretons dans l'entourage de Lamartine et de Michelet*, 1993

Léonce de Lavergne, *L'agriculture et la population*, 1865

Lucas, A., *Les clubs et les clubistes*, 1851

Magen, H., *Histoire de la terreur bonapartiste*, Brussels 1852

Le Pilori: listes par départements des proscripteurs, Brussels 1854

Malcaze, E., *Les agitateurs*, 1869
Manzut, *Le paysan socialiste*, 1869
Marchal, L., *Des chemins de fer envisagés sous le rapport de la question des subsistances*, Avranches 1847
Marqfoy, G., *De l'abaissement des tarifs des chemins de fer en France*, 1863
Martinelli, J. *Un mot sur la situation*, Bordeaux 1848
Marx, K. *The Eighteenth Brumaire of Louis Bonaparte* in *Marx–Engels Selected Works*, vol. 1, Moscow 1962
Maudit, Capitaine H. de, *Révolution militaire du 2 décembre*, 1852
Maupas, M. de, *Mémoires sur le Second Empire*, 2 vols., 1884
Mayer, P. *Histoire du deux décembre*, 1852
Mérimée, P., *Correspondance générale*, vol. 1: *1853–55*, Toulouse 1953
Michon, Abbé, *De la crise de l'Empire*, 1860
Modeste, V., *De la cherté des grains et des préjuges populaires*, 1862
Moilin, T., *La liquidation sociale*, 1869
Montigny, L., *Lettres à un électeur rural*, 1869
Mullois, Abbé, *Confiance! Il y aura du pain pour tous*, 1854
Nadaud, M., *Mémoires de Léonard*, 1948
Normanby, Lord, *Journal of the Year of Revolution*, 2 vols., London 1851
Ollivier, E., *L'Empire libéral*, 17 vols., 1895–1918
    Journal 1846–1869, 2 vols., ed. T. Zeldin and A. Troisier de Diaz, 1961
Ordinaire, E., *Des candidatures officielles et de leurs conséquences*, 1869
Pélicier, E., *Statistique du télégraphe privé depuis son origine en France*, 1858
Perdiguier, A., *Mémoires d'un compagnon*, 1964
Persigny, Duc de, *Mémoires*, 1896
Petitin, A. (prefect Haute-Savoie), *Discussion de politique démocratique.*, 1862
Peut, H., *Des chemins de fer et des tarifs différentiels*, 1858
Pichat, O., *L'Empereur devant le peuple*, 1870
Pinet, A., *L'enseignement primaire en présence de l'enquête agricole*, 1873
Pointu, J., *Histoire de la chute de l'Empire*, 1874
Pompery, E. de, *La question sociale dans les réunions publiques. Revendication du prolétaire*, 1869
Prévost-Paradol, L., *Du gouvernement parlementaire. Le décret du 24 novembre*, 1860
    La France nouvelle, 1868
Procès de sociétés secrètes. Etudiants et ouvriers, 1867
Proudhon, P-J., *Les confessions d'un révolutionnaire* 1929
Pyat, F., Rougée, and Jourdain, *Lettre à Marianne*, London 1856
Randon, Maréchal, *Mémoires*, vol. II., 1877
Rémusat, C. de, *Mémoires de ma vie*, vols. IV, V, 1962
Renouvier, C. *Manuel républicain de l'homme et du citoyen*, 1848
Réunion démocratique des représentants du Palais national, *Simples avis aux électeurs*, 1849
Réunion des journalistes conservateur des départements, 7–10 octobre 1869, Hôtel du Louvre, Paris, *Déclaration*, 1869
Rivière, A., *Les petites misères de la vie politique en Touraine*, Tours 1863

Robert, C. (secrétaire-général du Ministère de l'Instruction publique), *De l'ignorance des populations ouvrières et rurales de la France et des causes qui tendent à la perpétuer*, Montbéliard 1862

   Les améliorations sociales du Second Empire, 1868

Romieu, M., *Le spectre rouge de 1852*, Berlin 1851

Saint-Arnaud, Maréchal de, *Lettres*, 2 vols. 1858

Say, H., 'Misère ou charité', *Journal des Economistes*, 1847

Schmit, J., *Aux ouvriers: du pain, du travail et la vérité*, Bordeaux n.d.

Schoelcher, V., *Histoire des crimes du deux décembre*, London 1852

Sections parisiens fédérés de l'Internationale et de la Chambre fédérale des sociétés ouvrières, *Manifeste antiplébiscitaire*, 1870

Sempé, J., *Grèves et grévistes*, 1870

Senior, N. W., *Journals Kept in France and Italy from 1848 to 1852*, 2 vols. London 1871

   Conversations with M. Thiers, M. Guizot and other Distinguished Persons during the Second Empire, 2 vols. London 1878

Sibour, Mgr, *Mandements, lettres et instructions pastorales*, 1853

Société fraternelle de solidarité et de crédit mutuel, *Procès des ouvriers tailleurs. Grève de mars–avril 1867. Association de plus de 20 personnes, non autorisée*, 1868

Stern, D., *Histoire de la Révolution de 1848*, 2 vols., 1850–1

Talès, M., *L'Empire, c'est la souveraineté du peuple*, 1852

Tallon, E., *Les intérêts des campagnes*, 1869

Tardif, J.-A., *Le réveil de l'opinion. Antagonisme des idées fusionnistes, césariennes et radicales*, Marseilles 1865

Ténot, E., *Le suffrage universel et les paysans*, 1865

   Paris en décembre 1851 : Etude historique sur le Coup d'Etat, 1868

   La province en décembre 1851, 1868

Thiers-Dosne, A., *Correspondance 1841–65*, 1904

Thomas, E., *Histoire des Ateliers nationaux*, 1848

Tocqueville, A. de, *Oeuvres complètes*, vols., VI(1), VII, VIII(2), VIII(3), IX, XI, XII, XIII, 1959-

Tolain, H., *Quelques vérités sur les élections de Paris (31 mai 1863)*, 1863

Trochu, Général, *L'armée française en 1867*, 1868

Vallès, F. (ingénieur en chef ponts et chaussées), *Des chemins de fer et des routes impériales au point de vue de l'importance de leurs transports respectifs*, Laon 1857

Valori, C. de, *La fusion et les partis*, 1849

Vée, M., *Considérations sur le décroissement graduel du paupérisme à Paris ... et les causes des progrès moraux et économiques des classes ouvrières*, 1862

Vermorel, A., *Le parti socialiste*, 1870

Véron, Dr L., *Mémoires d'un bourgeois de Paris*, vol. V, 1856

Vitu, A., *Les réunions électorales à Paris*, 1869

   Les réunions publiques à Paris, 1868–69, 1869

Warmington, E., *Qu'est-ce que le Bonapartisme? Le salut de France*, 1852

Wolowski, M., *La liberté commerciale et les résultats du traité de commerce de 1860*, 1869

SECONDARY SOURCES

(Place of publication Paris unless otherwise stated)

Adriance, T., *The Last Gaiter Button. A Study of the Mobilization and Concentration of the French Army in the War of 1870*, London 1987

Agulhon, M., *Une ville ouvrière au temps du socialisme utopique. Toulon de 1815 à 1851*, 1970

    Marianne au combat. L'imagerie et la symbolique républicaine, 1979

    The Republic in the Village, Cambridge 1982

    The Republican Experiment, 1848–52, Cambridge 1983

Agulhon, M., 'L'Empire libéral. Emile Ollivier et les irréconciliables' in Hamon, *Les républicains*

    (ed.), *Histoire de la France urbaine*, vol. IV, 1983

Agulhon, M. and Bodiguel, M. (eds.), *Les associations au village*, Le Paradou 1981

Agulhon, M., Désert, G., and Specklin, R., *Histoire de la France rurale*, vol. III, 1976

Agulhon, M. *et al.*, *Monsieur Thiers d'une république à l'autre*, 1998

Albert, P., 'La presse et le télégraphe électrique au 19ᵉ siècle' in C. Bertho-Lavenir (ed.), *L'Etat et les télécommunications en France et à l'étranger, 1837–1987*, Geneva 1991

Albertini, J., 'Le rapporteur de la loi des coalitions' in Troisier de Diaz (ed.), *Ollivier*

Aminzade, R., *Ballots and Barricades. Class Formation and Republican Politics in France, 1830–71*, London 1993

Anceau, E., *Dictionnaire des députés du Second Empire*, Rennes 1999

    Les députés du second empire, 2000

Anderson, R., *Education in France, 1848–70*, Oxford 1975

Antonmattei, P., *Gambetta*, 1999

Archer, J., 'La naissance de la 3ᵉ République à Lyon,' *Cahiers d'histoire*, 1971

Ardaillou, P., *Les républicains du Havre au 19ᵉ siècle*, Rouen 1999

Armengaud, A, *Les populations de l'est-Aquitain au début de l'époque contemporain (vers 1845–vers 1871)*, 1961

    L'opinion publique en France et la crise nationale allemande en 1866, Dijon 1962

Aronson, D., *Adolphe Crémieux*, 1988

Aubert, J., *et al.*, *Les préfets en France (1800–1914)*, Geneva 1978

    L'état et sa police en France (1789–1914), Geneva 1979

Audoin-Rouzeau, S., *1870. La France dans la guerre*, 1989

    'French public opinion in 1870–1 and the emergence of total war' in Förster and Nagler, *On the Road*

Barbier, F., *Finance et politique. La dynastie des Fould*, 1991

    'Genres et niveaux de vie en France sous le Second Empire' in Tulard, *Pourquoi*

Barral, P., 'Les forces politiques sous le Second Empire dans le département de l'Isère' in *Actes du 77ᵉ CNSS Grenoble 1952*, 1952

    Les Perier dans l'Isère au 19ᵉ siècle d'après leur correspondance familiale, 1964

    Les fondateurs de la 3ᵉ République, 1968

'Le Bonapartisme vu par Gambetta' in K. Hammer and P. Hartmann (eds.), *Der Bonapartismus. Historischen Phänomen und politische Mythos*, Munich 1977

Bastid, P., *Doctrines et institutions politiques de la Seconde République*, 2 vols. 1945

Bebelon, J.-P., 'Les cités ouvrières à Paris', *Monuments historiques*, 1977

Bécanuer, J., 'Noblesse et représentation parlementaire (1871–1968)', *Revue française de science politique*, 1973

Becker, J.-J. (ed.), *Eugène Rouher*, Clermont-Ferrand 1985

Bédry, B., 'L'instruction primaire dans l'arrondissement de Toulouse sous le Second Empire', *Annales du Midi*, 1979

Bellanger, C., Godechot, J., Guiral, P., and Terrou, F., *Histoire générale de la presse française*, vol. II, 1972

Bellet, R., *Presse et journalisme sous le Second Empire*, 1967

Benoit, B., 'Les enjeux politiques de la révolution de 1848 à Lyon,' *Revue d'histoire du 19ᵉ siècle*, 1998

Berenson, E., *Populist Religion and Left-Wing Politics in France, 1830–52*, Princeton 1984

Bernard, M., 'La réorganisation de la police sous le Second Empire (1851–58)' in Vigier *et al.*, *Maintien de l'ordre*

'Les populations du Puy-de-Dôme face à la nouvelle république', *Cahiers d'histoire*, 1998

Bertho, C., *Histoire des télécommunications en France*, Toulouse 1984

Bertocci, P., *Jules Simon. Republican anticlericalism and cultural politics in France, 1848–86*, London 1978

Bianchi, S., 'Le phénomène électoral dans le sud de l'Ile-de-France sous la Seconde République', *Revue d'histoire du 19ᵉ siècle*, 1998

Bidegain, V., 'L'origine d'une réputation: l'image de l'impératrice Eugénie dans la société française du Second Empire' in Corbin, Lalouette, and Riot-Sarcey, *Femmes dans la cité*

Bidegaray, C., 'Les caprices de Marianne 24 février–20 décembre 1848' in Isoart and Bidegaray, *Des républiques*

Blayau, N., *Billault, ministre de Napoléon III*, 1969

Bluche, F. (ed.), *Le prince, le peuple et le droit. Autour des plébiscites de 1851 et 1852*, 2000

'L' adhésion plébiscitaire' in Bluche, *Le Prince*

Blum, A., 'La caricature politique en France sous le Second Empire', *Revue des études napoléoniennes*, 1919

Boivin, M., *Le mouvement ouvrier dans la région de Rouen, 1851–76*, 2 vols., Rouen 1989

Bouillon, J., 'Les démocrates-socialistes aux élections de 1849', *Revue française de science politique*, 1956

Bourachot, C., *Bibliographie critique des mémoires sur le Second Empire*, n.d.

Bourbuinat, N., 'De la question frumentaire à l'idée d'une *économie morale* sous la Seconde République,' *Cahiers d'histoire*, 1998

Bourgin, G., 'La législation ouvrière du Second Empire,' *Revue des études napoléoniennes*, 1913

'Les préfets de Napoléon III, historiens du *coup d'état*', *Revue historique*, 1931

Boutry, P., 'La légitimité et l'église en France au 19ᵉ siècle' in P. Boutry, *Catholiques entre monarchie et république. Mgr. Freppel et son temps*, n.d.

Bouvier, J., 'Lyon la républicaine à la veille de la guerre de 1870,' *1848*, 1971

Brelot, C.-I., *La noblesse réinventée. Nobles de Franche-Comté de 1814 à 1870*, 2 vols., 1992

Bruchat, M., 'Le *coup d'état* dans le Nord', *Revue du Nord*, 1925

Bury, J., *Napoleon III and the Second Empire*, London 1964

Bury, J. and Tombs, R., *Thiers, 1797–1877. A Political Life*, London 1986

Campbell, S., *The Second Empire Revisited: A Study in French Historiography*, London 1978

Carel, H., 'Le département de la Haute-Saône de 1850 à 1914', Doctorat ès lettres, Université de Paris-Sorbonne 1970

Caron, F., *La France des patriotes de 1851 à 1914*, 1985
Histoire des chemins de fer en France, 1740–1883, 1997

Caron-Deneuféglise, C., 'Le personnel politique bonapartiste du Pas-de-Calais sous le Second Empire', *Revue du Nord*, 1993

Carr, W., *The Origins of the Wars of German Unification*, 1991

Carrot, G., *Le maintien de l'ordre en France depuis la fin de l'Ancien Régime jusqu'à 1968*, 2 vols., 1986

Case, L., 'New sources for the study of French opinion during the Second Empire', *South Western Social Science Quarterly*, 1937
French Opinion on War and Diplomacy during the Second Empire, Philadelphia 1954

Casewitz, J., *Une loi manquée, La loi Niel, 1866–68. L'Armée française à la veille de la guerre de 1870*, 1960

Cayez, P., *Crises et croissance de l'industrie lyonnaise, 1850–1900*, 1980

Chaline, J.-P., *Les bourgeois de Rouen: une élite urbaine au 19ᵉ siècle*, 1982

Chalmin, P., *et al.*, *L'armée et la Seconde République*, 1955
L'officier français de 1815 à 1870, 1957

Charbon, P., 'Comment les français furent informés des événements guerriers de juillet à septembre 1870', *Relais. Revue des amis du musée de la poste*, 1994

Charbonnier, J., *Un grand préfet du Second Empire: Denis Gavini*, Nice 1995

Charle, C., *Les hauts fonctionnaires en France au 19ᵉ siècle*, 1980
Histoire sociale de la France au 19e siècle, 1991
'Les spécificités de la magistrature française en Europe,' *Crises*, 1994

Chassagne, S., 'Une affaire de longue durée. La production d'un grand notable républicain angevin des débuts de la 3ᵉ République: Henri Allain-Targé' in J.-L. Mayaud (ed.), *Clio dans les vignes*, 1998

Chatelain, A., 'Les migrants temporaires et la propagation des idées révolutionnaires en France au 19ᵉ siècle', *1848*, 1951

Chatelard, C., *Crime et criminalité dans l'arrondissement de St-Etienne au 19e siècle*, St-Etienne 1981

Chauvaud, F., 'L'usure au 19ᵉ siècle: le fléau des campagnes', *Etudes rurales*, 1984
Les passions villageoises au 19ᵉ siècle, 1995
'La magistrature du parquet et la diabolisation du politique, 1830–70', *Droit et société*, 1996

Chavot, F., 'Les sociétés de secours mutuels sous le Second Empire', *Cahiers d'histoire de l'Institut Maurice Thorez*, 1977

Chevalier, L., 'Les fondements économiques et sociaux de l'histoire politique de la région parisienne', Doctorat ès lettres, Université de Paris 1950

Choisel, F., 'L'image de Napoléon III et du Second Empire' in Tulard, *et al.*, *Pourquoi*

Cholvy, G., *Religion et société au 19ᵉ siècle. Le diocèse de Montpellier*, 2 vols., Lille 1973

Clavier, L. and Hinckner, L., 'La barricade de juin 1848: une construction politique' in Corbin and Mayeur (eds.), *La barricade*

Cloitre, M.-T., 'Aspects de la vie politique dans le département de Finistère de 1848 à 1870', *Bulletin de la Société archéologique du Finistère*, 1973

Collingham, H., *The July Monarchy: A Political History of France, 1830–48*, 1988

Constant, E., 'Notes sur la presse dans le département du Var sous le Second Empire', *Provence historique*, 1960

    'Quelques observations sur l'audience et l'évolution politique d'Emile Ollivier au début de l'Empire libéral (1864–65)' in *Actes du 90ᵉ CNSS. Nice 1965*, vol. III, 1966

    'Image du républicain varois à la fin du Second Empire' in J. Viard, *L'esprit républicain*, 1972

    'Le département du Var sous le Second Empire et au début de la 3ᵉ République', Doctorat ès lettres, Université de Provence-Aix 1977

    'Emile Ollivier et la décentralisation sous le Second Empire' in Troisier de Diaz (ed.), *Regards*

Copin, J., 'La presse dans l'Yonne sous le Second Empire' in Hamon (ed.), *Les républicains*

Corbin, A., *Archaïsme et modernité en Limousin au 19ᵉ siècle*, 2 vols., 1975

    The Village of Cannibals: Rage and Murder in France, 1870, Oxford 1992

Corbin, A., Lalouette, J., and Riot-Sarcey, M., *Femmes dans la cité*, 1997

Corbin, A. and Mayeur, J.-M. (eds.), *La barricade*, 1997

Cornu, P., *Une économie rurale dans la débâcle. Cévenne vivaraise 1852–92*, 1993

Crapo, P., 'Art and politics in the Côte-d'Or: Gustave Courbet's Dijon exhibition of May 1870', *French History*, 1995

Crepin, A., *La conscription en débat ou le triple apprentissage de la nation, de la citoyenneté, de la république (1798–1889)*, Arras 1998

Dagnan, J., *Le Gers sous la Seconde République*, Auch 1928

Dalotel, A., Faure, A., and Frieiermuth, J.-C., *Aux origines de la Commune. Le mouvement des réunions publiques à Paris 1868–70*, 1980

Dansette, A., *Deuxième république et second empire*, 1942

Darmon, J.-J., *Le colportage de librairie en France sous le second empire*, 1972

Daumard, A., *La bourgeoisie parisienne de 1815 à 1848*, 1963

    'Les fondements de la société bourgeoise en France au 19ᵉ siècle' in Roche, D. and Labrousse, E. (eds.), *Ordres et classes*, 1967

Dauphin, C., Lebrun-Pezerat, P., and Poublas, D., *Ces bonnes lettres. Une correspondance familiale au 19ᵉ siècle*, 1995

Debré, J.-L., *La justice au 19ᵉ siècle*, 1981

Decaux, A., 'Police et provocation sous le Second Empire' in G. Conac *et al.*, *Itinéraires*, 1982

Decormeille, P., 'La philosophie républicaine sous le Second Empire' in Hamon, *Les républicains*

Delhommeau, L., 'Un évêque légitimiste sous le Second Empire. Mgr J.-M.-J. Baillès, évêque de Luçon' in *Mélanges Charles Molette*, vol. II, Abbeville 1989

Delmas, J., Blanchard, A., and Bodinier, G., *Histoire militaire de la France*, vol. II, 1992

Deloyé, Y., 'Se présenter pour représenter. Enquête sur les professions de foi électorales de 1848' in M.Offerlé (ed.) *La profession politique*, 1999

Delpal, B., *Entre paroisse et commune. Les catholiques de la Drôme au milieu du 19ᵉ siècle*, Valence 1989

Démier, F., '*Comment naissent les révolutions*. 50 ans après', *Revue d'histire du 19ᵉ siècle*, 1997

Démier, F. and Mayaud, J.-L., 'Un bilan de 50 années de recherches sur 1848 et la Seconde République,' *Revue d'histoire du 19ᵉ siècle*, 1997

Denis, M., 'Les royalistes de la Mayenne et le monde moderne', Doctorat d'Etat, Université de Paris-Sorbonnne

Derobert-Ratel, C., *Les Arts et l'Amitié et le rayonnement maçonnique dans la société aixoise de 1848 à 1871*, Aix-en-Provence 1987

Désert, G., *Une société rurale au 19ᵉ siècle: les paysans de Calvados, 1815–95*, 3 vols., Lille 1975

Desmarest, J., 'L'état économique de la France à la fin du Second Empire', *Revue des travaux de l'Académie des sciences morales et politiques*, 1967

Dessal, M., 'Le complot de Lyon et la résistance au coup d'état dans les départements du sud-est', *1848*, 1951

   Un révolutionnaire jacobin: Charles Deleslcuze 1809–71, 1952

Dorandeu, R., 'Eléments pour une étude des élites et des organisations politiques. L'Hérault à la fin du Second Empire' in R. Dorandeu (ed.), *L'Hérault à la fin du Second Empire*, 1989

Duffour, P., 'Le soldat français de 1870', *Revue historique de l'Armée*, 1971

Dupeux, G., *Aspects de l'histoire sociale et politique du Loir-et-Cher*, 1962

Dupuy, A., *1870–1871. La guerre, la Commune et la presse*, 1959

Duroselle, J.-B., *Les débuts du catholicisme social en France, 1822–70*, 1951

Dutacq, F., 'La police politique et les partis d'opposition à Lyon et dans le Midi en 1852,' *1848*, 1923

Dutailly, H., 'L'armée du Second Empire' in J. Perot, *et al.*, *Une visite au camp de Châlons sous le Second Empire*, 1996

Duveau, G., *La vie ouvrière en France sous le Second Empire*, 1946

Echard, W., *Napoleon III and the Concert of Europe*, 1983

   (ed.) *Historical Dictionary of the French Second Empire*, 1985

Elwitt, S., *The Making of the 3rd Republic: Class and Politics in France 1868–84*, London 1975

Emerit, M., 'Les sources des idées sociales et coloniales de Napoléon III', *Revue d'Alger*, 1945

Emsley, C., *Gendarmes and the State in 19th Century Europe*, Oxford 1999

Farcy, J.-C., 'Les archives judiciaires et l'histoire rurale: l'exemple de la Beauce au 19e siècle', *Revue historique*, 1973

    Les paysans beaucerons au 19e siècle, 2 vols., Chartres 1989

    Magistrats en majesté. Les discours de rentré aux audiences solennelles des cours d'appel, 1998

Faury, J., *Cléricalisme et anticléricalisme dans le Tarn*, Toulouse 1980

Fohlen, C., *L'industrie textile au temps du Second Empire*, 1956

Forstenzer, T., *French Provincial Police and the Fall of the Second Republic: Social Fear and Counter-revolution*, Princeton 1981

Förster, S. and Nagler, J. (eds.), *On the Road to Total War. The American Civil War and the German Wars of Unification 1861–75*, Cambridge, 1997

Fortescue, W., *Alphonse de Lamartine: A Political Biography*, London 1983

Fougère, L., *et al*, *Histoire de l'administration française depuis 1800*, Geneva 1975

Furet, F., 'Jules Ferry et l'histoire de la Révolution française: la polémique autour du livre d'Edgar Quinet, 1865–6' in F. Furet (ed.), *Jules Ferry fondateur de la République*, 1985

Gachot, H., 'Le rôle politique du télégraphe à Strasbourg en 1851 et 1852: le règne des dépêches politiques', *Annuaire de la société des amis du Vieux-Strasbourg*, 1983

Gadille, J., *La pensée et l'action politique des évêques français au début de la 3e République*, 1967

Gaillard, J., 'Notes sur l'opposition au monopole des compagnies de chemins de fer entre 1850 et 1860', *1848*, 1950

    Paris, la ville, 1977

Garrigou, A., *Le vote et la vertu. Comment les français sont devenus électeurs*, 1992

Garrigues, J., *La République des hommes d'affaires, 1870–1900*, 1997

Gaudin, O., 'Les élections dans la Sarthe sous le Second Empire', *Province du Maine*, 1997

George, J. *Histoire des maires, 1789–1939*, 1989

Gerbod, P. *et al.*, *Les épurations administratives, 19e–20e siècles*, Geneva 1977

Gibson, R., *A Social History of French Catholicism 1789–1914*, London 1989

Gildea, R., *Education in Provincial France, 1800–1914*, Oxford 1983

    The Past in French History, London 1994

Girard, L., *La politique des travaux publics du Second Empire*, 1952

    Nouvelle histoire de Paris. La Deuxième République et le Second Empire, 1981

    'L'Empire libéral (1860–70)' in L. Hamon, *Mort de dictature*, 1982

    'La cour de Napoléon III' in K. Werner (ed.), *Hof, Kultur und Politik im 19. Jahrhundert*, Bonn 1985

    Les libéraux français, 1814–75, 1985

    'Jules Ferry et la génération des républicains du second empire' in Furet (ed.), *Jules Ferry*

    Napoléon III, 1986

    Problèmes politiques et constitutionnels du Second Empire, n.d.

    Questions politiques et constitutionnels du Second Empire, n.d.

'Le troupe face aux insurrections parisiennes (1830–48)' in Vigier, *Maintien* (ed.) *Les élections de 1869*, 1960

Girard, L., Prost, A., and Gossez, R., *Les conseillers généraux en 1870*, 1967

Goldstein, R., *Censorship of Political Caricature in 19th Century France*, London 1989

Gonnet, P., 'La société dijonnaise au 19ᵉ siècle. Esquisse de l'évolution économique, sociale et politique d'un milieu urbain contemporain (1815–90)', Doctorat d'Etat, Université de Paris IV, 1974

Gontard, M., *Les écoles primaires de la France bourgeoise (1833–78)*, Toulouse n.d.

Gorce, P. de la, *Histoire du Second Empire*, 7 vols., 1894–1904

Gordon, D., 'Industrialization and republican politics: the bourgeoisie of Reims and Saint-Etienne under the Second Empire' in J. Merriman (ed.), *French Cities in the 19th Century*, London 1982

Merchants and Capitalists. Industrialization and Provincial Politics in mid-19th-Century France, London 1985

Gosselin, R., *Les almanachs républicains. Traditions révolutionnaires et culture politique des masses populaires de Paris*, 1992

Gossez, A.-M., 'Un procès pour l'introduction frauduleuse de livres prohibés à Lille en 1853', *Révolution de 1848*, 1907–8

Gossez, R., 'La proscription et les origines de l'Internationale', *1848*, 1951

'Le 4 septembre 1870: initiatives et spontanéité,' *Actes du 77ᵉ CNSS*, 1952

Gouallou, H., 'Le plébiscite du 8 mai 1870 en Ille-et-Vilaine', *Annales de Bretagne*, 1970

Goueffon, J., 'La candidature officielle sous le Second Empire: le rôle des considérations locales' in A. Mabileau (ed.), *Les facteurs locaux de la vie politique nationale*, n.d.

'Le parti républicain dans le Loiret à la fin du Second Empire' in Viard, *L'esprit...*

Gough, A., 'The conflict in politics' in C. Zeldin (ed.), *Conflicts*

Paris and Rome: The Gallican Church and the Ultramontane Campaign 1848–53, Oxford 1986

Goujon, P., *Le vignoble de Saône-et-Loire au 19ᵉ siècle*, Lyons 1974

Le vigneron citoyen. Mâconnais et Châlonnais (1848–1914), 1993

Les révélations du suffrage universel: comportements électoraux et politisation des populations de Saône-et-Loire sous la Seconde République', *Cahiers d'histoire*, 1998

Gould, R., *Insurgent Identities. Class, Community, and Protest in Paris from 1848 to the Commune*, London 1995

Grothe, C., *Le Duc de Morny*, 1961

Guillemin, A., 'Le pouvoir de l'innovation. Les notables de la Manche et le développement de l'agriculture (1830–75), Doc.de 3ᵉ cycle, EHESS 1980

Guionnet, C., *L'apprentissage de la politique moderne*, 1998

Guiral, P., 'Prévost-Paradol ou l'apparent désaveu de soi-même' in Hamon (ed.), *Les républicains...*

Adolphe Thiers ou De la nécessité en politique, 1986

'Emile Ollivier et la politique extérieure' in Troisier de Diaz, *Regards*

Guthrie, C., 'Reactions to the *coup d'état* in the Narbonnais', *French Historical Studies*, 1983–4

Hamon, L. (ed.), *Les républicains sous le Second Empire*, 1993

Harvey, D., *Consciousness and the Urban Experience*, London 1985

Hatzfeld, H., *Du paupérisme à la sécurité sociale, 1850–1940*, 1970

Hazareesingh, S., 'Defining the republican good life: Second Empire municipalism and the emergence of the 3rd Republic', *French History*, 1997
From Subject to Citizen. The Second Empire and the Emergence of Modern French Democracy, Princeton, 1998

Heywood, C., *Childhood in Nineteenth-Century France. Work, Health and Education among the Classes Populaires*, Cambridge 1988

Heywood, O. and Heywood, C., 'Rethinking the 1848 Revolution in France: the Provisional Government and its enemies', *History*, 1994

Higgs, D., *Ultraroyalism in Toulouse*, London 1973

Hilaire, Y.-M., 'La vie religieuse des populations du diocèse d'Arras, 1840–1914', Doctorat d'Etat, Université de Paris IV, 1976

Hincker, L., 'La politicisation des milieux populaires en France au 19ᵉ siècle', *Revue d'histoire du 19ᵉ siècle*, 1997

Holmes, R., *The Road to Sedan: The French Army 1866–70*, London 1984

Hovarth-Peterson, S., *Victor Duruy and French Education. Liberal Reform in the Second Empire*, London 1984

Howard, M., *The Franco-Prussian War*, London 1967

Huard, R., 'La préhistoire des partis. Le parti républicain et l'opinion républicaine dans le Gard de 1848 à 1888', Doctorat d'Etat, Université de Paris IV, 1977
Le mouvement républicain en Bas-Languedoc, 1848–81, 1982
'Un parti en mutation: le parti républicain (1848–51)' in Isoart and Bidegaray (eds.), *Des républiques*
La naissance du parti politique en France, 1996
'Le *suffrage universel* sous la Seconde République. Etat des travaux, questions en attente', *Revue d'histoire du 19ᵉ siècle*, 1997

Hubscher, R., 'L'agriculture et la société rurale dans le Pas-de-Calais du milieu du 19ᵉ siècle à 1914', Doctorat d'Etat, Université de Paris 1978

Hutton, P., *The Cult of the Revolutionary Tradition*, Berkeley 1981

Igersheim, F., *Politique et administration dans le Bas-Rhin 1848–70*, 1993

Isoart, P. and Bidegaray, C. (eds.), *Des républiques françaises*, 1988

Isser, N., *The Second Empire and the Press*, The Hague 1974

Jacquemet, G., *Belleville au 19ᵉ siècle. Du faubourg à la ville*, 1984

Jacquier, B., *Le Légitimisme dauphinois 1830–70*, Grenoble 1976

Jardin, A., *Histoire du libéralisme politique, de la crise de l'absolutisme à la constitution de 1875*, 1985
Alexis de Tocqueville, 1988

Jeambrun, P., *Jules Grévy*, 1991

Jeloubovskaïa, F., *La chute du Second Empire et la naissance de la 3ᵉ République*, Moscou 1959

Johnson, C., *The Life and Death of Industrial Languedoc, 1700–1920*, Oxford 1995

Jones, P., *Politics and Rural Society. The Southern Massif Central c.1750–1880*, Cambridge 1985

Kale, S., *Legitimism and the Reconstruction of French Society, 1852–83*, London 1992

Krakovitch, O., 'La mise en pièces des théâtres: la censure des spectacles au 19ᵉ siècle' in Vigier *et al.*, *Maintien de l'ordre*

Kulstein, D., 'The attitude of French workers towards the Second Empire', *French Historical Studies*, 1962

    'Government propaganda and the press during the Second Empire', *Gazette*, 1964

    Napoleon III and the Working Class: A Study of Government Propaganda under the Second Empire, London 1969

Labrousse, E., (ed.) *Aspects de la crise et de la dépression de l'économie française au milieu du 19ᵉ siècle, 1846–51*, 1956

Lagoueyte, P., 'Candidature officielle et pratiques électorales sous le Second Empire,' Doctorat d' Etat, Université de Paris I, 1990

    'Le rôle des femmes dans les élections législatives sous le Second Empire' in Corbin, Lalouette, and Riot-Sarcey, *Femmes dans la cité*

Latta, C., 'Le maintien de l'ordre à Lyon' in Vigier, *et al.*, *Maintien*

Launay, M., *Le diocèse de Nantes sous le Second Empire*, 2 vols., Nantes 1983

Laurent, R., *Les vignerons de la Côte-d'Or au 19ᵉ siècle*, 1958

    L'octroi de Dijon au 19ᵉ siècle, 1960

Lavoie, E., 'Les élections municipales sous le second empire' in *Europe et Etat*, Aix-en-Provence 1993

Le Clère, B. and Wright, V., *Les préfets du Second Empire*, 1973

Lentz, T., 'Le plébiscite du 8 mai 1870 en Moselle,' *Cahiers lorraine*, 1988

Lequin, Y., *La formation de la classe ouvrière régionale: les ouvriers de la région lyonnaise (1848–1914)*, 2 vols., Lyons 1977

    'La France, une et indivisible. L'achèvement de l'unité française' in Y. Lequin (ed.), *Histoire des français 19ᵉ–20ᵉ siècles*, 3 vols., 1983–4

Lévêque, P., *Société en crise. La Bourgogne de la Monarchie de Juillet au Second Empire*, 2 vols., 1983

    'Conservatisme sans cléricalisme. L'évolution politique du Châtillonnais aux 19ᵉ et 20ᵉ siècles' in A. Faure, A. Plessis, and J.-C. Farcy, *La terre et la cité*, 1994

    'Les campagnes françaises et la Deuxième République. 50 ans d'historiographie', *Revue d'histoire du 19ᵉ siècle*, 1997

    'Les élections d'Avril 1848 en Bourgogne' in A. Bleton-Ruget and S. Wolikow (eds.), *Voter et élire à l'époque contemporaine*, Dijon 1999

Levy, C., 'Notes sur les fondements sociaux de l'insurrection de décembre 1851 en province,' *Information historique*, 1954

    'Les proscrits du 2 décembre' in Hamon (ed.), *Les républicains...*

Lévy-Leboyer, M., 'Histoire économique et histoire de l'administration' in *Histoire de l'administration française depuis 1800*, Geneva 1975

L'Huillier, F., *La lutte ouvrière à la fin du Second Empire*, 1957
  (ed.) *L'Alsace en 1870–71*, Gap 1971
Locke, R., *French Legitimists and the Politics of Moral Order in the Early Third Republic*, London 1974
  Les fonderies et forges d'Alais à l'époque des premiers chemins de fer, 1978
Lorcin, J., 'Le souvenir de la Révolution française dans la chanson ouvrier stéphanoise' in Société d'histoire de la Révolution de 1848, *Le 19ᵉ siècle et la Révolution française*, 1992
Lucas-Dubreton, J., *Le culte de Napoléon*, 1960
Luna, F. de, *The French Republic under Cavaignac, 1848*, London 1969
Machin, H., 'The prefects and political repression: Feb.1848 to Dec.1851' in Price, *Revolution and Reaction*
Machu, L., 'Deux aspects de la répression policière dans le Nord à l'époque du Second Empire', *Revue du Nord*, 1964
McMillan, J., *Napoleon III*, 1991
McPhee, P., *The Politics of Rural Life: Political Mobilisation in the French Countryside, 1846–52*, Oxford 1992
Magraw, R., *A History of the French Working Class*, vol. I, Oxford 1992
Maire, C., 'Crise agricole et misère en Lorraine au milieu du 19ᵉ siècle,' *La Revue lorraine populaire*, 1985
Maitron, J. (ed.), *Dictionnaire biographique du mouvement ouvrier français*, vol. I, 1964
Malon, C., *Jules Le Cesne. Député du Havre*, Luneray 1995
Maneglier, H., *Paris impérial. La vie quotidienne sous le Second Empire*, 1990
Marcilhacy, C., *Le diocèse d'Orléans sous l'épiscopat de Mgr Dupanloup, 1849–79*, 1962
  Le diocèse d'Orléans au milieu du 19ᵉ siècle, 1964
Margadant, T., *French Peasants in Revolt: The Insurrection of 1851*, London 1979
Marle, G., *Emile Combes*, 1995
Marlin, R., 'L'opinion franc-comtoise devant la guerre de Crimée', *Annales littéraires de l'Université de Besançon*, 1957
Maurain, J., *La politique ecclésiastique du Second Empire de 1852 à 1869*, 1930
  Un bourgeois français au 19ᵉ siècle: Baroche, ministre de Napoléon III, 1936
Mayaud, J.-L., *Les secondes républiques du Doubs*, 1986
  'Le Second Empire: faîte économique ou épisode négligeable?' in Tulard et al., *Pourquoi*
  'Ruralité et politique dans la France du 19ᵉ siècle,' *Histoire et sociétés rurales*, 1999
Ménager, B., 'La vie politique dans le département du Nord de 1851 à 1877', Doctorat D'Etat, Université de Paris IV, 1979
  'La vie politique dans le département du Nord de 1851 à 1877,' *Revue du Nord*, 1980
  'Rouher et la politique sociale du second empire' in Becker (ed.), *Eugène Rouher Les Napoléons du peuple*, 1988
  'Le bonapartisme pouvait-il être parlementaire?' in Tulard et al., *Pourquoi*
Merley, J., *La Haute-Loire de la fin de l'Ancien Régime au début de la 3ᵉ République*, Le Puy 1975

Merlin, P., 'Image, tradition religieuse et politique. Analyse de deux caricatures antibonapartistes', *Société d'émulation du Jura. Travaux*, 1993
'Le *coup* d 'état du 2 décembre 1851 dans le Jura', *Société d'émulation du Jura. Travaux*, 1994
Merriman, J., *The Agony of the Republic: The Repression of the Left in Revolutionary France, 1848–51*, London 1978
The Red City. Limoges and the French 19th century, Oxford 1986
(ed.), *French Cities in the 19th century*, London 1982
Mollier, J.-Y., 'Noël Parfait: une trajectoire républicaine au 19ᵉ siècle' in A. Faure, A. Plessis, and J.-C. Farcy, *La terre et la cité*, 1994
'De l'orléanisme à la République conservatrice, la volonté de pouvoir de Monsieur Thiers' in Agulhon *et al.*, *Monsieur Thiers*
'Ambiguïtés et réalités du commerce des livres entre la France et la Belgique au 19ᵉ siècle' in M. Quaghebeur and N. Savy, *France-Belgique (1848–1914)*, Brussels 1997
Morabito, M., 'Maintien de l'ordre et intégration politique en Bretagne: l'Ille-et-Vilaine sous le Second Empire', *Revue historique du droit français et étranger*, 1998
Neveu, B., 'Pour une histoire du gallicanisme administratif' in Gaudemat *et al.*, *Administration et église, du Concordat à la séparation de l'état*, Geneva 1987
Nicolet, C., *L'idée républicaine en France*, 1982
Nord, R., *The Republican Movement. Struggle for Democracy in 19th Century France*, London 1995
Nordmann, J., *La France radicale*, 1977
Olivesi, A., *La Commune de 1871 à Marseille et ses origines*, 1950
Pairault, F., 'Les personnalités bonapartistes charentaises d'après l'œuvre du baron Eschasserieux', *Annales du groupe de recherches et d'études historiques de la Charente saintongeaise*, 1992
Palard, J., 'Ultramontanisme et contre-révolution en France au 19ᵉ siècle', *La Revue Tocqueville*, 1989–90
Palmade, G., 'Le département du Gers à la fin du Second Empire', *Bulletin de la Société archéologique, historique et scientifique du Gers*, 1961
Payne, H., *The Police State of Louis-Napoleon Bonaparte, 1851–60*, Seattle 1966
'Preparation of a *coup d'état* – administrative centralisation and police powers in France 1849–51' in F. Cox (ed.), *Studies in Modern European History in Honor of F. C. Palm*, New York 1966
Pécout, G., 'La politisation des paysans au 19ᵉ siècle', *Histoire et sociétés rurales*, 1994
Pelletier, O., '*Figures imposées*. Pratiques et représentations de la barricade pendant les journées de décembre 1851' in A. Corbin and J.-M. Mayeur (eds.), *La barricade*, 1997
Pellissier, C., 'Les sociabilités patriciennes à Lyon du milieu du 19ᵉ siècle à 1914', Doctorat de l'Université de Lyon III, 1993
Perrot, M., *Les ouvriers en grève. France 1871–90*, 2 vols., 1974
Phélippeau, E., 'La fin des notables revisitée' in M. Offerlé, *La profession politique, 19ᵉ–20 siècles*, 1999

Pierrard, P., *La vie ouvrière à Lille sous le Second Empire*, 1965
Pilbeam, P., *Republicanism in 19th Century France, 1814–71*, London 1995
Pinard, L., *Les mentalités religieuses du Morvan au 19ᵉ siècle (1830–1914)*, Dijon 1997
Pinkney, D., *Napoleon III and the Rebuilding of Paris*, Princeton 1958
Pinol, J.-L., 'L'exercice du pouvoir' in Y. Lequin (ed.), *Histoire des français*, vol. III, 1984
Plessis, A., 'La Banque de France sous le Second Empire', 3 vols., Doctorat d'Etat, Université de Paris I, 1980
   The Rise and Fall of the Second Empire, Cambridge 1985
   'Rouher et les grands choix économiques du Second Empire' in Becker (ed.), *Eugène Rouher*
   'Pouvait-on penser librement sous le Second Empire?' in Tulard, *et al.*, *Pourquoi*
   'La République était-elle dans l'Empire?' in Tulard, *et al.*, *Pourquoi*
Ponsot, P., *Les grèves de 1870 et la Commune de 1871 au Creusot*, 1957
Pottinger, E., *Napoleon III and the German Crisis, 1865–66*, 1966
Pourcher, Y., 'Parenté et représentation politique en Lozère', *Terrain*, 1985
Price, R., *The French Second Republic. A Social History*, London 1972
   'The onset of labour shortage in French agriculture in the 19th century', *Economic History Review*, 1975
   'Techniques of repression. The control of popular protest in mid-19th-century France', *Historical Journal*, 1982
   The Modernisation of Rural France: Communications Networks and Agricultural Market Structures in 19th Century France, London 1983
   'Poor relief and social crisis in mid-19th-century France', *European Studies review*, 1983
   A Social History of 19th Century France, London 1987
   Napoleon III and the Second Empire, London 1997
   (ed.), *Revolution and Reaction. 1848 and the Second French Republic*, 1975
Prothero, I., *Radical Artisans in England and France, 1830–70*, Cambridge 1997
Prudhomme, A., 'Les sociétés secrètes républicains sous le Second Empire (1852–60),' *Mémoires Sciences Sociales, Lettres Loir-et-Cher*, 1984
Puech, L., *Essai sur la candidature officielle en France depuis 1851*, Mende 1922
Ratcliffe, B., 'Napoleon III and the Anglo-French commercial treaty of 1860: a reconsideration' in B. Ratcliffe (ed.), *Great Britain and Her World*, London 1975
Regnault, J., 'Le haut commandement et les généraux français en 1870', *Revue historique de l'Armée*, 1971
Remy, M., 'Le mauvais calcul de l'empereur Napoléon III', *Annales de l'Est*, 1993
Rials, S., *Révolution et contre-révolution au 19ᵉ siècle*, 1987
Rivet, D., *La vie politique dans le département de la Haute-Loire*, Le Puy 1979
Robert, V., *Les chemins de la manifestation 1848–1914*, Lyons 1996
Rocher, J.-P., 'Les élections dans l'Yonne de 1848 à 1871' in Hamon, *Les républicains*
Rohr, J., *Victor Duruy, ministre de Napoléon III*, 1967

Roncaylo, M., 'La production de la ville' in Agulhon (ed.), *Histoire de la France urbaine* IV

Rosanvallon, P., *Le sacre du citoyen. Histoire du suffrage universel en France*, 1992

Le peuple introuvable. Histoire de la représentation démocratique en France, 1998

Roth, F., *La guerre de 1870*, 1990

'Napoléon III et la déclaration de la guerre en 1870' in Tulard *et al.*, *Pourquoi*

Rougerie, J., 'La Ire Internationale à Lyon (1865–70): Problèmes d'histoire du mouvement ouvrier français,' *Annali Instituto Giangiacomo Feltrinelli*, 1961

'Les sections françaises de l'Association Internationale des travailleurs' in J. Rougerie *et al.*, *La Ire Internationale, l'institution, l'implantation, le rayonnement*, 1964

'Le Second Empire' in G. Duby (ed.), *Histoire de la France*, vol. III, 1972

Royer, J.-P., Martinage, R., and Lecocq, P., *Juges et notables au 19e siècle*, 1982

Rubel, M., *Karl Marx devant le bonapartisme*, 1960

Rudel, O., 'L'élaboration de la constitution de 1848' in Isoart and Bidegaray, *Des républiques*

Rütten, R., Jung, R., and Schneider, G., *La caricature entre République et censure. L'imagerie satirique en France de 1830 à 1880*, Lyons 1996

Salmon, F., 'La *gauche avancée* en 1849 et en 1870: le pourquoi de la chute' in Hamon, *Les républicains*

Sanson, R. 'Le 15 Août: fête nationale du Second Empire' in A. Corbin, *et al.*, (eds.), *Les usages politiques des fêtes au 19e siècle*, 1994

Saurel, C., 'La gendarmerie dans la société de la Deuxième République et du Second Empire,' Doctorat d'Etat, Université de Paris-Sorbonne 1956

Schnerb, R., *Rouher et le Second Empire*, 1949

Seignebos, C., *La Révolution de 1848–Le Second Empire*, 1921

Selig, J.-M., 'Misère et malnutrition dans les campagnes alsaciennes du 19e siècle,' *Revue d'Alsace*, 1988

Serman, W., 'Les généraux français de 1870', *Revue de défense nationale*, 1970

'Le corps des officiers français sous la deuxième république et le second empire', Doctorat d'Etat, Université de Paris-Sorbonne 1976

'Les français et la force armée prussienne de 1860 à 1866' in H.-O. Poidevin, and R. Siegburg, *Aspects des relations franco-allemands à l'époque du Second Empire*, Metz 1982

La noblesse dans l'armée française au 19e siècle' in G. Delille (ed.), *Les noblesses européennes au 19e siècle*, Rome 1988

'French mobilisation in 1870' in Förster and Nagler, *On the Road to Total War*

Sherman, D., 'Government policy towards joint-stock business organisation in mid-19th-century France', *Journal of European Economic History*, 1974

'Governmental responses to economic modernisation in mid-19th-century France,' *Journal of European Economic History*, 1977

Simon, F., *La Marianne, société secrète au pays d'Anjou*, Angers 1939

Simpson, F., *The Rise of Louis Napoleon*, 1909

Singer, B., *Village Notables in 19th Century France. Priests, Mayors, Schoolmasters*, Albany, N.Y. 1983

Smith, M., *Tariff Reform in France, 1860–1900: The Politics of Economic Interest*, London 1980

Smith, W., *Second Empire and Commune: France 1848–71*, London 1985

'La constitution de 1870 et la crise Hohenzollern' in Troisier de Diaz (ed.), *Regards*

'Le rôle politique de Rouher sous le Second Empire' in Becker (ed.), *Eugène Rouher*

Eugénie, impératrice et femme, 1989

Napoleon III. The pursuit of prestige, 1995

'L'évolution constitutionnelle était-elle imposée à l'Empire? ' in Tulard, *et al.*, *Pourquoi*

'La politique extérieure de Napoléon III: une politique des nationalités', in Tulard,' *et al.*, *Pourquoi*

Soulet, J.-F., *Les Pyrénées au 19ᵉ siècle*, 2 vols., 1987

Steefel, L., *Bismarck, the Hohenzollern Candidacy, and the Origins of the Franco-German War*, London 1962

Stewart-McDougall, M.-L., *Artisan Kingdom: Revolution, Reaction and Resistance in Lyon, 1848–51*, Gloucester 1984

Strauss, L., 'Opinion publique et forces politiques en Alsace à la fin du Second Empire. Le plébiscite du 8 mai 1870 dans le Haut-Rhin' in F. L'Huillier, *L'Alsace en 1870–71*, Gap 1971

Tchernoff, I., *Associations et sociétés secrètes sous la Deuxième République*, 1905

Le parti républicain au coup d'état et sous le Second Empire, 1906

Thibon, C., *Pays de Sault. Les Pyrénées audoises au 19ᵉ siècle: les villes et l'Etat*, 1988

Thuillier G. and Tulard, J., *Histoire de l'administration française depuis 1800*, Geneva 1975

Tollu, P., 'Démocratie et liberté' in Troisier de Diaz (ed.), *Regards*

Tombs, R., *The War against Paris, 1871*, London 1981

Toulotte, M., *Etienne Arago 1802–92*, Perpignan 1993

Traugott, M., 'The mid-19th-century crisis in France and England', *Theory and Society*, 1983

Armies of the Poor. Determinants of Working-Class Participation in the Parisian Insurrection of June 1848, Princeton 1985

Truesdell, M., *Spectacular Politics. Louis-Napoleon Bonaparte and the Fête Impériale, 1849–70*, Oxford 1997

Troisier de Diaz, A. (ed.), *Regards sur Emile Ollivier*, 1985

Tudesq, A. J. 'La légende napoléonienne en France en 1848', *Revue historique*, 1957

L'Election présidentielle de Louis-Napoléon Bonaparte, 10 décembre 1848, 1965

Tudesq, A. J., *Les grands notables en France (1840–49): Etude historique d'une psychologie sociale*, 2 vols., 1964

Tulard, J. (ed.), *Dictionnaire du second empire*, 1995

Tulard, J. (ed.), *Pourquoi réhabiliter le second empire?*, 1997

Verjus, A., 'Le suffrage universel, le chef de famille et la question de l'exclusion des femmes en 1848' in Corbin, Lalouette, and Riot-Sarcey, *Femmes dans la cité*

Vernon, J., *Politics and the People. A Study in English Political Culture c. 1815–67*, Cambridge 1993

Vidalenc, J., 'Histoire militaire et histoire de l'administration' in *Histoire de l'administration depuis 1800*, Geneva 1975

Vigier, P., *La Seconde République dans la région alpine*, 2 vols., 1953

'Lyon et l'évolution politique de la province française au 19ᵉ siècle', *Cahiers d'histoire*, 1967

'Le parti républicain en 1870' in Viard, J., *L'esprit républicain*, 1972

'Le parti républicain en 1869–70' in Hamon (ed.), *Les républicains*

Vigier P. *et al.*, *Maintien de l'ordre et police en France et en Europe au 19ᵉ siècle*, 1987

Vigreux, M., 'Des paysans républicains à la fin du second empire: les élections de 1869 dans le Morvan nivernais', *Revue d'histoire moderne et contemporaine*, 1978

Paysans et notables du Morvan au 19ᵉ siècle, Château-Chinon 1987

'Comment fait-on un *coup d'état?*' in Tulard (ed.), *Pourquoi*

Vuilleumier, M., 'La sous-préfecture de Gex et la surveillance politique de Genève (1848–70)', *Cahiers d'histoire*, 1964

Wahl, A., *Les françaises et la France (1859–99)*, 1986

Waquet, S., 'La politique étrangère de Napoléon III et l'opinion publique dans la Nièvre', *Annales de Bourgogne*, 1996

Wawro, G., *The Austro-Prussian War*, Cambridge 1996

Weber, E., *Peasants into Frenchmen. The Modernisation of Rural France, 1870–1914*, London 1976

'Comment la politique vint aux paysans: a second look at peasant politicisation', *American Historical Review*, 1982

Weill, G., *Histoire du parti républicain 1814–70*, 1928

Williams, R., *The mortal Napoleon III*, London 1971

Wirth, L., *Un équilibre perdu. Evolution démographique, économique et sociale du monde paysan dans le Cantal au 19ᵉ siècle*, Clermont-Ferrand 1996

Wiscart, J.-M., *La noblesse de la Somme au 19ᵉ siècle*, 1994

Wolfe, R., 'The Origins of the Paris Commune: The Popular Organizations of 1868–71', PhD thesis, Harvard University, 1965

Wolff, J., 'Napoleon III face à la crise économique de 1857–8', *Souvenir napoléonien*, 1997

Wright, G., 'Public opinion and conscription in France, 1866–70', *Journal of Modern History*, 1942

Wright, V., 'La loi de sûreté générale de 1858', *Revue d'histoire moderne et contemporaine*, 1969

Le Conseil d'Etat sous le Second Empire, 1972

'The *coup d'état* of December 1851: repression and the limits to repression' in Price (ed.) *Revolution and Reaction*

'Les directeurs et secrétaires généraux des administrations centrales sous le Second Empire' in F. de. Baecque, *et al.*, *Les directeurs de ministère en France*, Geneva 1976

'Les préfets de police pendant le Second Empire: personnalités et problèmes' in J. Aubert (ed.), *L'Etat et sa police en France (1789–1914)*, Geneva 1979

Zaniewicki, W., 'L'armée française en 1848', thèse de 3ᵉ cycle, Université de Paris, 1966

Zanten, D. van, *Rebuilding Paris. Architectural Institutions and the Transformation of the French Capital, 1830–70*, Cambridge 1994

Zeldin, T., *The Political System of Napoleon III*, Oxford 1958

'Government policy in the French general election of 1849', *English Historical Review*, 1959

Emile Ollivier and the Liberal Empire, 1963

France 1848–1945, 1972

(ed.) *Conflicts in French Society: Anti-Clericalism, Education and Morals in the 19th Century*, London 1970

Zind, P., *L'enseignement religieux dans l'instruction primaire publique en France de 1850 à 1873*, Lyons 1971

Zins, R., *Les maréchaux de Napoléon III. Dictionnaire*, 1996

Index

498